Maryland Public Service Records
1775-1783

A Compendium of Men and Women of Maryland Who Rendered Aid in Support of the American Cause Against Great Britain During the Revolutionary War

Henry C. Peden Jr.

HERITAGE BOOKS
2007

HERITAGE BOOKS
AN IMPRINT OF HERITAGE BOOKS, INC.

Books, CDs, and more—Worldwide

For our listing of thousands of titles see our website at
www.HeritageBooks.com

Published 2007 by
HERITAGE BOOKS, INC.
Publishing Division
65 East Main Street
Westminster, Maryland 21157-5026

Copyright © 2002 Henry C. Peden Jr.

All rights reserved. No part of this book may be reproduced or transmitted in any form or by any means, electronic or mechanical, including photocopying, recording or by any information storage and retrieval system without written permission from the author, except for the inclusion of brief quotations in a review.

International Standard Book Number: 978-1-58549-809-3

INTRODUCTION

Between 1775 and 1783 many men and women of Maryland rendered aid to the military in support of the American cause against Great Britain during the Revolutionary War. Their patriotic services, which are recanted in this compendium, entitle their descendants to become members in The National Society of the Sons of the American Revolution and The National Society of the Daughters of the American Revolution.

The names of these men and women who rendered aid to the Maryland government and all branches of the military by furnishing flour, corn, wheat, rye, hay, beef, mutton, pork, bacon, and other provisions, nursing the sick and wounded, boarding and clothing soldiers, riding express, repairing guns, manufacturing salt, milling grain, loaning money, providing boats, wagons, horses and cattle for the public use, and making weapons, among other things, have been gleaned from the following records:

(1) Original records courtesy of the Maryland State Archives in Annapolis, primarily Maryland State Papers (Series A), S1004;

(2) *An Inventory of Maryland State Papers, Volume I*, by Edward C. Papenfuse, Gregory A. Stiverson, Mary D. Donaldson, et al., courtesy of the Maryland State Archives;

(3) Original records courtesy of the Manuscripts Division of the Maryland Historical Society in Baltimore, primarily Revolutionary War Collection MS.1814; and,

(4) Journals, records, and proceedings of the Council of Maryland and Council of Safety published in the *Archives of Maryland* (Volumes 11, 12, 16, 21, 43, 45, 47, 48).

My appreciation is extended to those institutions and their staff for promoting awareness of Maryland's heritage by supporting historical, cultural and genealogical publications.

The information contained herein consists of the names of the patriots, counties of residence, nature of their service(s) and date(s) rendered, and the sources for that data. This information is in an abbreviated form and, therefore, the reader should always consult the original records for more details. This is not only important unto itself for the sake of accuracy in research, but also because it was discovered in the compilation of this book that a certificate may have been issued in one person's name, yet the actual aid was rendered by another person, or two persons, which was indicated on the reverse of the certificate or receipt from the purchasing agent. Most of the time a patriot either received a receipt or his or her name appeared on a list of returns, but oftentimes a certificate was issued as shown in the following example:

"_____ County, to wit: I hereby certify that I have taken into my possession, in virtue of the Act of Assembly, entitled An Act for the immediate supply of flour and other provisions for the Army, the articles expressed in the margin and the bearer thereof is entitled to receive from the State of Maryland the current market price on this day, with six percent interest thereon. Witness my hand this ____ day of _____ 17__." [Signed by the commissary or purchasing agent who also indicated the name of the person to whom it was issued].

In the preparation of this book the entire State of Maryland was scanned county by county to identify the men and women who rendered material aid and other supportive services to the government and the military during the Revolutionary War. The intent has been to assist people in finding an ancestor who served in a non-military capacity and whose public service would make their descendants eligible for membership in the SAR and DAR.

One should also consult the many other books I have compiled on Maryland patriots in the Revolutionary War, 1775-1783. While works such these may never be complete due to missing or unavailable records, I trust that they will be appreciated and used in the spirit intended. As we gain a renewed respect for our country, its flag, and our freedoms, we must honor our patriotic ancestors as we recognize the heroes on this first anniversary of the terrorist attack on America on September 11, 2001. Then as now, we will never forget.

                                        Henry C. Peden, Jr.
                                        Bel Air, Maryland
                                        September 11, 2002

MARYLAND PUBLIC SERVICE RECORDS, 1775-1783

ACKHEART, HENRY (Washington County) was appointed by the Council of Maryland as one of thirty men to be "Agents for Purchasing Provisions" on 30 Mar 1779 {Ref: Archives of Maryland 21:332}

ACTON, OSBON (Charles County) received receipts from the Purchasing Agent for furnishing wheat on 14 Aug and 18 Aug 1782 {Ref: Maryland State Archives MdHR-6636-42-18}

ADAIR, WILLIAM (Montgomery County) received a receipt from the Purchasing Agent for furnishing wheat on 26 Jan 1781 {Ref: Maryland State Archives MdHR-6636-24-9}

ADAM, VALENTINE (Frederick County) received a certificate from the Purchasing Agent for furnishing wheat on 1 Aug 1782 {Ref: Maryland State Archives MdHR-6636-42-36}

ADAMS, ANDREW (Wicomico Hundred, Somerset County) received a receipt from the Purchasing Agent for furnishing pork on 13 Mar 1781 {Ref: Maryland State Archives MdHR-6636-24-45}; received a receipt for furnishing pork on 21 May 1782 {Ref: Maryland State Archives MdHR-6636-43-21}

ADAMS, DANIEL (Baltimore County) received payment by order of the Council of Safety on 26 Jun 1776 "for detention of the schooner *Hawk* and wages for his seamen" when said vessel was sunk at Whetstone Point for the defence of Baltimore Town (which occurred in March, 1776 for the purpose of preventing any of the British Ships of War from coming up to Baltimore Town) {Ref: Archives of Maryland 11:521}

ADAMS, GEORGE (Montgomery County) received money from the Council of Maryland "to be delivered over to Thomas Richardson, Esqr., Commissary of Montgomery County [for the use of his Department] on Account" on 31 Aug 1781 {Ref: Archives of Maryland 45:593}

ADAMS, GERTRUDE (Somerset County) received a receipt from the Purchasing Agent for furnishing beef on 6 Dec 1781 {Ref: Maryland State Archives MdHR-6636-24-44}

ADAMS, IGNATIUS (Charles County) received a receipt from the Purchasing Agent for furnishing wheat on 8 May 1783 {Ref: Maryland State Archives MdHR-6636-42-22}

ADAMS, ISAAC (Somerset County) received a receipt from the Purchasing Agent for furnishing beef on 5 Dec 1781 {Ref: Maryland State Archives MdHR-6636-24-44}

ADAMS, JESSE (Prince George's County) received a receipt from the Purchasing Agent for furnishing wheat on 8 Jun 1782 {Ref: Maryland State Archives

MdHR-6636-50-135}

ADAMS, JOHN (Somerset County) received a receipt from the Purchasing Agent for furnishing pork on 4 Jun 1781 {Ref: Maryland State Archives MdHR-6636-24-43}

ADAMS, LEONARD (Charles County) received a receipt from the Purchasing Agent for furnishing wheat on 6 Sep 1782 {Ref: Maryland State Archives MdHR-6636-42-18}

ADAMS, RHODAH (Charles County) received a receipt from the Purchasing Agent for furnishing wheat on 10 May 1783 {Ref: Maryland State Archives MdHR-6636-42-22}

ADAMS, SAMUEL (Somerset County) received a receipt from the Purchasing Agent for furnishing beef on 5 Dec 1781 {Ref: Maryland State Archives MdHR-6636-24-44}

ADAMS, WILLIAM (Wicomico Hundred, Somerset County) was appointed by the Council of Safety to collect all the gold and silver coin that could be procured in the county in compliance with the Resolve of Congress on 27 Jan 1776 {Ref: Archives of Maryland 11:132}; received a receipt from the Purchasing Agent for furnishing pork on 13 Mar 1781 {Ref: Maryland State Archives MdHR-6636-24-45}; received a receipt for furnishing beef on 6 Dec 1781 {Ref: Maryland State Archives MdHR-6636-24-44}; received a loan certificate for £252.10.4 due from the Council of Maryland "agreeable to the Act proposing to the Citizens of this State, Creditors of Congress on Loan Office Certificates, Etc." on 20 Dec 1783 for services rendered during the war {Ref: Archives of Maryland 48:495}

ADAMS, WILLIAM SR. (Somerset County) received a receipt from the Purchasing Agent for furnishing beef on 6 Dec 1781 {Ref: Maryland State Archives MdHR-6636-24-44}

ADAMSON, JOHN (Montgomery County) received receipts from the Purchasing Agent for furnishing wheat on 10 Apr and 17 Apr 1781 {Ref: Maryland State Archives MdHR-6636-42-11}

ADKINSON, BENJAMIN (Somerset County) received receipts from the Purchasing Agent for furnishing bacon and pork on 10 Jun and 14 Jul 1781 {Ref: Maryland State Archives MdHR-6636-24-43}

ADLUM, JOHN (Frederick County) submitted an account for furnishing beef on 21 May 1781 {Ref: Maryland State Archives MdHR-6636-23-6}

AISQUITH, WILLIAM (Baltimore Town) was appointed by the Council of Maryland to be one of three "Superintendants of the Press, or Presses in Baltimore Town, employed in printing the Continental Bills of Credit" on 28 May 1777 {Ref: Archives of Maryland 16:261}; received a loan certificate for £16.8.5 due from the Council of Maryland "agreeable to the Act proposing to the Citizens of this State, Creditors of Congress on Loan Office Certificates,

Etc." on 30 Oct 1783 for services rendered during the war {Ref: Archives of Maryland 48:476}

AKERS (ACRES), WILLIAM (Talbot County) received payment by order of the Council of Safety for the hire of his boat for the Flying Camp on 30 Aug 1776 and for furnishing boatage on 3 Sep and 18 Sep 1776 {Ref: Archives of Maryland 12:248, 255, 280}

ALBRITTON, WILLIAM (Charles County) received a receipt from the Purchasing Agent for furnishing wheat on 28 Sep 1782 {Ref: Maryland State Archives MdHR-6636-42-19}

ALDRICE, ELISABETH (Talbot County) received a receipt from the Purchasing Agent for furnishing bacon on 29 May 1778 {Ref: Maryland State Archives MdHR-6636-12-15}

ALEXANDER, HANNAH (Talbot County) received a receipt from the Purchasing Agent for purchasing bacon on 12 Jun 1778 {Ref: Maryland State Archives MdHR-6636-12-15}

ALEXANDER, MARK (Baltimore Town) pledged a loan in the amount of £250 to the State of Maryland under the Act for the Emission of Bills of Credit "to defray the expences of the present campaign" in June, 1781 {Ref: Archives of Maryland 47:327}

ALEXANDER, ROBERT (Charles County) received a receipt from the Purchasing Agent for furnishing wheat on 8 May 1783 {Ref: Maryland State Archives MdHR-6636-42-22}

ALLCOCK, JAMES (Annapolis) received payment by order of the Council of Safety for engineering services rendered on 6 Sep 1776 {Ref: Archives of Maryland 12:259}

ALLEIN, WILLIAM (Calvert County) received payment by order of the Council of Maryland on 5 Aug 1777 for erecting a salt works {Ref: Archives of Maryland 16:325}

ALLEN, AUSTIN (Prince George's County) received a receipt from the Purchasing Agent for furnishing wheat on 12 Apr 1783 {Ref: Maryland State Archives MdHR-6636-43-9}

ALLEN, JOHN (county not stated) received a loan certificate for £13.9.4 due from the Council of Maryland "agreeable to the Act proposing to the Citizens of this State, Creditors of Congress on Loan Office Certificates, Etc." on 7 Nov 1783 for services rendered during the war {Ref: Archives of Maryland 48:478}

ALLEN, JOSEPH (Prince George's County) received a receipt from the Purchasing Agent for furnishing wheat on 29 Apr 1783 {Ref: Maryland State Archives MdHR-6636-43-9}

ALLEN, MICHAEL (Frederick County) received a receipt from the Purchasing Agent for furnishing beef on 8 Jan 1781; received a receipt from the Purchasing Agent for furnishing tallow and candles on 17 Jan 1781 {Ref: Maryland State

Archives MdHR-6636-23-2}; submitted an account for furnishing beef on 21 May 1781 {Ref: Maryland State Archives MdHR-6636-23-6}; submitted an account for goods supplied for the Maryland troops on 9 Jan 1782 {Ref: Maryland State Archives MdHR-6636-23-8}

ALLEN, MILFORD (Frederick County) received a receipt from the Purchasing Agent for furnishing beef and pork on 17 Jan 1781 {Ref: Maryland State Archives MdHR-6636-23-2}

ALLEN, SOLOMON (Baltimore County) received a loan certificate for £1038.7.11 due from the Council of Maryland "agreeable to the Act proposing to the Citizens of this State, Creditors of Congress on Loan Office Certificates, Etc." on 18 Dec 1783 for services rendered during the war {Ref: Archives of Maryland 48:491}

ALLEN, WILLIAM (Worcester County) received a receipt from the Purchasing Agent for furnishing corn on 20 Feb 1780 {Ref: Maryland State Archives MdHR-6636-24-52}; his name appeared on "A List of Sundry Persons Corn Purchased of for the use of the State of Maryland" by the Commissary on 19 Jun 1780 {Ref: Archives of Maryland 45:9-10}; received payment for furnishing beef on 10 Oct 1781 {Ref: Maryland State Archives MdHR-6636-43-28NNN}

ALLEN, ZACHARIAH (Charles County) received payment by order of the Council of Maryland for furnishing a gun on 13 Sep 1776 {Ref: Archives of Maryland 16:375}

ALLENDER, NICHOLAS (Harford County) received payment for furnishing a gun to the Committee of Safety on 18 Jun 1776 {Ref: Preston's History of Harford County, p. 330}

ALLISON, CHARLES (Montgomery County) received a receipt from the Purchasing Agent for furnishing wheat on 1 Aug 1780 {Ref: Maryland State Archives MdHR-6636-43-7}; received a receipt for furnishing wheat on 10 Aug 1780 {Ref: Maryland State Archives MdHR-6636-24-6}; received a receipt for furnishing wheat on 12 May 1781 {Ref: Maryland State Archives MdHR-6636-24-18}

ALLISON, ELIZABETH (Montgomery County) received a receipt from the Purchasing Agent for furnishing wheat on 31 May 1781 {Ref: Maryland State Archives MdHR-6636-24-18}

ALLISON, HENRY (Prince George's County) received a receipt from the Purchasing Agent for furnishing wheat on 1 Feb 1783 {Ref: Maryland State Archives MdHR-6636-50-135}

ALLISON, HENRY (Montgomery County) received a receipt from the Purchasing Agent for shelling corn on 23 Apr 1780 {Ref: Maryland State Archives MdHR-6636-24-2}

ALLISON, JOHN (Montgomery County) received a receipt from the Purchasing

Agent for furnishing wheat on 27 Sep 1780 {Ref: Maryland State Archives MdHR-6636-24-7}; received a receipt for furnishing wheat on 27 Oct 1780 {Ref: Maryland State Archives MdHR-6636-24-8}

ALLISON, JONATHAN (Montgomery County) received a receipt from the Purchasing Agent for furnishing wheat on 26 May 1781 {Ref: Maryland State Archives MdHR-6636-24-18}

ALLISON, RICHARD (Montgomery County) received a receipt from the Purchasing Agent for furnishing wheat on 24 Jul 1780 {Ref: Maryland State Archives MdHR-6636-24-5}; received a receipt for furnishing wheat on 1 Aug 1780 {Ref: Maryland State Archives MdHR-6636-43-7}

ALLISON, WILLIAM (Anne Arundel County) received a receipt from the Purchasing Agent for furnishing powder on 16 Apr 1777 {Ref: Maryland State Archives MdHR-6636-9-14A}

ALLNUT, JESSE (Frederick County) received a receipt from the Purchasing Agent for furnishing rye on 25 Apr 1780 {Ref: Maryland State Archives MdHR-6636-24-1}

ALLOWAY, WILLIAM (Talbot County) received a certificate from the Purchasing Agent for furnishing corn on 2 Mar 1780 {Ref: Maryland State Archives MdHR-6636-24-46}

AMBER, JOHN (Annapolis) received payment by order of the Council of Safety for attending the hospital on 2 Sep 1776 {Ref: Archives of Maryland 12:252}

AMBROSE, CATHERINE (Frederick County) received a certificate from the Purchasing Agent for furnishing beef on 28 Sep 1781 {Ref: Maryland State Archives MdHR-6636-23-28}

AMBROSE (AMBROSS), MALACHI (Kent County) received a certificate from the Purchasing Agent for hauling corn to Delaware on 15 Jun 1780 {Ref: Maryland State Archives MdHR-6636-43-1}; received payment from the Purchasing Agent for furnishing cattle for the public use in September, 1781 {Ref: Maryland State Archives MdHR-6636-43-3}

ANDERSON, CHARLES (Montgomery County) received a receipt from the Purchasing Agent for furnishing wheat on 11 Aug 1781 {Ref: Maryland State Archives MdHR-6636-24-15}

ANDERSON, ISAAC (Somerset County) received a receipt from the Purchasing Agent for furnishing pork on 27 Apr 1782 {Ref: Maryland State Archives MdHR-6636-43-21}

ANDERSON, ISAAC (Caroline County) received a receipt from the Purchasing Agent for furnishing wheat on 5 Aug 1782 {Ref: Maryland State Archives MdHR-6636-42-7}

ANDERSON, JAMES (Queen Anne's County) received a certificate from the Purchasing Agent for furnishing wheat on 24 Feb 1780 {Ref: Maryland State Archives MdHR-6636-24-28}

ANDERSON, JAMES JR. (Kent County) received a loan certificate for £16.19.2 due from the Council of Maryland "agreeable to the Act proposing to the Citizens of this State, Creditors of Congress on Loan Office Certificates, Etc." on 19 Dec 1783 for services rendered during the war {Ref: Archives of Maryland 48:494}

ANDERSON, PRISSILLA OR PRICELLA (Montgomery County) received a receipt from the Purchasing Agent for furnishing wheat on 29 Jul 1780 {Ref: Maryland State Archives MdHR-6636-24-5}; received a receipt for furnishing wheat on 1 Aug 1780 {Ref: Maryland State Archives MdHR-6636-43-7}

ANDERSON, ROBERT (Somerset County) received a receipt from the Purchasing Agent for furnishing bacon on 20 Jul 1781 {Ref: Maryland State Archives MdHR-6636-24-43}

ANDERSON, ROBERT (Baltimore County) received payment by order of the Council of Maryland for furnishing sails for the snow *Champion* on 7 May 1778 {Ref: Archives of Maryland 21:69}

ANDREW, CURTIS (Caroline County) received receipts from the Purchasing Agent for furnishing wheat on 5 Aug and 22 Aug 1782 {Ref: Maryland State Archives MdHR-6636-42-7}

ANDREW, GEORGE (Caroline County) received a receipt from the Purchasing Agent for furnishing wheat on 22 Aug 1782 {Ref: Maryland State Archives MdHR-6636-42-7}

ANDREW, ISAAC (Caroline County) received receipts from the Purchasing Agent for furnishing wheat on 31 May and 22 Aug 1782 {Ref: Maryland State Archives MdHR-6636-42-7}

ANDREW, JEREMIAH (Caroline County) received a receipt from the Purchasing Agent for furnishing wheat on 18 Jun 1782 {Ref: Maryland State Archives MdHR-6636-42-7}

ANDREW, JOHN (Caroline County) received a receipt from the Purchasing Agent for furnishing wheat on 22 Aug 1782 {Ref: Maryland State Archives MdHR-6636-42-7}

ANDREW, JOHN SR. (Caroline County) received a receipt from the Purchasing Agent for furnishing wheat on 31 May 1782 {Ref: Maryland State Archives MdHR-6636-42-7}

ANDREW, LUKE (Caroline County) received receipts from the Purchasing Agent for furnishing wheat on 5 Aug 1782 {Ref: Maryland State Archives MdHR-6636-42-7}

ANDREW, MARK (Caroline County) received receipts from the Purchasing Agent for furnishing wheat on 5 Aug 1782 {Ref: Maryland State Archives MdHR-6636-42-7}

ANDREW, WILLIAM (Caroline County) received receipts from the Purchasing Agent for furnishing wheat on 5 Aug and 22 Aug 1782 {Ref: Maryland State

Archives MdHR-6636-42-7}

ANDREWS, ABRAHAM (Harford County) delivered 166 blankets in his wagon to the Head of Elk in Cecil County for Col. Hall's Battalion on 2 Sep 1776 {Ref: Preston's History of Harford County, pp. 335-336}

ANDREWS, JOHN (Dorchester County) received a receipt from the Purchasing Agent for furnishing wheat on 1 Oct 1782 {Ref: Maryland State Archives MdHR-6636-42-23}

ANGEL, CHARLES (Frederick County) received a certificate from the Purchasing Agent for furnishing wheat on 30 Jun 1782 {Ref: Maryland State Archives MdHR-6636-42-36}

ANKENNEY, JOHN (Anne Arundel County) received a receipt from the Purchasing Agent for furnishing powder on 16 Apr 1777 {Ref: Maryland State Archives MdHR-6636-9-14A}

ANNIS, JOHN (Baltimore County) received payment by order of the Council of Safety for making a coffin for, and burying, a sergeant in Capt. Adams' Company on 9 Apr 1776 {Ref: Archives of Maryland 11:317}; received payment for burying a soldier on 31 Jan 1778 and 3 Apr 1779 {Ref: Archives of Maryland 16:481, 21:335}

ANTHONY, NATHAN (Caroline County) received a receipt from the Purchasing Agent for wheat on 10 Sep 1782 {Ref: Maryland State Archives MdHR-6636-42-7}

APPLEGARTH, THOMAS (Talbot County) was one of twenty-six people who contacted the Governor and Council of Maryland in 1781 and pledged to support and maintain at their own expense the Barge *Experiment* so it can patrol the bay between Kent Point and Tilghman's Island in order to protect them against the enemy, stating in part, "whereas from the present exhausted state of the public treasury the government cannot immediately give that protection to every individual which is become necessary from the cruel and savage mode in which the war is now carried on against us" {Ref: Archives of Maryland 47:584-585}

ARMSTRONG, DAVID (Baltimore County) submitted an account and receipt for furnishing whiskey on 27 Jun 1781 {Ref: Maryland State Archives MdHR-6636-43-38RR}

ARMSTRONG, JOHN (Harford County) received a loan certificate for £35.10.0 due from the Council of Maryland "agreeable to the Act proposing to the Citizens of this State, Creditors of Congress on Loan Office Certificates, Etc." on 8 Nov 1783 for services rendered during the war {Ref: Archives of Maryland 48:479}

ARMSTRONG, ROBERT (Harford County) received a loan certificate for £35.10.0 due from the Council of Maryland "agreeable to the Act proposing to the Citizens of this State, Creditors of Congress on Loan Office Certificates,

Etc." on 8 Nov 1783 for services rendered during the war {Ref: Archives of Maryland 48:479}

ARMSTRONG, WILLIAM (Baltimore County) submitted an account and received payment for stowing flour for two days on 24 Mar 1780 {Ref: Maryland Historical Society MS.1814, Box 6}

ARCHER, JOHN (Harford County) contracted with the Maryland Council of Safety to carry on a linen manufactory in partnership with James Harris on or about 16 Feb 1776 {Ref: Archives of Maryland 11:163}; as a major, he was appointed by the Committee of Safety to be one of four men to serve on "a Committee for Examination of Guns and report of their Sufficiency be a Guide for this Committee to receive them by" on 11 Jul 1776 {Ref: Preston's History of Harford County, p. 331}

ARNOLD, JOHN (Frederick County) received a certificate from the Purchasing Agent for furnishing flour on 8 Jun 1782 {Ref: Maryland State Archives MdHR-6636-42-35}

ARVIN, THOMAS (Charles County) received a receipt from the Purchasing Agent for furnishing wheat on 28 Dec 1782 {Ref: Maryland State Archives MdHR-6636-42-21}

ASHMEAD, JOSEPH (Anne Arundel County) received a receipt from the Purchasing Agent for furnishing beef on 17 Mar 1777 {Ref: Maryland State Archives MdHR-6636-5-189}

ASHMEAD, SAMUEL (Harford County) was appointed by the Committee of Safety "to ride in Bush River Upper, Spesutia & Eden Hundreds and purchase guns and blankets agreeable to the request of the [Maryland] Council of Safety" on 19 Aug 1776 {Ref: Preston's History of Harford County, pp. 333-334}

ASWORTH, HENRY (Somerset County) received a receipt from the Purchasing Agent for furnishing beef on 20 Sep 1781 {Ref: Maryland State Archives MdHR-6636-24-44}

ASWORTH, RICHARD (Somerset County) received a receipt from the Purchasing Agent for furnishing a hog on 18 Feb 1782 {Ref: Maryland State Archives MdHR-6636-43-21}

ATKINSON, ELIZABETH (Somerset County) received a receipt from the Purchasing Agent for furnishing bacon on 14 Aug 1780 {Ref: Maryland State Archives MdHR-6636-24-41}

ATKINSON, JOHN (Kent County) received a certificate from the Purchasing Agent for furnishing corn on 18 Jan 1780 {Ref: Maryland State Archives MdHR-6636-23-42}

AUBBER, JOHN (Annapolis) received payment by order of the Council of Safety for attending the hospital on 1 Oct 1776 {Ref: Archives of Maryland 12:313}

AULD, JOHN (Queen Anne's County) received a receipt from the Purchasing Agent for furnishing beef on 29 Sep 1780 {Ref: Maryland State Archives

MdHR-6636-24-33}; received a receipt for furnishing beef on 8 Oct 1781 {Ref: Maryland State Archives MdHR-6636-24-34}

AUNY, ELIZABETH (Dorchester County) received a receipt from the Purchasing Agent for furnishing wheat on 1 Nov 1782 {Ref: Maryland State Archives MdHR-6636-42-23}

AUSTIN, JOHN (Montgomery County) received a receipt from the Purchasing Agent for furnishing wheat on 19 Jul 1780 {Ref: Maryland State Archives MdHR-6636-24-5}; received a receipt for furnishing wheat on 1 Aug 1780 {Ref: Maryland State Archives MdHR-6636-43-7}; received a receipt for furnishing wheat on 14 Aug 1780 {Ref: Maryland State Archives MdHR-6636-24-6}

AYDELOTT, BENJAMIN (Worcester County) submitted an account and receipt for rendering lodging services and provisions on 20 Sep 1781 {Ref: Maryland State Archives MdHR-6636-43-27}

AYDELOTT, GEORGE HAYWARD (Worcester County) received a receipt from the Purchasing Agent for furnishing corn on 26 Aug 1780 {Ref: Maryland State Archives MdHR-6636-24-53}

AYDELOTT, HOWARD (Worcester County) received a receipt from the Purchasing Agent for furnishing corn on 19 Jun 1780 {Ref: Maryland State Archives MdHR-6636-24-53}

AYDELOTT (AYDELET), WILLIAM (Worcester County) received a receipt from the Purchasing Agent for furnishing corn on 27 Mar 1780 {Ref: Maryland State Archives MdHR-6636-24-52}; his name appeared on "A List of Corn Purchased in Worcester County for the use of the State of Maryland" by the Commissary in July, 1780 {Ref: Archives of Maryland 45:10}

AYRES, HENRY (Worcester County) received payment for furnishing beef on 5 Oct 1781 {Ref: Maryland State Archives MdHR-6636-43-28SSS}

AYRES, J. (Worcester County) received a receipt from the Purchasing Agent for furnishing corn on 1 Apr 1780 {Ref: Maryland State Archives MdHR-6636-24-52}

AYRES, JOHN (Worcester County) received payment for furnishing beef on 20 Sep 1781 {Ref: Maryland State Archives MdHR-6636-43-28ZZZ}

BABLEN, JOHN (Annapolis) received payment by order of the Council of Safety for furnishing necessaries for the hospital on 4 Oct 1776 {Ref: Archives of Maryland 12:318}

BACHER, CHRISTIAN (Harford County) received a receipt from the Purchasing Agent for furnishing wheat on 23 May 1780(?) {Ref: Maryland State Archives MdHR-6636-23-35}

BAGGOT, SAMUEL (Charles County) received a receipt from the Purchasing Agent for furnishing wheat on 11 Dec 1781 {Ref: Maryland State Archives MdHR-6636-42-15}

BAGGS, PEBBLES OR PIBBLES (Caroline County) received a receipt from the Purchasing Agent for furnishing wheat on 1 Sep 1782 {Ref: Maryland State Archives MdHR-6636-42-7}

BAILEY, JOHN SR. (Montgomery County) received a receipt from the Purchasing Agent for furnishing wheat on 19 Apr 1781 {Ref: Maryland State Archives MdHR-6636-42-11}

BAILEY, JOHN (Montgomery County) received a receipt from the Purchasing Agent for furnishing wheat on 15 Sep 1780 {Ref: Maryland State Archives MdHR-6636-24-7}

BAILEY, MOUNTJOY (Frederick County) submitted an account for furnishing provisions on 21 May 1781 {Ref: Maryland State Archives MdHR-6636-23-6}; submitted an account for furnishing hay and corn on 29 May 1781 {Ref: Maryland State Archives MdHR-6636-23-6}; submitted an account for furnishing beef and flour on 29 May 1781 {Ref: Maryland State Archives MdHR-6636-23-6}

BAILEY, NATHAN (Harford County) received payment for furnishing a gun to the Committee of Safety on 2 Sep 1776 {Ref: Preston's History of Harford County, p. 336}

BAILEY, NICKOLS (Montgomery County) received a receipt from the Purchasing Agent for furnishing wheat on 20 Apr 1781 {Ref: Maryland State Archives MdHR-6636-42-11}

BAILEY, SAMUEL (Harford County) received a receipt from the Purchasing Agent for furnishing flour on 28 Mar 1780 {Ref: Maryland State Archives MdHR-6636-23-35}

BAILEY, WILLIAM (Montgomery County) received a receipt from the Purchasing Agent for furnishing wheat on 23 Oct 1780 {Ref: Maryland State Archives MdHR-6636-24-8}; also see "William Baley," q.v.

BAIRD, ALEXANDER (Kent County) received payment from the Purchasing Agent for furnishing cattle for the public use in September, 1781 {Ref: Maryland State Archives MdHR-6636-43-3}

BAIRD, JAMES (Somerset County) received a receipt from the Purchasing Agent for furnishing pork on 20 May 1782 {Ref: Maryland State Archives MdHR-6636-43-21}

BAIRD, WILLIAM (Frederick County) was appointed by the Council of Safety to collect all the gold and silver coin that could be procured in the county in compliance with the Resolve of Congress on 27 Jan 1776 {Ref: Archives of Maryland 11:132}

BAKER, BENJAMIN (Somerset County) received a receipt from the Purchasing Agent for furnishing pork on 15 Apr 1782 {Ref: Maryland State Archives MdHR-6636-43-21}

BAKER, CHARLES (Kent County) received a certificate from the Purchasing

Agent for furnishing wheat on 14 Jan 1780 {Ref: Maryland State Archives MdHR-6636-23-41}; received a certificate for furnishing wheat on 22 Jan 1780 {Ref: Maryland State Archives MdHR-6636-23-42}

BAKER, FRANCIS (Skipton Hill, Talbot County) was a Commissary Agent who received payment by order of the Council of Maryland via Col. George Dashiell "to purchase beef for the Continental Army" on 14 Jan and 31 Jan 1778 {Ref: Archives of Maryland 16:466, 481}; submitted an account of purchase of pork for the militia on 7 Jul 1778 {Ref: Maryland State Archives MdHR-4585-61}; received payment "to be expended in the purchase of pork for the use of this State" on 3 Dec 1778 {Ref: Archives of Maryland 21:257}; submitted an account of purchase of provisions on 19 Dec 1778 {Ref: Maryland State Archives MdHR-4586-87}; ordered by the Council on 2 Oct 1781 to deliver flour to Barnesville Ferry on the James River in Virginia {Ref: Maryland State Archives MdHR-6636-31-74}

BAKER, FREDERICK (Frederick County) received a certificate from the Purchasing Agent for furnishing wheat on 28 May 1782 {Ref: Maryland State Archives MdHR-6636-42-33}

BAKER, JEREMIAH (Cecil County) was appointed by the Council of Maryland as one of thirty men to be "Agents for Purchasing Provisions" on 30 Mar 1779 {Ref: Archives of Maryland 21:332}

BAKER, JOHN (Caroline County) submitted an account of wheat received on 20 Sep 1782 {Ref: Maryland State Archives MdHR-6636-42-7}

BAKER, JOHN (Montgomery County) received a receipt from the Purchasing Agent for furnishing wheat on 1 Aug 1780 {Ref: Maryland State Archives MdHR-6636-43-7}

BAKER, MORRIS (Harford County) received a receipt from the Purchasing Agent for furnishing wheat on 30 Jun 1780 {Ref: Maryland State Archives MdHR-6636-23-35}

BALDWIN, JAMES (Anne Arundel County) received payment from the Council of Maryland for furnishing wood on 24 Feb 1783 {Ref: Archives of Maryland 48:366}

BAKER, THOMAS (Queenstown, Queen Anne's County) received a receipt from the Purchasing Agent for furnishing beef on 18 Dec 1779 {Ref: Maryland State Archives MdHR-6636-17-73}

BAKER, WILLIAM (county not stated) was a doctor who received a loan certificate for £1021.14.6 due from the Council of Maryland "agreeable to the Act proposing to the Citizens of this State, Creditors of Congress on Loan Office Certificates, Etc." on 15 Aug 1783 for services rendered during the war {Ref: Archives of Maryland 48:447, 485}

BALEY, NATHAN (Caroline County) received a receipt from the Purchasing Agent for furnishing wheat on 1 Sep 1782 {Ref: Maryland State Archives

MdHR-6636-42-7}

BALEY, WILLIAM (Montgomery County) delivered two cattle to the Purchasing Agent for the use of the State of Maryland in October, 1780 {Ref: Archives of Maryland 45:149}

BALLARD, RICHARD (Montgomery County) received a certificate of employment by the commissary of purchases on 13 Jun 1782 {Ref: Maryland State Archives MdHR-6636-50-91}

BALLARD, SARAH (Montgomery County) received a loan certificate for £28.4.11 due from the Council of Maryland "agreeable to the Act proposing to the Citizens of this State, Creditors of Congress on Loan Office Certificates, Etc." on 26 Jul 1783 for services rendered during the war {Ref: Archives of Maryland 48:440}

BALMYER, MICHAEL (Frederick County) received a certificate from the Purchasing Agent for furnishing wheat on 17 Sep 1781 {Ref: Maryland State Archives MdHR-6636-23-28}

BALSER, JOHN (Frederick County) received payment by order of the Council of Maryland "for 54 cattle purchased of him" on 22 Oct 1777 {Ref: Archives of Maryland 16:401}; received a receipt for furnishing beef on 27 Dec 1780 {Ref: Maryland State Archives MdHR-6636-23-1}; received a receipt for furnishing beef on 7 Jan 1781 {Ref: Maryland State Archives MdHR-6636-23-2}; received a certificate and receipt for furnishing beef and veal on 12 Mar and 2 Apr 1781 {Ref: Maryland State Archives MdHR-6636-23-4}

BALT, GEORGE (Frederick County) received a certificate from the Purchasing Agent for furnishing wheat on 18 Apr 1782 {Ref: Maryland State Archives MdHR-6636-42-34}

BAMBURGH, GEORGE (Frederick County) received a receipt from the Purchasing Agent for delivering fresh pork on 5 May 1781 {Ref: Maryland State Archives MdHR-6636-23-31}

BANE, GEORGE (Frederick County) received payment by order of the Council of Safety via Capt. George Stricker "for the waggonage of lead from Frederick Town to Port Tobacco" on 4 Apr 1776 {Ref: Archives of Maryland 11:308}

BANKS, JAMES (Caroline County) received a receipt from the Purchasing Agent for furnishing wheat on 1 Sep 1782 {Ref: Maryland State Archives MdHR-6636-42-7}

BANNING, ANTHONY (Kent County) received a certificate from the Purchasing Agent for furnishing wheat on 29 Jan 1780 {Ref: Maryland State Archives MdHR-6636-23-41}; received a loan certificate for £248.15.8 due from the Council of Maryland "agreeable to the Act proposing to the Citizens of this State, Creditors of Congress on Loan Office Certificates, Etc." on 12 Dec 1783 for services rendered during the war {Ref: Archives of Maryland 48:489}

BANNING, ASA (Caroline County) received a receipt from the Purchasing Agent for furnishing wheat on 17 Aug 1782 {Ref: Maryland State Archives MdHR-6636-42-7}

BARBER, JOHN (Montgomery County) received a receipt from the Purchasing Agent for furnishing wheat on 1 Aug 1780 {Ref: Maryland State Archives MdHR-6636-43-7}; received a receipt for furnishing wheat on 7 Apr 1781 {Ref: Maryland State Archives MdHR-6636-42-11}

BARBER, JOHN JR. (Montgomery County) received a receipt from the Purchasing Agent for furnishing wheat on 1 Aug 1780 {Ref: Maryland State Archives MdHR-6636-43-7}

BARBER, JOHN SR. (Montgomery County) received a receipt from the Purchasing Agent for furnishing wheat on 7 Apr 1781 {Ref: Maryland State Archives MdHR-6636-42-11}

BARD, ERWIN (Montgomery County) received a receipt from the Purchasing Agent for furnishing wheat on 25 Apr 1781 {Ref: Maryland State Archives MdHR-6636-24-14}

BARD, JESSE (Somerset County) received a receipt from the Purchasing Agent for furnishing beef on 2 Nov 1781 {Ref: Maryland State Archives MdHR-6636-24-44}

BARGER, FREDERICK (Frederick County) received a certificate from the Purchasing Agent for furnishing wheat on 14 Feb 1783 {Ref: Maryland State Archives MdHR-6636-42-38}

BARGER, PHILIP (Frederick County) received a certificate for money loaned to the state on 3 Jun 1780 {Ref: Maryland State Archives MdHR-6636-48-60}

BARKER, ANANIS (Montgomery County) received a receipt from the Purchasing Agent for furnishing wheat on 11 May 1781 {Ref: Maryland State Archives MdHR-6636-24-18}

BARKER, WILLIAM (Charles County) received a receipt from the Purchasing Agent for furnishing wheat on 15 Feb 1782 {Ref: Maryland State Archives MdHR-6636-42-16}

BARKER, WILLIAM (Prince George's County) received a receipt from the Purchasing Agent for furnishing wheat on 7 Jan 1782 {Ref: Maryland State Archives MdHR-6636-42-14}

BARLEY, JOHN (Harford County) received a receipt from the Purchasing Agent for furnishing flour at Susquehanna Lower Ferry on 7 Feb 1780 {Ref: Maryland State Archives MdHR-6636-23-37}

BARLOW, ZACHARIAS (Montgomery County) received a receipt from the Purchasing Agent for shelling corn on 17 Apr 1780 {Ref: Maryland State Archives MdHR-6636-24-2}

BARNABY, JOHN (Cecil County) appeared on 19 Feb 1781 on a "Return [of] Flour forwarded and Delivered at the Head of Elk the Purchase of different Persons for the use of the United States" in the year 1780 {Ref: Archives of

Maryland 47:77}

BARNABY, RICHARD (Talbot County) received payment by order of the Council of Safety for furnishing boatage on 5 Sep 1776 {Ref: Archives of Maryland 12:257}; submitted an account and receipt for furnishing flour on 18 Aug 1780 {Ref: Maryland State Archives MdHR-6636-24-49}

BARNABY (BARNEBY), WILLIAM (Kent County) received payments for driving cattle on 27 Oct and 12 Nov 1780 {Ref: Maryland State Archives MdHR-6636-23-49}; received payment from the Purchasing Agent for collecting cattle for the public use in November, 1782 {Ref: Maryland State Archives MdHR-6636-43-3}

BARNES, CATHERINE (Charles County) received a receipt from the Purchasing Agent for furnishing wheat on 4 Jan 1782 {Ref: Maryland State Archives MdHR-6636-42-16}

BARNES, JOHN (Montgomery County)received a receipt from the Purchasing Agent for furnishing wheat on 30 Jul 1781 {Ref: Maryland State Archives MdHR-6636-24-18}

BARNES, JOHN (county not stated) pledged a loan in the amount of £500 to the State of Maryland under the Act for the Emission of Bills of Credit "to defray the expences of the present campaign" in June, 1781 {Ref: Archives of Maryland 47:327}

BARNES, JOSEPH (Montgomery County) received a receipt from the Purchasing Agent for furnishing wheat on 21 Jul 1780 {Ref: Maryland State Archives MdHR-6636-24-5}; received a receipt for furnishing wheat on 1 Aug 1780 {Ref: Maryland State Archives MdHR-6636-43-7}; received a receipt for furnishing wheat on 12 May 1781 {Ref: Maryland State Archives MdHR-6636-24-18}

BARNES, RICHARD (St. Mary's County) was a colonel who was appointed by the Council of Safety to collect all the gold and silver coin that could be procured in the county in compliance with the Resolve of Congress on 27 Jan 1776 {Ref: Archives of Maryland 11:132}; his name appeared on "A Return of Beef on the Hoof Purchased by Joseph Ford Commissary of Purchases" on 14 Oct 1780 when he delivered 36 steers for the use of the state {Ref: Archives of Maryland 45:156}; received a loan certificate for £170.6.11 due from the Council of Maryland "agreeable to the Act proposing to the Citizens of this State, Creditors of Congress on Loan Office Certificates, Etc." on 13 May 1783 for services rendered during the war {Ref: Archives of Maryland 48:412}

BARNES, WILLIAM (Charles County) received receipts from the Purchasing Agent for furnishing wheat on 3 May and 10 May 1783 {Ref: Maryland State Archives MdHR-6636-42-22}

BARNETT, RICHARD (Talbot County) received a loan certificate for £14.17.6 due from the Council of Maryland "agreeable to the Act proposing to the

Citizens of this State, Creditors of Congress on Loan Office Certificates, Etc." on 19 May 1783 for services rendered during the war {Ref: Archives of Maryland 48:417}

BARNETT, THOMAS (Talbot County) submitted an account and receipt for furnishing bacon and pork on 29 Jul 1778 {Ref: Maryland State Archives MdHR-6636-12-15}

BARNS, JOHN (Frederick County) received a certificate from the Purchasing Agent for furnishing wheat on 29 May 1781 {Ref: Maryland State Archives MdHR-6636-42-34}

BARNWELL, JAMES (Talbot County) received a receipt from the Purchasing Agent for purchasing bacon on 19 May 1778 {Ref: Maryland State Archives MdHR-6636-12-15}

BARR, ISAAC (Baltimore Town) received payment for furnishing linen on 18 Oct 1779 {Ref: Maryland State Archives MdHR-19970-3-8}

BARRETT, NING (Montgomery County) received a receipt from the Purchasing Agent for furnishing wheat on 3 Nov 1781 {Ref: Maryland State Archives MdHR-6636-24-14}

BARRICK, CHRISTIAN (Frederick County) received a receipt from the Purchasing Agent for furnishing pork on 8 Mar 1781 {Ref: Maryland State Archives MdHR-6636-23-4}; received a certificate for furnishing wheat on 30 May 1782 {Ref: Maryland State Archives MdHR-6636-42-34}

BARRICK, HANDEL (Frederick County) submitted an account for furnishing bacon on 29 May 1781 {Ref: Maryland State Archives MdHR-6636-23-6}

BARRICK, JACOB (Frederick County) submitted an account for furnishing hay on 28 Apr 1781 {Ref: Maryland State Archives MdHR-6636-23-5}; received a certificate from the Purchasing Agent for furnishing wheat on 29 May 1782 {Ref: Maryland State Archives MdHR-6636-42-34}

BARRICK, JOHN (Frederick County) received a receipt from the Purchasing Agent for furnishing hay on 16 Jan 1781 {Ref: Maryland State Archives MdHR-6636-23-2}; submitted an account for furnishing beef on 29 May 1781 {Ref: Maryland State Archives MdHR-6636-23-6}

BARRINGTON, RICHARD (Kent County) furnished flour for the use of the state as reported to the Council of Maryland on a "Return of Provisions, Etc., received at the Head of Elk" on 22 Jun 1781 {Ref: Archives of Maryland 47:409}

BARRON, THOMAS (Charles County) received a certificate for a loan to the state on 14 Jun 1780 {Ref: Maryland State Archives MdHR-6636-54-20}

BARROW, JAMES (Talbot County) was one of twenty-six people who contacted the Governor and Council of Maryland in 1781 and pledged to support and maintain at their own expense the Barge *Experiment* so it can patrol the bay between Kent Point and Tilghman's Island in order to protect them against the enemy, stating in part, "whereas from the present exhausted state of the public treasury the government cannot immediately give that protection to every individual which is become necessary from the cruel and savage mode in which the war is now carried on against us" {Ref: Archives of Maryland 47:584-585}

BARROW, SAMUEL (Talbot County) received a receipt from the Purchasing Agent for purchasing bacon on 6 Jun 1778 {Ref: Maryland State Archives MdHR-6636-12-15}

BARROW, THOMAS (Talbot County) submitted an account and receipt for transporting bacon on 6 Jun 1778 {Ref: Maryland State Archives MdHR-6636-12-15}; he was one of twenty-six people who contacted the Governor and Council of Maryland in 1781 and pledged to support and maintain at their own expense the Barge *Experiment* so it can patrol the bay between Kent Point and Tilghman's Island in order to protect them against the enemy, stating in part, "whereas from the present exhausted state of the public treasury the government cannot immediately give that protection to every individual which is become necessary from the cruel and savage mode in which the war is now carried on against us" {Ref: Archives of Maryland 47:584-585}

BARRY, BENJAMIN (Charles County) received a receipt from the Purchasing Agent for furnishing wheat on 2 Nov 1782 {Ref: Maryland State Archives MdHR-6636-42-19}

BARTH, ANDREW (Montgomery County) received a receipt from the Purchasing Agent for furnishing wheat on 4 May 1781 {Ref: Maryland State Archives MdHR-6636-24-18}

BARTLETT, DANIEL (Caroline County) received a receipt from the Purchasing Agent for furnishing wheat on 17 Aug 1782 {Ref: Maryland State Archives MdHR-6636-42-7}

BARTLETT (BARTLET), JAMES (Caroline County) received receipts from the Purchasing Agent for furnishing wheat on 1 Aug, 31 Aug and 20 Sep 1782 {Ref: Maryland State Archives MdHR-6636-42-7}

BARTON, JAMES (Caroline County) received a receipt from the Purchasing Agent for furnishing wheat on 5 Aug 1782 {Ref: Maryland State Archives MdHR-6636-42-7}

BARTON, JOSEPH (Prince George's County) received a receipt from the Purchasing Agent for furnishing wheat on 24 Feb 1783 {Ref: Maryland State Archives MdHR-6636-50-135}

BARWICK, EDWARD (Caroline County) received a receipt from the Purchasing Agent for furnishing wheat on 1 Sep 1782 {Ref: Maryland State Archives MdHR-6636-42-7}

BARWICK, JAMES (Caroline County) received a receipt from the Purchasing Agent for furnishing wheat on 4 Jul 1782 {Ref: Maryland State Archives MdHR-6636-42-7}

17

BARWICK, JOHN (Frederick County) received a certificate for money loaned to the state on 1 Jun 1780 {Ref: Maryland State Archives MdHR-6636-18-119B}

BARWICK, MARGARET (Caroline County) received a receipt from the Purchasing Agent for furnishing wheat on 17 Aug 1782 {Ref: Maryland State Archives MdHR-6636-42-7}

BAWNEL, ELIJAH (Charles County) received a receipt from the Purchasing Agent for furnishing wheat on 28 Dec 1782 {Ref: Maryland State Archives MdHR-6636-42-21}

BAXTER, JOSEPH (county not stated) received a loan certificate for £137.9.1 due from the Council of Maryland "agreeable to the Act proposing to the Citizens of this State, Creditors of Congress on Loan Office Certificates, Etc." on 10 Jun 1783 for services rendered during the war {Ref: Archives of Maryland 48:429}

BAYLEY, WILLIAM (Frederick County) received loan certificates for £41.0.2 and £89.4.1 due from the Council of Maryland "agreeable to the Act proposing to the Citizens of this State, Creditors of Congress on Loan Office Certificates, Etc." on 15 Aug and 17 Oct 1783 for services rendered during the war {Ref: Archives of Maryland 48:447, 48:469-470}

BAYLEY, WILLIAM JR. (Frederick County) pledged a loan in the amount of £100 to the State of Maryland under the Act for the Emission of Bills of Credit "to defray the expences of the present campaign" in June, 1781 {Ref: Archives of Maryland 47:327}

BAYNARD, LEVIN (Caroline County) received a receipt from the Purchasing Agent for furnishing wheat on 1 Sep 1782 {Ref: Maryland State Archives MdHR-6636-42-7}

BAYNARD, THOMAS (Caroline County) received a receipt from the Purchasing Agent for furnishing wheat on 1 Sep 1782 {Ref: Maryland State Archives MdHR-6636-42-7}

BEACH, JERE (Caroline County) received a receipt from the Purchasing Agent for furnishing wheat on 5 Aug 1782 {Ref: Maryland State Archives MdHR-6636-42-7}

BEAL, ELINER (Charles County) received a receipt from the Purchasing Agent for furnishing wheat on 15 Apr 1783 {Ref: Maryland State Archives MdHR-6636-42-22}

BEALE, ELEANOR (Charles County) received a receipt from the Purchasing Agent for furnishing wheat on 21 Dec 1781 {Ref: Maryland State Archives MdHR-6636-42-15}

BEALL, ALEXANDER (Montgomery County) received a receipt from the Purchasing Agent for furnishing wheat on 25 Apr 1781 {Ref: Maryland State Archives MdHR-6636-42-11}

BEALL, ANDREW (Prince George's County) received payment by order of the Council of Maryland for furnishing 65 cattle on 22 Oct 1777 and for recruiting services on 10 Mar 1778 {Ref: Archives of Maryland 16:401, 532}

BEALL, ARCHIBALD (Montgomery County) received a receipt from the Purchasing Agent for furnishing wheat on 1 Aug 1780 {Ref: Maryland State Archives MdHR-6636-43-7}

BEALL, BASIL (Frederick County) received a receipt from the Purchasing Agent for furnishing hay on 20 Nov 1780 {Ref: Maryland State Archives MdHR-6636-23-5}; received a receipt for furnishing beef on 28 Dec 1780 {Ref: Maryland State Archives MdHR-6636-23-1}; received a receipt for furnishing beef on 5 Jan 1781 {Ref: Maryland State Archives MdHR-6636-23-2}; received a receipt for furnishing beef on 18 Feb 1781 {Ref: Maryland State Archives MdHR-6636-23-3}

BEALL, BASIL (Montgomery County) received a receipt from the Purchasing Agent for furnishing wheat on 9 Jun 1781 {Ref: Maryland State Archives MdHR-6636-24-18}

BEALL, BROOKE (Montgomery County) was appointed Purchaser of Clothing in his county by the Council of Maryland on 5 Jun 1781 {Ref: Archives of Maryland 45:462}

BEALL, CHARLES (Frederick County) received a receipt from the Purchasing Agent for furnishing beef on 23 Dec 1780 {Ref: Maryland State Archives MdHR-6636-23-1}; received a receipt for furnishing hay on 5 Feb 1781 {Ref: Maryland State Archives MdHR-6636-23-3}; received a certificate for furnishing wheat on 14 Jun 1782 {Ref: Maryland State Archives MdHR-6636-50-91}

BEALL, JACOB (Baltimore County) received payment for furnishing beef on 11 Nov 1780 {Ref: Maryland State Archives MdHR-6636-43-38BBBBB}

BEALL, JAMES, OF JAMES (Montgomery County) received a receipt from the Purchasing Agent for furnishing wheat on 1 Aug 1780 {Ref: Maryland State Archives MdHR-6636-43-7}

BEALL, JOHN (Montgomery County) received a receipt from the Purchasing Agent for furnishing wheat on 26 Oct 1780 {Ref: Maryland State Archives MdHR-6636-24-8}; received a receipt for furnishing wheat on 25 Apr 1781 {Ref: Maryland State Archives MdHR-6636-42-11}; received a receipt for furnishing wheat on 5 Oct 1781 {Ref: Maryland State Archives MdHR-6636-24-15}; received a certificate of employment by the commissary of purchases on 10 Jun 1782 {Ref: Maryland State Archives MdHR-6636-50-91}

BEALL, JOHN (Prince George's County) received payment by order of the Council of Maryland for his use as Contractor for Horses in Prince George's County on 29 Aug 1780 {Ref: Archives of Maryland 43:270}

BEALL, JOHN (county not stated) received a loan certificate for £153.2.2 due from the Council of Maryland "agreeable to the Act proposing to the Citizens of this State, Creditors of Congress on Loan Office Certificates, Etc." on 17 Oct

1783 for services rendered during the war {Ref: Archives of Maryland 48:470}

BEALL, JOS'A. (Prince George's County) served as county lieutenant and was listed in possession of powder, lead, and shot "at my own house" on a "Return of Armes and Ammunition in Prince George's County Belonging to the Publick" on 3 Jul 1780 {Ref: Archives of Maryland 45:4}

BEALL, JOSEPH (Montgomery County) received a receipt from the Purchasing Agent for furnishing wheat on 26 Sep 1780 {Ref: Maryland State Archives MdHR-6636-24-13}

BEALL, JOSEPH (Somerset County) received receipts from the Purchasing Agent for furnishing beef on 6 Nov and 6 Dec 1781 {Ref: Maryland State Archives MdHR-6636-24-44}

BEALL, JOSIAS (Prince George's County) received a loan certificate for £150.4.5 due from the Council of Maryland "agreeable to the Act proposing to the Citizens of this State, Creditors of Congress on Loan Office Certificates, Etc." on 17 Oct 1783 for services rendered during the war {Ref: Archives of Maryland 48:470}

BEALL, ROBERT (Montgomery County) received a receipt from the Purchasing Agent for furnishing wheat on 12 Dec 1780 {Ref: Maryland State Archives MdHR-6636-24-8}; received a receipt for furnishing wheat on 26 May 1781 {Ref: Maryland State Archives MdHR-6636-24-18}

BEALL, SAMUEL (Montgomery County) received a receipt from the Purchasing Agent for furnishing wheat on 29 Jul 1780 {Ref: Maryland State Archives MdHR-6636-24-5}; received a receipt for furnishing wheat on 1 Aug 1780 {Ref: Maryland State Archives MdHR-6636-43-7}

BEALL, THOMAS (Prince George's County) received a receipt from the Purchasing Agent for furnishing corn on 3 Jul 1780 {Ref: Maryland State Archives MdHR-6636-19-79F}; received a receipt for furnishing corn on 12 Jul 1780 {Ref: Maryland State Archives MdHR-6636-19-79B}

BEALL, WILLIAM (Frederick County) received a certificate from the Purchasing Agent for furnishing wheat on 11 Feb 1783 {Ref: Maryland State Archives MdHR-6636-42-38}

BEALL, ZACHARIAH (Montgomery County) received a receipt from the Purchasing Agent for furnishing wheat on 1 Aug 1780 {Ref: Maryland State Archives MdHR-6636-43-7}; received a receipt for furnishing wheat on 3 Aug 1780 {Ref: Maryland State Archives MdHR-6636-24-13}

BEALT, HIGASON OR HIGGINSON (Montgomery County) received receipts from the Purchasing Agent for furnishing wheat on 28 Apr and 4 May 1781 {Ref: Maryland State Archives MdHR-6636-42-11}

BEAN, JOSIAH (Montgomery County) received a certificate of employment by the commissary of purchases on 24 Apr 1782 {Ref: Maryland State Archives MdHR-6636-50-91}

BEANE, BENJAMIN (Montgomery County) received a receipt from the Purchasing Agent for furnishing wheat on 3 Aug 1781 {Ref: Maryland State Archives MdHR-6636-24-18}

BEANS, WILLIAM (Charles County) was a doctor who was appointed by the Council of Maryland to serve as a "Surgeon to the Maryland Marching Militia" on 4 Sep 1777 {Ref: Archives of Maryland 16:362}

BEAR, GEORGE (Frederick County) received payment by order of the Council of Safety for the hire of himself and his wagon on 28 Mar 1778 {Ref: Archives of Maryland 16:556}; received a certificate for money loaned to the state on 1 Jun 1780 {Ref: Maryland State Archives MdHR-6636-18-119C}

BEARD, JOHN (Prince George's County) received receipts from the Purchasing Agent for furnishing wheat on 25 Apr 1782, 4 Sep 1782 and 5 Sep 1783 {Ref: Maryland State Archives MdHR-6636-50-135}

BEARD, PAUL (Frederick County) received a receipt from the Purchasing Agent for furnishing wheat on 16 May 1782 {Ref: Maryland State Archives MdHR-6636-42-34}

BEARD, RICHARD JR. (Anne Arundel County) was given permission by the Council of Maryland on 14 Dec 1782 "to go into New York by Dobb's Ferry to carry his Son Necessaries who is a Prisoner" {Ref: Archives of Maryland 48:322}

BEASLEY, JOHN (Kent County) received payment for furnishing bacon on 21 Jul 1780 {Ref: Maryland State Archives MdHR-6636-23-49}; received payment from the Purchasing Agent for furnishing cattle for the public use in September, 1781 {Ref: Maryland State Archives MdHR-6636-43-3}

BEATTY, CHARLES (Frederick County) received payment by order of the Council of Maryland for beef cattle purchased for the militia on 25 Sep 1777 {Ref: Archives of Maryland 16:385}

BEATTY, ELIJAH (Frederick County) received a loan certificate for £226.5.2 due from the Council of Maryland "agreeable to the Act proposing to the Citizens of this State, Creditors of Congress on Loan Office Certificates, Etc." on 19 May 1783 for services rendered during the war {Ref: Archives of Maryland 48:417}

BEATTY, JAMES (Frederick County) received a certificate for money loaned to the state on 1 Jun 1780 {Ref: Maryland State Archives MdHR-6636-18-119A}

BEATTY, JOHN (Frederick County) received a loan certificate for £67.17.0 due from the Council of Maryland "agreeable to the Act proposing to the Citizens of this State, Creditors of Congress on Loan Office Certificates, Etc." on 19 May 1783 for services rendered during the war {Ref: Archives of Maryland 48:417}

BEATTY, THOMAS (Frederick County) received certificates from the Purchasing Agent for furnishing wheat, rye and corn on 26 Jan on 9 Feb on 11 Feb on 12

Feb on 9 Apr on 10 Apr and 26 Sep 1780 {Ref: Maryland State Archives MdHR-6636-42-29}; received a receipt for wheat and corn on 24 Feb 1780 {Ref: Maryland State Archives MdHR-19970-19-23&24}; delivered flour, Indian corn and rye to the commissary at Baltimore Town for the use of the State of Maryland in the summer of 1780 {Ref: Archives of Maryland 45:84}; pledged a loan in the amount of £800 to the State of Maryland under the Act for the Emission of Bills of Credit "to defray the expences of the present campaign" in June, 1781 {Ref: Archives of Maryland 47:327}; served as sheriff and submitted his account and receipt "for conveying mail for the State" on 23 May 1782 {Ref: Maryland State Archives MdHR-6636-40-66}

BEATTY, WILLIAM (Frederick County) was appointed by the Council of Maryland on 25 Mar 1778 as one of eighteen men to be "Agents for Purchasing Provisions for the Army of the United States Agreeable to an Act of Assembly passed the 23rd Inst." {Ref: Archives of Maryland 16:551}; received a receipt for furnishing beef on 19 Jan 1781 {Ref: Maryland State Archives MdHR-6636-23-2}

BEAUCHAMP (BEACHAMP), ANN (Caroline County) received a receipt from the Purchasing Agent for furnishing wheat on 22 Aug 1782 {Ref: Maryland State Archives MdHR-6636-42-7}

BEAUCHAMP, JOHN (Caroline County) received a receipt from the Purchasing Agent for furnishing wheat on 11 Jun and 12 Jun 1782 {Ref: Maryland State Archives MdHR-6636-42-7}

BEAVENS, THOMAS (Worcester County) received payment for furnishing pork on 4 Jan 1781 {Ref: Maryland State Archives MdHR-43-28KKKK}

BEAVIN, BENJAMIN (Charles County) received a receipt from the Purchasing Agent for furnishing wheat on 20 Dec 1782 {Ref: Maryland State Archives MdHR-6636-42-20}

BECK, AQUILA (Caroline County) received a receipt from the Purchasing Agent for furnishing wheat on 1 Sep 1782 {Ref: Maryland State Archives MdHR-6636-42-7}

BECK, ALEXANDER (Kent County) received certificates from the Purchasing Agent for furnishing wheat on 18 Jan and 19 Jan 1780 {Ref: Maryland State Archives MdHR-6636-23-42}

BECK, SAMUEL (Kent County) received a certificate from the Purchasing Agent for furnishing wheat on 10 Mar 1780 {Ref: Maryland State Archives MdHR-6636-23-45}

BECKETT, WILLIAM (Frederick County) received a certificate from the Purchasing Agent for furnishing flour on 21 Aug 1781 {Ref: Maryland State Archives MdHR-6636-23-28}

BECKWITH (BECKWORTH), JOHN (Montgomery County) received a receipt from the Purchasing Agent for furnishing wheat on 29 Jul 1780 {Ref: Maryland

State Archives MdHR-6636-24-5}; received a receipt for furnishing wheat on 1 Aug 1780 {Ref: Maryland State Archives MdHR-6636-43-7}; received a receipt for furnishing wheat on 22 May 1781 {Ref: Maryland State Archives MdHR-6636-42-11}; received a receipt for furnishing wheat on 7 Oct 1781 {Ref: Maryland State Archives MdHR-6636-24-15}

BECKWITH (BECKWORTH), VOLINDER OR VOLENDAR (Montgomery County) received a receipt from the Purchasing Agent for furnishing wheat on 29 Jul 1780 {Ref: Maryland State Archives MdHR-6636-24-5}; received a receipt for furnishing wheat on 1 Aug 1780 {Ref: Maryland State Archives MdHR-6636-43-7}; received a receipt for furnishing wheat on 4 Oct 1781 {Ref: Maryland State Archives MdHR-6636-42-11}

BECRAFT, BENJAMIN (Montgomery County) received a certificate of employment by the commissary of purchases on 31 May 1782 {Ref: Maryland State Archives MdHR-6636-50-91}

BECRAFT, CHARLES PETER (Montgomery County) received a receipt from the Purchasing Agent for furnishing wheat on 10 Oct 1780 {Ref: Maryland State Archives MdHR-6636-24-8}

BECRAFT, PETER (Montgomery County) received a receipt from the Purchasing Agent for furnishing wheat on 8 Aug 1780 {Ref: Maryland State Archives MdHR-6636-24-6}; received a receipt for furnishing wheat on 1 Aug 1780 {Ref: Maryland State Archives MdHR-6636-43-7}

BEEDEN, JOHN, see "John Murdock," q.v.

BEEDING, JOSEPH (Montgomery County) received a receipt from the Purchasing Agent for shelling corn on 15 May 1780 {Ref: Maryland State Archives MdHR-6636-24-2}

BEEMER, ADAM (Frederick County) received a receipt from the Purchasing Agent for furnishing wheat on 29 May 1782 {Ref: Maryland State Archives MdHR-6636-42-34}

BEETLE, JOHN (Cecil County) furnished corn on 3 Apr 1781 for the use of the State of Maryland {Ref: Archives of Maryland 47:250}

BEGGARLY, BENJAMIN (Montgomery County) received receipts from the Purchasing Agent for furnishing wheat on 5 Oct and 3 Nov 1780 {Ref: Maryland State Archives MdHR-6636-24-8}

BELL, BASIL (Charles County) received a receipt from the Purchasing Agent for furnishing wheat on 29 Dec 1782 {Ref: Maryland State Archives MdHR-6636-42-21}

BELL, NINGEL (Montgomery County) received a receipt from the Purchasing Agent for furnishing wheat on 16 May 1781 {Ref: Maryland State Archives MdHR-6636-24-18}

BELL, WILLIAM (Somerset County) received a receipt from the Purchasing Agent for furnishing bacon on 9 Aug 1780 {Ref: Maryland State Archives

MdHR-6636-24-41}
BELL, WILLIAM SR. (Caroline County) received a receipt from the Purchasing Agent for furnishing wheat on 17 Aug 1782 {Ref: Maryland State Archives MdHR-6636-42-7}
BELT, CARLTON (Prince George's County) received a receipt from the Purchasing Agent for furnishing wheat on 1 May 1783 {Ref: Maryland State Archives MdHR-6636-50-142}; received receipts from the Purchasing Agent for furnishing wheat on 8 Jun 1782 and 15 Aug 1783 {Ref: Maryland State Archives MdHR-6636-50-135}
BELT, HIGGINSON JR. (Prince George's County) received a receipt from the Purchasing Agent for furnishing wheat on 6 Aug 1783 {Ref: Maryland State Archives MdHR-6636-50-142}
BELT, HIGGINSON (Prince George's County) received a receipt from the Purchasing Agent for furnishing wheat on 6 Aug 1783 {Ref: Maryland State Archives MdHR-6636-50-135}
BELT, JEREMIAH (Frederick County) received a certificate from the Purchasing Agent for furnishing wheat on 27 May 1782 {Ref: Maryland State Archives MdHR-6636-42-35}
BELT, LEONARD (Montgomery County) received a receipt from the Purchasing Agent for furnishing wheat on 25 Jul 1780 {Ref: Maryland State Archives MdHR-6636-24-5}; received a receipt for furnishing wheat on 1 Aug 1780 {Ref: Maryland State Archives MdHR-6636-43-7}; received a receipt for furnishing wheat on 5 Aug 1780 {Ref: Maryland State Archives MdHR-6636-24-6}; received a receipt for furnishing wheat on 14 Sep 1780 {Ref: Maryland State Archives MdHR-6636-24-7}; received a receipt for furnishing wheat on 6 Feb 1781 {Ref: Maryland State Archives MdHR-6636-24-9}
BELT, THOMAS (Montgomery County) received a receipt from the Purchasing Agent for furnishing wheat on 13 Dec 1780 {Ref: Maryland State Archives MdHR-6636-24-8}
BELWOOD (BALWOOD), WILLIAM (Annapolis) received payments by order of the Council of Safety for the hire of his boat on 15 Aug and 29 Aug 1776 and for boatage on 3 Sep 1776 {Ref: Archives of Maryland 12:205, 247, 255}; received payment for the hire of his boat for the Flying Camp on 23 Aug 1776 {Ref: Archives of Maryland 12:233}
BENDEN, THOMAS (Caroline County) received a receipt from the Purchasing Agent for furnishing wheat on 22 Aug 1782 {Ref: Maryland State Archives MdHR-6636-42-7}
BENNETT, JAMES (Somerset County) received payment by order of the Council of Maryland "of the New Emission of this State to be delivered over to Henry Jackson, Commissary for Somerset County" on 4 Oct 1780 {Ref: Archives of Maryland 43:312}

BENNETT, JOHN (Prince George's County) received a receipt from the Purchasing Agent for furnishing wheat on 20 May 1782 {Ref: Maryland State Archives MdHR-6636-50-135}

BENNETT, RICHARD (Prince George's County) received a receipt from the Purchasing Agent for furnishing wheat on 24 May 1782 {Ref: Maryland State Archives MdHR-6636-50-135}

BENNITT, JOHN (Frederick County) received a receipt from the Purchasing Agent for furnishing pork and meal on 6 Apr 1781 {Ref: Maryland State Archives MdHR-6636-23-5}

BENNY, BENJAMIN (Talbot County) received a receipt from the Purchasing Agent for furnishing wheat on 9 Oct 1780 {Ref: Maryland State Archives MdHR-6636-24-47}

BENSON, BENJAMIN (Charles County) received a receipt from the Purchasing Agent for furnishing wheat on 20 Dec 1782 {Ref: Maryland State Archives MdHR-6636-42-20}

BENSON, T.? (Talbot County) was one of twenty-six people who contacted the Governor and Council of Maryland in 1781 and pledged to support and maintain at their own expense the Barge *Experiment* so it can patrol the bay between Kent Point and Tilghman's Island in order to protect them against the enemy, stating in part, "whereas from the present exhausted state of the public treasury the government cannot immediately give that protection to every individual which is become necessary from the cruel and savage mode in which the war is now carried on against us" {Ref: Archives of Maryland 47:584-585}

BENSON, WILLIAM (Montgomery County) received a receipt from the Purchasing Agent for furnishing wheat on 28 May 1781 {Ref: Maryland State Archives MdHR-6636-42-11}

BENSON, WILLIAM (Frederick County) received a receipt from the Purchasing Agent for furnishing corn and rye on 27 Jun 1780 {Ref: Maryland State Archives MdHR-6636-24-1}

BENSON, WILLIAM THOMAS (Montgomery County) received a receipt from the Purchasing Agent for furnishing wheat on 10 Apr 1781 {Ref: Maryland State Archives MdHR-6636-42-11}

BENTON, JOSEPH (Prince George's County) received a receipt from the Purchasing Agent for furnishing wheat in 1783 {Ref: Maryland State Archives MdHR-6636-50-135}

BENTON, JOSEPH (Montgomery County) received a receipt from the Purchasing Agent for furnishing wheat on 30 Aug 1780 {Ref: Maryland State Archives MdHR-6636-24-6}

BENTON, WILLIAM (Montgomery County) received a receipt from the Purchasing Agent for furnishing wheat on 30 Aug 1780 {Ref: Maryland State Archives MdHR-6636-24-6}

BERRY, BENJAMIN (Charles County) received a receipt from the Purchasing Agent for furnishing wheat on 9 May 1783 {Ref: Maryland State Archives MdHR-6636-42-22}

BERRY, JOHN (Montgomery County) received a receipt from the Purchasing Agent for furnishing wheat on 1 Aug 1780 {Ref: Maryland State Archives MdHR-6636-43-7}; received receipts from the Purchasing Agent for furnishing wheat on 4 Aug and 9 Aug 1780 {Ref: Maryland State Archives MdHR-6636-24-6}

BERRY, JOHN (Annapolis) received payment from the Council of Maryland "for riding expresses" on 30 May 1782 {Ref: Archives of Maryland 48:178}

BERRY, PRYOR, see "John Halkerston," q.v.

BERRY, RICHARD (Montgomery County) served the Maryland Council of Safety by 30 Aug 1776 when they "ordered and granted him permission to procure coal from Virginia for the use of this state" {Ref: Archives of Maryland 12:248}; received a receipt from the Purchasing Agent for furnishing wheat on 16 Sep 1780 {Ref: Maryland State Archives MdHR-6636-24-7}

BERRYMAN, JOHN (Baltimore Town) received payment by order of the Council of Maryland "for taking care of the state ship *Defence*" on 30 May 1778 {Ref: Archives of Maryland 21:116}

BESWICKS, GEORGE (Talbot County) submitted an account and receipt for hauling and purchasing bacon on 16 Jun 1778 {Ref: Maryland State Archives MdHR-6636-12-15}

BETHARD, JARMAN (Worcester County) submitted an account and receipt for hauling salt on 3 Mar 1782 {Ref: Maryland State Archives MdHR-6636-43-28ZZ}

BETS, ROBERT (Worcester County) received payment for furnishing beef on 20 Sep 1781 {Ref: Maryland State Archives MdHR-6636-43-28WWW}

BETTS, JOHN (Baltimore County) received a receipt from the Purchasing Agent for furnishing pork and beef on 8 May 1780 {Ref: Maryland State Archives MdHR-6636-40-46C}

BEVAN, CHARLES (Harford County) received a receipt from the Purchasing Agent for furnishing wheat on 24 Mar 1780 {Ref: Maryland State Archives MdHR-6636-17-116}

BIDDELL, GILBERT (Worcester County) submitted an account and receipt for collecting cattle on 30 Sep 1781 {Ref: Maryland State Archives MdHR-6636-43-27}

BIDDLE, JOHN (Cecil County) received receipts from the Purchasing Agent for furnishing wheat on 19 Aug, 24 Aug and 4 Sep 1782 and for furnishing flour on 30 Nov 1782 and 3 Apr, 5 Apr and 9 Apr 1783 {Ref: Maryland State Archives MdHR-6636-42-9}

BIGG, JOHN (Montgomery County) received a receipt from the Purchasing Agent for furnishing wheat on 23 Sep 1780 {Ref: Maryland State Archives MdHR-6636-24-7}

BIGGS, JOHN (Montgomery County) received a receipt from the Purchasing Agent for furnishing wheat on 9 Sep 1780 {Ref: Maryland State Archives MdHR-6636-24-7}

BILLINGSLY, JOHN (St. Mary's County) received payment from the Purchasing Agent on 2 Jan 1782 for feeding corn and fodder to 106 head of public cattle for 3 days and nights {Ref: Maryland State Archives MdHR-6636-43-23}

BIRD, BENJAMIN (Somerset County) received a loan certificate for £18.18.3 due from the Council of Maryland "agreeable to the Act proposing to the Citizens of this State, Creditors of Congress on Loan Office Certificates, Etc." on 7 Nov 1783 for services rendered during the war {Ref: Archives of Maryland 48:478}

BIRDWHISTLE (BIRDWHISTELL), THOMAS (Montgomery County) received a receipt from the Purchasing Agent for furnishing wheat on 18 Oct 1781 {Ref: Maryland State Archives MdHR-6636-42-11}; received a receipt for furnishing wheat on 21 Oct 1781 {Ref: Maryland State Archives MdHR-6636-24-15}

BIRELY, LODWICK (Frederick County) received a certificate from the Purchasing Agent for furnishing wheat on 30 May 1782 {Ref: Maryland State Archives MdHR-6636-42-35}

BIRELY, MICHAEL (Frederick County) received a certificate from the Purchasing Agent for furnishing wheat on 30 May 1782 {Ref: Maryland State Archives MdHR-6636-42-35}

BIRKHEAD, CHRISTOPHER (Anne Arundel County) received a loan certificate for £116.9.5 due from the Council of Maryland "agreeable to the Act proposing to the Citizens of this State, Creditors of Congress on Loan Office Certificates, Etc." on 29 Apr 1783 for services rendered during the war {Ref: Archives of Maryland 48:403-404}; also see "John Chever," q.v.

BIRNIE, HUGH (Baltimore County) submitted an account and received payment for furnishing barrels and hoops on 22 Jan 1780 {Ref: Maryland Historical Society MS.1814, Box 6}

BISER, JACOB (Frederick County) received a certificate from the Purchasing Agent for furnishing wheat on 9 Jan 1781 {Ref: Maryland State Archives MdHR-6636-42-32}

BISHOP, HENRY (Frederick County) received a receipt from the Purchasing Agent for furnishing wheat on 16 May 1782 {Ref: Maryland State Archives MdHR-6636-42-34}

BISHOP, JACOB (Anne Arundel County) received a receipt from the Purchasing Agent for furnishing powder on 16 Apr 1777 {Ref: Maryland State Archives MdHR-6636-9-14A}

BISHOP, MARY ANN (Caroline County) received a receipt from the Purchasing Agent for furnishing wheat on 1 Sep 1782 {Ref: Maryland State Archives

MdHR-6636-42-7}

BISHOP, WILLIAM (Worcester County) was a doctor who received a receipt in payment for furnishing beef on 10 Oct 1781 {Ref: Maryland State Archives MdHR-6636-43-28LLL}

BISSETT, THOMAS (Baltimore County) received payment by order of the Council of Maryland for providing waggonage on 28 Mar 1778 {Ref: Archives of Maryland 16:557}

BIVEN, BENJAMIN (Charles County) received a receipt from the Purchasing Agent for furnishing wheat on 2 Nov 1782 {Ref: Maryland State Archives MdHR-6636-42-19}

BLACK, ADAM (Frederick County) received a receipt from the Purchasing Agent for furnishing wheat on 16 May 1782 {Ref: Maryland State Archives MdHR-6636-42-34}

BLACK & McCONNELL (county not stated) received payment by order of the Council of Safety for furnishing clothing for the troops on 17 Apr 1776 {Ref: Archives of Maryland 11:336}

BLACKLOCK, RICHARD (Montgomery County) received a receipt from the Purchasing Agent for furnishing wheat on 1 Aug 1780 {Ref: Maryland State Archives MdHR-6636-43-7}

BLACKMORE, SAMUEL (Montgomery County) received a receipt from the Purchasing Agent for hauling corn on 30 Dec 1780 {Ref: Maryland State Archives MdHR-6636-24-2}

BLACKMORE, WILLIAM (Montgomery County) received a receipt from the Purchasing Agent for shelling corn on 17 Jul 1780 {Ref: Maryland State Archives MdHR-6636-24-2}

BLADES, JAMES (Caroline County) received receipts from the Purchasing Agent for furnishing wheat on 17 Aug 1782 {Ref: Maryland State Archives MdHR-6636-42-7}

BLAINE, DUNCAN (Somerset County) received a receipt from the Purchasing Agent for furnishing bacon on 12 Aug 1780 {Ref: Maryland State Archives MdHR-6636-24-41}

BLAIR, CHARLES (Baltimore County) received payment for furnishing beef on 1 May 1781 {Ref: Maryland State Archives MdHR-6636-43-38BBB}; received payment for furnishing beef on 13 Jun 1781 {Ref: Maryland State Archives MdHR-6636-43-38FF}

BLAISE, DAVID (Montgomery County) received a receipt from the Purchasing Agent for furnishing wheat on 21 Apr 1781 {Ref: Maryland State Archives MdHR-6636-24-14}

BLAISE, WILLIAM (Montgomery County) received a receipt from the Purchasing Agent for furnishing wheat on 21 Apr 1781 {Ref: Maryland State Archives MdHR-6636-24-14}

BLAKE, CHARLES (Queen Anne's County) received a certificate from the Purchasing Agent for furnishing corn on 4 Jan 1780 {Ref: Maryland State Archives MdHR-6636-24-33}; received certificates for furnishing wheat on 26 Jan and 24 Feb 1780 {Ref: Maryland State Archives MdHR-6636-24-28, MdHR-6636-24-32}; appointed Commissary of Purchases for Queen Anne's County by the Council of Maryland on 18 Jul 1780 {Ref: Archives of Maryland 43:223, 475}; appointed Purchaser of Clothing in his county by the Council of Maryland on 5 Jun 1781 {Ref: Archives of Maryland 45:462}; received a receipt for furnishing beef on 28 Dec 1781 {Ref: Maryland State Archives MdHR-6636-43-37K}; certification of wheat received in 1782 {Ref: Maryland State Archives MdHR-6636-43-11}; received a certificate for furnishing flour on 15 Apr 1782 {Ref: Maryland State Archives MdHR-6636-43-37}; received a loan certificate for £36.10.9 due from the Council of Maryland "agreeable to the Act proposing to the Citizens of this State, Creditors of Congress on Loan Office Certificates, Etc." on 26 Jun 1783 for services rendered during the war {Ref: Archives of Maryland 48:435}; also see "Conrad T. Wederstrandt," q.v.

BLAKE, HENRIETTA (Queen Anne's County) received a loan certificate for £33.8.9 due from the Council of Maryland "agreeable to the Act proposing to the Citizens of this State, Creditors of Congress on Loan Office Certificates, Etc." on 26 Jun 1783 for services rendered during the war {Ref: Archives of Maryland 48:435}

BLAKE, JOSEPH JR. (Calvert County) received payment for services rendered on 5 Feb 1782 {Ref: Maryland State Archives MdHR-6636-50-37}

BLAKE, LEVIN (Worcester County) submitted an account and receipt for expenses while collecting cattle from 9 Oct to 6 Nov 1781 {Ref: Maryland State Archives MdHR-6636-43-27}

BLAKE, NED (Worcester County) submitted an account and receipt for butchering beef on 15 Oct 1781 {Ref: Maryland State Archives MdHR-6636-43-27}

BLAKEWAY, JOHN (Kent County) submitted an account and receipt for hauling flour in 1781 {Ref: Maryland State Archives MdHR-6636-43-5}

BLAND, JOSEPH (Caroline County) received a receipt from the Purchasing Agent for furnishing wheat on 17 Aug 1782 {Ref: Maryland State Archives MdHR-6636-42-7}

BLUNT, BENJAMIN (Caroline County) received a receipt from the Purchasing Agent for furnishing wheat on 31 Aug 1782 {Ref: Maryland State Archives MdHR-6636-42-7}

BLUNT, SAMUEL (Queen Anne's County) submitted an account and receipt for storing wheat in 1782 {Ref: Maryland State Archives MdHR-6636-43-12}

BOARMAN, RALPH (Charles County) received a receipt from the Purchasing Agent for furnishing wheat on 11 Apr 1782 {Ref: Maryland State Archives

MdHR-6636-42-18}

BOGHMAN, ANDREW (Frederick County) received a receipt from the Purchasing Agent for delivering flour on 15 Feb 1781 {Ref: Maryland State Archives MdHR-6636-23-30}

BOKEY, MATTHIAS (Frederick County) received a certificate from the Purchasing Agent for furnishing wheat on 31 Jul 1782 {Ref: Maryland State Archives MdHR-6636-42-36}

BOLT, THOMAS (county not stated) received a loan certificate for £40.17.1 due from the Council of Maryland "agreeable to the Act proposing to the Citizens of this State, Creditors of Congress on Loan Office Certificates, Etc." on 8 Nov 1783 for services rendered during the war {Ref: Archives of Maryland 48:479}

BOLTON, JOHN (Baltimore County) received a loan certificate for £169.0.6 due from the Council of Maryland "agreeable to the Act proposing to the Citizens of this State, Creditors of Congress on Loan Office Certificates, Etc." on 8 Dec 1783 for services rendered during the war {Ref: Archives of Maryland 48:486}

BOLTON, WILLIAM (Baltimore County) submitted an account and received payment for stowing flour on 23 Mar 1780 {Ref: Maryland Historical Society MS.1814, Box 6}

BOLTZ, CONRAD (Frederick County) submitted an account for furnishing beef on 29 May 1781 {Ref: Maryland State Archives MdHR-6636-23-6}

BOMAN, JACOB (Montgomery County) received a receipt from the Purchasing Agent for furnishing wheat on 29 May 1781 {Ref: Maryland State Archives MdHR-6636-24-15}

BOND, BENJAMIN (Harford County) received a loan certificate for £24.11.5 due from the Council of Maryland "agreeable to the Act proposing to the Citizens of this State, Creditors of Congress on Loan Office Certificates, Etc." on 23 Oct 1783 for services rendered during the war {Ref: Archives of Maryland 48:472}

BOND, JACOB (Harford County) received payment by order of the Council of Safety for furnishing a blunderbuss on 28 Aug 1776 {Ref: Archives of Maryland 12:245}

BOND, RICHARD (Cecil County) received a certificate from the Purchasing Agent for the hire of his wagon on 10 May 1780 {Ref: Maryland State Archives MdHR-6636-23-22}

BOND, WILLIAM, OF JOSHUA (Harford County) was appointed by the Council of Maryland on 25 Mar 1778 as one of eighteen men to be "Agents for Purchasing Provisions for the Army of the United States Agreeable to an Act of Assembly passed the 23rd Inst." {Ref: Archives of Maryland 16:551}

BONHAM, ABSOLOM (Frederick County) submitted an account for boarding services on 3 Apr 1777 {Ref: Maryland State Archives MdHR-19970-2-4}

BONIFANT, JAMES (Prince George's County) received a receipt from the Purchasing Agent for furnishing wheat on 10 May 1783 {Ref: Maryland State

Archives MdHR-6636-43-9}

BONIFIELD, SAMUEL (Montgomery County) received a receipt from the Purchasing Agent for furnishing wheat on 1 Aug 1780 {Ref: Maryland State Archives MdHR-6636-43-7}

BONN, CHARLES (Montgomery County) received a receipt from the Purchasing Agent for furnishing wheat on 14 Nov 1781 {Ref: Maryland State Archives MdHR-6636-24-15}

BONWELL, GEORGE (Dorchester County) was a miller who submitted an account of wheat availability at his mill on 21 Apr 1781 {Ref: Maryland State Archives MdHR-6636-43-15}; received receipts from the Purchasing Agent for furnishing wheat on 1 Oct and 1 Nov 1782 {Ref: Maryland State Archives MdHR-6636-42-23}

BOOGHER, BARTHOLOMEW (Frederick County) received a certificate from the Purchasing Agent for furnishing wheat on 11 Jun 1782 {Ref: Maryland State Archives MdHR-6636-42-35}

BOOGHER, JOHN (Frederick County) received a certificate from the Purchasing Agent for furnishing wheat on 18 May 1782 {Ref: Maryland State Archives MdHR-6636-42-33}

BOON, FOSTER (Caroline County) received a receipt from the Purchasing Agent for furnishing wheat on 20 Sep 1782 {Ref: Maryland State Archives MdHR-6636-42-7}

BOON, ISAAC (Caroline County) received receipts from the Purchasing Agent for furnishing wheat on 17 Aug and 1 Sep 1782 {Ref: Maryland State Archives MdHR-6636-42-7}

BOON, JAMES (Caroline County) received a receipt from the Purchasing Agent for furnishing wheat on 1 Sep 1782 {Ref: Maryland State Archives MdHR-6636-42-7}

BOON, JOHN (Caroline County) received a receipt from the Purchasing Agent for furnishing wheat on 1 Sep 1782 {Ref: Maryland State Archives MdHR-6636-42-7}

BOON, JOSEPH (Caroline County) received a receipt from the Purchasing Agent for furnishing wheat on 31 Aug 1782 {Ref: Maryland State Archives MdHR-6636-42-7}

BOON, LETAETIA (Caroline County) received a receipt from the Purchasing Agent for furnishing wheat on 1 Sep 1782 {Ref: Maryland State Archives MdHR-6636-42-7}

BOON, MOSES (Caroline County) received a receipt from the Purchasing Agent for furnishing wheat on 1 Sep 1782 {Ref: Maryland State Archives MdHR-6636-42-7}

BOON, THOMAS (Caroline County) received a receipt from the Purchasing Agent for furnishing wheat on 31 Aug 1782 {Ref: Maryland State Archives

MdHR-6636-42-7}
BOON, WILLIAM (Caroline County) received a receipt from the Purchasing Agent for furnishing wheat on 31 Aug 1782 {Ref: Maryland State Archives MdHR-6636-42-7}
BOON, WILLIAM (Caroline County) was a joiner (carpenter) who received a receipt from the Purchasing Agent for furnishing wheat on 20 Sep 1782 {Ref: Maryland State Archives MdHR-6636-42-7}
BOONE, SAMUEL (Frederick County) received a receipt from the Purchasing Agent for hauling flour on 17 Feb 1783 {Ref: Maryland State Archives MdHR-6636-42-28}
BOOTH, JONATHAN (Cecil County) received a receipt from the Purchasing Agent for furnishing wheat on 15 Aug 1782 {Ref: Maryland State Archives MdHR-6636-42-9}
BOOTH, ROBERT (Frederick County) received a receipt from the Purchasing Agent for furnishing whiskey on 3 Feb 1781 {Ref: Maryland State Archives MdHR-6636-23-3}
BORDLEY, JAMES (Queen Anne's County) received a certificate from the Purchasing Agent for furnishing corn on 17 Jan 1780 {Ref: Maryland State Archives MdHR-6636-24-30}; received a receipt for furnishing bacon on 7 Apr 1781 {Ref: Maryland State Archives MdHR-6636-24-34}
BORDLEY, JOHN BEALL (Talbot County) received a receipt from the Purchasing Agent for furnishing a cow on 1 Apr 1778 {Ref: Maryland State Archives MdHR-4587-41}; received a receipt for furnishing wheat on 14 Oct 1780 {Ref: Maryland State Archives MdHR-6636-24-49}
BORDLEY, WILLIAM (Kent County) received a certificate from the Purchasing Agent for furnishing wheat on 26 Jan 1780 {Ref: Maryland State Archives MdHR-6636-43-1}; received a certificate for furnishing flour on 14 Apr 1780 {Ref: Maryland State Archives MdHR-6636-23-45}
BORDLEY, WILLIAM (Talbot County) received a receipt from the Purchasing Agent for furnishing wheat on 7 Oct 1780 {Ref: Maryland State Archives MdHR-6636-24-47}
BORK, PARKET (Annapolis) received payment by order of the Council of Safety "for his cart, horses, etc. with artillery baggage" on 10 Jan 1778 {Ref: Archives of Maryland 16:465}
BORMAN, ADAM (Frederick County) submitted an account for hauling flour on 20 Mar 1781 {Ref: Maryland State Archives MdHR-6636-23-8}
BOSMAN, EDWARD (Baltimore County) received a certificate from the Purchasing Agent for furnishing flour on 9 Jan 1780 {Ref: Maryland State Archives MdHR-6636-23-15}
BOSSEL, JOHN (Charles County) received a receipt from the Purchasing Agent for furnishing wheat on 2 Nov 1782 {Ref: Maryland State Archives MdHR-

6636-42-19}

BOSWELL, MATTHEW (Charles County) received a receipt from the Purchasing Agent for furnishing wheat on 20 Dec 1782 {Ref: Maryland State Archives MdHR-6636-42-20}

BOSWELL, WALTER (Charles County) received a receipt from the Purchasing Agent for furnishing wheat on 28 Sep 1782 {Ref: Maryland State Archives MdHR-6636-42-19}; received a receipt for furnishing wheat on 20 Dec 1782 {Ref: Maryland State Archives MdHR-6636-42-20}

BOUCHEL, JOSEPH (Kent County) received a certificate from the Purchasing Agent for furnishing corn on 15 Feb 1780 {Ref: Maryland State Archives MdHR-6636-43-1}

BOULDERSON, ISAIAH (Harford County) received money from the Committee of Safety to carry on the business of gun making in partnership with Cuthbert Warner on 27 Nov 1775 {Ref: Preston's History of Harford County, p. 317}

BOURK, PATRICK (Annapolis) received payment by order of the Council of Safety for riding express on 19 Sep 1776 {Ref: Archives of Maryland 12:284}; also see "Parket Bork," q.v.

BOWDLE, STEPHEN (Talbot County) submitted an account and receipt for furnishing bacon on 23 Apr 1778 {Ref: Maryland State Archives MdHR-6636-12-15}

BOWEN, JETHRO (Worcester County) received a receipt from the Purchasing Agent for furnishing corn on 1 Feb 1780 {Ref: Maryland State Archives MdHR-6636-24-52}; his name appeared on "A List of Corn Purchased in Worcester County for the use of the State of Maryland" by the Commissary in July, 1780 {Ref: Archives of Maryland 45:10}

BOWEN, WHITNEY (Worcester County) submitted an account and receipt for packing pork on 19 May 1781 {Ref: Maryland State Archives MdHR-6636-43-27}

BOWEN, WHITTINGTON (Worcester County) submitted an account and receipt for preparing pork on 10 Jun 1782 {Ref: Maryland State Archives MdHR-6636-43-28M}

BOWEN, WILLIAM (Worcester County) submitted an account and receipt for furnishing salt on 15 Mar 1782 {Ref: Maryland State Archives MdHR-6636-43-28/OO}

BOWERS, THOMAS (Kent County) received payment from the Purchasing Agent for furnishing cattle and pasturage for the public use in September, 1781 {Ref: Maryland State Archives MdHR-6636-43-3}

BOWIE, ALLEN (Montgomery County) received a receipt from the Purchasing Agent for furnishing wheat on 23 Aug 1780 {Ref: Maryland State Archives MdHR-6636-24-6}

BOWIE, ROBERT (Prince George's County) served as Collector of Horses in his county and received payment from the Council of Maryland "to be expended in the Collection of the Horses and for employing persons to take care of them" on 25 Jul 1781 {Ref: Archives of Maryland 45:520}; appointed by the Council of Maryland to purchase thirteen horses on the Eastern Shore for the use of the Southern Army on 8 Jul 1782 {Ref: Archives of Maryland 48:208}

BOWING, JETHRO (Worcester County) received a receipt from the Purchasing Agent for furnishing beef on 11 Oct 1780 {Ref: Maryland State Archives MdHR-6636-24-54}

BOWLEY, DANIEL (Baltimore County) received a loan certificate for £1310.17.7 due from the Council of Maryland "agreeable to the Act proposing to the Citizens of this State, Creditors of Congress on Loan Office Certificates, Etc." on 24 Dec 1783 for services rendered during the war {Ref: Archives of Maryland 48:499}; also see "Thomas Harrison," q.v.

BOWMAN, JOHN (Frederick County) submitted an account for furnishing corn meal on 14 Apr 1781 {Ref: Maryland State Archives MdHR-6636-23-5}

BOWRY, OSWELL (Charles County) received a receipt from the Purchasing Agent for furnishing wheat on 8 Sep 1781 {Ref: Maryland State Archives MdHR-6636-42-15}

BOWYE, ISSABEL (Charles County) received a receipt from the Purchasing Agent for furnishing wheat on 10 May 1783 {Ref: Maryland State Archives MdHR-6636-42-22}

BOYD, ABRAHAM (Montgomery County) received a receipt from the Purchasing Agent for furnishing wheat on 1 Aug 1780 {Ref: Maryland State Archives MdHR-6636-43-7}; received receipts from the Purchasing Agent for furnishing wheat on 11 Aug and 18 Aug 1780 {Ref: Maryland State Archives MdHR-6636-24-6}; received a receipt for furnishing wheat on 12 Sep 1780 {Ref: Maryland State Archives MdHR-6636-24-7}; received receipts from the Purchasing Agent for furnishing wheat on 3 Nov and 23 Dec 1780 {Ref: Maryland State Archives MdHR-6636-24-8}; received a receipt for furnishing pork on 7 Apr 1781 {Ref: Maryland State Archives MdHR-6636-23-5}; received a receipt for furnishing wheat on 28 Aug 1781 {Ref: Maryland State Archives MdHR-6636-24-15}

BOYD, BENJAMIN (Montgomery County) received a receipt from the Purchasing Agent for furnishing wheat on 2 Sep 1780 {Ref: Maryland State Archives MdHR-6636-24-7}

BOYD, FRANCIS (Baltimore County) received payment for furnishing beef on 23 May 1781 {Ref: Maryland State Archives MdHR-6636-43-38GGG}

BOYD, JAMES (Harford County) received payment by order of the Council of Safety for furnishing bayonets on 31 Aug 1776 {Ref: Archives of Maryland 12:250}

BOYD, WILLIAM (Montgomery County) received a receipt from the Purchasing

Agent for furnishing wheat on 30 Aug 1780 {Ref: Maryland State Archives MdHR-6636-24-6}

BOYEL, JOSIAS (Charles County) received a receipt from the Purchasing Agent for furnishing wheat on 7 Sep 1782 {Ref: Maryland State Archives MdHR-6636-42-18}

BOZMAN, LUINITIA OR LUNITIA (Talbot County) received a receipt from the Purchasing Agent for furnishing beef on 28 Sep 1780 {Ref: Maryland State Archives MdHR-6636-24-49}

BOZMAN, RISDON (Worcester County) received a receipt from the Purchasing Agent for furnishing pork on 18 Jun 1782 {Ref: Maryland State Archives MdHR-6636-43-27}

BRADFORD, MARY (Worcester County) received a receipt from the Purchasing Agent for furnishing corn on 14 Jun 1780 {Ref: Maryland State Archives MdHR-6636-24-53}; his name appeared on "A List of Corn Purchased in Worcester County for the use of the State of Maryland" by the Commissary in July, 1780 {Ref: Archives of Maryland 45:10}

BRADLEY, CHRISTOPHER SHORT (Dorchester County) received a receipt from the Purchasing Agent for furnishing wheat on 1 Oct 1782 {Ref: Maryland State Archives MdHR-6636-42-23}

BRADLEY, EZEKIEL (Dorchester County) received a receipt from the Purchasing Agent for furnishing wheat on 1 Nov 1782 {Ref: Maryland State Archives MdHR-6636-42-23}

BRADLEY, RICHARD (Dorchester County) received a receipt from the Purchasing Agent for furnishing wheat on 1 Oct 1782 {Ref: Maryland State Archives MdHR-6636-42-23}

BRADLEY, THOMAS (Caroline County) received a receipt from the Purchasing Agent for furnishing wheat on 24 Aug 1782 {Ref: Maryland State Archives MdHR-6636-42-7}

BRADSHAW, JAMES (Kent County) received a receipt from the Purchasing Agent for furnishing flour on 18 Apr 1780 {Ref: Maryland State Archives MdHR-6636-24-1}; received a receipt for hauling flour on 15 May 1780 {Ref: Maryland State Archives MdHR-6636-24-41}

BRADY, JAMES (Kent County) received payment from the Purchasing Agent for furnishing cattle for the public use in September, 1781 {Ref: Maryland State Archives MdHR-6636-43-3}

BRAKENRIGE, ROBERT (Anne Arundel County) received a receipt from the Purchasing Agent for furnishing powder on 16 Apr 1777 {Ref: Maryland State Archives MdHR-6636-9-14F}

BRANDENBAUGH, WILLIAM (Frederick County) received certificates from the Purchasing Agent for hauling and delivering flour on 16 Feb and 13 Mar 1781 {Ref: Maryland State Archives MdHR-6636-23-30}

BRANGLE, LAWRENCE (Frederick County), executor of John Hummell, received a loan certificate due him for £21.19.0 due from the Council of Maryland "agreeable to the Act proposing to the Citizens of this State, Creditors of Congress on Loan Office Certificates, Etc." on 19 May 1783 for services rendered during the war {Ref: Archives of Maryland 48:417}

BRANS, DUNCAN (Somerset County) received a receipt from the Purchasing Agent for furnishing pork on 8 Jun 1781 {Ref: Maryland State Archives MdHR-6636-24-43}

BRATTON, WILLIAM (Worcester County) received a receipt from the Purchasing Agent for furnishing corn on 3 Jan 1780 {Ref: Maryland State Archives MdHR-6636-24-53}; his name appeared on "A List of Corn Purchased in Worcester County for the use of the State of Maryland" by the Commissary in July, 1780 {Ref: Archives of Maryland 45:10}

BRAUGHAN, PATRICK (Dorchester County) received a receipt from the Purchasing Agent for furnishing wheat on 1 Nov 1782 {Ref: Maryland State Archives MdHR-6636-42-23}

BRAVARD, BENJAMIN (Cecil County) received a certificate for money loaned to the state on 1 May 1782 {Ref: Maryland State Archives MdHR-6636-40-54}

BRAWNER, BASIL (Charles County) received a receipt from the Purchasing Agent for furnishing wheat on 28 Dec 1782 {Ref: Maryland State Archives MdHR-6636-42-21}

BRAWNER, BENJAMIN (Charles County) received a receipt from the Purchasing Agent for furnishing wheat on 26 Jun 1782 {Ref: Maryland State Archives MdHR-6636-42-18}; received a receipt for furnishing wheat on 10 May 1783 {Ref: Maryland State Archives MdHR-6636-42-22}

BRAWNER, WILLIAM (Charles County) received a receipt from the Purchasing Agent for furnishing wheat on 27 Apr 1782 {Ref: Maryland State Archives MdHR-6636-42-18}; received a receipt for furnishing wheat on 10 May 1783 {Ref: Maryland State Archives MdHR-6636-42-22}

BREDLE, JOHN (Cecil County) submitted an account and receipt for freight charges on 23 Dec 1782 {Ref: Maryland State Archives MdHR-6636-42-9}

BREESE, HENRY (Kent County) received payment from the Purchasing Agent for furnishing cattle for the public use in September, 1781 {Ref: Maryland State Archives MdHR-6636-43-3}

BREMER, PETER (Frederick County) submitted an account for furnishing hay on 29 May 1781 {Ref: Maryland State Archives MdHR-6636-23-6}

BRENT, RICHARD (Charles County) received a receipt from the Purchasing Agent for furnishing wheat on 28 Dec 1782 {Ref: Maryland State Archives MdHR-6636-42-21}

BRENT, ROBERT (Charles County) received a receipt from the Purchasing Agent for furnishing wheat on 21 Jan 1782 {Ref: Maryland State Archives MdHR-

6636-42-16}

BREVARD, ADAM (Worcester County) received a receipt from the Purchasing Agent for furnishing corn on 15 Aug 1780 {Ref: Maryland State Archives MdHR-6636-24-53}

BREVARD, BENJAMIN (Worcester County) received a loan certificate for £126.7.10 due from the Council of Maryland "agreeable to the Act proposing to the Citizens of this State, Creditors of Congress on Loan Office Certificates, Etc." on 13 May 1783 for services rendered during the war {Ref: Archives of Maryland 48:411}

BREWER, JOHN SR. (Anne Arundel County) received a loan certificate for £27.4.0 due from the Council of Maryland "agreeable to the Act proposing to the Citizens of this State, Creditors of Congress on Loan Office Certificates, Etc." on 4 Jul 1783 for services rendered during the war {Ref: Archives of Maryland 48:436}

BREWER, JOSEPH (Anne Arundel County) received payment by order of the Council of Safety for furnishing a musquet on 21 Aug 1776 {Ref: Archives of Maryland 12:226}

BRIAN, DANIEL (Baltimore County) was a captain who received a receipt from the Purchasing Agent for furnishing flour on 29 Nov 1781 {Ref: Maryland State Archives MdHR-6636-43-38I}; received a receipt for the delivery of flour on 21 Apr 1782 {Ref: Maryland State Archives MdHR-6636-43-37J}

BRICE, ANN (Anne Arundel County) received a loan certificate for £8.15.10 due from the Council of Maryland "agreeable to the Act proposing to the Citizens of this State, Creditors of Congress on Loan Office Certificates, Etc." on 26 Apr 1783 for services rendered during the war {Ref: Archives of Maryland 48:403}

BRICE, BENEDICT (Caroline County) received a certificate from the Purchasing Agent for hauling corn on 1 Jun 1780 {Ref: Maryland State Archives MdHR-6636-23-20}

BRICE, DAVID (Frederick County) received a certificate from the Purchasing Agent for furnishing wheat on 20 Sep 1781 {Ref: Maryland State Archives MdHR-6636-23-28}

BRICE, JAMES (Anne Arundel County) received a loan certificate for £10.11.0 due from the Council of Maryland "agreeable to the Act proposing to the Citizens of this State, Creditors of Congress on Loan Office Certificates, Etc." on 26 Apr 1783 for services rendered during the war {Ref: Archives of Maryland 48:403}

BRICE, JOHN (Anne Arundel County) received payment by order of the Council of Safety for furnishing walnut plank on 20 Mar 1776 {Ref: Archives of Maryland 11:269}; received payment for the hire of his horse on 15 Aug 1776 {Ref: Archives of Maryland 12:208}

BRIGG, EDWARD (Harford County) received a receipt from the Purchasing Agent for furnishing wheat on 24 Mar 1780 {Ref: Maryland State Archives MdHR-6636-23-35}

BRIGGS, EDMOND (Montgomery County) received a receipt from the Purchasing Agent for furnishing wheat on 1 Sep 1781 {Ref: Maryland State Archives MdHR-6636-24-15}

BRILEY, WILLIAM (Caroline County) received a receipt from the Purchasing Agent for furnishing wheat on 1 Sep 1782 {Ref: Maryland State Archives MdHR-6636-42-7}

BRINGLE, CHRISTIAN (Frederick County) received a receipt from the Purchasing Agent for furnishing pork on 12 Mar 1781 {Ref: Maryland State Archives MdHR-6636-23-4}

BRINGLE, LAWRENCE (Frederick County) received a certificate for money loaned to the state on 3 Jun 1780 {Ref: Maryland State Archives MdHR-6636-18-128}

BRINSFIELD, ELIZABETH (Dorchester County) received a receipt from the Purchasing Agent for furnishing wheat on 1 Jun 1782 {Ref: Maryland State Archives MdHR-6636-42-23}

BRISCOE, ALEXANDER (Kent County) submitted an account and receipt for furnishing nails on 8 Mar 1782 {Ref: Maryland State Archives MdHR-6636-43-5}

BRISCOE (BRISCO), BENJAMIN (Kent County) received payment from the Purchasing Agent for furnishing cattle for the public use in September, 1781 {Ref: Maryland State Archives MdHR-6636-43-3}

BRISCOE, HANSON (St. Mary's County) was appointed by the Council of Safety to collect all the gold and silver coin that could be procured in the county in compliance with the Resolve of Congress on 27 Jan 1776 {Ref: Archives of Maryland 11:132}; his name appeared on "A Return of Beef on the Hoof Purchased by Joseph Ford Commissary of Purchases" on 8 Oct 1780 when he delivered two steers for the use of the state {Ref: Archives of Maryland 45:156}; Council of Maryland recorded that "Mr. Hanson Briscoe of Chaptico, St. Mary's County, has Vessels and will engage to transport all the Wheat in that County, and perhaps in the neighbouring ones" on 1 Dec 1781 {Ref: Archives of Maryland 48:9}

BRISCOE (BRISCO), ISAAC (Kent County) received payment from the Purchasing Agent for furnishing cattle for the public use in September, 1781 {Ref: Maryland State Archives MdHR-6636-43-3}

BRISCOE, JAMES (Charles County) received a receipt from the Purchasing Agent for furnishing wheat on 31 Oct 1782 {Ref: Maryland State Archives MdHR-6636-42-19}; received a receipt for furnishing wheat on 8 May 1783 {Ref: Maryland State Archives MdHR-6636-42-22}

BRISCOE, ROBERT (Montgomery County) received a receipt from the Purchasing Agent for furnishing wheat on 9 Oct 1781 {Ref: Maryland State Archives MdHR-6636-24-15}; received a loan certificate for £119.0.8 due from the Council of Maryland "agreeable to the Act proposing to the Citizens of this State, Creditors of Congress on Loan Office Certificates, Etc." on 13 May 1783 for services rendered during the war {Ref: Archives of Maryland 48:412}

BRISCOE, THOMAS (St. Mary's County) received payment by order of the Council of Safety "for going express on account of North Carolina prisoners" on 25 Jun 1776 {Ref: Archives of Maryland 11:515}

BRITE, JONES (Caroline County) received a receipt from the Purchasing Agent for furnishing wheat on 17 Aug 1782 {Ref: Maryland State Archives MdHR-6636-42-7}

BRITTINGHAM, SAMUEL (Worcester County) submitted an account and receipt for furnishing pork barrels on 20 Mar 1782 {Ref: Maryland State Archives MdHR-6636-43-28LL}

BROADY, JAMES (Caroline County) received a receipt from the Purchasing Agent for furnishing wheat on 20 Sep 1782 {Ref: Maryland State Archives MdHR-6636-42-7}

BROCKHART, GEORGE (Frederick County) received a receipt from the Purchasing Agent for furnishing beef on 27 Dec 1780 {Ref: Maryland State Archives MdHR-6636-23-1}

BROGDON, WILLIAM (Anne Arundel County) was appointed by the Council of Maryland as one of thirty men to be "Agents for Purchasing Provisions" on 30 Mar 1779 {Ref: Archives of Maryland 21:332}

BRONBAUGH, JACOB (Anne Arundel County) received a receipt from the Purchasing Agent for furnishing powder on 16 Apr 1777 {Ref: Maryland State Archives MdHR-6636-9-14G}

BROOK, HENRY (Montgomery County) received a receipt from the Purchasing Agent for furnishing wheat on 27 May 1781 {Ref: Maryland State Archives MdHR-6636-42-11}

BROOKE (BROOK), BAKER (Charles County) received a receipt from the Purchasing Agent for furnishing wheat on 28 Dec 1782 {Ref: Maryland State Archives MdHR-6636-42-21}; received a receipt for furnishing wheat on 9 May 1782 {Ref: Maryland State Archives MdHR-6636-42-18}

BROOKE, CATHARINE (county not stated) received a loan certificate for £20.5.7 due from the Council of Maryland "agreeable to the Act proposing to the Citizens of this State, Creditors of Congress on Loan Office Certificates, Etc." on 20 May 1783 for services rendered during the war {Ref: Archives of Maryland 48:418}

BROOKE, CLEMENT (Montgomery County) received a receipt from the

Purchasing Agent for furnishing wheat on 14 Sep 1780 {Ref: Maryland State Archives MdHR-6636-24-7}

BROOKE, HENRY (Prince George's County) received a receipt from the Purchasing Agent for furnishing wheat on 30 Apr 1783 {Ref: Maryland State Archives MdHR-6636-43-9}

BROOKE (BROOKES), JOHN SMITH (Prince George's County) was appointed by the Council of Maryland as one of thirty men to be "Agents for Purchasing Provisions" on 30 Mar 1779 {Ref: Archives of Maryland 21:332}; submitted an account and receipt for delivery of pork on 25 May 1780 {Ref: Maryland State Archives MdHR-6636-18-105}; appointed Commissary of Purchases for Prince George's County by the Council of Maryland on 8 Jul 1780 {Ref: Archives of Maryland 43:215}; submitted an account for purchase of fish on 24 Jul 1780 {Ref: Maryland State Archives MdHR-6636-19-47}; ordered by the Council of Maryland to give certificates in payment for salt meat procured by the "Act to Procure a Supply of Salt Meat for the Use of the Army" on 14 Oct 1780 {Ref: Archives of Maryland 43:328; Maryland State Archives MdHR-6636-20-109}; submitted an account for beef and request for barrels from the commissary on 28 Feb 1781 {Ref: Maryland State Archives MdHR-6636-15-120}; "John Smith Brookes & Company" received payment from the Purchasing Agent for furnishing material for clothing ("oznaburgs and rusha sheeting") on 11 Jun 1781 {Ref: Archives of Maryland 47:288}; also see "John Pool," q.v.

BROOKE, MARGARET, Mrs. (Prince George's County) received a receipt from the Purchasing Agent for furnishing wheat on 30 Apr 1783 {Ref: Maryland State Archives MdHR-6636-43-9}; received a loan certificate for £244.18.6 due from the Council of Maryland "agreeable to the Act proposing to the Citizens of this State, Creditors of Congress on Loan Office Certificates, Etc." on 20 Dec 1783 for services rendered during the war {Ref: Archives of Maryland 48:494}

BROOKE, NICHOLAS (Prince George's County) received a receipt from the Purchasing Agent for furnishing wheat on 10 May 1783 {Ref: Maryland State Archives MdHR-6636-43-9}

BROOKE, RICHARD (Montgomery County) was appointed by the Council of Maryland as one of thirty men to be "Agents for Purchasing Provisions" on 30 Mar 1779 {Ref: Archives of Maryland 21:332}; purchased provisions for the army on 9 May 1779 {Ref: Maryland State Archives MdHR-6636-14-11}

BROOKS, DENNIS (Baltimore County) received payment for furnishing corn on 25 Jan 1781 {Ref: Maryland State Archives MdHR-6636-43-38QQQQ}; received payment for furnishing corn on 25 Apr 1781 {Ref: Maryland State Archives MdHR-6636-43-38RRR}

BROOKS, ISAAC (Montgomery County) received a receipt from the Purchasing

Agent for furnishing wheat on 29 Oct 1780 {Ref: Maryland State Archives MdHR-6636-24-13}

BROOM & JOHNSON (Cecil County) appeared on 19 Feb 1781 on a "Return [of] Flour forwarded and Delivered at the Head of Elk the Purchase of different Persons for the use of the United States" in the year 1780 {Ref: Archives of Maryland 47:77}

BROWN, GEORGE (Worcester County) received a receipt from the Purchasing Agent for furnishing bacon on 15 Oct 1780 {Ref: Maryland State Archives MdHR-6636-24-54}

BROWN, HUMPHREY (Dorchester County) received a receipt from the Purchasing Agent for furnishing wheat on 1 Nov 1782 {Ref: Maryland State Archives MdHR-6636-42-23}

BROWN, JAMES (Harford County) received payment by order of the Council of Safety "for repairing a gun and the screws on two bayonets on two musketts (given to him by Col. Carvel Hall for repair)" on 21 Aug 1776 {Ref: Archives of Maryland 12:230}

BROWN, JOHN (Baltimore County) submitted an account and credit due for furnishing rum on 28 Aug 1781 {Ref: Maryland State Archives MdHR-6636-41-87}

BROWN, JOHN (Montgomery County) received a receipt from the Purchasing Agent for furnishing wheat on 13 Sep 1780 {Ref: Maryland State Archives MdHR-6636-24-13}

BROWN, LEVI (Caroline County) received a receipt from the Purchasing Agent for furnishing wheat on 3 Jun 1782 {Ref: Maryland State Archives MdHR-6636-42-7}

BROWN, NATHANIEL (Queen Anne's County) received a receipt from the Purchasing Agent for furnishing a cow and a steer on 1 Apr 1778 {Ref: Maryland State Archives MdHR-4587-40/41}

BROWN, NICHOLAS (Kent County) received a certificate from the Purchasing Agent for furnishing wheat on 14 Jan 1780 {Ref: Maryland State Archives MdHR-6636-23-43}

BROWN, PETER (Montgomery County) received a receipt from the Purchasing Agent for furnishing wheat on 29 Jul 1780 {Ref: Maryland State Archives MdHR-6636-24-5}; received a receipt for furnishing wheat on 1 Aug 1780 {Ref: Maryland State Archives MdHR-6636-43-7}; received a receipt for furnishing wheat on 1 Sep 1780 {Ref: Maryland State Archives MdHR-6636-24-7}

BROWN, ROBERT (Frederick County) received a certificate from the Purchasing Agent for furnishing wheat on 30 Jul 1782 {Ref: Maryland State Archives MdHR-6636-42-36}

BROWN, WILLIAM (Queen Anne's County) received a receipt from the

Purchasing Agent for furnishing steers on 29 Apr 1778 {Ref: Maryland State Archives MdHR-4587-35}

BROWN, WILLIAM (Annapolis) received payment from the Maryland Council of Safety for "the expence of guarding the records at his house" on 16 Feb 1776 {Ref: Archives of Maryland 11:163}

BROWNE, NICHOLAS (Kent County) received payment from the Purchasing Agent for furnishing cattle and pasturage for the public use in September, 1781 {Ref: Maryland State Archives MdHR-6636-43-3}

BROWNER, BASIL (Charles County) received a receipt from the Purchasing Agent for furnishing wheat on 31 Dec 1781 {Ref: Maryland State Archives MdHR-6636-42-15}

BROWNER, WILLIAM (Charles County) received a receipt from the Purchasing Agent for furnishing wheat on 16 Feb 1782 {Ref: Maryland State Archives MdHR-6636-42-16}

BROWNING, EDWARD (Montgomery County) received a receipt from the Purchasing Agent for furnishing wheat on 26 May 1781 {Ref: Maryland State Archives MdHR-6636-42-11}

BROWNING, JOHN W. (Kent County) received payment for hauling flour and bacon on 28 Jul 1780 {Ref: Maryland State Archives MdHR-6636-23-49}

BROWNING, JONATHAN (Montgomery County) received a receipt from the Purchasing Agent for furnishing wheat on 25 May 1781 {Ref: Maryland State Archives MdHR-6636-24-15}; received a receipt for furnishing wheat on 26 May 1781 {Ref: Maryland State Archives MdHR-6636-42-11}

BROWNING, NATHAN (Montgomery County) received a receipt from the Purchasing Agent for furnishing wheat on 25 May 1781 {Ref: Maryland State Archives MdHR-6636-42-11}; received a certificate of employment by the commissary of purchases on 10 Jun 1782 {Ref: Maryland State Archives MdHR-6636-50-91}

BROWNING, THOMAS (Kent County) received a receipt from the Purchasing Agent for furnishing flour on 28 Jul 1780 {Ref: Maryland State Archives MdHR-6636-23-49}

BRUCE, JOHN (Charles County) received a receipt from the Purchasing Agent for furnishing wheat on 10 May 1783 {Ref: Maryland State Archives MdHR-6636-42-22}

BRUCE, NORMAN OR NORMAND (Frederick County) was appointed by the Council of Maryland as one of thirty men to be "Agents for Purchasing Provisions" on 30 Mar 1779 {Ref: Archives of Maryland 21:332}; received a certificate for confiscated flour on 27 Feb 1780 {Ref: Maryland State Archives MdHR-6636-42-25}; delivered flour to the commissary at Baltimore Town for the use of the State of Maryland in the summer of 1780 {Ref: Archives of Maryland 45:84}; received a receipt for furnishing beef and pork on 23 Mar

1781 {Ref: Maryland State Archives MdHR-6636-23-4}

BRUCE, TOWNLEY (Frederick County) was appointed by the Council of Maryland as one of thirty men to be "Agents for Purchasing Provisions" on 30 Mar 1779 {Ref: Archives of Maryland 21:332}

BRUESBANK, FRANCIS (Baltimore Town or County) received payment by order of the Council of Safety for furnishing boatage on 4 Sep 1776 {Ref: Archives of Maryland 12:256}

BRUFF, JOSEPH (Talbot County) was appointed Collector of Clothing in the room of James Hindman by the Council of Maryland on 27 Jan 1778 {Ref: Archives of Maryland 16:474}; received a receipt from the Purchasing Agent for furnishing cattle on 12 Apr 1781 {Ref: Maryland State Archives MdHR-6636-31-127}; appointed Purchaser of Clothing in his county by the Council of Maryland on 5 Jun 1781 {Ref: Archives of Maryland 45:462}; received a receipt for furnishing wheat on 19 Mar 1782 {Ref: Maryland State Archives MdHR-6636-43-25}

BRUFF, W. (Talbot County) pledged a loan in the amount of £250 to the State of Maryland under the Act for the Emission of Bills of Credit "to defray the expences of the present campaign" in June, 1781 {Ref: Archives of Maryland 47:327}

BRUINGTON, WILLIAM (Somerset County) received a receipt from the Purchasing Agent for furnishing beef on 20 Oct 1781 {Ref: Maryland State Archives MdHR-6636-24-44}

BRUNER, JOHN (Frederick County) received a certificate from the Purchasing Agent for furnishing wheat on 28 Jan 1783 {Ref: Maryland State Archives MdHR-6636-42-38}

BRUNER, PETER (Frederick County) received a certificate from the Purchasing Agent for furnishing wheat on 28 May 1782 {Ref: Maryland State Archives MdHR-6636-42-34}

BRUNNER, JOHN (Frederick County) received a receipt from the Purchasing Agent for delivering flour on 23 Apr 1781 {Ref: Maryland State Archives MdHR-6636-23-31}; received a receipt for hauling flour on 24 Aug 1783 {Ref: Maryland State Archives MdHR-6636-42-28}

BRUNNER, STEPHEN (Frederick County) received a certificate from the Purchasing Agent for furnishing wheat on 3 Oct 1781 {Ref: Maryland State Archives MdHR-6636-23-28}

BRYAN, ARTHUR (Talbot County) received a loan certificate for £42.14.0 due from the Council of Maryland "agreeable to the Act proposing to the Citizens of this State, Creditors of Congress on Loan Office Certificates, Etc." on 2 Jun 1783 for services rendered during the war {Ref: Archives of Maryland 48:424-425}

BRYAN, RICHARD (Dorchester County) received payment by order of the

Council of Safety "for going express" on 16 Oct 1776 {Ref: Archives of Maryland 12:354}; received a supply of lead and gun flints by order of the Council of Maryland on 24 May 1779 to be delivered to Henry Hooper, county lieutenant in Dorchester County {Ref: Archives of Maryland 21:413}

BUCHANAN, ROBERT (Baltimore Town) was an Assistant Commissary Agent in 1778 and purchased bread for the army on 24 Dec 1778 {Ref: Maryland State Archives MdHR-4586-89}; appointed by the Council of Maryland as one of thirty men to be "Agents for Purchasing Provisions" on 30 Mar 1779 {Ref: Archives of Maryland 21:332, 452}; commissioned an Assistant Deputy Commissary of Purchases for Baltimore County on 10 Sep 1779 {Ref: Archives of Maryland 21:518}

BUCHANAN, ROBERT (Kent County) received payment from the Purchasing Agent for furnishing cattle and pasturage for the public use in September, 1781 {Ref: Maryland State Archives MdHR-6636-43-3}

BUCKALOW, JOHN (Harford County) submitted an account for grinding wheat on 8 Mar 1780 {Ref: Maryland State Archives MdHR-6636-23-35}

BULL, JOHN (Harford County) received receipts from the Purchasing Agent for furnishing wheat on 12 Feb and 10 Mar 1780 {Ref: Maryland State Archives MdHR-6636-23-35}

BULLEN, JOHN (Anne Arundel County) received payment by order of the Council of Safety for the hire of his teams for six days on 6 Apr 1776 {Ref: Archives of Maryland 11:314}; received payment for furnishing two horses and a team on 5 Aug and 16 Sep 1776 {Ref: Archives of Maryland 12:166, 274}; appointed by the Council of Maryland as "Commissary of Stores for this State in the room of Charles Wallace Howard who has resigned" on 1 Nov 1777 {Ref: Archives of Maryland 16:407}; received from the Council a "warrant to impress teams sufficient to remove the public stores and records" on 17 May 1779 {Ref: Archives of Maryland 21:395}; received payment by order of the Council of Maryland "to be expended in the purchase of straw and plank for the accommodation of the officers and soldiers now encamped near this city [Annapolis] to be accounted for" on 31 Jul 1780 {Ref: Archives of Maryland 43:243}; served as Quartermaster in 1781 {Ref: Archives of Maryland 45:429}; also see "William Yielding" and "Frederick Green" and "Thomas Rutland" and "Joshua Lackland," q.v.

BULLEN, WILLIAM (Talbot County) received a receipt from the Purchasing Agent for purchasing bacon on 19 May 1778 {Ref: Maryland State Archives MdHR-6636-12-15}

BUNBURY, BENJAMIN (Queen Anne's County) was a Deputy Commissary Agent in 1782-1783 and submitted an account and receipt for storing wheat in 1782 {Ref: Maryland State Archives MdHR-6636-43-12/13}; received certificates from the Purchasing Agent for the receipt of wheat, pork and beef on 1 Mar and 3 Apr 1783 {Ref: Maryland State Archives MdHR-6636-43-14}

BURBIG, SALATHIEL (Worcester County) received a receipt from the Purchasing Agent for furnishing salt on 22 Dec 1782 {Ref: Maryland State Archives MdHR-19970-3-23}

BURCH, REBECCAH (Charles County) received a receipt from the Purchasing Agent for furnishing wheat on 28 Sep 1782 {Ref: Maryland State Archives MdHR-6636-42-19}

BURCH, RICHARD (Charles County) received a receipt from the Purchasing Agent for furnishing wheat on 28 Sep 1782 {Ref: Maryland State Archives MdHR-6636-42-19}

BURCH, WALTER (Charles County) received a loan certificate for £216.8.8 due from the Council of Maryland "agreeable to the Act proposing to the Citizens of this State, Creditors of Congress on Loan Office Certificates, Etc." on 21 Oct 1783 for services rendered during the war {Ref: Archives of Maryland 48:472}

BURCHNELL, WILLIAM, see "William Burtchnell," q.v.

BURDET (BURDIT), BENJAMIN (Montgomery County) received a receipt from the Purchasing Agent for furnishing wheat on 15 May 1781 {Ref: Maryland State Archives MdHR-6636-42-11}; received a receipt for furnishing wheat on 9 Oct 1781 {Ref: Maryland State Archives MdHR-6636-24-15}

BURGESS, ALLEN (Talbot County) received a receipt from the Purchasing Agent for furnishing bacon for the use of the army on 30 Apr 1778 {Ref: Maryland State Archives MdHR-4587-76}; submitted an account and receipt for hauling on 30 Apr 1778 {Ref: Maryland State Archives MdHR-6636-12-15}

BURGESS, ELIAS (Montgomery County) received payment due for driving cattle received by Simon Nicholls on 29 Apr 1782 {Ref: Maryland State Archives MdHR-6636-43-6}

BURGESS, RICHARD (Prince George's County) received a receipt from the Purchasing Agent for furnishing wheat on 30 Apr 1783 {Ref: Maryland State Archives MdHR-6636-43-9}

BURK, EDWARD (Caroline County) received a receipt from the Purchasing Agent for furnishing wheat on 17 Aug 1782 {Ref: Maryland State Archives MdHR-6636-42-7}

BURK, JOHN (Kent County) received payment from the Purchasing Agent for furnishing cattle and pasturage for the public use in September, 1781 {Ref: Maryland State Archives MdHR-6636-43-3}

BURK, THOMAS (Caroline County) received a receipt from the Purchasing Agent for furnishing wheat on 17 Aug 1782 {Ref: Maryland State Archives MdHR-6636-42-7}

BURKE, WILLIAM (Cecil County) received a certificate from the Purchasing Agent for furnishing flour on 17 Jan 1780 {Ref: Maryland State Archives MdHR-6636-23-22}

BURKHAM, JOHN (Talbot County) submitted an account and receipt for hiring a team on 19 May 1778 {Ref: Maryland State Archives MdHR-6636-12-15}

BURKHART, CHRISTIAN (Frederick County) received a certificate from the Purchasing Agent for furnishing whiskey on 31 Jan 1781 {Ref: Maryland State Archives MdHR-6636-23-2}

BURNITT, ELIJAH (Worcester County) submitted an account and receipt for processing pork on 10 May 1782 {Ref: Maryland State Archives MdHR-6636-43-28Z}; submitted an account and receipt for processing and hauling wheat on 1 Aug 1782 {Ref: Maryland State Archives MdHR-6636-43-28I}

BURNS (BURNES), JAMES (Montgomery County) received a receipt from the Purchasing Agent for furnishing wheat on 1 Aug 1780 {Ref: Maryland State Archives MdHR-6636-43-7}; received receipts from the Purchasing Agent for furnishing wheat on 3 Aug and 4 Aug 1780 {Ref: Maryland State Archives MdHR-6636-24-6}

BURNS, JOHN (Montgomery County) received a receipt from the Purchasing Agent for furnishing wheat on 31 Mar 1781 {Ref: Maryland State Archives MdHR-6636-42-11}

BURROUGHS, MATTHEW (St. Mary's County) received payment from the Purchasing Agent on 30 Dec 1781 for collecting and driving public cattle for 17 days {Ref: Maryland State Archives MdHR-6636-43-23}

BURRAGE, NINAN (Charles County) received a receipt from the Purchasing Agent for furnishing wheat on 29 Dec 1782 {Ref: Maryland State Archives MdHR-6636-42-21}

BURT, HENRY (Caroline County) received a receipt from the Purchasing Agent for furnishing wheat on 31 Aug 1782 {Ref: Maryland State Archives MdHR-6636-42-7}

BURT, WILLIAM (Caroline County) received a receipt from the Purchasing Agent for furnishing wheat on 31 Aug 1782 {Ref: Maryland State Archives MdHR-6636-42-7}

BURTCHNELL, WILLIAM (Kent County) received payment from the Purchasing Agent for furnishing cattle and pasturage for the public use in September, 1781 {Ref: Maryland State Archives MdHR-6636-43-3}

BUSH, HARMAN (Frederick County) received a certificate from the Purchasing Agent for furnishing wheat on 27 May 1782 {Ref: Maryland State Archives MdHR-6636-42-33}

BUSSEY, CHARLES (Montgomery County) received a receipt from the Purchasing Agent for furnishing wheat on 12 Oct 1781 {Ref: Maryland State Archives MdHR-6636-24-15}

BUSSEY, JOHN (Prince George's County) received a receipt from the Purchasing Agent for furnishing wheat on 10 Oct 1781 {Ref: Maryland State Archives MdHR-6636-24-14}

BUSSEY, JOHN (Montgomery County) received a receipt from the Purchasing Agent for furnishing wheat on 17 Jul 1780 {Ref: Maryland State Archives MdHR-6636-24-14}

BUSSEY, SAMUEL (Montgomery County) received a receipt from the Purchasing Agent for furnishing wheat on 20 Jul 1780 {Ref: Maryland State Archives MdHR-6636-24-13}

BUTCHER, JAMES (Kent County) received payment from the Purchasing Agent for furnishing cattle for the public use in September, 1781 {Ref: Maryland State Archives MdHR-6636-43-3}

BUTLER, EDWARD (Frederick County) received a certificate from the Purchasing Agent for furnishing wheat on 27 May 1782 {Ref: Maryland State Archives MdHR-6636-42-33}

BUTLER, JAMES (Montgomery County) received receipts from the Purchasing Agent for furnishing wheat on 19 Apr and 26 Apr 1781 {Ref: Maryland State Archives MdHR-6636-42-11}

BUTLER, JOHN (Baltimore County) received money from the Council of Maryland "to be delivered over to David Poe and by him expended in procuring Forage for the Post of Baltimore" on 12 Nov 1781 {Ref: Archives of Maryland 45:666}

BUTLER, MOSES (Talbot County) received a receipt from the Purchasing Agent for furnishing wheat on 19 Mar 1782 {Ref: Maryland State Archives MdHR-6636-43-25}

BUTTERS (RUTTERS?), JAMES (Harford County) received payment for furnishing a gun to the Committee of Safety on 18 Jun 1776 {Ref: Preston's History of Harford County, p. 330}

BUTTS, CLEMENT (Charles County) received a receipt from the Purchasing Agent for furnishing wheat on 10 May 1783 {Ref: Maryland State Archives MdHR-6636-42-22}

BUXTON, JOHN (Montgomery County) received a receipt from the Purchasing Agent for shelling corn on 11 Jul 1780 {Ref: Maryland State Archives MdHR-6636-24-2}; received a receipt for furnishing wheat on 11 Sep 1780 {Ref: Maryland State Archives MdHR-6636-24-7}; received a receipt for furnishing wheat on 2 Jul 1781 {Ref: Maryland State Archives MdHR-6636-42-11}

BUXTON, THOMAS (Montgomery County) received a receipt from the Purchasing Agent for furnishing wheat on 10 Apr 1781 {Ref: Maryland State Archives MdHR-6636-42-11}; received a receipt for furnishing wheat on 7 Oct 1781 {Ref: Maryland State Archives MdHR-6636-24-15}

BUZZARD, JACOB (Frederick County) received a certificate from the Purchasing Agent for furnishing wheat on 29 May 1782 {Ref: Maryland State Archives MdHR-6636-42-35}

BYARD, JAMES (Harford County) received payment for furnishing a gun to the

47

Committee of Safety on 2 Sep 1776 {Ref: Preston's History of Harford County, p. 335}

BYE, JOHN (Frederick County) received a certificate from the Purchasing Agent for furnishing wheat on 29 May 1782 {Ref: Maryland State Archives MdHR-6636-42-34}

BYERS, JAMES (Baltimore Town or County) received payment by order of the Council of Safety for furnishing boatage on 2 Sep 1776 {Ref: Archives of Maryland 12:253}

CADWALADER, JOHN (Kent County) pledged a loan in the amount of £1000 to the State of Maryland under the Act for the Emission of Bills of Credit "to defray the expences of the present campaign" in June, 1781 {Ref: Archives of Maryland 47:326}

CAHOW, WILLIAM (Montgomery County) received a receipt from the Purchasing Agent for furnishing wheat on 7 Aug 1781 {Ref: Maryland State Archives MdHR-6636-42-11}

CAILE, JOHN HALL (Dorchester County) submitted an account for provisions purchased for the army on 15 Dec 1780 {Ref: Maryland State Archives MdHR-6636-21-104}

CALDELEUGH, JANE, Mrs. (county not stated) received a loan certificate for £86.12.2 due from the Council of Maryland "agreeable to the Act proposing to the Citizens of this State, Creditors of Congress on Loan Office Certificates, Etc." on 22 May 1783 for services rendered during the war {Ref: Archives of Maryland 48:419}

CALDWELL, SAMUEL (Harford County) was a captain who was appointed by the Committee of Safety to be one of four men to serve on "a Committee for Examination of Guns and report of their Sufficiency be a Guide for this Committee to receive them by" on 11 Jul 1776 {Ref: Preston's History of Harford County, p. 331}

CALHOUN, ISAAC (Somerset County) received a receipt from the Purchasing Agent for furnishing beef on 7 Nov 1781 {Ref: Maryland State Archives MdHR-6636-24-44}

CALHOUN, JAMES (Baltimore Town) was appointed one of eighteen Collectors of Clothing by the Council of Maryland under "An Act to Procure Cloathing for the Quota of this State of the American Army" on 27 Nov 1777 {Ref: Archives of Maryland 16:426}; appointed Commissary of Purchases for Baltimore County by the Council of Maryland on 5 Sep 1780 {Ref: Archives of Maryland 43:276}; received payment for ship's provisions on 31 Mar 1781 {Ref: Maryland State Archives MdHR-6636-43-38VVV}; received a receipt for furnishing beef on 19 Jun 1781 {Ref: Maryland State Archives MdHR-6636-43-38EE}; received a receipt of supplies by Continental storekeepers on 12 Jul 1781 {Ref: Maryland State Archives MdHR-6636-28-16}; received a receipt for supplies on 30 Nov 1781 {Ref: Maryland State Archives MdHR-6636-28-16}; received a receipt for wheat on 30 Mar 1782 {Ref: Maryland State Archives MdHR-6636-42-3}; received a loan certificate for £479.8.6 due from the Council of Maryland "agreeable to the Act proposing to the Citizens of this State, Creditors of Congress on Loan Office Certificates, Etc." on 18 Dec 1783 for services rendered during the war {Ref: Archives of Maryland 48:491}

CALHOUN, JOSEPH (Somerset County) received a receipt from the Purchasing Agent for furnishing beef on 5 Nov 1781 {Ref: Maryland State Archives MdHR-6636-24-44}

CALHOUN, NATHAN (Somerset County) received a receipt from the Purchasing Agent for furnishing beef on 6 Nov 1781 {Ref: Maryland State Archives MdHR-6636-24-44}

CALLAHAN, JOHN (Anne Arundel County) was appointed by the Council of Maryland to be one of six "Signers of the Bills emitted in Virtue of the Act to enable the Treasurer of the Western Shore to draw and sell Bills of Exchange and for an Emission of Bills of Credit if necessary" on 8 Sep 1780 {Ref: Archives of Maryland 43:281}

CALLAHAN, THOMAS (Anne Arundel County) received a loan certificate for £73.17.9 due from the Council of Maryland "agreeable to the Act proposing to the Citizens of this State, Creditors of Congress on Loan Office Certificates, Etc." on 24 Jun 1783 for services rendered during the war {Ref: Archives of Maryland 48:434}

CALLISTER, HARRIOT (Talbot County) was one of twenty-six people who contacted the Governor and Council of Maryland in 1781 and pledged to support and maintain at their own expense the Barge *Experiment* so it can patrol the bay between Kent Point and Tilghman's Island in order to protect them against the enemy, stating in part, "whereas from the present exhausted state of the public treasury the government cannot immediately give that protection to every individual which is become necessary from the cruel and savage mode in which the war is now carried on against us" {Ref: Archives of Maryland 47:584-585}

CAMBURN, THOMAS (Montgomery County) received a receipt from the Purchasing Agent for furnishing wheat on 25 Apr 1781 {Ref: Maryland State Archives MdHR-6636-24-14}

CAMM, JOHN (Worcester County) submitted an account and receipt for furnishing cattle on 16 Dec 1781 {Ref: Maryland State Archives MdHR-6636-31-127}

CAMM, JOHN J. (Cecil County) received a receipt from the Purchasing Agent for furnishing wheat on 6 May 1783 and account of wheat for Col. Henry Hollingsworth on 18 Aug 1783 {Ref: Maryland State Archives MdHR-6636-

42-9}

CAMPBELL, ALEXANDER (Montgomery County) received a receipt from the Purchasing Agent for furnishing wheat on 14 May 1781 {Ref: Maryland State Archives MdHR-6636-24-18}

CAMPBELL, DANIEL (Harford County) received payment by order of the Council of Safety for furnishing a gun on 12 Sep 1776 {Ref: Archives of Maryland 12:267}

CAMPBELL, JOHN (Montgomery County) received a receipt from the Purchasing Agent for furnishing wheat on 18 Apr 1781 {Ref: Maryland State Archives MdHR-6636-24-18}

CAMPBELL, JOHN (Baltimore Town or County) received payment by order of the Council of Safety for furnishing nails on 2 Apr 1776 {Ref: Archives of Maryland 11:303}

CAMPBELL, SOLOMON (Worcester County) received a receipt from the Purchasing Agent for furnishing corn on 14 Jun 1780 {Ref: Maryland State Archives MdHR-6636-24-53}; his name appeared on "A List of Corn Purchased in Worcester County for the use of the State of Maryland" by the Commissary in July, 1780 {Ref: Archives of Maryland 45:10}

CAMPBELL, WILLIAM (Worcester County) received a receipt from the Purchasing Agent for furnishing corn on 20 Aug 1780 {Ref: Maryland State Archives MdHR-6636-24-53}; received a receipt for hauling supplies on 1 Mar 1783 {Ref: Maryland State Archives MdHR-19970-4-1}

CANNON, JOHN (Talbot County) received a receipt from the Purchasing Agent for furnishing cattle on 12 Apr 1781 {Ref: Maryland State Archives MdHR-6636-31-127}

CANNON, MATTHEW (Somerset County) received a receipt from the Purchasing Agent for furnishing pork on 20 Apr 1782 {Ref: Maryland State Archives MdHR-6636-43-21}

CANNON, WILLIAM (Caroline County) furnished corn and bacon on 21 Apr 1781 for the use of the State of Maryland {Ref: Archives of Maryland 47:250}; received a receipt from the Purchasing Agent for furnishing wheat on 20 Sep 1782 {Ref: Maryland State Archives MdHR-6636-42-7}

CAREY, DENNIS (Queen Anne's County) received a certificate from the Purchasing Agent for furnishing wheat on 18 Jan 1780 {Ref: Maryland State Archives MdHR-6636-24-30}

CAREY, HANNAH (Caroline County) received a receipt from the Purchasing Agent for furnishing wheat on 22 Aug 1782 {Ref: Maryland State Archives MdHR-6636-42-7}

CARICOE, IGNATIUS (Montgomery County) received a receipt from the Purchasing Agent for furnishing wheat on 28 May 1781 {Ref: Maryland State Archives MdHR-6636-24-18}

CARLAN, GEORGE (Baltimore Town) received payment for furnishing linen on 2 Oct 1779 {Ref: Maryland State Archives MdHR-19970-3-8}
CARMAN, JAMES (Dorchester County) received a receipt from the Purchasing Agent for furnishing wheat on 1 Oct 1782 {Ref: Maryland State Archives MdHR-6636-42-23}
CARMICHAEL, RICHARD B. (Queen Anne's County) received a certificate from the Purchasing Agent for furnishing wheat on 10 Jan 1780 {Ref: Maryland State Archives MdHR-6636-24-29}
CARMICHAEL, RUTH (Queen Anne's County) received a receipt from the Purchasing Agent for furnishing a bull on 1 Mar 1778 {Ref: Maryland State Archives MdHR-4587-50}
CARPENTER, WILLIAM (Charles County) received a receipt from the Purchasing Agent for furnishing wheat on 18 Sep 1781 {Ref: Maryland State Archives MdHR-6636-23-24}; received a receipt for furnishing wheat on 14 Nov 1781 {Ref: Maryland State Archives MdHR-6636-42-15}; received a receipt for furnishing wheat on 10 May 1783 {Ref: Maryland State Archives MdHR-6636-42-22}
CARRADINE, WILLIAM (Queen Anne's County) received a certificate from the Purchasing Agent for furnishing corn on 23 Jan 1780 {Ref: Maryland State Archives MdHR-6636-24-29}
CARRICO, JOSEPH (Charles County) received a receipt from the Purchasing Agent for furnishing wheat on 20 Dec 1782 {Ref: Maryland State Archives MdHR-6636-42-20}
CARRINGTON, JOHN (Charles County) received a receipt from the Purchasing Agent for furnishing wheat on 22 Dec 1781 {Ref: Maryland State Archives MdHR-6636-42-15}
CARROLL, CHARLES (Frederick County) received a certificate from the Purchasing Agent for furnishing wheat on 29 Aug 1781 {Ref: Maryland State Archives MdHR-6636-23-28}
CARROLL, CHARLES, OF CARROLLTON (Anne Arundel County) was appointed by the Council of Safety to collect all the gold and silver coin that could be procured in the county in compliance with the Resolve of Congress on 27 Jan 1776 {Ref: Archives of Maryland 11:132}
CARROLL, CHARLES, THE BARRISTER (Anne Arundel County) received payment by order of the Council of Safety on 3 Jul 1776 for iron furnished to George Gordon for gun carriages {Ref: Archives of Maryland 11:545}
CARROLL, ELINOR (Montgomery County) received a receipt from the Purchasing Agent for furnishing wheat on 16 Oct 1780 {Ref: Maryland State Archives MdHR-6636-24-8}
CARSON, RICHARD (Baltimore County) submitted an account and receipt for purchase of goods on 21 Apr 1781 {Ref: Maryland State Archives MdHR-

6636-26-138B}
CARTER, EDWARD (Caroline County) received a receipt from the Purchasing Agent for furnishing wheat on 20 Sep 1782 {Ref: Maryland State Archives MdHR-6636-42-7}
CARTER, EDWARD SR. (Caroline County) received a receipt from the Purchasing Agent for furnishing wheat on 20 Sep 1782 {Ref: Maryland State Archives MdHR-6636-42-7}
CARTER, JOHN (Dorchester County) received a receipt from the Purchasing Agent for furnishing wheat on 25 Mar 1783 {Ref: Maryland State Archives MdHR-6636-42-24}
CARTER, MARGARET (Baltimore Town) received payment by order of the Council of Maryland for services rendered (not specified) on 12 Jul 1778 {Ref: Archives of Maryland 21:158}
CARTER, SOLOMON (Caroline County) received a receipt from the Purchasing Agent for furnishing wheat on 1 Sep 1782 {Ref: Maryland State Archives MdHR-6636-42-7}
CARTRITE, JOHN (Prince George's County) received a receipt from the Purchasing Agent for furnishing wheat in 1782 {Ref: Maryland State Archives MdHR-6636-42-16}
CARTES (CARTY?), JOHN (Baltimore County) submitted an account and received payment for driving a wagon for six days and for forwarding flour to the army on 19 Feb 1780 {Ref: Maryland Historical Society MS.1814, Box 6}
CARTY, JOHN (Cecil County) received a receipt from the Purchasing Agent for furnishing flour on 12 Jun 1783 {Ref: Maryland State Archives MdHR-6636-42-9}
CARVILL, JOHN (Kent County) received a loan certificate for £8.8.9 due from the Council of Maryland "agreeable to the Act proposing to the Citizens of this State, Creditors of Congress on Loan Office Certificates, Etc." on 16 May 1783 for services rendered during the war {Ref: Archives of Maryland 48:414}
CARY, MARY, Mrs. (Frederick County) received a certificate from the Purchasing Agent for furnishing wheat on 7 Feb 1783 {Ref: Maryland State Archives MdHR-6636-42-38}
CASDON, JAMES (Cecil County) submitted an account for hauling wheat on 2 Sep 1783 {Ref: Maryland State Archives MdHR-6636-42-9}
CASE, SHADRACH (Montgomery County) received a receipt from the Purchasing Agent for furnishing wheat on 7 Jun 1781 {Ref: Maryland State Archives MdHR-6636-42-11}
CASEY, PHILIP (Montgomery County) received a receipt from the Purchasing Agent for furnishing wheat on 1 Aug 1780 {Ref: Maryland State Archives MdHR-6636-43-7}
CASEY, ROBERT (Annapolis) received payment by order of the Council of

Safety for riding express on 10 Jul 1777 {Ref: Archives of Maryland 16:316}

CASH, CALEB (Montgomery County) received a certificate from the Purchasing Agent for indebtedness owed to him by the state for services rendered to the commissary of purchases on 18 Mar 1782 {Ref: Maryland State Archives MdHR-6636-50-91}

CASSON, PHILIP (Caroline County) was appointed Purchaser of Clothing in his county by the Council of Maryland on 5 Jun 1781 {Ref: Archives of Maryland 45:462}; submitted an account for procurement of horses on 1 Aug 1781 {Ref: Maryland State Archives MdHR-6636-28-67}

CASTER, JAMES (Montgomery County) received a receipt from the Purchasing Agent for furnishing wheat on 16 Sep 1780 {Ref: Maryland State Archives MdHR-6636-24-7}

CASTER, JOHN (Montgomery County) received a receipt from the Purchasing Agent for furnishing wheat on 9 Sep 1780 {Ref: Maryland State Archives MdHR-6636-24-7}

CATON, CHARLES (Montgomery County) received receipts from the Purchasing Agent for furnishing wheat on 9 Sep and 22 Sep 1780 {Ref: Maryland State Archives MdHR-6636-24-7}; received a receipt for furnishing wheat in 1780 {Ref: Maryland State Archives MdHR-6636-24-8}

CATON, JOSHUA (Montgomery County) received a receipt from the Purchasing Agent for shelling corn on 7 Apr 1780 {Ref: Maryland State Archives MdHR-6636-24-2}

CATROP, LAMBERT (Talbot County) received a receipt from the Purchasing Agent for furnishing bacon for the use of the army on 6 May 1778 {Ref: Maryland State Archives MdHR-4587-84}

CATTILIT, ALEXANDER (Montgomery County) received a receipt from the Purchasing Agent for furnishing wheat on 25 May 1781 {Ref: Maryland State Archives MdHR-6636-42-11}

CAULK, FRANCES (Caroline County) received a receipt from the Purchasing Agent for furnishing wheat on 5 Aug 1782 {Ref: Maryland State Archives MdHR-6636-42-7}

CAULK, FRANCIS (Caroline County) received a receipt from the Purchasing Agent for furnishing wheat on 31 May 1782 {Ref: Maryland State Archives MdHR-6636-42-7}

CAULK, LAWRENCE (Caroline County) received a receipt from the Purchasing Agent for furnishing wheat on 16 Aug 1782 {Ref: Maryland State Archives MdHR-6636-42-7}

CAULK, LEVIN (Caroline County) received a receipt from the Purchasing Agent for furnishing wheat on 5 Aug 1782 {Ref: Maryland State Archives MdHR-6636-42-7}

CAULK, SUSANNAH (Kent County) received payment from the Purchasing

Agent for furnishing cattle and pasturage for the public use in September, 1781 {Ref: Maryland State Archives MdHR-6636-43-3}

CAUSIN, GERRARD B. (Charles County) pledged a loan in the amount of £350 to the State of Maryland under the Act for the Emission of Bills of Credit "to defray the expences of the present campaign" in June, 1781 {Ref: Archives of Maryland 47:326}; received a receipt from the Purchasing Agent for furnishing wheat on 7 Sep 1782 {Ref: Maryland State Archives MdHR-6636-42-18}; received a receipt for furnishing wheat on 28 Dec 1782 {Ref: Maryland State Archives MdHR-6636-42-21}

CAWSEY, BEACHAM (Caroline County) received a receipt from the Purchasing Agent for furnishing wheat on 5 Aug 1782 {Ref: Maryland State Archives MdHR-6636-42-7}

CAWSEY, FREDERICK (Caroline County) received a receipt from the Purchasing Agent for furnishing wheat on 5 Aug 1782 {Ref: Maryland State Archives MdHR-6636-42-7}

CAWSEY, ISAAC (Caroline County) received a receipt from the Purchasing Agent for furnishing wheat on 5 Aug 1782 {Ref: Maryland State Archives MdHR-6636-42-7}

CAWSEY, SOLOMON (Caroline County) received a receipt from the Purchasing Agent for furnishing wheat on 5 Aug 1782 {Ref: Maryland State Archives MdHR-6636-42-7}

CAWSEY, THOMAS (Caroline County) received a receipt from the Purchasing Agent for furnishing wheat on 5 Aug 1782 {Ref: Maryland State Archives MdHR-6636-42-7}

CAWSEY, ZEBULON (Caroline County) received a receipt from the Purchasing Agent for furnishing wheat on 5 Aug 1782 {Ref: Maryland State Archives MdHR-6636-42-7}

CAYTON, WILLIAM (Baltimore County) received payment by order of the Council of Safety for the hire of his cart on 17 Aug 1776 and for cartage for the Flying Camp on 2 Sep 1776 {Ref: Archives of Maryland 12:215, 252}

CEASY, PHILLIP (Montgomery County) received a receipt from the Purchasing Agent for furnishing wheat on 7 Apr 1780 {Ref: Maryland State Archives MdHR-6636-24-5}; received a receipt for furnishing wheat on 8 Aug 1780 {Ref: Maryland State Archives MdHR-6636-24-6}; received a receipt for furnishing wheat on 8 Sep 1780 {Ref: Maryland State Archives MdHR-6636-24-7}

CECIL, ARCHIBALD (Prince George's County) received a receipt from the Purchasing Agent for furnishing wheat on 12 Feb 1783 {Ref: Maryland State Archives MdHR-6636-50-135}

CECIL, SAMUEL (Montgomery County) received receipts from the Purchasing Agent for furnishing wheat on 25 Apr and 14 Oct 1781 {Ref: Maryland State

Archives MdHR-6636-24-14}

CECIL, WILLIAM (Prince George's County) received receipts from the Purchasing Agent for furnishing wheat on 12 Feb and 27 Apr 1783 {Ref: Maryland State Archives MdHR-6636-50-135}

CERRICO, IGNATIUS (Montgomery County) received a receipt from the Purchasing Agent for furnishing wheat on 1 Aug 1780 {Ref: Maryland State Archives MdHR-6636-43-7}

CHAILLE, PETER (Worcester County) was a colonel who was appointed by the Council of Safety to collect all the gold and silver coin that could be procured in the county in compliance with the Resolve of Congress on 27 Jan 1776 {Ref: Archives of Maryland 11:132}; served as a Commissary Agent in 1780-1782; received a receipt for furnishing corn on 29 Feb 1780 {Ref: Maryland State Archives MdHR-6636-24-52}; his name appeared on "A List of Corn Purchased in Worcester County for the use of the State of Maryland" by the Commissary in July, 1780 {Ref: Archives of Maryland 45:9}; appointed Purchaser of Clothing in his county by the Council of Maryland on 5 Jun 1781 {Ref: Archives of Maryland 45:462}; submitted an account for procuring horses and clothing on 16 Jul 1781 {Ref: Maryland State Archives MdHR-6636-28-22}; submitted an account for commissary disbursements on 15 Dec 1782 {Ref: Maryland State Archives MdHR-6636-43-29B}

CHALMERS, JOHN (Anne Arundel County) received payment by order of the Council of Maryland "for fish purchased of him by this Board for the Continental Troops in this city [Annapolis] and delivered to Mr. Crisall" on 2 May 1780 {Ref: Archives of Maryland 43:160}

CHAMBERLAINE, JAMES (Talbot County) received a certificate from the Purchasing Agent for furnishing wheat on 14 Mar 1780 {Ref: Maryland State Archives MdHR-6636-24-46}

CHAMBERLAINE, JAMES LLOYD (Talbot County) was appointed by the Council of Safety to collect all the gold and silver coin that could be procured in the county in compliance with the Resolve of Congress on 27 Jan 1776 {Ref: Archives of Maryland 11:132}

CHAMBERLAINE, SAMUEL (Talbot County) received a certificate from the Purchasing Agent for furnishing wheat on 25 Mar 1780 {Ref: Maryland State Archives MdHR-6636-24-46}; submitted an account and receipt of payment due for cattle on 29 Sep 1780 {Ref: Maryland State Archives MdHR-6636-24-49}

CHAMBERS, CLEMENT (Montgomery County) received a receipt from the Purchasing Agent for furnishing wheat on 23 Apr 1781 {Ref: Maryland State Archives MdHR-6636-24-14}

CHAMBERS, JOHN (Worcester County) submitted an account and receipt for hauling salt on 5 Jan 1782 {Ref: Maryland State Archives MdHR-6636-43-

28GGG}

CHAMBERS, JOHN (Montgomery County) received a receipt from the Purchasing Agent for furnishing wheat on 4 May 1781 {Ref: Maryland State Archives MdHR-6636-24-18}

CHANCE, ABSALOM (Caroline County) received a receipt from the Purchasing Agent for furnishing wheat on 31 Aug 1782 {Ref: Maryland State Archives MdHR-6636-42-7}

CHANCE, THOMAS (Caroline County) received a receipt from the Purchasing Agent for furnishing wheat on 1 Sep 1782 {Ref: Maryland State Archives MdHR-6636-42-7}

CHANE, JUDITH (Charles County) received a receipt from the Purchasing Agent for furnishing wheat on 28 Dec 1782 {Ref: Maryland State Archives MdHR-6636-42-21}

CHANEY, HEZEKIAH (Montgomery County) received receipts from the Purchasing Agent for furnishing wheat on 14 Oct and 20 Oct 1780 {Ref: Maryland State Archives MdHR-6636-24-13}

CHAPLIN, THOMAS (Talbot County) received a receipt from the Purchasing Agent for purchasing bacon on 12 Jun 1778 {Ref: Maryland State Archives MdHR-6636-12-15}

CHAPLINE, JAMES (Washington County) pledged a loan in the amount of £250 to the State of Maryland under the Act for the Emission of Bills of Credit "to defray the expences of the present campaign" in June, 1781 {Ref: Archives of Maryland 47:327}

CHAPLINE, JOSEPH (Washington County) submitted an account of purchase of grain for the use of the state on 31 Mar 1780 {Ref: Maryland State Archives MdHR-4590-76}

CHAPMAN, HENRY (Anne Arundel County) submitted an account for delivery of candles on 16 May 1782 {Ref: Maryland State Archives MdHR-6636-36-92A}

CHAPMAN, JOHN JR. (Charles County) received a receipt from the Purchasing Agent for furnishing wheat on 6 Oct 1781 {Ref: Maryland State Archives MdHR-6636-42-15}

CHAPMAN, JOHN (Charles County) received a receipt from the Purchasing Agent for furnishing wheat on 1 Sep 1781 {Ref: Maryland State Archives MdHR-6636-42-15}; received a receipt for furnishing wheat on 6 Sep 1782 {Ref: Maryland State Archives MdHR-6636-42-18}; received a receipt for furnishing wheat on 29 Nov 1782 {Ref: Maryland State Archives MdHR-6636-42-20}

CHAPMAN, PEARSON (Charles County) received a receipt from the Purchasing Agent for furnishing wheat on 18 Aug 1782 {Ref: Maryland State Archives MdHR-6636-42-18}; received a receipt for furnishing wheat on 31 Oct 1782

{Ref: Maryland State Archives MdHR-6636-42-19}

CHAPPELL, ARCHIBALD (Montgomery County) received a receipt from the Purchasing Agent for furnishing wheat on 26 May 1781 {Ref: Maryland State Archives MdHR-6636-24-18}

CHARLES, ISAAC (Dorchester County) received a receipt from the Purchasing Agent for furnishing wheat on 25 Mar 1783 {Ref: Maryland State Archives MdHR-6636-42-24}

CHARLES, SOLOMON (Dorchester County) received a receipt from the Purchasing Agent for furnishing wheat on 25 Mar 1783 {Ref: Maryland State Archives MdHR-6636-42-24}

CHARLETON, JOHN W. (Frederick County) received a receipt from the Purchasing Agent for furnishing beef on 4 Jan 1781 {Ref: Maryland State Archives MdHR-6636-42-26}; received receipts from the Purchasing Agent for delivering flour and furnishing pork on 24 Feb and 1 Mar 1781 {Ref: Maryland State Archives MdHR-6636-23-30}; received certificates from the Purchasing Agent for delivering and furnishing flour on 1 Dec, 27 Dec and 30 Dec 1780 {Ref: Maryland State Archives MdHR-6636-23-29}

CHARLETON, JOHN (Frederick County) received a receipt from the Purchasing Agent for delivering flour on 29 Dec 1780 {Ref: Maryland State Archives MdHR-6636-23-29}

CHARTWRIGHT, GUSTAVUS (Charles County) received a receipt from the Purchasing Agent for furnishing wheat on 28 Sep 1782 {Ref: Maryland State Archives MdHR-6636-42-19}

CHASE, JEREMIAH T. (Baltimore County) submitted an account for purchase of blankets and shoes on 1 Aug 1780 {Ref: Maryland State Archives MdHR-4599-22}

CHASE, JUDITH (Charles County) received receipts from the Purchasing Agent for furnishing wheat on 5 Nov and 11 Dec 1781 {Ref: Maryland State Archives MdHR-6636-42-15}

CHASE, SAMUEL (Anne Arundel County) pledged a loan in the amount of £500 to the State of Maryland under the Act for the Emission of Bills of Credit "to defray the expences of the present campaign" in June, 1781 {Ref: Archives of Maryland 47:327}

CHAVEL, EZEKIEL (Worcester County) submitted an account and receipt for cutting beef and guarding a sloop on 1 Oct 1781 {Ref: Maryland State Archives MdHR-6636-43-27}

CHENEY, SAMUEL (Anne Arundel County) received a loan certificate for £14 due from the Council of Maryland "agreeable to the Act proposing to the Citizens of this State, Creditors of Congress on Loan Office Certificates, Etc." on 21 Oct 1783 for services rendered during the war {Ref: Archives of Maryland 48:472}

57

CHENWORTH, RICHARD (Baltimore County) received a receipt from the Purchasing Agent for hauling flour on 1 Sep 1781 {Ref: Maryland State Archives MdHR-6636-43-38BB}

CHEVER, JOHN (Talbot County) was a lieutenant who received a supply of gun flints and cartridge paper by order of the Council of Maryland on 21 May 1779 to be delivered to Christopher Birkhead, county lieutenant in Talbot County {Ref: Archives of Maryland 21:408, 453}

CHEW, WILLIAM (Calvert County) was appointed by the Council of Maryland as one of thirty men to be "Agents for Purchasing Provisions" on 30 Mar 1779 {Ref: Archives of Maryland 21:332}

CHILCOT, ROBERT (Baltimore County) received payment for furnishing mutton on 13 Jun 1781 {Ref: Maryland State Archives MdHR-6636-43-38SS}

CHILCUT, THOMAS (Caroline County) received a receipt from the Purchasing Agent for furnishing wheat on 5 Aug 1782 {Ref: Maryland State Archives MdHR-6636-42-7}

CHILLAM, JOHN (Prince George's County) received a receipt from the Purchasing Agent for furnishing wheat on 14 Jul 1781 {Ref: Maryland State Archives MdHR-6636-24-20}

CHILTON, JOHN S. (Charles County) received a receipt from the Purchasing Agent for furnishing wheat on 8 Nov 1782 {Ref: Maryland State Archives MdHR-6636-42-19}

CHILTON, WILLIAM (Caroline County) received a receipt from the Purchasing Agent for furnishing wheat on 17 Aug 1782 {Ref: Maryland State Archives MdHR-6636-42-7}

CHINN, EDWARD (Montgomery County) received a receipt from the Purchasing Agent for furnishing wheat on 12 May 1781 {Ref: Maryland State Archives MdHR-6636-24-18}

CHIPCHASE, THOMAS (Baltimore County) received a receipt from the Purchasing Agent for furnishing veal on 31 May 1781 {Ref: Maryland State Archives MdHR-6636-43-38XX}

CHISELL, JOSEPH NEWTON (Montgomery County) received a receipt from the Purchasing Agent for furnishing wheat on 23 Aug 1781 {Ref: Maryland State Archives MdHR-6636-24-15}

CHISHOLM, ARCHIBALD (Anne Arundel County) received payments by order of the Council of Safety "for stocking musquets" on 16 Apr and 8 May 1776 {Ref: Archives of Maryland 11:333, 417}

CHISWELL, JOSEPH (Prince George's County) received a receipt from the Purchasing Agent for furnishing wheat on 8 May 1782 {Ref: Maryland State Archives MdHR-6636-50-135}; received a receipt for furnishing wheat on 1 Aug 1783 {Ref: Maryland State Archives MdHR-6636-50-142}; received a receipt for furnishing wheat on 13 Aug 1783 {Ref: Maryland State Archives

MdHR-6636-50-135}

CHISWELL, NEWTON (Montgomery County) received a receipt from the Purchasing Agent for shelling corn on 1 Jul 1780 {Ref: Maryland State Archives MdHR-6636-24-2}

CHRIST, PHILIP (Frederick County) received a certificate from the Purchasing Agent for furnishing hay on 21 Dec 1781 {Ref: Maryland State Archives MdHR-6636-42-32}; received a certificate for wintering a bull on 27 May 1782 {Ref: Maryland State Archives MdHR-6636-42-33}

CHRISTIE, GABRIEL (Harford County) received payment by order of the Council of Safety for furnishing a gun on 21 Aug 1776 {Ref: Archives of Maryland 12:230}

CHRISTIE, ROBERT (Baltimore Town) received payment by order of the Council of Safety on 10 Oct 1776 "for the detention of two vessels sunk at *Otter* alarm" at Whetstone Point in March, 1776 for the purpose of preventing any of the British Ships of War from coming up to Baltimore Town {Ref: Archives of Maryland 12:330, 333}

CHRISTIE, ROBERT JR. (Baltimore Town) received payment by order of the Council of Safety on 10 Oct 1776 "for the detention of two vessels sunk at *Otter* alarm" at Whetstone Point in March, 1776 for the purpose of preventing any of the British Ships of War from coming up to Baltimore Town {Ref: Archives of Maryland 12:330, 333}

CLACKSON, NOTLEY (Montgomery County) received a receipt from the Purchasing Agent for furnishing wheat on 1 Aug 1780 {Ref: Maryland State Archives MdHR-6636-43-7}

CLAGETT, HENRY (Frederick County) received a receipt from the Purchasing Agent for furnishing beef on 14 Mar 1781 {Ref: Maryland State Archives MdHR-6636-23-4}

CLAGETT, HEZEKIAH (Montgomery County) received a receipt from the Purchasing Agent for furnishing wheat on 20 Oct 1780 {Ref: Maryland State Archives MdHR-6636-24-8}

CLAGETT, JAMES (Charles County) received a receipt from the Purchasing Agent for furnishing wheat on 28 Dec 1782 {Ref: Maryland State Archives MdHR-6636-42-21}

CLAGETT, JOHN (Montgomery County) received a receipt from the Purchasing Agent for furnishing wheat on 23 Sep 1780 {Ref: Maryland State Archives MdHR-6636-24-7}; received a receipt for furnishing wheat on 8 Dec 1780 and 17 Jan 1782 {Ref: Maryland State Archives MdHR-6636-43-8}

CLAGETT (CLAGGET), JOSEPH (Montgomery County) received a receipt from the Purchasing Agent for furnishing wheat on 28 Jul 1780 {Ref: Maryland State Archives MdHR-6636-24-5}; received a receipt from the Purchasing Agent for furnishing wheat on 1 Aug 1780 {Ref: Maryland State Archives MdHR-6636-

43-7}; received a receipt for furnishing wheat on 18 Jan 1781 {Ref: Maryland State Archives MdHR-6636-24-9}

CLAGETT, NATHAN (Montgomery County) received receipts from the Purchasing Agent for furnishing wheat on 7 Aug, 10 Aug and 28 Aug 1780 {Ref: Maryland State Archives MdHR-6636-24-6}; received a receipt for furnishing wheat on 15 Nov 1780 {Ref: Maryland State Archives MdHR-6636-24-8}

CLAGETT, NINIAN (Prince George's County) received a receipt from the Purchasing Agent for furnishing wheat on 17 Aug 1782 {Ref: Maryland State Archives MdHR-6636-50-135}

CLAGETT (CLAGGET), R. K. (Montgomery County) received a receipt from the Purchasing Agent for furnishing wheat on 1 Aug 1780 {Ref: Maryland State Archives MdHR-6636-43-7}

CLAGETT, RICHARD CAIN (Montgomery County) received a receipt from the Purchasing Agent for furnishing wheat on 12 Aug 1780 {Ref: Maryland State Archives MdHR-6636-24-6}

CLAGETT (CLAGGETT), THOMAS (Prince George's County) was appointed by the Council of Maryland on 25 Mar 1778 as one of eighteen men to be "Agents for Purchasing Provisions for the Army of the United States Agreeable to an Act of Assembly passed the 23rd Inst." {Ref: Archives of Maryland 16:551}; purchased bacon and beef for the army on 25 Jun 1778 {Ref: Maryland State Archives MdHR-4587-57}; appointed by the Council of Maryland as one of thirty men to be "Agents for Purchasing Provisions" on 30 Mar 1779 {Ref: Archives of Maryland 21:332}; his name appeared as "Thomas Clegetts Store Piscatoway" when he was listed in possession of Powder, Balls, and "F" [unexplained initial] on a "Return of Armes and Ammunition in Prince George's County Belonging to the Publick" on 3 Jul 1780 {Ref: Archives of Maryland 45:4}; "Thomas Clagett & Co." (Thomas noted as being the brother of William Clagett, Purchaser of Clothing) offered for the use of the state "a few linens and a few hatts" on 12 Jun 1781 {Ref: Archives of Maryland 47:288}; pledged a loan in the amount of £250 to the State of Maryland under the Act for the Emission of Bills of Credit "to defray the expences of the present campaign" in June, 1781 {Ref: Archives of Maryland 47:327}; also see "Charles Lansdale," q.v.

CLAGETT, WILLIAM (Prince George's County) was appointed Purchaser of Clothing in his county by the Council of Maryland on 5 Jun 1781 {Ref: Archives of Maryland 45:462, 47:287}

CLAGETT (CLAGGETT), WISEMAN (Prince George's County) received payment by order of the Council of Safety for furnishing a gun on 5 Sep 1776 {Ref: Archives of Maryland 12:257}

CLAGETT, ZACHARIAH (Montgomery County) received a receipt from the

Purchasing Agent for furnishing wheat on 18 Jan 1781 {Ref: Maryland State Archives MdHR-6636-24-9}

CLAREY, JOHN (Frederick County) received certificates from the Purchasing Agent for furnishing wheat on 7 Jan and 14 Feb 1783 {Ref: Maryland State Archives MdHR-6636-42-38}

CLARK, JEAMS OR JEAMES (Harford County) received a receipt from the Purchasing Agent for furnishing wheat on 13 Jun 1780 {Ref: Maryland State Archives MdHR-6636-23-39}

CLARK, JOHN (Kent County) submitted a transmittal of a return for provisions to the commissary on 22 Apr 1779 {Ref: Maryland State Archives MdHR-6636-13-125}

CLARK, WILLIAM (Back Creek, Cecil County) purchased flour for the use of the state on 19 Jan 1780 {Ref: Maryland State Archives MdHR-4590-82}

CLARKE, DANIEL (Prince George's County) received a loan certificate for £121.5.10 due from the Council of Maryland "agreeable to the Act proposing to the Citizens of this State, Creditors of Congress on Loan Office Certificates, Etc." on 25 Oct 1783 for services rendered during the war {Ref: Archives of Maryland 48:473}

CLARKE, JAMES (Baltimore County) received payment by order of the Council of Safety on 10 Oct 1776 "for sinkage of vessels at *Otter* alarm" at Whetstone Point in March, 1776 for the purpose of preventing any of the British Ships of War from coming up to Baltimore Town {Ref: Archives of Maryland 12:330, 333}

CLARKE, THOMAS (Montgomery County) received a receipt from the Purchasing Agent for furnishing wheat on 13 Oct 1781 {Ref: Maryland State Archives MdHR-6636-24-15}

CLARKSON, NOTLEY (Montgomery County) received a receipt from the Purchasing Agent for furnishing wheat on 4 Aug 1780 {Ref: Maryland State Archives MdHR-6636-24-6}

CLEGETT, THOMAS, see "Thomas Clagett," q.v.

CLEMENT, FRANCES (Montgomery County) received a receipt from the Purchasing Agent for furnishing wheat on 1 Aug 1780 {Ref: Maryland State Archives MdHR-6636-43-7}

CLEMENTS, CLEMENT (Charles County) received a receipt from the Purchasing Agent for furnishing wheat on 8 May 1783 {Ref: Maryland State Archives MdHR-6636-42-22}

CLEMENTS, FRANCIS (Montgomery County) received a receipt from the Purchasing Agent for furnishing wheat on 7 Aug 1780 {Ref: Maryland State Archives MdHR-6636-24-6}

CLEMENTS, JOHN (Charles County) received receipts from the Purchasing Agent for furnishing wheat on 25 May and 18 Aug 1782 {Ref: Maryland State

Archives MdHR-6636-42-18}; received a receipt for furnishing wheat on 28 Sep 1782 {Ref: Maryland State Archives MdHR-6636-42-19}

CLEMENTS, LEONARD (Charles County) received a receipt from the Purchasing Agent for furnishing wheat on 14 Sep 1782 {Ref: Maryland State Archives MdHR-6636-42-18}

CLEMENTS, OSWALD (Montgomery County) received a receipt from the Purchasing Agent for furnishing wheat on 14 May 1781 {Ref: Maryland State Archives MdHR-6636-24-18}

CLEMENTS, THOMAS (Charles County) received a receipt from the Purchasing Agent for furnishing wheat on 8 Dec 1781 {Ref: Maryland State Archives MdHR-6636-42-15}; received receipts from the Purchasing Agent for furnishing wheat on 10 Sep and 10 Oct 1782 {Ref: Maryland State Archives MdHR-6636-42-19}

CLEMENTS, WALTER (Charles County) received a receipt from the Purchasing Agent for furnishing wheat on 15 Apr 1783 {Ref: Maryland State Archives MdHR-6636-42-22}

CLEMENTS, WILLIAM (Montgomery County) received a receipt from the Purchasing Agent for furnishing wheat on 1 Aug 1780 {Ref: Maryland State Archives MdHR-6636-43-7}

CLEMM, WILLIAM (Baltimore County) was a lieutenant who received payment for furnishing beef on 30 Apr 1781 {Ref: Maryland State Archives MdHR-6636-43-38/OOO}

CLEMMENTS, JOHN, OF FRANCIS (Charles County) received a receipt from the Purchasing Agent for furnishing wheat on 26 Apr 1783 {Ref: Maryland State Archives MdHR-6636-42-22}

CLIGET, NONOMAN (Prince George's County) received a receipt from the Purchasing Agent for furnishing wheat in 1783 {Ref: Maryland State Archives MdHR-6636-50-135}

CLOW, JOHN (Caroline County) received a receipt from the Purchasing Agent for furnishing wheat on 17 Aug 1782 {Ref: Maryland State Archives MdHR-6636-42-7}

CLUNIE, JAMES (Baltimore Town) received payment for furnishing linen on 19 Nov 1779 {Ref: Maryland State Archives MdHR-19970-3-8}

CLYMA, PETER (Frederick County) received a certificate from the Purchasing Agent for furnishing wheat on 1 Feb 1783 {Ref: Maryland State Archives MdHR-6636-42-38}

COALE, SKIPWITH (Harford County) received a receipt from the Purchasing Agent for furnishing wheat on 1 Apr 1780 {Ref: Maryland State Archives MdHR-6636-23-35}

COATMAN, JOSEPH (Somerset County) received a receipt from the Purchasing Agent for furnishing pork on 1 Aug 1781 {Ref: Maryland State Archives

MdHR-6636-24-43}

COBLENCE, PETER (Frederick County) received a certificate from the Purchasing Agent for furnishing wheat on 30 May 1782 {Ref: Maryland State Archives MdHR-6636-42-35}

COCHINDERFER, MICHAEL (Frederick and Montgomery Counties) received payment by order of the Council of Safety to enable him to carry on a stocking manufactory on 29 Jul 1776 {Ref: Archives of Maryland 12:109}

COCKAYNE, SAMUEL (Talbot County) was a captain who received a loan certificate for £9.13.2 due from the Council of Maryland "agreeable to the Act proposing to the Citizens of this State, Creditors of Congress on Loan Office Certificates, Etc." on 16 Jun 1783 for services rendered during the war {Ref: Archives of Maryland 48:431-432}

COCKERELL, JOHN (Frederick County) received a receipt from the Purchasing Agent for furnishing pork on 14 Mar 1781 {Ref: Maryland State Archives MdHR-6636-23-4}

COCKEY, JOHN (Baltimore County) received payment by order of the Council of Maryland for his use as Contractor for Wagons and Teams in Baltimore County on 4 Sep 1780 {Ref: Archives of Maryland 43:275}; delivered a wagon and gears with nine horses for the use of the state on 5 Dec 1780 {Ref: Archives of Maryland 45:198}

COCKRAN, JAMES (Dorchester County) received a receipt from the Purchasing Agent for furnishing wheat on 1 Oct 1782 {Ref: Maryland State Archives MdHR-6636-42-23}

COCKRAN, WILLIAM (Dorchester County) received a receipt from the Purchasing Agent for furnishing wheat on 1 Oct 1782 {Ref: Maryland State Archives MdHR-6636-42-23}

COCKS, JOHN (Charles County) received a receipt from the Purchasing Agent for furnishing wheat on 2 Nov 1782 {Ref: Maryland State Archives MdHR-6636-42-19}

COILE, ADAM, see "Nicholas White," q.v.

COLAGIN, MICHAEL (Montgomery County) received a receipt from the Purchasing Agent for furnishing wheat on 11 Oct 1781 {Ref: Maryland State Archives MdHR-6636-24-15}

COLBURN, ELIJAH (Somerset County) received a receipt from the Purchasing Agent for furnishing beef on 6 Nov 1781 {Ref: Maryland State Archives MdHR-6636-24-44}

COLBURN, JOHN (Worcester County) submitted an account and receipt for furnishing pork barrels on 12 Mar 1782 {Ref: Maryland State Archives MdHR-6636-43-28SS}

COLBURN, ROBERT (Somerset County) received a receipt from the Purchasing Agent for furnishing beef on 2 Sep 1781 {Ref: Maryland State Archives

MdHR-6636-24-44}
COLBURN, SARAH (Somerset County) received a receipt from the Purchasing Agent for furnishing beef on 1 Nov 1781 {Ref: Maryland State Archives MdHR-6636-24-44}
COLBURN, STEPHEN (Somerset County) received a receipt from the Purchasing Agent for furnishing beef on 5 Dec 1781 {Ref: Maryland State Archives MdHR-6636-24-44}
COLE, ELIJAH (Cecil County) submitted an account for grain purchased on 1 Jun 1780 {Ref: Maryland State Archives MdHR-4590-81}; submitted an account of flour for use of the army in 1780 {Ref: Maryland State Archives MdHR-4595-9}
COLE, JOHN (county not stated) received a loan certificate for £56.11.1 due from the Council of Maryland "agreeable to the Act proposing to the Citizens of this State, Creditors of Congress on Loan Office Certificates, Etc." on 3 Dec 1783 for services rendered during the war {Ref: Archives of Maryland 48:485}
COLE, SARAH (Charles County) received a receipt from the Purchasing Agent for furnishing wheat on 31 Oct 1782 {Ref: Maryland State Archives MdHR-6636-42-19}
COLEY, JOHN (Kent County) received payment from the Purchasing Agent for furnishing cattle for the public use in September, 1781 {Ref: Maryland State Archives MdHR-6636-43-3}
COLLETT, ROBERT (Baltimore Town or County) received payments by order of the Council of Safety for painting gun carriages on 16 Apr and 31 Jul 1776 {Ref: Archives of Maryland 11:333, 12:148}
COLLEY, THOMAS (Montgomery County) received a receipt from the Purchasing Agent for furnishing wheat on 30 May 1781 {Ref: Maryland State Archives MdHR-6636-42-11}
COLLIER, SARAH (Worcester County) received a receipt from the Purchasing Agent for furnishing corn on 14 Jun 1780 {Ref: Maryland State Archives MdHR-6636-24-53}; her name appeared on "A List of Corn Purchased in Worcester County for the use of the State of Maryland" by the Commissary in July, 1780 {Ref: Archives of Maryland 45:10}; received a receipt for furnishing beef on 20 Sep 1780 {Ref: Maryland State Archives MdHR-6636-24-54}; submitted an account and receipt for furnishing salt on 1 Feb 1782 {Ref: Maryland State Archives MdHR-6636-43-28DDD}
COLLIER (COLLIAR), WILLIAM (Montgomery County) received a receipt from the Purchasing Agent for furnishing wheat on 1 Aug 1780 {Ref: Maryland State Archives MdHR-6636-43-7}; received a receipt for furnishing wheat on 31 Aug 1780 {Ref: Maryland State Archives MdHR-6636-24-6}; received a receipt for furnishing wheat on 27 Sep 1780 {Ref: Maryland State Archives MdHR-6636-24-7}; received a receipt for furnishing wheat on 15 Nov 1780

{Ref: Maryland State Archives MdHR-6636-24-8}

COLLINS, ABRAHAM (Caroline County) received receipts from the Purchasing Agent for furnishing wheat on 31 May, 17 Aug and 22 Aug 1782 {Ref: Maryland State Archives MdHR-6636-42-7}

COLLINS, SAMUEL (Somerset County) received a receipt from the Purchasing Agent for furnishing beef on 5 Dec 1781 {Ref: Maryland State Archives MdHR-6636-24-44}

COLLINS, SARAH (Montgomery County) was a widow who received a receipt from the Purchasing Agent for furnishing wheat on 6 Jun 1781 {Ref: Maryland State Archives MdHR-6636-24-14}

COLLISON, PETER (Caroline County) received a receipt from the Purchasing Agent for furnishing wheat on 5 Aug 1782 {Ref: Maryland State Archives MdHR-6636-42-7}

COLLISON, WILLIAM (Caroline County) received receipts from the Purchasing Agent for furnishing wheat on 5 Aug 1782 {Ref: Maryland State Archives MdHR-6636-42-7}

COLSCOTT, WILLIAM (Caroline County) received a receipt from the Purchasing Agent for wheat on 29 Aug 1782 {Ref: Maryland State Archives MdHR-6636-42-7}

COLSTON, JEREMIAH (Caroline County) received a receipt from the Purchasing Agent for wheat on 16 Sep 1782 {Ref: Maryland State Archives MdHR-6636-42-7}

COMBERS, ANN (Montgomery County) received a receipt from the Purchasing Agent for furnishing wheat on 27 Apr 1781 {Ref: Maryland State Archives MdHR-6636-24-18}

COMBS, RICHARD (Charles County) received a receipt from the Purchasing Agent for furnishing wheat on 27 Jul 1782 {Ref: Maryland State Archives MdHR-6636-42-18}

COMEGYS, JACOB (Kent County) received a certificate from the Purchasing Agent for hauling wheat on 15 Feb 1780 {Ref: Maryland State Archives MdHR-6636-43-1}

COMPTON, STEPHEN (Charles County) submitted an account for purchasing beef on 23 Sep 1780 {Ref: Maryland State Archives MdHR-6636-20-61B}; received a receipt for furnishing wheat on 29 Dec 1782 {Ref: Maryland State Archives MdHR-6636-42-21}; received a loan certificate for £76.10.6 due from the Council of Maryland "agreeable to the Act proposing to the Citizens of this State, Creditors of Congress on Loan Office Certificates, Etc." on 14 Aug and 14 Oct 1783 for services rendered during the war {Ref: Archives of Maryland 48:446, 464}

COMPTON, WILLIAM S. (Charles County) received a receipt from the Purchasing Agent for furnishing wheat on 7 Jul 1781 {Ref: Maryland State

Archives MdHR-6636-42-15}

CONES, RICHARD (Montgomery County) received receipts from the Purchasing Agent for furnishing wheat on 15 Oct and 22 Oct 1781 {Ref: Maryland State Archives MdHR-6636-42-11}

CONN, JANE (Montgomery County) received a receipt from the Purchasing Agent for furnishing wheat on 2 Oct 1780 {Ref: Maryland State Archives MdHR-6636-24-13}

CONNAWAY, BENJAMIN (Caroline County) received a receipt from the Purchasing Agent for furnishing wheat on 1 Sep 1782 {Ref: Maryland State Archives MdHR-6636-42-7}

CONNAWAY, SAMUEL (Caroline County) received receipts from the Purchasing Agent for furnishing wheat on 1 Sep and 20 Sep 1782 {Ref: Maryland State Archives MdHR-6636-42-7}

CONNELLY, DENNIS (Dorchester County) received a receipt from the Purchasing Agent for furnishing wheat on 1 Oct 1782 {Ref: Maryland State Archives MdHR-6636-42-23}

CONNELLY, JEREMIAH (Dorchester County) received a receipt from the Purchasing Agent for furnishing wheat on 1 Oct 1782 {Ref: Maryland State Archives MdHR-6636-42-23}

CONNELLY (CONNELY), THOMAS (Montgomery County) received receipts from the Purchasing Agent for furnishing wheat on 15 Sep and 19 Sep 1780 {Ref: Maryland State Archives MdHR-6636-24-7}

CONNER, RICHARD (Montgomery County) received a receipt from the Purchasing Agent for furnishing wheat on 5 May 1781 {Ref: Maryland State Archives MdHR-6636-42-11}

CONNER, THOMAS (Montgomery County) received a receipt from the Purchasing Agent for furnishing wheat on 5 May 1781 {Ref: Maryland State Archives MdHR-6636-42-11}

CONNOWAY, TIMOTHY (Anne Arundel County) received a receipt from the Purchasing Agent for furnishing powder on 16 Apr 1777 {Ref: Maryland State Archives MdHR-6636-9-14A}

CONTEE, ALEXANDER (Nottingham, Prince George's County) received payment from the Purchasing Agent for furnishing material for clothing ("brown drugget and brown serge") on 12 Jun 1781 {Ref: Archives of Maryland 47:288}

CONTEE, THOMAS (Prince George's County) was appointed by the Council of Safety to collect all the gold and silver coin that could be procured in the county in compliance with the Resolve of Congress on 27 Jan 1776 {Ref: Archives of Maryland 11:132}; received payment for furnishing rugs and blankets for the troops on 7 May 1776 {Ref: Archives of Maryland 11:414}; his name appeared as "Thomas Contees Nottingham" when he was listed in possession of one gun, some powder, and F" [unexplained initial] on a "Return of Armes and Ammunition in Prince George's County Belonging to the Publick" on 3 Jul 1780 {Ref: Archives of Maryland 45:4}

CONWAY, JOHN SPAN (Somerset County) received a receipt from the Purchasing Agent for furnishing bacon on 11 Aug 1780 {Ref: Maryland State Archives MdHR-6636-24-41}

COOK, ADAM (Baltimore Town) submitted an account and received payment for turning out flour of stores for two days and stowing for the commission in Baltimore on 28 Jan 1780; received payment for measuring wheat for four days on 3 Feb 1780 {Ref: Maryland Historical Society MS.1814, Box 6}

COOK, GEORGE, see "Margaret Lucas," q.v.

COOK, HENRY (Frederick County) received payment by order of the Council of Maryland for furnishing pasturage, hay and wood on 25 Mar 1778 {Ref: Archives of Maryland 16:550-551}

COOMES, WILLIAM JR. (Charles County) received a receipt from the Purchasing Agent for delivering wheat on 20 Oct 1781 {Ref: Maryland State Archives MdHR-6636-42-15}

COOPER, ADAM (Frederick County) received a receipt from the Purchasing Agent for furnishing beef on 3 Jan 1781 {Ref: Maryland State Archives MdHR-6636-23-2}

COOPER, ARCHIBALD (Frederick County) received a certificate from the Purchasing Agent for furnishing wheat on 29 May 1782 {Ref: Maryland State Archives MdHR-6636-42-37}

COOPER, CHARLES (Kent County) received a certificate from the Purchasing Agent for furnishing wheat on 20 Apr 1780 {Ref: Maryland State Archives MdHR-6636-23-44}

COOPER, ELISHA (Kent County) received payment from the Purchasing Agent for collecting cattle for the public use in November, 1782 {Ref: Maryland State Archives MdHR-6636-43-3}

COOPER, JOHN (Caroline County) received receipts from the Purchasing Agent for wheat on 20 Aug and 1 Sep 1782 {Ref: Maryland State Archives MdHR-6636-42-7}

COOPER, GEORGE (Frederick County) received a certificate from the Purchasing Agent for furnishing wheat on 7 Dec 1782 {Ref: Maryland State Archives MdHR-6636-42-37}

COOPER, MARK G. (Caroline County) received a receipt from the Purchasing Agent for furnishing wheat on 1 Sep 1782 {Ref: Maryland State Archives MdHR-6636-42-7}

COOPER, OWEN (Caroline County) received a receipt from the Purchasing Agent for furnishing wheat on 31 Aug 1782 {Ref: Maryland State Archives MdHR-6636-42-7}

COPAGE, PHILEMON (Kent County) received a certificate from the Purchasing Agent for the use of his horse and cart by the military on 19 Apr 1778 {Ref: Maryland State Archives MdHR-6636-54-31}

COPKINS, JOHN (Baltimore County) submitted an account and received payment for five days of "conducing flower" to Susquehanna Lower Ferry for the use of the army on 1 Feb 1780 {Ref: Maryland Historical Society MS.1814, Box 6}

COPPER, GEORGE (Kent County) received payment from the Purchasing Agent for furnishing cattle and pasturage for the public use in September, 1781 {Ref: Maryland State Archives MdHR-6636-43-3}

COPPER, PHILLIP (Kent County) received payment from the Purchasing Agent for furnishing cattle and pasturage for the public use in September, 1781 {Ref: Maryland State Archives MdHR-6636-43-3}

CORKE, DANIEL (Baltimore County) was a captain who received a receipt from the Purchasing Agent for flour on 26 Jun 1782 {Ref: Maryland State Archives MdHR-6636-43-37H}

CORNELIUS, DANIEL (Kent County) received payments from the Purchasing Agent for furnishing cattle for the public use in September, 1781 and for purchasing beef cattle for the public use in October, 1782 {Ref: Maryland State Archives MdHR-6636-43-3}; received a loan certificate for £83.4.1 due from the Council of Maryland "agreeable to the Act proposing to the Citizens of this State, Creditors of Congress on Loan Office Certificates, Etc." on 20 May 1783 for services rendered during the war {Ref: Archives of Maryland 48:418}

CORRIE, JOHN (Talbot County) received a receipt from the Purchasing Agent for furnishing wheat on 21 Feb 1781 {Ref: Maryland State Archives MdHR-6636-24-49}

COSTIN, JAMES (Queen Anne's County) received a receipt from the Purchasing Agent for furnishing wheat on 12 Oct 1781 {Ref: Maryland State Archives MdHR-6636-24-34}

COTTINGHAM, JOHN (Somerset County) received a receipt from the Purchasing Agent for furnishing pork and barrels on 1 May 1782 {Ref: Maryland State Archives MdHR-6636-43-21}

COTTINGHAM, THOMAS (Somerset and Worcester Counties) received a receipt from the Purchasing Agent for furnishing pork on 29 Apr 1782 {Ref: Maryland State Archives MdHR-6636-43-21}; submitted an account and receipt for furnishing pork on 10 Jun 1782 {Ref: Maryland State Archives MdHR-6636-43-28S}

COTTMAN, BENJAMIN (Somerset County) received a certificate from the Purchasing Agent for furnishing corn on 24 Jan 1780 {Ref: Maryland State Archives MdHR-6636-24-38}

COTTMAN (COTMAN), JOSEPH (Somerset County) received a certificate from the Purchasing Agent for furnishing pork on 22 Jan 1782 {Ref: Maryland State

Archives MdHR-6636-43-21}

COUDEN, ROBERT (Baltimore County) submitted an account for delivery of flour on 17 May 1782 {Ref: Maryland State Archives MdHR-6636-43-35B}; received a loan certificate for £32.13.2 due from the Council of Maryland "agreeable to the Act proposing to the Citizens of this State, Creditors of Congress on Loan Office Certificates, Etc." on 4 Mar 1783 for services rendered during the war {Ref: Archives of Maryland 48:373}; also see "Richard Tootle," q.v.

COULTER, DANIEL (Baltimore Town or County) received payment by order of the Council of Safety for attending the hospital on 19 Aug 1776 {Ref: Archives of Maryland 12:220}

COURSEY, EDWARD (Queen Anne's County) received a certificate from the Purchasing Agent for furnishing corn on 18 Jan 1780 {Ref: Maryland State Archives MdHR-6636-24-30}; received a certificate for furnishing wheat on 4 Jan 1780 {Ref: Maryland State Archives MdHR-6636-24-32}

COURSEY, THOMAS (Queen Anne's County) received a certificate from the Purchasing Agent for furnishing wheat on 4 Jan 1780 {Ref: Maryland State Archives MdHR-6636-24-28}

COURSEY, WILLIAM (Caroline County) received a receipt from the Purchasing Agent for furnishing wheat on 1 Sep 1782 {Ref: Maryland State Archives MdHR-6636-42-7}

COURTENAY, HERCULES (Baltimore Town) received payment via Richard Ridgely for £206.7.11 due from the Council of Maryland on 23 Oct 1783, "being for Clothing Contracted for by the Governor and Council" during the war {Ref: Archives of Maryland 48:472}

COURTS, WILLIAM (Charles County) received a receipt from the Purchasing Agent for furnishing wheat on 29 Dec 1782 {Ref: Maryland State Archives MdHR-6636-42-21}; received a receipt for furnishing wheat on 10 May 1783 {Ref: Maryland State Archives MdHR-6636-42-22}

COUSTEN, MATTHEW (Somerset County) received a receipt from the Purchasing Agent for furnishing beef on 4 Oct 1782 {Ref: Maryland State Archives MdHR-6636-43-21}

COVELIME, HARMON (Frederick County) received a certificate from the Purchasing Agent for furnishing wheat on 30 May 1782 {Ref: Maryland State Archives MdHR-6636-42-35}

COVENTON, THOMAS (Caroline County) received a receipt from the Purchasing Agent for furnishing wheat on 5 Aug 1782 {Ref: Maryland State Archives MdHR-6636-42-7}

COVENTRY, CHARLES (Montgomery County) received a receipt from the Purchasing Agent for furnishing wheat on 25 Apr 1781 {Ref: Maryland State Archives MdHR-6636-24-14}

69

COVEY, FRANCIS (Caroline County) received a receipt from the Purchasing Agent for furnishing wheat on 5 Aug 1782 {Ref: Maryland State Archives MdHR-6636-42-7}

COVEY, HENRY (Dorchester County) received a receipt from the Purchasing Agent for furnishing wheat on 1 Oct 1782 {Ref: Maryland State Archives MdHR-6636-42-23}

COVINGTON, THOMAS (Caroline County) received a receipt from the Purchasing Agent for furnishing wheat on 22 Aug 1782 {Ref: Maryland State Archives MdHR-6636-42-7}

COWARD, JOHN (Talbot County) received a receipt from the Purchasing Agent for furnishing bacon for the use of the army on 27 Apr 1778 {Ref: Maryland State Archives MdHR-4587-73}; submitted an account and receipt for hauling on 28 Apr 1778 {Ref: Maryland State Archives MdHR-6636-12-15}

COWMAN, JOSEPH (Anne Arundel County) was appointed by the Council of Maryland to be one of six "Signers of the Bills emitted in Virtue of the Act to enable the Treasurer of the Western Shore to draw and sell Bills of Exchange and for an Emission of Bills of Credit if necessary" on 8 Sep 1780 {Ref: Archives of Maryland 43:281}

COWMAN, RICHARD (Anne Arundel County) served as Contractor for Wagons and Teams in his county by 12 Dec 1780 at which time he received payment from the Council of Maryland for his services {Ref: Archives of Maryland 45:241}

COX (COXE), ABRAHAM, see "John Wynn," q.v.

COX, JOHN (Cecil County) submitted an account of flour for the use of the army in 1780 {Ref: Maryland State Archives MdHR-4595-9}; received a certificate from the Purchasing Agent for furnishing wheat on 20 Jan 1780 {Ref: Maryland State Archives MdHR-6636-23-21A}; submitted an account for wheat, flour and grain on 1 Mar 1780 {Ref: Maryland State Archives MdHR-4590-78}; submitted an account for grain purchased on 1 Jun 1780 {Ref: Maryland State Archives MdHR-4590-81}; he was a captain who was appointed by the Council of Maryland to be one of five men in Cecil County "to carry the Act to prohibit for a limited time the Exportation of Indian Corn, Etc., by Land" on 22 Dec 1780 {Ref: Archives of Maryland 45:250}

COX, JOHN (Montgomery County) received a receipt from the Purchasing Agent for furnishing wheat on 8 Sep 1780 {Ref: Maryland State Archives MdHR-6636-24-7}

COX, THOMAS (Charles County) received a receipt from the Purchasing Agent for furnishing wheat on 15 Apr 1783 {Ref: Maryland State Archives MdHR-6636-42-22}

COX, WILLIAM (Somerset County) received a receipt from the Purchasing Agent for furnishing beef on 4 Dec 1781 {Ref: Maryland State Archives MdHR-

6636-24-44}

COXTONE, HENRY WILLIAM (Prince George's County) received a receipt from the Purchasing Agent for furnishing wheat on 16 Jul 1782 {Ref: Maryland State Archives MdHR-6636-50-135}

CRABB, RICHARD (Frederick County) received payment by order of the Council of Maryland for providing waggonage on 21 Nov 1777 {Ref: Archives of Maryland 16:421}

CRABIN, WILLIAM (Kent County) received a certificate from the Purchasing Agent for furnishing corn on 10 Apr 1780 {Ref: Maryland State Archives MdHR-6636-23-43}

CRABS, JOHN (Frederick County) received a certificate from the Purchasing Agent for furnishing wheat on 5 Feb 1783 {Ref: Maryland State Archives MdHR-6636-42-38}

CRACKELLS, THOMAS (Prince George's County) received payment from the Maryland Council of Safety "for riding express from Marlborough to Annapolis" on 19 Feb 1776 {Ref: Archives of Maryland 11:169}

CRAFTON, JOSEPH (Caroline County) received a receipt from the Purchasing Agent for furnishing wheat on 1 Sep 1782 {Ref: Maryland State Archives MdHR-6636-42-7}

CRAIG, ROBERT (Baltimore County) received payment by order of the Council of Safety for repairing a musquet on 27 Mar 1776 {Ref: Archives of Maryland 11:292}

CRAIK, JAMES (Charles County) served as "Chief Physician in the Hospital Department" by 18 Dec 1780 at which time he was paid by the Council of Maryland for his services {Ref: Archives of Maryland 45:245}

CRAMBLIT, JACOB (Montgomery County) received a receipt from the Purchasing Agent for furnishing wheat on 10 Apr 1781 {Ref: Maryland State Archives MdHR-6636-42-11}; received a receipt for furnishing wheat on 14 Aug 1781 {Ref: Maryland State Archives MdHR-6636-24-15}

CRAMER (CREMER), GEORGE (Frederick County) received a loan certificate for £10.7.9 due from the Council of Maryland "agreeable to the Act proposing to the Citizens of this State, Creditors of Congress on Loan Office Certificates, Etc." on 30 Sep 1783 for services rendered during the war {Ref: Archives of Maryland 48:458}

CRAMER, WILLIAM (Frederick County) received a certificate from the Purchasing Agent for furnishing wheat on 1 Mar 1781 {Ref: Maryland State Archives MdHR-6636-28-39}

CRAMPHIN, THOMAS JR. (Frederick County) pledged a loan in the amount of £400 to the State of Maryland under the Act for the Emission of Bills of Credit "to defray the expences of the present campaign" in June, 1781 {Ref: Archives of Maryland 47:327}

CRAMPTON, JOSEPH (Prince George's County) received a receipt from the Purchasing Agent for furnishing wheat on 24 May 1782 {Ref: Maryland State Archives MdHR-6636-50-135}

CRAMPTON, THOMAS (Montgomery County) received a certificate of services rendered to the commissary of purchases on 8 Jun 1782 {Ref: Maryland State Archives MdHR-6636-50-91}

CRANDALL, JOHN (Anne Arundel County) received payment by order of the Council of Safety for furnishing a gun on 4 Sep 1776 {Ref: Archives of Maryland 12:256}

CRANER, JOSHUA (Caroline County) received a receipt from the Purchasing Agent for furnishing wheat on 17 Aug 1782 {Ref: Maryland State Archives MdHR-6636-42-7}

CRAPPER, JOHN (Worcester County) submitted an account and receipt for collecting cattle on 23 Oct 1781 {Ref: Maryland State Archives MdHR-6636-43-27}

CRAPPER, VINCENT (Worcester County) received payment for furnishing beef on or about 21 Sep 1781 {Ref: Maryland State Archives MdHR-6636-43-28XXX}

CRAUFURD (CRAWFURD), DAVID (Prince George's County) was appointed one of eighteen Collectors of Clothing by the Council of Maryland under "An Act to Procure Cloathing for the Quota of this State of the American Army" on 27 Nov 1777 {Ref: Archives of Maryland 16:426}; pledged a loan in the amount of £500 to the State of Maryland under the Act for the Emission of Bills of Credit "to defray the expences of the present campaign" in June, 1781 {Ref: Archives of Maryland 47:327}

CRAYCRAFT (CRACROFT), BLADEN (Charles County) received a loan certificate for £36.4.3 due from the Council of Maryland "agreeable to the Act proposing to the Citizens of this State, Creditors of Congress on Loan Office Certificates, Etc." on 16 Oct 1783 for services rendered during the war {Ref: Archives of Maryland 48:469}

CRAYCRAFT, CHARITY (Charles County) received a receipt from the Purchasing Agent for furnishing wheat on 8 May 1783 {Ref: Maryland State Archives MdHR-6636-42-22}

CRAYCRAFT (CRAYCROFT), IGNATIUS (Charles County) was employed by the Council of Maryland to purchase cattle for the public on 8 Sep 1777 {Ref: Archives of Maryland 16:366}; received a loan certificate for £266.13.2 due from the Council of Maryland "agreeable to the Act proposing to the Citizens of this State, Creditors of Congress on Loan Office Certificates, Etc." on 12 Apr 1783 for services rendered during the war {Ref: Archives of Maryland 48:397}

CRAYCRAFT, THOMAS (Charles County) received a receipt from the

Purchasing Agent for furnishing wheat on 11 Apr 1782 {Ref: Maryland State Archives MdHR-6636-42-18}

CREAGER, ADAM (Frederick County) submitted an account for furnishing mutton on 29 May 1781 {Ref: Maryland State Archives MdHR-6636-23-6}

CREAGER, CONRAD (Frederick County) submitted an account for furnishing bacon on 29 May 1781 {Ref: Maryland State Archives MdHR-6636-23-6}

CREAGER, GEORGE (Frederick County) submitted an account for furnishing veal on 29 May 1781 {Ref: Maryland State Archives MdHR-6636-23-6}

CREAGER, HENRY (Frederick County) submitted an account for furnishing mutton and bacon on 29 May 1781 {Ref: Maryland State Archives MdHR-6636-23-6}

CRETON, THOMAS (Harford County) received a receipt from the Purchasing Agent for furnishing wheat on 23 Mar 1780 {Ref: Maryland State Archives MdHR-6636-23-35}

CREW, EDWARD (Kent County) received payment from the Purchasing Agent for furnishing cattle for the public use in September, 1781 {Ref: Maryland State Archives MdHR-6636-32-3}

CREWE, EDWARD JR. (Montgomery County) received a receipt from the Purchasing Agent for furnishing wheat on 1 Oct 1781 {Ref: Maryland State Archives MdHR-6636-42-11}

CRISALL, JOHN (Baltimore County) received payment by order of the Council of Maryland "for beef purchased of him for the State" on 6 Feb 1778 {Ref: Archives of Maryland 16:484}; served as Issuing Commissary in 1780 {Ref: Archives of Maryland 43:252}; received a receipt from the Purchasing Agent for furnishing beef on 19 Jun 1781 {Ref: Maryland State Archives MdHR-6636-43-38EE}; received payment "to purchase necessaries for the Hospital and to be Accounted for" on 23 Jul 1781 {Ref: Archives of Maryland 45:515}; received payment "for the purpose of procuring Necessaries for the Sick Soldiers in the Hospital on Account" on 20 Jan 1783 {Ref: Archives of Maryland 48:346}; received a loan certificate for £28.2.7 due from the Council of Maryland "agreeable to the Act proposing to the Citizens of this State, Creditors of Congress on Loan Office Certificates, Etc." on 10 Jun 1783 for services rendered during the war {Ref: Archives of Maryland 48:429}; also see "John Sellman" and "John Chalmers," q.v.

CROCK, GEORGE (Caroline County) received a certificate from the Purchasing Agent for the use of his wagon and team on 22 Jun 1780 {Ref: Maryland State Archives MdHR-6636-23-20}

CROOKE, GEORGE (Caroline County) received payment by order of the Council of Safety for providing waggonage on 18 Oct 1776 {Ref: Archives of Maryland 12:364}

CROMEAN, JOHN (Caroline County) was a tailor who received receipts from the

Purchasing Agent for furnishing wheat on 17 Aug and 22 Aug 1782 {Ref: Maryland State Archives MdHR-6636-42-7}

CROON, THOMAS (Kent County) received payment from the Purchasing Agent for furnishing cattle and pasturage for the public use in September, 1781 {Ref: Maryland State Archives MdHR-6636-32-3}

CROPPER, NATHAN (Worcester County) received a receipt from the Purchasing Agent for furnishing beef on 12 Oct 1780 {Ref: Maryland State Archives MdHR-6636-24-54}

CROSS, JEREMIAH (Prince George's County) received a receipt from the Purchasing Agent for furnishing wheat on 16 Aug 1781 {Ref: Maryland State Archives MdHR-6636-24-20}

CROW, EDWARD (Montgomery County) received a receipt from the Purchasing Agent for furnishing wheat on 30 Mar 1781 {Ref: Maryland State Archives MdHR-6636-42-11}

CROW, SAMUEL (Montgomery County) received a receipt from the Purchasing Agent for furnishing wheat on 30 Mar 1781 {Ref: Maryland State Archives MdHR-6636-42-11}

CRYSALL, JOHN, see "John Sellman," q.v.

CUDY, PHILIP (Frederick County) received a certificate from the Purchasing Agent for furnishing wheat on 30 Jul 1782 {Ref: Maryland State Archives MdHR-6636-42-36}

CULLEN, JACOB (Somerset County) received a receipt from the Purchasing Agent for furnishing beef on 6 Nov 1781 {Ref: Maryland State Archives MdHR-6636-24-44}

CULVER, HENRY (Montgomery County) received a receipt from the Purchasing Agent for furnishing wheat on 1 Aug 1780 {Ref: Maryland State Archives MdHR-6636-43-7}; received a receipt for furnishing wheat on 4 Aug 1780 {Ref: Maryland State Archives MdHR-6636-24-6}

CUMMINGS, WILLIAM (Frederick County) received a certificate from the Purchasing Agent for furnishing wheat on 1 Jun 1782 {Ref: Maryland State Archives MdHR-6636-42-34}

CUNES, JACOB (Anne Arundel County) made an agreement to deliver bacon and pork to Col. Henry Hollingsworth on 12 Jun 1780 {Ref: Maryland State Archives MdHR-6636-18-141}

CUTMORE, JOSHUA (Montgomery County) received a receipt from the Purchasing Agent for furnishing wheat on 24 Aug 1781 {Ref: Maryland State Archives MdHR-6636-42-11}

CYPHERT, HUGH (Montgomery County) received a receipt from the Purchasing Agent for furnishing wheat on 10 May 1781 {Ref: Maryland State Archives MdHR-6636-24-18}

DALE, JONATHAN (Worcester County) received a receipt from the Purchasing

Agent for hauling on 1 Oct 1780 {Ref: Maryland State Archives MdHR-6636-24-54}

DALE, JOSIAH (Worcester County) received a receipt from the Purchasing Agent for furnishing corn on 14 Jun 1780 {Ref: Maryland State Archives MdHR-6636-24-53}; his name appeared on "A List of Corn Purchased in Worcester County for the use of the State of Maryland" by the Commissary in July, 1780 {Ref: Archives of Maryland 45:10}

DALLAM, RICHARD (Harford County) was appointed by the Council of Safety to collect all the gold and silver coin that could be procured in the county in compliance with the Resolve of Congress on 27 Jan 1776 {Ref: Archives of Maryland 11:132}; appointed one of eighteen Collectors of Clothing by the Council of Maryland under "An Act to Procure Cloathing for the Quota of this State of the American Army" on 27 Nov 1777 {Ref: Archives of Maryland 16:426}; appointed by the Council of Maryland as one of thirty men to be "Agents for Purchasing Provisions" on 30 Mar 1779 {Ref: Archives of Maryland 21:332, 423}; commissioned an Assistant Deputy Commissary of Purchases on 10 Sep 1779 {Ref: Archives of Maryland 21:518}; received certificates for furnishing corn on 19 Jan 1780 and for furnishing wheat on 16 Apr 1780 {Ref: Maryland State Archives MdHR-6636-23-36}; appointed Commissary of Purchases for Harford County by the Council of Maryland on 8 Jul 1780 {Ref: Archives of Maryland 43:215, 43:475}; his name was listed as "Richd. Dulham" when he delivered 64 barrels of flour and "12 bales of ship stuff" to the commissary at Baltimore Town for the use of the State of Maryland in the summer of 1780, and was listed as "Richd. Dalham" when he delivered flour on 18 Sep 1780 {Ref: Archives of Maryland 45:84, 109}; also see "John Gilmore," q.v.

DARBY, GEORGE (Montgomery County) received receipts from the Purchasing Agent for furnishing wheat on 13 Apr and 28 Apr 1781 {Ref: Maryland State Archives MdHR-6636-24-18}; received a loan certificate for £42.19.9 due from the Council of Maryland "agreeable to the Act proposing to the Citizens of this State, Creditors of Congress on Loan Office Certificates, Etc." on 20 Dec 1783 for services rendered during the war {Ref: Archives of Maryland 48:494}

DARBY, JOHN (Dorchester County) received a receipt from the Purchasing Agent for furnishing wheat on 25 Mar 1783 {Ref: Maryland State Archives MdHR-6636-42-24}

DARDIN, JOSEPH (Talbot County) submitted an account and receipt for furnishing bacon on 23 Apr 1778 {Ref: Maryland State Archives MdHR-6636-12-15}

DARNALL, ROBERT (Frederick County) received a loan certificate for £13.8.9 due from the Council of Maryland "agreeable to the Act proposing to the

Citizens of this State, Creditors of Congress on Loan Office Certificates, Etc." on 23 Oct 1783 for services rendered during the war {Ref: Archives of Maryland 48:472}

DARNALL, THOMAS (Frederick County) received a certificate from the Purchasing Agent for furnishing wheat on 25 May 1782 {Ref: Maryland State Archives MdHR-6636-42-33}

DARRINGTON, JAMES (Kent County) received a certificate from the Purchasing Agent for furnishing wheat on 20 Apr 1780 {Ref: Maryland State Archives MdHR-6636-23-44}

DASHIELL, GEORGE (Somerset County) was appointed one of eighteen Collectors of Clothing by the Council of Maryland under "An Act to Procure Cloathing for the Quota of this State of the American Army" on 27 Nov 1777 {Ref: Archives of Maryland 16:426}; appointed by the Council of Safety to collect all the gold and silver coin that could be procured in the county in compliance with the Resolve of Congress on 27 Jan 1776 {Ref: Archives of Maryland 11:132}; received certificates from the Purchasing Agent for furnishing corn on 15 Jan to 22 Jan 1780 {Ref: Maryland State Archives MdHR-6636-24-38}; also see "Francis Baker," q.v.

DASHIELL, JOSEPH (Worcester County) was appointed one of eighteen Collectors of Clothing by the Council of Maryland under "An Act to Procure Cloathing for the Quota of this State of the American Army" on 27 Nov 1777 {Ref: Archives of Maryland 16:426}; appointed by the Council of Maryland on 25 Mar 1778 as one of eighteen men to be "Agents for Purchasing Provisions for the Army of the United States Agreeable to an Act of Assembly passed the 23rd Inst." {Ref: Archives of Maryland 16:551}; appointed Commissary of Purchases for Worcester County by the Council of Maryland on 8 Jul 1780 {Ref: Archives of Maryland 43:215}; pledged a loan in the amount of £200 to the State of Maryland under the Act for the Emission of Bills of Credit "to defray the expences of the present campaign" in June, 1781 {Ref: Archives of Maryland 47:327}

DASHIELL, JOSIAH (Somerset County) received a receipt from the Purchasing Agent for furnishing beef on 14 May 1781 {Ref: Maryland State Archives MdHR-6636-24-43}; received a loan certificate for £51.6.9 due from the Council of Maryland "agreeable to the Act proposing to the Citizens of this State, Creditors of Congress on Loan Office Certificates, Etc." on 22 May 1783 for services rendered during the war {Ref: Archives of Maryland 48:419}

DASHIELL, LEVIN (Somerset County) received a certificate from the Purchasing Agent for furnishing corn on 15 Jan 1780 {Ref: Maryland State Archives MdHR-6636-24-38}; received a loan certificate for £1086.12.11 due from the Council of Maryland "agreeable to the Act proposing to the Citizens of this State, Creditors of Congress on Loan Office Certificates, Etc." on 19 Dec 1783 for services rendered during the war {Ref: Archives of Maryland 48:493}

DASHIELL, ROBERT (Somerset County) was a captain who received a receipt from the Purchasing Agent for furnishing beef on 26 May 1781 {Ref: Maryland State Archives MdHR-6636-24-43}

DAVENPORT, JAMES (Frederick County) was an assistant commissary who submitted a bill and receipt for furnishing beef and flour on 2 Mar 1781 {Ref: Maryland State Archives MdHR-6636-23-4}; received a receipt for furnishing corn meal on 5 Apr 1781 {Ref: Maryland State Archives MdHR-6636-23-33}

DAVENPORT, JOSEPH (Kent County) received payment for furnishing flour and beef on 1 Jan 1781 {Ref: Maryland State Archives MdHR-6636-23-49}

DAVEY, ALEXANDER W. (Baltimore County) submitted an account and receipt for furnishing salt and for cooperage on 13 May 1782 {Ref: Maryland State Archives MdHR-6636-43-38E}

DAVID, JOHN (Worcester County) submitted an account and receipt for packing and storing pork on 20 May 1781 {Ref: Maryland State Archives MdHR-6636-43-27}

DAVID, RANDOLPH (Charles County) received a receipt from the Purchasing Agent for furnishing wheat on 28 Sep 1782 {Ref: Maryland State Archives MdHR-6636-42-19}

DAVIDSON, HENRY (Montgomery County) received a receipt from the Purchasing Agent for furnishing wheat on 29 Aug 1780 {Ref: Maryland State Archives MdHR-6636-24-6}

DAVIDSON, JOHN (Anne Arundel County) received payment by order of the Council of Safety for furnishing boatage on 30 Sep 1776 {Ref: Archives of Maryland 12:310}

DAVIDSON, SAMUEL (Baltimore County) received a loan certificate for £541.6.0 due from the Council of Maryland "agreeable to the Act proposing to the Citizens of this State, Creditors of Congress on Loan Office Certificates, Etc." on 13 Jun 1783 for services rendered during the war {Ref: Archives of Maryland 48:430}

DAVIDSON, THOMAS (Frederick County) received a certificate from the Purchasing Agent for furnishing beef on 29 May 1782 {Ref: Maryland State Archives MdHR-6636-42-34}

DAVIS, BENJAMIN (Charles County) received a receipt from the Purchasing Agent for furnishing wheat on 2 Nov 1782 {Ref: Maryland State Archives MdHR-6636-42-19}

DAVIS, BETSY (Montgomery County) received a receipt from the Purchasing Agent for furnishing wheat on 4 May 1781 {Ref: Maryland State Archives MdHR-6636-42-11}

DAVIS, BIRCHAMP (Somerset County) received a receipt from the Purchasing Agent for furnishing pork on 21 Jan 1782 {Ref: Maryland State Archives

MdHR-6636-43-21}

DAVIS, CHARLES (Somerset County) received a receipt from the Purchasing Agent for furnishing beef on 29 Nov 1781 {Ref: Maryland State Archives MdHR-6636-24-44}

DAVIS, ELIZABETH (Charles County) received a receipt from the Purchasing Agent for furnishing wheat on 20 Dec 1782 {Ref: Maryland State Archives MdHR-6636-42-20}

DAVIS, GEORGE (Somerset County) received payment from the Council of Maryland for riding express on 14 Jul 1781 {Ref: Archives of Maryland 45:502}

DAVIS, GRIFFITH (Montgomery County) received a receipt from the Purchasing Agent for furnishing wheat on 1 Aug 1780 {Ref: Maryland State Archives MdHR-6636-43-7}; received a receipt for furnishing wheat on 9 Apr 1781 {Ref: Maryland State Archives MdHR-6636-42-11}

DAVIS, IGNATIUS (Montgomery County) received a receipt from the Purchasing Agent for shelling corn on 10 Jun 1780 {Ref: Maryland State Archives MdHR-6636-24-2}; received a receipt for furnishing wheat on 3 Mar 1781 {Ref: Maryland State Archives MdHR-6636-24-18}; received a receipt for hauling flour on 17 May 1783 {Ref: Maryland State Archives MdHR-6636-42-28}

DAVIS, JAMES (Kent County) furnished flour, lard, beef, and wheat for the use of the state as reported to the Council of Maryland on a "Return of Provisions, Etc., received at the Head of Elk" on 9 Jul 1781 {Ref: Archives of Maryland 47:409}

DAVIS, JARRARD OR GERARD (Frederick County) received a certificate from the Purchasing Agent for furnishing wheat on 1 Jun 1782 {Ref: Maryland State Archives MdHR-6636-42-36}

DAVIS, JOHN (Charles County) received a receipt from the Purchasing Agent for furnishing wheat on 20 Dec 1782 {Ref: Maryland State Archives MdHR-6636-42-20}

DAVIS, JOHN (Worcester County) submitted an account and receipt for processing pork on 15 May 1782 {Ref: Maryland State Archives MdHR-6636-43-28Y}

DAVIS (DAVISS), JOSEPH (St. Mary's County) received payment from the Purchasing Agent on 29 Dec 1781 for collecting and driving public cattle for 10 days {Ref: Maryland State Archives MdHR-6636-32-23}

DAVIS, LEONARD (Montgomery County) received a receipt from the Purchasing Agent for furnishing wheat on 29 Jul 1780 {Ref: Maryland State Archives MdHR-6636-24-5}; received a receipt for furnishing wheat on 1 Aug 1780 {Ref: Maryland State Archives MdHR-6636-43-7}; received a receipt for furnishing wheat on 4 Sep 1780 {Ref: Maryland State Archives MdHR-6636-24-7}

DAVIS, LEVI (Frederick County) received a receipt from the Purchasing Agent for furnishing corn on 12 Jan 1781 {Ref: Maryland State Archives MdHR-6636-23-2}

DAVIS, LEVIN (Worcester County) received a receipt from the Purchasing Agent for furnishing pork on 1 Oct 1780 {Ref: Maryland State Archives MdHR-6636-24-54}; submitted an account and receipt for furnishing pork on 10 Oct 1782 {Ref: Maryland State Archives MdHR-6636-43-30B}

DAVIS, LOANHART (Montgomery County) received a certificate from the Purchasing Agent for furnishing wheat on 29 May 1781 {Ref: Maryland State Archives MdHR-6636-24-18}

DAVIS, PHILIP (Kent County) received a receipt from the Purchasing Agent for furnishing wheat on 29 Jul 1780 {Ref: Maryland State Archives MdHR-6636-23-49}

DAVIS, RICHARD (Prince George's County) received a receipt from the Purchasing Agent for furnishing wheat on 9 Aug 1783 {Ref: Maryland State Archives MdHR-6636-50-135}

DAVIS, RICHARD (Montgomery County) received a receipt from the Purchasing Agent for furnishing wheat on 30 Aug 1780 {Ref: Maryland State Archives MdHR-6636-24-6}

DAVIS, RICHARD (Washington County) was appointed one of eighteen Collectors of Clothing by the Council of Maryland under "An Act to Procure Cloathing for the Quota of this State of the American Army" on 27 Nov 1777 {Ref: Archives of Maryland 16:426}; appointed by the Council of Maryland on 25 Mar 1778 as one of eighteen men to be "Agents for Purchasing Provisions for the Army of the United States Agreeable to an Act of Assembly passed the 23rd Inst." {Ref: Archives of Maryland 16:551}; served as a Commissary Agent in 1782 and received a receipt from the Purchasing Agent for furnishing wheat on 19 Dec 1782 {Ref: Maryland State Archives MdHR-6636-43-26}

DAVIS, THOMAS (Annamessex Hundred, Somerset County) was a captain who received a receipt from the Purchasing Agent for furnishing pork on 16 Apr 1781 {Ref: Maryland State Archives MdHR-6636-24-45}

DAVISON, THOMAS (Dorchester County) received a receipt from the Purchasing Agent for furnishing wheat on 3 Sep 1782 {Ref: Maryland State Archives MdHR-6636-42-23}

DAW, ROBERT (Montgomery County) received a receipt from the Purchasing Agent for furnishing wheat on 19 Apr 1781 {Ref: Maryland State Archives MdHR-6636-42-11}

DAWSEL, RICHARD (Baltimore County) submitted an account and received payment for hauling three loads of flour on 28 Jan 1780 {Ref: Maryland Historical Society MS.1814, Box 6}

DAWSON, BENONI (Frederick County) received a receipt from the Purchasing

Agent for furnishing corn and rye on 3 May 1780 {Ref: Maryland State Archives MdHR-6636-24-1}

DAWSON, JOHN (Frederick County) received a receipt from the Purchasing Agent for furnishing beef on 27 Feb 1781 {Ref: Maryland State Archives MdHR-6636-23-3}

DAWSON, JOHN (Talbot County) was one of twenty-six people who contacted the Governor and Council of Maryland in 1781 and pledged to support and maintain at their own expense the Barge *Experiment* so it can patrol the bay between Kent Point and Tilghman's Island in order to protect them against the enemy, stating in part, "whereas from the present exhausted state of the public treasury the government cannot immediately give that protection to every individual which is become necessary from the cruel and savage mode in which the war is now carried on against us" {Ref: Archives of Maryland 47:584-585}

DAWSON, JONAS (Caroline County) received a receipt from the Purchasing Agent for furnishing wheat on 5 Aug 1782 {Ref: Maryland State Archives MdHR-6636-42-7}

DAWSON, NICHOLAS (Frederick County) received a receipt from the Purchasing Agent for furnishing hay on 18 Dec 1780 {Ref: Maryland State Archives MdHR-6636-23-1}

DAWSON, ROBERT (Queen Anne's County) received a receipt from the Purchasing Agent for furnishing beef on 10 Sep 1781 {Ref: Maryland State Archives MdHR-6636-24-34}

DAWSON, THOMAS (Talbot County) was an assistant purchasing agent in 1778 {Ref: Maryland State Archives MdHR-4587-71}; submitted an account of provisions purchased for the use of the state on 18 May 1778 {Ref: Maryland State Archives MdHR-4587-87}; submitted an account for the transport of provisions on 18 Jun 1778 {Ref: Maryland State Archives MdHR-4587-58}

DAWSON, WILLIAM (Talbot County) received certificates from the Purchasing Agent for furnishing wheat on 16 Jan and 10 Feb 1780 {Ref: Maryland State Archives MdHR-6636-24-46}

DAY, RICHARD (Caroline County) received receipts from the Purchasing Agent for furnishing wheat on 5 Aug, 17 Aug and 22 Aug 1782 {Ref: Maryland State Archives MdHR-6636-42-7}

DEAKINS, FRANCIS (Prince George's County) received a receipt from the Purchasing Agent for furnishing wheat on 3 Apr 1782 {Ref: Maryland State Archives MdHR-6636-50-135}; received receipts from the Purchasing Agent for furnishing wheat on 6 Jul and 13 Aug 1783 {Ref: Maryland State Archives MdHR-6636-50-135}

DEAKINS, WILLIAM (Prince George's County) was appointed one of eighteen Collectors of Clothing by the Council of Maryland under "An Act to Procure Cloathing for the Quota of this State of the American Army" on 27 Nov 1777

{Ref: Archives of Maryland 16:426}; received a receipt for furnishing wheat on 25 Jul 1783 {Ref: Maryland State Archives MdHR-6636-50-135}
DEAN, CHARLES (Dorchester County) received a receipt from the Purchasing Agent for furnishing wheat on 1 Oct 1782 {Ref: Maryland State Archives MdHR-6636-42-23}
DEAN, EDWARD (Dorchester County) received a receipt from the Purchasing Agent for furnishing wheat on 1 Oct 1782 {Ref: Maryland State Archives MdHR-6636-42-23}
DEAN, JOHN (Baltimore Town) received payment by order of the Council of Safety on 27 Jun 1776 "for 12 lb. cask powder supplied the militia at *Otter* alarm" at Whetstone Point in March, 1776 for the purpose of preventing any of the British Ships of War from coming up to Baltimore Town {Ref: Archives of Maryland 11:523}
DEAN, JOHN (Kent County) received payment from the Purchasing Agent for pasturing public cattle on 26 Sep 1781 {Ref: Maryland State Archives MdHR-6636-43-3}
DEANES, JAMES (Frederick County) received a certificate from the Purchasing Agent for furnishing wheat on 29 May 1782 {Ref: Maryland State Archives MdHR-6636-42-34}
DEARDS, WILLIAM (Annapolis) received payment by order of the Council of Safety for furnishing straw for the use of the troops on 6 Apr 1776 {Ref: Archives of Maryland 11:314}
DEEDLER, EMORY (Kent County) received a certificate from the Purchasing Agent for furnishing wheat on 20 Mar 1780 {Ref: Maryland State Archives MdHR-6636-23-43}
DEGAN, THOMAS (Kent County) received a certificate from the Purchasing Agent for hauling wheat on 29 Mar 1780 and a receipt for freight charges on 21 Apr 1780 {Ref: Maryland State Archives MdHR-6636-23-42}
DEGAN, WILLIAM (Kent County) received a certificate from the Purchasing Agent for furnishing wheat on 3 Feb 1780 {Ref: Maryland State Archives MdHR-6636-23-43}
DELANY, BENJAMIN (Frederick County) was a doctor who received a certificate from the Purchasing Agent for furnishing wheat on 318 May 1783 {Ref: Maryland State Archives MdHR-6636-42-38}
DELASHMIT, ELIAS (Frederick County) received a receipt from the Purchasing Agent for furnishing corn meal on 20 Mar 1781 {Ref: Maryland State Archives MdHR-6636-23-4}
DELASHMUTT, LINSEY (Frederick County) received a certificate from the Purchasing Agent for furnishing wheat and mutton on 17 Jun 1782 {Ref: Maryland State Archives MdHR-6636-42-35}
DELLY, HARISON (Montgomery County) received a receipt from the Purchasing

Agent for furnishing wheat on 7 May 1781 {Ref: Maryland State Archives MdHR-6636-24-18}

DELOZIER, JOHN (Charles County) received a receipt from the Purchasing Agent for furnishing wheat on 8 May 1783 {Ref: Maryland State Archives MdHR-6636-42-22}

DEMENT, CHARLES (Charles County) received a receipt from the Purchasing Agent for furnishing wheat on 24 Oct 1782 {Ref: Maryland State Archives MdHR-6636-42-19}

DEMENT, JOHN (Charles County) received a receipt from the Purchasing Agent for furnishing wheat on 28 Sep 1782 {Ref: Maryland State Archives MdHR-6636-42-19}

DEMENT, WILLIAM (Charles County) received a receipt from the Purchasing Agent for furnishing wheat on 31 Oct 1782 {Ref: Maryland State Archives MdHR-6636-42-19}

DENNIS, HENRY (Worcester County) received a receipt from the Purchasing Agent for furnishing corn on 7 Apr 1780 {Ref: Maryland State Archives MdHR-6636-24-52}; his name appeared as "H. Denis & Selby" on "A List of Corn Purchased in Worcester County for the use of the State of Maryland" by the Commissary in July, 1780 {Ref: Archives of Maryland 45:10}

DENNIS, JOHN (Worcester County) was a colonel who submitted an account and receipt for furnishing salt on 1 Jan 1782 {Ref: Maryland State Archives MdHR-6636-43-28YY}

DENNIS, JOHNSON (Worcester County) received a certificate from the Purchasing Agent for furnishing pork barrels on 11 Mar 1781 {Ref: Maryland State Archives MdHR-6636-43-27}

DENNIS, SUSANNAH (Worcester County) received a receipt from the Purchasing Agent for furnishing beef on 5 Oct 1780 {Ref: Maryland State Archives MdHR-6636-24-54}; received a receipt for furnishing pork on 1 Apr 1782 {Ref: Maryland State Archives MdHR-6636-43-21}

DENNIS, WILLIAM (Montgomery County) received a receipt from the Purchasing Agent for furnishing wheat on 18 May 1781 {Ref: Maryland State Archives MdHR-6636-24-18}; received a loan certificate for £38.16.11 due from the Council of Maryland "agreeable to the Act proposing to the Citizens of this State, Creditors of Congress on Loan Office Certificates, Etc." on 19 May 1783 for services rendered during the war {Ref: Archives of Maryland 48:417}

DENNY, JAMES EARL (Talbot County) received a receipt from the Purchasing Agent for furnishing bacon on 10 Jun 1778 {Ref: Maryland State Archives MdHR-6636-12-15}; he was one of twenty-six people who contacted the Governor and Council of Maryland in 1781 and pledged to support and maintain at their own expense the Barge *Experiment* so it can patrol the bay between Kent Point and Tilghman's Island in order to protect them against the enemy, stating in part, "whereas from the present exhausted state of the public treasury the government cannot immediately give that protection to every individual which is become necessary from the cruel and savage mode in which the war is now carried on against us" {Ref: Archives of Maryland 47:584-585}

DENT, GEORGE (Charles County) received a receipt from the Purchasing Agent for furnishing wheat on 10 Oct and 31 Oct 1782 {Ref: Maryland State Archives MdHR-6636-42-19}; received a receipt for furnishing wheat on 8 May 1783 {Ref: Maryland State Archives MdHR-6636-42-22}

DENT, GEORGE (St. Mary's County) received payment from the Purchasing Agent on 2 Jan 1782 for collecting and driving public cattle for 17 days {Ref: Maryland State Archives MdHR-6636-32-23}

DENT, HATCH (Charles County) received a receipt from the Purchasing Agent for furnishing wheat on 28 Dec 1782 {Ref: Maryland State Archives MdHR-6636-42-21}

DENT, HEZEKIAH (Charles County) received a receipt from the Purchasing Agent for furnishing wheat on 28 Dec 1782 {Ref: Maryland State Archives MdHR-6636-42-21}

DENT, JOHN (Montgomery County) received a receipt from the Purchasing Agent for furnishing wheat on 9 Jun 1781 {Ref: Maryland State Archives MdHR-6636-24-18}

DENT, JOHN (Charles County) was appointed by the Council of Safety to collect all the gold and silver coin that could be procured in the county in compliance with the Resolve of Congress on 27 Jan 1776 {Ref: Archives of Maryland 11:132}; received a receipt for furnishing wheat on 2 Nov 1782 {Ref: Maryland State Archives MdHR-6636-42-19}

DENT, MARY (Somerset County) received a receipt from the Purchasing Agent for furnishing beef on 5 Nov 1781 {Ref: Maryland State Archives MdHR-6636-24-44}

DENT, MICHAEL (Charles County) received a receipt from the Purchasing Agent for furnishing wheat on 29 Dec 1782 {Ref: Maryland State Archives MdHR-6636-42-21}

DENT, RICHARD (Charles County) received a receipt from the Purchasing Agent for furnishing wheat on 11 Apr 1782 {Ref: Maryland State Archives MdHR-6636-42-18}; received a receipt for furnishing wheat on 31 Oct 1782 {Ref: Maryland State Archives MdHR-6636-42-19}

DENT, SARAH (Charles County) received a receipt from the Purchasing Agent for furnishing wheat on 31 Oct 1782 {Ref: Maryland State Archives MdHR-6636-42-19}

DENT, WARREN (Charles County) pledged a loan in the amount of £200 to the State of Maryland under the Act for the Emission of Bills of Credit "to defray the expences of the present campaign" in June, 1781 {Ref: Archives of Maryland 47:326}; received a receipt from the Purchasing Agent for furnishing wheat on 29 Dec 1782 {Ref: Maryland State Archives MdHR-6636-42-21}; received a receipt for furnishing wheat on 10 May 1783 {Ref: Maryland State Archives MdHR-6636-42-22}

DENWOOD, JOHN (Somerset County) received a receipt from the Purchasing Agent for furnishing pork on 21 May 1782 {Ref: Maryland State Archives MdHR-6636-43-21}

DENWOOD, LEVIN (Somerset County) was a doctor who served as surgeon to the 7th Maryland Line in 1780 {Ref: Archives of Maryland 43:339}

DERBY, BASIL (Frederick County) received a receipt from the Purchasing Agent for furnishing corn and rye on 23 Mar 1780 {Ref: Maryland State Archives MdHR-6636-24-1}

DERN, JOHN (Frederick County) received a receipt from the Purchasing Agent for furnishing pork on 17 Mar 1781 {Ref: Maryland State Archives MdHR-6636-23-4}

DERN, WILLIAM (Frederick County) received a receipt from the Purchasing Agent for furnishing meal on 12 Feb 1781 {Ref: Maryland State Archives MdHR-6636-23-3}

DEVENISH, HELLEN (Kent County) received payment by order of the Council of Maryland for services rendered (not specified) on 27 Jul 1778 {Ref: Archives of Maryland 21:167}

DEVILBISS, GEORGE (Frederick County) received a certificate from the Purchasing Agent for hauling flour on 28 May 1782 {Ref: Maryland State Archives MdHR-6636-42-33}; received a loan certificate for £62.8.0 due from the Council of Maryland "agreeable to the Act proposing to the Citizens of this State, Creditors of Congress on Loan Office Certificates, Etc." on 30 Apr 1783 for services rendered during the war {Ref: Archives of Maryland 48:404}

DEYE, THOMAS COCKEY (Baltimore County) received receipts from the Purchasing Agent for furnishing wheat on 23 Jul, 8 Aug and 3 Sep 1779 {Ref: Maryland State Archives MdHR-6636-21-67}

DHUGE (DHUGIE), MONSIEUR PETICUSON OR PETICUENET (Annapolis) was a French engineer who received payment from the Maryland Council of Safety for his services on 24 Aug 1776 and by a letter to Gen. George Washington which noted he was "a native of France and a gentleman of character and experience in the management of artillery who has served in the Artillery of his most Christian Majesty and came as a passenger in an armed brigantine purchased for the Province of Maryland by Vanbibber & Harrison our agents in Statia and Martinique." {Ref: Archives of Maryland 12:235, 236}

DICK, JAMES (Baltimore Town or County) received payment by order of the Council of Safety for furnishing iron pots on 11 May 1776 {Ref: Archives of

Maryland 11:420}

DICK, ROBERT (Prince George's County) appeared as "Robert Dicks Store Bladenburgh" when he was listed in possession of Powder, Lead, Balls, Shot, and "F" [unexplained initial] on a "Return of Armes and Ammunition in Prince George's County Belonging to the Publick" on 3 Jul 1780 {Ref: Archives of Maryland 45:4}; received a loan certificate for £190.6.11 due from the Council of Maryland "agreeable to the Act proposing to the Citizens of this State, Creditors of Congress on Loan Office Certificates, Etc." on 25 Mar 1783 for services rendered during the war {Ref: Archives of Maryland 48:389}

DICKASON, JOHN (Montgomery County) received a receipt from the Purchasing Agent for furnishing wheat on 17 Apr 1781 {Ref: Maryland State Archives MdHR-6636-42-11}

DICKASON (DICKESON, DICKENSON), SERRETT OR SERRATT (Montgomery County) received a receipt from the Purchasing Agent for furnishing wheat on 1 Aug 1780 {Ref: Maryland State Archives MdHR-6636-43-7}; received a receipt for furnishing wheat on 4 Aug 1780 {Ref: Maryland State Archives MdHR-6636-24-6}; received a receipt for furnishing wheat on 17 Apr 1781 {Ref: Maryland State Archives MdHR-6636-42-11}

DICKASON, SOLLAMON (Montgomery County) received a receipt from the Purchasing Agent for furnishing wheat on 7 Apr 1781 {Ref: Maryland State Archives MdHR-6636-42-11}

DICKENS, THOMAS (Anne Arundel County) submitted a bill and receipt for furnishing pork and beef on 12 Mar 1777 {Ref: Maryland State Archives MdHR-6636-9-1}

DICKINSON, HENRY (Caroline County) was appointed by the Council of Safety to collect all the gold and silver coin that could be procured in the county in compliance with the Resolve of Congress on 27 Jan 1776 {Ref: Archives of Maryland 11:132}

DICKINSON, SAMUEL (Talbot County) received a receipt from the Purchasing Agent for furnishing pork for the use of the army on 2 May 1778 {Ref: Maryland State Archives MdHR-4587-78}

DICKINSON, WILLIAM (Montgomery County) received a receipt from the Purchasing Agent for furnishing wheat on 7 May 1781 {Ref: Maryland State Archives MdHR-6636-24-18}

DICKSON, THOMAS (Baltimore County) submitted an account and received payment for furnishing cask nails for the use of the state on 29 Feb 1780 {Ref: Maryland Historical Society MS.1814, Box 6}

DICKSON, WILLIAM (Baltimore County) received a loan certificate for £43.7.0 due from the Council of Maryland "agreeable to the Act proposing to the Citizens of this State, Creditors of Congress on Loan Office Certificates, Etc." on 29 Mar 1783 for services rendered during the war {Ref: Archives of

Maryland 48:391}

DIGGANS, JOHN (Caroline County) received a receipt from the Purchasing Agent for wheat on 10 Sep 1782 {Ref: Maryland State Archives MdHR-6636-42-7}

DIGGES, EDWARD (Charles County) received a loan certificate for £591.1.17 due from the Council of Maryland "agreeable to the Act proposing to the Citizens of this State, Creditors of Congress on Loan Office Certificates, Etc." on 12 Aug 1783 for services rendered during the war {Ref: Archives of Maryland 48:446}

DIGGES, GEORGE (Charles County) reported at Warburton the loss of a receipt for beef supplied at Charlestown in Cecil County to the Commissary of Provisions in Charles County on 1 Nov 1781 {Ref: Maryland State Archives MdHR-19969-1-58}; reported at Port Tobacco the loss of an affidavit for beef supplies and offered to supply wheat to the Commissary of Provisions in Charles County on 28 Dec 1781 {Ref: Maryland State Archives MdHR-19969-1-100}; received a loan certificate for £99.2.3 due from the Council of Maryland "agreeable to the Act proposing to the Citizens of this State, Creditors of Congress on Loan Office Certificates, Etc." on 10 Dec 1783 for services rendered during the war {Ref: Archives of Maryland 48:486-487}

DIGGS, HENRY (Charles County) received a receipt from the Purchasing Agent for furnishing wheat on 2 Nov 1782 {Ref: Maryland State Archives MdHR-6636-42-19}

DIGGS, JOSEPH (Charles County) was a doctor who was appointed by the Council of Maryland to serve as a "Surgeon to the Maryland Marching Militia" on 4 Sep 1777 {Ref: Archives of Maryland 16:362}

DIGGS, WILLIAM (Charles County) received a receipt from the Purchasing Agent for furnishing wheat on 29 Dec 1782 {Ref: Maryland State Archives MdHR-6636-42-21}

DILLAHAY, WILLIAM (Caroline County) received a receipt from the Purchasing Agent for furnishing wheat on 1 Sep 1782 {Ref: Maryland State Archives MdHR-6636-42-7}

DILLON, JAMES (Caroline County) received a receipt from the Purchasing Agent for furnishing wheat on 5 Aug 1782 {Ref: Maryland State Archives MdHR-6636-42-7}

DILLON, JOSHUA (Caroline County) received a receipt from the Purchasing Agent for furnishing wheat on 5 Aug 1782 {Ref: Maryland State Archives MdHR-6636-42-7}

DISNEY, RACHEL (Anne Arundel County) received a loan certificate for £25.13.6 due from the Council of Maryland "agreeable to the Act proposing to the Citizens of this State, Creditors of Congress on Loan Office Certificates, Etc." on 23 May 1783 for services rendered during the war {Ref: Archives of

Maryland 48:420}

DIXON, AMBROSE (Annamessex Hundred, Somerset County) received a receipt from the Purchasing Agent for furnishing pork on 27 Mar 1781 {Ref: Maryland State Archives MdHR-6636-24-45}; received a receipt for furnishing beef on 1 Nov 1781 {Ref: Maryland State Archives MdHR-6636-24-44}

DIXON, GEORGE (Charles County) received a receipt from the Purchasing Agent for furnishing wheat on 8 May 1783 {Ref: Maryland State Archives MdHR-6636-42-22}

DIXON, GEORGE JR. (Charles County) received a receipt from the Purchasing Agent for furnishing wheat on 28 Dec 1782 {Ref: Maryland State Archives MdHR-6636-42-21}

DIXON, ISAAC SR. (Somerset County) received a receipt from the Purchasing Agent for furnishing bacon on 7 Sep 1780 {Ref: Maryland State Archives MdHR-6636-24-41}

DIXON, THOMAS JR. (Somerset County) received receipts from the Purchasing Agent for furnishing pork on 1 May and 4 Jun 1782 {Ref: Maryland State Archives MdHR-6636-43-21}

DIXON, THOMAS (Somerset County) received a receipt from the Purchasing Agent for furnishing beef on 1 Nov 1781 {Ref: Maryland State Archives MdHR-6636-24-44}

DOBSON, ISAAC (Annapolis) received payment by order of the Council of Maryland for riding express for the justices and the governor on 25 Feb 1778 {Ref: Archives of Maryland 16:520}

DODSON, JACOB (Charles County) received a receipt from the Purchasing Agent for furnishing wheat on 28 Dec 1782 {Ref: Maryland State Archives MdHR-6636-42-21}

DODSON, MICHAEL (Frederick County) received a certificate from the Purchasing Agent for furnishing wheat on 19 Jul 1782 {Ref: Maryland State Archives MdHR-6636-42-37}

DOHERTY, JOHN (Montgomery County) received a receipt from the Purchasing Agent for furnishing wheat on 9 Apr 1781 {Ref: Maryland State Archives MdHR-6636-42-11}

DOLL, CONROD (Frederick County) received a loan certificate for £24.1.7 due from the Council of Maryland "agreeable to the Act proposing to the Citizens of this State, Creditors of Congress on Loan Office Certificates, Etc." on 19 Aug 1783 for services rendered during the war {Ref: Archives of Maryland 48:448}

DONALDSON, ALEXANDER (Baltimore County) received payment for furnishing corn on 24 Apr 1781 {Ref: Maryland State Archives MdHR-6636-43-38PPP}

DONALDSON, JOSEPH (Baltimore County) received payment for furnishing

corn on 24 Apr 1781 {Ref: Maryland State Archives MdHR-6636-43-38PPP}
DONAR, GEORGE (Frederick County) received a certificate from the Purchasing Agent for furnishing wheat on 22 May 1782 {Ref: Maryland State Archives MdHR-6636-42-33}
DONE, JOHN (Worcester County) was appointed by the Council of Safety to collect all the gold and silver coin that could be procured in the county in compliance with the Resolve of Congress on 27 Jan 1776 {Ref: Archives of Maryland 11:132}
DONE, ROBERT (Worcester County) submitted an account and receipt of payment due for beef on 1 Oct 1781 {Ref: Maryland State Archives MdHR-6636-43-28TTT}
DONNELLAN, THOMAS (Baltimore Town) submitted an account for delivery of fish on 23 Jun 1780 {Ref: Maryland State Archives MdHR-4594-35}; submitted to the Council of Maryland a "Return of Provisions belonging to the State of Maryland from the time of his Appointment in June last to this 7th Septr. 1780 inclusive" {Ref: Archives of Maryland 45:84-85}; submitted an account and receipt for processing beef on 11 Nov 1780 {Ref: Maryland State Archives MdHR-6636-43-38ZZZZ}; received payment for storing bread on 31 May 1781 {Ref: Maryland State Archives MdHR-6636-43-38YY}; received payment for furnishing beef on 31 May 1781 {Ref: Maryland State Archives MdHR-6636-43-38QQ}; also see "David Poe," q.v.
DONNINGTON, JAMES (Baltimore County) received payment for furnishing beef on 30 Mar 1781 {Ref: Maryland State Archives MdHR-6636-43-38EEEE}
DORSET, JAMES (Baltimore County) contracted with the Council of Safety on 29 Jul 1776 to erect a paper mill and received payment accordingly {Ref: Archives of Maryland 11:465}
DORSEY, CALEB (Baltimore County) submitted an account and receipt for furnishing flour on 29 Sep 1782 {Ref: Maryland State Archives MdHR-6636-43-38V}
DORSEY, EDWARD (Frederick County) received a receipt from the Purchasing Agent for furnishing beef on 4 Jan 1781 {Ref: Maryland State Archives MdHR-6636-23-2}; received a certificate for furnishing wheat on 28 Jan 1782 {Ref: Maryland State Archives MdHR-6636-42-38}; received a certificate for furnishing wheat on 15 Jun 1782 {Ref: Maryland State Archives MdHR-6636-42-35}; received a receipt for furnishing wheat in payment for hauling flour on 30 May 1783 {Ref: Maryland State Archives MdHR-6636-42-28}
DORSEY, JOHN (Baltimore County) delivered rum to the commissary at Baltimore Town for the use of the State of Maryland in the summer of 1780 {Ref: Archives of Maryland 45:84}; received a certificate from the Purchasing Agent for transmittal of sugar on 12 Nov 1780 {Ref: Maryland State Archives

MdHR-4594-69}; received payment for furnishing beef on 31 May 1781 {Ref: Maryland State Archives MdHR-6636-43-38AAA}

DORSEY, JOHN (Anne Arundel County) was a lieutenant who received payment by order of the Council of Safety for furnishing a musquet and bayonet on 20 Aug 1776 {Ref: Archives of Maryland 12:223}

DORSEY, JOSEPH (Montgomery County) received a receipt from the Purchasing Agent for furnishing wheat on 21 Jun 1781 {Ref: Maryland State Archives MdHR-6636-24-15}

DORSEY (DORSAY), JOSEPH (Anne Arundel County) received payment by order of the Council of Safety for furnishing boatage on 2 Sep 1776 {Ref: Archives of Maryland 12:253}

DORSEY, JOSHUA (Anne Arundel County) was Contractor for Horses in his county by 9 Jan 1781 at which time he was paid for his services by the Council of Maryland {Ref: Archives of Maryland 45:268}; received payment from the Council of Maryland as "appropriated for the payment of Expresses, Etc., his allowance on the Journal of May Session 1781" on 16 Jul 1781 {Ref: Archives of Maryland 45:503}

DORSEY, JOSIAH (Anne Arundel County) received payments by order of the Council of Safety for the hire of his boat for the Flying Camp on 15 Aug and 23 Aug 1776 {Ref: Archives of Maryland 12:205, 233}

DORSEY, NICHOLAS (Montgomery County) received a receipt from the Purchasing Agent for furnishing wheat on 12 May 1781 {Ref: Maryland State Archives MdHR-6636-42-11}

DORSEY, NICHOLAS, OF HENRY (Anne Arundel County) received payment by order of the Council of Maryland for providing waggonage on 28 Mar 1778 {Ref: Archives of Maryland 16:557}

DORSEY, SAMUEL (Anne Arundel County) received payment by order of the Council of Safety for furnishing tents on 2 Oct 1776 {Ref: Archives of Maryland 12:316}

DORSEY, THOMAS (Charles County) received a receipt from the Purchasing Agent for furnishing wheat on 23 Oct 1781 {Ref: Maryland State Archives MdHR-6636-23-24}

DORSEY, THOMAS (Anne Arundel County) was a colonel who was appointed by the Council of Safety to collect all the gold and silver coin that could be procured in the county in compliance with the Resolve of Congress on 27 Jan 1776 {Ref: Archives of Maryland 11:132}; received payment by order of the Council of Maryland "for the hire of his waggon, etc." on 7 Jan 1778 {Ref: Archives of Maryland 16:456}; appointed by the Council of Maryland on 25 Mar 1778 as one of eighteen men to be "Agents for Purchasing Provisions for the Army of the United States Agreeable to an Act of Assembly passed the 23rd Inst." {Ref: Archives of Maryland 16:551}; also see "Ephraim Howard" and

"Walter Warfield," q.v.

DORSEY, WILLIAM (Frederick County) received a receipt from the Purchasing Agent for furnishing pork on 27 Feb 1781 {Ref: Maryland State Archives MdHR-6636-23-3}

DOUGHERTY, JOHN (Montgomery County) received a receipt from the Purchasing Agent for furnishing wheat on 7 Oct 1781 {Ref: Maryland State Archives MdHR-6636-24-15}

DOUGHERTY, PHILLIP (Montgomery County) received a receipt from the Purchasing Agent for furnishing wheat on 10 Apr 1781 {Ref: Maryland State Archives MdHR-6636-24-15}

DOUGHTY, RUBEN (Frederick County) received a certificate from the Purchasing Agent for furnishing pork on 14 Mar 1781 {Ref: Maryland State Archives MdHR-6636-23-4}; received receipts from the Purchasing Agent for furnishing beef and pork on 6 Apr and 17 Apr 1781 {Ref: Maryland State Archives MdHR-6636-23-5}

DOUGLAS, SAMUEL (Prince George's County) received a receipt from the Purchasing Agent for furnishing wheat on 9 Aug 1783 {Ref: Maryland State Archives MdHR-6636-50-135}

DOUGLASS, BENJAMIN (Charles County) received a receipt from the Purchasing Agent for furnishing wheat on 24 Nov 1781 {Ref: Maryland State Archives MdHR-6636-42-15}; received a receipt for furnishing wheat on 31 Oct 1782 {Ref: Maryland State Archives MdHR-6636-42-19}

DOUGLASS, HUGH (Frederick County) submitted an account for furnishing pork and beef on 7 Apr 1781 {Ref: Maryland State Archives MdHR-6636-23-5}

DOUGLASS, JESSE (Charles County) received a receipt from the Purchasing Agent for furnishing wheat on 28 Dec 1782 {Ref: Maryland State Archives MdHR-6636-42-21}

DOUGLASS, THOMAS (Charles County) received a receipt from the Purchasing Agent for furnishing wheat on 8 May 1783 {Ref: Maryland State Archives MdHR-6636-42-22}

DOUGLASS, WILLIAM (Caroline County) received a receipt from the Purchasing Agent for furnishing wheat on 22 Aug 1782 {Ref: Maryland State Archives MdHR-6636-42-7}; received a loan certificate for £571.3.2 due from the Council of Maryland "agreeable to the Act proposing to the Citizens of this State, Creditors of Congress on Loan Office Certificates, Etc." on 29 Jul 1783 for services rendered during the war {Ref: Archives of Maryland 48:441}

DOWDEN, MICHAEL (Frederick County) received receipts from the Purchasing Agent for furnishing corn and rye on 7 Apr, 14 Apr, 18 Apr, 16 Jun and 27 Jun 1780 {Ref: Maryland State Archives MdHR-6636-24-1}

DOWDEN, THOMAS (Montgomery County) received a receipt from the Purchasing Agent for furnishing wheat on 1 Sep 1780 {Ref: Maryland State

Archives MdHR-6636-24-7}

DOWDEN, THOMAS (Frederick County) received receipts from the Purchasing Agent for furnishing corn on 22 Mar, 11 Apr, 19 Apr and 10 May 1780; received a receipt for furnishing corn and rye on 16 Jun 1780 {Ref: Maryland State Archives MdHR-6636-24-1}

DOWDEN, ZACHARIAH (Montgomery County) received receipts from the Purchasing Agent for furnishing wheat on 2 May and 9 May 1781 {Ref: Maryland State Archives MdHR-6636-24-18}

DOWLES, SAMUEL (Baltimore County) submitted an account and received payment for hauling five loads of flour on 28 Jan 1780 {Ref: Maryland Historical Society MS.1814, Box 6}

DOWN, WILLIAM (Harford County) received payment for furnishing two musquets to the Committee of Safety on 10 Jun 1776 {Ref: Preston's History of Harford County, p. 329}

DOWNES, CHARLES (Queen Anne's County) was appointed by the Council of Maryland on 25 Mar 1778 as one of eighteen men to be "Agents for Purchasing Provisions for the Army of the United States Agreeable to an Act of Assembly passed the 23rd Inst." {Ref: Archives of Maryland 16:551}; submitted an account for furnishing cattle and bacon on 8 May 1778 {Ref: Maryland State Archives MdHR-4587-49/50}; also see "Pat O'Bryan," q.v.

DOWNES, EDWARD (Queen Anne's County) received a certificate from the Purchasing Agent for furnishing corn on 19 Feb 1780 {Ref: Maryland State Archives MdHR-6636-24-29}; received a receipt for furnishing bacon on 10 Apr 1781 {Ref: Maryland State Archives MdHR-6636-24-34}

DOWNES, MICHAEL (Prince George's County) received a receipt from the Purchasing Agent for furnishing wheat on 5 Mar 1782 {Ref: Maryland State Archives MdHR-6636-50-142}

DOWNES, HENRY (Caroline County) was appointed by the Council of Maryland as one of thirty men to be "Agents for Purchasing Provisions" on 30 Mar 1779 {Ref: Archives of Maryland 21:332}

DOWNES, VACHEL (Queen Anne's County) was appointed by the Council of Maryland to be one of three men in Queen Anne's County "to carry the Act to prohibit for a limited time the Exportation of Indian Corn, Etc., by Land" on 22 Dec 1780 {Ref: Archives of Maryland 45:251}

DOWNS, WILLIAM (Charles County) received a receipt from the Purchasing Agent for furnishing wheat on 20 Dec 1782 {Ref: Maryland State Archives MdHR-6636-42-20}

DOWSON, JOSEPH (Frederick County) received money from the Council of Maryland "to be delivered over to Col. Thomas Price, Commissary of Frederick County, for the use of his Department on Account" on 30 Aug 1781 {Ref: Archives of Maryland 45:587}

91

DOXON, GEORGE SR. (Charles County) received a receipt from the Purchasing Agent for furnishing wheat on 31 Oct 1782 {Ref: Maryland State Archives MdHR-6636-42-19}

DOYLE, JAMES (Montgomery County) received a certificate of employment by the commissary of purchases on 7 Aug 1782 {Ref: Maryland State Archives MdHR-6636-50-91}

DRAKE, FRANCIS (Baltimore County) submitted an account and received payment for measuring wheat for two days on 3 Feb 1780 {Ref: Maryland Historical Society MS.1814, Box 6}

DRANE, THOMAS (Montgomery County) received a receipt from the Purchasing Agent for furnishing wheat on 29 Jul 1780 {Ref: Maryland State Archives MdHR-6636-24-5}; received a receipt for furnishing wheat on 1 Aug 1780 {Ref: Maryland State Archives MdHR-6636-43-7}; received a receipt for furnishing wheat on 7 Jun 1781 {Ref: Maryland State Archives MdHR-6636-24-18}

DRAPER, JUDREK OR JUDREH (Caroline County) received a receipt from the Purchasing Agent for furnishing wheat on 17 Aug 1782 {Ref: Maryland State Archives MdHR-6636-42-7}

DRAPER, SAMUEL (Caroline County) received a receipt from the Purchasing Agent for furnishing wheat on 31 Aug 1782 {Ref: Maryland State Archives MdHR-6636-42-7}

DROWN, THOMAS (Prince George's County) received payment by order of the Council of Safety "for making cloaths" on 3 Sep 1776 {Ref: Archives of Maryland 12:255}

DRURY, ENOCH (St. Mary's County) received payment from the Purchasing Agent on 30 Dec 1781 for collecting and driving public cattle for 13 days {Ref: Maryland State Archives MdHR-6636-43-23}

DRURY, IGNATIUS (St. Mary's County) received payment from the Purchasing Agent on 30 Dec 1781 for collecting and driving public cattle for 13 days {Ref: Maryland State Archives MdHR-6636-43-23}

DRYDEN, JOHN (Worcester County) submitted an account and receipt for furnishing pork barrels on 10 Mar 1782 {Ref: Maryland State Archives MdHR-6636-43-28TT}

DUBBERLY (DUBERLY), JOHN (Worcester County) received a receipt from the Purchasing Agent for furnishing corn on 14 Jun 1780 {Ref: Maryland State Archives MdHR-6636-24-53}; his name appeared on "A List of Corn Purchased in Worcester County for the use of the State of Maryland" by the Commissary in July, 1780 {Ref: Archives of Maryland 45:10}

DUCKER, JEREMIAH (Montgomery County) received a receipt from the Purchasing Agent for furnishing wheat on 1 Aug 1780 {Ref: Maryland State Archives MdHR-6636-43-7}; received a receipt for furnishing wheat on 3 Aug

1780 {Ref: Maryland State Archives MdHR-6636-24-6}

DUCKER, NATHANIEL (Montgomery County) received a receipt from the Purchasing Agent for furnishing wheat on 3 Apr 1781 {Ref: Maryland State Archives MdHR-6636-42-11}; received a receipt for furnishing wheat on 5 Oct 1781 {Ref: Maryland State Archives MdHR-6636-24-15}

DUCKETT, JACOB (Prince George's County) was appointed as a Commissary by the Council of Maryland on 5 Jan 1778 "to procure Supplies and Distribute them to the Quota of Troops of the American Army agreeable to a Resolve of the General Assembly" on 13 Dec 1777 {Ref: Archives of Maryland 16:454}

DUCKETT, RICHARD JR. (Prince George's County) received a certificate from the Purchasing Agent for furnishing rye on 8 Jan 1780 {Ref: Maryland State Archives MdHR-6636-19-3}; received a certificate for providing supplies for the army on 28 Mar 1780 {Ref: Maryland State Archives MdHR-6636-17-117}

DUCKETT, RIGNALL (Prince George's County) was a doctor who was appointed by the Council of Maryland to serve as "Surgeon's Mate to the 11th Battalion of Militia whilst in actual service" on 17 Feb 1778 {Ref: Archives of Maryland 16:503}

DUCKETT, THOMAS (Prince George's County) was appointed by the Council of Maryland to purchase pork in his county on 5 Jan 1778 {Ref: Archives of Maryland 16:454}; as sheriff he submitted an account due to the state "for conveying public letters" on 11 May 1780 {Ref: Maryland State Archives MdHR-6636-18-78}; pledged a loan in the amount of £200 to the State of Maryland under the Act for the Emission of Bills of Credit "to defray the expences of the present campaign" in June, 1781 {Ref: Archives of Maryland 47:327}

DUER, JAMES JR. (Worcester County) submitted an account and receipt for furnishing salt on 10 Oct 1781 {Ref: Maryland State Archives MdHR-6636-43-27}

DUFFEY, THOMAS (Baltimore County) received payment for furnishing flour on 12 Jul 1781 {Ref: Maryland State Archives MdHR-6636-43-38LL}

DUGAN, CUMBERLAND (Baltimore Town) was a merchant and baker who received payment by order of the Council of Maryland "for flour purchased according to the direction of the Convention" on 26 Jun 1776 and "delivered 2000 wt. of bisquit by him baked for provincial use" on 28 Jun 1776 {Ref: Archives of Maryland 11:521, 529}

DUKE, ISAAC (Caroline County) received a receipt from the Purchasing Agent for furnishing wheat on 5 Aug 1782 {Ref: Maryland State Archives MdHR-6636-42-7}

DUKE, ZEBULON (Caroline County) received receipts from the Purchasing Agent for furnishing wheat on 5 Aug and 22 Aug 1782 {Ref: Maryland State Archives MdHR-6636-42-7}

DULANY, JAMES (Talbot County) received a certificate from the Purchasing Agent for furnishing wheat on 2 May 1780 {Ref: Maryland State Archives MdHR-6636-24-51}

DULEY, WILLIAM (Montgomery County) received a receipt from the Purchasing Agent for furnishing wheat on 31 Oct 1780 {Ref: Maryland State Archives MdHR-6636-24-13}

DUNE, ELIZABETH (county not stated) received payment by order of the Council of Safety for services rendered (not specified) on 14 Oct 1776 {Ref: Archives of Maryland 12:349}

DUNN, HEZEKIAH (Kent County) received certificates from the Purchasing Agent for milling on 15 Mar and 20 Apr 1780, and for hauling flour on 10 Apr 1780 {Ref: Maryland State Archives MdHR-6636-23-41}

DUNN, JAMES (Kent County) received a certificate from the Purchasing Agent for furnishing flour on 18 Feb 1780 {Ref: Maryland State Archives MdHR-6636-23-46}

DUNN, JOHN (Charles County) received a receipt from the Purchasing Agent for furnishing wheat on 31 Oct 1782 {Ref: Maryland State Archives MdHR-6636-42-19}

DUNN, ROBERT (Kent County) received certificates from the Purchasing Agent for milling on 15 Mar and 20 Apr 1780 {Ref: Maryland State Archives MdHR-6636-23-41}

DUNN (DUN), WILLIAM (Montgomery County) received a receipt from the Purchasing Agent for furnishing wheat on 7 Aug 1780 {Ref: Maryland State Archives MdHR-6636-24-6}; received a receipt for furnishing wheat on 1 Aug 1780 {Ref: Maryland State Archives MdHR-6636-43-7}

DUNNINGTON, PETER (Charles County) received a receipt from the Purchasing Agent for furnishing wheat on 10 May 1783 {Ref: Maryland State Archives MdHR-6636-42-22}

DURBIN, DANIEL (Harford County) was certified and appointed as county purchasing agent to receive flour at Susquehanna Lower Ferry for the Continental Army on 4 Nov 1780 {Ref: Maryland State Archives MdHR-6636-23-37}

DURBIN, FRANCIS (Harford County) was appointed by the Committee of Safety "to ride in Susquehanna Hundred and purchase guns and blankets agreeable to the request of the [Maryland] Council of Safety" on 19 Aug 1776 and submitted his account on 2 Sep 1776 {Ref: Preston's History of Harford County, pp. 333-334, 336}

DURHAM, PATRICK (Montgomery County) received a receipt from the Purchasing Agent for furnishing wheat on 20 Apr 1781 {Ref: Maryland State Archives MdHR-6636-42-11}

DUTTERO, JOHN (Frederick County) received a certificate from the Purchasing

Agent for furnishing hay on 27 Oct 1781 {Ref: Maryland State Archives MdHR-6636-42-32}

DUTTON, LEVI (Worcester County) submitted an account for slaughtering beef and receipt for a negro's wages on 31 Oct 1781 {Ref: Maryland State Archives MdHR-6636-43-27}

DUVALL, WILLIAM (Frederick County) was a captain who received a receipt from the Purchasing Agent for salt pork delivery on 27 Mar 1781 {Ref: Maryland State Archives MdHR-6636-23-30}

DWIGANS, JOHN (Caroline County) received a receipt from the Purchasing Agent for furnishing wheat on 17 Aug 1782 {Ref: Maryland State Archives MdHR-6636-42-7}

DWIGGINS, ROBERT (Talbot County) received a receipt from the Purchasing Agent for furnishing wheat on 23 Oct 1780 {Ref: Maryland State Archives MdHR-6636-24-47}

DYAN, ANNACLATUS (Charles County) received a certificate from the Purchasing Agent for furnishing wheat on 11 Apr 1782 {Ref: Maryland State Archives MdHR-6636-42-18}

DYER, JOHN (Charles County) received a receipt from the Purchasing Agent for furnishing rum and cider on 12 Apr 1781 {Ref: Maryland State Archives MdHR-19970-3-16}

DYER, THOMAS (Montgomery County) received a receipt from the Purchasing Agent for furnishing wheat on 9 Sep 1780 {Ref: Maryland State Archives MdHR-6636-24-7}

DYMACK, WILLIAM (Somerset County) received a receipt from the Purchasing Agent for furnishing pork on 14 May 1781 {Ref: Maryland State Archives MdHR-6636-24-43}

DYSON, BENNETT (Charles County) made a shipment of corn to Head of Elk in Cecil County on 20 Jun 1780 {Ref: Maryland State Archives MdHR-6636-18-159}

DYSON, GARRARD (Charles County) received a receipt from the Purchasing Agent for furnishing wheat on 28 Dec 1782 {Ref: Maryland State Archives MdHR-6636-42-21}

DYSON, MARY (Montgomery County) received a receipt from the Purchasing Agent for furnishing wheat on 19 May 1781 {Ref: Maryland State Archives MdHR-6636-24-18}

DYSON, ROSWELL (Frederick County) received a certificate from the Purchasing Agent for furnishing pork on 22 Oct 1781 {Ref: Maryland State Archives MdHR-6636-50-91}

DYSON, SAMUEL (Montgomery County) received receipts from the Purchasing Agent for furnishing wheat on 28 Apr and 19 May 1781 {Ref: Maryland State Archives MdHR-6636-24-18}

EARLE, JAMES (Queen Anne's County) received a certificate from the Purchasing Agent for furnishing wheat on 4 Jan 1780 {Ref: Maryland State Archives MdHR-6636-24-28}; received a certificate for furnishing wheat on 18 Jan 1780 {Ref: Maryland State Archives MdHR-6636-24-30}

EARLE, JOSEPH (Kent County) was appointed by the Council of Safety to collect all the gold and silver coin that could be procured in the county in compliance with the Resolve of Congress on 27 Jan 1776 {Ref: Archives of Maryland 11:132}

EARLE, MICHAEL (Cecil County) submitted an account for hauling wheat on 29 Nov 1783 {Ref: Maryland State Archives MdHR-6636-42-9}

EASTMAN, JOSEPH (county not stated) received payment by order of the Council of Safety for furnishing a musquet on 10 Aug 1776 {Ref: Archives of Maryland 12:179}; Eastman & Neth received payment by order of the Council of Maryland for services rendered (not specified) on 5 Aug 1777 and also received payment via Joseph Eastman on 31 Aug 1778 {Ref: Archives of Maryland 16:325, 21:192}

EASUM, JONATHAN SR. (Dorchester County) received a receipt from the Purchasing Agent for furnishing wheat on 1 Nov 1782 {Ref: Maryland State Archives MdHR-6636-42-23}

EATON, PETER (Caroline County) received receipts from the Purchasing Agent for furnishing wheat on 31 May and 5 Aug 1782 {Ref: Maryland State Archives MdHR-6636-42-7}

EATON, THOMAS (Caroline County) received receipts from the Purchasing Agent for furnishing wheat on 31 May and 5 Aug 1782 {Ref: Maryland State Archives MdHR-6636-42-7}

EBERT, ADAM (Frederick County) received a receipt from the Purchasing Agent for furnishing beef on 7 Jan 1781 {Ref: Maryland State Archives MdHR-6636-23-2}; submitted an account for furnishing beef on 23 Apr 1781 {Ref: Maryland State Archives MdHR-6636-23-5}; submitted an account for furnishing beef on 21 May 1781 and an account for furnishing mutton on 29 May 1781 {Ref: Maryland State Archives MdHR-6636-23-6}; received a receipt for cash to commissary of provisions on 2 Mar 1782 {Ref: Maryland State Archives MdHR-6636-42-27}

EBERT, ANDREW (Frederick County) received a certificate from the Purchasing Agent for transportation of flour on 19 May 1782 {Ref: Maryland State Archives MdHR-6636-42-26}

ECCLESTON, CHARLES (Dorchester County) received a receipt from the Purchasing Agent for furnishing wheat on 25 Mar 1783 {Ref: Maryland State Archives MdHR-6636-42-24}

ECCLESTON, JOHN (Kent County) received payment from the Purchasing Agent for furnishing cattle for the public use in September, 1781 {Ref: Maryland

State Archives MdHR-6636-43-3}

EDELIN (EDELEN), BENEDICT (Prince George's County) received a loan certificate for £35.14.10 due from the Council of Maryland "agreeable to the Act proposing to the Citizens of this State, Creditors of Congress on Loan Office Certificates, Etc." on 4 Apr 1783 for services rendered during the war {Ref: Archives of Maryland 48:394}

EDELIN (EDELEN), BENJAMIN (Charles County) received a receipt from the Purchasing Agent for furnishing wheat on 20 Dec 1782 {Ref: Maryland State Archives MdHR-6636-42-20}

EDELIN (EDELEN), CHRISTOPHER (Frederick County) was appointed Purchaser of Clothing in his county by the Council of Maryland on 5 Jun 1781 {Ref: Archives of Maryland 45:462}

EDELIN (EDELEN), EDWARD JR. (Prince George's County) received a receipt from the Purchasing Agent for furnishing wheat on 9 May 1783 {Ref: Maryland State Archives MdHR-6636-43-9}

EDELIN (EDELEN), FRANCIS (Charles County) received a receipt from the Purchasing Agent for furnishing wheat on 26 Jan 1782 {Ref: Maryland State Archives MdHR-6636-42-16}; received a receipt for furnishing wheat on 20 Dec 1782 {Ref: Maryland State Archives MdHR-6636-42-20}

EDELIN (EDELEN), JOHN (Charles County) received a receipt from the Purchasing Agent for furnishing wheat on 4 Oct 1781 {Ref: Maryland State Archives MdHR-6636-43-45G}; received a receipt for furnishing wheat on 23 Nov 1781 {Ref: Maryland State Archives MdHR-6636-42-15}

EDELIN (EDELEN), JOSEPH (Prince George's County) received a receipt from the Purchasing Agent for furnishing wheat on 9 May 1783 {Ref: Maryland State Archives MdHR-6636-43-9}

EDELIN (EDELEN), RICHARD (Charles County) received a receipt from the Purchasing Agent for furnishing wheat on 17 Jun 1782 {Ref: Maryland State Archives MdHR-6636-42-18}; received a receipt for furnishing wheat on 20 Dec 1782 {Ref: Maryland State Archives MdHR-6636-42-20}

EDELIN (EDELEN), SUSANNAH (Charles County) received a receipt from the Purchasing Agent for furnishing wheat on 10 May 1783 {Ref: Maryland State Archives MdHR-6636-42-22}

EDEN, JOHN (St. Mary's County) was appointed by the Council of Maryland as one of thirty men to be "Agents for Purchasing Provisions" on 30 Mar 1779 {Ref: Archives of Maryland 21:332}; his name appeared on "A Return of Beef on the Hoof Purchased by Joseph Ford Commissary of Purchases" on 10 Oct 1780 when he delivered two steers for the use of the state {Ref: Archives of Maryland 45:156}

EDGE, JESSE (Caroline County) received a receipt from the Purchasing Agent for furnishing wheat on 17 Aug 1782 {Ref: Maryland State Archives MdHR-6636-

42-7}

EDGELL, DANIEL (Caroline County) received a receipt from the Purchasing Agent for furnishing wheat on 22 Aug 1782 {Ref: Maryland State Archives MdHR-6636-42-7}

EDMONDSON, POLLARD (Queen Anne's County) received payment by order of the Council of Safety for the hire of his boat for the Flying Camp on 22 Aug 1776 {Ref: Archives of Maryland 12:232}; received a receipt for furnishing wheat on 10 Nov 1781 {Ref: Maryland State Archives MdHR-6636-24-34}; received a receipt for furnishing wheat on 26 Mar 1783 {Ref: Maryland State Archives MdHR-6636-43-14}

EDWARDS, JOHN (Prince George's County) received a receipt from the Purchasing Agent for furnishing wheat on 20 May 1782 {Ref: Maryland State Archives MdHR-6636-50-135}

EGLIN, BENEDICT, see "Benedict Elgin," q.v.

ELBERT, JOHN L. (Talbot County) was a doctor who served as Assistant Surgeon to the Maryland Line and received payment from the Council of Maryland for £13.10.0 as "part of the Advance directed to be made by the Act relating to public Creditors" on 21 May 1782 for services rendered during the war {Ref: Archives of Maryland 48:419}

ELDER, GUY (Frederick County) received a certificate from the Purchasing Agent for furnishing wheat on 27 Mar 1782 {Ref: Maryland State Archives MdHR-6636-42-34}

ELDER, HUGH (Montgomery County) received a receipt from the Purchasing Agent for furnishing wheat on 16 Nov 1780 {Ref: Maryland State Archives MdHR-6636-24-8}; received a receipt for furnishing wheat on 5 Feb 1781 {Ref: Maryland State Archives MdHR-6636-24-9}

ELGIN (EGLIN?), BENEDICT (Charles County) received payment from the Council of Maryland "for forage found 11 Horses on their way to join the Southern Army" on 24 Feb 1783 {Ref: Archives of Maryland 48:366}

ELGIN, RICHARD (Charles County) received a receipt from the Purchasing Agent for furnishing wheat in or about 1780 {Ref: Maryland State Archives MdHR-6636-23-24}

ELGIN, WILLIAM SR. (Charles County) received a receipt from the Purchasing Agent for furnishing wheat on 20 Dec 1782 {Ref: Maryland State Archives MdHR-6636-42-20}

ELLESS, JOHN (Montgomery County) received a receipt from the Purchasing Agent for furnishing wheat on 30 Apr 1781 {Ref: Maryland State Archives MdHR-6636-42-11}

ELLIOT, BENJAMIN (Queen Anne's County) furnished cattle on 11 Apr 1781 for the use of the State of Maryland {Ref: Archives of Maryland 47:250}

ELLIS, JOHN (Prince George's County) received a receipt from the Purchasing

Agent for furnishing wheat in 1783 {Ref: Maryland State Archives MdHR-6636-50-135}

ELLIS, RICHARD (Cecil County) was a captain who also served as Deputy Commissary and Purchasing Agent for the Continental Army in 1782-1783 {Ref: Maryland State Archives MdHR-6636-42-9}

ELLIS, ZACHARIAH (Montgomery County) received a receipt from the Purchasing Agent for shelling corn on 17 May 1780 {Ref: Maryland State Archives MdHR-6636-24-2}

ELLIS, ZACHARIAH (Prince George's County) received a receipt from the Purchasing Agent for furnishing wheat on 17 Jan 1783 {Ref: Maryland State Archives MdHR-6636-50-135}

ELMORE, CLIFFORD (Worcester County) received a receipt from the Purchasing Agent for furnishing corn on 21 Apr 1780 {Ref: Maryland State Archives MdHR-6636-24-52}

ELMORE, COMFORT (Worcester County) appeared on "A List of Corn Purchased in Worcester County for the use of the State of Maryland" by the Commissary in July, 1780 {Ref: Archives of Maryland 45:10}

ELSBURY, LAMBERT (Cecil County) submitted an account for hauling wheat on 30 Nov 1782 {Ref: Maryland State Archives MdHR-6636-42-9}

ELZEY, ANN (Somerset County) received a loan certificate for £75.4.10 due from the Council of Maryland "agreeable to the Act proposing to the Citizens of this State, Creditors of Congress on Loan Office Certificates, Etc." on 19 Dec 1783 for services rendered during the war {Ref: Archives of Maryland 48:493}

ELZEY, ARNOLD (Somerset County) was a doctor who received a loan certificate for £9.8.5 due from the Council of Maryland "agreeable to the Act proposing to the Citizens of this State, Creditors of Congress on Loan Office Certificates, Etc." on 22 May 1783 for services rendered during the war {Ref: Archives of Maryland 48:419}

ELZEY, JAMES (Somerset County) received a loan certificate for £741.1.3 due from the Council of Maryland "agreeable to the Act proposing to the Citizens of this State, Creditors of Congress on Loan Office Certificates, Etc." on 31 Jul 1783 for services rendered during the war {Ref: Archives of Maryland 48:442}

ELZEY, MARGARET, Mrs. (Calvert County) received certificates for loans to the Continental Congress on 28 Feb and 6 Mar 1778 {Ref: Maryland State Archives MdHR-6636-11-119B/C}; received a loan certificate for £226.1.10 due from the Council of Maryland "agreeable to the Act proposing to the Citizens of this State, Creditors of Congress on Loan Office Certificates, Etc." on 24 Sep 1783 for services rendered during the war {Ref: Archives of Maryland 48:456}

ELZEY, ROBERT (Somerset County) received a receipt from the Purchasing Agent for furnishing pork on 28 May 1782 {Ref: Maryland State Archives

MdHR-6636-43-21}

EMMIT, SAMUEL (Frederick County) received a certificate from the Purchasing Agent for furnishing wheat on 26 Nov 1782 {Ref: Maryland State Archives MdHR-6636-42-37}

EMORY, ARTHUR (Queen Anne's County) was appointed one of eighteen Collectors of Clothing by the Council of Maryland under "An Act to Procure Cloathing for the Quota of this State of the American Army" on 27 Nov 1777 {Ref: Archives of Maryland 16:426}; received a certificate from the Purchasing Agent for furnishing wheat on 8 Jan 1780 {Ref: Maryland State Archives MdHR-6636-24-30}; received a receipt for furnishing beef on 15 Dec 1781 {Ref: Maryland State Archives MdHR-6636-24-34}

EMORY, GIDEON (Queen Anne's County) received a receipt from the Purchasing Agent for furnishing beef on 8 Oct 1781 {Ref: Maryland State Archives MdHR-6636-24-34}

EMORY, JOHN R. (Queen Anne's County) received a receipt from the Purchasing Agent for furnishing bacon on 15 Apr 1781 {Ref: Maryland State Archives MdHR-6636-24-34}

EMORY, THOMAS L. (Queen Anne's County) received a certificate from the Purchasing Agent for furnishing wheat on 18 Jan 1780 {Ref: Maryland State Archives MdHR-6636-24-30}

EMORY, THOMAS (Queen Anne's County) received a certificate from the Purchasing Agent for furnishing wheat on 24 Jan 1780 {Ref: Maryland State Archives MdHR-6636-24-28}

EMORY, WILLIAM WILSON (Queen Anne's County) received a certificate from the Purchasing Agent for furnishing wheat on 24 Jan 1780 {Ref: Maryland State Archives MdHR-6636-24-32}

EMORY, WILLIAM W. (Queen Anne's County) received a certificate from the Purchasing Agent for furnishing wheat on 24 Jan 1780 {Ref: Maryland State Archives MdHR-6636-24-28}

ENBLETON, WILLIAM (Kent County) received payment from the Purchasing Agent for furnishing cattle for the public use in September, 1781 {Ref: Maryland State Archives MdHR-6636-43-3}

ENGLEMAN, LODWICK (Frederick County) received a certificate from the Purchasing Agent for furnishing wheat on 23 Mar 1782 {Ref: Maryland State Archives MdHR-6636-42-35}

ENNALLS, BARTHOLOMEW JR. (Dorchester County) submitted a bill and receipt for transporting flour on 1 Sep 1778 {Ref: Maryland State Archives MdHR-6636-23-26}

ENNALLS, HENRY (Dorchester County) submitted an account and receipt for driving cattle on 12 May 1778 {Ref: Maryland State Archives MdHR-6636-23-26}

ENNALLS, JOHN (Dorchester County) was appointed one of eighteen Collectors of Clothing by the Council of Maryland under "An Act to Procure Cloathing for the Quota of this State of the American Army" on 27 Nov 1777 {Ref: Archives of Maryland 16:426}; also see "Joseph Ennalls," q.v.

ENNALLS, JOSEPH (Dorchester County) was appointed Collector of Clothing in the room of John Ennalls (incapable of acting due to sickness) by the Council of Maryland on 3 Feb 1778 {Ref: Archives of Maryland 16:482}

ENNALLS, WILLIAM (Dorchester County) was appointed by the Council of Safety to collect all the gold and silver coin that could be procured in the county in compliance with the Resolve of Congress on 27 Jan 1776 {Ref: Archives of Maryland 11:132}

ERGS, ASSIRIAH (Prince George's County) received a receipt from the Purchasing Agent for furnishing wheat on 12 Jun 1782 {Ref: Maryland State Archives MdHR-6636-50-135}

EUBANKS, JOHN (Caroline County) received a receipt from the Purchasing Agent for furnishing wheat on 1 Sep 1782 {Ref: Maryland State Archives MdHR-6636-42-7}

EVANS, ELIZABETH (Worcester County) received a receipt from the Purchasing Agent for furnishing beef on 12 Oct 1780 {Ref: Maryland State Archives MdHR-6636-24-54}

EVANS, EPHRAIM (Somerset County) received a receipt from the Purchasing Agent for furnishing beef on 5 Dec 1781 {Ref: Maryland State Archives MdHR-6636-24-44}

EVANS, ISAAC (Worcester County) received a receipt from the Purchasing Agent for furnishing corn on 14 Jun 1780 {Ref: Maryland State Archives MdHR-6636-24-53}; his name appeared on "A List of Corn Purchased in Worcester County for the use of the State of Maryland" by the Commissary in July, 1780 {Ref: Archives of Maryland 45:9}

EVANS, JOHN SR. (Somerset County) received a receipt from the Purchasing Agent for furnishing bacon on 17 Aug 1780 {Ref: Maryland State Archives MdHR-6636-24-41}

EVANS, JOHN (Frederick County) received a certificate from the Purchasing Agent for furnishing wheat on 4 Mar 1782 {Ref: Maryland State Archives MdHR-6636-42-36}

EVANS, THOMAS, see "John Halkerston," q.v.

EVANS, WILLIAM (Montgomery County) received receipts from the Purchasing Agent for furnishing wheat on 28 Apr and 18 May 1781 {Ref: Maryland State Archives MdHR-6636-24-18}

EVARS, JOHN (Frederick County) received a certificate from the Purchasing Agent for furnishing wheat on 29 Aug 1782 {Ref: Maryland State Archives MdHR-6636-42-37}

EVERET, HAILES (Kent County) received payment from the Purchasing Agent for furnishing cattle and pasturage for the public use in September, 1781 {Ref: Maryland State Archives MdHR-6636-43-3}

EVERITT, BENJAMIN (Kent County) submitted an account and receipt for carting supplies on 30 Mar 1782 {Ref: Maryland State Archives MdHR-6636-43-5}

EVERLY, JACOB (Frederick County) received a certificate from the Purchasing Agent for furnishing wheat on 7 Jun 1782 {Ref: Maryland State Archives MdHR-6636-42-34}

EVINS, ELEXANDER (Charles County) received a receipt from the Purchasing Agent for furnishing wheat on 10 May 1783 {Ref: Maryland State Archives MdHR-6636-42-22}

EVINS, WARRINGTON (Caroline County) received a receipt from the Purchasing Agent for furnishing wheat on 5 Aug 1782 {Ref: Maryland State Archives MdHR-6636-42-7}

EWING, JAMES (Caroline County) received a receipt from the Purchasing Agent for furnishing wheat on 22 Aug 1782 {Ref: Maryland State Archives MdHR-6636-42-7}

EWING, PATRICK (Cecil County) was commissioned an Assistant Deputy Commissary of Purchases for Cecil and Kent Counties on 10 Sep 1779 {Ref: Archives of Maryland 21:518; Maryland State Archives MdHR-6636-15-145A}; received a receipt for furnishing flour on 23 Apr 1783 {Ref: Maryland State Archives MdHR-6636-42-9}

FAIRBROTHER, FRANCIS (Anne Arundel County) received payment by order of the Council of Safety for the freight of linen from Edward Parker's factory in Cecil County to Annapolis on 3 Jul 1776 {Ref: Archives of Maryland 11:545}; received payment for furnishing bar iron to Capt. Conway for the sloop *Molly* on 28 Mar 1778 {Ref: Archives of Maryland 16:556}

FAIRFAX, JONATHAN (Charles County) received a receipt from the Purchasing Agent for furnishing wheat on 3 May 1783 {Ref: Maryland State Archives MdHR-6636-42-22}

FALCONAR, ABRAHAM (Kent County) received certificates from the Purchasing Agent for furnishing flour and wheat on 16 Jan, 10 Mar, 10 May and 20 May 1780 {Ref: Maryland State Archives MdHR-6636-43-1}; received payment by order of the Council of Maryland for his use as Contractor for Horses and Wagons in Kent County on 23 Aug 1780 {Ref: Archives of Maryland 43:262}; received a contract to deliver Indian corn on 7 Jul 1781 {Ref: Maryland State Archives MdHR-6636-28-8A}

FALCONER, GILBERT (Kent County) was appointed by the Council of Maryland to be one of three men in Kent County "to carry the Act to prohibit for a limited time the Exportation of Indian Corn, Etc., by Land" on 22 Dec 1780 {Ref:

Archives of Maryland 45:251}; received a certificate from the Purchasing Agent for furnishing wheat on 21 May 1782 {Ref: Maryland State Archives MdHR-6636-42-34}

FARFAX, WILLIAM (Charles County) received a receipt from the Purchasing Agent for furnishing wheat on 22 Jul 1782 {Ref: Maryland State Archives MdHR-6636-42-18}

FARIS (FARRIS), WILLIAM (Annapolis) received a loan certificate for £230.10.0 due from the Council of Maryland "agreeable to the Act proposing to the Citizens of this State, Creditors of Congress on Loan Office Certificates, Etc." on 25 Oct 1783 for services rendered during the war {Ref: Archives of Maryland 48:474}

FARMER, JOHN (Montgomery County) received a receipt from the Purchasing Agent for furnishing wheat on 11 Nov 1781 {Ref: Maryland State Archives MdHR-6636-24-15}

FARMER, WILLIAM (Somerset County) received a receipt from the Purchasing Agent for furnishing pork on 6 Jul 1781 {Ref: Maryland State Archives MdHR-6636-24-43}

FARNANDIS, ELENOR (Charles County) received a receipt from the Purchasing Agent for furnishing wheat on 14 Aug 1782 {Ref: Maryland State Archives MdHR-6636-42-18}; received a receipt for furnishing wheat on 28 Dec 1782 {Ref: Maryland State Archives MdHR-6636-42-21}

FARNANDIS, PETER (Charles County) received a receipt from the Purchasing Agent for furnishing wheat on 28 Dec 1782 {Ref: Maryland State Archives MdHR-6636-42-21}; received a receipt for furnishing wheat on 10 May 1783 {Ref: Maryland State Archives MdHR-6636-42-22}

FASHOUR, JACOB (Frederick County) received a certificate from the Purchasing Agent for furnishing hay on 12 Dec 1781 {Ref: Maryland State Archives MdHR-6636-42-32}

FASSETT (FASSITT), DAVID (Worcester County) received a receipt from the Purchasing Agent for furnishing corn on 19 May 1780 {Ref: Maryland State Archives MdHR-6636-24-53}; his name appeared twice on "A List of Corn Purchased in Worcester County for the use of the State of Maryland" by the Commissary in July, 1780 {Ref: Archives of Maryland 45:10}

FASSETT (FASSITT), JOHN (Worcester County) was a captain who received a receipt from the Purchasing Agent for furnishing corn on 14 Jun 1780 {Ref: Maryland State Archives MdHR-6636-24-53}; his name appeared on "A List of Corn Purchased in Worcester County for the use of the State of Maryland" by the Commissary in July, 1780 {Ref: Archives of Maryland 45:10}; received a receipt for furnishing wheat on 12 Oct 1780 and for hauling corn on 15 Oct 1780 {Ref: Maryland State Archives MdHR-6636-24-54}

FASSETT (FASSITT), WILLIAM (Worcester County) received a receipt from the

Purchasing Agent for furnishing corn on 14 Jun 1780 {Ref: Maryland State Archives MdHR-6636-24-53}; his name appeared on "A List of Corn Purchased in Worcester County for the use of the State of Maryland" by the Commissary in July, 1780 {Ref: Archives of Maryland 45:10}

FAUNTLEROY, GRIFFIN (Queen Anne's County) received a receipt from the Purchasing Agent for feeding cattle on 27 Nov 1781 {Ref: Maryland State Archives MdHR-6636-24-34}

FAW, ABRAHAM (Frederick County) was appointed by the Council of Maryland to superintend the building of the barracks in Frederick on or about 27 Jun 1777 {Ref: Archives of Maryland 16:300}; appointed one of eighteen Collectors of Clothing by the Council of Maryland under "An Act to Procure Cloathing for the Quota of this State of the American Army" on 27 Nov 1777 {Ref: Archives of Maryland 16:426}; purchased clothing for the use of the state on or about 25 Mar 1778 {Ref: Archives of Maryland 16:550}; purchased clothing for the use of the army on 2 Feb 1780 {Ref: Maryland State Archives MdHR-4603-23}

FAWNER, JACOB (Frederick County) received a certificate from the Purchasing Agent for furnishing wheat on 28 May 1782 {Ref: Maryland State Archives MdHR-6636-42-34}

FEDDEMAN, BARTHOLOMEW (Caroline County) received a receipt from the Purchasing Agent for wheat on 16 Sep 1782 {Ref: Maryland State Archives MdHR-6636-42-7}

FEDDEMAN (FIDDEMAN), PHILIP (Queen Anne's County) received payment by order of the Council of Maryland for his use as Contractor for Horses in Queen Anne's County on 11 Sep 1780 {Ref: Archives of Maryland 43:285}

FEE, WILLIAM (Montgomery County) received a receipt from the Purchasing Agent for furnishing wheat on 13 Oct 1780 {Ref: Maryland State Archives MdHR-6636-24-8}

FEILOS, JOHN (Montgomery County) received a receipt from the Purchasing Agent for furnishing wheat on 28 Apr 1781 {Ref: Maryland State Archives MdHR-6636-24-18}

FELTIN (FELTON), HENRY (Frederick County) received a receipt from the Purchasing Agent for furnishing beef on 24 Mar 1781 {Ref: Maryland State Archives MdHR-6636-23-4}; received a certificate for furnishing wheat on 29 May 1782 {Ref: Maryland State Archives MdHR-6636-42-34}

FENDALL, BENJAMIN (Charles County) received a receipt from the Purchasing Agent for furnishing wheat on 19 Jan 1782 {Ref: Maryland State Archives MdHR-6636-42-16}; received a receipt for furnishing wheat on 31 Oct 1782 {Ref: Maryland State Archives MdHR-6636-42-19}; received a loan certificate for £151.4.3 due from the Council of Maryland "agreeable to the Act proposing to the Citizens of this State, Creditors of Congress on Loan Office Certificates,

Etc." on 20 Oct 1783 for services rendered during the war {Ref: Archives of Maryland 48:471}

FENWICK, IGNATIUS (St. Mary's County) was a captain who received payment from the Council of Maryland on 30 Apr 1783 "for 17,350 pounds of nett Tobacco at George Town and Bladensburgh Warehouses due him for the like Quantity lent the State in November 1780" {Ref: Archives of Maryland 48:405}

FERGUSON, JOSEPH (Montgomery County) received a receipt from the Purchasing Agent for shelling corn on 17 Apr 1780 {Ref: Maryland State Archives MdHR-6636-24-2}

FERGUSON, ROBERT (Charles County) received a receipt from the Purchasing Agent for furnishing wheat on 18 Sep 1781 {Ref: Maryland State Archives MdHR-6636-23-24}; received a receipt for furnishing wheat on 18 Nov 1782 {Ref: Maryland State Archives MdHR-6636-42-19}; received a receipt for furnishing wheat on 20 Dec 1782 {Ref: Maryland State Archives MdHR-6636-42-20}

FERRELL, HENRY (Montgomery County) received a receipt from the Purchasing Agent for furnishing wheat on 21 Oct 1780 {Ref: Maryland State Archives MdHR-6636-24-8}

FERRELL, JOHN (Montgomery County) received a receipt from the Purchasing Agent for furnishing wheat on 27 Oct 1780 {Ref: Maryland State Archives MdHR-6636-24-8}

FERVER, PHILIP (Frederick County) received a certificate from the Purchasing Agent for furnishing wheat on 7 Feb 1783 {Ref: Maryland State Archives MdHR-6636-42-38}

FIELDS, ABRAHAM (Montgomery County) received a receipt from the Purchasing Agent for furnishing wheat on 10 Apr 1781 {Ref: Maryland State Archives MdHR-6636-42-11}

FIELDS, MATTHEW (Montgomery County) received a receipt from the Purchasing Agent for furnishing wheat on 17 Oct 1781 {Ref: Maryland State Archives MdHR-6636-24-15}

FIEREW, HENRY SR. (Frederick County) received a certificate from the Purchasing Agent for hauling flour on 27 Oct 1781 {Ref: Maryland State Archives MdHR-6636-42-32}

FIFE, JACOB (Frederick County) received a receipt from the Purchasing Agent for furnishing corn on 2 May 1780 {Ref: Maryland State Archives MdHR-6636-24-1}

FILPUT, BARTON (Frederick County) received a certificate from the Purchasing Agent for furnishing corn on 26 Jan 1780 {Ref: Maryland State Archives MdHR-6636-42-29}

FIMMS, JOHN (Charles County) received a receipt from the Purchasing Agent for furnishing wheat on 18 Aug 1782 {Ref: Maryland State Archives MdHR-6636-42-18}

FINNAY, MORRIS (Harford County) received a receipt from the Purchasing Agent for furnishing wheat on 28 Mar 1780 {Ref: Maryland State Archives MdHR-6636-17-116}

FISCHER, ADAM (Frederick County) received a receipt from the Purchasing Agent for furnishing beef on 29 May 1781 {Ref: Maryland State Archives MdHR-6636-23-6}

FISHER, MARTIN (Montgomery County) received a receipt from the Purchasing Agent for furnishing wheat on 1 Aug 1780 {Ref: Maryland State Archives MdHR-6636-43-7}; received a receipt for furnishing wheat on 12 Aug 1780 {Ref: Maryland State Archives MdHR-6636-24-6}

FISHER, RICHARD (Queen Anne's County) received a certificate from the Purchasing Agent for furnishing wheat on 17 Feb 1780 {Ref: Maryland State Archives MdHR-6636-24-29}

FITZGERALD, JOHN (Montgomery County) received a receipt from the Purchasing Agent for furnishing wheat on 5 Oct 1780 {Ref: Maryland State Archives MdHR-6636-24-8}

FITZPATRICK, HUGH (Frederick County) received payment for driving cattle on 29 Mar 1781 {Ref: Maryland State Archives MdHR-6636-23-30}

FLACKALL, THOMAS (Montgomery County) received a receipt from the Purchasing Agent for shelling corn on 20 Oct 1780 {Ref: Maryland State Archives MdHR-6636-24-2}

FLEETWOOD, BENJAMIN, see "John Stump, Jr.," q.v.

FLEMING, JAMES (Somerset County) received a receipt from the Purchasing Agent for furnishing beef on 6 Dec 1781 {Ref: Maryland State Archives MdHR-6636-24-44}

FLEMING, RICHARD (Anne Arundel County) received payment by order of the Council of Safety for furnishing a gun on 20 Aug 1776 {Ref: Archives of Maryland 12:223}

FLEMMING, JOHN (Worcester County) submitted an account and receipt for furnishing pork barrels on 10 Mar 1782 {Ref: Maryland State Archives MdHR-6636-43-28WW}

FLEMMING, SAMUEL (Frederick County) received a certificate from the Purchasing Agent for furnishing wheat on 29 May 1782 {Ref: Maryland State Archives MdHR-6636-42-36}

FLETCHALL, THOMAS (Montgomery County) received a receipt from the Purchasing Agent for furnishing wheat on 19 May 1781 {Ref: Maryland State Archives MdHR-6636-24-18}

FLETCHALL, THOMAS (Prince George's County) received a receipt from the Purchasing Agent for furnishing wheat on 9 Aug 1783 {Ref: Maryland State

Archives MdHR-6636-50-135}

FLETCHER, GEORGE (Somerset County) received a certificate from the Purchasing Agent for furnishing corn on 10 Feb 1780 {Ref: Maryland State Archives MdHR-6636-24-39}

FLOLA, JACOB (Frederick County) received a certificate from the Purchasing Agent for furnishing beef on 13 Jun 1781 {Ref: Maryland State Archives MdHR-6636-23-28}

FLOYD, AARON (Caroline County) received a receipt from the Purchasing Agent for wheat on 20 Aug 1782 {Ref: Maryland State Archives MdHR-6636-42-7}

FLUKE, JOHN (Frederick County) received payment from the Maryland Council of Safety for providing waggonage on 20 Mar 1776 {Ref: Archives of Maryland 11:269}

FLURRY, JOHN (Charles County) received a receipt from the Purchasing Agent for furnishing wheat on 31 Oct 1782 {Ref: Maryland State Archives MdHR-6636-42-19}; received a receipt for furnishing wheat on 11 Dec 1782 {Ref: Maryland State Archives MdHR-6636-42-20}

FOGLE, ANDREW (Frederick County) received a certificate for money loaned to the state on 13 Mar 1782 {Ref: Maryland State Archives MdHR-6636-40-42}

FOOKS (FOOKES), THOMAS (Worcester County) received a receipt from the Purchasing Agent for furnishing corn on 10 Mar 1780 {Ref: Maryland State Archives MdHR-6636-24-52}; his name appeared on "A List of Corn Purchased in Worcester County for the use of the State of Maryland" by the Commissary in July, 1780 {Ref: Archives of Maryland 45:10}

FORBES, JOHN (Charles County) received a loan certificate for £456.16.6 due from the Council of Maryland "agreeable to the Act proposing to the Citizens of this State, Creditors of Congress on Loan Office Certificates, Etc." on 4 Apr 1783 for services rendered during the war {Ref: Archives of Maryland 48:394}

FORD, ATHANASIUS (St. Mary's County) received payment "of the New Emission of this State to be delivered over to Joseph Ford, Commissary for St. Mary's County" by order of the Council of Maryland on 20 Sep 1780 {Ref: Archives of Maryland 43:297}

FORD, CHARLES (Charles County) received a receipt from the Purchasing Agent for furnishing wheat on 29 Dec 1782 {Ref: Maryland State Archives MdHR-6636-42-21}; received a receipt for furnishing wheat on 15 Apr 1783 {Ref: Maryland State Archives MdHR-6636-42-22}

FORD, JOSEPH (St. Mary's County) was appointed Commissary of Purchases for St. Mary's County by the Council of Maryland on 8 Jul 1780 {Ref: Archives of Maryland 43:215}; submitted an account for wheat purchased from 25 Jul to 5 Oct 1780 {Ref: Maryland State Archives MdHR-4595-42}; submitted an account of forage purchased for the Continental Army from 4 Aug to 10 Aug 1780 {Ref: Maryland State Archives MdHR-4595-41}; received payment by order of the Council of Maryland for his use as Contractor for Horses in St. Mary's County on 8 Sep 1780 {Ref: Archives of Maryland 43:281}; submitted an account for purchasing beef from 5 Oct to 14 Oct 1780 {Ref: Maryland State Archives MdHR-4595-39; Archives of Maryland 45:156}; submitted an account for furnishing beef on 6 Nov 1780 {Ref: Maryland State Archives MdHR-4595-33}; submitted an account for furnishing wheat on 10 Dec 1780 {Ref: Maryland State Archives MdHR-4595-34}; served as Purchaser of Horses in his county by 12 Jan 1781 at which time he was paid for his services by the Council of Maryland {Ref: Archives of Maryland 45:271}; appointed Purchaser of Clothing in his county by the Council of Maryland on 5 Jun 1781 {Ref: Archives of Maryland 45:462}; submitted an account of expenses for collecting and driving cattle from Dec 1781 to Jan 1782 {Ref: Maryland State Archives MdHR-6636-43-23}; also see "Athanasius Ford," q.v.

FORD, NOTLEY (Charles County) received a receipt from the Purchasing Agent for furnishing wheat on 15 Dec 1781 {Ref: Maryland State Archives MdHR-6636-42-15}

FOREMAN, CHARLES (Kent County) received payment from the Purchasing Agent for furnishing cattle and pasturage for the public use in September, 1781 {Ref: Maryland State Archives MdHR-6636-43-3}

FOREMAN, JOHN (Queen Anne's County) received a receipt from the Purchasing Agent for furnishing beef on 28 Sep 1781 {Ref: Maryland State Archives MdHR-6636-24-34}

FORMAN, EZEKIEL (Queen Anne's County) was appointed one of eighteen Collectors of Clothing by the Council of Maryland under "An Act to Procure Cloathing for the Quota of this State of the American Army" on 27 Nov 1777 {Ref: Archives of Maryland 16:426}; received a receipt for furnishing a steer on 2 May 1778 {Ref: Maryland State Archives MdHR-4587-38}

FORMAN, SAMUEL (Talbot County) received a receipt from the Purchasing Agent for furnishing wheat on 20 Oct 1780 {Ref: Maryland State Archives MdHR-6636-24-47}

FORMAN, THOMAS (Dorchester County) received a receipt from the Purchasing Agent for furnishing bacon for the use of the army on 18 May 1778 {Ref: Maryland State Archives MdHR-4588-2}

FORTUNE, GEORGE (Somerset County) received a receipt from the Purchasing Agent for furnishing pork on 6 Feb 1782 {Ref: Maryland State Archives MdHR-6636-43-21}

FORREST, ZACHARIAH (St. Mary's County) received a loan certificate for £120.7.0 due from the Council of Maryland "agreeable to the Act proposing to the Citizens of this State, Creditors of Congress on Loan Office Certificates, Etc." on 16 May 1783 for services rendered during the war {Ref: Archives of Maryland 48:414}

FOSSETT (FOSSITT), DAVID (Worcester County) received a receipt from the Purchasing Agent for furnishing corn on 15 Apr 1780 {Ref: Maryland State Archives MdHR-6636-24-52}; submitted an account and receipt for furnishing salt on 10 Jan 1782 {Ref: Maryland State Archives MdHR-6636-43-28EEE}

FOUNTAIN, ANDREW (Caroline County) received a receipt from the Purchasing Agent for furnishing wheat on 1 Sep 1782 {Ref: Maryland State Archives MdHR-6636-42-7}

FOUNTAIN, JAMES (Caroline County) received a receipt from the Purchasing Agent for furnishing wheat on 24 Aug 1782 {Ref: Maryland State Archives MdHR-6636-42-7}

FOUNTAIN, THOMAS (Somerset County) received a receipt from the Purchasing Agent for furnishing bacon on 9 Aug 1780 {Ref: Maryland State Archives MdHR-6636-24-41}

FOUNTAIN, THOMAS (Caroline County) received a receipt from the Purchasing Agent for furnishing wheat on 1 Sep 1782 {Ref: Maryland State Archives MdHR-6636-42-7}

FOUNTAIN, THOMAS SR. (Caroline County) received a receipt from the Purchasing Agent for furnishing wheat on 1 Sep 1782 {Ref: Maryland State Archives MdHR-6636-42-7}

FOUNTAIN, WILLIAM (Caroline County) received receipts from the Purchasing Agent for furnishing wheat on 7 Jun and 5 Aug 1782 {Ref: Maryland State Archives MdHR-6636-42-7}

FOUTZ, HENRY (Frederick County) received payment by order of the Council of Maryland for furnishing pasturage, hay and wood on 25 Mar 1778 {Ref: Archives of Maryland 16:550-551}

FOWKE, ROGER (Charles County) received a receipt from the Purchasing Agent for furnishing wheat on 28 Dec 1782 {Ref: Maryland State Archives MdHR-6636-42-21}

FOWLER, DANIEL (Anne Arundel County) received payment by order of the Council of Safety for furnishing a gun on 10 Sep 1776 {Ref: Archives of Maryland 12:263}

FOWLER, JEREMIAH (Frederick County) received a receipt from the Purchasing Agent for furnishing beef and corn on 2 Feb 1781 {Ref: Maryland State Archives MdHR-6636-23-3}

FOWLER, JUB OR JUBB (Anne Arundel County) was appointed Messenger to the Governor and Council of Maryland on 6 Feb 1781 and serviced to at least 8 Nov 1783 {Ref: Archives of Maryland 45:302, 48:479}; submitted an account for flour on 19 Jan 1782 {Ref: Maryland State Archives MdHR-19970-5-8}; received payment from the Council of Maryland "for the Purpose of procuring Wood for the Public" on 7 Oct 1782 {Ref: Archives of Maryland 48:276}

FOWLER, THOMAS (Caroline County) received a receipt from the Purchasing

Agent for furnishing wheat on 22 Aug 1782 {Ref: Maryland State Archives MdHR-6636-42-7}

FRADEN, HENRY (Somerset County) received a receipt from the Purchasing Agent for furnishing bacon on 20 Jul 1781 {Ref: Maryland State Archives MdHR-6636-24-43}

FRAIZIER, JOHNATHON (Frederick County) received a receipt from the Purchasing Agent for furnishing wheat on 29 May 1782 {Ref: Maryland State Archives MdHR-6636-42-34}

FRANCES (FRANCIS), JOSEPH (Montgomery County) received a receipt from the Purchasing Agent for furnishing wheat on 5 Sep 1780 {Ref: Maryland State Archives MdHR-6636-24-13}; received a receipt for furnishing wheat on 30 Apr 1781 {Ref: Maryland State Archives MdHR-6636-24-14}

FRANKLIN, FRANCIS B. (Charles County) received a receipt from the Purchasing Agent for furnishing wheat on 24 Oct 1781 {Ref: Maryland State Archives MdHR-6636-23-24}

FRANKLIN, HENRY (Worcester County) appeared on "A List of Corn Purchased in Worcester County for the use of the State of Maryland" by the Commissary in July, 1780 {Ref: Archives of Maryland 45:10}; submitted an account and receipt for furnishing salt on 14 Jan 1782 {Ref: Maryland State Archives MdHR-6636-43-28III}

FRANKLIN, PRISCILLA OR PRESILA (Charles County) received a receipt from the Purchasing Agent for furnishing wheat on 20 Oct 1781 {Ref: Maryland State Archives MdHR-6636-42-15}; received a loan certificate for £22.9.9 due from the Council of Maryland "agreeable to the Act proposing to the Citizens of this State, Creditors of Congress on Loan Office Certificates, Etc." on 26 Mar 1783 for services rendered during the war {Ref: Archives of Maryland 48:390}; received a receipt for furnishing wheat on 9 May 1783 {Ref: Maryland State Archives MdHR-6636-42-22}

FRANKLIN, WILLIAM (Charles County) received a receipt from the Purchasing Agent for wheat on 14 Nov 1781 {Ref: Maryland State Archives MdHR-6636-42-15}

FRANKLIN (FRANKLING), ZEPHANIAH (Charles County) received receipts from the Purchasing Agent for furnishing wheat on 14 Sep and 20 Oct 1781 {Ref: Maryland State Archives MdHR-6636-42-15}; received a receipt for furnishing wheat on 15 Apr 1782 {Ref: Maryland State Archives MdHR-6636-42-18}; received a receipt for furnishing wheat on 9 May 1783 {Ref: Maryland State Archives MdHR-6636-42-22}

FRANTOM, JOSEPH (Talbot County) received a receipt from the Purchasing Agent for furnishing bacon for the use of the army on 30 Apr 1778 {Ref: Maryland State Archives MdHR-4587-75}; submitted an account and receipt for hauling on 2 May 1778 {Ref: Maryland State Archives MdHR-6636-12-

15}

FRAWLEY, EDWARD (Caroline County) received a receipt from the Purchasing Agent for furnishing wheat on 20 Sep 1782 {Ref: Maryland State Archives MdHR-6636-42-7}

FRAZIER, JAMES (Caroline County) received a receipt from the Purchasing Agent for furnishing wheat on 1 Sep 1782 {Ref: Maryland State Archives MdHR-6636-42-7}

FRAZIER, JOHN (Kent County) received a certificate from the Purchasing Agent for furnishing wheat on 20 Feb 1780 {Ref: Maryland State Archives MdHR-6636-43-1}

FRAZIER, SOLOMON (Dorchester County) was a captain who received a loan certificate for £53.7.1 due from the Council of Maryland "agreeable to the Act proposing to the Citizens of this State, Creditors of Congress on Loan Office Certificates, Etc." on 7 Apr 1783 for services rendered during the war {Ref: Archives of Maryland 48:395}

FREELAND, FRISBY (Prince George's County) pledged a loan in the amount of £200 to the State of Maryland under the Act for the Emission of Bills of Credit "to defray the expences of the present campaign" in June, 1781 {Ref: Archives of Maryland 47:326}

FREEMAN, AARON (Montgomery County) received a receipt from the Purchasing Agent for furnishing wheat on 1 Aug 1780 {Ref: Maryland State Archives MdHR-6636-43-7}; received a receipt for furnishing wheat on 10 Aug 1780 {Ref: Maryland State Archives MdHR-6636-24-6}; received a receipt for furnishing wheat on 12 May 1781 {Ref: Maryland State Archives MdHR-6636-42-11}

FREEMAN, ISAAC (Kent County) received certificates from the Purchasing Agent for furnishing wheat on 28 Feb and 28 Mar 1780 {Ref: Maryland State Archives MdHR-6636-43-1}; received payment from the Purchasing Agent for furnishing cattle for the public use in September, 1781 {Ref: Maryland State Archives MdHR-6636-43-3}

FREEMAN, JOHN (Caroline County) received a receipt from the Purchasing Agent for wheat on 16 Sep 1782 {Ref: Maryland State Archives MdHR-6636-42-7}

FREEMAN, RICHARD (Prince George's County) received receipts from the Purchasing Agent for furnishing wheat on 16 May, 1 Aug and 22 Dec 1782 {Ref: Maryland State Archives MdHR-6636-50-135}

FRENCH, ZURABABEL (Kent County) received payment from the Purchasing Agent for furnishing cattle for the public use in September, 1781 {Ref: Maryland State Archives MdHR-6636-43-3}

FRIBEL, GEORGE (Baltimore County) received payment for butter on 16 May 1781 {Ref: Maryland State Archives MdHR-6636-43-38III}

FRISBY, JAMES (Kent County) received a certificate from the Purchasing Agent for furnishing wheat on 24 Jan 1780 {Ref: Maryland State Archives MdHR-6636-23-45}; received payment from the Purchasing Agent for furnishing cattle and pasturage for the public use in September, 1781 {Ref: Maryland State Archives MdHR-6636-43-3}

FRISBY, RICHARD (Kent County) received a certificate from the Purchasing Agent for furnishing wheat on 24 Jan 1780 {Ref: Maryland State Archives MdHR-6636-23-45}; received payment from the Purchasing Agent for furnishing cattle and pasturage for the public use in September, 1781 {Ref: Maryland State Archives MdHR-6636-43-3}

FRY, JONATHAN (Frederick County) received a certificate from the Purchasing Agent for furnishing wheat on 27 Jun 1782 {Ref: Maryland State Archives MdHR-6636-42-36}

FRYER, WALTER (Montgomery County) received a receipt from the Purchasing Agent for furnishing wheat on 6 Sep 1780 {Ref: Maryland State Archives MdHR-6636-24-7}; received a receipt for furnishing wheat on 8 Oct 1781 {Ref: Maryland State Archives MdHR-6636-24-15}

FUDDLE, JOHN (Frederick County) was a miller who submitted an account for flour on 22 Jun 1782 {Ref: Maryland State Archives MdHR-6636-42-27}

FULFORD, JOHN (Annapolis) was a captain who was empowered by the Council of Safety "to purchase and provide a scow, boats, and intrenching tools sufficient to carry on, prosecute and compleat the fortifications at Annapolis" on 16 Aug 1776 {Ref: Archives of Maryland 12:209}

FULTON, JEREMIAH (St. Mary's County) submitted an account of expenses for collecting and driving cattle on 22 Nov 1781 {Ref: Maryland State Archives MdHR-19970-3-17}

FUNK, HENRY (Frederick County) received a receipt from the Purchasing Agent for furnishing a gun on 4 Jun 1776 {Ref: Maryland State Archives MdHR-6636-49-126}

FYFFE, JAMES (Montgomery County) received a receipt from the Purchasing Agent for furnishing wheat on 18 May 1781 {Ref: Maryland State Archives MdHR-6636-24-18}

GAEA(?), JOHN (Montgomery County) received a receipt from the Purchasing Agent for furnishing wheat on 1 Aug 1780 {Ref: Maryland State Archives MdHR-6636-43-7}

GAITHER, EDWARD (Anne Arundel County) was a colonel who submitted an account for provisions on 29 Jan 1780 {Ref: Maryland State Archives MdHR-6636-23-9}; appointed Commissary of Purchases for Anne Arundel County by the Council of Maryland on 8 Jul 1780 {Ref: Archives of Maryland 43:215}; his name was listed as "Edwd. Gather" when he delivered flour, Indian corn and rye to the commissary at Baltimore Town for the use of the State of

Maryland in the summer of 1780 {Ref: Archives of Maryland 45:84}; received a receipt for delivery of cattle on 21 Mar 1781 {Ref: Maryland State Archives MdHR-6636-26-48}; received certification of wheat manufactured at Nicholas Maccubbin's mill on 21 Aug 1781 {Ref: Maryland State Archives MdHR-6636-23-9}; received certification of livestock purchased from John Worthington on 4 Dec 1781 {Ref: Maryland State Archives MdHR-6636-23-9}; requested payment for hauling provisions on 22 Dec 1781 {Ref: Maryland State Archives MdHR-6636-31-115}

GAITHER, EDWARD JR. (Elk Ridge, Anne Arundel County) was commissary of provisions on 1 Apr 1781 {Ref: Maryland State Archives MdHR-6636-26-74}; submitted an account for the acquisition of cattle on 27 Jul 1781 {Ref: Maryland State Archives MdHR-6636-28-52}; received certification of the purchase of cattle on 10 Aug 1781 {Ref: Maryland State Archives MdHR-6636-42-1}

GAITHER, GREENBURY (Montgomery County) received a receipt from the Purchasing Agent for furnishing wheat on 1 Aug 1780 {Ref: Maryland State Archives MdHR-6636-43-7}

GAITHER, SETH (Prince George's County) received a receipt from the Purchasing Agent for furnishing wheat in 1782 {Ref: Maryland State Archives MdHR-6636-50-135}

GALE, ELIZABETH (Somerset County) received a receipt from the Purchasing Agent for furnishing pork on 15 Mar 1782 {Ref: Maryland State Archives MdHR-6636-43-21}

GALLOWAY, BENJAMIN (Frederick County) received a payment by order of the Council of Maryland "to be delivered over to Messrs. Beatty, Hanson and Johnson, Superintendants of the Gunlock Manufactory" on 16 Aug 1777; appointed Attorney General of Maryland on 6 Jan 1778 {Ref: Archives of Maryland 16:335, 455}; also see "Luther Martin," q.v.

GALLOWAY, CHARLES (Dorchester County) received a receipt from the Purchasing Agent for furnishing wheat on 1 Nov 1782 {Ref: Maryland State Archives MdHR-6636-42-23}

GALLOWAY (GALLAWAY), JOHN (Kent County) received a certificate from the Purchasing Agent for furnishing wheat on 18 Feb 1780 {Ref: Maryland State Archives MdHR-6636-23-41}; received payment from the Purchasing Agent for furnishing cattle and pasturage for the public use in September, 1781 {Ref: Maryland State Archives MdHR-6636-43-3}

GALLOWAY & STEUARD (Annapolis) arranged and agreed to a payment allowance with the Council of Safety "for all the iron, which they shall furnish, and use in building the gondolas contracted for, on behalf of this province" on 29 Jun 1776 {Ref: Archives of Maryland 11:533}

GAMBELL, RICHARDSON (Dorchester County) received a receipt from the

Purchasing Agent for furnishing wheat on 25 Mar 1783 {Ref: Maryland State Archives MdHR-6636-42-24}

GAMBER, JACOB (Frederick County) received a certificate for money loaned to the state on 3 Jun 1780 {Ref: Maryland State Archives MdHR-6636-18-128}

GAMBRA, RICHARD (Charles County) received a receipt from the Purchasing Agent for furnishing wheat on 28 Dec 1782 {Ref: Maryland State Archives MdHR-6636-42-21}

GANNON, PERRY (Caroline County) received a receipt from the Purchasing Agent for furnishing wheat on 5 Aug 1782 {Ref: Maryland State Archives MdHR-6636-42-7}

GANTT, FIEDLER (Frederick County) received a receipt from the Purchasing Agent for hauling flour on 20 Aug 1783 {Ref: Maryland State Archives MdHR-6636-42-28}

GANTT, THOMAS (Calvert County) received payment by order of the Council of Maryland on 5 Aug 1777 for erecting a salt works {Ref: Archives of Maryland 16:325}

GANTT, THOMAS (Prince George's County) pledged a loan in the amount of £250 to the State of Maryland under the Act for the Emission of Bills of Credit "to defray the expences of the present campaign" in June, 1781 {Ref: Archives of Maryland 47:326}

GARDENER, IGNATIUS (Charles County) received a receipt from the Purchasing Agent for furnishing wheat on 28 Sep 1782 {Ref: Maryland State Archives MdHR-6636-42-19}

GARDNER, THOMAS (Montgomery County) received a receipt from the Purchasing Agent for furnishing wheat on 11 Aug 1781 {Ref: Maryland State Archives MdHR-6636-24-15}

GARNER, HEZEKIAH (Charles County) received a receipt from the Purchasing Agent for furnishing wheat on 9 May 1783 {Ref: Maryland State Archives MdHR-6636-42-22}

GARNETT, MARY (Kent County) received payment from the Purchasing Agent for furnishing cattle and pasturage for the public use in September, 1781 {Ref: Maryland State Archives MdHR-6636-43-3}

GARRETSON, CORNELIUS (Baltimore County) received payment by order of the Council of Safety for sounding the depth of the river between Greenbury's Point and Horn Point on 11 Apr 1776 {Ref: Archives of Maryland 11:326}; received payment for tipping 78 bayonets on 16 Jul 1776 {Ref: Archives of Maryland 12:53}

GARRETT, AMOS (Harford County) received payment for furnishing a musquet to the Committee of Safety on 2 Sep 1776 {Ref: Preston's History of Harford County, p. 335}

GARROTT, ALLEN (Frederick County) received a certificate from the Purchasing

Agent for furnishing wheat on 10 Jun 1782 {Ref: Maryland State Archives MdHR-6636-42-35}

GARROTT, EDWARD (Montgomery County) received a receipt from the Purchasing Agent for furnishing wheat on 22 Jan 1781 {Ref: Maryland State Archives MdHR-6636-24-9}

GARSTON, GEORGE (Anne Arundel County) received payment by order of the Council of Safety for pilotage on 14 Sep 1776 {Ref: Archives of Maryland 12:349}

GARTAIN, RICHARD (Montgomery County) received a receipt from the Purchasing Agent for furnishing wheat on 31 Aug 1780 {Ref: Maryland State Archives MdHR-6636-24-6}

GARTIN, WILLIAM (Charles County) received a receipt from the Purchasing Agent for furnishing wheat on 8 Nov 1782 {Ref: Maryland State Archives MdHR-6636-42-19}

GARTRELL, RICHARD (Montgomery County) received a receipt from the Purchasing Agent for furnishing wheat on 5 May 1781 {Ref: Maryland State Archives MdHR-6636-42-11}

GARTRELL, SARAH (Montgomery County) received a receipt from the Purchasing Agent for furnishing wheat on 4 Aug 1781 {Ref: Maryland State Archives MdHR-6636-42-11}

GASH, THOMAS (Baltimore County) received payment for furnishing beef on 30 Apr 1781 {Ref: Maryland State Archives MdHR-6636-43-38MM}

GASSAWAY, CHARLES (Frederick County) received receipts from the Purchasing Agent for furnishing corn and rye on 15 Mar, 17 Mar, 25 Apr, 1 May, 3 May and 20 May 1780 {Ref: Maryland State Archives MdHR-6636-24-1}

GASSAWAY, CHARLES (Prince George's County) was a wagoner who received a receipt from the Purchasing Agent for furnishing wheat on 9 May 1783 {Ref: Maryland State Archives MdHR-6636-50-142}

GASSAWAY, CHARLES (Prince George's County) was a captain who received a receipt from the Purchasing Agent for furnishing wheat on 3 Sep 1783 {Ref: Maryland State Archives MdHR-6636-50-135}

GATTON, JAMES (Montgomery County) received a receipt from the Purchasing Agent for furnishing wheat on 9 Sep 1780 {Ref: Maryland State Archives MdHR-6636-24-7}

GATTON, JAMES (Prince George's County) received a receipt from the Purchasing Agent for furnishing wheat on 11 Feb 1783 {Ref: Maryland State Archives MdHR-6636-50-135}

GATTON, RICHARD (Montgomery County) received a receipt from the Purchasing Agent for furnishing wheat on 12 May 1781 {Ref: Maryland State Archives MdHR-6636-24-18}

GATTON, WILLIAM (Montgomery County) received a receipt from the Purchasing Agent for furnishing wheat on 14 Aug 1781 {Ref: Maryland State Archives MdHR-6636-24-18}

GATTON, ZACHARIAH (Montgomery County) received a receipt from the Purchasing Agent for furnishing wheat on 12 May 1781 {Ref: Maryland State Archives MdHR-6636-24-18}

GAVER, JOHN (Frederick County) submitted an account for flour delivery on 10 Apr 1781 {Ref: Maryland State Archives MdHR-6636-23-32}; submitted an account for furnishing pork on 29 May 1781 {Ref: Maryland State Archives MdHR-6636-23-6}

GAVIN, GEORGE (Worcester County) submitted an account and receipt for furnishing pork barrels on 10 Apr 1782 {Ref: Maryland State Archives MdHR-6636-43-28HH}

GAYLORD, JAMES (Harford County) received a receipt from the Purchasing Agent for furnishing wheat on 18 Feb 1780 {Ref: Maryland State Archives MdHR-6636-23-39}

GAZE, SAMUEL (Montgomery County) received a receipt from the Purchasing Agent for furnishing wheat on 7 Aug 1780 {Ref: Maryland State Archives MdHR-6636-24-6}

GEIGER, ANDREW (Baltimore County) submitted an account and receipt for furnishing beef on 11 Nov 1780 {Ref: Maryland State Archives MdHR-6636-43-38YYYY}

GENTILE, STEPHEN (Prince George's County) received a receipt from the Purchasing Agent for furnishing wheat on 23 May 1782 {Ref: Maryland State Archives MdHR-6636-50-135}

GEOGHEGAN, WILLIAM (Baltimore County) received a receipt from the Purchasing Agent for furnishing flour on 13 Oct 1781 {Ref: Maryland State Archives MdHR-6636-43-38S}

GEORGE, JOSHUA (Cecil County) received a certificate from the Purchasing Agent for furnishing wheat on 22 Jan 1780 {Ref: Maryland State Archives MdHR-6636-23-42}; received a receipt for delivery of provisions on 1 Jun 1781 {Ref: Maryland State Archives MdHR-6636-27-59}; received a receipt of salt on 12 Dec 1781 {Ref: Maryland State Archives MdHR-6636-29-136}

GEORGE, RICHARD (Talbot County) received a receipt from the Purchasing Agent for furnishing wheat on 23 Oct 1780 {Ref: Maryland State Archives MdHR-6636-24-47}

GEROCK, JOHN (Baltimore Town) received payment by order of the Council of Maryland "to be expended for the use of the hospital in Baltimore Town" on 21 Nov 1777 {Ref: Archives of Maryland 16:421}

GEROCK, SAMUEL (Baltimore Town) received payment by order of the Council of Maryland "for the use of the hospital in Baltimore Town" on 23 Dec 1777

{Ref: Archives of Maryland 16:444}

GETTETT, JOHN (Worcester County) received a receipt from the Purchasing Agent for furnishing corn on 12 Apr 1780 {Ref: Maryland State Archives MdHR-6636-24-52}

GHISELIN, MARY, Mrs. (Anne Arundel County) received payment by order of the Council of Maryland "for the hire of her Negro man to work at the Tanyard" on 5 Jun 1778 {Ref: Archives of Maryland 21:123}; received payment for an unspecified service "due her account passed by the Auditor General" on 29 Mar 1780 {Ref: Archives of Maryland 43:123}

GIBSON, JOHN (Harford County) was appointed Purchaser of Clothing in his county by the Council of Maryland on 5 Jun 1781 {Ref: Archives of Maryland 45:462}

GIBSON, JOHN (Talbot County) received payments by order of the Council of Safety for the hire of his boat on 11 Apr and 5 Jul 1776 {Ref: Archives of Maryland 11:326, 550}; submitted an account of wheat collected at Gibson's Granary on the Wye River on 18 Sep 1781 {Ref: Maryland State Archives MdHR-6636-24-47}; received a receipt for furnishing wheat on 19 Mar 1782 {Ref: Maryland State Archives MdHR-6636-43-25}

GIBSON, WOOLMAN JR. (Talbot County) received payment for hauling wheat on 7 Nov 1780 {Ref: Maryland State Archives MdHR-6636-24-49}

GIDDINGS, THOMAS (Charles County) received a receipt from the Purchasing Agent for furnishing wheat on 31 Oct 1782 {Ref: Maryland State Archives MdHR-6636-42-19}

GIDEN, HENRY (Montgomery County) received a receipt from the Purchasing Agent for furnishing wheat on 3 Sep 1780 {Ref: Maryland State Archives MdHR-6636-24-13}

GILBERT, GEORGE (Kent County) received a certificate from the Purchasing Agent for milling on 14 Mar 1780 {Ref: Maryland State Archives MdHR-6636-23-41}

GILCHREST, DANIEL (Kent County) received payment for furnishing wheat on 1 Nov 1780 {Ref: Maryland State Archives MdHR-6636-23-49}; Gilchriest & Richardson received payment by order of the Council of Safety for furnishing boatage on 10 Oct 1776 {Ref: Archives of Maryland 12:329}

GILES, JACOB (Harford County) was licensed Assistant Commissary of Purchases by the Council of Maryland on 19 Nov 1779 {Ref: Archives of Maryland 43:20}

GILES, JAMES (Harford County) pledged a loan in the amount of £300 to the State of Maryland under the Act for the Emission of Bills of Credit "to defray the expences of the present campaign" in June, 1781 {Ref: Archives of Maryland 47:327}

GILES, JOHN (Worcester County) submitted an account and receipt for furnishing pork barrels on 5 Mar 1782 {Ref: Maryland State Archives MdHR-6636-43-28}

GILES, NATHANIEL, see "John Stump, Jr.," q.v.

GILES, THOMAS (Cecil County) received payment by order of the Council of Maryland "for express from the Head of Elk ... to be charged to the Continent" on 6 Sep 1780 {Ref: Archives of Maryland 43:278}; requested payment for riding express for Col. Henry Hollingsworth on 16 Nov 1780 and was paid on 19 Nov 1780 {Ref: Maryland State Archives MdHR-6636-21-32; Archives of Maryland 45:186, 217}

GILES, THOMAS (Harford County) received a loan certificate for £105.10.8 due from the Council of Maryland "agreeable to the Act proposing to the Citizens of this State, Creditors of Congress on Loan Office Certificates, Etc." on 9 Dec 1783 for services rendered during the war {Ref: Archives of Maryland 48:486}

GILES, WILLIAM (Harford County) received a receipt from the Purchasing Agent for furnishing wheat on 14 Feb 1780 {Ref: Maryland State Archives MdHR-6636-23-39}

GILES & SMITH (Harford County) receipt payment from the Committee of Safety for furnishing carting, powder, and arms on 2 Sep 1776 {Ref: Preston's History of Harford County, p. 335}

GILL, JOSEPH (Montgomery County) received a receipt from the Purchasing Agent for furnishing wheat on 23 Aug 1780 {Ref: Maryland State Archives MdHR-6636-24-6}

GILLETT, AYRES (Worcester County) submitted an account and receipt for grazing cattle on 10 Sep 1782 {Ref: Maryland State Archives MdHR-6636-43-28G}

GILLISS, EZEKIEL (Somerset County) received a loan certificate for £130.10.6 due from the Council of Maryland "agreeable to the Act proposing to the Citizens of this State, Creditors of Congress on Loan Office Certificates, Etc." on 24 Sep 1783 for services rendered during the war {Ref: Archives of Maryland 48:456}

GILLISS, JOSEPH (Somerset County) received a loan certificate for £34.7.7 due from the Council of Maryland "agreeable to the Act proposing to the Citizens of this State, Creditors of Congress on Loan Office Certificates, Etc." on 22 May 1783 for services rendered during the war {Ref: Archives of Maryland 48:419}

GILLISS, NELLY (Somerset County) received a loan certificate for £45.14.7 due from the Council of Maryland "agreeable to the Act proposing to the Citizens of this State, Creditors of Congress on Loan Office Certificates, Etc." on 19 Dec 1783 for services rendered during the war {Ref: Archives of Maryland 48:494}

GILLISS, WILLIAM (Somerset County) received a loan certificate for

£99.13.10½ due from the Council of Maryland "agreeable to the Act proposing to the Citizens of this State, Creditors of Congress on Loan Office Certificates, Etc." on 22 May 1783 for services rendered during the war {Ref: Archives of Maryland 48:419}

GILLITT, JOHN (Worcester County) appeared on "A List of Corn Purchased in Worcester County for the use of the State of Maryland" by the Commissary in July, 1780 {Ref: Archives of Maryland 45:10}

GILMORE, JOHN (Harford County) received from the Council of Maryland a payment "of the new Emission to be delivered over to Richard Dallam, Esqr. on Account of Expresses employed by him at the request of this Board and agreeable to the Recommendation of Congress" on 1 Dec 1780 {Ref: Archives of Maryland 45:230}

GILPIN, JOSEPH (Cecil County) was appointed by the Council of Safety to collect all the gold and silver coin that could be procured in the county in compliance with the Resolve of Congress on 27 Jan 1776 {Ref: Archives of Maryland 11:132}; received payment by order of the Council of Safety for providing waggonage on 2 Sep 1776 {Ref: Archives of Maryland 12:256}; appointed one of eighteen Collectors of Clothing by the Council of Maryland under "An Act to Procure Cloathing for the Quota of this State of the American Army" on 27 Nov 1777 {Ref: Archives of Maryland 16:426}; received a certificate from the Purchasing Agent for furnishing wheat on 9 Jan 1780 {Ref: Maryland State Archives MdHR-6636-23-22}; pledged a loan in the amount of £250 to the State of Maryland under the Act for the Emission of Bills of Credit "to defray the expences of the present campaign" in October, 1781 {Ref: Archives of Maryland 47:533}

GILPIN, SAMUEL (Cecil County) was appointed by the Council of Maryland on 25 Mar 1778 as one of eighteen men to be "Agents for Purchasing Provisions for the Army of the United States Agreeable to an Act of Assembly passed the 23rd Instant" {Ref: Archives of Maryland 16:551}; appointed by the Council of Maryland as one of thirty men to be "Agents for Purchasing Provisions" on 30 Mar 1779 {Ref: Archives of Maryland 21:332}; submitted an account of flour for use of the army in 1780 {Ref: Maryland State Archives MdHR-4595-9}; submitted an account for flour purchased on 19 Jan 1780 {Ref: Maryland State Archives MdHR-4590-82}; received certificates for furnishing flour on 26 Jan 1780 and for hauling provisions on 4 Feb 1780 {Ref: Maryland State Archives MdHR-6636-23-22}; submitted an account for flour and wheat purchased on 3 Mar 1780 {Ref: Maryland State Archives MdHR-4590-80}; submitted an account for grain purchased on 1 Jun 1780 {Ref: Maryland State Archives MdHR-4590-81}; appointed by the Council of Maryland to be one of five men in Cecil County "to carry the Act to prohibit for a limited time the Exportation of Indian Corn, Etc., by Land" on 22 Dec 1780 {Ref: Archives of Maryland

45:250}; requested compensation for procuring provisions on 28 Feb 1781 {Ref: Maryland State Archives MdHR-4601-54}; pledged a loan in the amount of £100 to the State of Maryland under the Act for the Emission of Bills of Credit "to defray the expences of the present campaign" in October, 1781 {Ref: Archives of Maryland 47:533}

GINN, JOHN (Caroline County) received a receipt from the Purchasing Agent for furnishing wheat on 1 Sep 1782 {Ref: Maryland State Archives MdHR-6636-42-7}

GITTINGS, BASIL (Montgomery County) received a receipt from the Purchasing Agent for furnishing wheat on 21 Oct 1780 {Ref: Maryland State Archives MdHR-6636-24-8}

GITTINGS, BENJAMIN (Montgomery County) received a receipt from the Purchasing Agent for furnishing wheat on 14 Aug 1780 {Ref: Maryland State Archives MdHR-6636-24-6}; received a receipt for furnishing wheat on 9 Feb 1781 {Ref: Maryland State Archives MdHR-6636-24-9}

GITTINGS (GETINGS), BENJAMIN JR. (Montgomery County) received a receipt from the Purchasing Agent for furnishing wheat on 1 Aug 1780 {Ref: Maryland State Archives MdHR-6636-43-7}

GITTINGS, JAMES (Baltimore County) received receipts from the Purchasing Agent for furnishing currency and cash on 22 May and 28 May 1779 {Ref: Maryland State Archives MdHR-6636-21-67}

GITTINGS, THOMAS (Montgomery County) received a receipt from the Purchasing Agent for furnishing wheat on 29 Aug 1780 {Ref: Maryland State Archives MdHR-6636-24-6}

GLANVILLE, JAMES (Kent County) received a certificate from the Purchasing Agent for furnishing flour on 18 Feb 1780 {Ref: Maryland State Archives MdHR-6636-23-41}

GLASGOE, WILLIAM (Charles County) received a receipt from the Purchasing Agent for furnishing wheat on 28 Dec 1782 {Ref: Maryland State Archives MdHR-6636-42-21}

GLASGOW, ANN (Charles County) received a loan certificate for £40.13.8 due from the Council of Maryland "agreeable to the Act proposing to the Citizens of this State, Creditors of Congress on Loan Office Certificates, Etc." on 24 Sep 1783 for services rendered during the war {Ref: Archives of Maryland 48:456}

GLAZE, JOSEPH (Montgomery County) received a receipt from the Purchasing Agent for furnishing wheat on 19 Jul 1780 {Ref: Maryland State Archives MdHR-6636-24-5}; received a receipt for furnishing wheat on 1 Aug 1780 {Ref: Maryland State Archives MdHR-6636-43-7}; received a receipt for furnishing wheat on 1 Sep 1780 {Ref: Maryland State Archives MdHR-6636-24-7}

GLAZE, NATHAN (Montgomery County) received a receipt from the Purchasing

Agent for furnishing wheat on 16 Oct 1780 {Ref: Maryland State Archives MdHR-6636-24-8}

GLAZE, SAMUEL (Montgomery County) received a receipt from the Purchasing Agent for furnishing wheat on 1 Aug 1780 {Ref: Maryland State Archives MdHR-6636-43-7}; received a receipt for furnishing wheat on 7 Aug 1780 {Ref: Maryland State Archives MdHR-6636-24-6}

GLENN (GLEN), SAMUEL (Cecil County) was appointed by the Council of Maryland to be one of five men in Cecil County "to carry the Act to prohibit for a limited time the Exportation of Indian Corn, Etc., by Land" on 22 Dec 1780 {Ref: Archives of Maryland 45:250}; submitted an account for furnishing wheat from 22 Jun to 1 Jul 1782 {Ref: Maryland State Archives MdHR-6636-42-9}

GLEVES, THOMAS (Baltimore County) submitted an account and received payment for stowing flour for one and a quarter days on 28 Jan 1780 {Ref: Maryland Historical Society MS.1814, Box 6}

GLOVER, JOHN (Montgomery County) received a receipt from the Purchasing Agent for furnishing wheat on 2 Sep 1780 {Ref: Maryland State Archives MdHR-6636-24-13}

GLOVER, RICHART (Frederick County) received a certificate from the Purchasing Agent for furnishing wheat on 30 Jul 1782 {Ref: Maryland State Archives MdHR-6636-42-36}

GODDARD, MARY K. (Baltimore Town) submitted an account and received payment for printing 1400 blank certificates for the commission in Baltimore on 14 Feb 1780 {Ref: Maryland Historical Society MS.1814, Box 6}

GODDARD, WILLIAM (Somerset County) received a certificate from the Purchasing Agent for furnishing corn on 29 Jan 1780 {Ref: Maryland State Archives MdHR-6636-24-39}

GODFREY, CHARLES (Worcester County) received a receipt from the Purchasing Agent for furnishing bacon on 19 Sep 1780 {Ref: Maryland State Archives MdHR-6636-24-54}

GODMAN, HUMPHREY (Frederick County) received receipts from the Purchasing Agent for furnishing corn on 31 Mar, 3 May and 7 Jun 1780 {Ref: Maryland State Archives MdHR-6636-24-1}

GODMAN, SAMUEL (Baltimore County) received payment for hauling tallow on 13 Jun 1781 {Ref: Maryland State Archives MdHR-6636-43-38WW}

GOENALL, FRONTZ H. (Baltimore County) received a receipt from the Purchasing Agent for furnishing meal on 15 Jun 1781 {Ref: Maryland State Archives MdHR-6636-43-38PP}; received payment for furnishing veal on 18 Jun 1781 {Ref: Maryland State Archives MdHR-6636-43-38TT}

GOLD, WILLIAM (Baltimore County) submitted an account and received payment for stowing flour for one and three-quarter days on 28 Jan and 1 Feb

1780 {Ref: Maryland Historical Society MS.1814, Box 6}
GOLDEN (GOLDIN), SAMUEL (Montgomery County) received a receipt from the Purchasing Agent for furnishing wheat on 19 May 1781 {Ref: Maryland State Archives MdHR-6636-42-11}; received a receipt for furnishing wheat on 10 Oct 1781 {Ref: Maryland State Archives MdHR-6636-24-15}
GOLDSBOROUGH, GREENBURY (Talbot County) was appointed by the Council of Safety to collect all the gold and silver coin that could be procured in the county in compliance with the Resolve of Congress on 27 Jan 1776 {Ref: Archives of Maryland 11:132}
GOLDSBOROUGH, RACHEL (Caroline County) received a receipt from the Purchasing Agent for furnishing wheat on 17 Aug 1782 {Ref: Maryland State Archives MdHR-6636-42-7}
GOLDSBOROUGH, ROBERT JR. (Talbot County) was one of twenty-six people who contacted the Governor and Council of Maryland in 1781 and pledged to support and maintain at their own expense the Barge *Experiment* so it can patrol the bay between Kent Point and Tilghman's Island in order to protect them against the enemy, stating in part, "whereas from the present exhausted state of the public treasury the government cannot immediately give that protection to every individual which is become necessary from the cruel and savage mode in which the war is now carried on against us" {Ref: Archives of Maryland 47:584-585}
GOLDSBOROUGH, THOMAS (Caroline County) received a receipt from the Purchasing Agent for furnishing corn and certificate for furnishing wheat on 25 Feb 1780 {Ref: Maryland State Archives MdHR-6636-23-19}; received a certificate for storage of grain on 21 Jun 1780 {Ref: Maryland State Archives MdHR-6636-23-20}; received a receipt for furnishing wheat on 1 Aug 1782 {Ref: Maryland State Archives MdHR-6636-42-7}
GOLDSBOROUGH, WILLIAM (Talbot County) received a receipt from the Purchasing Agent for furnishing beef on 30 Sep 1780 {Ref: Maryland State Archives MdHR-6636-24-49}
GOLDSMITH, HENRY (Anne Arundel County) received a loan certificate for £5.14.3 due from the Council of Maryland "agreeable to the Act proposing to the Citizens of this State, Creditors of Congress on Loan Office Certificates, Etc." on 1 Jul 1783 for services rendered during the war {Ref: Archives of Maryland 48:435}
GOLDSMITH, JOHN (Anne Arundel County) received a certificate from the Purchasing Agent for furnishing beef hides on 18 Dec 1780 {Ref: Maryland State Archives MdHR-6636-21-133}
GOODRICH, RICHARD (Charles County) received a receipt from the Purchasing Agent for furnishing wheat on 11 Oct 1782 {Ref: Maryland State Archives MdHR-6636-42-19}

GORDON, GEORGE (Anne Arundel County) received payment by order of the Council of Safety for furnishing iron work for gun carriages on 6 Apr 1776 {Ref: Archives of Maryland 11:314}; received payment "for repairing a dungeon wherein to confine culprit soldiers" on 9 May 1776 {Ref: Archives of Maryland 11:418}; contracted to repair muskets for the Council of Safety in July and August, 1776, and received payments on 5 Aug and 3 Sep 1776; contracted for the making of cartouch belts, bayonet belts and gun slings on 24 Sep 1776 {Ref: Archives of Maryland 12:47, 166, 255, 297}; received payment for furnishing guns on 11 Feb and 18 Apr 1777 {Ref: Archives of Maryland 16:130, 219}; also see "Charles Carroll, Barrister," q.v.

GORDON (GORDEN), JAMES (Harford County) received a receipt from the Purchasing Agent for furnishing wheat on 9 Mar 1780 {Ref: Maryland State Archives MdHR-6636-23-39}

GORDON, JOHN (Cecil County) received a receipt from the Purchasing Agent for furnishing wheat on 8 Aug 1782 and submitted an account for storing wheat on 1 Sep 1782 {Ref: Maryland State Archives MdHR-6636-42-9}

GORDON, JOHN (Baltimore Town or County) received payment for the balance of his contract with the Council of Maryland for making cartouch boxes on 11 Apr 1777 {Ref: Archives of Maryland 16:206}

GORSUCH, BENJAMIN (Baltimore Town) was a wagon master who submitted an account and received payment for furnishing flour to Susquehanna Lower Ferry in Harford County on 28 Jan 1780 and received payment for six days as wagon master for the Commission in Baltimore on 10 Feb 1780 {Ref: Maryland Historical Society MS.1814, Box 6; Maryland State Archives MdHR-6636-23-37}

GORSUCH, NICHOLAS (Baltimore County) received payment by order of the Council of Maryland for riding express on 8 Jan 1778 {Ref: Archives of Maryland 16:460; Maryland State Archives MdHR-6636-10-53}

GOTHARD, WILLIAM (Somerset County) received a receipt from the Purchasing Agent for furnishing beef on 18 Nov 1781 {Ref: Maryland State Archives MdHR-6636-24-44}; received a receipt for furnishing a hog on 15 Feb 1782 {Ref: Maryland State Archives MdHR-6636-43-21}

GOTHERY, JOSHUA (Worcester County) submitted an account and receipt for furnishing pork on 3 May 1782 {Ref: Maryland State Archives MdHR-6636-43-28AA}

GOTTING, PHILLIP (Worcester County) submitted an account for coopering on 20 Jun 1781 {Ref: Maryland State Archives MdHR-6636-43-27}

GOUGH, GEORGE (Baltimore County) received payment by order of the Council of Safety for the hire of his boat on 15 Aug 1776 {Ref: Archives of Maryland 12:205}

GOVANE, JAMES (Baltimore County) was a doctor who was appointed by the

Council of Maryland as one of thirty men to be "Agents for Purchasing Provisions" on 30 Mar 1779 {Ref: Archives of Maryland 21:332}; received payment by order of the Council "to be expended in the purchase of wheat, bread and flour for the use of the Continental Army" on 8 May 1779 {Ref: Archives of Maryland 21:383}; submitted an account for disbursements from 21 May 1779 to 1 Nov 1780 {Ref: Maryland State Archives MdHR-6636-21-67}; submitted an account of supplies from 21 May 1779 to 8 Nov 1780 {Ref: Maryland State Archives MdHR-6636-21-67}; served as Contractor for Horses in Baltimore County and submitted an account on condition of horses and their provisions on 19 Jan 1781 {Ref: Maryland State Archives MdHR-6636-25-42}; ordered by the Council of Maryland "to deliver all the public horses in his possession" to John Bullen on 11 Apr 1781 {Ref: Archives of Maryland 45:391}

GRABEL, PETER (Frederick County) received a certificate from the Purchasing Agent for furnishing wheat on 28 May 1782 {Ref: Maryland State Archives MdHR-6636-42-34}

GRACE, ABEL (Talbot County) received a receipt from the Purchasing Agent for furnishing wheat on 18 Oct 1780 {Ref: Maryland State Archives MdHR-6636-24-47}

GRACE, JOHN (Anne Arundel County) received payment by order of the Council of Safety for the carriage of powder and arms from Philadelphia to the magazine near Capt. Tootles at Annapolis on 2 Aug 1776 {Ref: Archives of Maryland 12:159}

GRACE, SOLOMON (Caroline County) received a receipt from the Purchasing Agent for furnishing wheat on 5 Aug 1782 {Ref: Maryland State Archives MdHR-6636-42-7}

GRAHAM, OWEN (Baltimore Town) submitted a bill and receipt for furnishing linen on 17 Nov 1779 {Ref: Maryland State Archives MdHR-19970-3-8}

GRAHAME, ASENATH, Mrs. (Calvert County) received a loan certificate for £21.3.9 due from the Council of Maryland "agreeable to the Act proposing to the Citizens of this State, Creditors of Congress on Loan Office Certificates, Etc." was also paid £48 for one year's interest on four certificates issued on 20 May 1783 for services rendered during the war {Ref: Archives of Maryland 48:418}

GRAMMER, FREDERICK (Baltimore County) received a loan certificate for £142.1.11½ due from the Council of Maryland "agreeable to the Act proposing to the Citizens of this State, Creditors of Congress on Loan Office Certificates, Etc." on 19 Dec 1783 for services rendered during the war {Ref: Archives of Maryland 48:493}

GRANGER, WILLIAM (Kent County) received a certificate from the Purchasing Agent for furnishing wheat on 18 Jan 1780 {Ref: Maryland State Archives

MdHR-6636-23-41}; received a certificate for furnishing wheat on 18 Jan 1780 {Ref: Maryland State Archives MdHR-6636-23-46}; received payment from the Purchasing Agent for furnishing cattle and pasturage for the public use in September, 1781 {Ref: Maryland State Archives MdHR-6636-43-3}

GRANGETT, ANDREW, see "Elizabeth Husk," q.v.

GRANT, JAMES (Queen Anne's County) submitted an account and receipt for hauling wheat from Sep 1782 to Feb 1783 {Ref: Maryland State Archives MdHR-6636-43-12}

GRANT, JOHN (Charles County) received a receipt from the Purchasing Agent for furnishing wheat on 17 Jun 1782 {Ref: Maryland State Archives MdHR-6636-42-18}; received a receipt for furnishing wheat on 8 May 1783 {Ref: Maryland State Archives MdHR-6636-42-22}

GRASON, RICHARD (Queen Anne's County) received a certificate of payment due for furnishing beef on 19 Oct 1781 {Ref: Maryland State Archives MdHR-6636-24-34}; received a loan certificate for £479.12.9 due from the Council of Maryland "agreeable to the Act proposing to the Citizens of this State, Creditors of Congress on Loan Office Certificates, Etc." on 3 Dec 1783 for services rendered during the war {Ref: Archives of Maryland 48:485}

GRAVES, WILLIAM (Frederick County) submitted an account for furnishing pork on 10 Apr 1781 {Ref: Maryland State Archives MdHR-6636-23-5}; received a certificate from the Purchasing Agent for furnishing wheat on 8 Oct 1781 {Ref: Maryland State Archives MdHR-6636-23-28}

GRAY, ADAM (Queen Anne's County) received a certificate from the Purchasing Agent for furnishing wheat on 6 Feb 1780 {Ref: Maryland State Archives MdHR-6636-24-31}; received a loan certificate for £782.14.0 due from the Council of Maryland "agreeable to the Act proposing to the Citizens of this State, Creditors of Congress on Loan Office Certificates, Etc." on 16 May 1783 for services rendered during the war {Ref: Archives of Maryland 48:414}

GRAY, ADIN (Montgomery County) received a receipt from the Purchasing Agent for furnishing wheat on 21 Jun 1781 {Ref: Maryland State Archives MdHR-6636-24-15}

GRAY, ANDREW (Dorchester County) received a receipt from the Purchasing Agent for furnishing wheat on 1 Oct 1782 {Ref: Maryland State Archives MdHR-6636-42-23}

GRAY, BENJAMIN (Montgomery County) received a receipt from the Purchasing Agent for furnishing wheat on 1 Aug 1780 {Ref: Maryland State Archives MdHR-6636-43-7}; received a receipt for furnishing wheat on 7 Aug 1780 {Ref: Maryland State Archives MdHR-6636-24-6}; received a receipt for furnishing wheat on 7 Nov 1781 {Ref: Maryland State Archives MdHR-6636-24-15}

GRAY, EDWARD (Charles County) received a receipt from the Purchasing Agent for furnishing wheat on 24 Nov 1781 {Ref: Maryland State Archives MdHR-6636-23-24}; received a receipt for furnishing wheat on 8 Jan 1782 {Ref: Maryland State Archives MdHR-6636-42-16}; received a receipt for furnishing wheat on 10 May 1783 {Ref: Maryland State Archives MdHR-6636-42-22}

GRAY, GEORGE (Charles County) received a receipt from the Purchasing Agent for furnishing wheat on 10 May 1783 {Ref: Maryland State Archives MdHR-6636-42-22}

GRAY, JEREMIAH (Charles County) received a receipt from the Purchasing Agent for furnishing wheat on 29 Dec 1782 {Ref: Maryland State Archives MdHR-6636-42-21}

GRAY, JOHN (Kent County) received payment for furnishing beef on 14 Dec 1780 {Ref: Maryland State Archives MdHR-6636-23-49}

GRAY, JOHN N. (Charles County) received a receipt from the Purchasing Agent for furnishing wheat on 30 Nov 1781 {Ref: Maryland State Archives MdHR-6636-42-15}

GRAY, MOSES (Charles County) received a receipt from the Purchasing Agent for furnishing wheat on 10 May 1783 {Ref: Maryland State Archives MdHR-6636-42-22}

GRAY, RUBEN (Talbot County) received a receipt from the Purchasing Agent for furnishing wheat on 30 Oct 1780 {Ref: Maryland State Archives MdHR-6636-24-47}

GRAY, THOMAS (Caroline County) submitted his collector's account of wheat received in 1782 {Ref: Maryland State Archives MdHR-6636-42-6}

GRAY, THOMAS JR. (Worcester County) received a receipt from the Purchasing Agent for furnishing corn on 14 Jun 1780 {Ref: Maryland State Archives MdHR-6636-24-53}; his name appeared on "A List of Corn Purchased in Worcester County for the use of the State of Maryland" by the Commissary in July, 1780 {Ref: Archives of Maryland 45:10}

GRAY, THOMAS SR. (Worcester County) received a receipt from the Purchasing Agent for furnishing corn on 26 Sep 1780 {Ref: Maryland State Archives MdHR-6636-24-54}; his name appeared on "A List of Corn Purchased in Worcester County for the use of the State of Maryland" by the Commissary in July, 1780 {Ref: Archives of Maryland 45:10}

GRAYBILL, PHILIP (Baltimore County) submitted an account and receipt for furnishing liquor on 17 Apr 1781 {Ref: Maryland State Archives MdHR-6636-43-38XXX}

GRAYLESS, JESSE (Caroline County) received a receipt from the Purchasing Agent for furnishing wheat on 5 Aug 1782 {Ref: Maryland State Archives MdHR-6636-42-7}

GREEN, BENEDICT (Montgomery County) received a receipt from the Purchasing Agent for shelling corn on 18 Jul 1780 {Ref: Maryland State

Archives MdHR-6636-24-2}

GREEN, BENNETT (Montgomery County) received a receipt from the Purchasing Agent for furnishing wheat on 7 Sep 1781 {Ref: Maryland State Archives MdHR-6636-24-15}

GREEN, EDWARD (Charles County) received a receipt from the Purchasing Agent for furnishing wheat on 28 Dec 1782 {Ref: Maryland State Archives MdHR-6636-42-21}; received a receipt for furnishing wheat on 10 May 1783 {Ref: Maryland State Archives MdHR-6636-42-22}

GREEN, FREDERICK (Annapolis) was a printer who contracted with the Maryland Council of Safety "for printing the new Emission of Money according to the Resolves of the last Convention" on 30 Apr 1776 {Ref: Archives of Maryland 11:394}; received payment for printing Bills of Credit on 5 Aug 1776 {Ref: Archives of Maryland 12:166}; received from John Bullen, the Issuing Commissary, "one of the public horses to go to Baltimore" by order of the Council of Maryland on 28 Aug 1780 {Ref: Archives of Maryland 43:267}; appointed by the Council of Maryland to be one of six "Signers of the Bills emitted in Virtue of the Act to enable the Treasurer of the Western Shore to draw and sell Bills of Exchange and for an Emission of Bills of Credit if necessary" on 8 Sep 1780 {Ref: Archives of Maryland 43:281}

GREEN, GILES (Charles County) received a receipt from the Purchasing Agent for furnishing wheat on 24 Nov 1781 {Ref: Maryland State Archives MdHR-6636-23-25}

GREEN, HUGH (Montgomery County) received a receipt from the Purchasing Agent for furnishing pork on 10 Mar 1781 {Ref: Maryland State Archives MdHR-6636-24-15}

GREEN, JACOB (Kent County) received a certificate from the Purchasing Agent for furnishing wheat on 17 Mar 1780 {Ref: Maryland State Archives MdHR-6636-23-42}

GREEN, LANHART (Montgomery County) received a receipt from the Purchasing Agent for furnishing wheat on 15 May 1781 {Ref: Maryland State Archives MdHR-6636-24-18}

GREEN, PETER (Baltimore County) submitted an account and received payment for stowing flour on 28 Jan and 1 Feb 1780 {Ref: Maryland Historical Society MS.1814, Box 6}

GREEN, PETER (Charles County) received a receipt from the Purchasing Agent for furnishing wheat on 28 Dec 1782 {Ref: Maryland State Archives MdHR-6636-42-21}

GREEN, PHILIP (Prince George's County) received a receipt from the Purchasing Agent for furnishing wheat on 1 Feb 1783 {Ref: Maryland State Archives MdHR-6636-50-135}

GREEN, RICHARD (Montgomery County) received a receipt from the Purchasing

Agent for furnishing wheat on 10 Apr 1781 {Ref: Maryland State Archives MdHR-6636-42-11}

GREEN, VALENTINE (Caroline County) received a receipt from the Purchasing Agent for furnishing wheat on 1 Sep 1782 {Ref: Maryland State Archives MdHR-6636-42-7}

GREENFIELD, WALTER (Montgomery County) received a receipt from the Purchasing Agent for furnishing wheat on 1 Aug 1780 {Ref: Maryland State Archives MdHR-6636-43-7}; received receipts from the Purchasing Agent for furnishing wheat on 9 Aug and 10 Aug 1780 {Ref: Maryland State Archives MdHR-6636-24-6}

GREENFIELD, WILLIAM (Prince George's County) received a receipt from the Purchasing Agent for furnishing wheat on 16 Aug 1781 {Ref: Maryland State Archives MdHR-6636-24-20}

GREENHAWK, JONATHAN (Caroline County) received a receipt from the Purchasing Agent for furnishing wheat on 24 Aug 1782 {Ref: Maryland State Archives MdHR-6636-42-7}

GREENWELL, BENNET (Montgomery County) received a receipt from the Purchasing Agent for furnishing wheat on 1 Aug 1780 {Ref: Maryland State Archives MdHR-6636-43-7}

GREENWOOD, THOMAS (Baltimore County) received a receipt from the Purchasing Agent for furnishing flour on 17 Jan 1780 {Ref: Maryland State Archives MdHR-6636-17-15}; submitted an account and received payment for taking care of four wagons to Susquehanna on 25 Mar 1780 {Ref: Maryland Historical Society MS.1814, Box 6}

GREGG, JOSHUA (Montgomery County) received a receipt from the Purchasing Agent for furnishing wheat on 30 Jun 1780 {Ref: Maryland State Archives MdHR-6636-24-2}; received a receipt for furnishing wheat on 1 Aug 1780 {Ref: Maryland State Archives MdHR-6636-43-7}

GRESHAM, ANN (Kent County) received a certificate from the Purchasing Agent for furnishing wheat on 14 Jan 1780 {Ref: Maryland State Archives MdHR-6636-23-47}; received a certificate for furnishing wheat on 28 Jan 1780 {Ref: Maryland State Archives MdHR-6636-23-43}

GREYTON (GUYTON?), ROBERT (Baltimore County) submitted an account and received payment for hauling eight loads of flour on 28 Jan 1780 {Ref: Maryland Historical Society MS.1814, Box 6}

GRIEST (GRIST), ISAAC (Baltimore Town) received receipts from the Purchasing Agent for furnishing flour on 11 Jan, 17 Jan and 19 Jan 1780 {Ref: Maryland State Archives MdHR-6636-23-37}; directed by the Council of Maryland "to impress vessels sufficient to transport three hundred troops of the Regiment Extra from Annapolis to the Head of Elk" in Cecil County on 25 Aug 1780 {Ref: Archives of Maryland 43:264, 475}

GRIFFIN, GEORGE (Montgomery County) received a receipt from the Purchasing Agent for furnishing wheat on 14 May 1781 {Ref: Maryland State Archives MdHR-6636-24-18}
GRIFFIN, JOHN (Calvert County) received payment for transporting cattle on 23 Jan 1782 {Ref: Maryland State Archives MdHR-6636-50-37}
GRIFFIN, LUKE (Kent County) received payment from the Purchasing Agent for furnishing cattle and pasturage for the public use in September, 1781 {Ref: Maryland State Archives MdHR-6636-43-3}
GRIFFIN, SARAH (Charles County) received a receipt from the Purchasing Agent for furnishing wheat on 27 Oct 1781 {Ref: Maryland State Archives MdHR-6636-42-15}
GRIFFITH, BENJAMIN (Baltimore County) was a Commissary Agent who submitted an account of provisions on 1 Aug 1781 (Ref: Courtesy of the Maryland State Archives MdHR-6636-23-16}; received a receipt for flour and meal on 31 Aug 1781 {Ref: Maryland State Archives MdHR-6636-43-38CC}; received a receipt for flour on 30 Sep 1781 {Ref: Maryland State Archives MdHR-6636-42-3}; requested flour delivery to Captain Keeports on 1 Nov 1781 {Ref: Maryland State Archives MdHR-6636-43-38T}; submitted an account of a receipt and disbursements of provisions in 1782 {Ref: Maryland State Archives MdHR-6636-42-5}; received a receipt for wheat on 30 Mar 1782 {Ref: Maryland State Archives MdHR-6636-42-3}
GRIFFITH, CHARLES G. (Montgomery County) was a colonel who received a certificate from the Purchasing Agent for purchasing a horse on 2 Aug 1780 {Ref: Maryland State Archives MdHR-6636-24-50}; received a receipt for furnishing wheat on 10 Apr 1781 {Ref: Maryland State Archives MdHR-6636-42-11}
GRIFFITH, GREENBURY JR. (Montgomery County) received a receipt from the Purchasing Agent for furnishing wheat on 1 Aug 1780 {Ref: Maryland State Archives MdHR-6636-43-7}
GRIFFITH, HENRY (Montgomery County) received a receipt from the Purchasing Agent for furnishing wheat on 4 Oct 1781 {Ref: Maryland State Archives MdHR-6636-42-11}
GRIFFITH, HENRY (Frederick County) was appointed by the Council of Safety to collect all the gold and silver coin that could be procured in the county in compliance with the Resolve of Congress on 27 Jan 1776 {Ref: Archives of Maryland 11:132}; received payment by order of the Council of Safety for furnishing musquets on 7 Aug 1776 {Ref: Archives of Maryland 12:179}
GRIFFITH, JOHN (Baltimore County) received a receipt from the Purchasing Agent for furnishing casks on 1 Apr 1781 {Ref: Maryland State Archives MdHR-6636-52-52}
GRIFFITH, SAUNDERS (Caroline County) received a receipt from the

Purchasing Agent for furnishing wheat on 5 Aug 1782 {Ref: Maryland State Archives MdHR-6636-42-7}

GRINDALL, WILLIAM (Prince George's County) received a receipt from the Purchasing Agent for furnishing wheat in 1782 {Ref: Maryland State Archives MdHR-6636-42-16}

GRISLAR, SAMUEL FRIFOSSEL (Baltimore County) received payment for furnishing veal on 11 Jun 1781 {Ref: Maryland State Archives MdHR-6636-43-38VV}

GRIST, JACOB (Frederick County) received a receipt from the Purchasing Agent for furnishing whiskey on 23 Mar 1781 {Ref: Maryland State Archives MdHR-6636-23-4}

GRIST, MICHAEL (Frederick County) received a receipt from the Purchasing Agent for furnishing hay on 23 Dec 1780 {Ref: Maryland State Archives MdHR-6636-23-1}; received a receipt for furnishing whiskey on 12 Jan 1781 {Ref: Maryland State Archives MdHR-6636-23-2}

GROOM, CHARLES (Kent County) received payment from the Purchasing Agent for furnishing cattle and pasturage for the public use in September, 1781 {Ref: Maryland State Archives MdHR-6636-43-3}

GROSSNICKLE, PETER (Frederick County) received a certificate from the Purchasing Agent for furnishing beef on 26 Jul 1781 {Ref: Maryland State Archives MdHR-6636-23-28}; received certificates from the Purchasing Agent for furnishing beef and hauling flour on 2 Aug and 3 Aug 1782 {Ref: Maryland State Archives MdHR-6636-42-36}

GROVE, JACOB (Frederick County) received a certificate for money loaned to the state on 3 Jun 1780 {Ref: Maryland State Archives MdHR-6636-18-126}

GUE, GEORGE (Montgomery County) received a receipt from the Purchasing Agent for furnishing wheat on 17 May 1781 {Ref: Maryland State Archives MdHR-6636-42-11}

GUE, REBAKAH (Montgomery County) received a receipt from the Purchasing Agent for furnishing wheat on 17 May 1781 {Ref: Maryland State Archives MdHR-6636-42-11}

GUMP, JOHN (Frederick County) received a certificate for money loaned to the state on 3 Jun 1780 {Ref: Maryland State Archives MdHR-6636-18-127}

GUNBY, JOHN (Somerset County) was a colonel who received a loan certificate for £30.12.10 due from the Council of Maryland "agreeable to the Act proposing to the Citizens of this State, Creditors of Congress on Loan Office Certificates, Etc." on 9 Apr 1783 for services rendered during the war {Ref: Archives of Maryland 48:395}

GURGE, ROBERT (Kent County) received payment from the Purchasing Agent for furnishing cattle and pasturage for the public use in September, 1781 {Ref: Maryland State Archives MdHR-6636-43-3}

GUTHERY, PHILIP (Worcester County) submitted an account and receipt for processing beef in 1782 {Ref: Maryland State Archives MdHR-6636-43-28PP}; submitted an account and receipt for coopering in 1782 {Ref: Maryland State Archives MdHR-6636-43-28GG}

GUTRA, ANN (Baltimore Town) submitted an account for rendering lodging services on 12 Apr 1777 {Ref: Maryland State Archives MdHR-19970-2-1}

GUTTON, ISAAC (Somerset County) received a receipt from the Purchasing Agent for furnishing beef on 6 Nov 1781 {Ref: Maryland State Archives MdHR-6636-24-44}

GUTTON, PURNELL (Somerset County) received a receipt from the Purchasing Agent for furnishing beef on 6 Nov 1781 {Ref: Maryland State Archives MdHR-6636-24-44}

GUY, JOHN (Charles County) received a receipt from the Purchasing Agent for furnishing wheat on 20 Dec 1782 {Ref: Maryland State Archives MdHR-6636-42-20}

GUY, WILLIAM (Charles County) received a receipt from the Purchasing Agent for furnishing wheat on 20 Dec 1782 {Ref: Maryland State Archives MdHR-6636-42-20}

GUYTON (GREYTON?), ROBERT (Baltimore County) submitted an account and received payment for hauling eight loads of flour on 28 Jan 1780 {Ref: Maryland Historical Society MS.1814, Box 6}

GWINN, JOSEPH (Frederick County) received a receipt from the Purchasing Agent for furnishing pork on 17 Mar 1781 {Ref: Maryland State Archives MdHR-6636-23-4}

HACKETT, CHARLES (Kent County) received gun locks from the Armourer by order of the Council of Maryland "to be delivered over to William Bordley, Esqr., Lieutenant of Kent County" on 11 Apr 1781 {Ref: Archives of Maryland 45:391}

HACKETT, OLIVER JR. (Caroline County) received a receipt from the Purchasing Agent for furnishing wheat on 5 Jun 1782 {Ref: Maryland State Archives MdHR-6636-42-7}

HACKETT, OLIVER SR. (Caroline County) received a receipt from the Purchasing Agent for furnishing wheat on 5 Jun 1782 {Ref: Maryland State Archives MdHR-6636-42-7}

HACKETT, THEOPHILUS (Dorchester County) received a receipt from the Purchasing Agent for furnishing wheat on 1 Nov 1782 {Ref: Maryland State Archives MdHR-6636-42-23}

HACKETT, THOMAS (Dorchester County) received a receipt from the Purchasing Agent for furnishing wheat on 1 Nov 1782 {Ref: Maryland State Archives MdHR-6636-42-23}

HADDOCK, JOHN (Baltimore County) received flour from the commissary in

Baltimore Town for delivery to Col. Henry Hollingsworth on 15 Jul 1780 {Ref: Archives of Maryland 45:85}

HAFF, ABRAHAM (Frederick County) received a certificate from the Purchasing Agent for furnishing wheat on 29 May 1782 {Ref: Maryland State Archives MdHR-6636-42-36}; received a loan certificate for £9.13.2 due from the Council of Maryland "agreeable to the Act proposing to the Citizens of this State, Creditors of Congress on Loan Office Certificates, Etc." on 17 Jun 1783 for services rendered during the war {Ref: Archives of Maryland 48:432}

HAGAN (HAGON), HENRY (Charles County) received a receipt from the Purchasing Agent for furnishing wheat on 11 Dec 1781 {Ref: Maryland State Archives MdHR-6636-42-15}; received a receipt for furnishing wheat on 31 Oct 1782 {Ref: Maryland State Archives MdHR-6636-42-19}; received a receipt for furnishing wheat on 20 Dec 1782 {Ref: Maryland State Archives MdHR-6636-42-20}

HAGEN, BENNET (Frederick County) received certificates from the Purchasing Agent for furnishing wheat on 24 Jan and 30 Nov 1782 {Ref: Maryland State Archives MdHR-6636-42-37}

HAILE, GEORGE JR. (Baltimore County) received a receipt from the Purchasing Agent for hauling wheat on 19 Jun 1779 {Ref: Maryland State Archives MdHR-6636-21-67}

HAILE, NICHOLAS (Baltimore County) received a receipt from the Purchasing Agent for hauling flour on 20 Sep 1779 {Ref: Maryland State Archives MdHR-6636-21-67}

HAILY, JOHN (Kent County) received payment from the Purchasing Agent for furnishing cattle for the public use in September, 1781 {Ref: Maryland State Archives MdHR-6636-43-3}

HAIS, WILLIAM (Charles County) received a receipt from the Purchasing Agent for furnishing wheat on 14 Sep 1782 {Ref: Maryland State Archives MdHR-6636-42-18}

HALE, FRANCIS (Queen Anne's County) submitted an account and receipt for hauling wheat on 30 Aug 1782 {Ref: Maryland State Archives MdHR-6636-43-12}

HALEY, ANN (county not stated) received a loan certificate for £105.15.0 due from the Council of Maryland "agreeable to the Act proposing to the Citizens of this State, Creditors of Congress on Loan Office Certificates, Etc." on 10 Jun 1783 for services rendered during the war {Ref: Archives of Maryland 48:429}

HALKERSTON, JOHN (Charles and Prince George's Counties) was a Commissary Agent and Quartermaster in 1781: received a request for beef from Capt. Richard B. Mitchell on 29 Apr 1781 {Ref: Maryland State Archives MdHR-6636-43-44L}; received a request for flour from Thomas Evans, Quartermaster on 29 Apr 1781 {Ref: Maryland State Archives MdHR-6636-

43-44P}; received a request for beef from Capt. Samuel Smallwood on 30 Apr 1781 {Ref: Maryland State Archives MdHR-6636-43-44N}; received a request for beef from Capt. William McPherson on 30 Apr 1781 {Ref: Maryland State Archives MdHR-6636-43-44M}; received a request for beef and flour from Thomas Evans, Quartermaster on 30 Apr 1781 {Ref: Maryland State Archives MdHR-6636-43-44/O}; received a request for beef from Capt. Richard B. Mitchell on 1 May 1781 {Ref: Maryland State Archives MdHR-6636-43-44L}; received a request for beef and flour from Capt. Benjamin Harwood on 1 May 1781 {Ref: Maryland State Archives MdHR-6636-43-44J}; received a request for beef from Pryor Berry, Sergeant of the Guard on 2 May 1781 {Ref: Maryland State Archives MdHR-6636-43-44G}; received a request for beef from Philip Spalding, Sergeant of the Magazine Guards on 3 May 1781 {Ref: Maryland State Archives MdHR-6636-43-44D}; received a request from Sgt. John B. Turner to deliver beef and flour to Joseph Turner on 3 May 1781 {Ref: Maryland State Archives MdHR-6636-43-44E}; received a request from Sgt. Pryor Berry to deliver beef to the magazine guards on 3 May 1781 {Ref: Maryland State Archives MdHR-6636-43-44F}

HALKETT, WILLIAM (Queen Anne's County) received a certificate of payment due for furnishing beef on 15 Nov 1781 {Ref: Maryland State Archives MdHR-6636-24-34}

HALL, AQUILA (Harford County) was a colonel who was appointed by the Council of Safety to collect all the gold and silver coin that could be procured in his county in compliance with the Resolve of Congress on 27 Jan 1776 {Ref: Archives of Maryland 11:132}

HALL, AQUILA, Esquire (Harford County) received a loan certificate for £423.6.1 due from the Council of Maryland "agreeable to the Act proposing to the Citizens of this State, Creditors of Congress on Loan Office Certificates, Etc." on 24 Oct 1783 for services rendered during the war {Ref: Archives of Maryland 48:473}

HALL, BENEDICT EDWARD (Harford County) received payment for furnishing a gun, bayonet, and gun barrel to the Committee of Safety on 1 Jul 1776 {Ref: Preston's History of Harford County, p. 331}

HALL, CHRISTOPHER (Kent County) received a receipt from the Purchasing Agent for furnishing wheat on 3 Nov 1780 {Ref: Maryland State Archives MdHR-6636-23-49}

HALL, DOCTOR (Cecil County) received payment by order of the Council of Maryland "for sick militia in Cecil County under his care" on 6 Oct 1777 {Ref: Archives of Maryland 16:392}

HALL, JOHN (Baltimore County) pledged a loan in the amount of £500 to the State of Maryland under the Act for the Emission of Bills of Credit "to defray the expences of the present campaign" in June, 1781 {Ref: Archives of

Maryland 47:326}; received a loan certificate for £243.12.6 due from the Council of Maryland "agreeable to the Act proposing to the Citizens of this State, Creditors of Congress on Loan Office Certificates, Etc." on 13 May 1783 for services rendered during the war {Ref: Archives of Maryland 48:411}

HALL, JOSEPH (Frederick County) was a doctor who was appointed by the Council of Maryland to serve as "Surgeon to Col. Murdock's Battalion of Marching Militia" on 4 Sep 1777 {Ref: Archives of Maryland 16:362}

HALL, JOSIAS CARVIL (Harford County) was a doctor and colonel who offered a mare to the Committee of Safety for the public use on 3 May 1775 {Ref: Preston's History of Harford County, p. 297}; received payment by order of the Maryland Council of Safety for furnishing two guns on 21 Aug 1776 and a rifle on 27 Aug 1776 {Ref: Archives of Maryland 12:230, 243}; also see "James Brown," q.v.

HALL, ELIHU (Cecil County) received a certificate from the Purchasing Agent for furnishing wheat for the use of the state on 7 Mar 1780 {Ref: Maryland State Archives MdHR-6636-23-22}

HALL, FRANCIS (Queenstown, Queen Anne's County) received a receipt from the Purchasing Agent for furnishing beef on 12 Dec 1779 {Ref: Maryland State Archives MdHR-6636-17-73}

HALL, GABRIEL (Frederick County) received a certificate from the Purchasing Agent for furnishing wheat on 8 Jun 1782 {Ref: Maryland State Archives MdHR-6636-42-34}

HALL, JOHN (Harford County) received payment by order of the Council of Safety for furnishing a gun on 21 Aug 1776 {Ref: Archives of Maryland 12:230}

HALL, NICHOLAS (Frederick County) received a receipt from the Purchasing Agent for furnishing corn on 29 Feb 1781 {Ref: Maryland State Archives MdHR-6636-23-3}; received a certificate for furnishing wheat on 10 Jun 1782 {Ref: Maryland State Archives MdHR-6636-42-36}

HALL, RICHARD (Annapolis) received payment from the Maryland Council of Safety "to defray the expence of carting the records" on 8 Mar 1776 {Ref: Archives of Maryland 11:214}

HALL ROBERT (Kent County) received payment from the Purchasing Agent for collecting cattle for the public use in November, 1782 {Ref: Maryland State Archives MdHR-6636-43-3}

HALL, ROBERT C. (Charles County) received a receipt from the Purchasing Agent for furnishing wheat on 8 May 1783 {Ref: Maryland State Archives MdHR-6636-42-22}

HALL, WILLIAM (Frederick County) received a certificate from the Purchasing Agent for furnishing wheat on 8 Jun 1782 {Ref: Maryland State Archives MdHR-6636-42-36}

HALL, WILLIAM (Harford County) received payment for furnishing a musquet to the Committee of Safety on 18 Jun 1776 {Ref: Preston's History of Harford County, p. 329}

HAMELTON, LEONARD (Charles County) received a receipt from the Purchasing Agent for furnishing wheat on 28 Sep 1782 {Ref: Maryland State Archives MdHR-6636-42-19}; received a receipt for furnishing wheat on 28 Dec 1782 {Ref: Maryland State Archives MdHR-6636-42-21}

HAMELTON, MARMADUKE (Charles County) received a receipt from the Purchasing Agent for furnishing wheat on 8 May 1783 {Ref: Maryland State Archives MdHR-6636-42-22}

HAMELTON, SAMUEL (Charles County) received receipts from the Purchasing Agent for furnishing wheat on 28 Sep and 12 Oct 1782 {Ref: Maryland State Archives MdHR-6636-42-19}

HAMERSLEY, FRANCIS (Charles County) received a receipt from the Purchasing Agent for furnishing wheat on 29 Dec 1782 {Ref: Maryland State Archives MdHR-6636-42-21}

HAMILTON, EDWARD (Frederick County) received a receipt from the Purchasing Agent for furnishing corn on 2 Jan 1781 {Ref: Maryland State Archives MdHR-6636-23-2}

HAMILTON, PATRICK (Charles County) received a receipt from the Purchasing Agent for furnishing wheat on 31 Dec 1781 {Ref: Maryland State Archives MdHR-6636-42-15}

HAMM, JOHN (Kent County) received receipts from the Purchasing Agent for furnishing flour on 9 Jan and 19 Dec 1780, for furnishing cattle on 25 Oct and 10 Nov 1780 and 13 Sep and 26 Oct 1781, and for furnishing beef on 7 Nov 1780 and 8 Sep, 20 Oct, 14 Nov and 21 Nov 1781 {Ref: Maryland State Archives MdHR-6636-23-48}

HAMMOND, CHARLES (Frederick County) received a certificate from the Purchasing Agent for furnishing wheat on 16 Dec 1780 {Ref: Maryland State Archives MdHR-6636-23-27}; received a certificate for furnishing wheat on 8 Jun 1782 {Ref: Maryland State Archives MdHR-6636-42-35}; received a certificate for furnishing wheat on 28 Jun 1782 {Ref: Maryland State Archives MdHR-6636-42-36}; received certificates from the Purchasing Agent for furnishing wheat on 24 Sep and 12 Dec 1782 {Ref: Maryland State Archives MdHR-6636-42-37}

HAMMOND, EDWARD (Worcester County) received a receipt from the Purchasing Agent for furnishing corn on 28 Apr 1780 {Ref: Maryland State Archives MdHR-6636-24-52}; his name appeared on "A List of Corn Purchased in Worcester County for the use of the State of Maryland" by the Commissary in July, 1780 {Ref: Archives of Maryland 45:10}

HAMMOND, JOHN (Baltimore or Annapolis) received payment by order of the

Council of Safety for furnishing plank on 24 Aug 1776 {Ref: Archives of Maryland 12:235}

HAMMOND, RACHAEL (Baltimore or Annapolis) received payment by order of the Council of Safety for making shirts on 14 Mar 1777 {Ref: Archives of Maryland 16:173}

HAMMOND, THOMAS (Frederick County) received a certificate from the Purchasing Agent for furnishing wheat on 12 Sep 1782 {Ref: Maryland State Archives MdHR-6636-42-37}

HAMMOND, WILLIAM (Baltimore Town) was a merchant who received "six of the four-pounders [cannons] belonging to this State now at Dorsey's Works, he having engaged to return guns of the same size and quality to this State when required" per order of the Council of Maryland on 22 Jan 1778 {Ref: Archives of Maryland 16:471}

HAMMOURSLY, FRANCIS (Charles County) received a receipt from the Purchasing Agent for furnishing wheat on 14 Sep 1782 {Ref: Maryland State Archives MdHR-6636-42-18}

HAMPTON, DAVID (Harford County) received payment by order of the Council of Maryland for providing waggonage on 3 Nov 1777 {Ref: Archives of Maryland 16:408}

HANCE, JOHN (Cecil County) received a receipt from the Purchasing Agent for furnishing flour on 29 Nov 1782 {Ref: Maryland State Archives MdHR-6636-42-9}

HANCOCK, JOHN (Talbot County) submitted an account and receipt for hiring a cart and team on 12 Jun 1778 {Ref: Maryland State Archives MdHR-6636-12-15}

HANCOCK, THOMAS (Charles County) received a receipt from the Purchasing Agent for furnishing wheat on 5 Oct 1781 {Ref: Maryland State Archives MdHR-6636-43-45M}

HANCOCK, WILLIAM (Charles County) received a receipt from the Purchasing Agent for furnishing wheat on 30 Nov 1781 {Ref: Maryland State Archives MdHR-6636-43-45C}; received a receipt for furnishing wheat on 8 Dec 1781 {Ref: Maryland State Archives MdHR-6636-42-15}

HANDY, ANN (Somerset County) received a loan certificate for £318.19.11 due from the Council of Maryland "agreeable to the Act proposing to the Citizens of this State, Creditors of Congress on Loan Office Certificates, Etc." on 19 Dec 1783 for services rendered during the war {Ref: Archives of Maryland 48:493}

HANDY, EBENEZER (Somerset County) received payment by order of the Council of Maryland for furnishing a blanket on 17 Apr 1777 {Ref: Archives of Maryland 16:216}; received a receipt for storage of pork on 28 Jul 1781 {Ref: Maryland State Archives MdHR-6636-24-43}

HANDY, ELIZABETH (Somerset County) received a loan certificate for £318.19.11 due from the Council of Maryland "agreeable to the Act proposing to the Citizens of this State, Creditors of Congress on Loan Office Certificates, Etc." on 19 Dec 1783 for services rendered during the war {Ref: Archives of Maryland 48:494}

HANDY, GEORGE (Somerset County) was a captain who received a receipt from the Purchasing Agent for furnishing beef on 18 Nov 1781 {Ref: Maryland State Archives MdHR-6636-24-44}; received a receipt for furnishing wheat on 20 Feb 1782 {Ref: Maryland State Archives MdHR-6636-43-21}

HANDY, HENRY (Somerset County) received receipts from the Purchasing Agent for furnishing pork on 14 May and 10 Jul 1781 {Ref: Maryland State Archives MdHR-6636-24-43}

HANDY, ISAAC (Somerset County) received a receipt from the Purchasing Agent for furnishing beef on 7 Nov 1781 {Ref: Maryland State Archives MdHR-6636-24-44}; received a loan certificate for £450.9.7 due from the Council of Maryland "agreeable to the Act proposing to the Citizens of this State, Creditors of Congress on Loan Office Certificates, Etc." on 19 Dec 1783 for services rendered during the war {Ref: Archives of Maryland 48:493}

HANDY, LEVIN (Somerset County) received a receipt from the Purchasing Agent for furnishing flour and storage of corn on 12 Apr 1780 {Ref: Maryland State Archives MdHR-6636-24-39}; submitted an account and payment due for storage and delivery of corn on 19 Feb 1781 {Ref: Maryland State Archives MdHR-6636-24-38}

HANDY, NELLY (Somerset County) received a loan certificate for £362.6.8 due from the Council of Maryland "agreeable to the Act proposing to the Citizens of this State, Creditors of Congress on Loan Office Certificates, Etc." on 19 Dec 1783 for services rendered during the war {Ref: Archives of Maryland 48:493}

HANDY, SAMUEL (Worcester County) was appointed by the Council of Safety to collect all the gold and silver coin that could be procured in the county in compliance with the Resolve of Congress on 27 Jan 1776 {Ref: Archives of Maryland 11:132}; served as Commissary in 1780 {Ref: Archives of Maryland 45:9}; submitted an account and receipt for furnishing salt in 1781-1782 {Ref: Maryland State Archives MdHR-6636-43-28P}; submitted an account and receipt for furnishing pork on 10 Oct 1782 {Ref: Maryland State Archives MdHR-6636-43-30E}

HANDY, THOMAS (Somerset County) was a captain who received a receipt from the Purchasing Agent for furnishing pork on 10 Jun 1781 {Ref: Maryland State Archives MdHR-6636-24-43}

HANDY, THOMAS SR. (Somerset County) received a receipt from the Purchasing Agent for furnishing beef on 6 Nov 1781 {Ref: Maryland State

Archives MdHR-6636-24-44}

HANDY, WILLIAM (Worcester County) received receipts from the Purchasing Agent for furnishing corn on 29 Jan and 7 Mar 1780 {Ref: Maryland State Archives MdHR-6636-24-52}; his name appeared on "A List of Sundry Persons Corn Purchased of for the use of the State of Maryland" by the Commissary on 19 Jun 1780 {Ref: Archives of Maryland 45:9}; his name appeared twice on "A List of Corn Purchased in Worcester County for the use of the State of Maryland" by the Commissary in July, 1780 {Ref: Archives of Maryland 45:9-10}; submitted an account for renting a warehouse in 1782 {Ref: Maryland State Archives MdHR-6636-43-28W}; submitted an account and receipt for furnishing pork on 10 Oct 1782 {Ref: Maryland State Archives MdHR-6636-43-30D}

HANDY, WILLIAM (Somerset County) received a receipt from the Purchasing Agent for furnishing beef on 10 Dec 1781 {Ref: Maryland State Archives MdHR-6636-24-44}; received a loan certificate for £276.4.7 due from the Council of Maryland "agreeable to the Act proposing to the Citizens of this State, Creditors of Congress on Loan Office Certificates, Etc." on 19 Dec 1783 for services rendered during the war {Ref: Archives of Maryland 48:493}

HANES, MICHAEL (Frederick County) received a certificate from the Purchasing Agent for hauling flour on 4 Nov 1781 {Ref: Maryland State Archives MdHR-6636-42-32}

HANEY(?), JOHN (Caroline County) received a receipt from the Purchasing Agent for furnishing wheat on 5 Aug 1782 {Ref: Maryland State Archives MdHR-6636-42-7}

HANNAH (HANAH), PATRICK (Baltimore County) received payments by order of the Council of Safety for furnishing tent poles on 17 Aug and 2 Sep 1776 and 28 May 1777 {Ref: Archives of Maryland 12:214, 12:252, 16:261}

HANSON, GEORGE (Kent County) received payment by order of the Council of Safety for cleaning guns on 9 Oct 1776 {Ref: Archives of Maryland 12:327}; received payment from the Purchasing Agent for furnishing cattle and pasturage for the public use in September, 1781 and for purchasing beef cattle for the public use in October, 1782 {Ref: Maryland State Archives MdHR-6636-43-3}; appointed by the Council of Maryland to purchase seven horses on the Eastern Shore for the use of the Southern Army on 8 Jul 1782 {Ref: Archives of Maryland 48:208}

HANSON, HENRY (Charles County) submitted an account of payment due for furnishing wheat and for weaving cloth on 6 Aug 1782 {Ref: Maryland State Archives MdHR-6636-47-2}

HANSON, HENRY M. (Charles County) received receipts from the Purchasing Agent for furnishing wheat on 15 Sep and 21 Dec 1781 {Ref: Maryland State Archives MdHR-6636-42-15}

HANSON, JOHN (Charles County) received payment by order of the Council of Safety on 29 Jul 1776 to enable him and Walter Hanson the youngest to erect a powder mill agreeable to the Resolutions of the late Convention {Ref: Archives of Maryland 11:463}

HANSON, JOHN JR. (Frederick County) was appointed by the Council of Safety to collect all the gold and silver coin that could be procured in the county in compliance with the Resolve of Congress on 27 Jan 1776 {Ref: Archives of Maryland 11:132}

HANSON, MARY (Baltimore Town) submitted an account and receipt for making beds on the state ship *Defence* on 12 Mar 1777 {Ref: Maryland State Archives MdHR-19970-2-1}

HANSON, SAMUEL (Frederick County) was a doctor who was appointed by the Council of Maryland to serve as "Surgeon to Col. Baker Johnson's Battalion of Marching Militia" on 4 Sep 1777 {Ref: Archives of Maryland 16:362}

HANSON, SAMUEL (Charles County) was a colonel who received a receipt from the Purchasing Agent for furnishing wheat on 28 Sep 1782 {Ref: Maryland State Archives MdHR-6636-42-19}

HANSON, SAMUEL JR. (Charles County) received a receipt from the Purchasing Agent for furnishing wheat on 6 Sep 1782 {Ref: Maryland State Archives MdHR-6636-42-18}

HANSON, THOMAS (Charles County) was a captain who received a receipt from the Purchasing Agent for furnishing wheat on 1 Jun 1781 {Ref: Maryland State Archives MdHR-6636-42-15}

HANSON, WALTER (Charles County) received receipts from the Purchasing Agent for furnishing wheat on 12 Oct and 2 Nov 1782 {Ref: Maryland State Archives MdHR-6636-42-19}; also see "John Hanson," q.v.

HANSON, WALTER JR. (Charles County) received payment by order of the Council of Maryland for his use as Contractor for Horses in Charles County on 6 Sep 1780 {Ref: Archives of Maryland 43:278}

HANSON, WILLIAM (Kent County) received certificates from the Purchasing Agent for furnishing wheat on 29 Jan and 17 Feb 1780 {Ref: Maryland State Archives MdHR-6636-43-1}; appointed by the Council of Maryland to be one of three men in Kent County "to carry the Act to prohibit for a limited time the Exportation of Indian Corn, Etc., by Land" on 22 Dec 1780 {Ref: Archives of Maryland 45:251}; received payment from the Purchasing Agent for furnishing cattle for the public use in September, 1781 {Ref: Maryland State Archives MdHR-6636-43-3}

HARBIN, GERRARD (Frederick County) received a receipt from the Purchasing Agent for furnishing corn on 25 Apr 1780; received a receipt for furnishing corn and rye on 29 Apr 1780 {Ref: Maryland State Archives MdHR-6636-24-1}

HARBIN, JAMES (Frederick County) received payment by order of the Council of Maryland for providing waggonage on 21 Nov 1777 {Ref: Archives of Maryland 16:421}; received receipts from the Purchasing Agent for furnishing corn on 16 Jun and 20 Jun 1780 {Ref: Maryland State Archives MdHR-6636-24-1}

HARBIN, JOSHUA (Frederick County) received payment by order of the Council of Maryland "for waggon hire for the Virginia Troops" on 27 Mar 1778 {Ref: Archives of Maryland 16:554}; received receipts from the Purchasing Agent for furnishing corn on 11 Apr and 22 Apr 1780 {Ref: Maryland State Archives MdHR-6636-24-1}

HARDASTAY (HARDAYSTAY), SAMUEL (Montgomery County) received receipts from the Purchasing Agent for furnishing corn on 9 Mar and 19 Mar 1781 {Ref: Maryland State Archives MdHR-6636-42-11}; received a receipt for furnishing wheat on 29 May 1781 {Ref: Maryland State Archives MdHR-6636-24-15}

HARDCASTLE, JOHN (Caroline County) received a receipt from the Purchasing Agent for furnishing wheat on 1 Sep 1782 {Ref: Maryland State Archives MdHR-6636-42-7}

HARDCASTLE, ROBERT (Caroline County) received a certificate from the Purchasing Agent for storage of grain on 5 Jun 1780 {Ref: Maryland State Archives MdHR-6636-23-20}

HARDCASTLE, SOLOMON (Caroline County) received a receipt from the Purchasing Agent for furnishing wheat on 1 Sep 1782 {Ref: Maryland State Archives MdHR-6636-42-7}

HARDCASTLE, THOMAS (Caroline County) received receipts from the Purchasing Agent for furnishing corn and provisions on 10 Feb and 11 Feb 1780 {Ref: Maryland State Archives MdHR-6636-23-19}; received a certificate for storage of corn on 18 Jun 1780 {Ref: Maryland State Archives MdHR-6636-23-20}; received a receipt for furnishing wheat on 1 Aug 1782 {Ref: Maryland State Archives MdHR-6636-42-7}

HARDEN, ELIHU (Frederick County) received a certificate from the Purchasing Agent for furnishing pork on 14 Mar 1781 {Ref: Maryland State Archives MdHR-6636-23-4}

HARDEN, JOSIAH (Prince George's County) received a receipt from the Purchasing Agent for furnishing wheat in 1782 {Ref: Maryland State Archives MdHR-6636-50-135}; received a receipt for furnishing wheat on 14 Dec 1782 {Ref: Maryland State Archives MdHR-6636-50-142}

HARDEN, THOMAS (Caroline County) received a receipt from the Purchasing Agent for furnishing wheat on 5 Aug 1782 {Ref: Maryland State Archives MdHR-6636-42-7}

HARDESTY, GEORGE (Calvert County) received payment for driving cattle on

25 Dec 1781 {Ref: Maryland State Archives MdHR-6636-50-37}

HARDIN, JUDITH (Dorchester County) received a receipt from the Purchasing Agent for furnishing wheat on 1 Oct 1782 {Ref: Maryland State Archives MdHR-6636-42-23}

HARDIN, MARY (Dorchester County) received a loan certificate for £50.10.9 due from the Council of Maryland "agreeable to the Act proposing to the Citizens of this State, Creditors of Congress on Loan Office Certificates, Etc." on 19 May 1783 for services rendered during the war {Ref: Archives of Maryland 48:417}

HARDING, EDWARD (Montgomery County) received a receipt from the Purchasing Agent for furnishing wheat on 19 Aug 1780 {Ref: Maryland State Archives MdHR-6636-24-6}

HARDING, ELIAS (Montgomery County) received a receipt from the Purchasing Agent for furnishing wheat on 29 Jul 1780 {Ref: Maryland State Archives MdHR-6636-24-5}; received a receipt for furnishing wheat on 1 Aug 1780 {Ref: Maryland State Archives MdHR-6636-43-7}

HARDING, JOSEPH (Talbot County) received a receipt from the Purchasing Agent for furnishing bacon for the use of the army on 27 Apr 1778 {Ref: Maryland State Archives MdHR-4587-74}; submitted an account and receipt for hauling on 30 Apr 1778 {Ref: Maryland State Archives MdHR-6636-12-15}

HARDING, JOSIAH (Prince George's County) received a receipt from the Purchasing Agent for furnishing wheat on 9 Dec 1782 {Ref: Maryland State Archives MdHR-6636-50-142}

HARDING, PHILIP (Frederick County) received a certificate from the Purchasing Agent for furnishing wheat on 15 Jun 1782 {Ref: Maryland State Archives MdHR-6636-42-35}

HARDING, WALTER (Frederick County) received receipts from the Purchasing Agent for furnishing corn on 7 Apr, 20 Apr, 3 May and 23 May 1780; received a receipt for furnishing corn and rye on 13 Jun 1780 {Ref: Maryland State Archives MdHR-6636-24-1}

HARDMAN, DANIEL (Frederick County) received a certificate from the Purchasing Agent for furnishing wheat on 28 Jul 1782 {Ref: Maryland State Archives MdHR-6636-42-36}

HARDY, BAPTIST (Montgomery County) received a receipt from the Purchasing Agent for furnishing wheat on 4 Sep 1780 {Ref: Maryland State Archives MdHR-6636-24-7}

HARDY, JOHN (Prince George's County) received a receipt from the Purchasing Agent for furnishing wheat on 9 May 1782 {Ref: Maryland State Archives MdHR-6636-50-135}

HARDY, KINS (Prince George's County) received a receipt from the Purchasing

Agent for furnishing wheat on 9 Dec 1782 {Ref: Maryland State Archives MdHR-6636-50-142}

HARGADINE, JOHN (Queen Anne's County) received a receipt from the Purchasing Agent for furnishing bacon on 1 Apr 1778 {Ref: Maryland State Archives MdHR-4587-47}

HARGADINE, JOHN TAYLOR (Queen Anne's County) received a certificate from the Purchasing Agent for furnishing wheat on 19 Feb 1780 {Ref: Maryland State Archives MdHR-6636-24-28}

HARGRAVE (HARGRAVES), GEORGE (Charles County) received a receipt from the Purchasing Agent for furnishing wheat on 14 Sep 1782 {Ref: Maryland State Archives MdHR-6636-42-18}; received a receipt for furnishing wheat on 20 Dec 1782 {Ref: Maryland State Archives MdHR-6636-42-20}

HARLYNTIS, NALY (Montgomery County) received a receipt from the Purchasing Agent for furnishing wheat on 18 May 1781 {Ref: Maryland State Archives MdHR-6636-24-18}

HARPER, WILLIAM (Caroline County) received a receipt from the Purchasing Agent for furnishing wheat on 1 Sep 1782 {Ref: Maryland State Archives MdHR-6636-42-7}

HARRAWOOD, ROBERT (Kent County) submitted an account and receipt for hauling flour on 30 Mar 1782 {Ref: Maryland State Archives MdHR-6636-43-5}

HARRINGTON, ABIGAIL (Caroline County) received a receipt from the Purchasing Agent for furnishing wheat on 1 Sep 1782 {Ref: Maryland State Archives MdHR-6636-42-7}

HARRINGTON, JAMES (Caroline County) received payment by order of the Council of Safety for furnishing boatage on 6 Sep 1776 {Ref: Archives of Maryland 12:259}

HARRINGTON, JOHN (Caroline County) received a receipt from the Purchasing Agent for furnishing wheat on 1 Sep 1782 {Ref: Maryland State Archives MdHR-6636-42-7}

HARRINGTON, LEVIN (Baltimore County) received a receipt from the Purchasing Agent for furnishing beef and pork on 10 May 1780 {Ref: Maryland State Archives MdHR-6636-40-46F}

HARRINGTON, PETER (Caroline County) was a Commissary Agent who submitted an account on 20 Sep 1782 of wheat received on 17 Aug 1782 {Ref: Maryland State Archives MdHR-6636-42-7}; also see "William Harrington," q.v.

HARRINGTON, REBECCA (Caroline County) received a receipt from the Purchasing Agent for furnishing wheat on 1 Sep 1782 {Ref: Maryland State Archives MdHR-6636-42-7}

HARRINGTON, WILLIAM (Caroline County) received payment by order of the

Council of Maryland via Peter Harrington for services rendered (not specified) on 27 Oct 1778 {Ref: Archives of Maryland 21:225}

HARRIS, DANIEL (Harford County) received a certificate from the Purchasing Agent for furnishing wheat on 31 Jan 1780 {Ref: Maryland State Archives MdHR-6636-17-75}

HARRIS, DAVID (Baltimore County) submitted an account for furnishing rum and sugar on 18 May 1780 {Ref: Maryland State Archives MdHR-6636-18-91}

HARRIS, ISAAC (Anne Arundel County) was appointed "Armourer to the Troops stationed in Annapolis" by the Maryland Council of Safety on 7 Mar 1776 {Ref: Archives of Maryland 11:206}; received payment for his services as armourer on 17 Aug 1776 {Ref: Archives of Maryland 12:214}

HARRIS, JAMES (Harford County) contracted with the Maryland Council of Safety to carry on a linen manufactory in partnership with John Archer on or about 16 Feb 1776 {Ref: Archives of Maryland 11:163}

HARRIS, JAMES (Kent County) received payment from the Purchasing Agent for furnishing cattle and pasturage for the public use in September, 1781 {Ref: Maryland State Archives MdHR-6636-43-3}

HARRIS, JOHN (Prince George's County) received a receipt from the Purchasing Agent for furnishing wheat on 8 Jun 1782 {Ref: Maryland State Archives MdHR-6636-50-135}

HARRIS, JOHN (Baltimore County) received payment for furnishing flour on 24 Mar 1781 {Ref: Maryland State Archives MdHR-6636-43-38FFFF}; received payment for furnishing barrels on 23 Apr 1781 {Ref: Maryland State Archives MdHR-6636-43-38SSS}

HARRIS, JOHN (Somerset County) received a receipt from the Purchasing Agent for furnishing pork on 3 Jul 1781 {Ref: Maryland State Archives MdHR-6636-24-45}

HARRIS, JOHN (Caroline County) received a receipt from the Purchasing Agent for furnishing wheat on 1 Jun 1782 {Ref: Maryland State Archives MdHR-6636-42-7}

HARRIS, JOSEPH (Prince George's County) received a receipt from the Purchasing Agent for furnishing wheat on 12 Apr 1782 {Ref: Maryland State Archives MdHR-6636-50-135}

HARRIS, JOSEPH (Montgomery County) received a receipt from the Purchasing Agent for shelling corn on 9 Jul 1780 {Ref: Maryland State Archives MdHR-6636-24-2}

HARRIS, NATHAN (Prince George's County) received receipts from the Purchasing Agent for furnishing wheat on 21 Jan 1782, 28 May 1782 and 13 Sep 1783 {Ref: Maryland State Archives MdHR-6636-50-135}

HARRIS, SPENCER (Somerset County) received a receipt from the Purchasing Agent for furnishing pork on 3 Apr 1781 {Ref: Maryland State Archives

MdHR-6636-24-45}; received a receipt for furnishing pork on 28 May 1782 {Ref: Maryland State Archives MdHR-6636-43-21}

HARRIS (HARRESS), THOMAS (Charles County) was a colonel who received a receipt from the Purchasing Agent for delivering wheat on 31 Dec 1781 {Ref: Maryland State Archives MdHR-6636-42-15}; received a receipt for furnishing wheat on 29 Dec 1782 {Ref: Maryland State Archives MdHR-6636-42-21}

HARRIS, THOMAS (Frederick County) received a certificate from the Purchasing Agent for furnishing wheat on 11 Feb 1783 {Ref: Maryland State Archives MdHR-6636-42-38}

HARRIS, ZADOCK (Montgomery County) received receipts from the Purchasing Agent for furnishing wheat on 25 Jul and 25 Aug 1780 {Ref: Maryland State Archives MdHR-6636-24-13}; received receipts from the Purchasing Agent for furnishing wheat on 22 Oct and 3 Nov 1781 {Ref: Maryland State Archives MdHR-6636-24-14}

HARRIS, ZEPHANIAH (Montgomery County) received a receipt from the Purchasing Agent for furnishing wheat on 10 Apr 1781 {Ref: Maryland State Archives MdHR-6636-42-11}; received a receipt for furnishing wheat on 10 Oct 1781 {Ref: Maryland State Archives MdHR-6636-24-15}

HARRISON, BENJAMIN (Montgomery County) received a receipt from the Purchasing Agent for furnishing wheat on 10 Apr 1781 {Ref: Maryland State Archives MdHR-6636-24-15}

HARRISON, JAMES (Montgomery County) received a receipt from the Purchasing Agent for furnishing wheat on 14 Apr 1781 {Ref: Maryland State Archives MdHR-6636-24-14}

HARRISON, JOHN CAILE (Cambridge, Dorchester County) was appointed Commissary of Purchases for Dorchester County by the Council of Maryland on 8 Jul 1780 {Ref: Archives of Maryland 43:215, 239}; requested cash from the state to purchase provisions for the military and to pay for provisions purchased by certificates on 9 Aug 1780 {Ref: Maryland State Archives MdHR-6636-19-105}

HARRISON, JOSEPH HANSON (Charles County) received payment by order of the Council of Safety, "he having given bond with security for erecting a Salt Works" on 22 Jun 1776 {Ref: Archives of Maryland 11:506}

HARRISON, JOSIAS (Montgomery County) received a receipt from the Purchasing Agent for furnishing wheat on 7 Apr 1781 {Ref: Maryland State Archives MdHR-6636-42-11}

HARRISON, NATHAN (Montgomery County) received a receipt from the Purchasing Agent for furnishing wheat on 1 Aug 1780 {Ref: Maryland State Archives MdHR-6636-43-7}; received a receipt for furnishing wheat on 10 Apr 1781 {Ref: Maryland State Archives MdHR-6636-42-11}

HARRISON, RICHARD (Baltimore County) received a receipt from the

144

Purchasing Agent for furnishing flour and bread on 31 May 1781 {Ref: Maryland State Archives MdHR-6636-43-38DDD}

HARRISON, THOMAS (Frederick County) received a receipt from the Purchasing Agent for hauling flour on 26 Jun 1783 {Ref: Maryland State Archives MdHR-6636-42-28}

HARRISON, THOMAS (Baltimore County) received via his executors Daniel Bowley, William West and Richard Ridgely, a loan certificate for £586.1.6 due from the Council of Maryland "agreeable to the Act proposing to the Citizens of this State, Creditors of Congress on Loan Office Certificates, Etc." on 18 Dec 1783 for his services rendered during the war {Ref: Archives of Maryland 48:491}

HARRISON, WILLIAM (Charles County) received a receipt from the Purchasing Agent for furnishing wheat on 29 Dec 1782 {Ref: Maryland State Archives MdHR-6636-42-21}

HARRY, RICHARD (Montgomery County) received a receipt from the Purchasing Agent for furnishing wheat on 11 Sep 1780 {Ref: Maryland State Archives MdHR-6636-24-7}

HART, MORGAN (Kent County) received a certificate from the Purchasing Agent for furnishing corn on 8 Feb 1780 {Ref: Maryland State Archives MdHR-6636-23-41}

HART, SAMUEL (county not stated) received payment from the Council of Maryland on 11 Nov 1782 "for a horse purchased by A. McLane for Colonel Lee's Corps agreeable to a Resolve of the Assembly of December 1st 1780" {Ref: Archives of Maryland 48:301}

HARTSOCK, PETER (Frederick County) received a certificate from the Purchasing Agent for furnishing wheat on 5 Mar 1782 {Ref: Maryland State Archives MdHR-6636-42-37}

HARVEY, JOHN (Caroline County) received receipts from the Purchasing Agent for furnishing wheat on 5 Aug and 22 Aug 1782 {Ref: Maryland State Archives MdHR-6636-42-7}

HARVEY, SAMUEL (Caroline County) received receipts from the Purchasing Agent for furnishing wheat on 4 Jun, 6 Jun and 5 Aug 1782 {Ref: Maryland State Archives MdHR-6636-42-7}

HARVEY, THOMAS (Caroline County) received a receipt from the Purchasing Agent for furnishing wheat on 1 Sep 1782 {Ref: Maryland State Archives MdHR-6636-42-7}

HARVEY, WILLIAM (Montgomery County) received a receipt from the Purchasing Agent for furnishing wheat on 5 Oct 1781 {Ref: Maryland State Archives MdHR-6636-24-15}

HARVEY, WILLIAM SR. (Montgomery County) received a receipt from the Purchasing Agent for furnishing wheat on 25 Apr 1781 {Ref: Maryland State

Archives MdHR-6636-42-11}

HARWIN, EDWARD (Montgomery County) received a receipt from the Purchasing Agent for furnishing wheat on 14 Aug 1781 {Ref: Maryland State Archives MdHR-6636-24-14}

HARWOOD, BENJAMIN (Prince George's County) received a loan certificate for £217.1.7 due from the Council of Maryland "agreeable to the Act proposing to the Citizens of this State, Creditors of Congress on Loan Office Certificates, Etc." on 18 Oct 1783 for services rendered during the war {Ref: Archives of Maryland 48:470}; also see "John Halkerston," q.v.

HARWOOD, JOHN (Prince George's County) was a major who received a receipt from the Purchasing Agent for furnishing wheat in 1782 {Ref: Maryland State Archives MdHR-6636-50-135}

HARWOOD, NICHOLAS (Anne Arundel County) was appointed by the Council of Maryland to be one of six "Signers of the Bills emitted in Virtue of the Act to enable the Treasurer of the Western Shore to draw and sell Bills of Exchange and for an Emission of Bills of Credit if necessary" on 8 Sep 1780 {Ref: Archives of Maryland 43:281}

HARWOOD, THOMAS (Anne Arundel County) was a captain who contracted with the Maryland Council of Safety for a linen manufactory on 24 Aug 1776 {Ref: Archives of Maryland 12:236}

HASKINS, JOSEPH (Baltimore County) received a receipt from the Purchasing Agent for furnishing corn on 10 Sep 1781 {Ref: Maryland State Archives MdHR-6636-43-38AA}

HASKINS, SARAH (Baltimore County) received a loan certificate for £33.8.6 due from the Council of Maryland "agreeable to the Act proposing to the Citizens of this State, Creditors of Congress on Loan Office Certificates, Etc." on 16 May 1783 for services rendered during the war {Ref: Archives of Maryland 48:415}

HASLET, WILLIAM (Caroline County) received a certificate from the Purchasing Agent for storing wheat in his granary on 29 Apr 1780 {Ref: Maryland State Archives MdHR-6636-23-20}

HASTINGS, GEORGE (Queen Anne's County) received payment for furnishing beef on 18 Dec 1779 {Ref: Maryland State Archives MdHR-6636-17-73}; received a certificate from the Purchasing Agent for furnishing corn on 18 Jan 1780 {Ref: Maryland State Archives MdHR-6636-24-29}

HATCHESON, NATHANIEL (Kent County) received a certificate from the Purchasing Agent for furnishing wheat on 1 Mar 1780 {Ref: Maryland State Archives MdHR-6636-23-41}

HATTON, WILLIAM (Somerset County) furnished cattle on 12 Apr 1781 for the use of the State of Maryland {Ref: Archives of Maryland 47:250}; received a receipt from the Purchasing Agent for driving cattle on 28 Jul 1781 {Ref:

Maryland State Archives MdHR-6636-24-43}

HAUCK, JOHN (Frederick County) received a certificate from the Purchasing Agent for furnishing wheat on 29 Jul 1782 {Ref: Maryland State Archives MdHR-6636-42-36}

HAWKER, SAMUEL (Montgomery County) received a receipt from the Purchasing Agent for furnishing wheat on 1 Aug 1780 {Ref: Maryland State Archives MdHR-6636-43-7}; received a receipt for furnishing wheat on 10 Aug 1780 {Ref: Maryland State Archives MdHR-6636-24-6}

HAWKER, NICHOLAS (Montgomery County) received a receipt from the Purchasing Agent for furnishing wheat on 1 Aug 1780 {Ref: Maryland State Archives MdHR-6636-43-7}

HAWKER, WILLIAM (Prince George's County) received a receipt from the Purchasing Agent for furnishing wheat on 22 Jul 1782 {Ref: Maryland State Archives MdHR-6636-50-135}

HAWKINS, CATHARINE OR CATHERINE (Charles County) received a receipt from the Purchasing Agent for furnishing wheat on 15 Sep 1781 {Ref: Maryland State Archives MdHR-6636-43-45P}; received a receipt for furnishing wheat on 3 Nov 1781 {Ref: Maryland State Archives MdHR-6636-42-15}

HAWKINS, DOROTHY (Montgomery County) received a receipt from the Purchasing Agent for furnishing wheat on 22 May 1781 {Ref: Maryland State Archives MdHR-6636-24-18}

HAWKINS, HENRY S. (Charles County) received a receipt from the Purchasing Agent for furnishing wheat on 18 Nov 1782 {Ref: Maryland State Archives MdHR-6636-42-19}; received a receipt for furnishing wheat on 29 Dec 1782 {Ref: Maryland State Archives MdHR-6636-42-21}

HAWKINS, JOHN (Montgomery County) received a receipt from the Purchasing Agent for furnishing wheat on 21 Dec 1781 {Ref: Maryland State Archives MdHR-6636-24-14}; received a receipt for furnishing wheat on 2 Mar 1782 {Ref: Maryland State Archives MdHR-6636-43-8}

HAWKINS, JOSIAS (Charles County) was a colonel who received a receipt from the Purchasing Agent for furnishing wheat on 8 Dec 1781 {Ref: Maryland State Archives MdHR-6636-42-15}; received a receipt for furnishing wheat on 29 Jun 1782 {Ref: Maryland State Archives MdHR-6636-42-18}; received a receipt for furnishing wheat on 2 Nov 1782 {Ref: Maryland State Archives MdHR-6636-42-19}

HAWKINS, PHILIP (Baltimore Town) received payment for furnishing linen on 14 Oct 1779 {Ref: Maryland State Archives MdHR-19970-3-8}

HAWKINS, SAMUEL (Harford County) received a receipt from the Purchasing Agent for furnishing wheat on 24 Mar 1780 {Ref: Maryland State Archives MdHR-6636-17-116}

HAWKINS, THOMAS (Baltimore County) received a certificate from the Purchasing Agent for furnishing corn on 6 Mar 1780 {Ref: Maryland State Archives MdHR-6636-23-33}

HAWKINS, THOMAS (Frederick County) received a certificate from the Purchasing Agent for furnishing wheat on 16 Jul 1781 {Ref: Maryland State Archives MdHR-6636-23-28}

HAYLEY, GEORGE (Frederick County) received a receipt from the Purchasing Agent for furnishing corn meal on 28 Feb 1781 {Ref: Maryland State Archives MdHR-6636-23-3}; submitted an account for furnishing beef on 21 Apr 1781 {Ref: Maryland State Archives MdHR-6636-23-5}

HAYLEY, JOHN (Frederick County) received a certificate from the Purchasing Agent for furnishing corn meal on 28 Feb 1781 {Ref: Maryland State Archives MdHR-6636-23-3}

HAYMAN, CHARLES (Frederick County) received a certificate from the Purchasing Agent for furnishing wheat on 9 Aug 1782 {Ref: Maryland State Archives MdHR-6636-42-37}

HAYMAN, CHARLES JR. (Worcester County) received payment for furnishing bacon on 5 Aug 1781 {Ref: Maryland State Archives MdHR-6636-43-28FFFF}

HAYMAN, CHARLES SR. (Worcester County) received a receipt from the Purchasing Agent for furnishing bacon on 15 Oct 1780 {Ref: Maryland State Archives MdHR-6636-24-54}

HAYMAN, RACHEL (Worcester County) received a receipt from the Purchasing Agent for furnishing pork on 15 Oct 1780 {Ref: Maryland State Archives MdHR-6636-24-54}

HAYNIE, JAMES (Somerset County) received a receipt from the Purchasing Agent for furnishing pork on 26 May 1781 {Ref: Maryland State Archives MdHR-6636-24-43}

HAYS, CHARLES (Prince George's County) received a receipt from the Purchasing Agent for furnishing wheat in 1783 {Ref: Maryland State Archives MdHR-6636-50-135}

HAYS, GEORGE (Prince George's County) received a receipt from the Purchasing Agent for furnishing wheat in 1783 {Ref: Maryland State Archives MdHR-6636-50-135}

HAYS, JEREMIAH (Montgomery County) received a receipt from the Purchasing Agent for furnishing wheat on 7 May 1781 {Ref: Maryland State Archives MdHR-6636-24-15}

HAYS, JERIAH (Prince George's County) received a receipt from the Purchasing Agent for furnishing wheat on 15 Jul 1782 {Ref: Maryland State Archives MdHR-6636-50-135}

HAYS, LEONARD (Prince George's County) received a receipt from the

Purchasing Agent for furnishing wheat in 1783 {Ref: Maryland State Archives MdHR-6636-50-135}

HAYS, THOMAS (Prince George's County) received a receipt from the Purchasing Agent for furnishing wheat in 1783 {Ref: Maryland State Archives MdHR-6636-50-135}

HAYWARD, SARAH (Worcester County) received payment for furnishing beef on 25 Oct 1781 {Ref: Maryland State Archives MdHR-6636-43-28/OOO}

HEAD, BIGGER (Frederick County) received a certificate from the Purchasing Agent for furnishing wheat on 11 Jun 1782 {Ref: Maryland State Archives MdHR-6636-42-34}

HEAD, WILLIAM (Frederick County) received a receipt from the Purchasing Agent for delivering flour on 21 Apr 1781 {Ref: Maryland State Archives MdHR-6636-23-31}

HEADLEY, JAMES (Montgomery County) received a receipt from the Purchasing Agent for furnishing wheat on 9 Feb 1782 {Ref: Maryland State Archives MdHR-6636-43-7}

HEARDING, PHILIP (Anne Arundel County) received a receipt from the Purchasing Agent for furnishing powder on 16 Apr 1777 {Ref: Maryland State Archives MdHR-6636-9-14E}

HEARN, BENJAMIN (Somerset County) received receipts from the Purchasing Agent for furnishing pork and bacon on 2 May and 10 May 1781 {Ref: Maryland State Archives MdHR-6636-24-43}; received a receipt for furnishing pork on 6 Jun 1782 {Ref: Maryland State Archives MdHR-6636-43-21}

HEARSAY, JOHN (Cecil County) submitted an account for storing wheat on 22 Nov 1782 {Ref: Maryland State Archives MdHR-6636-42-9}

HEATH, WILLIAM (Somerset County) received a receipt from the Purchasing Agent for furnishing bacon on 1 Aug 1780 {Ref: Maryland State Archives MdHR-6636-24-41}; received a receipt for furnishing pork and wheat on 30 Apr 1782 {Ref: Maryland State Archives MdHR-6636-43-21}

HEATHER, MICHAEL (Dorchester County) received a receipt from the Purchasing Agent for furnishing wheat on 1 Oct 1782 {Ref: Maryland State Archives MdHR-6636-42-23}

HEATHERS, EDWARD (Queen Anne's County) received a receipt from the Purchasing Agent for furnishing bacon on 23 Apr 1778 {Ref: Maryland State Archives MdHR-4587-50}

HECK, BALSER, see "John Lingenfelter," q.v.

HEDGE, MARY (Frederick County) received a receipt from the Purchasing Agent for furnishing pork on 7 Apr 1781 {Ref: Maryland State Archives MdHR-6636-42-26}

HEDGES, CHARLES (Frederick County) received a receipt from the Purchasing Agent for furnishing pork on 24 Jul 1782 {Ref: Maryland State Archives

MdHR-6636-23-3}

HEDGES, PETER (Frederick County) received a certificate from the Purchasing Agent for furnishing wheat on 24 Jul 1782 {Ref: Maryland State Archives MdHR-6636-42-36}

HEDLEY, JACOB (Montgomery County) received a receipt from the Purchasing Agent for furnishing wheat on 15 May 1781 {Ref: Maryland State Archives MdHR-6636-24-18}

HEFFER, CHRISTIAN (Frederick County) received a certificate from the Purchasing Agent for furnishing mutton on 11 Jun 1781 {Ref: Maryland State Archives MdHR-6636-23-28}

HEFFERSON, ROBERT (Caroline County) received receipts from the Purchasing Agent for furnishing wheat on 24 Aug and 1 Sep 1782 {Ref: Maryland State Archives MdHR-6636-42-7}

HEFFINOW, LAWRENCE (Frederick County) received a receipt from the Purchasing Agent for delivering flour on 21 Apr 1781 {Ref: Maryland State Archives MdHR-6636-23-31}

HEFNER (HEFFNER), MICHAEL (Frederick County) received a receipt from the Purchasing Agent for furnishing beef on 5 Jan 1781 {Ref: Maryland State Archives MdHR-6636-23-2}; received a receipt for furnishing beef on 24 Mar 1781 {Ref: Maryland State Archives MdHR-6636-23-4}

HEINZMAN, SAMUEL (Baltimore County) received payment for furnishing beef on 11 Nov 1780 {Ref: Maryland State Archives MdHR-6636-43-38AAAAA}

HEIRS, ABRAHAM (Caroline County) received a receipt from the Purchasing Agent for furnishing wheat on 20 Sep 1781 {Ref: Maryland State Archives MdHR-6636-42-7}

HELLEN, WILLIAM (Annapolis) received payment from the Council of Maryland "for transporting three soldiers from Baltimore" on 14 Nov 1782 {Ref: Archives of Maryland 48:302}

HEMASTY, HENRY (Charles County) received a receipt from the Purchasing Agent for furnishing wheat on 29 Dec 1782 {Ref: Maryland State Archives MdHR-6636-42-21}

HEMSLEY, WILLIAM (Queen Anne's County) was appointed by the Council of Safety to collect all the gold and silver coin that could be procured in the county in compliance with the Resolve of Congress on 27 Jan 1776 {Ref: Archives of Maryland 11:132}; appointed by the Council of Maryland as one of thirty men to be "Agents for Purchasing Provisions" on 30 Mar 1779 {Ref: Archives of Maryland 21:332}; submitted an account for purchasing wheat on 30 May 1779 {Ref: Maryland State Archives MdHR-6636-14-64}; received a certificate from the Purchasing Agent for furnishing corn on 12 Jan 1780 {Ref: Maryland State Archives MdHR-6636-24-31}; received certificates for furnishing wheat on 27 Jan and 7 Apr 1780 {Ref: Maryland State Archives

MdHR-6636-24-46}; received receipts for furnishing wheat on 13 Sep 1780 and 19 Feb 1781 {Ref: Maryland State Archives MdHR-6636-24-49}; he was one of twenty-six people who contacted the Governor and Council of Maryland in 1781 and pledged to support and maintain at their own expense the Barge *Experiment* so it can patrol the bay between Kent Point and Tilghman's Island in order to protect them against the enemy, stating in part, "whereas from the present exhausted state of the public treasury the government cannot immediately give that protection to every individual which is become necessary from the cruel and savage mode in which the war is now carried on against us" {Ref: Archives of Maryland 47:584-585}

HENLY, JOHN (Montgomery County) received a receipt from the Purchasing Agent for furnishing wheat on 27 Oct 1780 {Ref: Maryland State Archives MdHR-6636-24-8}

HENRICKS, EDWARD (Talbot County) received a receipt from the Purchasing Agent for furnishing wheat on 9 Oct 1780 {Ref: Maryland State Archives MdHR-6636-24-47}

HENRY, JAMES (Kent County) submitted an account and receipt for hauling flour on 1 Dec 1781 {Ref: Maryland State Archives MdHR-6636-43-5}

HENRY, JOHN, Esquire (Worcester County) was a colonel who received a receipt from the Purchasing Agent for furnishing corn on 15 Jan 1780 {Ref: Maryland State Archives MdHR-6636-24-52}; his name appeared on "A List of Corn Purchased in Worcester County for the use of the State of Maryland" by the Commissary in July, 1780 {Ref: Archives of Maryland 45:10}; received a receipt for hauling corn on 4 Oct 1780 {Ref: Maryland State Archives MdHR-6636-24-54}; received a receipt for furnishing wheat on 14 May 1781 {Ref: Maryland State Archives MdHR-6636-24-43}; received a loan certificate for £96.14.5 due from the Council of Maryland "agreeable to the Act proposing to the Citizens of this State, Creditors of Congress on Loan Office Certificates, Etc." on 17 May 1783 for services rendered during the war {Ref: Archives of Maryland 48:416}

HENRY, MARTIN (St. Mary's County) received payment from the Purchasing Agent on 23 Dec 1781 for collecting and driving public cattle for 24 days {Ref: Maryland State Archives MdHR-6636-43-23}

HENRY, THOMAS (Harford County) received a receipt from the Purchasing Agent for furnishing wheat on 22 Mar 1780 {Ref: Maryland State Archives MdHR-6636-23-35}

HENRY, WILLIAM (Georgetown, Kent County) was a colonel who served as Commissary by 1779 {Ref: Maryland State Archives MdHR-6636-13-125}; appointed by the Council of Maryland as one of thirty men to be "Agents for Purchasing Provisions" on 30 Mar 1779 {Ref: Archives of Maryland 21:332, 413}; purchased wheat and flour on 17 Apr 1779 {Ref: Maryland State

151

Archives MdHR-6636-13-119}; served as a Purchasing Agent throughout 1779 {Ref: Maryland State Archives MdHR-6636-14-38A}; received a certificate for furnishing wheat on 26 Jan 1780 {Ref: Maryland State Archives MdHR-6636-43-1}

HEPBURN, SAMUEL (Montgomery County) received receipts from the Purchasing Agent for furnishing wheat on 2 Sep and 8 Sep 1780 {Ref: Maryland State Archives MdHR-6636-24-7}

HERD, JOSEPH (Caroline County) received a receipt from the Purchasing Agent for furnishing wheat on 1 Sep 1782 {Ref: Maryland State Archives MdHR-6636-42-7}

HERLEN, JOHN (Frederick County) received a certificate from the Purchasing Agent for furnishing wheat on 24 Jan 1782 {Ref: Maryland State Archives MdHR-6636-42-37}

HERON, PETER (Kent or Queen Anne's County) received payment by order of the Council of Safety for ferriage on 10 Oct 1776 {Ref: Archives of Maryland 12:329}

HERMSLEY (HERMESLEY), HENRY (Charles County) received a receipt from the Purchasing Agent for furnishing wheat on 2 Feb 1782 {Ref: Maryland State Archives MdHR-6636-42-16}; received a receipt for furnishing wheat on 29 Dec 1782 {Ref: Maryland State Archives MdHR-6636-42-21}

HERRINGTON, JOHN (Caroline County) received a receipt from the Purchasing Agent for furnishing wheat on 1 Sep 1782 {Ref: Maryland State Archives MdHR-6636-42-7}

HERRINGTON, WILLIAM (Caroline County) received a receipt from the Purchasing Agent for furnishing wheat on 1 Sep 1782 {Ref: Maryland State Archives MdHR-6636-42-7}

HERSHBERG, BARNET (Frederick County) received a certificate from the Purchasing Agent for furnishing beef on 1 May 1782 {Ref: Maryland State Archives MdHR-6636-42-33}

HEWS, DANIEL (Caroline County) received a receipt from the Purchasing Agent for furnishing wheat on 1 Sep 1782 {Ref: Maryland State Archives MdHR-6636-42-7}

HEWES, JAMES (Talbot County) was one of twenty-six people who contacted the Governor and Council of Maryland in 1781 and pledged to support and maintain at their own expense the Barge *Experiment* so it can patrol the bay between Kent Point and Tilghman's Island in order to protect them against the enemy, stating in part, "whereas from the present exhausted state of the public treasury the government cannot immediately give that protection to every individual which is become necessary from the cruel and savage mode in which the war is now carried on against us" {Ref: Archives of Maryland 47:584-585}

HICK, BALSER (Frederick County) received a certificate for loaning paper money to the state on 31 May 1780 {Ref: Maryland State Archives MdHR-6636-48-39}

HICKMAN, ELIHU (Prince George's County) received a receipt from the Purchasing Agent for furnishing wheat on 3 Sep 1783 {Ref: Maryland State Archives MdHR-6636-50-135}

HICKMAN, PHILIP (Frederick County) submitted an account for furnishing pork on 29 Apr 1781 {Ref: Maryland State Archives MdHR-6636-23-5}

HICKMAN, WILLIAM (Prince George's County) received a receipt from the Purchasing Agent for furnishing wheat on 9 Aug 1783 {Ref: Maryland State Archives MdHR-6636-50-135}

HICKS, GILES III (Caroline County) was a Commissary Agent who submitted an account of wheat received on 27 May 1782 {Ref: Maryland State Archives MdHR-6636-42-7}

HICKS, ISAAC (Baltimore County) received a certificate from the Purchasing Agent for furnishing flour on 29 Jan 1780 {Ref: Maryland State Archives MdHR-6636-23-15}

HICKS, JAMES SR. (Caroline County) received a receipt from the Purchasing Agent for furnishing wheat on 17 Aug 1782 {Ref: Maryland State Archives MdHR-6636-42-7}

HICKS, RICHARD (Talbot County) submitted an account and receipt for purchasing bacon on 23 Apr 1778 {Ref: Maryland State Archives MdHR-6636-12-15}

HICKSON, RICHARD (Talbot County) received payment for purchasing bacon on 30 Jul 1778 {Ref: Maryland State Archives MdHR-6636-12-15}

HIFIELD, JEREMIAH (Charles County) received a receipt from the Purchasing Agent for furnishing wheat on 28 Sep 1782 {Ref: Maryland State Archives MdHR-6636-42-19}

HIGDON, IGNATIUS (Charles County) received a receipt from the Purchasing Agent for furnishing wheat on 10 May 1783 {Ref: Maryland State Archives MdHR-6636-42-22}

HIGDON, THOMAS (Prince George's County) received a receipt from the Purchasing Agent for furnishing wheat on 3 Sep 1783 {Ref: Maryland State Archives MdHR-6636-50-135}

HIGENS, JOHN (Montgomery County) received a receipt from the Purchasing Agent for furnishing wheat on 10 Apr 1781 {Ref: Maryland State Archives MdHR-6636-42-11}

HIGGINS, JOHN (Talbot County) received a receipt from the Purchasing Agent for purchasing bacon on 12 Jun 1778 {Ref: Maryland State Archives MdHR-6636-12-15}

HIGNIT, THOMAS (Baltimore County) submitted an account and received payment for one day's drayage of flour for use of the army on 28 Jan 1780

{Ref: Maryland Historical Society MS.1814, Box 6}

HIGNUT, THOMAS (Caroline County) received a receipt from the Purchasing Agent for furnishing wheat on 5 Aug 1782 {Ref: Maryland State Archives MdHR-6636-42-7}

HILAND, JOHN (Baltimore Town) received payment from the Council of Maryland in Annapolis for riding "Express from Baltimore with Dispatches from Messrs. Lee, Carroll and Hemsley, Delegates in Congress" on 17 Mar 1783 {Ref: Archives of Maryland 48:383}

HILDEBRAND, N. (Frederick County) received a receipt from the Purchasing Agent for delivering flour on 18 Apr 1781 {Ref: Maryland State Archives MdHR-6636-23-31}

HILES, LEONARD (Prince George's County) received a receipt from the Purchasing Agent for furnishing wheat on 26 Aug 1783 {Ref: Maryland State Archives MdHR-6636-50-135}

HILL, CLEMENT (Charles County) received a loan certificate for £178.5.0 due from the Council of Maryland "agreeable to the Act proposing to the Citizens of this State, Creditors of Congress on Loan Office Certificates, Etc." on 16 May 1783 for services rendered during the war {Ref: Archives of Maryland 48:414}

HILL, LEVIN (Worcester County) submitted an account and receipt for furnishing salt on 20 Feb 1782 {Ref: Maryland State Archives MdHR-6636-43-28AAA}

HILL, NATHAN (Caroline County) received a receipt from the Purchasing Agent for furnishing wheat on 22 Aug 1782 {Ref: Maryland State Archives MdHR-6636-42-7}

HILLARY, HENRY (Montgomery County) received a receipt from the Purchasing Agent for furnishing wheat on 1 Oct 1781 {Ref: Maryland State Archives MdHR-6636-24-15}

HILLARY, JOHN (Montgomery County) received a receipt from the Purchasing Agent for furnishing wheat on 29 Jul 1780 {Ref: Maryland State Archives MdHR-6636-24-5}; received a receipt for furnishing wheat on 1 Aug 1780 {Ref: Maryland State Archives MdHR-6636-43-7}; received a receipt for furnishing wheat on 15 Sep 1781 {Ref: Maryland State Archives MdHR-6636-42-18}

HILMAN, JOSHUA (Somerset County) received a receipt from the Purchasing Agent for furnishing beef on 18 Nov 1781 {Ref: Maryland State Archives MdHR-6636-24-44}

HILTON, LOOK? (Prince George's County) received a receipt from the Purchasing Agent for furnishing wheat on 13 Feb 1783 {Ref: Maryland State Archives MdHR-6636-50-135}

HILTON, WILLIAM (Montgomery County) received a receipt from the Purchasing Agent for furnishing wheat on 9 Sep 1781 {Ref: Maryland State

Archives MdHR-6636-24-15}

HINDMAN, ELIZA (Talbot County) was one of twenty-six people who contacted the Governor and Council of Maryland in 1781 and pledged to support and maintain at their own expense the Barge *Experiment* so it can patrol the bay between Kent Point and Tilghman's Island in order to protect them against the enemy, stating in part, "whereas from the present exhausted state of the public treasury the government cannot immediately give that protection to every individual which is become necessary from the cruel and savage mode in which the war is now carried on against us" {Ref: Archives of Maryland 47:584-585}

HINDMAN, JAMES (Talbot County) was a colonel who was appointed one of eighteen Collectors of Clothing by the Council of Maryland under "An Act to Procure Cloathing for the Quota of this State of the American Army" on 27 Nov 1777 {Ref: Archives of Maryland 16:426}; appointed Commissary of Purchases for Talbot County by the Council of Maryland on 8 Jul 1780 {Ref: Archives of Maryland 43:215}; served as Contractor for Horses in Talbot County in 1780 {Ref: Archives of Maryland 43:256}; submitted an account of the purchase of flour and horses on 22 Aug 1780 {Ref: Maryland State Archives MdHR-6636-19-136}; submitted an account for purchasing provisions for the Continental Army on 27 Sep 1780 {Ref: Maryland State Archives MdHR-6636-20-65C}; received receipts for furnishing beef and wheat on 13 Sep 1780 and 16 Feb 1781 {Ref: Maryland State Archives MdHR-6636-24-49}; he was one of twenty-six people who contacted the Governor and Council of Maryland in 1781 and pledged to support and maintain at their own expense the Barge *Experiment* so it can patrol the bay between Kent Point and Tilghman's Island in order to protect them against the enemy, stating in part, "whereas from the present exhausted state of the public treasury the government cannot immediately give that protection to every individual which is become necessary from the cruel and savage mode in which the war is now carried on against us" {Ref: Archives of Maryland 47:584-585}; also see "Joseph Bruff," q.v.

HINDMAN, WILLIAM (Talbot County) received a certificate from the Purchasing Agent for furnishing wheat on 10 Feb 1780 {Ref: Maryland State Archives MdHR-6636-24-46}; received a receipt for furnishing beef and wheat on 5 Oct and 10 Oct 1780 {Ref: Maryland State Archives MdHR-6636-24-49}; he was one of twenty-six people who contacted the Governor and Council of Maryland in 1781 and pledged to support and maintain at their own expense the Barge *Experiment* so it can patrol the bay between Kent Point and Tilghman's Island in order to protect them against the enemy, stating in part, "whereas from the present exhausted state of the public treasury the government cannot immediately give that protection to every individual which is become necessary from the cruel and savage mode in which the war is now carried on against us"

155

{Ref: Archives of Maryland 47:584-585}

HINECK, THOMAS (Charles County) received a receipt from the Purchasing Agent for furnishing wheat on 29 Dec 1782 {Ref: Maryland State Archives MdHR-6636-42-21}

HISSEY, CHARLES (Baltimore County) received payment for hauling flour on 31 Aug 1781 {Ref: Maryland State Archives MdHR-6636-43-38DD}

HITCH, BENJAMIN (Somerset County) received a receipt from the Purchasing Agent for furnishing pork on 17 May 1781 {Ref: Maryland State Archives MdHR-6636-24-43}

HITCH, JOSHUA (Somerset County) received a receipt from the Purchasing Agent for furnishing pork on 14 May 1781 {Ref: Maryland State Archives MdHR-6636-24-43}

HITCH, SALLY (Somerset County) received a receipt from the Purchasing Agent for furnishing beef on 2 Sep 1781 {Ref: Maryland State Archives MdHR-6636-24-44}

HOBBS, JOSEPH (Frederick County) received a certificate from the Purchasing Agent for furnishing wheat on 28 Jun 1782 {Ref: Maryland State Archives MdHR-6636-42-35}; received a receipt for furnishing wheat on 17 Aug 1782 {Ref: Maryland State Archives MdHR-6636-42-7}; received a certificate for furnishing wheat on 25 Jan 1783 {Ref: Maryland State Archives MdHR-6636-42-38}

HOBBS, JOSEPH JR. (Anne Arundel County) received payment by order of the Council of Safety for furnishing a musquet on 7 Aug 1776 {Ref: Archives of Maryland 12:179}

HOBBS, JOSHUA (Caroline County) received a receipt from the Purchasing Agent for furnishing wheat on 17 Aug 1782 {Ref: Maryland State Archives MdHR-6636-42-7}

HOBBS, JOY (Caroline County) received receipts from the Purchasing Agent for furnishing wheat on 5 Aug 1782 {Ref: Maryland State Archives MdHR-6636-42-7}

HOBBS, NICHOLAS (Frederick County) received a certificate from the Purchasing Agent for furnishing wheat on 9 Dec 1782 {Ref: Maryland State Archives MdHR-6636-42-37}

HOBBS, SAMUEL (Prince George's County) received a receipt from the Purchasing Agent for furnishing wheat on 21 May 1782 {Ref: Maryland State Archives MdHR-6636-50-135}

HOBBS, WILLIAM (Caroline County) received a receipt from the Purchasing Agent for furnishing wheat on 5 Aug 1782 {Ref: Maryland State Archives MdHR-6636-42-7}

HOBS, SAMUEL (Montgomery County) received a receipt from the Purchasing Agent for furnishing wheat on 9 Apr 1781 {Ref: Maryland State Archives

MdHR-6636-42-11}

HOCKER, JOHN (Baltimore County) submitted an account and received payment for riding to hire and compress wagons for three days on 27 Jan 1780 {Ref: Maryland Historical Society MS.1814, Box 6}

HOCKER, NICHOLAS (Montgomery County) received a receipt from the Purchasing Agent for furnishing wheat on 10 Aug 1780 {Ref: Maryland State Archives MdHR-6636-24-6}

HOCKER, PHILIP (Montgomery County) received a receipt from the Purchasing Agent for furnishing wheat on 10 Apr 1781 {Ref: Maryland State Archives MdHR-6636-42-11}

HODGKIN (HODGSKIN), THOMAS BROOKS (Anne Arundel County) received payment by order of the Council of Safety for furnishing cartouch paper on 2 Sep 1776 {Ref: Archives of Maryland 12:253}; Council of Maryland ordered on 1 Feb 1781 "that the public records be immediately packed up with care and removed by land to Elkridge Landing, there kept safe by Mr. Thomas Hodgkin and this Board hereby engage to make the said Mr. Hodgkin a reasonable satisfaction for his care of the Records and for the extraordinary expence he must necessarily incur in removing his Family to the place of Deposit" {Ref: Archives of Maryland 45:296, 303}; received payment on 9 May 1782 "for his trouble in superintending the Public Records at Elkridge from March 1781 to March 1782 including Extra house Rent incurred by his removal from Annapolis on the above Service" {Ref: Archives of Maryland 48:160}

HOGGINS, RICHARD (Montgomery County) received a receipt from the Purchasing Agent for furnishing wheat on 10 Apr 1781 {Ref: Maryland State Archives MdHR-6636-42-11}

HOLLAND, ABRAHAM (Montgomery County) received a receipt from the Purchasing Agent for furnishing wheat on 21 Apr 1781 {Ref: Maryland State Archives MdHR-6636-42-11}

HOLLAND, BENJAMIN (Montgomery County) received a receipt from the Purchasing Agent for furnishing wheat on 12 May 1781 {Ref: Maryland State Archives MdHR-6636-42-11}; received a receipt for furnishing wheat on 9 Oct 1781 {Ref: Maryland State Archives MdHR-6636-24-15}

HOLLAND, EPHRAIM (Baltimore County) received payment for furnishing beef on 11 Nov 1780 {Ref: Maryland State Archives MdHR-6636-43-38EEEEE}

HOLLAND, FRANCIS, Esquire (Harford County) was appointed by the Committee of Safety to be one of four men to serve on "a Committee for Examination of Guns and report of their Sufficiency be a Guide for this Committee to receive them by" on 11 Jul 1776 {Ref: Preston's History of Harford County, p. 331}; received a loan certificate for £3145.11.1 due from the Council of Maryland "agreeable to the Act proposing to the Citizens of this State, Creditors of Congress on Loan Office Certificates, Etc." on 18 Oct 1783

for services rendered during the war {Ref: Archives of Maryland 48:471}
HOLLAND, ISAAC (Somerset County) received a receipt from the Purchasing Agent for furnishing pork on 3 Apr 1781 {Ref: Maryland State Archives MdHR-6636-24-43}; received a loan certificate for £37.4.10 due from the Council of Maryland "agreeable to the Act proposing to the Citizens of this State, Creditors of Congress on Loan Office Certificates, Etc." on 2 May 1783 for services rendered during the war {Ref: Archives of Maryland 48:405}
HOLLAND, JOHN (Worcester County) received a receipt from the Purchasing Agent for furnishing corn on 14 Jun 1780 {Ref: Maryland State Archives MdHR-6636-24-53}; his name appeared on "A List of Corn Purchased in Worcester County for the use of the State of Maryland" by the Commissary in July, 1780 {Ref: Archives of Maryland 45:10}; received a receipt for hauling corn on 7 Oct 1780 {Ref: Maryland State Archives MdHR-6636-24-54}
HOLLAND, NATHAN (Montgomery County) received a receipt from the Purchasing Agent for furnishing wheat on 1 Aug 1780 {Ref: Maryland State Archives MdHR-6636-43-7}; received a receipt for furnishing wheat on 9 Aug 1780 {Ref: Maryland State Archives MdHR-6636-24-6}
HOLLAND, NEHEMIAH (Worcester County) received a receipt from the Purchasing Agent for furnishing corn on 4 Mar 1780 {Ref: Maryland State Archives MdHR-6636-24-52}; his name appeared on "A List of Corn Purchased in Worcester County for the use of the State of Maryland" by the Commissary in July, 1780 {Ref: Archives of Maryland 45:9}; submitted an account and receipt for furnishing pork on 7 Oct 1782 {Ref: Maryland State Archives MdHR-6636-43-30I}
HOLLAND, WILLIAM (Montgomery County) received receipts from the Purchasing Agent for furnishing wheat on 21 Apr and 27 Apr 1781 {Ref: Maryland State Archives MdHR-6636-42-11}; received a certificate of employment by the commissary of purchases on 10 Jun 1782 {Ref: Maryland State Archives MdHR-6636-50-91}
HOLLAND, WILLIAM (Worcester County) received a receipt from the Purchasing Agent for furnishing corn on 4 Mar 1780 {Ref: Maryland State Archives MdHR-6636-24-52}; his name appeared on "A List of Corn Purchased in Worcester County for the use of the State of Maryland" by the Commissary in July, 1780 {Ref: Archives of Maryland 45:9}; submitted an account and receipt for furnishing pork on 6 Oct 1782 {Ref: Maryland State Archives MdHR-6636-43-30C}
HOLLIDAY, JAMES (Queen Anne's County) received a receipt from the Purchasing Agent for furnishing steers on 8 May 1778 {Ref: Maryland State Archives MdHR-4587-37}
HOLLINGSWORTH, HENRY (Head of Elk, Cecil County) was a colonel who received a certificate from the Purchasing Agent for furnishing wheat on 18

Mar 1780 {Ref: Maryland State Archives MdHR-6636-24-21A}; received a receipt for furnishing cattle on 13 Nov 1780 {Ref: Maryland State Archives MdHR-6636-21-24}; appointed by the Council of Maryland to be one of five men in Cecil County "to carry the Act to prohibit for a limited time the Exportation of Indian Corn, Etc., by Land" on 22 Dec 1780 {Ref: Archives of Maryland 45:250}; submitted an account of provisions received on 1 Feb 1781 {Ref: Maryland State Archives MdHR-6636-30-40}; his name appeared on 19 Feb 1781 on a "Return [of] Flour forwarded and Delivered at the Head of Elk the Purchase of different Persons for the use of the United States" in the year 1780 {Ref: Archives of Maryland 47:77}; pledged a loan in the amount of £500 to the State of Maryland under the Act for the Emission of Bills of Credit "to defray the expences of the present campaign" in October, 1781 {Ref: Archives of Maryland 47:533}; received a receipt for furnishing flour on 21 Jun 1782 {Ref: Maryland State Archives MdHR-6636-43-42F}; submitted an account for furnishing wheat and flour on 15 Sep 1783 {Ref: Maryland State Archives MdHR-6636-42-9}; also see "John J. Camm" and "Jacob Cunes" and "Thomas Giles" and "John Haddock" and "John Pitt" and "John Stump, Jr." and "Baruch Williams" and "Matthew Wills", q.v.

HOLLINGSWORTH, JESSE (Baltimore Town) received payment by order of the Council of Safety on 26 Jun 1776 "for expences incurred in raising and refitting the vessels sunk at Whetstone Point for the defence of Baltimore Town" (which occurred in March, 1776 for the purpose of preventing any of the British Ships of War from coming up to Baltimore Town) {Ref: Archives of Maryland 11:520}; submitted an account for furnishing coffee on 18 May 1780 {Ref: Maryland State Archives MdHR-6636-18-92}; received payment of £79.10.8 from the Council of Maryland on 30 Jul 1783 "for the like Sum (including Interest) lent the State the 12th May 1780" {Ref: Archives of Maryland 48:441}

HOLLINGSWORTH, SAMUEL (Baltimore County) submitted an account and receipt for furnishing salt on 20 Feb 1782 {Ref: Maryland State Archives MdHR-6636-43-38D}

HOLLINGSWORTH, THOMAS (Baltimore County) submitted an account and receipt for furnishing salt on 20 Feb 1782 {Ref: Maryland State Archives MdHR-6636-43-38D}

HOLLINGSWORTH, ZEBULON (Cecil County) received a certificate from the Purchasing Agent for furnishing wheat on 18 Mar 1780 {Ref: Maryland State Archives MdHR-6636-40-46B}; his name appeared on 19 Feb 1781 on a "Return [of] Flour forwarded and Delivered at the Head of Elk the Purchase of different Persons for the use of the United States" in the year 1780 {Ref: Archives of Maryland 47:77}

HOLLINS, EDWARD (Baltimore County) received a receipt from the Purchasing

159

Agent for furnishing pork and flour on 18 Sep 1782 {Ref: Maryland State Archives MdHR-6636-43-37D}

HOLLIS, CLARK (Caroline County) received receipts from the Purchasing Agent for furnishing wheat on 5 Aug 1782 {Ref: Maryland State Archives MdHR-6636-42-7}

HOLLYDAY, HENRY (Talbot County) received a certificate from the Purchasing Agent for furnishing wheat on 1 Feb 1780 {Ref: Maryland State Archives MdHR-6636-24-46}

HOLLYDAY, LEONARD (Prince George's County) was a doctor who received a loan certificate for £72.1.3 due from the Council of Maryland "agreeable to the Act proposing to the Citizens of this State, Creditors of Congress on Loan Office Certificates, Etc." on 2 Jul 1783 for services rendered during the war {Ref: Archives of Maryland 48:436}

HOLSON, WILLIAM (Caroline County) received a receipt from the Purchasing Agent for furnishing wheat on 24 Aug 1782 {Ref: Maryland State Archives MdHR-6636-42-7}

HONOKER, WILLIAM (Prince George's County) received a receipt from the Purchasing Agent for furnishing wheat on 10 Dec 1782 {Ref: Maryland State Archives MdHR-6636-50-135}

HOOE, ROBERT TOWNSEND (Charles County) was appointed by the Council of Safety to collect all the gold and silver coin that could be procured in the county in compliance with the Resolve of Congress on 27 Jan 1776 {Ref: Archives of Maryland 11:132}

HOOK, JAMES (Talbot County) received a loan certificate for £31.16.4 due from the Council of Maryland "agreeable to the Act proposing to the Citizens of this State, Creditors of Congress on Loan Office Certificates, Etc." on 18 Oct 1783 for services rendered during the war {Ref: Archives of Maryland 48:471}

HOOK, JOHN SNOWDEN (Frederick County) received a receipt from the Purchasing Agent for furnishing wheat on 10 Jun 1782 {Ref: Maryland State Archives MdHR-6636-42-34}

HOOPER, HENRY, see "Richard Bryan," q.v.

HOOPER, ROGER A. (Dorchester County) submitted a bill and receipt for hauling flour on 1 Dec 1778 {Ref: Maryland State Archives MdHR-6636-23-26}

HOOVER, NENTIL (Frederick County) received a certificate from the Purchasing Agent for furnishing wheat on 2 Jan 1782 {Ref: Maryland State Archives MdHR-6636-42-37}

HOPE, THOMAS (Harford County) received payment due him from the Council of Maryland on 14 Oct 1783 for furnishing wheat during the war {Ref: Archives of Maryland 48:464}

HOPEWELL, HUGH (St. Mary's or Calvert County) received payments by order of the Council of Safety for furnishing boatage on 29 Aug 1776 {Ref: Archives of Maryland 12:247}

HOPEWELL, THOMAS (Charles County) received a receipt from the Purchasing Agent for furnishing beef on 14 Nov 1781 and submitted an account for collecting cattle on 20 Nov 1781 {Ref: Maryland State Archives MdHR-6636-23-25}; received a receipt for furnishing wheat on 10 May 1783 {Ref: Maryland State Archives MdHR-6636-42-22}

HOPKINS, GEORGE COLLIER (Somerset County) received a receipt from the Purchasing Agent for furnishing pork on 8 Aug 1780 {Ref: Maryland State Archives MdHR-6636-24-41}

HOPKINS, HAMPTON (Worcester County) submitted an account and receipt for furnishing salt on 27 Dec 1781 {Ref: Maryland State Archives MdHR-6636-43-27}

HOPKINS, JOHN (Harford County) received a receipt from the Purchasing Agent for furnishing flour at Susquehanna Lower Ferry on 27 Jan 1780 {Ref: Maryland State Archives MdHR-6636-23-37}

HORNER, NATHAN (Harford County) received payment for furnishing a gun to the Committee of Safety on 18 Jun 1776 {Ref: Preston's History of Harford County, p. 330}

HORNER, THOMAS (Frederick County) received a receipt from the Purchasing Agent for furnishing pork on 10 Jan 1781 {Ref: Maryland State Archives MdHR-6636-23-2}

HORSEY, ISAAC, see "William Horsey," q.v.

HORSEY, JOHN (Somerset County) received a receipt from the Purchasing Agent for furnishing beef on 1 Nov 1781 {Ref: Maryland State Archives MdHR-6636-24-44}

HORSEY, OUTERBRIDGE (Somerset County) received a receipt from the Purchasing Agent for furnishing pork on 10 Jul 1781 {Ref: Maryland State Archives MdHR-6636-24-43}; received a receipt for furnishing beef on 2 Nov 1781 {Ref: Maryland State Archives MdHR-6636-24-44}; received a loan certificate for £1275 due from the Council of Maryland "agreeable to the Act proposing to the Citizens of this State, Creditors of Congress on Loan Office Certificates, Etc." on 18 Dec 1783 for services rendered during the war {Ref: Archives of Maryland 48:491}

HORSEY, REVILL (Somerset County) received a receipt from the Purchasing Agent for furnishing bacon on 15 Aug 1780 {Ref: Maryland State Archives MdHR-6636-24-41}; received a receipt for furnishing beef on 8 Mar 1781 {Ref: Maryland State Archives MdHR-6636-24-45}; received a receipt for furnishing pork on 1 May 1781 {Ref: Maryland State Archives MdHR-6636-24-43}

HORSEY, SARAH (Somerset County) received a receipt from the Purchasing Agent for furnishing beef on 6 Nov 1781 {Ref: Maryland State Archives

MdHR-6636-24-44}
HORSEY, SMITH (Annamessex Hundred, Somerset County) received a receipt from the Purchasing Agent for furnishing pork on 24 Jun 1781 {Ref: Maryland State Archives MdHR-6636-24-43}; received a receipt for furnishing pork on 3 Jul 1781 {Ref: Maryland State Archives MdHR-6636-24-45}
HORSEY, THOMAS (Monie Hundred, Somerset County) received a receipt from the Purchasing Agent for furnishing pork on 27 Mar 1781 {Ref: Maryland State Archives MdHR-6636-24-45}
HORSEY, WILLIAM (Somerset County) was a Commissary Agent who received a receipt from the Purchasing Agent for payment for supplies for a ship carrying beef to Head of Elk in Cecil County on 3 Jan 1782 {Ref: Maryland State Archives MdHR-6636-43-15}; submitted an account and receipt for processing pork on 21 May 1782 {Ref: Maryland State Archives MdHR-6636-43-22}; William and Isaac Horsey received a loan certificate for £562.3.6 due from the Council of Maryland "agreeable to the Act proposing to the Citizens of this State, Creditors of Congress on Loan Office Certificates, Etc." on 18 Dec 1783 for services rendered during the war {Ref: Archives of Maryland 48:491}
HOSKIN, HUGH (Frederick County) received a receipt from the Purchasing Agent for furnishing mutton on 29 Mar 1781 {Ref: Maryland State Archives MdHR-6636-23-4}
HOSKINS, GEORGE (Prince George's County) received a receipt from the Purchasing Agent for furnishing wheat on 9 Jan 1782 {Ref: Maryland State Archives MdHR-6636-50-142}; received a receipt for furnishing wheat on 12 Feb 1783 {Ref: Maryland State Archives MdHR-6636-50-135}
HOUSE, JOHN (Montgomery County) received a receipt from the Purchasing Agent for furnishing wheat on 14 Aug 1781 {Ref: Maryland State Archives MdHR-6636-24-15}
HOUSER, PHILIP (Montgomery County) received payment by order of the Council of Maryland for the hire of his wagon on 14 Apr 1778 {Ref: Archives of Maryland 21:34}; received a receipt from the Purchasing Agent for furnishing wheat on 7 May 1781 {Ref: Maryland State Archives MdHR-6636-24-18}
HOUSSER, MARTIN (Montgomery County) received a receipt from the Purchasing Agent for furnishing wheat on 18 Jul 1781 {Ref: Maryland State Archives MdHR-6636-24-18}
HOUSTON, ISAAC (Worcester County) received a certificate from the Purchasing Agent for furnishing beef on or about 10 Oct 1781 {Ref: Maryland State Archives MdHR-6636-43-28PPP}; submitted an account and receipt for grazing cattle on 8 Nov 1781 {Ref: Maryland State Archives MdHR-6636-43-27}

HOUSTON, JAMES (Somerset County) received a receipt of wages for hauling beef by ship on 8 Jan 1782 {Ref: Maryland State Archives MdHR-6636-43-15}

HOUSTON, JAMES (Somerset County) was a doctor who received a receipt from the Purchasing Agent for furnishing pork on 14 May 1781 {Ref: Maryland State Archives MdHR-6636-24-43}

HOUSTON, JAMES (Worcester County) received a receipt from the Purchasing Agent for furnishing corn on 18 Feb 1780 {Ref: Maryland State Archives MdHR-6636-24-52}; his name appeared on "A List of Corn Purchased in Worcester County for the use of the State of Maryland" by the Commissary in July, 1780 {Ref: Archives of Maryland 45:10}; submitted an account and receipt for preparing pork and bacon on 20 May 1781 {Ref: Maryland State Archives MdHR-6636-43-27}

HOUSTON, WILLIAM (Kent County) was appointed by the Council of Maryland on 25 Mar 1778 as one of eighteen men to be "Agents for Purchasing Provisions for the Army of the United States Agreeable to an Act of Assembly passed the 23rd Inst." {Ref: Archives of Maryland 16:551}

HOWARD, CHARLES WALLACE, see "John Bullen," q.v.

HOWARD, ELEANOR, Mrs. (Baltimore Town) received payment by order of the Council of Maryland for making shirts on 28 Feb and 27 Mar 1777 {Ref: Archives of Maryland 16:153, 190}

HOWARD, EPHRAIM (Anne Arundel County) was a doctor who was appointed by the Council of Maryland to serve as "Surgeon to Col. Thomas Dorsey's Battalion of Marching Militia" on 3 Sep 1777 {Ref: Archives of Maryland 16:359}; also see "Walter Warfield," q.v.

HOWARD, HARRY, see "Francis Kelsimer," q.v.

HOWARD, JACOB (Montgomery County) received a receipt from the Purchasing Agent for furnishing and shelling corn on 18 Apr 1780 {Ref: Maryland State Archives MdHR-6636-24-2}; received a receipt for furnishing wheat on 12 Dec 1780 {Ref: Maryland State Archives MdHR-6636-24-8}; received a receipt for furnishing wheat on 9 Apr 1781 {Ref: Maryland State Archives MdHR-6636-42-11}

HOWARD, JACOB (Prince George's County) received a receipt from the Purchasing Agent for furnishing wheat on 20 Aug 1783 {Ref: Maryland State Archives MdHR-6636-50-142}

HOWARD, JACOB (Frederick County) received receipts from the Purchasing Agent for furnishing corn on 22 Mar, 6 Apr, 18 Apr, 25 Apr, 4 May and 19 May 1780; received receipts from the Purchasing Agent for furnishing corn and rye on 8 Apr and 4 May 1780; received a receipt for furnishing rye on 14 May 1780; received receipts from the Purchasing Agent for furnishing rye and flour on 9 Jun, 23 Jun and 4 Aug 1780 {Ref: Maryland State Archives MdHR-6636-

24-1}; received certification of weight of wheat on 1 May 1780 {Ref: Maryland State Archives MdHR-6636-24-3}

HOWARD, JAMES (Anne Arundel County) was appointed by the Council of Maryland as one of thirty men to be "Agents for Purchasing Provisions" on 30 Mar 1779 {Ref: Archives of Maryland 21:332}; received payment by order of the Council "to be expended in the purchase of wheat, etc., for the Continental Army" on 18 May 1779 {Ref: Archives of Maryland 21:399}

HOWARD, JOSEPH JR. (Anne Arundel County) received a loan certificate for £21.5.1 due from the Council of Maryland "agreeable to the Act proposing to the Citizens of this State, Creditors of Congress on Loan Office Certificates, Etc." on 20 Oct 1783 for services rendered during the war {Ref: Archives of Maryland 48:471}

HOWARD, MARY (county not stated) received payment of £3.7.7 from the Council of Maryland on 14 Oct 1783 for "one Year's Interest on a [loan] Certificate issued 23 Aug 1782 with interest from 15 Aug 1782" {Ref: Archives of Maryland 48:463}

HOWARD, THOMAS (Baltimore County) received a receipt from the Purchasing Agent for furnishing beef on 1 Apr 1781 {Ref: Maryland State Archives MdHR-6636-52-52}

HOWARD, THOMAS (Anne Arundel County) was a doctor who was appointed by the Council of Maryland to serve as "Assistant Surgeon to the Matross Companies in Annapolis" on 9 May 1777 {Ref: Archives of Maryland 16:381}

HOWARD, THOMAS J. (Charles County) received a receipt from the Purchasing Agent for furnishing wheat on 28 Dec 1782 {Ref: Maryland State Archives MdHR-6636-42-21}

HOWARD, WILLIAM (Montgomery County) received a receipt from the Purchasing Agent for furnishing wheat on 5 May 1781 {Ref: Maryland State Archives MdHR-6636-42-11}

HOWARD, WILLIAM (Baltimore County) received payment by order of the Council of Safety for furnishing a musquet on 29 Jul 1776 {Ref: Archives of Maryland 12:134}

HOWELL, MARY (Charles County) received a receipt from the Purchasing Agent for furnishing wheat on 2 Feb 1782 {Ref: Maryland State Archives MdHR-6636-42-16}

HOWELL, RICHARD (Frederick County) received a receipt from the Purchasing Agent for furnishing wheat on 8 Jun 1782 {Ref: Maryland State Archives MdHR-6636-42-34}

HOWELL, THOMAS (Charles County) received a receipt from the Purchasing Agent for furnishing wheat on 24 Nov 1781 {Ref: Maryland State Archives MdHR-6636-42-15}; received a receipt for furnishing wheat on 27 Apr 1782 {Ref: Maryland State Archives MdHR-6636-42-18}; received a receipt for furnishing wheat on 28 Dec 1782 {Ref: Maryland State Archives MdHR-6636-42-21}

HOWELL, WILLIAM (Kent County) furnished flour and pork for the use of the state as reported to the Council of Maryland on a "Return of Provisions, Etc., received at the Head of Elk" on 22 Jun and 2 Jul 1781 {Ref: Archives of Maryland 47:409}

HOWER, EDWARD (Montgomery County) received a receipt from the Purchasing Agent for furnishing wheat on 14 Aug 1781 {Ref: Maryland State Archives MdHR-6636-24-15}

HOWER, NICHOLAS (Frederick County) received a certificate for money loaned to the state on 3 Jun 1780 {Ref: Maryland State Archives MdHR-6636-48-39}; submitted an account for furnishing meal on 29 May 1781 {Ref: Maryland State Archives MdHR-6636-23-6}

HOY, PAUL (Montgomery County) received a receipt from the Purchasing Agent for furnishing wheat on 24 Nov and 29 Nov 1780 {Ref: Maryland State Archives MdHR-6636-24-8}

HOZIER, RICHARD (Kent County) received payment from the Purchasing Agent for furnishing cattle and pasturage for the public use in September, 1781 {Ref: Maryland State Archives MdHR-6636-43-3}

HUBBERD, JESSE (Caroline County) received a receipt from the Purchasing Agent for furnishing wheat on 5 Aug 1782 {Ref: Maryland State Archives MdHR-6636-42-7}

HUBBERT, SOLOMON (Caroline County) received a receipt from the Purchasing Agent for furnishing wheat on 5 Aug 1782 {Ref: Maryland State Archives MdHR-6636-42-7}

HUBBERT, THOMAS (Caroline County) received a receipt from the Purchasing Agent for furnishing wheat on 5 Aug 1782 {Ref: Maryland State Archives MdHR-6636-42-7}

HUDSON, JAMES (Dorchester County) submitted an account and receipt for caring for cattle on 12 May 1778 {Ref: Maryland State Archives MdHR-6636-23-26}

HUDSON, JONATHAN (Baltimore County) contracted for purchasing flour for the use of the state on 21 Jul 1780 {Ref: Maryland State Archives MdHR-6636-19-37}; delivered barrels of shad and herring to the commissary at Baltimore Town for the use of the State of Maryland in the summer of 1780 {Ref: Archives of Maryland 45:84, 119}

HUDSON, SETH (Worcester County) submitted an account and receipt for driving cattle on 30 Sep 1781 {Ref: Maryland State Archives MdHR-6636-43-27}

HUFF, JACOB (Frederick County) received a receipt from the Purchasing Agent for delivering flour on 29 Dec 1780 {Ref: Maryland State Archives MdHR-6636-23-29}; received a receipt for delivering flour on 4 Jan 1781 {Ref:

Maryland State Archives MdHR-6636-23-30}

HUGGINS, JOHN (Montgomery County) received a receipt from the Purchasing Agent for furnishing wheat on 24 Nov 1780 {Ref: Maryland State Archives MdHR-6636-24-8}

HUGGINS, THOMAS (Cecil County) pledged a loan in the amount of £150 to the State of Maryland under the Act for the Emission of Bills of Credit "to defray the expences of the present campaign" in October, 1781 {Ref: Archives of Maryland 47:533}

HUGGINS, PETER (Frederick County) received receipts from the Purchasing Agent for furnishing corn on 21 Mar, 4 Apr and 4 May 1780 {Ref: Maryland State Archives MdHR-6636-24-1}

HUGHES, ANDREW (Montgomery County) received a receipt from the Purchasing Agent for furnishing wheat on 27 Sep 1780 {Ref: Maryland State Archives MdHR-6636-24-7}; received a receipt for furnishing wheat on 10 Nov 1780 {Ref: Maryland State Archives MdHR-6636-24-8}

HUGHES (HUGHS), DANIEL (Baltimore Town) received by order of the Council of Safety "whatever quantity of powder that may be necessary for the proof of cannon to be supplied this province according to his contract" (in partnership with Samuel Hughes) on 23 May 1776 {Ref: Archives of Maryland 11:438, 439}

HUGHES, GEORGE (Frederick County) received a certificate from the Purchasing Agent for furnishing wheat on 7 Dec 1781 {Ref: Maryland State Archives MdHR-6636-23-28}

HUGHES (HUGHS), JAMES (Frederick County) received a certificate from the Purchasing Agent for furnishing wheat on 23 May 1782 {Ref: Maryland State Archives MdHR-6636-42-34}

HUGHES, LEVY (Frederick County) received a certificate from the Purchasing Agent for furnishing wheat on 17 Sep 1781 {Ref: Maryland State Archives MdHR-6636-23-28}

HUGHES (HUGHS), SAMUEL (Baltimore Town) received by order of the Council of Safety "whatever quantity of powder that may be necessary for the proof of cannon to be supplied this province according to his contract" (in partnership with Daniel Hughes) on 23 May 1776 {Ref: Archives of Maryland 11:438, 439}

HUGHES, SARAH (Montgomery County) received a receipt from the Purchasing Agent for furnishing wheat on 30 Aug 1781 {Ref: Maryland State Archives MdHR-6636-42-11}

HUGHES (HUGHS), THOMAS (Baltimore County) submitted an account and received payment for stowing flour for one and a quarter days on 28 Jan 1780; submitted an account and received payment for measuring wheat for four days on 3 Feb 1780 {Ref: Maryland Historical Society MS.1814, Box 6}

HUGHES (HUGHS), WILLIAM (Baltimore County) submitted an account and received payment for turning out and stowing flour for one and a quarter days on 28 Jan 1780 {Ref: Maryland Historical Society MS.1814, Box 6}

HUGHSTON, WILLIAM (Kent County) received payment from the Purchasing Agent for purchasing beef cattle for the public use in October, 1782 {Ref: Maryland State Archives MdHR-6636-43-3}

HUGHLETT, THOMAS, Esquire (Caroline County) received a certificate from the Purchasing Agent for furnishing wheat on 14 Feb 1780 {Ref: Maryland State Archives MdHR-6636-23-19}; appointed by the Council of Maryland to be one of two men in Caroline County "to carry the Act to prohibit for a limited time the Exportation of Indian Corn, Etc., by Land" on 22 Dec 1780 {Ref: Archives of Maryland 45:251}; received a loan certificate for £42.8.0 due from the Council of Maryland "agreeable to the Act proposing to the Citizens of this State, Creditors of Congress on Loan Office Certificates, Etc." on 10 Dec 1783 for services rendered during the war {Ref: Archives of Maryland 48:487}

HULTZAPPLE, FREDERICK (Frederick County) received a certificate from the Purchasing Agent for furnishing wheat on 15 Jun 1782 {Ref: Maryland State Archives MdHR-6636-42-35}

HUMBERT, JACOB (Frederick County) received a receipt from the Purchasing Agent for delivering flour on 3 Mar 1781 {Ref: Maryland State Archives MdHR-6636-23-30}; received receipts from the Purchasing Agent for delivering flour on 2 May, 12 May, 16 May and 21 May 1781 {Ref: Maryland State Archives MdHR-6636-23-31}

HUMMEL, CHRISTIANA (Frederick County) received a receipt from the Purchasing Agent for delivering flour on 16 May 1781 {Ref: Maryland State Archives MdHR-6636-23-31}

HUMMELL, JOHN, see "Lawrence Brangle," q.v.

HUMPHRIES, PHILLIP (Somerset County) received a receipt from the Purchasing Agent for furnishing a hog on 6 Feb 1782 {Ref: Maryland State Archives MdHR-6636-43-21}

HUNT, JOSEPH (Charles County) received a receipt from the Purchasing Agent for furnishing wheat on 2 Feb 1782 {Ref: Maryland State Archives MdHR-6636-42-16}

HUNT(?), GEORGE (Baltimore County) submitted an account and received payment for fourteen days as an assistant to collect wagons and forward flour to the army on 19 Feb 1780 {Ref: Maryland Historical Society MS.1814, Box 6}

HUNTER, ELIZABETH (county not stated) received payment by order of the Council of Safety "for ferriage of General Lee" on 5 Oct 1776 {Ref: Archives of Maryland 12:321}

HUNTER, NATHAN (Caroline County) received a receipt from the Purchasing Agent for furnishing wheat on 1 Sep 1782 {Ref: Maryland State Archives

MdHR-6636-42-7}

HUNTER, SUSANNA (Prince George's County) received a receipt from the Purchasing Agent for furnishing wheat in 1783 {Ref: Maryland State Archives MdHR-6636-50-135}

HURLOCK, THOMAS (Dorchester County) received a receipt from the Purchasing Agent for furnishing wheat on 1 Nov 1782 {Ref: Maryland State Archives MdHR-6636-42-23}

HURLOCK, WILLIAM (Dorchester County) received a receipt from the Purchasing Agent for furnishing wheat on 1 Nov 1782 {Ref: Maryland State Archives MdHR-6636-42-23}

HURT, JOHN (Kent County) received payment by order of the Council of Safety for the hire of his boat in transporting troops to the Head of Elk (in Cecil County) on 16 Jul 1776 {Ref: Archives of Maryland 12:53}

HUSK (HUSH?), ELIZABETH (Baltimore County) received payment by order of the Council of Maryland for the use of Andrew Grangett (for services not specified) on 17 Sep 1778 {Ref: Archives of Maryland 21:204}

HUSTON, WILLIAM (Kent County) received payment from the Purchasing Agent for collecting cattle for the public use in November, 1782 {Ref: Maryland State Archives MdHR-6636-43-3}

HUTCHINGS, JAMES (Kent County) received a certificate from the Purchasing Agent for furnishing wheat on 10 Mar 1780 {Ref: Maryland State Archives MdHR-6636-23-44}

HUTCHINS, AQUILLA (Caroline County) received a receipt from the Purchasing Agent for furnishing wheat on 5 Aug 1782 {Ref: Maryland State Archives MdHR-6636-42-7}

HUTCHINS, NICHOLAS (Baltimore County) received a certificate from the Purchasing Agent for furnishing flour on 29 Jan 1780 {Ref: Maryland State Archives MdHR-6636-23-15}

HUTCHINSON, GEORGE (Charles County) received a receipt from the Purchasing Agent for furnishing wheat on 12 Nov 1782 {Ref: Maryland State Archives MdHR-6636-42-19}

HUTCHINSON, JOHN (Caroline County) received a receipt from the Purchasing Agent for furnishing wheat on 24 Aug 1782 {Ref: Maryland State Archives MdHR-6636-42-7}

HUTCHINSON, VINCENT (Kent County) received payment from the Purchasing Agent for furnishing cattle for the public use in September, 1781 {Ref: Maryland State Archives MdHR-6636-43-3}

HUTCHISON, BENJAMIN (Kent County) received payment from the Purchasing Agent for furnishing cattle and pasturage for the public use in September, 1781 and for purchasing beef cattle for the public use in October, 1782 {Ref: Maryland State Archives MdHR-6636-43-3}

HUTSON, THOMAS (Caroline County) received a receipt from the Purchasing Agent for furnishing wheat on 20 Sep 1782 {Ref: Maryland State Archives MdHR-6636-42-7}

HUTTON, MARY (Caroline County) received a receipt from the Purchasing Agent for furnishing wheat on 1 Jun 1782 {Ref: Maryland State Archives MdHR-6636-42-7}

HUTTON, WILLIAM (Caroline County) received a receipt from the Purchasing Agent for furnishing wheat on 1 Sep 1782 {Ref: Maryland State Archives MdHR-6636-42-7}

HYDE, THOMAS (Anne Arundel County) received payment from the Maryland Council of Safety for furnishing lead on 8 Mar 1776 {Ref: Archives of Maryland 11:214}; received payment from the Council of Maryland on 19 Dec 1782 "for House Rent" for the use of the state {Ref: Archives of Maryland 48:324}

HYDE, WILLIAM (Anne Arundel County) received payment from the Council of Maryland as "appropriated for the payment of Expresses, Etc., on Account" on 18 Jul 1781 {Ref: Archives of Maryland 45:508}

HYLAND, LAMBERT (Somerset County) received a loan certificate for £23.12.8 due from the Council of Maryland "agreeable to the Act proposing to the Citizens of this State, Creditors of Congress on Loan Office Certificates, Etc." on 19 Dec 1783 for services rendered during the war {Ref: Archives of Maryland 48:493}

HYLAND, STEPHEN (Cecil County) pledged a loan in the amount of £100 to the State of Maryland under the Act for the Emission of Bills of Credit "to defray the expences of the present campaign" in October, 1781 {Ref: Archives of Maryland 47:533}

HYNSON, CHARLES (Kent County) received payment from the Purchasing Agent for furnishing cattle and pasturage for the public use in September, 1781 {Ref: Maryland State Archives MdHR-6636-43-3}

HYNSON, JAMES (Kent County) was appointed by the Council of Maryland to be one of three men in Kent County "to carry the Act to prohibit for a limited time the Exportation of Indian Corn, Etc., by Land" on 22 Dec 1780 {Ref: Archives of Maryland 45:251}; received payment from the Purchasing Agent for furnishing cattle for the public use in September, 1781 {Ref: Maryland State Archives MdHR-6636-43-3}

HYNSON, JOHN CARVIL (Kent County) received payment from the Purchasing Agent for furnishing cattle and pasturage for the public use in September, 1781 {Ref: Maryland State Archives MdHR-6636-43-3}

IJAMS, SARAH (Anne Arundel County) received a loan certificate for £107.17.4 due from the Council of Maryland "agreeable to the Act proposing to the Citizens of this State, Creditors of Congress on Loan Office Certificates, Etc."

on 22 Mar 1783 for services rendered during the war {Ref: Archives of Maryland 48:389}

INCH, PETER (Frederick County) received a certificate from the Purchasing Agent for furnishing wheat on 15 Jun 1781 {Ref: Maryland State Archives MdHR-6636-23-28}

INSLEY, NABOTH (Dorchester County) was given permission by the Council of Maryland on 26 Dec 1782 "to go into the City of New York for the purpose of carrying necessaries to his Brother who is a Prisoner in New York" {Ref: Archives of Maryland 48:327-328}

IRELAND, JONATHAN (Caroline County) received a receipt from the Purchasing Agent for furnishing wheat on 29 May 1782 {Ref: Maryland State Archives MdHR-6636-42-7}

IRELAND, JOHN (Queen Anne's County) submitted an account and receipt for hauling wheat from Nov 1782 to Feb 1783 {Ref: Maryland State Archives MdHR-6636-43-12}

IRELAND, SAMUEL (Caroline County) received a receipt from the Purchasing Agent for furnishing wheat on 5 Aug 1782 {Ref: Maryland State Archives MdHR-6636-42-7}

IRONSHIRE, JOSEPH (Worcester County) received a receipt from the Purchasing Agent for furnishing corn on 14 Jun 1780 {Ref: Maryland State Archives MdHR-6636-24-53}; his name appeared on "A List of Corn Purchased in Worcester County for the use of the State of Maryland" by the Commissary in July, 1780 {Ref: Archives of Maryland 45:10}

IRONSHIRE (IRONSHARE), WILLIAM (Worcester County) received a receipt from the Purchasing Agent for furnishing corn on 1 Jun 1780 {Ref: Maryland State Archives MdHR-6636-24-53}; his name appeared on "A List of Corn Purchased in Worcester County for the use of the State of Maryland" by the Commissary in July, 1780 {Ref: Archives of Maryland 45:9}

IRVING, JOHN (Somerset County) received a receipt from the Purchasing Agent for furnishing bacon on 16 Aug 1780 {Ref: Maryland State Archives MdHR-6636-24-41}

IRVING, LEVIN (Somerset County) received a loan certificate for £276.4.7 due from the Council of Maryland "agreeable to the Act proposing to the Citizens of this State, Creditors of Congress on Loan Office Certificates, Etc." on 19 Dec 1783 for services rendered during the war {Ref: Archives of Maryland 48:494}

ISEMINGER, ADAM (Frederick County) received a certificate from the Purchasing Agent for furnishing wheat on 22 May 1782 {Ref: Maryland State Archives MdHR-6636-42-33}

JAC(?), DAVID (Montgomery County) received a receipt from the Purchasing Agent for furnishing wheat on 1 Aug 1780 {Ref: Maryland State Archives

MdHR-6636-43-7}

JACKSON, BENNET (Montgomery County) received a receipt from the Purchasing Agent for furnishing wheat on 8 Sep 1780 {Ref: Maryland State Archives MdHR-6636-24-13}

JACKSON, HENRY (Somerset County) received certificates from the Purchasing Agent for furnishing and hauling corn on 21 Jan, 9 Feb, 15 Apr, 25 May and 1 Jul 1780 {Ref: Maryland State Archives MdHR-6636-24-41}; appointed Commissary of Purchases for Somerset County by the Council of Maryland on 8 Jul 1780 {Ref: Archives of Maryland 43:215}; submitted an account for salt on 25 Oct 1780 {Ref: Maryland State Archives MdHR-6636-24-40}; submitted an account for providing the Dorchester County militia with fodder and corn in Somerset County on 18 Mar 1781 {Ref: Maryland State Archives MdHR-6636-43-15}; received a receipt for storage and preparation of pork on 6 Feb 1782 {Ref: Maryland State Archives MdHR-6636-43-20}; received a receipt for furnishing fodder and corn on 23 Apr 1782 {Ref: Maryland State Archives MdHR-6636-43-15}; received a loan certificate for £13.4.9 due from the Council of Maryland "agreeable to the Act proposing to the Citizens of this State, Creditors of Congress on Loan Office Certificates, Etc." on 19 Dec 1783 for services rendered during the war {Ref: Archives of Maryland 48:493}; also see "James Bennett," q.v.

JACKSON, JAMES (Montgomery County) received a receipt from the Purchasing Agent for furnishing wheat on 19 Oct 1780 {Ref: Maryland State Archives MdHR-6636-24-8}; received a receipt for furnishing wheat on 12 Mar 1781 {Ref: Maryland State Archives MdHR-6636-24-14}

JACKSON, JAMES (Caroline County) received a receipt from the Purchasing Agent for furnishing wheat on 1 Sep 1782 {Ref: Maryland State Archives MdHR-6636-42-7}

JACKSON, JOHN (Talbot County) submitted an account and receipt for hauling on 18 Jun 1778 {Ref: Maryland State Archives MdHR-6636-12-15}

JACKSON, MARY (Kent County) received payment from the Purchasing Agent for furnishing cattle and pasturage for the public use in September, 1781 {Ref: Maryland State Archives MdHR-6636-43-3}

JACKSON, MRS. (Queen Anne's County) received a receipt from the Purchasing Agent for furnishing beef on 14 Nov 1781 {Ref: Maryland State Archives MdHR-6636-24-34}

JACKSON, PETER (Caroline County) received a receipt from the Purchasing Agent for furnishing wheat on 1 Sep 1782 {Ref: Maryland State Archives MdHR-6636-42-7}

JACKSON, SAMUEL (Somerset County) received a receipt from the Purchasing Agent for furnishing beef on 10 Dec 1781 {Ref: Maryland State Archives MdHR-6636-24-44}

JACKSON, SARAH (Talbot County) received a receipt from the Purchasing Agent for furnishing wheat on 1 Oct 1780 {Ref: Maryland State Archives MdHR-6636-24-47}

JACKSON, WILLIAM (Caroline County) received a receipt from the Purchasing Agent for furnishing wheat on 5 Aug 1782 {Ref: Maryland State Archives MdHR-6636-42-7}

JACOB, JOHN CONRAD (Frederick County) received a certificate from the Purchasing Agent for furnishing wheat on 22 Jun 1782 {Ref: Maryland State Archives MdHR-6636-42-35}

JACOB, WILLIAM (Annapolis) received payments by order of the Council of Safety for tent making on 10 Aug and 26 Aug 1776 {Ref: Archives of Maryland 12:192, 240}; Council of Maryland ordered him "to deliver to Richard Murrow the coarse linen belonging to public heretofore put into his hands to make into tents which he thinks is not proper for that purpose" on 14 Oct 1777 {Ref: Archives of Maryland 16:397}

JACOBS, ELIZABETH (Frederick County) received a certificate from the Purchasing Agent for furnishing wheat on 5 Oct 1781 {Ref: Maryland State Archives MdHR-6636-23-28}

JACQUES, LANCELOT (Frederick County) received payment by order of the Council of Safety for furnishing steel and bar iron on 4 Apr 1776 {Ref: Archives of Maryland 11:308}; received payment for "weights purchased of him for the State" on 15 Oct 1777 {Ref: Archives of Maryland 16:399}

JADWIN, ROBERT (Talbot County) received a receipt from the Purchasing Agent for furnishing beef on 30 Sep 1780 {Ref: Maryland State Archives MdHR-6636-24-49}

JAMES, JOHN (Worcester County) received a receipt from the Purchasing Agent for furnishing corn on 14 Jun 1780 {Ref: Maryland State Archives MdHR-6636-24-53}

JAMES, THOMAS (Charles County) received a receipt from the Purchasing Agent for furnishing wheat on 29 Dec 1782 {Ref: Maryland State Archives MdHR-6636-42-21}

JAMES, THOMAS (Montgomery County) received a receipt from the Purchasing Agent for furnishing wheat on 1 Aug 1780 {Ref: Maryland State Archives MdHR-6636-43-7}

JAMES, WILLIAM (Dorchester County) received a receipt from the Purchasing Agent for furnishing wheat on 1 Nov 1782 {Ref: Maryland State Archives MdHR-6636-42-23}

JAMESON, HENRY (Frederick County) received a certificate from the Purchasing Agent for furnishing wheat on 8 Jun 1782 {Ref: Maryland State Archives MdHR-6636-42-35}

JAMESTON, BENJAMIN (Charles County) received a receipt from the

Purchasing Agent for furnishing wheat on 26 Jun 1782 {Ref: Maryland State Archives MdHR-6636-42-18}

JAQUETT, PETER (Baltimore County) received payment for freight charges on 23 Feb 1782 {Ref: Maryland State Archives MdHR-6636-43-38H}

JENIFER, DANIEL OF ST. THOMAS (Charles County) received a receipt from the Purchasing Agent for furnishing wheat on 27 Oct 1781 {Ref: Maryland State Archives MdHR-6636-42-15}

JENIFER, DANIEL (Charles County) was appointed one of eighteen Collectors of Clothing by the Council of Maryland under "An Act to Procure Cloathing for the Quota of this State of the American Army" on 27 Nov 1777 {Ref: Archives of Maryland 16:426}; appointed by the Council of Maryland on 25 Mar 1778 as one of eighteen men to be "Agents for Purchasing Provisions for the Army of the United States Agreeable to an Act of Assembly passed the 23rd Inst." {Ref: Archives of Maryland 16:551}; appointed Commissary of Purchases for Charles County by the Council of Maryland on 8 Jul 1780 {Ref: Archives of Maryland 43:215}; submitted an account for purchasing barrels for storage of fish on 9 Nov 1780 {Ref: Maryland State Archives MdHR-4589-7}; served as "Surgeon in the Hospital Department" by 18 Dec 1780 at which time he was paid by the Council of Maryland for his services {Ref: Archives of Maryland 45:245}; appointed Purchaser of Clothing in his county by the Council of Maryland on 5 Jun 1781 {Ref: Archives of Maryland 45:462}; submitted an account for purchase and appraisal of horses on 10 Sep 1781 {Ref: Maryland State Archives MdHR-4599-36}; received a receipt for furnishing wheat on 3 Aug 1782 {Ref: Maryland State Archives MdHR-6636-42-18}; received a receipt of repayment of money lent during the war to the state on 22 Dec 1784 {Ref: Maryland State Archives MdHR-6636-50-71}

JENIFER, DANIEL JR. (Charles County) received payment by order of the Council of Safety for his medical attendance at St. George's Camp on 3 Sep 1776 {Ref: Archives of Maryland 12:255}

JENIFER, WALTER (Charles County) was a doctor who received a receipt from the Purchasing Agent for furnishing wheat on 14 Aug 1782 {Ref: Maryland State Archives MdHR-6636-42-18}

JENKINS, ENOCH (Prince George's County) received a loan certificate for £7.3.2 due from the Council of Maryland "agreeable to the Act proposing to the Citizens of this State, Creditors of Congress on Loan Office Certificates, Etc." on 29 Oct 1783 for services rendered during the war {Ref: Archives of Maryland 48:475}

JENKINS, RICHARD (Caroline County) received a receipt from the Purchasing Agent for furnishing wheat on 6 Jun 1782 {Ref: Maryland State Archives MdHR-6636-42-7}

JENKINS, THOMAS (Charles County) was a captain who received a receipt from the Purchasing Agent for furnishing wheat on 28 Dec 1782 {Ref: Maryland State Archives MdHR-6636-42-21}

JENKINS, THOMAS (Charles County) received a receipt from the Purchasing Agent for furnishing wheat on 28 Dec 1782 {Ref: Maryland State Archives MdHR-6636-42-21}

JENKINS, WALTER (Charles County) received a loan certificate for £15.14.2 due from the Council of Maryland "agreeable to the Act proposing to the Citizens of this State, Creditors of Congress on Loan Office Certificates, Etc." on 29 Apr 1783 for services rendered during the war {Ref: Archives of Maryland 48:403}

JENKINS, WILLIAM (Charles County) received a receipt from the Purchasing Agent for furnishing wheat on 2 Feb 1782 {Ref: Maryland State Archives MdHR-6636-42-16}

JENKINS, WILLIAM (Prince George's County) received payment by order of the Council of Safety for the hire of his wagon on 26 Aug 1776 {Ref: Archives of Maryland 12:241}

JENNINGS, JOHN (Montgomery County) received a receipt from the Purchasing Agent for furnishing wheat on 7 Sep 1780 {Ref: Maryland State Archives MdHR-6636-24-7}; received receipts from the Purchasing Agent for furnishing wheat on 4 Nov and 11 Nov 1780 {Ref: Maryland State Archives MdHR-6636-24-8}

JEWELL, CORNELIUS (Harford County) furnished wheat for the use of the state as reported to the Council of Maryland on a "Return of Provisions, Etc., received at the Head of Elk" on 20 Jul 1781 {Ref: Archives of Maryland 47:409}

JOBSON, MICHAEL (Kent County) received payment for furnishing wheat and flour on 7 Dec 1780 {Ref: Maryland State Archives MdHR-6636-23-49}; submitted an account and receipt for furnishing flour barrels and grinding wheat on 30 Mar 1782 {Ref: Maryland State Archives MdHR-6636-43-5}

JOHNS, BENJEMOND (Harford County) received a receipt from the Purchasing Agent for furnishing flour on 4 Jul 1780 {Ref: Maryland State Archives MdHR-6636-23-39}

JOHNS, RICHARD (Talbot County) was appointed by the Council of Maryland as one of thirty men to be "Agents for Purchasing Provisions" on 30 Mar 1779 {Ref: Archives of Maryland 21:332}

JOHNS, THOMAS (Montgomery County) received a receipt from the Purchasing Agent for furnishing wheat on 1 Aug 1780 {Ref: Maryland State Archives MdHR-6636-43-7}; received a receipt for furnishing wheat on 10 Aug 1780 {Ref: Maryland State Archives MdHR-6636-24-6}; delivered dried beef to the Purchasing Agent for the use of the State of Maryland in October, 1780 {Ref: Archives of Maryland 45:149}

JOHNSON, BAKER, see "Samuel Hanson," q.v.

JOHNSON, BARNET (Harford County) received receipts from the Purchasing Agent for furnishing wheat on 17 Jan, 14 Apr and 28 Jun 1780 {Ref: Maryland State Archives MdHR-6636-23-35}

JOHNSON, BENJAMIN (Frederick County) submitted an account of sales at the gun factory on 10 Nov 1778 {Ref: Maryland State Archives MdHR-4570-99}

JOHNSON, BENJAMIN (Montgomery County) received a receipt from the Purchasing Agent for furnishing wheat on 24 Apr 1781 {Ref: Maryland State Archives MdHR-6636-42-11}; received a receipt for furnishing wheat on 11 Aug 1781 {Ref: Maryland State Archives MdHR-6636-24-15}

JOHNSON, CORNELIUS (Caroline County) received a receipt from the Purchasing Agent for furnishing wheat on 5 Aug 1782 {Ref: Maryland State Archives MdHR-6636-42-7}

JOHNSON, E. (county not stated) pledged a loan in the amount of £200 to the State of Maryland under the Act for the Emission of Bills of Credit "to defray the expences of the present campaign" in June, 1781 {Ref: Archives of Maryland 47:326}

JOHNSON, HENRY (Caroline County) received a receipt from the Purchasing Agent for furnishing wheat on 1 Sep 1782 {Ref: Maryland State Archives MdHR-6636-42-7}

JOHNSON, HEZEKIAH (Charles County) received a receipt from the Purchasing Agent for furnishing wheat on 28 Sep 1782 {Ref: Maryland State Archives MdHR-6636-42-19}

JOHNSON, JAMES (Frederick County) received a certificate from the Purchasing Agent for furnishing wheat on 10 Feb 1783 {Ref: Maryland State Archives MdHR-6636-42-38}

JOHNSON, JAMES (Worcester County) submitted an account and receipt for driving cattle and salting beef on 10 Oct 1781 {Ref: Maryland State Archives MdHR-6636-43-27}

JOHNSON, JOHN (Montgomery County) received receipts from the Purchasing Agent for furnishing wheat on 2 Aug and 28 Aug 1780 {Ref: Maryland State Archives MdHR-6636-24-6}; received a receipt for furnishing wheat on 25 Sep 1780 {Ref: Maryland State Archives MdHR-6636-24-7}

JOHNSON, JOHN (Talbot County) received a receipt from the Purchasing Agent for furnishing wheat on 29 Nov 1780 {Ref: Maryland State Archives MdHR-6636-24-49}

JOHNSON, JOHN (Head of Elk, Cecil County) submitted his quartermaster's account of provisions received on 15 Nov 1780 {Ref: Maryland State Archives MdHR-6636-21-24}

JOHNSON, JOHN (Frederick County) received a certificate from the Purchasing Agent for furnishing wheat on 17 Sep 1781 {Ref: Maryland State Archives

MdHR-6636-23-28}; received a certificate for furnishing wheat on 30 May 1782 {Ref: Maryland State Archives MdHR-6636-42-34}; received a certificate for furnishing wheat on 31 May 1782 {Ref: Maryland State Archives MdHR-6636-42-35}

JOHNSON, JOHN (county not stated) received a loan certificate for £21.1.6 due from the Council of Maryland "agreeable to the Act proposing to the Citizens of this State, Creditors of Congress on Loan Office Certificates, Etc." on 17 Jul 1783 for services rendered during the war {Ref: Archives of Maryland 48:440}

JOHNSON, JOSEPH (Frederick County) received a certificate from the Purchasing Agent for furnishing wheat on 8 Oct 1781 {Ref: Maryland State Archives MdHR-6636-23-28}

JOHNSON, JOSIAH (Kent County) received certificates from the Purchasing Agent for furnishing flour, wheat and corn on 15 Jan, 20 Jan, 26 Jan, 29 Jan, 31 Jan, 1 Feb, 20 Feb and 28 Feb 1780 {Ref: Maryland State Archives MdHR-6636-43-1}

JOHNSON, PETER (Frederick County) received a certificate from the Purchasing Agent for furnishing wheat on 28 Oct 1782 {Ref: Maryland State Archives MdHR-6636-42-37}

JOHNSON, ROBERT (county not stated) received payment from the Council of Maryland as "appropriated for the payment of Expresses due him per Account passed by the Auditor General" on 19 Jul 1781 {Ref: Archives of Maryland 45:509}

JOHNSON (JOHNSTON), ROBERT (Baltimore County) received payment by order of the Council of Safety on 10 Oct 1776 "for sinkage of vessels at *Otter* alarm" at Whetstone Point in March, 1776 for the purpose of preventing any of the British Ships of War from coming up to Baltimore Town {Ref: Archives of Maryland 12:330, 333}

JOHNSON, SAMUEL (Montgomery County) received a receipt from the Purchasing Agent for furnishing wheat on 7 Apr 1781 {Ref: Maryland State Archives MdHR-6636-42-11}; received a receipt for furnishing wheat on 11 Aug 1781 {Ref: Maryland State Archives MdHR-6636-24-15}

JOHNSON, SIMON (Worcester County) received a receipt from the Purchasing Agent for hauling and storing pork on 13 Oct 1780 {Ref: Maryland State Archives MdHR-6636-24-54}

JOHNSON, THOMAS (Anne Arundel County) pledged a loan in the amount of £800 to the State of Maryland under the Act for the Emission of Bills of Credit "to defray the expences of the present campaign" in June, 1781 {Ref: Archives of Maryland 47:327}

JOHNSON, THOMAS (Harford County) received a receipt from the Purchasing Agent for furnishing wheat and corn on 8 Mar 1780 {Ref: Maryland State Archives MdHR-6636-23-35}

JOHNSON, THOMAS (Clifts, Calvert County) received payment by order of the Council of Maryland on 5 Aug 1777 for erecting a salt works {Ref: Archives of Maryland 16:326}

JOHNSON, THOMAS JR. (Anne Arundel County) was appointed by the Council of Maryland to be one of six "Signers of the Bills emitted in Virtue of the Act to enable the Treasurer of the Western Shore to draw and sell Bills of Exchange and for an Emission of Bills of Credit if necessary" on 8 Sep 1780 {Ref: Archives of Maryland 43:281}

JOHNSON, WILLIAM (Calvert County) received payment for driving cattle on 19 Jan 1782 {Ref: Maryland State Archives MdHR-6636-50-37}

JOHNSON, WILLIAM (Caroline County) received a receipt from the Purchasing Agent for furnishing wheat on 5 Aug 1782 {Ref: Maryland State Archives MdHR-6636-42-7}

JOHNSON, WILLIAM (Somerset County) received a receipt from the Purchasing Agent for furnishing pork on 20 Apr 1782 {Ref: Maryland State Archives MdHR-6636-43-21}

JOHNSON, WILLIAM (county not stated) received payment by order of the Council of Safety for making tents on 22 Jul 1776; received materials ("15 pieces cruder") to be made into tents on 25 Jul 1776; received payment for tent making on 21 Aug 1776 {Ref: Archives of Maryland 12:88, 113, 227}

JOHNSTON, DIANNA (Worcester County) received a receipt from the Purchasing Agent for furnishing flour and corn on 16 Mar 1780 {Ref: Maryland State Archives MdHR-6636-24-52}

JOHNSTON, JAMES (Caroline County) received receipts from the Purchasing Agent for furnishing wheat on 30 May and 22 Aug 1782 {Ref: Maryland State Archives MdHR-6636-42-7}

JONES, BENJAMIN (Baltimore Town) submitted an account and receipt for furnishing labor on 30 Oct 1779 {Ref: Maryland State Archives MdHR-19970-3-8}; also see "Benjemond Johns," q.v.

JONES, CHARLES (Montgomery County) received a receipt from the Purchasing Agent for furnishing wheat on 9 Jun 1781 {Ref: Maryland State Archives MdHR-6636-24-14}; received a receipt for furnishing wheat on 21 Feb 1782 {Ref: Maryland State Archives MdHR-6636-43-7}; received a receipt for furnishing wheat on 2 Mar 1782 {Ref: Maryland State Archives MdHR-6636-43-8};2

JONES, DANIEL (Somerset County) received a receipt from the Purchasing Agent for furnishing pork on 20 Sep 1780 {Ref: Maryland State Archives MdHR-6636-24-41}

JONES, EDWARD (Prince George's County) received a receipt from the Purchasing Agent for furnishing wheat in 1782 {Ref: Maryland State Archives MdHR-6636-50-135}; received a receipt for furnishing wheat on 9 Aug 1783

{Ref: Maryland State Archives MdHR-6636-50-135}

JONES, ELIZABETH (Somerset County) received a loan certificate for £38.5.0 due from the Council of Maryland "agreeable to the Act proposing to the Citizens of this State, Creditors of Congress on Loan Office Certificates, Etc." on 19 Dec 1783 for services rendered during the war {Ref: Archives of Maryland 48:493}

JONES, EVAN (Montgomery County) received a receipt from the Purchasing Agent for furnishing wheat on 31 Aug 1780 {Ref: Maryland State Archives MdHR-6636-24-6}

JONES, GEORGE (Frederick County) received a receipt from the Purchasing Agent for furnishing corn on 23 Jan 1781 {Ref: Maryland State Archives MdHR-6636-23-2}; received a receipt for furnishing corn meal on 28 Feb 1781 {Ref: Maryland State Archives MdHR-6636-23-3}; received a receipt for furnishing corn meal on 21 Mar 1781 {Ref: Maryland State Archives MdHR-6636-23-4}; received a receipt for furnishing meal on 5 Apr 1781 {Ref: Maryland State Archives MdHR-6636-23-5}

JONES, GRIFFIN (Kent County) received payment from the Purchasing Agent for furnishing cattle and pasturage for the public use in September, 1781 {Ref: Maryland State Archives MdHR-6636-43-3}

JONES, HENRY (Caroline County) received a receipt from the Purchasing Agent for wheat on 21 Aug 1782 {Ref: Maryland State Archives MdHR-6636-42-7}

JONES, HUGH (Prince George's County) received receipts from the Purchasing Agent for furnishing wheat on 2 Jan and 9 Aug 1783 {Ref: Maryland State Archives MdHR-6636-50-135}; received receipts from the Purchasing Agent for furnishing wheat on 12 Feb, 24 Feb and 1 May 1783 {Ref: Maryland State Archives MdHR-6636-50-142}

JONES, JAMES (Calvert County) received payment for driving cattle on 21 Jan 1782 {Ref: Maryland State Archives MdHR-6636-50-37}

JONES, JAMES (Kent County) received payments for furnishing cattle on 20 Oct 1780 and for furnishing wheat on 24 Oct 1780 {Ref: Maryland State Archives MdHR-6636-23-49}

JONES, JESSE (Worcester County) submitted an account and receipt for furnishing salt on 11 Feb 1782 {Ref: Maryland State Archives MdHR-6636-43-28BBB}

JONES, JOHN (Kent County) received a certificate from the Purchasing Agent for hauling flour on 10 Jun 1780 {Ref: Maryland State Archives MdHR-6636-23-42}

JONES, JOHN (Somerset County) received a receipt from the Purchasing Agent for furnishing pork on 3 Aug 1780 {Ref: Maryland State Archives MdHR-6636-24-41}; received a loan certificate for £27.7.5 due from the Council of Maryland "agreeable to the Act proposing to the Citizens of this State,

Creditors of Congress on Loan Office Certificates, Etc." on 19 Dec 1783 for services rendered during the war {Ref: Archives of Maryland 48:493}

JONES, JOHN, farmer (Somerset County) received a certificate from the Purchasing Agent for provisions and fodder used by the Dorchester County militia in Somerset County on 7 Mar 1781 {Ref: Maryland State Archives MdHR-6636-43-15}

JONES, JOHN (Montgomery County) received a receipt from the Purchasing Agent for furnishing wheat on 12 Sep 1780 {Ref: Maryland State Archives MdHR-6636-24-7}; received a receipt for furnishing wheat on 11 Aug 1781 {Ref: Maryland State Archives MdHR-6636-24-15}

JONES, JOHN (Worcester County) appeared on "A List of Corn Purchased in Worcester County for the use of the State of Maryland" by the Commissary in July, 1780 {Ref: Archives of Maryland 45:10}; submitted an account and receipt for furnishing pork barrels on 5 Apr 1782 {Ref: Maryland State Archives MdHR-6636-43-28II}

JONES, JOHN JR. (Worcester County) received a receipt from the Purchasing Agent for furnishing beef on 14 Oct 1780 {Ref: Maryland State Archives MdHR-6636-24-54}

JONES, JOHN N. (Frederick County) received a certificate from the Purchasing Agent for furnishing wheat on 18 Sep 1781 {Ref: Maryland State Archives MdHR-6636-23-28}

JONES, JOHN RAYMOND (Frederick County) received a certificate from the Purchasing Agent for furnishing corn on 26 Jan 1781 {Ref: Maryland State Archives MdHR-6636-23-2}

JONES, JONATHAN (Anne Arundel County) received a loan certificate for £129.1.0 due from the Council of Maryland "agreeable to the Act proposing to the Citizens of this State, Creditors of Congress on Loan Office Certificates, Etc." on 4 Oct 1783 for services rendered during the war {Ref: Archives of Maryland 48:459}

JONES, P. (Montgomery County) received a receipt from the Purchasing Agent for shelling corn on 1 Jul 1780 {Ref: Maryland State Archives MdHR-6636-24-2}

JONES, PETER (Frederick County) received a receipt from the Purchasing Agent for furnishing corn meal on 1 Feb 1781 {Ref: Maryland State Archives MdHR-6636-23-3}; received a receipt for furnishing corn meal on 27 Mar 1781 {Ref: Maryland State Archives MdHR-6636-23-4}; received a receipt for furnishing meal on 3 Apr 1781 {Ref: Maryland State Archives MdHR-6636-23-5}

JONES, ROBERT (Baltimore County) received payment for hauling barrels on 19 Feb 1782 {Ref: Maryland State Archives MdHR-6636-43-38L}

JONES, SAMUEL (Montgomery County) received a certificate of employment by the commissary of purchases on 21 May 1782 {Ref: Maryland State Archives MdHR-6636-50-91}

JONES, THOMAS (Annamessex Hundred, Somerset County) was appointed by the Council of Maryland to purchase provisions for the public on or about 26 Jun 1777 {Ref: Archives of Maryland 16:300}; received a certificate and receipt for furnishing bacon on 7 Sep 1780 {Ref: Maryland State Archives MdHR-6636-24-41}; received a receipt for furnishing pork on 3 Jul 1781 {Ref: Maryland State Archives MdHR-6636-24-45}

JONES, THOMAS (Calvert County) received payment by order of the Council of Maryland for his use as Contractor for Horses in Calvert County on 26 Aug 1780 {Ref: Archives of Maryland 43:265}

JONES, WILLIAM (Harford County) was appointed by the Committee of Safety "to ride in Harford Upper and Lower and Speustia Lower Hundreds and purchase guns and blankets agreeable to the request of the [Maryland] Council of Safety" on 19 Aug 1776 and submitted his account on 2 Sep 1776 {Ref: Preston's History of Harford County, pp. 333-334, 336}

JONES, WILLIAM (Dorchester County) received a receipt from the Purchasing Agent for furnishing wheat on 1 Oct 1782 {Ref: Maryland State Archives MdHR-6636-42-23}

JONES, WILLIAM (Somerset County) received certificates from the Purchasing Agent for furnishing corn on 14 Jan and 15 Jan 1780 {Ref: Maryland State Archives MdHR-6636-24-38}

JONES, WILLIAM SR. (Charles County) received a receipt from the Purchasing Agent for furnishing wheat on 7 Sep 1782 {Ref: Maryland State Archives MdHR-6636-42-18}

JORDAN (JORDON), JAMES (Montgomery County) received a receipt from the Purchasing Agent for furnishing wheat on 1 Aug 1780 {Ref: Maryland State Archives MdHR-6636-43-7}; received a receipt for furnishing wheat on 11 Jun 1781 {Ref: Maryland State Archives MdHR-6636-42-11}

JORDAN, JOSHUA (Montgomery County) received a certificate from the Purchasing Agent for furnishing wheat on 29 Jul 1780 {Ref: Maryland State Archives MdHR-6636-24-5}

JOSEPH, JOSEPH (Montgomery County) received a receipt from the Purchasing Agent for furnishing wheat on 25 May 1781 {Ref: Maryland State Archives MdHR-6636-42-11}

JOSEPH & ANDREW (two Frenchmen) received payment by order of the Council of Maryland for furnishing a musquet, a broken musquet and three cutlasses on 13 Aug 1777 {Ref: Archives of Maryland 16:332}

JOWL, JOSEPH (Baltimore County) received payment for furnishing beef on 11 Nov 1780 {Ref: Maryland State Archives MdHR-6636-43-38FFFFF}

JOY, IGNATIUS (St. Mary's County) received payment from the Purchasing Agent on 29 Dec 1781 for collecting and driving public cattle for 16 days {Ref: Maryland State Archives MdHR-6636-43-23}

JOYE, JOSEPH (Charles County) received a receipt from the Purchasing Agent for furnishing wheat on 29 Dec 1782 {Ref: Maryland State Archives MdHR-6636-42-21}

JUDAH, WILLIAM (Baltimore County) purchased provisions and submitted a settlement of his account on 28 Aug 1779 {Ref: Maryland State Archives MdHR-4593-53}; also see "Samuel Sadler," q.v.

JUMP, ANDREW (Caroline County) received receipts from the Purchasing Agent for furnishing wheat on 1 Sep and 20 Sep 1782 {Ref: Maryland State Archives MdHR-6636-42-7}

JUMP, JACOB (Caroline County) received receipts from the Purchasing Agent for furnishing wheat on 1 Sep and 20 Sep 1782 {Ref: Maryland State Archives MdHR-6636-42-7}

JUMP, SOLOMON (Caroline County) received a receipt from the Purchasing Agent for furnishing wheat on 20 Sep 1782 {Ref: Maryland State Archives MdHR-6636-42-7}

JUMP, WILLIAM (Caroline County) received a receipt from the Purchasing Agent for furnishing wheat on 1 Sep 1782 {Ref: Maryland State Archives MdHR-6636-42-7}

KAFMAN, JOHN (Frederick County) received a receipt from the Purchasing Agent for caring for cattle on 22 Nov 1781 {Ref: Maryland State Archives MdHR-6636-23-31}

KEARSLEY, JOHN (Frederick County) received a receipt from the Purchasing Agent for furnishing corn meal on 1 Mar 1781 {Ref: Maryland State Archives MdHR-6636-23-4}

KECKETHORN, GEORGE (Frederick County) received a certificate from the Purchasing Agent for furnishing wheat on 4 Feb 1783 {Ref: Maryland State Archives MdHR-6636-42-38}

KEECH, GEORGE (Charles County) received a receipt from the Purchasing Agent for furnishing wheat on 26 Jun 1782 {Ref: Maryland State Archives MdHR-6636-42-18}

KEEFAUVER, PHILIP (Frederick County) received a certificate from the Purchasing Agent for furnishing wheat on 28 May 1782 {Ref: Maryland State Archives MdHR-6636-42-33}

KEENE, CHARLES (Caroline County) received a receipt from the Purchasing Agent for furnishing corn on 28 Feb 1780 {Ref: Maryland State Archives MdHR-6636-23-19}; received a certificate for employing his cart and driver on 24 Jun 1780 {Ref: Maryland State Archives MdHR-6636-23-20}

KEENE, EDMOND (Caroline County) received a certificate of employment by the commissary for transporting public stores on 10 May 1780 {Ref: Maryland State Archives MdHR-6636-23-20}

KEENE, JOHN (Queen Anne's County) received a certificate from the Purchasing

Agent for furnishing bacon on 10 Apr 1781 {Ref: Maryland State Archives MdHR-6636-24-34}

KEENE, JOHN (Caroline County) received a receipt from the Purchasing Agent for furnishing wheat on 17 Aug 1782 {Ref: Maryland State Archives MdHR-6636-42-7}

KEENE, MARCELLUS (Caroline County) received a receipt from the Purchasing Agent for furnishing corn on 9 Feb 1780 {Ref: Maryland State Archives MdHR-6636-23-19}

KEENE, POLLARD (Caroline County) received a receipt from the Purchasing Agent for furnishing wheat on 20 Sep 1782 {Ref: Maryland State Archives MdHR-6636-42-7}

KEENE, RICHARD (Caroline County) received receipts from the Purchasing Agent for furnishing corn, wheat and flour on 10 Feb, 12 Feb, 22 Feb and 24 Feb 1780 {Ref: Maryland State Archives MdHR-6636-23-19}; received a certificate for furnishing corn on 18 Mar 1780 {Ref: Maryland State Archives MdHR-6636-23-20}

KEENE, THOMAS B. (Caroline County) received receipts from the Purchasing Agent for furnishing wheat on 1 Sep and 20 Sep 1782 {Ref: Maryland State Archives MdHR-6636-42-7}

KEENE, WILLIAM (Caroline County) received a receipt from the Purchasing Agent for furnishing corn on 7 Feb 1780 {Ref: Maryland State Archives MdHR-6636-23-19}

KEENE, YOUNG (Caroline County) received a receipt from the Purchasing Agent for furnishing wheat on 1 Sep 1782 {Ref: Maryland State Archives MdHR-6636-42-7}

KEENER, MELCHER (Baltimore Town) received payment by order of the Council of Safety on 10 Oct 1776 "for the detention of two vessels sunk at *Otter* alarm" at Whetstone Point in March, 1776 for the purpose of preventing any of the British Ships of War from coming up to Baltimore Town {Ref: Archives of Maryland 12:330, 333}

KEENER, PETER (Baltimore Town) was a gunsmith who contracted to make arms for the Council of Maryland on or about 17 Sep 1777 and was still manufacturing arms on 12 Jan 1781 {Ref: Archives of Maryland 16:377, 47:14}

KEENER, SAMUEL (Baltimore Town) was a gunsmith who contracted to repair guns for the Council of Safety on or about 7 Feb 1776 {Ref: Archives of Maryland 11:155}

KEEPORTS, GEORGE P. (Baltimore Town) received payment by order of the Council of Maryland via Capt. Alexander Truman "to be expended in the making of soldiers cloathing" on 8 Apr 1778 {Ref: Archives of Maryland 21:16}; he was a captain who purchased provisions and submitted an account for stockings and hats on 26 Oct 1779 {Ref: Maryland State Archives MdHR-4586-113/114}; ordered by the Council "to collect and receive into his charge all the arms and accoutrements in Baltimore County belonging to this State that they may be ready for service occasionally and that the officers of the militia assist him in the said collection" on 12 Jun 1779; on the same day he was "appointed Armourer at Baltimore, where the principal part of the arms now are" {Ref: Archives of Maryland 21:452}; received a certificate for furnishing wagons on 8 Jan 1780 {Ref: Maryland State Archives MdHR-4600-19}; received payment for hauling provisions on 1 Jun 1782 {Ref: Maryland State Archives MdHR-19970-3-28}; received a receipt for flour on 30 Jul 1782 {Ref: Maryland State Archives MdHR-19970-42-3}; also see "Benjamin Griffith," q.v.

KEEPORTS (KEMPOTS?), JACOB (Baltimore Town) received payment by order of the Council of Safety "for house rent for boarding soldiers" on 23 Aug 1776 {Ref: Archives of Maryland 12:233}

KEESE, FRANCES (Dorchester County) received a receipt from the Purchasing Agent for furnishing wheat on 25 Mar 1783 {Ref: Maryland State Archives MdHR-6636-42-24}

KEITLY (KEITHLY), JAMES (Talbot County) was one of twenty-six people who contacted the Governor and Council of Maryland in 1781 and pledged to support and maintain at their own expense the Barge *Experiment* so it can patrol the bay between Kent Point and Tilghman's Island in order to protect them against the enemy, stating in part, "whereas from the present exhausted state of the public treasury the government cannot immediately give that protection to every individual which is become necessary from the cruel and savage mode in which the war is now carried on against us" {Ref: Archives of Maryland 47:584-585}

KELLAR, ANDREW (Frederick County) received a certificate from the Purchasing Agent for furnishing wheat on 9 Aug 1782 {Ref: Maryland State Archives MdHR-6636-42-37}

KELLER, ADAM (Frederick County) received a receipt from the Purchasing Agent for delivering flour on 28 Apr 1781 {Ref: Maryland State Archives MdHR-6636-23-31}

KELLER (KELLAR), JACOB (Frederick County) received a receipt from the Purchasing Agent for furnishing pork on 21 Mar 1781 {Ref: Maryland State Archives MdHR-6636-23-4}; submitted an account for furnishing mutton on 29 May 1781 {Ref: Maryland State Archives MdHR-6636-23-6}; received a certificate for furnishing wheat on 28 May 1782 {Ref: Maryland State Archives MdHR-6636-42-33}; received a certificate for furnishing wheat on 10 Jun 1782 {Ref: Maryland State Archives MdHR-6636-42-34}

KELLY, BEN (Caroline County) received a receipt from the Purchasing Agent for furnishing wheat on 5 Aug 1782 {Ref: Maryland State Archives MdHR-6636-42-7}

KELLY, EDWARD OR RICHARD (Baltimore County) whose first name is unclear in the record (signature smudged), submitted an account and received payment for stowing flour for two days on 24 Mar 1780 {Ref: Maryland Historical Society MS.1814, Box 6}

KELLY, JAMES (Prince George's County) received a receipt from the Purchasing Agent for furnishing wheat on 31 Mar 1783 {Ref: Maryland State Archives MdHR-6636-50-135}

KELLY, JOSEPH (Caroline County) received a receipt from the Purchasing Agent for furnishing wheat on 5 Aug 1782 {Ref: Maryland State Archives MdHR-6636-42-7}

KELLY, THOMAS (Montgomery County) received a certificate from the Purchasing Agent for services rendered on 24 Oct 1781 {Ref: Maryland State Archives MdHR-6636-50-91}

KELSIMER (KILSIMER), FRANCIS (Baltimore County) submitted an account and received payment for driving Harry Howard's wagon for five days and stowing flour for two days on 1 Feb 1780 {Ref: Maryland Historical Society MS.1814, Box 6}; received payment from the Council of Maryland as "appropriated for the payment of Expresses" on 24 Jul 1781 {Ref: Archives of Maryland 45:518}

KEMP, CHRISTIAN (Frederick County) received a certificate from the Purchasing Agent for furnishing flour on 29 May 1782 {Ref: Maryland State Archives MdHR-6636-42-34}

KEMP (CAMP), LODOWICK OR LUDWICK (Frederick County) received payments by order of the Council of Maryland for furnishing pasturage, hay and wood on 25 Mar 1778 and services rendered (not specified) on 22 Apr 1779 {Ref: Archives of Maryland 16:550-551, 21:361}; received a receipt from the Purchasing Agent for hauling flour on 10 Aug 1783 {Ref: Maryland State Archives MdHR-6636-42-28}

KEMP, PETER (Frederick County) received a receipt from the Purchasing Agent for delivering flour on 21 Apr 1781 {Ref: Maryland State Archives MdHR-6636-23-31}; received a certificate for furnishing wheat on 9 Oct 1781 {Ref: Maryland State Archives MdHR-6636-42-32}

KEMPOTS, JACOB, see "Jacob Keeports," q.v.

KENARD, JOHN (Caroline County) received a receipt from the Purchasing Agent for furnishing corn on 28 Feb 1780 {Ref: Maryland State Archives MdHR-6636-23-19}

KENDALL, WILLIAM (Kent County) received payment from the Purchasing Agent for furnishing cattle and pasturage for the public use in September, 1781 {Ref: Maryland State Archives MdHR-6636-43-3}

KENICKOUSER (KENINGHOUSER), GEORGE (Frederick County) received a certificate from the Purchasing Agent for furnishing wheat on 29 Jun 1782 {Ref: Maryland State Archives MdHR-6636-42-36}

KENNARD, D. (Cecil County) received a receipt from the Purchasing Agent for furnishing flour on 2 Dec 1782 {Ref: Maryland State Archives MdHR-6636-42-9}

KENNARD, JOHN (Kent County) received payment from the Purchasing Agent for furnishing cattle and pasturage for the public use in September, 1781 {Ref: Maryland State Archives MdHR-6636-43-3}

KENNEDY, JOHN (Frederick County) received receipts from the Purchasing Agent for furnishing corn on 7 Jan and 18 Jan 1781 {Ref: Maryland State Archives MdHR-6636-23-2}

KENNEDY, WILLIAM (Kent County) received a certificate from the Purchasing Agent for furnishing wheat on 14 Jan 1780 {Ref: Maryland State Archives MdHR-6636-23-41}

KENNER, NATHANIEL JR. (Baltimore County) delivered barrels of shad and herring to the commissary at Baltimore Town for the use of the State of Maryland in the summer of 1780 {Ref: Archives of Maryland 45:84, 45:119}

KENNETT, PRESGRAVE (Worcester County) submitted an account and receipt for furnishing salt on 16 Mar 1782 {Ref: Maryland State Archives MdHR-6636-43-28MM}

KENNY, JAMES (Frederick County) received a receipt from the Purchasing Agent for furnishing whiskey on 10 Feb 1781 {Ref: Maryland State Archives MdHR-6636-23-3}

KENT, JACOB LAMBETH (Queen Anne's County) received a certificate from the Purchasing Agent for furnishing wheat on 18 Jan 1780 {Ref: Maryland State Archives MdHR-6636-24-30}

KENT, JAMES (Queen Anne's County) pledged a loan in the amount of £200 to the State of Maryland under the Act for the Emission of Bills of Credit "to defray the expences of the present campaign" in June, 1781 {Ref: Archives of Maryland 47:327}

KERR, DAVID (Anne Arundel County) received payment for supplying vinegar for the hospital on 29 Jul 1776 {Ref: Archives of Maryland 12:134}; received payment from the Council of Maryland "for the transportation of five Continental Soldiers from Baltimore" on 30 Jan 1783 {Ref: Archives of Maryland 48:351}

KERR, MR. (Queen Anne's County) received a receipt from the Purchasing Agent for furnishing beef on 1 Dec 1779 {Ref: Maryland State Archives MdHR-6636-17-73}

KERR, NEVIN (Harford County) received payment for furnishing a musquet with bayonet and steel rammer to the Committee of Safety on 2 Sep 1776 {Ref:

Preston's History of Harford County, p. 335}

KERRICK, EDWARD (Charles County) delivered cattle to Annapolis for the use of the state troops on 23 Aug 1781 and returned to Charles County with five horses to take care of in the public use on 24 Aug 1781 {Ref: Archives of Maryland 45:579}; submitted an account and receipt for dressing cattle on 22 Oct 1781 {Ref: Maryland State Archives MdHR-6636-23-25}

KEY, PHILIP (St. Mary's County) pledged a loan in the amount of £500 to the State of Maryland under the Act for the Emission of Bills of Credit "to defray the expences of the present campaign" in June, 1781 {Ref: Archives of Maryland 47:326}; received a certificate from the Purchasing Agent for furnishing wheat on 9 Jul 1781 {Ref: Maryland State Archives MdHR-6636-24-36}; received a loan certificate for £7.11.8 due from the Council of Maryland "agreeable to the Act proposing to the Citizens of this State, Creditors of Congress on Loan Office Certificates, Etc." on 19 Dec 1783 for services rendered during the war {Ref: Archives of Maryland 48:493}

KEYER, HENRY (Frederick County) received a receipt from the Purchasing Agent for furnishing beef on 3 Apr 1781 {Ref: Maryland State Archives MdHR-6636-23-5}

KIBORD, THOMAS (Charles County) received a receipt from the Purchasing Agent for furnishing wheat on 12 Nov 1782 {Ref: Maryland State Archives MdHR-6636-42-19}

KILGORE, WILLIAM (St. Mary's County) received a receipt from the Purchasing Agent for furnishing wheat on 3 Feb 1780 {Ref: Maryland State Archives MdHR-6636-24-37}

KINDERDINE, COOPER (Caroline County) received receipts from the Purchasing Agent for furnishing wheat on 1 Sep 1782 {Ref: Maryland State Archives MdHR-6636-42-7}

KING, ABRAM (Frederick County) received a certificate from the Purchasing Agent for furnishing wheat on 30 May 1782 {Ref: Maryland State Archives MdHR-6636-42-35}

KING, FRANCIS (Somerset County) received a receipt from the Purchasing Agent for furnishing bacon on 19 Aug 1780 {Ref: Maryland State Archives MdHR-6636-24-41}; received a loan certificate for £130.12.3 due from the Council of Maryland "agreeable to the Act proposing to the Citizens of this State, Creditors of Congress on Loan Office Certificates, Etc." on 19 Dec 1783 for services rendered during the war {Ref: Archives of Maryland 48:493}

KING, JOHN (Anne Arundel County) received payment by order of the Council of Safety "for going express to Antietam Forge" on 1 Apr 1776 {Ref: Archives of Maryland 11:301}; received payment "for riding express for Congress" on 30 Aug 1776 {Ref: Archives of Maryland 12:248}; received payment "for riding express from Baltimore" on 14 Jul 1778 {Ref: Archives of Maryland 21:159};

received payment from the Council of Maryland for riding express on 13 Jul 1781 {Ref: Archives of Maryland 45:500}

KING, MARY (Harford County) received a receipt from the Purchasing Agent for furnishing wheat on 25 Feb 1780 {Ref: Maryland State Archives MdHR-6636-17-116}

KING, NEHEMIAH (Somerset County) received a receipt from the Purchasing Agent for furnishing bacon on 19 Aug 1780 {Ref: Maryland State Archives MdHR-6636-24-41}

KING, ROBERT (Somerset County) received a receipt from the Purchasing Agent for furnishing beef on 5 Dec 1781 {Ref: Maryland State Archives MdHR-6636-24-44}

KING, THOMAS (Talbot County) furnished cattle on 12 Apr 1781 for the use of the State of Maryland {Ref: Archives of Maryland 47:250}

KING, UPSHER (Baltimore County) delivered bacon and pork to the commissary at Baltimore Town for the use of the State of Maryland in the summer of 1780 {Ref: Archives of Maryland 45:84}

KINGSLEY, PATRICK (Frederick County) submitted an account for furnishing corn on 2 Nov 1780 {Ref: Maryland State Archives MdHR-6636-23-8}

KININGER, ULRICH (Frederick County) received a certificate from the Purchasing Agent for furnishing wheat on 1 Aug 1782 {Ref: Maryland State Archives MdHR-6636-42-36}

KINNARD, JOSHUA (Talbot and Queen Anne's Counties) submitted an account and receipt for hauling supplies on 25 Sep 1780 {Ref: Maryland State Archives MdHR-6636-24-49}; submitted an account and receipt for furnishing pork barrels and hauling provisions on 14 Mar 1783 {Ref: Maryland State Archives MdHR-6636-43-13}

KIRBY, ELEANOR (Baltimore Town) received payment by order of the Council of Safety for attending the hospital on 28 Aug 1776 {Ref: Archives of Maryland 12:245}

KIRK, THOMAS (Frederick County) received receipts from the Purchasing Agent for furnishing beef on 19 Jan and 25 Jan 1781 {Ref: Maryland State Archives MdHR-6636-23-2}

KIRK, THOMAS (Prince George's County) received a receipt from the Purchasing Agent for furnishing wheat in 1783 {Ref: Maryland State Archives MdHR-6636-50-135}

KIRK, TIMOTHY (county not stated) pledged a loan in the amount of £100 to the State of Maryland under the Act for the Emission of Bills of Credit "to defray the expences of the present campaign" in June, 1781 {Ref: Archives of Maryland 47:327}

KIRKMAN, ELISHA (Dorchester County) received a receipt from the Purchasing Agent for furnishing wheat on 1 Nov 1782 {Ref: Maryland State Archives

MdHR-6636-42-23}

KIRKMAN, GEORGE (Caroline County) received a receipt from the Purchasing Agent for furnishing wheat on 31 May 1782 {Ref: Maryland State Archives MdHR-6636-42-7}

KIRKMAN, JAMES (Caroline County) received a receipt from the Purchasing Agent for furnishing wheat on 5 Aug 1782 {Ref: Maryland State Archives MdHR-6636-42-7}

KIRKMAN, LEVIN (Dorchester County) submitted a bill and receipt for hauling pork on 17 May 1778 {Ref: Maryland State Archives MdHR-6636-23-26}

KIRKPATRICK, HUGH (Harford County) was appointed by the Committee of Safety to be one of four men to serve on "a Committee for Examination of Guns and report of their Sufficiency be a Guide for this Committee to receive them by" on 11 Jul 1776 {Ref: Preston's History of Harford County, p. 331}

KITE, JOHN (Caroline County) received receipts from the Purchasing Agent for furnishing wheat on 1 Sep and 20 Sep 1782 {Ref: Maryland State Archives MdHR-6636-42-7}

KLEIN, JACOB (Frederick County) received a receipt from the Purchasing Agent for slaughtering cattle on 11 Nov 1781 {Ref: Maryland State Archives MdHR-6636-42-26}

KNAPP, JOHN (Annapolis) received payment from the Council of Maryland as "appropriated for the payment of Expresses, Etc., his allowance on the Journal of May Session 1781" on 16 Jul 1781 {Ref: Archives of Maryland 45:504}; received payment "for four Days assisting the Council Coppying" on 4 May 1782 {Ref: Archives of Maryland 48:155}

KNOLES, EDWARD (Baltimore County) received a receipt from the Purchasing Agent for furnishing flour on 18 Aug 1781 {Ref: Maryland State Archives MdHR-6636-28-121B}

KNOTT, JOHN (Dorchester County) received a receipt from the Purchasing Agent for furnishing wheat on 1 Nov 1782 {Ref: Maryland State Archives MdHR-6636-42-23}

KNOTT, JUSTINIAN (Charles County) received a receipt from the Purchasing Agent for furnishing wheat on 24 Nov 1781 {Ref: Maryland State Archives MdHR-6636-42-15}

KNOTT, RALPH (Montgomery County) received a receipt from the Purchasing Agent for furnishing wheat on 20 Oct 1780 {Ref: Maryland State Archives MdHR-6636-24-8}; received a receipt for furnishing wheat on 3 Jan 1781 {Ref: Maryland State Archives MdHR-6636-24-9}

KNOTT, THOMAS (Montgomery County) received a receipt from the Purchasing Agent for furnishing wheat on 30 Apr 1781 {Ref: Maryland State Archives MdHR-6636-42-11}

KNOTT, ZACHARIAH (Montgomery County) received a receipt from the

Purchasing Agent for furnishing wheat on 10 Apr and 4 May 1781 {Ref: Maryland State Archives MdHR-6636-42-11}

KNOX, ROSE T. (Charles County) received a receipt from the Purchasing Agent for furnishing wheat on 9 May 1783 {Ref: Maryland State Archives MdHR-6636-42-22}

KOONTZ, GEORGE (Frederick County) received a receipt from the Purchasing Agent for furnishing beef on 22 Dec 1780 {Ref: Maryland State Archives MdHR-6636-23-1}

KOONTZ, HENRY (Frederick County) received a receipt from the Purchasing Agent for delivering flour on 3 Jan 1781 {Ref: Maryland State Archives MdHR-6636-23-30}

KOONTZ, JACOB (Frederick County) received a certificate from the Purchasing Agent for furnishing wheat on 29 May 1782 {Ref: Maryland State Archives MdHR-6636-42-34}

KORTZ, GEORGE (Frederick County) received a certificate from the Purchasing Agent for furnishing wheat on 24 Sep 1781 {Ref: Maryland State Archives MdHR-6636-23-28}

KREPS(?), JACOB (Baltimore Town) submitted an account and received payment for furnishing two padlocks for the commission's wagon yard in Baltimore on 25 Mar 1780 {Ref: Maryland Historical Society MS.1814, Box 6}

KUHN, PHILIP (Frederick County) received payment for driving cattle on 29 Mar 1781 {Ref: Maryland State Archives MdHR-6636-23-30}

KYZER, STOFIELD (Montgomery County) received a receipt from the Purchasing Agent for furnishing wheat on 26 Sep 1780 {Ref: Maryland State Archives MdHR-6636-24-7}

LACEY, JOHN (Montgomery County) delivered wheat from his mill to the Purchasing Agent for the use of the State of Maryland in October, 1780 {Ref: Archives of Maryland 45:149}; received a receipt from the Purchasing Agent for furnishing wheat on 12 May 1781 {Ref: Maryland State Archives MdHR-6636-24-14}

LACKLAND, JOSHUA (Anne Arundel County) received payment by order of the Council of Maryland "to be delivered over to John Bullen, Commissary of Stores for Anne Arundel County" on 16 Feb 1782 {Ref: Archives of Maryland 48:78}

LAMB, JOHN (Kent County) received payment by order of the Council of Safety for furnishing boatage on 8 Oct 1776 {Ref: Archives of Maryland 12:326}

LAMB, PEARCE (Kent County) received a certificate from the Purchasing Agent for furnishing wheat on 28 Jan 1780 {Ref: Maryland State Archives MdHR-6636-23-47}; received a certificate for furnishing wheat on 5 Apr 1780 {Ref: Maryland State Archives MdHR-6636-23-45}; received a certificate for delivering wheat on 17 Apr 1781 {Ref: Maryland State Archives MdHR-6636-

23-40}

LAMPARD, THOMAS (Montgomery County) received a receipt from the Purchasing Agent for furnishing wheat on 20 Apr 1781 {Ref: Maryland State Archives MdHR-6636-42-11}

LANAM, SHADRICK (Montgomery County) received a receipt from the Purchasing Agent for furnishing wheat on 29 Sep 1780 {Ref: Maryland State Archives MdHR-6636-24-13}; received a receipt for furnishing wheat on 3 Nov 1781 {Ref: Maryland State Archives MdHR-6636-24-14}

LANCASTER, JOHN (Charles County) received a receipt from the Purchasing Agent for furnishing wheat on 29 Dec 1782 {Ref: Maryland State Archives MdHR-6636-42-21}

LANDHORN, AARON (Montgomery County) received a receipt from the Purchasing Agent for furnishing wheat on 31 Aug 1780 {Ref: Maryland State Archives MdHR-6636-24-6}

LANDISS, HENRY (Frederick County) received a certificate from the Purchasing Agent for furnishing barrels on 16 Mar 1781 {Ref: Maryland State Archives MdHR-6636-23-28}

LANDON, GEORGE (Baltimore County) received a receipt from the Purchasing Agent for furnishing flour to Susquehanna Lower Ferry on 23 Jan 1780 {Ref: Maryland State Archives MdHR-6636-23-37}

LANDRA, JOHN (Baltimore County) submitted an account and received payment for taking care of four wagons to Susquehanna for the use of the army on 25 Jan 1780 {Ref: Maryland Historical Society MS.1814, Box 6}

LANGDEN, JOHN, see "John Longden," q.v.

LANHAM, AARON (Montgomery County) received a receipt from the Purchasing Agent for furnishing wheat on 2 Sep 1780 {Ref: Maryland State Archives MdHR-6636-24-7}; received a receipt for furnishing wheat on 23 Nov and 28 Nov 1780 {Ref: Maryland State Archives MdHR-6636-24-8}

LANHAM, NOTLEY (Montgomery County) received a receipt from the Purchasing Agent for furnishing wheat on 17 Oct 1780 {Ref: Maryland State Archives MdHR-6636-24-8}

LANHAM, SHADRICK (Montgomery County) received a receipt from the Purchasing Agent for furnishing wheat on 26 Aug and 29 Sep 1780 {Ref: Maryland State Archives MdHR-6636-24-13}

LANKFORD, BENJAMIN (Somerset County) received a receipt from the Purchasing Agent for furnishing beef on 1 Nov 1781 {Ref: Maryland State Archives MdHR-6636-24-44}

LANKFORD, EZEKIEL (Somerset County) received a receipt from the Purchasing Agent for furnishing pork on 1 May 1782 {Ref: Maryland State Archives MdHR-6636-43-21}

LANKFORD, WILLIAM (Somerset County) received a receipt from the

Purchasing Agent for furnishing pork on 15 Jul 1781 {Ref: Maryland State Archives MdHR-6636-24-43}; received a receipt for furnishing beef on 4 Nov 1781 {Ref: Maryland State Archives MdHR-6636-24-44}

LANNEMS (SANNEMS?), JACOB (Baltimore County) submitted an account and received payment for hauling three loads of flour for the use of the army and for one and a half days drayage on 28 Jan 1780 {Ref: Maryland Historical Society MS.1814, Box 6}

LANSDALE, CHARLES (Prince George's County) received payment by order of the Council of Maryland "out of the money remitted by Congress for the Purchase of Provisions to be delivered over to Thomas Claggett, Purchaser for Prince George's County" on 24 Apr 1778 {Ref: Archives of Maryland 21:56}; submitted an account for riding express on 1 Jul 1780 {Ref: Maryland State Archives MdHR-6636-19-72}; received payment by order of the Council of Maryland "of the New Emission of this State to be delivered over to Daniel Jenifer, Commissary for Charles County" on 29 Sep 1780 {Ref: Archives of Maryland 43:308}

LANSDALE, THOMAS AND ELEANOR (Prince George's County) received a loan certificate for £162.9.6 due from the Council of Maryland "agreeable to the Act proposing to the Citizens of this State, Creditors of Congress on Loan Office Certificates, Etc." on 7 Jul 1783 for services rendered during the war {Ref: Archives of Maryland 48:437}

LANSLEY, THOMAS (Montgomery County) received a certificate from the Purchasing Agent for furnishing wheat on 29 Jul 1780 {Ref: Maryland State Archives MdHR-6636-24-5}; received a receipt for furnishing wheat on 1 Aug 1780 {Ref: Maryland State Archives MdHR-6636-43-7}

LANTZ, CANNON (Somerset County) received a receipt from the Purchasing Agent for furnishing pork on 26 May 1781 {Ref: Maryland State Archives MdHR-6636-24-43}

LAREY, JAMES (Caroline County) received a receipt from the Purchasing Agent for wheat on 20 Sep 1782 {Ref: Maryland State Archives MdHR-6636-42-7}

LARKINGS, JOHN (Frederick County) received a certificate from the Purchasing Agent for furnishing wheat on 31 May 1782 {Ref: Maryland State Archives MdHR-6636-42-35}

LATON, URIAH (Montgomery County) received a receipt from the Purchasing Agent for furnishing wheat on 28 Apr 1781 {Ref: Maryland State Archives MdHR-6636-42-11}

LATTAMORE, THOMAS (Charles County) received a receipt from the Purchasing Agent for furnishing wheat on 18 May 1782 {Ref: Maryland State Archives MdHR-6636-42-18}

LAUMAN, LUDWICK (Frederick County) received a certificate from the Purchasing Agent for furnishing flour on 15 Mar 1781 {Ref: Maryland State

Archives MdHR-6636-23-31}

LAVAY, WILLIAM (Montgomery County) received a receipt from the Purchasing Agent for furnishing wheat on 8 Oct 1781 {Ref: Maryland State Archives MdHR-6636-42-11}

LAVELY, WILLIAM (Baltimore Town) received payment by order of the Council of Safety for furnishing bread to the hospital in Baltimore Town on 8 Aug 1776 {Ref: Archives of Maryland 12:187}

LAW, DAVID (Montgomery County) received a receipt from the Purchasing Agent for furnishing wheat on 23 Sep 1780 {Ref: Maryland State Archives MdHR-6636-24-7}

LAWS, ELIJAH (Worcester County) received payment for furnishing beef on 26 Sep 1781 {Ref: Maryland State Archives MdHR-6636-43-28AAAA}

LAWS, JOHN (Worcester County) received a loan certificate for £13.13.8 due from the Council of Maryland "agreeable to the Act proposing to the Citizens of this State, Creditors of Congress on Loan Office Certificates, Etc." on 18 Dec 1783 for services rendered during the war {Ref: Archives of Maryland 48:491}

LAWS, MICHAH (Montgomery County) received a receipt from the Purchasing Agent for furnishing wheat on 11 Aug 1781 {Ref: Maryland State Archives MdHR-6636-24-15}

LAWSON, JOSEPH (Kent County) received a receipt from the Purchasing Agent for furnishing wheat on 29 Jan 1780 {Ref: Maryland State Archives MdHR-6636-23-48}

LAWSON, PETER (county not stated) pledged a loan in the amount of £200 to the State of Maryland under the Act for the Emission of Bills of Credit "to defray the expences of the present campaign" in June, 1781 {Ref: Archives of Maryland 47:327}

LAWSON, ROBERT (Charles County) received a receipt from the Purchasing Agent for furnishing wheat on 3 Nov 1781 {Ref: Maryland State Archives MdHR-6636-42-15}

LAYFIELD, WILLIAM (Worcester County) received a receipt from the Purchasing Agent for furnishing bacon on 7 Oct 1780 {Ref: Maryland State Archives MdHR-6636-24-54}

LAYRING, AARON (Baltimore Town) submitted a bill and receipt for furnishing linen on 11 Oct 1779 {Ref: Maryland State Archives MdHR-19970-3-8}

LAYTON, LEVIN (Dorchester County) received a receipt from the Purchasing Agent for furnishing wheat on 1 Oct 1782 {Ref: Maryland State Archives MdHR-6636-42-23}

LAZENBY, ELIAS (Montgomery County) received a certificate of employment by the commissary of purchases on 4 Jun 1782 {Ref: Maryland State Archives MdHR-6636-50-91}

LAZENBY, ROBERT (Frederick County) received receipts from the Purchasing Agent for furnishing corn on 31 Mar, 5 Apr, 11 Apr, 14 Apr, 18 Apr, 21 Apr, 25 Apr, 12 May, 16 May, 30 May and 13 Jun 1780 {Ref: Maryland State Archives MdHR-6636-24-1}

LEACH, JOSIAS (Montgomery County) received a receipt from the Purchasing Agent for furnishing wheat on 7 Jun 1781 {Ref: Maryland State Archives MdHR-6636-42-11}

LEACH, MARY (Montgomery County) received a receipt from the Purchasing Agent for furnishing wheat on 1 Aug 1780 {Ref: Maryland State Archives MdHR-6636-43-7}; received a receipt for furnishing wheat on 29 Jul 1781 {Ref: Maryland State Archives MdHR-6636-42-11}; received a receipt for furnishing wheat on 2 Mar 1782 {Ref: Maryland State Archives MdHR-6636-43-7}

LEACH, WILLIAM (Montgomery County) received a receipt from the Purchasing Agent for furnishing wheat on 18 Oct 1780 {Ref: Maryland State Archives MdHR-6636-24-8}; received a receipt for furnishing wheat on 14 Aug 1781 {Ref: Maryland State Archives MdHR-6636-24-15}

LEAKEN, JOHN (Frederick County) received a certificate from the Purchasing Agent for furnishing wheat on 27 May 1782 {Ref: Maryland State Archives MdHR-6636-42-33}

LEAS, WILLIAM (Baltimore County) submitted an account and receipt for furnishing flour and casks on 11 Nov 1780 {Ref: Maryland State Archives MdHR-6636-43-38KKKKK}

LEASE, WILLIAM (Frederick County) received a certificate from the Purchasing Agent for furnishing wheat on 1 Jul 1782 {Ref: Maryland State Archives MdHR-6636-42-36}

LEATEN, HUGHRIAH (Montgomery County) received a receipt from the Purchasing Agent for furnishing wheat on 29 May 1781 {Ref: Maryland State Archives MdHR-6636-42-11}

LEATH, ALEXANDER (Caroline County) received receipts from the Purchasing Agent for furnishing wheat on 17 Aug and 1 Sep 1782 {Ref: Maryland State Archives MdHR-6636-42-7}

LEATH, SAMUEL (Frederick County) received a certificate from the Purchasing Agent for furnishing wheat on 10 Jun 1782 {Ref: Maryland State Archives MdHR-6636-42-34}

LEATHER, JOHN (Frederick County) received a certificate from the Purchasing Agent for furnishing wheat on 24 Sep 1781 {Ref: Maryland State Archives MdHR-6636-23-28}

LEATHERBURY, JOSEPH (Somerset County) received a receipt from the Purchasing Agent for furnishing pork on 20 May 1782 {Ref: Maryland State Archives MdHR-6636-43-21}

LEATHERMAN, DANIEL (Frederick County) received a certificate from the Purchasing Agent for furnishing flour on 8 Jun 1782 {Ref: Maryland State Archives MdHR-6636-42-35}

LEATHERMAN, HENRY (Frederick County) submitted an account for furnishing pork on 28 May 1781 {Ref: Maryland State Archives MdHR-6636-23-6}

LEAVERTON, ELISABETH (Caroline County) received a receipt from the Purchasing Agent for wheat on 19 Sep 1782 {Ref: Maryland State Archives MdHR-6636-42-7}

LECOMPT, JAMES (Caroline County) received receipts from the Purchasing Agent for furnishing wheat on 1 Sep and 1 Sep 1782 {Ref: Maryland State Archives MdHR-6636-42-7}

LECOMPT, THOMAS (Caroline County) received a receipt from the Purchasing Agent for furnishing wheat on 1 Sep 1782 {Ref: Maryland State Archives MdHR-6636-42-7}

LECOMPT, WILLIAM (Caroline County) received a receipt from the Purchasing Agent for furnishing wheat on 1 Sep 1782 {Ref: Maryland State Archives MdHR-6636-42-7}

LEE, COLONEL, see "Samuel Hart," q.v.

LEE, DANIEL (Prince George's County) received a receipt from the Purchasing Agent for furnishing wheat in 1782 {Ref: Maryland State Archives MdHR-6636-50-135}

LEE, DANIEL (Montgomery County) received a receipt from the Purchasing Agent for furnishing wheat on 6 Sep and 8 Sep 1780 {Ref: Maryland State Archives MdHR-6636-24-7}

LEE, GENERAL, see "Elizabeth Hunter," q.v.

LEE, JAMES (Montgomery County) received a receipt from the Purchasing Agent for furnishing wheat on 23 Oct 1780 {Ref: Maryland State Archives MdHR-6636-24-8}; received a certificate of employment by the commissary of purchases on 1 Jun 1782 {Ref: Maryland State Archives MdHR-6636-50-91}

LEE, JOHN (Montgomery County) received a receipt from the Purchasing Agent for furnishing wheat on 25 Sep 1780 {Ref: Maryland State Archives MdHR-6636-24-7}

LEE, MARY (Dorchester County) received a receipt from the Purchasing Agent for furnishing wheat on 12 Aug 1782 {Ref: Maryland State Archives MdHR-6636-42-23}

LEE, WILLIAM (Charles County) received a receipt from the Purchasing Agent for furnishing wheat on 17 Oct 1781 {Ref: Maryland State Archives MdHR-6636-43-45K}

LEEK, ELIZABETH (Montgomery County) received a receipt from the Purchasing Agent for furnishing wheat on 9 Apr 1781 {Ref: Maryland State Archives MdHR-6636-42-11}

LEFAVOR, CHRISTIAN (Frederick County) received a certificate from the Purchasing Agent for furnishing hay on 27 May 1782 {Ref: Maryland State Archives MdHR-6636-42-33}

LEGG, THOMAS (Montgomery County) received a receipt from the Purchasing Agent for furnishing wheat on 4 Sep 1780 {Ref: Maryland State Archives MdHR-6636-24-7}

LEGGIT, JOSHUA (Baltimore County) received a receipt from the Purchasing Agent for furnishing flour on 12 Feb 1780 {Ref: Maryland State Archives MdHR-6636-23-15}

LEIGH, WILLIAM (Charles County) received a receipt from the Purchasing Agent for furnishing wheat on 8 May 1783 {Ref: Maryland State Archives MdHR-6636-42-22}

LEMAR, CHARLES (Caroline County) received a receipt from the Purchasing Agent for furnishing wheat on 1 Sep 1782 {Ref: Maryland State Archives MdHR-6636-42-7}

LEMAR, JOHN (Caroline County) received a receipt from the Purchasing Agent for furnishing wheat on 24 Aug 1782 {Ref: Maryland State Archives MdHR-6636-42-7}

LEMARR, GALEE (Caroline County) received a receipt from the Purchasing Agent for furnishing wheat on 24 Aug 1782 {Ref: Maryland State Archives MdHR-6636-42-7}

LEMARR, LEMUEL (Caroline County) received a receipt from the Purchasing Agent for furnishing wheat on 24 Aug 1782 {Ref: Maryland State Archives MdHR-6636-42-7}

LEMMON, ELEXIS SR. (Baltimore County) received a receipt from the Purchasing Agent for furnishing wheat on 4 Oct 1779 {Ref: Maryland State Archives MdHR-6636-21-67}

LEMMON, LODWICK (Frederick County) received a certificate from the Purchasing Agent for furnishing wheat on 31 May 1782 {Ref: Maryland State Archives MdHR-6636-42-37}

LEMMON, RICHARD (Baltimore County) submitted an account and receipt for furnishing nails on 27 Dec 1780 {Ref: Maryland State Archives MdHR-6636-43-38/OOOO}; submitted an account and receipt for furnishing nails on 7 Mar 1781 {Ref: Maryland State Archives MdHR-6636-43-38CCCC}; submitted an account and receipt for furnishing nails on 8 May 1781 {Ref: Maryland State Archives MdHR-6636-43-38JJJ}

LEMMON, ROBERT (Baltimore County) submitted an account and received payment for furnishing nails on 21 Jan and 25 Mar 1780 {Ref: Maryland Historical Society MS.1814, Box 6}

LEONARD, JOHN (Somerset County) received a receipt from the Purchasing Agent for furnishing bacon on 14 Jul 1781 {Ref: Maryland State Archives

MdHR-6636-24-43}

LERNER, VAL (Frederick County) received a receipt from the Purchasing Agent for furnishing beef on 30 Dec 1780 {Ref: Maryland State Archives MdHR-6636-23-1}; received a receipt for furnishing beef on 16 Jan 1781 {Ref: Maryland State Archives MdHR-6636-23-2}

LESLIE, PATRICK (Frederick County) received a receipt from the Purchasing Agent for furnishing beef on 13 Feb 1781 {Ref: Maryland State Archives MdHR-6636-23-3}; received a certificate for furnishing pork on 14 Mar 1781 {Ref: Maryland State Archives MdHR-6636-23-4}

LESSHON, PAUL (Anne Arundel County) received a receipt from the Purchasing Agent for furnishing powder on 16 Apr 1777 {Ref: Maryland State Archives MdHR-6636-9-14C}

LEWIS, DAVID (Frederick County) received receipts from the Purchasing Agent for furnishing beef on 23 Dec 1780 and for furnishing corn on 29 Dec 1780 {Ref: Maryland State Archives MdHR-6636-23-1}; received a receipt for furnishing corn on 3 Jan 1781 {Ref: Maryland State Archives MdHR-6636-23-2}

LEWIS, HENRY HOPKINS (Frederick County) received a receipt from the Purchasing Agent for furnishing beef on 4 Mar 1781 {Ref: Maryland State Archives MdHR-6636-23-4}

LEWIS, HOPKINS (Frederick County) received a receipt from the Purchasing Agent for furnishing bulls on 28 Feb 1781 {Ref: Maryland State Archives MdHR-6636-23-3}; submitted an account for furnishing pork on 21 Apr 1781 {Ref: Maryland State Archives MdHR-6636-23-5}

LEWIS, JEREMIAH (Montgomery County) received a receipt from the Purchasing Agent for furnishing wheat on 30 Apr 1781 {Ref: Maryland State Archives MdHR-6636-42-11}

LEWIS, MARY (Montgomery County) received a receipt from the Purchasing Agent for furnishing wheat on 30 Apr 1781 {Ref: Maryland State Archives MdHR-6636-42-11}

LEWIS, THOMAS (Montgomery County) received a receipt from the Purchasing Agent for furnishing wheat on 27 Apr 1781 {Ref: Maryland State Archives MdHR-6636-24-18}; submitted an account for hauling on 1 May 1781 {Ref: Maryland State Archives MdHR-6636-50-91}; received a certificate of employment by the commissary of purchases on 24 Apr 1782 {Ref: Maryland State Archives MdHR-6636-50-91}

LEYPOLD, JOHN (Baltimore Town) received payment by order of the Council of Safety for three days service in examining flour in Baltimore Town on 8 Aug 1776 and for riding express on 17 Sep 1776 {Ref: Archives of Maryland 12:187, 276}

LIBRANT, CHRISTIAN (county not stated) received payment by order of the

Council of Safety for providing waggonage on 28 Aug 1776 {Ref: Archives of Maryland 12:245}

LICKLITER, CONRAD (Frederick County) received a certificate for money loaned to the state on 2 Jun 1780 {Ref: Maryland State Archives MdHR-6636-61-17}

LIDEN, RICHARD (Baltimore County) received a receipt from the Purchasing Agent for furnishing Indian corn on 9 Oct 1781 {Ref: Maryland State Archives MdHR-6636-43-38Q}

LIDEN, SHADRACH (Caroline County) received a receipt from the Purchasing Agent for furnishing wheat on 5 Aug 1782 {Ref: Maryland State Archives MdHR-6636-42-7}

LINCK, ADAM (Frederick County) received a certificate from the Purchasing Agent for furnishing wheat on 23 Mar 1782 {Ref: Maryland State Archives MdHR-6636-42-35}

LINDENBERGER, GEORGE (Baltimore Town) had his house occupied as a laboratory and guard house by the military and since it was damaged while in the public service, the Council of Maryland ordered the damages to be certified on 11 Apr 1777 and a reasonable annual rent be ascertained {Ref: Archives of Maryland 16:206}

LINDSAY, JOHN CAMPBELL (Charles or Prince George's County) received payment by order of the Council of Safety for furnishing a musquet on 1 Jul 1776 {Ref: Archives of Maryland 11:539}

LINDSAY, WILLIAM (Charles County) received payment by order of the Council of Safety "for furnishing waggonage" on 26 Aug 1776 {Ref: Archives of Maryland 12:241}

LINE, JACOB (Anne Arundel County) received a receipt from the Purchasing Agent for furnishing powder on 16 Apr 1777 {Ref: Maryland State Archives MdHR-6636-9-14A}

LINGENFELTER, JOHN (Frederick County) received via his executors Ann Lingenfelter and Balser Heck, a loan certificate for £74.9.2 due from the Council of Maryland "agreeable to the Act proposing to the Citizens of this State, Creditors of Congress on Loan Office Certificates, Etc." on 30 Sep 1783 for his services rendered during the war {Ref: Archives of Maryland 48:457}

LININTELLY, MR. (Frederick County) received a certificate from the Purchasing Agent for furnishing rye on 12 Feb 1780 {Ref: Maryland State Archives MdHR-6636-42-29}

LINSEY, DAVID (Charles County) received a receipt from the Purchasing Agent for furnishing wheat on 2 Nov 1782 {Ref: Maryland State Archives MdHR-6636-42-19}

LINSEY, OLIVER (Frederick County) received a certificate from the Purchasing Agent for furnishing wheat on 28 Nov 1782 {Ref: Maryland State Archives

MdHR-6636-42-37}
LINTHICUM (LINTHICUMB), FRANCIS (Anne Arundel County) received payment by order of the Council of Safety for furnishing a gun and bayonet on 12 Oct 1776 {Ref: Archives of Maryland 12:338}
LINTHICUM, NATHAN (Frederick County) received receipts from the Purchasing Agent for furnishing corn on 5 Apr and 11 Apr 1780 {Ref: Maryland State Archives MdHR-6636-24-1}
LIPHART, PETER (Frederick County) received a receipt from the Purchasing Agent for furnishing pork on 20 Jan 1781 {Ref: Maryland State Archives MdHR-6636-23-2}
LISTOR, JOSHUA (Caroline County) received a receipt from the Purchasing Agent for furnishing wheat on 24 Aug 1782 {Ref: Maryland State Archives MdHR-6636-42-7}
LITTIG (LETTIGG), PETER (Baltimore Town) was a gunsmith who contracted to make arms for the Council of Maryland on or about 17 Sep 1777 {Ref: Archives of Maryland 16:377}; submitted an account for making and testing guns on 6 Apr 1780 {Ref: Maryland State Archives MdHR-6636-66-69}; he was still manufacturing arms on 12 Jan 1781 {Ref: Archives of Maryland 47:14}
LITTLE, JOHN (Baltimore County) received payment by order of the Council of Safety for furnishing a musquet on 16 Oct 1776 {Ref: Archives of Maryland 12:354}
LIVINGSTON, LIEUTENANT (Frederick County) received a receipt from the Purchasing Agent for delivering flour on 4 May 1781 {Ref: Maryland State Archives MdHR-6636-23-31}
LLOYD, ANNA MARIE (Talbot County) received a certificate from the Purchasing Agent for furnishing wheat on 16 Jan 1780 {Ref: Maryland State Archives MdHR-6636-24-46}
LLOYD, EDWARD (Talbot County) was appointed by the Council of Safety to collect all the gold and silver coin that could be procured in the county in compliance with the Resolve of Congress on 27 Jan 1776 {Ref: Archives of Maryland 11:132}; submitted an account and receipt for furnishing cattle on 2 Oct 1780 {Ref: Maryland State Archives MdHR-6636-24-49}; pledged a loan in the amount of £2000 to the State of Maryland under the Act for the Emission of Bills of Credit "to defray the expences of the present campaign" in June, 1781 {Ref: Archives of Maryland 47:326}; he was one of twenty-six people who contacted the Governor and Council of Maryland in 1781 and pledged to support and maintain at their own expense the Barge *Experiment* so it can patrol the bay between Kent Point and Tilghman's Island in order to protect them against the enemy, stating in part, "whereas from the present exhausted state of the public treasury the government cannot immediately give that

protection to every individual which is become necessary from the cruel and savage mode in which the war is now carried on against us" {Ref: Archives of Maryland 47:584-585}

LLOYD, JAMES (Kent County) received payment from the Council of Maryland on 27 Sep 1782 for having furnished a horse for the use of the Southern Army {Ref: Archives of Maryland 48:270}

LLOYD, RICHARD (Kent County) received payment from the Purchasing Agent for furnishing cattle and pasturage for the public use in September, 1781 {Ref: Maryland State Archives MdHR-6636-43-3}

LLOYD, RICHARD B. (Kent County) received payment from the Purchasing Agent for furnishing cattle and pasturage for the public use in September, 1781 {Ref: Maryland State Archives MdHR-6636-43-3}

LOCKER, JOSEPH (Montgomery County) received a receipt from the Purchasing Agent for shelling corn on 17 Apr 1780 {Ref: Maryland State Archives MdHR-6636-24-2}; received a receipt for furnishing wheat on 12 Sep 1780 {Ref: Maryland State Archives MdHR-6636-24-7}

LOCKER, PHILIP (Montgomery County) received a receipt from the Purchasing Agent for furnishing wheat on 20 Oct 1781 {Ref: Maryland State Archives MdHR-6636-24-15}

LOGAN, MARY (county not stated) received payment by order of the Council of Maryland via William Logan for services rendered (not specified) on 24 Jun 1779 {Ref: Archives of Maryland 21:461}

LOGG, THOMAS (Montgomery County) received a receipt from the Purchasing Agent for furnishing wheat on 11 Jun 1781 {Ref: Maryland State Archives MdHR-6636-42-11}

LOLLAND, NATHAN (Montgomery County) received a receipt from the Purchasing Agent for furnishing wheat on 1 Aug 1780 {Ref: Maryland State Archives MdHR-6636-43-7}

LOMAX, THOMAS (Charles County) received a receipt from the Purchasing Agent for furnishing wheat on 8 Jan 1782 {Ref: Maryland State Archives MdHR-6636-42-16}

LONEY, JONATHAN (Queen Anne's County) received a receipt from the Purchasing Agent for furnishing a steer on 8 May 1778 {Ref: Maryland State Archives MdHR-4587-36}

LONEY, THOMAS (Caroline County) received a receipt from the Purchasing Agent for furnishing wheat on 1 Sep 1782 {Ref: Maryland State Archives MdHR-6636-42-7}

LONG, DANIEL (Worcester County) submitted an account and receipt for driving cattle on 15 Sep 1781 {Ref: Maryland State Archives MdHR-6636-43-27}

LONG, DAVID (Worcester County) received a receipt from the Purchasing Agent for furnishing beef on 11 Oct 1780 {Ref: Maryland State Archives MdHR-

6636-24-54}

LONG, ROBERT (Baltimore County) was empowered by the Council of Maryland "to remove the cannon at Indian Landing to Elk Ridge landing and any person who can is requested to give him assistance" on 4 Sep 1777 {Ref: Archives of Maryland 16:362}; submitted an account and received payment for procuring wagons for thirteen days and for forwarding supplies to the Continental Army on 3 Feb 1780 {Ref: Maryland Historical Society MS.1814, Box 6}

LONG, SOLOMON (Worcester County) was a major who received a receipt from the Purchasing Agent for furnishing corn on 14 Jun 1780 {Ref: Maryland State Archives MdHR-6636-24-53}; his name appeared on "A List of Corn Purchased in Worcester County for the use of the State of Maryland" by the Commissary in July, 1780 {Ref: Archives of Maryland 45:10}; received a receipt for hauling corn on 15 Nov 1780 {Ref: Maryland State Archives MdHR-6636-24-54}; received payment for furnishing beef on 9 Oct 1781 {Ref: Maryland State Archives MdHR-6636-43-28QQQ}; submitted an account and receipt for grazing cattle on 20 Oct 1781 {Ref: Maryland State Archives MdHR-6636-43-27}; submitted an account and receipt for furnishing pork in 1782 {Ref: Maryland State Archives MdHR-19970-4-1}

LONG, WILLIAM (Somerset County) received a receipt from the Purchasing Agent for furnishing beef on 29 Oct 1781 {Ref: Maryland State Archives MdHR-6636-24-44}

LONGDEN (LANGDEN), JOHN (Anne Arundel County) received payment from the Council of Maryland for riding express on 14 Jul 1781 {Ref: Archives of Maryland 45:501}

LOOCKERMAN, RICHARD (Caroline County) received a receipt from the Purchasing Agent for furnishing wheat on 17 Aug 1782 {Ref: Maryland State Archives MdHR-6636-42-7}

LORAH, JOHN (Baltimore County) submitted an account and received payment for "shoe and frosting" one of the wagon master's horses in Baltimore on 19 Jan 1780 {Ref: Maryland Historical Society MS.1814, Box 6}

LORD, JOHN JR. (Somerset County) received a receipt from the Purchasing Agent for furnishing pork on 8 Jun 1781 {Ref: Maryland State Archives MdHR-6636-24-43}

LORD, THOMAS (Montgomery County) received a receipt from the Purchasing Agent for furnishing wheat on 7 Sep 1780 {Ref: Maryland State Archives MdHR-6636-24-7}

LOVE, SAMUEL (Charles County) was appointed by the Council of Safety to collect all the gold and silver coin that could be procured in the county in compliance with the Resolve of Congress on 27 Jan 1776 {Ref: Archives of Maryland 11:132}

LOVE, THOMAS (Baltimore Town) was a doctor who submitted an account of his services rendered to Capt. James Bosley and the Council of Safety in November, 1776 {Ref: Archives of Maryland 16:96}

LOVE, WILLIAM (Caroline County) received receipts from the Purchasing Agent for furnishing wheat on 17 Aug, 31 Aug and 1 Sep 1782 {Ref: Maryland State Archives MdHR-6636-42-7}

LOVELESS, BENJAMIN (Montgomery County) received a receipt from the Purchasing Agent for shelling corn on 4 Jun 1780 {Ref: Maryland State Archives MdHR-6636-24-2}; received a receipt for furnishing wheat on 21 May 1781 {Ref: Maryland State Archives MdHR-6636-24-18}

LOWE, DANIEL (Montgomery County) received a receipt from the Purchasing Agent for furnishing wheat on 29 Jul 1780 {Ref: Maryland State Archives MdHR-6636-24-5}

LOWE (LOW), DAVID (Montgomery County) received a receipt from the Purchasing Agent for furnishing wheat on 29 Jul 1780 {Ref: Maryland State Archives MdHR-6636-24-5}; received a receipt for furnishing wheat on 1 Aug 1780 {Ref: Maryland State Archives MdHR-6636-43-7}

LOWE, HENRY (Talbot County) submitted an account and receipt for furnishing bacon on 14 May and 30 Jul 1778 {Ref: Maryland State Archives MdHR-6636-12-15}

LOWE, ISAAC, OF WILLIAM (Dorchester County) received a receipt from the Purchasing Agent for furnishing wheat on 1 Oct 1782 {Ref: Maryland State Archives MdHR-6636-42-23}

LOWES, HENRY (Somerset County) received a receipt from the Purchasing Agent for furnishing wheat on 29 Dec 1781 {Ref: Maryland State Archives MdHR-6636-24-44}

LOWNDES, CHRISTOPHER (Bladensburgh, Prince George's County) received payment from the Purchasing Agent for furnishing men's shoes on 11 Jun 1781 {Ref: Archives of Maryland 47:287}; received a loan certificate for £126.13.6 due from the Council of Maryland "agreeable to the Act proposing to the Citizens of this State, Creditors of Congress on Loan Office Certificates, Etc." on 12 Apr 1783 for services rendered during the war {Ref: Archives of Maryland 48:397}

LOY, ADAM (Frederick County) submitted an account for furnishing hay on 18 Nov 1780 {Ref: Maryland State Archives MdHR-6636-23-5}

LUCAS, BARTON (Montgomery County) was a colonel who received receipts from the Purchasing Agent for furnishing wheat on 13 Sep and 5 Oct 1780 {Ref: Maryland State Archives MdHR-6636-24-13}

LUCAS, MARGARET (Baltimore Town) submitted an account and receipt for making clothing for Capt. George Cook on the state ship *Defence* on 12 Apr 1777 {Ref: Maryland State Archives MdHR-19970-2-1}

LUCAS, MICHAEL (Caroline County) received a receipt from the Purchasing

Agent for furnishing wheat on 22 Aug 1782 {Ref: Maryland State Archives MdHR-6636-42-7}
LUCAS, WILLIAM (Baltimore County) submitted an account and received payment for driving a team for five days with continental flour to Susquehanna for the use of the army on 1 Jan and 25 Jan 1780 {Ref: Maryland Historical Society MS.1814, Box 6}
LUCK, MARY (Montgomery County) received a receipt from the Purchasing Agent for furnishing wheat on 26 Jul 1780 {Ref: Maryland State Archives MdHR-6636-24-5}
LUCK, THOMAS (Montgomery County) received a receipt from the Purchasing Agent for furnishing wheat on 26 Jul 1780 {Ref: Maryland State Archives MdHR-6636-24-5}
LUCK, WILLIAM JR. (Montgomery County) received a receipt from the Purchasing Agent for furnishing wheat on 21 Jul 1780 {Ref: Maryland State Archives MdHR-6636-24-5}
LUCKETT, IGNATIUS (Charles County) received a receipt from the Purchasing Agent for furnishing wheat on 24 Nov 1781 {Ref: Maryland State Archives MdHR-6636-42-15}; received a receipt for furnishing wheat on 18 Jan 1782 {Ref: Maryland State Archives MdHR-6636-42-16}
LUCKETT, LEVIN (Prince George's County) received a receipt from the Purchasing Agent for furnishing wheat on 26 Mar 1783 {Ref: Maryland State Archives MdHR-6636-50-135}
LUCKETT, THOMAS (Charles County) received a receipt from the Purchasing Agent for furnishing wheat on 28 Dec 1782 {Ref: Maryland State Archives MdHR-6636-42-21}
LUCKETT, THOMAS H. (Charles County) received a receipt from the Purchasing Agent for furnishing wheat on 10 May 1783 {Ref: Maryland State Archives MdHR-6636-42-22}
LUCKETT, WILLIAM (Prince George's County) received receipts from the Purchasing Agent for furnishing wheat on 12 May and 29 May 1782 {Ref: Maryland State Archives MdHR-6636-50-135}
LUESFORDE, JOHN (Montgomery County) received a receipt from the Purchasing Agent for furnishing wheat on 25 Apr 1781 {Ref: Maryland State Archives MdHR-6636-24-14}
LUSER, YOST (Frederick County) received a certificate from the Purchasing Agent for furnishing wheat on 31 Jul 1782 {Ref: Maryland State Archives MdHR-6636-42-36}
LUSER, ZACHARIAH (Frederick County) received a certificate from the Purchasing Agent for furnishing wheat on 1 Aug 1781 {Ref: Maryland State Archives MdHR-6636-23-28}
LUTCH, GEORGE (Frederick County) received a certificate from the Purchasing

Agent for furnishing wheat on 12 Sep 1782 {Ref: Maryland State Archives MdHR-6636-42-37}

LUTCH, THOMAS (Montgomery County) received a receipt from the Purchasing Agent for furnishing wheat on 1 Aug 1780 {Ref: Maryland State Archives MdHR-6636-43-7}

LUTCH, WILLIAM JR. (Montgomery County) received a receipt from the Purchasing Agent for furnishing wheat on 1 Aug 1780 {Ref: Maryland State Archives MdHR-6636-43-7}

LUTHER, JACOB (Frederick County) received payment for hauling provisions to Frederick Town on 17 Mar 1781 {Ref: Maryland State Archives MdHR-6636-23-4}

LUX, WILLIAM (Baltimore County) was appointed by the Council of Safety to collect all the gold and silver coin that could be procured in the county in compliance with the Resolve of Congress on 27 Jan 1776 {Ref: Archives of Maryland 11:131}; also see "Charles Wallace," q.v.

LUX & BOWLEY (Baltimore Town) received payment by order of the Council of Maryland for furnishing cordage and rigging for the galley *Chester* on 8 Oct 1777 {Ref: Archives of Maryland 16:392}

LYDDAN (LYDAN), NICHOLAS (Montgomery County) received a receipt from the Purchasing Agent for furnishing wheat on 24 Jul 1780 {Ref: Maryland State Archives MdHR-6636-24-5}; received receipts from the Purchasing Agent for furnishing wheat on 1 Sep and 12 Sep 1780 {Ref: Maryland State Archives MdHR-6636-24-7}; received a receipt for furnishing wheat on 16 Oct 1780 {Ref: Maryland State Archives MdHR-6636-24-8}

LYDICK, PETER (Baltimore Town) was a gunsmith who contracted to repair guns for the Council of Safety on or about 7 Feb 1776 {Ref: Archives of Maryland 11:155}

LYLES, WILLIAM (Prince George's County) was licensed Assistant Commissary of Purchases by the Council of Maryland on 19 Nov 1779 {Ref: Archives of Maryland 43:20}

LYNN, DAVID (Montgomery County) received a receipt from the Purchasing Agent for furnishing wheat on 23 Aug 1780 {Ref: Maryland State Archives MdHR-6636-24-6}

LYON, WILLIAM (Baltimore County) submitted an account and receipt for furnishing flour on 23 Apr 1781 {Ref: Maryland State Archives MdHR-6636-43-38UUU}

MABERRY, AARON (Caroline County) received a receipt from the Purchasing Agent for furnishing wheat on 5 Aug 1782 {Ref: Maryland State Archives MdHR-6636-42-7}

MACATEE, ELIZABETH (Charles County) received a receipt from the Purchasing Agent for furnishing wheat on 15 Apr 1783 {Ref: Maryland State

Archives MdHR-6636-42-22}

MACATEE, JOHN (Charles County) received a receipt from the Purchasing Agent for the use of a horse on 14 Apr 1781 {Ref: Maryland State Archives MdHR-19970-3-16}; received a receipt for furnishing wheat on 28 Sep 1782 {Ref: Maryland State Archives MdHR-6636-42-19}; received a receipt for furnishing wheat on 28 Dec 1782 {Ref: Maryland State Archives MdHR-6636-42-21}

MACATEE, JOSEPH (Charles County) received a loan certificate for £6.12.10 due from the Council of Maryland "agreeable to the Act proposing to the Citizens of this State, Creditors of Congress on Loan Office Certificates, Etc." on 18 Dec 1783 for services rendered during the war {Ref: Archives of Maryland 48:490}

MACATEE, THOMAS (Charles County) received a receipt from the Purchasing Agent for wheat on 14 Nov 1781 {Ref: Maryland State Archives MdHR-6636-42-15}

MACATEE, WALTER (Charles County) received a receipt from the Purchasing Agent for furnishing wheat on 29 Dec 1782 {Ref: Maryland State Archives MdHR-6636-42-21}; received a receipt for furnishing wheat on 3 May 1783 {Ref: Maryland State Archives MdHR-6636-42-22}

MACCUBBIN (MACKUBIN), ELIZABETH (Baltimore County) received a loan certificate for £9.8.5 due from the Council of Maryland "agreeable to the Act proposing to the Citizens of this State, Creditors of Congress on Loan Office Certificates, Etc." on 17 Oct 1783 for services rendered during the war {Ref: Archives of Maryland 48:470}

MACCUBBIN (MACKUBIN), JAMES (Baltimore County) received a certificate from the Purchasing Agent for furnishing beef on 26 Oct 1780 {Ref: Maryland State Archives MdHR-6636-21-133}; received a loan certificate for £52.14.6 due from the Council of Maryland "agreeable to the Act proposing to the Citizens of this State, Creditors of Congress on Loan Office Certificates, Etc." on 3 Jun 1783 for services rendered during the war {Ref: Archives of Maryland 48:425}

MACCUBBIN, THOMAS (Montgomery County) submitted an account for furnishing provisions on 1 Jul 1780 {Ref: Maryland State Archives MdHR-6636-50-91}

MACCUBBIN, NICHOLAS (Baltimore County) received payment by order of the Council of Safety "for Messrs. Nicholas Maccubbin & Son" for furnishing shoes for the troops on 25 Mar 1776 {Ref: Archives of Maryland 11:285}; Nicholas received a receipt from the Purchasing Agent for furnishing veal on 16 Jul 1781 {Ref: Maryland State Archives MdHR-6636-31-121}; received a loan certificate for £287.11.0 due from the Council of Maryland "agreeable to the Act proposing to the Citizens of this State, Creditors of Congress on Loan Office Certificates, Etc." on 6 Jun 1783 for services rendered during the war

{Ref: Archives of Maryland 48:427}; also see "Edward Gaither," q.v.

MACCUBBIN, ZACHARIAH (Montgomery County) was a captain who received payment by order of the Council of Safety for furnishing two musquets and bayonets on 29 Aug 1776 {Ref: Archives of Maryland 12:247}; received a receipt for furnishing wheat on 23 Aug 1780 {Ref: Maryland State Archives MdHR-6636-24-6}

MACCUBBIN, ZACHARIAH JR. (Baltimore County) was appointed by the Council of Maryland to be one of three "Superintendants of the Press, or Presses in Baltimore Town, employed in printing the Continental Bills of Credit" on 28 May 1777 {Ref: Archives of Maryland 16:261}

MACDADE, PATRICK (Prince George's County) received a receipt from the Purchasing Agent for furnishing wheat on 2 Sep 1782 {Ref: Maryland State Archives MdHR-6636-50-135}

MACDADE, PHILIP (Prince George's County) received a receipt from the Purchasing Agent for furnishing wheat on 1 Aug 1782 {Ref: Maryland State Archives MdHR-6636-50-135}

MACDOGLE, JOHN (Montgomery County) received a receipt from the Purchasing Agent for furnishing wheat on 10 Apr 1781 {Ref: Maryland State Archives MdHR-6636-42-11}

MACGILL, JAMES (Anne Arundel County) received payment by order of the Council of Safety via Patrick Macgill for the hire of his wagon on 10 Feb 1778 {Ref: Archives of Maryland 16:485}

MACKALL, BENJAMIN (Montgomery County) received a receipt from the Purchasing Agent for furnishing wheat on 19 May 1781 {Ref: Maryland State Archives MdHR-6636-24-18}

MACKALL, BENJAMIN (Calvert County) received a certificate for a loan to the Continental Congress on 12 Jun 1778 {Ref: Maryland State Archives MdHR-6636-11-119G}

MACKALL, BENJAMIN 4TH (Calvert County) was appointed by the Council of Safety to collect all the gold and silver coin that could be procured in the county in compliance with the Resolve of Congress on 27 Jan 1776 {Ref: Archives of Maryland 11:132}

MACKELFRESH, JOHN (Frederick County) received a certificate from the Purchasing Agent for furnishing wheat on 8 Jun 1782 {Ref: Maryland State Archives MdHR-6636-42-35}

MACKEY, JAMES (Worcester County) submitted an account and receipt for furnishing pork on 19 May 1781 {Ref: Maryland State Archives MdHR-6636-43-27}

MACKEY, JAMES (Dorchester County) furnished flour, pork, lard and beef for the use of the state as reported to the Council of Maryland on a "Return of Provisions, Etc., received at the Head of Elk" on 15 Jun 1781 {Ref: Archives of

Maryland 47:409}

MACKEY, WILLIAM (Frederick County) received a receipt from the Purchasing Agent for delivering flour on 29 Dec 1780 {Ref: Maryland State Archives MdHR-6636-23-29}; received a receipt for furnishing beef on 16 Jan 1781 {Ref: Maryland State Archives MdHR-6636-23-2}; received a receipt for furnishing corn meal on 7 Feb 1781 {Ref: Maryland State Archives MdHR-6636-23-3}; received a receipt for furnishing corn meal on 1 Mar 1781 {Ref: Maryland State Archives MdHR-6636-23-4}; received a receipt for furnishing wheat on 30 Oct 1781 {Ref: Maryland State Archives MdHR-6636-23-28}; received a receipt for hauling flour on 21 May 1783 {Ref: Maryland State Archives MdHR-6636-42-28}

MACKILFISH, RICHARD SR. (Montgomery County) received a receipt from the Purchasing Agent for furnishing wheat on 17 May 1781 {Ref: Maryland State Archives MdHR-6636-42-11}

MACKLEE, JAMES (Frederick County) received a receipt from the Purchasing Agent for furnishing hay on 13 Feb 1781 {Ref: Maryland State Archives MdHR-6636-23-3}

MADDEN, JOHN (Charles County) received a receipt from the Purchasing Agent for furnishing wheat on 29 Dec 1782 {Ref: Maryland State Archives MdHR-6636-42-21}

MADDEN, JONATHAN (Prince George's County) received a receipt from the Purchasing Agent for furnishing wheat on 19 Dec 1782 {Ref: Maryland State Archives MdHR-6636-50-142}

MADDOX, HEZEKIAH (Worcester County) received a receipt from the Purchasing Agent for furnishing bacon on 27 Aug 1780 {Ref: Maryland State Archives MdHR-6636-24-53}

MADDOX, JOHN (Charles County) received a receipt from the Purchasing Agent for furnishing wheat on 25 Sep 1781 {Ref: Maryland State Archives MdHR-6636-23-24}; received a receipt for furnishing wheat on 20 Nov 1781 {Ref: Maryland State Archives MdHR-6636-42-15}

MADDOX, NOTLEY (Charles County) received a receipt from the Purchasing Agent for furnishing wheat on 28 Dec 1782 {Ref: Maryland State Archives MdHR-6636-42-21}

MADDOX, SARAH (Charles County) received a receipt from the Purchasing Agent for furnishing wheat on 15 Apr 1783 {Ref: Maryland State Archives MdHR-6636-42-22}

MAFFITH (MAFFITT?), SAMUEL (Cecil County) pledged a loan in the amount of £100 to the State of Maryland under the Act for the Emission of Bills of Credit "to defray the expences of the present campaign" in October, 1781 {Ref: Archives of Maryland 47:533}

MAGRUDER, ARCHIBALD (Montgomery County) received receipts from the

Purchasing Agent for furnishing wheat on 30 Sep and 31 Oct 1780 {Ref: Maryland State Archives MdHR-6636-24-13}

MAGRUDER, EDWARD (Montgomery County) received a receipt from the Purchasing Agent for furnishing wheat on 6 Sep 1780 {Ref: Maryland State Archives MdHR-6636-24-13}; received a receipt for furnishing wheat on 18 Jul 1781 {Ref: Maryland State Archives MdHR-6636-24-14}

MAGRUDER, ELIAS (Montgomery County) received a receipt from the Purchasing Agent for furnishing wheat on 16 Dec 1780 {Ref: Maryland State Archives MdHR-6636-24-13}

MAGRUDER, GEORGE FRAZER (Montgomery County) received receipts from the Purchasing Agent for furnishing wheat on 2 Sep and 5 Sep 1780 {Ref: Maryland State Archives MdHR-6636-24-7}; received a receipt for furnishing wheat on 1 Oct 1781 {Ref: Maryland State Archives MdHR-6636-24-15}

MAGRUDER, GEORGE T. (Prince George's County) received a receipt from the Purchasing Agent for furnishing wheat on 26 Aug 1783 {Ref: Maryland State Archives MdHR-6636-50-135}

MAGRUDER, HEZEKIAH (Montgomery County) received a receipt from the Purchasing Agent for furnishing wheat on 24 Nov 1780 {Ref: Maryland State Archives MdHR-6636-24-13}

MAGRUDER, JAMES (Montgomery County) received a receipt from the Purchasing Agent for furnishing wheat on 5 Aug 1780 {Ref: Maryland State Archives MdHR-6636-24-2}

MAGRUDER, NATHANIEL (Montgomery County) received a receipt from the Purchasing Agent for furnishing wheat on 1 Aug 1780 {Ref: Maryland State Archives MdHR-6636-43-7}; received receipts from the Purchasing Agent for furnishing wheat on 8 Aug and 24 Aug 1780 {Ref: Maryland State Archives MdHR-6636-24-6}; received a receipt for furnishing wheat on 24 Oct 1780 {Ref: Maryland State Archives MdHR-6636-24-8}; received a receipt for furnishing wheat on 7 Nov 1780 {Ref: Maryland State Archives MdHR-6636-24-8}

MAGRUDER, SAMUEL (Montgomery County) received receipts from the Purchasing Agent for furnishing wheat on 29 Jul and 5 Sep 1780 {Ref: Maryland State Archives MdHR-6636-24-13}; received a receipt for furnishing wheat on 1 Aug 1780 {Ref: Maryland State Archives MdHR-6636-43-7}; received receipts from the Purchasing Agent for furnishing wheat on 10 May and 11 Aug 1781 {Ref: Maryland State Archives MdHR-6636-24-14}

MAGRUDER, SAMUEL (Montgomery County) received a loan certificate for £193.16.8 due from the Council of Maryland "agreeable to the Act proposing to the Citizens of this State, Creditors of Congress on Loan Office Certificates, Etc." on 16 Oct 1783 for services rendered during the war {Ref: Archives of Maryland 48:469}

207

MAGRUDER, SAMUEL BEALL (Montgomery County) received a receipt from the Purchasing Agent for furnishing wheat on 11 Dec 1780 {Ref: Maryland State Archives MdHR-6636-24-13}

MAGRUDER, SAMUEL WADE (Montgomery County) received a receipt from the Purchasing Agent for furnishing wheat on 12 Aug 1780 {Ref: Maryland State Archives MdHR-6636-24-6}; received receipts from the Purchasing Agent for furnishing wheat on 4 Nov, 11 Nov, 13 Nov, 15 Nov, 18 Nov, 21 Nov, 29 Nov, 4 Dec and 29 Dec 1780 {Ref: Maryland State Archives MdHR-6636-24-8}; received a receipt for furnishing wheat on 11 Dec 1780 {Ref: Maryland State Archives MdHR-6636-24-13}; received receipts from the Purchasing Agent for furnishing wheat on 1 Jan and 9 Feb 1781 {Ref: Maryland State Archives MdHR-6636-24-9}

MAGRUDER, THOMAS (Montgomery County) received a receipt from the Purchasing Agent for furnishing wheat on 20 Apr 1781 {Ref: Maryland State Archives MdHR-6636-24-18}

MAGRUDER, WALTER (Montgomery County) received a receipt from the Purchasing Agent for furnishing wheat on 22 Jul 1780 {Ref: Maryland State Archives MdHR-6636-24-13}; received a receipt for furnishing wheat on 1 Aug 1780 {Ref: Maryland State Archives MdHR-6636-43-7}

MAGRUDER, WILLIAM (Frederick County) received payment by order of the Council of Maryland for his use as Contractor for Horses in Frederick County on 31 Aug 1780 {Ref: Archives of Maryland 43:270}; received a certificate from the Purchasing Agent for furnishing wheat on 12 Jun 1782 {Ref: Maryland State Archives MdHR-6636-42-35}

MAGRUDER, WILLIAM B. (Montgomery County) received a receipt from the Purchasing Agent for shelling corn on 30 Jun 1780 {Ref: Maryland State Archives MdHR-6636-24-2}; received a receipt for furnishing wheat on 1 Sep 1780 {Ref: Maryland State Archives MdHR-6636-24-7}

MALL, THOMAS (Harford County) furnished flour for the use of the state as reported to the Council of Maryland on a "Return of Provisions, Etc., received at the Head of Elk" on 5 Jun 1781 {Ref: Archives of Maryland 47:409}

MALLORT, JACOB (Frederick County) submitted an account for furnishing veal and beef on 29 May 1781 {Ref: Maryland State Archives MdHR-6636-23-6}

MALTIMORE, JOHN (county not stated) received payment by order of the Council of Safety for furnishing boatage on 7 Sep 1776 {Ref: Archives of Maryland 12:260}

MANSFIELD, MRS. (Baltimore Town) submitted an account for rendering lodging services on 12 Apr 1777 {Ref: Maryland State Archives MdHR-19970-2-1}

MANLY, JOHN (Cecil County) received a loan certificate for £35.8.10 due from the Council of Maryland "agreeable to the Act proposing to the Citizens of this

State, Creditors of Congress on Loan Office Certificates, Etc." on 19 Dec 1783 for services rendered during the war {Ref: Archives of Maryland 48:494}

MANSHIP, CHARLES (Caroline County) received receipts from the Purchasing Agent for furnishing wheat on 5 Aug and 22 Aug 1782 {Ref: Maryland State Archives MdHR-6636-42-7}

MANSHIP, CHARLES JR. (Caroline County) received a receipt from the Purchasing Agent for furnishing wheat on 5 Aug 1782 {Ref: Maryland State Archives MdHR-6636-42-7}

MANSIL, RICHARD (Baltimore County) submitted an account and received payment for assisting to stow away flour on 28 Jan 1780 {Ref: Maryland Historical Society MS.1814, Box 6}

MANTZ, FRANCIS (Frederick County) received a certificate from the Purchasing Agent for furnishing wheat on 29 May 1782 {Ref: Maryland State Archives MdHR-6636-42-35}

MARBURY, FRANCIS H. (Charles County) received a receipt from the Purchasing Agent for furnishing wheat on 10 May 1782 {Ref: Maryland State Archives MdHR-6636-42-18}; received a receipt for furnishing wheat on 31 Oct 1782 {Ref: Maryland State Archives MdHR-6636-42-19}; received a receipt for furnishing wheat on 28 Dec 1782 {Ref: Maryland State Archives MdHR-6636-42-21}

MARBURY, HENRY (Charles County) received a receipt from the Purchasing Agent for furnishing wheat on 19 Jan 1782 {Ref: Maryland State Archives MdHR-6636-42-16}

MARBURY, WILLIAM (Charles County) received a receipt from the Purchasing Agent for furnishing wheat on 28 Dec 1782 {Ref: Maryland State Archives MdHR-6636-42-21}

MARLOW, JAMES (Charles County) received a receipt from the Purchasing Agent for furnishing wheat on 20 Dec 1782 {Ref: Maryland State Archives MdHR-6636-42-20}

MARSH, CHARLES HYNSON (Caroline County) received a receipt from the Purchasing Agent for furnishing wheat on 1 Sep 1782 {Ref: Maryland State Archives MdHR-6636-42-7}

MARSHALL, ANDREW (Dorchester County) received a receipt from the Purchasing Agent for furnishing wheat on 25 Mar 1783 {Ref: Maryland State Archives MdHR-6636-42-24}

MARSHALL, BENJAMIN (Charles County) received a receipt from the Purchasing Agent for furnishing wheat on 29 Dec 1782 {Ref: Maryland State Archives MdHR-6636-42-21}

MARSHALL, ELIJAH (Dorchester County) received a receipt from the Purchasing Agent for furnishing wheat on 25 Mar 1783 {Ref: Maryland State Archives MdHR-6636-42-24}

MARSHALL, ISAAC (Somerset County) received a receipt from the Purchasing Agent for furnishing beef on 5 Dec 1781 {Ref: Maryland State Archives MdHR-6636-24-44}

MARSHALL, JAMES (Dorchester County) received a receipt from the Purchasing Agent for furnishing wheat on 1 Oct 1782 {Ref: Maryland State Archives MdHR-6636-42-23}

MARSHALL, JOHN (Charles County) was a colonel who received payment for furnishing wheat on 5 Oct 1781 {Ref: Maryland State Archives MdHR-6636-43-45RRR}; received a receipt for furnishing wheat on 23 Oct 1781 {Ref: Maryland State Archives MdHR-6636-43-45E}; received a receipt for furnishing wheat on 27 Oct 1781 {Ref: Maryland State Archives MdHR-6636-42-15}; received a receipt for furnishing wheat on 11 Oct 1782 {Ref: Maryland State Archives MdHR-6636-42-19}

MARSHALL, JOHN (Worcester County) received a receipt from the Purchasing Agent for furnishing pork on 22 Sep 1780 {Ref: Maryland State Archives MdHR-6636-24-54}; received a receipt for furnishing pork on 20 Mar 1781 {Ref: Maryland State Archives MdHR-6636-24-56}; submitted an account and receipt of payment due for furnishing beef on 5 Oct 1781 {Ref: Maryland State Archives MdHR-6636-43-28R}

MARSHALL, RICHARD (Charles County) received a receipt from the Purchasing Agent for furnishing wheat on 11 Oct 1782 {Ref: Maryland State Archives MdHR-6636-42-19}

MARSHALL, SAMUEL (Dorchester County) received a receipt from the Purchasing Agent for furnishing wheat on 1 Oct 1782 {Ref: Maryland State Archives MdHR-6636-42-23}

MARSHALL, STEPHEN (Somerset County) received a receipt from the Purchasing Agent for furnishing beef on 5 Dec 1781 {Ref: Maryland State Archives MdHR-6636-24-44}

MARSHALL, THOMAS (Charles County) received a receipt from the Purchasing Agent for furnishing wheat on 31 Oct 1782 {Ref: Maryland State Archives MdHR-6636-42-19}

MARSHALL, THOMAS HANSON (Charles County) was a captain who received a receipt from the Purchasing Agent for furnishing wheat on 11 Apr 1782 {Ref: Maryland State Archives MdHR-6636-42-18}; received a loan certificate for £372.11.3 due from the Council of Maryland "agreeable to the Act proposing to the Citizens of this State, Creditors of Congress on Loan Office Certificates, Etc." on 14 May 1783 for services rendered during the war {Ref: Archives of Maryland 48:413}

MARSHALL, WILLIAM (Charles County) received a receipt from the Purchasing Agent for furnishing wheat on 23 Sep 1781 {Ref: Maryland State Archives MdHR-6636-43-45N}; received a receipt for furnishing wheat on 20 Dec 1782

{Ref: Maryland State Archives MdHR-6636-42-20}; received a loan certificate for £30.18.1 due from the Council of Maryland "agreeable to the Act proposing to the Citizens of this State, Creditors of Congress on Loan Office Certificates, Etc." on 15 May 1783 for services rendered during the war {Ref: Archives of Maryland 48:414}

MARSHALL, WILLIAM (Frederick County) received a certificate from the Purchasing Agent for furnishing wheat on 7 Sep 1781 {Ref: Maryland State Archives MdHR-6636-23-28}

MARTIN, JAMES (Worcester County) was a colonel who received receipts from the Purchasing Agent for furnishing and hauling corn on 10 May and 20 Aug 1780 {Ref: Maryland State Archives MdHR-6636-24-53}; received a receipt for hauling corn on 30 Sep 1780 {Ref: Maryland State Archives MdHR-6636-24-54}; submitted an account for storing and hauling provisions on 1 Jan 1782 {Ref: Maryland State Archives MdHR-6636-43-28C}; submitted an account and receipt for processing pork on 18 May 1782 {Ref: Maryland State Archives MdHR-6636-43-28U}; received a receipt for storing pork on 5 Jun 1783 {Ref: Maryland State Archives MdHR-19970-4-1}

MARTIN, JOHN (Cecil County) submitted an account for hauling, grinding and storing wheat on 1 Sep 1783 {Ref: Maryland State Archives MdHR-6636-42-9}

MARTIN, LUTHER (Somerset County) was appointed Attorney General of Maryland in the room of Benjamin Galloway (who had resigned) on 11 Feb 1778 {Ref: Archives of Maryland 16:487}; accepted his commission on 2 Mar 1778 {Ref: Maryland State Archives MdHR-4587-18}; received a loan certificate for £167.6.3 due from the Council of Maryland "agreeable to the Act proposing to the Citizens of this State, Creditors of Congress on Loan Office Certificates, Etc." on 29 Oct 1783 for services rendered during the war {Ref: Archives of Maryland 48:475}

MARTIN, ROBERT (Talbot County) received payment by order of the Council of Safety for furnishing boatage on 5 Sep 1776 {Ref: Archives of Maryland 12:257}

MARTIN, THOMAS JR. (Talbot County) received a receipt from the Purchasing Agent for furnishing bacon for the use of the army on 2 May 1778 {Ref: Maryland State Archives MdHR-4587-80}; received a receipt for purchasing pork on 13 Jun 1778 {Ref: Maryland State Archives MdHR-6636-12-15}

MARTIN, ZACHARIAH (Charles County) received a receipt from the Purchasing Agent for furnishing wheat on 22 Jul 1782 {Ref: Maryland State Archives MdHR-6636-42-18}

MASEBOUGH, JACOB B. (Frederick County) received a certificate from the Purchasing Agent for furnishing wheat on 24 Jun 1782 {Ref: Maryland State Archives MdHR-6636-42-35}

211

MASLIN, BERTRAM (Kent County) received a certificate from the Purchasing Agent for furnishing wheat on 29 Jan 1780 {Ref: Maryland State Archives MdHR-6636-23-42}

MASLIN, JAMES (Kent County) received a certificate from the Purchasing Agent for furnishing wheat on 20 Mar 1780 {Ref: Maryland State Archives MdHR-6636-23-44}

MASLIN, THOMAS (Kent County) received payment from the Purchasing Agent for furnishing cattle and pasturage for the public use in September, 1781 {Ref: Maryland State Archives MdHR-6636-43-3}

MASON, BENJAMIN (Baltimore County) submitted an account and received payment for hauling four loads of flour on 1 Feb 1780 {Ref: Maryland Historical Society MS.1814, Box 6}

MASON, GEORGE (Charles County) was a colonel who received a receipt from the Purchasing Agent for furnishing wheat on 22 Jul 1782 {Ref: Maryland State Archives MdHR-6636-42-18}; received a receipt for furnishing wheat on 29 Dec 1782 {Ref: Maryland State Archives MdHR-6636-42-21}

MASON, HANNAH (Caroline County) received a receipt from the Purchasing Agent for furnishing wheat on 1 Sep 1782 {Ref: Maryland State Archives MdHR-6636-42-7}

MASON, HENRY (Caroline County) received a receipt from the Purchasing Agent for furnishing wheat on 1 Sep 1782 {Ref: Maryland State Archives MdHR-6636-42-7}

MASON, RICHARD (Montgomery County) received a receipt from the Purchasing Agent for furnishing wheat on 1 Aug 1780 {Ref: Maryland State Archives MdHR-6636-43-7}; received a receipt for furnishing wheat on 10 Aug 1780 {Ref: Maryland State Archives MdHR-6636-24-6}

MASON, RICHARD (Charles County) received a receipt from the Purchasing Agent for furnishing wheat on 28 Dec 1782 {Ref: Maryland State Archives MdHR-6636-42-21}

MASON, RICHARD (county not stated) received a loan certificate for £7.15.2 due from the Council of Maryland "agreeable to the Act proposing to the Citizens of this State, Creditors of Congress on Loan Office Certificates, Etc." on 18 Dec 1783 for services rendered during the war {Ref: Archives of Maryland 48:491}

MASON, THOMAS (Prince George's County) received a receipt from the Purchasing Agent for furnishing wheat in 1782 {Ref: Maryland State Archives MdHR-6636-50-135}

MASON, WILLIAM (Kent County) received payment from the Purchasing Agent for furnishing cattle and pasturage for the public use in September, 1781 {Ref: Maryland State Archives MdHR-6636-43-3}

MASON, WILLIAM (Charles County) was a captain who received a receipt from the Purchasing Agent for furnishing wheat on 31 Oct 1782 {Ref: Maryland State Archives MdHR-6636-42-19}; received a receipt for furnishing wheat on 28 Dec 1782 {Ref: Maryland State Archives MdHR-6636-42-21}

MASON, WILLIAM (Charles County) was a colonel who received a receipt from the Purchasing Agent for furnishing wheat on 8 May 1783 {Ref: Maryland State Archives MdHR-6636-42-22}

MASSEY, EBENEZER (Kent County) received a certificate from the Purchasing Agent for furnishing wheat on 1 Apr 1780 {Ref: Maryland State Archives MdHR-6636-43-1}

MASSEY, ELIJAH (Kent County) received payment from the Purchasing Agent for furnishing cattle and pasturage for the public use on 29 Oct 1781 {Ref: Maryland State Archives MdHR-6636-43-3}

MASSEY, JOHN (Worcester County) received a receipt from the Purchasing Agent for furnishing corn on 14 Jun 1780 {Ref: Maryland State Archives MdHR-6636-24-53}; his name appeared on "A List of Corn Purchased in Worcester County for the use of the State of Maryland" by the Commissary in July, 1780 {Ref: Archives of Maryland 45:9}

MASSEY, STEPHEN (Queen Anne's County) received a receipt of hauling fees for the account of Spencer & Falconar on 19 Nov 1782 {Ref: Maryland State Archives MdHR-6636-43-12}

MASTEN, SARAH (Charles County) received a receipt from the Purchasing Agent for furnishing wheat on 22 Jul 1782 {Ref: Maryland State Archives MdHR-6636-42-18}

MATHERS, JAMES (Harford County) received payment for furnishing a musquet to the Committee of Safety on 5 Aug 1776 {Ref: Preston's History of Harford County, p. 332}

MATHEWS, DANIEL (Frederick County) received a certificate from the Purchasing Agent for furnishing wheat on 6 Aug 1782 {Ref: Maryland State Archives MdHR-6636-42-37}

MATHEWS, IGNATIUS (Charles County) was a minister who submitted an account and receipt of cash for the use of the state on 22 Sep 1780 {Ref: Maryland State Archives MdHR-6636-20-52}; received receipts from the Purchasing Agent for furnishing wheat on 30 May, 7 Sep, 8 Sep, 14 Sep, 15 Sep and 29 1781 {Ref: Maryland State Archives MdHR-6636-42-15}; received receipts from the Purchasing Agent for furnishing wheat on 9 Apr and 14 Sep 1782 {Ref: Maryland State Archives MdHR-6636-42-18}; received receipts from the Purchasing Agent for furnishing wheat on 26 Apr, 28 Dec and 29 Dec 1782 {Ref: Maryland State Archives MdHR-6636-42-21}; received a receipt for furnishing wheat on 3 May 1783 {Ref: Maryland State Archives MdHR-6636-42-22}

MATHEWS, MARY (Charles County) received a receipt from the Purchasing

Agent for furnishing wheat on 27 Apr 1782 {Ref: Maryland State Archives MdHR-6636-42-18}; received receipts from the Purchasing Agent for furnishing wheat on 28 Dec and 29 Dec 1782 {Ref: Maryland State Archives MdHR-6636-42-21}

MATTART, JACOB (Frederick County) received a receipt from the Purchasing Agent for furnishing veal on 26 Feb 1781 {Ref: Maryland State Archives MdHR-6636-23-3}

MATTHEWS, GEORGE (Baltimore Town) submitted a bill and receipt for furnishing flour on 11 Nov 1779 {Ref: Maryland State Archives MdHR-19970-3-8}

MATTHEWS, GREENBURY (Caroline County) received a receipt from the Purchasing Agent for furnishing wheat on 20 Sep 1782 {Ref: Maryland State Archives MdHR-6636-42-7}

MATTHEWS, THOMAS (Caroline County) received a receipt from the Purchasing Agent for furnishing wheat on 24 Aug 1782 {Ref: Maryland State Archives MdHR-6636-42-7}

MATTHEWS, WILLIAM (Kent County) received a certificate from the Purchasing Agent for storing flour on 22 May 1780 {Ref: Maryland State Archives MdHR-6636-23-42}; received payment from the Purchasing Agent for furnishing cattle and pasturage for the public use in September, 1781 {Ref: Maryland State Archives MdHR-6636-43-3}

MATTINGLY, LUKE (St. Mary's County) appeared on "A Return of Beef on the Hoof Purchased by Joseph Ford Commissary of Purchases" on 13 Oct 1780 when he delivered two steers for the use of the state {Ref: Archives of Maryland 45:156}

MAW, ELIZABETH (Baltimore Town) received payments by order of the Council of Maryland "for rent of her house as a barrack" on 27 Mar, 3 Jul and 21 Sep 1778 and 23 Mar 1779 {Ref: Archives of Maryland 16:554, 21:154, 209, 326}; Elizabeth Maw received payment via William Maw for services rendered on 15 Jun 1779 (Note: Their surname was mistakenly listed as "Man" instead of "Maw" in this record) {Ref: Archives of Maryland 21:455}

MAXWELL, ANN (Talbot County) was one of twenty-six people who contacted the Governor and Council of Maryland in 1781 and pledged to support and maintain at their own expense the Barge *Experiment* so it can patrol the bay between Kent Point and Tilghman's Island in order to protect them against the enemy, stating in part, "whereas from the present exhausted state of the public treasury the government cannot immediately give that protection to every individual which is become necessary from the cruel and savage mode in which the war is now carried on against us" {Ref: Archives of Maryland 47:584-585}

MAXWELL, ELIZABETH, Mrs. (Talbot County) received a receipt from the Purchasing Agent for furnishing wheat on 9 Oct 1780 {Ref: Maryland State

Archives MdHR-6636-24-49}; received a loan certificate for £377.19.10 due from the Council of Maryland "agreeable to the Act proposing to the Citizens of this State, Creditors of Congress on Loan Office Certificates, Etc." on 4 Mar 1783 for services rendered during the war {Ref: Archives of Maryland 48:373}

MAXWELL, ROBERT (Kent County) received payment from the Purchasing Agent for furnishing cattle for the public use in September, 1781 {Ref: Maryland State Archives MdHR-6636-43-3}

MAXWELL, WILLIAM JR. (Kent County) received payment from the Purchasing Agent for furnishing cattle for the public use in September, 1781 {Ref: Maryland State Archives MdHR-6636-43-3}

MAXWELL, WILLIAM SR. (Kent County) received payment from the Purchasing Agent for furnishing cattle for the public use in September, 1781 {Ref: Maryland State Archives MdHR-6636-43-3}

MAY, BENJAMIN (Montgomery County) received a receipt from the Purchasing Agent for furnishing wheat on 14 Sep 1781 {Ref: Maryland State Archives MdHR-6636-24-15}

MAY (MEY), JAMES (Harford County) was a gunsmith who furnished 19 guns and bayonets to the Committee of Safety from Richard Dallam's factory on 17 Feb 1777 {Ref: Preston's History of Harford County, p. 339}; contracted with the Maryland Council of Safety to make guns on 14 Mar 1777 {Ref: Archives of Maryland 16:173}; received a receipt for supplying musquets and bayonets on 22 Jun 1780 {Ref: Maryland State Archives MdHR-6636-18-165}; he was still manufacturing arms on 12 Jan 1781 {Ref: Archives of Maryland 47:14}

MAYBURY, BERIAH (Anne Arundel County) was a captain who received payment by order of the Council of Safety for sounding the depth of the river between Greenbury's Point and Horn Point on 11 Apr 1776 {Ref: Archives of Maryland 11:326, 16:337}; received payment for the hire of his boat on 4 Oct 1776 {Ref: Archives of Maryland 12:319}; received payment for the use of the hospital on 23 Jul 1778 {Ref: Archives of Maryland 21:164}

MAYHILL, ROBERT (Annapolis, Anne Arundel County) was a doctor and surgeon who received a receipt from the Purchasing Agent for furnishing bed sacks for use at the hospital on 3 Sep 1781 {Ref: Maryland State Archives MdHR-6636-31-76D}

MAYNADIER, WILLIAM (Talbot County) received payment for furnishing beef on 26 Sep 1780 {Ref: Maryland State Archives MdHR-6636-24-49}

MAYNARD, JAMES (Annapolis) served as messenger for the Council of Maryland from March to September, 1777 and was paid for his services on 2 Jul and 17 Sep 1777 {Ref: Archives of Maryland 16:306, 377}; received payment for furnishing a gun on 6 Aug 1777 {Ref: Archives of Maryland 16:326}

MAYO, JOSEPH (Anne Arundel County) received a loan certificate for £168.1.5

due from the Council of Maryland "agreeable to the Act proposing to the Citizens of this State, Creditors of Congress on Loan Office Certificates, Etc." on 12 Dec 1783 for services rendered during the war {Ref: Archives of Maryland 48:489}

McALISTER, ALEXANDER (Frederick County) received a certificate from the Purchasing Agent for furnishing wheat on 31 May 1782 {Ref: Maryland State Archives MdHR-6636-42-34}

McBRIDE, LAZARUS (Prince George's County) received receipts from the Purchasing Agent for furnishing wheat on 1 Nov 1782 and 26 Feb 1783 {Ref: Maryland State Archives MdHR-6636-50-135}; received receipts from the Purchasing Agent for furnishing wheat on 11 Dec and 15 Dec 1782 and 3 Jan 1783 {Ref: Maryland State Archives MdHR-6636-50-142}

McBRYDE (McBRIDE), WILLIAM (Somerset County) was appointed by the Council of Maryland as one of thirty men to be "Agents for Purchasing Provisions" on 30 Mar 1779 {Ref: Archives of Maryland 21:332, 423}; received a certificate of payment due for storing corn on 10 Jun 1780 {Ref: Maryland State Archives MdHR-6636-24-39}; served as Commissary by 1781 {Ref: Maryland State Archives MdHR-6636-24-43}; appointed Purchaser of Clothing in his county by the Council of Maryland on 5 Jun 1781 {Ref: Archives of Maryland 45:462}; submitted an account for slaughtering beef on 1 Oct 1781 {Ref: Maryland State Archives MdHR-6636-43-15}; certification of wheat ground on 6 Sep 1782 {Ref: Maryland State Archives MdHR-6636-42-18}

McCABE, JAMES (Queen Anne's County) submitted an account and receipt for storing wheat from Sep 1782 to Feb 1783 {Ref: Maryland State Archives MdHR-6636-43-12}; submitted an account for processing beef and pork on 7 Feb 1783 {Ref: Maryland State Archives MdHR-6636-43-13}

McCALLISTER, JOHN (Queen Anne's County) received a certificate from the Purchasing Agent for furnishing wheat on 4 Jan 1780 {Ref: Maryland State Archives MdHR-6636-24-30}

McCALLUM, ALEXANDER (Talbot County) received a receipt from the Purchasing Agent for furnishing bacon for the use of the army on 27 Apr 1778 {Ref: Maryland State Archives MdHR-4587-71}

McCAY, ABSALOM (Kent County) received payment from the Purchasing Agent for furnishing cattle and pasturage for the public use in September, 1781 {Ref: Maryland State Archives MdHR-6636-43-3}

McCLELLAN, NATHANIEL (Kent County) furnished flour for the use of the state as reported to the Council of Maryland on a "Return of Provisions, Etc., received at the Head of Elk" on 2 Jul 1781 {Ref: Archives of Maryland 47:409}

McCLAIN, JOHN (Worcester County) appeared on "A List of Corn Purchased in

Worcester County for the use of the State of Maryland" by the Commissary in July, 1780 {Ref: Archives of Maryland 45:10}

McCLEMMY, SAMUEL (Somerset County) received a loan certificate for £220.1.7 due from the Council of Maryland "agreeable to the Act proposing to the Citizens of this State, Creditors of Congress on Loan Office Certificates, Etc." on 19 Dec 1783 for services rendered during the war {Ref: Archives of Maryland 48:493}

McCLEMMY, WHITTY (Somerset County) received a loan certificate for £33.13.0½ due from the Council of Maryland "agreeable to the Act proposing to the Citizens of this State, Creditors of Congress on Loan Office Certificates, Etc." on 19 Dec 1783 for services rendered during the war {Ref: Archives of Maryland 48:493}

McCOMBS, JACOB (Caroline County) received a receipt from the Purchasing Agent for furnishing wheat on 20 Sep 1782 {Ref: Maryland State Archives MdHR-6636-42-7}

McCORMICK, DENNIS (Queen Anne's County) received a receipt from the Purchasing Agent for furnishing bacon on 1 Mar 1778 {Ref: Maryland State Archives MdHR-4587-50}

McCRASS, WILLIAM (Montgomery County) received a receipt from the Purchasing Agent for furnishing wheat on 1 Aug 1780 {Ref: Maryland State Archives MdHR-6636-43-7}

McCRAY, ISAAC (Somerset County) received a receipt from the Purchasing Agent for furnishing beef on 4 Dec 1781 {Ref: Maryland State Archives MdHR-6636-24-44}

McDADE, DANIEL (Montgomery County) received a receipt from the Purchasing Agent for furnishing wheat on 10 Apr 1781 {Ref: Maryland State Archives MdHR-6636-24-15}

McDADE, JOHN (Frederick County) received receipts from the Purchasing Agent for furnishing corn on 6 Mar, 1 Apr and 3 May 1780 {Ref: Maryland State Archives MdHR-6636-24-1}

McDANIEL, REDNUM (Frederick County) received a receipt from the Purchasing Agent for furnishing wheat on 18 Jan 1783 {Ref: Maryland State Archives MdHR-6636-42-28}

McDANIEL, WILLIAM (Prince George's County) received a receipt from the Purchasing Agent for furnishing wheat on 12 Feb 1783 {Ref: Maryland State Archives MdHR-6636-50-135}; received a receipt for furnishing wheat on 1 May 1783 {Ref: Maryland State Archives MdHR-6636-50-142}

McDERMOTT, PATRICK (Montgomery County) received a receipt from the Purchasing Agent for furnishing wheat on 8 May 1781 {Ref: Maryland State Archives MdHR-6636-42-11}

McDONAL, ZACARIAH (Charles County) received a receipt from the Purchasing

Agent for furnishing wheat on 26 Apr 1783 {Ref: Maryland State Archives MdHR-6636-42-22}

McDONALD, GEORGE (Montgomery County) received a receipt from the Purchasing Agent for shelling corn on 18 Apr 1780 {Ref: Maryland State Archives MdHR-6636-24-2}

McDONOLD, FRANCIS (Frederick County) received a receipt from the Purchasing Agent for furnishing wheat on 7 Jun 1782 {Ref: Maryland State Archives MdHR-6636-42-34}

McDONNOW, MORRIS J. (Charles County) received a receipt from the Purchasing Agent for furnishing wheat on 28 Dec 1782 {Ref: Maryland State Archives MdHR-6636-42-21}

McFADON, ALEXANDER (George Town, Frederick County, now Montgomery County) received payment by order of the Council of Safety to enable him to carry on a linen manufactory on 10 Jun 1776 {Ref: Archives of Maryland 11:473}

McFADON, ARTHUR (Worcester County) submitted an account and receipt for slaughtering beef on 1 Oct 1781 {Ref: Maryland State Archives MdHR-6636-43-28RR}

McFADON, JAMES (Worcester County) received payment by order of the Council of Safety to enable him to carry on a linen manufactory on 24 Jul 1776 {Ref: Archives of Maryland 12:109}

McGEE, SAMUEL (Dorchester County) received a receipt from the Purchasing Agent for furnishing wheat on 1 Nov 1782 {Ref: Maryland State Archives MdHR-6636-42-23}

McGINES, DANIEL (Caroline County) received a receipt from the Purchasing Agent for furnishing wheat on 1 Sep 1782 {Ref: Maryland State Archives MdHR-6636-42-7}

McGLALIN, ALEXANDER (Worcester County) received a receipt from the Purchasing Agent for furnishing bacon on 3 Aug 1780 {Ref: Maryland State Archives MdHR-6636-24-53}

McGOWAN, JAMES (Cecil County) received receipts from the Purchasing Agent for furnishing wheat on 20 Feb and 12 Mar 1783 {Ref: Maryland State Archives MdHR-6636-42-9}

McGOWAN, JOHN (Cecil County) submitted an account and receipt for storing wheat on 15 Sep 1783 {Ref: Maryland State Archives MdHR-6636-42-9}

McGOWEN, JAMES (Kent County) furnished flour for the use of the state as reported to the Council of Maryland on a "Return of Provisions, Etc., received at the Head of Elk" on 25 Jul 1781 {Ref: Archives of Maryland 47:409}

McGRAW, WILLIAM (Montgomery County) received a receipt from the Purchasing Agent for furnishing wheat on 9 Aug 1780 {Ref: Maryland State Archives MdHR-6636-24-6}

McGREGORY, JOHN (Kent County) received a certificate from the Purchasing Agent for furnishing wheat on 24 Jan 1780 {Ref: Maryland State Archives MdHR-6636-23-46}

McGUIRE, MICHAEL (Frederick County) received a receipt from the Purchasing Agent for furnishing beef on 10 Jan 1781, submitted an account for cattle for commissary of provisions on 2 Mar 1782, and received a receipt from the Purchasing Agent for cash from the commissary of provisions on 1 Apr 1782 {Ref: Maryland State Archives MdHR-6636-42-27}

McHARD, ISAAC (Annapolis, Anne Arundel County) was a Commissary Agent who received a receipt from the Purchasing Agent for furnishing powder on 16 Apr 1777 {Ref: Maryland State Archives MdHR-6636-9-14D}; received an order from the Maryland Council to supply and deliver salt on 1 May 1777 {Ref: Maryland State Archives MdHR-6636-7-76}; received an order from the Governor of Maryland to purchase leather and salt in Virginia on 10 Jun 1777 {Ref: Maryland State Archives MdHR-4590-37}; appointed by the Council of Maryland to be one of the two "Supervisors of the Press for superintending the printing of the [Continental] Bills of Credit" on 5 Sep 1780 {Ref: Archives of Maryland 43:276}; appointed by the Council of Maryland to be one of six "Signers of the Bills emitted in Virtue of the Act to enable the Treasurer of the Western Shore to draw and sell Bills of Exchange and for an Emission of Bills of Credit if necessary" on 8 Sep 1780 {Ref: Archives of Maryland 43:281}

McINTYRE, WILLIAM (Somerset County) received a receipt from the Purchasing Agent for furnishing pork on 20 Mar 1782 {Ref: Maryland State Archives MdHR-6636-43-21}

McKANON, DAVID (Montgomery County) received a receipt from the Purchasing Agent for furnishing wheat on 7 May 1781 {Ref: Maryland State Archives MdHR-6636-42-11}

McKENZIE, JAMES (Prince George's County) received payment by order of the Council of Safety for furnishing a musquet on 21 Aug 1776 {Ref: Archives of Maryland 12:226}

McKIMMY, GIDEON (Caroline County) received a receipt from the Purchasing Agent for furnishing wheat on 5 Aug 1782 {Ref: Maryland State Archives MdHR-6636-42-7}

McLAIN, JAMES (Kent County) received payment from the Purchasing Agent for furnishing cattle and pasturage for the public use in September, 1781 {Ref: Maryland State Archives MdHR-6636-43-3}

McLAMAR, DENNIS (Charles County) received a receipt from the Purchasing Agent for furnishing wheat on 15 Apr 1783 {Ref: Maryland State Archives MdHR-6636-42-22}

McLANE, A., see "Samuel Hart," q.v.

McLEAN, JOHN (Frederick County) received a certificate from the Purchasing

Agent for furnishing wheat on 3 Oct 1781 {Ref: Maryland State Archives MdHR-6636-23-28}

McLURE, JOHN (Baltimore County) received a loan certificate for £342.14.7 due from the Council of Maryland "agreeable to the Act proposing to the Citizens of this State, Creditors of Congress on Loan Office Certificates, Etc." on 18 Dec 1783 for services rendered during the war {Ref: Archives of Maryland 48:491}

McMECHEN, DAVID (Baltimore Town) pledged a loan in the amount of £100 to the State of Maryland under the Act for the Emission of Bills of Credit "to defray the expences of the present campaign" in June, 1781 {Ref: Archives of Maryland 47:327}

McNEALE, ARCHIBALD (Talbot County) received a loan certificate for £15.16.1 due from the Council of Maryland "agreeable to the Act proposing to the Citizens of this State, Creditors of Congress on Loan Office Certificates, Etc." on 19 May 1783 for services rendered during the war {Ref: Archives of Maryland 48:417}

McPHERSON, BASIL (Charles County) received a receipt from the Purchasing Agent for furnishing wheat on 21 Dec 1781 {Ref: Maryland State Archives MdHR-6636-42-15}; received a receipt for furnishing wheat on 15 Apr 1783 {Ref: Maryland State Archives MdHR-6636-42-22}

McPHERSON, CHLOE (Charles County) received a receipt from the Purchasing Agent for furnishing wheat on 28 Sep 1782 {Ref: Maryland State Archives MdHR-6636-42-19}

McPHERSON, DANIEL (Charles County) received a receipt from the Purchasing Agent for furnishing wheat on 7 Sep 1781 {Ref: Maryland State Archives MdHR-6636-42-15}; received receipts from the Purchasing Agent for furnishing wheat on 15 Apr and 10 May 1783 {Ref: Maryland State Archives MdHR-6636-42-22}

McPHERSON, JOHN (Charles County) received a receipt from the Purchasing Agent for furnishing wheat on 27 Oct 1781 {Ref: Maryland State Archives MdHR-6636-42-15}

McPHERSON, JOHN JR. (Charles County) was appointed by the Council of Maryland as one of thirty men to be "Agents for Purchasing Provisions" on 30 Mar 1779 {Ref: Archives of Maryland 21:332}; received a receipt for furnishing wheat on 15 Dec 1781 {Ref: Maryland State Archives MdHR-6636-42-15}

McPHERSON, WALTER (Charles County) received a receipt from the Purchasing Agent for furnishing wheat on 8 May 1783 {Ref: Maryland State Archives MdHR-6636-42-22}

McPHERSON, WILLIAM (Charles County) was a captain who received a receipt from the Purchasing Agent for furnishing wheat on 20 Dec 1782 {Ref:

Maryland State Archives MdHR-6636-42-20}; also see "John Halkerston," q.v.

MEAD, SAMUEL (Anne Arundel County) was one of the Deputy Collectors of Clothing who received payment by order of the Council of Maryland on 24 Feb 1778 {Ref: Archives of Maryland 16:519}

MEADS, BENJAMIN (Harford County) received payment for furnishing a gun to the Committee of Safety on 18 Jun 1776 {Ref: Preston's History of Harford County, p. 330}

MEATHARD, CHARLES (Frederick County) received a certificate from the Purchasing Agent for furnishing wheat on 30 Jul 1782 {Ref: Maryland State Archives MdHR-6636-42-36}

MEATON, SARAH (Baltimore Town) submitted an account for rendering lodging services on 12 Apr 1777 {Ref: Maryland State Archives MdHR-19970-2-1}

MEDFORD, MARMEDUKE (Kent County) received payment from the Purchasing Agent for furnishing cattle for the public use in September, 1781 {Ref: Maryland State Archives MdHR-6636-43-3}

MEDFORD, NATHANIEL (Dorchester County) received a receipt from the Purchasing Agent for furnishing wheat on 1 Oct 1782 {Ref: Maryland State Archives MdHR-6636-42-23}

MEDFORD, THOMAS (Kent County) received payment from the Purchasing Agent for furnishing cattle for the public use in September, 1781 {Ref: Maryland State Archives MdHR-6636-43-3}

MEDFORD, WILLIAM (Dorchester County) received a receipt from the Purchasing Agent for furnishing wheat on 1 Oct 1782 {Ref: Maryland State Archives MdHR-6636-42-23}

MEEDS, RACHEL (Caroline County) received a receipt from the Purchasing Agent for furnishing wheat on 17 Aug 1782 {Ref: Maryland State Archives MdHR-6636-42-7}

MELCHOR, VENDEL (Frederick County) received a certificate from the Purchasing Agent for furnishing wheat on 29 Jul 1782 {Ref: Maryland State Archives MdHR-6636-42-36}

MELVIL, DAVID (Dorchester County) received a receipt from the Purchasing Agent for furnishing wheat on 25 Mar 1783 {Ref: Maryland State Archives MdHR-6636-42-24}

MELVILL, JOHN (Caroline County) received a receipt from the Purchasing Agent for furnishing wheat on 3 Jun 1782 {Ref: Maryland State Archives MdHR-6636-42-7}

MENCH, ADAM (Frederick County) received a certificate from the Purchasing Agent for furnishing wheat on 1 Jul 1782 {Ref: Maryland State Archives MdHR-6636-42-36}

MENCH, JOHN (Frederick County) received a certificate from the Purchasing Agent for furnishing wheat on 25 May 1782 {Ref: Maryland State Archives

MdHR-6636-42-36}

MENSON, JAMES (Cecil County) received a receipt from the Purchasing Agent for furnishing wheat on 29 Jan 1783 {Ref: Maryland State Archives MdHR-6636-42-9}

MERCHANT, JOHN (Talbot County) received a receipt from the Purchasing Agent for furnishing bacon for the use of the army on 6 May 1778 {Ref: Maryland State Archives MdHR-4587-83}

MERCHANT, WILLIAM (Kent County) received a certificate from the Purchasing Agent for hauling wheat on 23 Feb 1780 {Ref: Maryland State Archives MdHR-6636-23-42}

MERIWETHER, REUBIN, see "Vachel Warfield," q.v.

MERRICK, ISAAC (Caroline County) received a receipt from the Purchasing Agent for furnishing wheat on 20 Sep 1782 {Ref: Maryland State Archives MdHR-6636-42-7}

MERRICK, ISRAEL (Caroline County) received a receipt from the Purchasing Agent for furnishing wheat on 17 Aug 1782 {Ref: Maryland State Archives MdHR-6636-42-7}

MERRICK, JOHN (Caroline County) received a receipt from the Purchasing Agent for furnishing wheat on 27 May 1782 {Ref: Maryland State Archives MdHR-6636-42-7}

MERRIKEN (MEREKIN), JOSEPH (Anne Arundel County) was appointed by the Council of Maryland as one of thirty men to be "Agents for Purchasing Provisions" on 30 Mar 1779 {Ref: Archives of Maryland 21:332}

MERRILL, LEVI (Worcester County) received payment for furnishing beef on 25 Sep 1781 {Ref: Maryland State Archives MdHR-6636-43-28VV}

MERRITT, L. (Kent County) received a certificate from the Purchasing Agent for furnishing flour on 20 Mar 1780 {Ref: Maryland State Archives MdHR-6636-43-1}

MERRITT, MARTHA (Kent County) received a certificate from the Purchasing Agent for furnishing wheat on 20 Mar 1780 {Ref: Maryland State Archives MdHR-6636-23-42}

MERRITT (MERRIT), SARAH (Kent County) received payment from the Purchasing Agent for furnishing cattle and pasturage for the public use in September, 1781 {Ref: Maryland State Archives MdHR-6636-43-3}

MERRITT, SYLVANUS (Baltimore County) submitted an account and received payment for turning out flour on 28 Jan and 3 Feb 1780 {Ref: Maryland Historical Society MS.1814, Box 6}

MERRITT (MERRIT), WILLIAM (Kent County) received payment from the Purchasing Agent for furnishing cattle for the public use in September, 1781 {Ref: Maryland State Archives MdHR-6636-43-3}

MERRYMAN, JOHN JR. (Baltimore County) received a loan certificate for

£505.2.5 due from the Council of Maryland "agreeable to the Act proposing to the Citizens of this State, Creditors of Congress on Loan Office Certificates, Etc." on 30 Sep 1783 for services rendered during the war {Ref: Archives of Maryland 48:457}

MESNISE, TYLER (Frederick County) received a certificate from the Purchasing Agent for hauling flour on 28 Sep 1781 {Ref: Maryland State Archives MdHR-6636-42-32}

MESSERSMITH, SAMUEL (Baltimore Town) was a gunsmith who contracted to repair guns for the Council of Safety on or about 7 Feb 1776 {Ref: Archives of Maryland 11:155}; received payment on 17 Jul 1776 and all guns left in his custody to be repaired were requested to be delivered to the military on 12 Sep 1776 {Ref: Archives of Maryland 12:63, 266}

MICHAEL, HENRY (Frederick County) received a receipt from the Purchasing Agent for furnishing pork on 23 Feb 1781 {Ref: Maryland State Archives MdHR-6636-23-3}

MIDDLETON, HORATIO (Charles County) received a receipt from the Purchasing Agent for furnishing wheat on 19 Jan 1782 {Ref: Maryland State Archives MdHR-6636-42-16}; received a receipt for furnishing wheat on 31 Oct 1782 {Ref: Maryland State Archives MdHR-6636-42-19}; received a receipt for furnishing wheat on 28 Dec 1782 {Ref: Maryland State Archives MdHR-6636-42-21}

MIDDLETON, JOSEPH (Anne Arundel County) received payment by order of the Council of Safety for furnishing a pilot boat for the purpose of gaining and communicating intelligence on 8 Apr 1776 {Ref: Archives of Maryland 11:316}; received payment for furnishing his look out boats on 12 Sep 1776 {Ref: Archives of Maryland 12:266}

MIFLIN, MARY (Kent County) received payment from the Purchasing Agent for furnishing cattle and pasturage for the public use in September, 1781 {Ref: Maryland State Archives MdHR-6636-43-3}

MILBURN, CALEB (Somerset County) received a receipt from the Purchasing Agent for furnishing beef on 5 Dec 1781 {Ref: Maryland State Archives MdHR-6636-24-44}

MILES, JOHN (Prince George's County) received a receipt from the Purchasing Agent for furnishing wheat on 17 Apr 1783 {Ref: Maryland State Archives MdHR-6636-43-9}

MILES, LEVIN (Somerset County) received a receipt from the Purchasing Agent for furnishing beef on 2 Nov 1781 {Ref: Maryland State Archives MdHR-6636-24-44}; received a receipt for furnishing pork on 12 May 1782 {Ref: Maryland State Archives MdHR-6636-43-21}

MILES, MATHIAS (Somerset County) received a receipt from the Purchasing Agent for furnishing pork on 12 May 1782 {Ref: Maryland State Archives

MdHR-6636-43-21}

MILES, ROBERT (St. Mary's County) received payment from the Council of Maryland for riding express on 16 Jul 1781 {Ref: Archives of Maryland 45:504}

MILLER, ANDREW (Anne Arundel County) received a receipt from the Purchasing Agent for furnishing powder on 16 Apr 1777 {Ref: Maryland State Archives MdHR-6636-9-14A}

MILLER, ANDREW (Cecil County) furnished flour for the use of the state as reported to the Council of Maryland on a "Return of Provisions, Etc., received at the Head of Elk" on 20 Jul 1781 {Ref: Archives of Maryland 47:409}

MILLER, ARTHUR (Kent County) received a certificate from the Purchasing Agent for furnishing wheat on 14 Jan 1780 {Ref: Maryland State Archives MdHR-6636-23-46}

MILLER, CHARLES (Kent County) received a certificate from the Purchasing Agent for storing wheat on 6 Jun 1780 {Ref: Maryland State Archives MdHR-6636-23-42}

MILLER, JACOB (Charles County) received a receipt from the Purchasing Agent for furnishing wheat on 8 May 1783 {Ref: Maryland State Archives MdHR-6636-42-22}

MILLER, MARTIN (Montgomery County) received a receipt from the Purchasing Agent for furnishing wheat on 9 May 1781 {Ref: Maryland State Archives MdHR-6636-24-18}

MILLER, MARTIN (Frederick County) received a certificate from the Purchasing Agent for furnishing wheat on 8 Feb 1782 {Ref: Maryland State Archives MdHR-6636-42-36}

MILLER, NATHANIEL (Kent County) received a certificate from the Purchasing Agent for furnishing wheat on 5 Apr 1780 {Ref: Maryland State Archives MdHR-6636-23-45}

MILLER, RICHARD (Kent County) received a certificate from the Purchasing Agent for furnishing wheat on 14 Jan 1780 {Ref: Maryland State Archives MdHR-6636-23-43}

MILLS, CORNELIUS (Anne Arundel County) received payment by order of the Council of Safety for supplying three cords of wood on 17 Aug 1776 {Ref: Archives of Maryland 12:216}

MILLS, JAMES (Caroline County) received a receipt from the Purchasing Agent for furnishing wheat on 22 Aug 1782 {Ref: Maryland State Archives MdHR-6636-42-7}

MILLS, JAMES (Dorchester County) received a receipt from the Purchasing Agent for furnishing wheat on 1 Nov 1782 {Ref: Maryland State Archives MdHR-6636-42-23}

MILLS, JAMES (St. Mary's County) appeared on "A Return of Beef on the Hoof

Purchased by Joseph Ford Commissary of Purchases" on 9 Oct 1780 when he delivered two steers for the use of the state {Ref: Archives of Maryland 45:156}

MILLS, MARY (Dorchester County) received a receipt from the Purchasing Agent for furnishing wheat on 1 Nov 1782 {Ref: Maryland State Archives MdHR-6636-42-23}

MILLS, RICHARD (Worcester County) received a receipt from the Purchasing Agent for furnishing corn on 5 Apr 1780 {Ref: Maryland State Archives MdHR-6636-24-52}; his name appeared on "A List of Corn Purchased in Worcester County for the use of the State of Maryland" by the Commissary in July, 1780 {Ref: Archives of Maryland 45:10}

MILLS, WILLIAM (Worcester County) submitted an account and receipt for packing and storing pork on 1 Aug 1781 {Ref: Maryland State Archives MdHR-6636-43-27}

MILSON, SAMUEL (Caroline County) received a receipt from the Purchasing Agent for furnishing wheat on 1 Sep 1782 {Ref: Maryland State Archives MdHR-6636-42-7}

MILSTEAD, WILLIAM (Charles County) received a certificate from the Purchasing Agent for furnishing wheat on 5 Dec 1782 {Ref: Maryland State Archives MdHR-6636-42-20}

MINSKEY (MINSKIE), CATHARINE, Mrs. (Anne Arundel County) received payment by order of the Council of Safety for attending the hospital on 3 Oct 1776 and 13 Feb 1777 {Ref: Archives of Maryland 12:317, 16:133}

MISSELL, FRED (Frederick County) submitted an account for furnishing beef on 29 May 1781 {Ref: Maryland State Archives MdHR-6636-23-6}

MITCHELL, JOHN (Marlbro, Prince George's County) was a captain who received payment from the Purchasing Agent for furnishing material for clothing ("light duck and heavy duck") on 11 Jun 1781 {Ref: Archives of Maryland 47:287}

MITCHELL, JOHN (Calvert County) received payment for driving cattle on 27 Feb 1782 {Ref: Maryland State Archives MdHR-6636-50-37}

MITCHELL, JOHN (Caroline County) received a receipt from the Purchasing Agent for furnishing wheat on 27 May 1782 {Ref: Maryland State Archives MdHR-6636-42-7}

MITCHELL, JOHN JR. (Dorchester County) received a receipt from the Purchasing Agent for furnishing wheat on 3 Sep 1782 {Ref: Maryland State Archives MdHR-6636-42-23}

MITCHELL, JOHN P. (Worcester County) was a captain who received a receipt from the Purchasing Agent for furnishing beef on 30 Sep 1780 {Ref: Maryland State Archives MdHR-6636-24-54}

MITCHELL, JOSEPH (Montgomery County) received a receipt from the

225

Purchasing Agent for furnishing wheat on 16 Sep 1780 {Ref: Maryland State Archives MdHR-6636-24-7}

MITCHELL, JOSIAH (Worcester County) submitted an account and receipt for furnishing salt in 1782 {Ref: Maryland State Archives MdHR-6636-43-28DD}; submitted an account and receipt for furnishing salt in 1782 {Ref: Maryland State Archives MdHR-6636-43-28VV}

MITCHELL, RACHAL (Charles County) received a receipt from the Purchasing Agent for furnishing wheat on 10 May 1783 {Ref: Maryland State Archives MdHR-6636-42-22}

MITCHELL, RICHARD B., see "John Halkerston," q.v.

MOALE, JOHN (Baltimore County) was appointed by the Council of Safety to collect all the gold and silver coin that could be procured in the county in compliance with the Resolve of Congress on 27 Jan 1776 {Ref: Archives of Maryland 11:131}; his name was listed as "Mr. John Moles" when he delivered flour to the commissary at Baltimore Town for the use of the State of Maryland in the summer of 1780 {Ref: Archives of Maryland 45:84}; received payment for furnishing corn on 23 Apr 1781 {Ref: Maryland State Archives MdHR-6636-43-38CCC}

MOALE, ROBERT (Baltimore County) received payment for furnishing veal on 25 May 1781 {Ref: Maryland State Archives MdHR-6636-43-38FFF}

MOALEN, WALTER (Charles County) received a receipt from the Purchasing Agent for furnishing wheat on 28 Dec 1782 {Ref: Maryland State Archives MdHR-6636-42-21}

MOBLEY, ARCHIBALD (Montgomery County) received a receipt from the Purchasing Agent for shelling corn on 11 Jul 1780 {Ref: Maryland State Archives MdHR-6636-24-2}

MOCK, VALENTINE (Frederick County) received a certificate from the Purchasing Agent for furnishing wheat on 31 May 1781 {Ref: Maryland State Archives MdHR-6636-42-34}

MOCKABEY, NINIAN (Montgomery County) received a receipt from the Purchasing Agent for furnishing wheat on 6 Apr 1781 {Ref: Maryland State Archives MdHR-6636-42-11}

MOFFATT, THOMAS (Anne Arundel County) received payment by order of the Council of Maryland "for going express to Virginia" on or about 3 Oct 1777 {Ref: Archives of Maryland 16:387}

MOFFETT, GEORGE JR. (Kent County) received a certificate from the Purchasing Agent for hauling flour on 10 Jun 1780 {Ref: Maryland State Archives MdHR-6636-43-1}

MOLAHARN, THOMAS (Charles County) received a receipt from the Purchasing Agent for furnishing wheat on 28 Dec 1782 {Ref: Maryland State Archives MdHR-6636-42-21}

MOLES, JOHN, see "John Moale," q.v.
MOLIN, LEDDY (Charles County) received a receipt from the Purchasing Agent for furnishing wheat on 31 Oct 1782 {Ref: Maryland State Archives MdHR-6636-42-19}
MOLIN, PHILIP (Charles County) received a receipt from the Purchasing Agent for furnishing wheat on 31 Oct 1782 {Ref: Maryland State Archives MdHR-6636-42-19}
MOLIN, SAMUEL (Charles County) received a receipt from the Purchasing Agent for furnishing wheat on 31 Oct 1782 {Ref: Maryland State Archives MdHR-6636-42-19}
MOLIN, WILLIAM (Charles County) received a receipt from the Purchasing Agent for furnishing wheat on 14 Sep 1782 {Ref: Maryland State Archives MdHR-6636-42-18}
MOLTING, THOMAS (Prince George's County) received a receipt from the Purchasing Agent for furnishing wheat on 31 Jul 1783 {Ref: Maryland State Archives MdHR-6636-50-135}
MONK, RICHARD (Harford County) received payment for furnishing a gun to the Committee of Safety on 18 Jun 1776 {Ref: Preston's History of Harford County, p. 330}
MONROE, THOMAS (Charles County) received a receipt from the Purchasing Agent for furnishing wheat on 26 Jun 1782 {Ref: Maryland State Archives MdHR-6636-42-18}; received receipts from the Purchasing Agent for furnishing wheat on 24 Oct and 31 Oct 1782 {Ref: Maryland State Archives MdHR-6636-42-19}
MONTGOMERY, JAMES (Charles County) received a receipt from the Purchasing Agent for furnishing wheat on 15 Apr 1783 {Ref: Maryland State Archives MdHR-6636-42-22}
MONTGOMERY, WILLIAM (Harford County) was appointed by the Council of Maryland to be one of five men in Harford County "to carry the Act to prohibit for a limited time the Exportation of Indian Corn, Etc., by Land" on 22 Dec 1780 {Ref: Archives of Maryland 45:251}
MOOD, JOHN (Frederick County) received a receipt from the Purchasing Agent for delivering flour on 9 Mar 1781 {Ref: Maryland State Archives MdHR-6636-23-30}
MOODY (MOODEY), ROBERT (Kent County) received payment from the Purchasing Agent for furnishing cattle for the public use in September, 1781 {Ref: Maryland State Archives MdHR-6636-43-3}; submitted an account and receipt for grinding wheat and carting supplies on 30 Mar 1782 {Ref: Maryland State Archives MdHR-6636-43-5}; received a loan certificate for £96.6.0 due from the Council of Maryland "agreeable to the Act proposing to the Citizens of this State, Creditors of Congress on Loan Office Certificates, Etc." on 20

227

May 1783 for services rendered during the war {Ref: Archives of Maryland 48:418}

MOORE, BARTON (Montgomery County) received a receipt from the Purchasing Agent for furnishing wheat on 7 Sep 1780 {Ref: Maryland State Archives MdHR-6636-24-7}

MOORE, GEORGE (Montgomery County) received a receipt from the Purchasing Agent for furnishing wheat on 2 Sep 1780 {Ref: Maryland State Archives MdHR-6636-24-13}

MOORE, JAMES (Montgomery County) received a receipt from the Purchasing Agent for furnishing wheat on 27 Apr 1781 {Ref: Maryland State Archives MdHR-6636-24-18}; received a receipt for furnishing wheat on 21 Feb 1782 {Ref: Maryland State Archives MdHR-6636-43-7}

MOORE, JAMES (Charles County) received a receipt from the Purchasing Agent for furnishing wheat on 28 May 1782 {Ref: Maryland State Archives MdHR-6636-42-18}

MOORE, JOHN (Anne Arundel County) received a receipt from the Purchasing Agent for furnishing powder on 16 Apr 1777 {Ref: Maryland State Archives MdHR-6636-9-14D}

MOORE, JOHN (Kent County) received payment from the Purchasing Agent for furnishing cattle and pasturage for the public use on 29 Oct 1781 and for purchasing beef cattle for the public use in October, 1782 {Ref: Maryland State Archives MdHR-6636-43-3}

MOORE, JOHN JR. (Kent County) received a certificate from the Purchasing Agent for furnishing flour on 6 Apr 1780 {Ref: Maryland State Archives MdHR-6636-23-43}

MOORE (MORE), JOHN IRONS OR ISONS (Caroline County) received a receipt from the Purchasing Agent for furnishing wheat on 1 Sep 1782 {Ref: Maryland State Archives MdHR-6636-42-7}

MOORE, JOSHUA (Somerset County) received a receipt from the Purchasing Agent for furnishing bacon on 17 Aug 1780 {Ref: Maryland State Archives MdHR-6636-24-41}

MOORE, NICHOLAS RUXTON (Baltimore County) was a lieutenant in 1776 who received payment from the Maryland Council of Safety "for his expences to and from Philadelphia to carry gold and silver coin for the operations in Canada" on 1 May 1776 {Ref: Archives of Maryland 11:395}

MOORE, ROBERT (Baltimore County) submitted an account and receipt for furnishing spirits on 26 Apr 1781 {Ref: Maryland State Archives MdHR-6636-43-38TTT}

MOORE, SHILES (county not stated) received payment by order of the Council of Safety for furnishing boatage on 2 Oct 1776 {Ref: Archives of Maryland 12:316}

MOORE, WILLIAM (Baltimore County) submitted an account and receipt for furnishing ship's provisions and casks on 1 Mar 1781 {Ref: Maryland State Archives MdHR-6636-43-38LLLL}

MOORE, WILLIAM (Montgomery County) received a receipt from the Purchasing Agent for furnishing wheat on 19 Oct 1780 {Ref: Maryland State Archives MdHR-6636-24-8}

MOORE, WILLIAM JR. (Baltimore County) submitted an account and receipt for furnishing corn on 6 Oct 1781 {Ref: Maryland State Archives MdHR-6636-43-38U}

MORAN, ANDREW (Charles County) received a receipt from the Purchasing Agent for furnishing wheat on 16 Nov 1782 {Ref: Maryland State Archives MdHR-6636-42-19}; received a receipt for furnishing wheat on 30 Nov 1782 {Ref: Maryland State Archives MdHR-6636-42-20}

MORELAND, PARTRICK (Charles County) received a receipt from the Purchasing Agent for furnishing wheat on 20 Dec 1782 {Ref: Maryland State Archives MdHR-6636-42-20}

MORELAND, WILLIAM (Charles County) received a receipt from the Purchasing Agent for furnishing wheat on 20 Dec 1782 {Ref: Maryland State Archives MdHR-6636-42-20}

MORGAN, BEN (Caroline County) received a receipt from the Purchasing Agent for furnishing wheat on 5 Aug 1782 {Ref: Maryland State Archives MdHR-6636-42-7}

MORGAN, DAVID (Caroline County) received a receipt from the Purchasing Agent for furnishing wheat on 17 Aug 1782 {Ref: Maryland State Archives MdHR-6636-42-7}

MORGAN, HAB? (Caroline County) received a receipt from the Purchasing Agent for furnishing wheat on 5 Aug 1782 {Ref: Maryland State Archives MdHR-6636-42-7}

MORGAN, JAMES (Dorchester County) received a receipt from the Purchasing Agent for furnishing wheat on 1 Nov 1782 {Ref: Maryland State Archives MdHR-6636-42-23}

MORGAN, JOHN (Caroline County) received receipts from the Purchasing Agent for wheat on 17 Aug and 20 Sep 1782 {Ref: Maryland State Archives MdHR-6636-42-7}

MORGAN, THOMAS (Talbot County) received a receipt from the Purchasing Agent for furnishing wheat on 9 Oct 1780 {Ref: Maryland State Archives MdHR-6636-24-47}

MORLING, FRANCIS (Talbot County) was one of twenty-six people who contacted the Governor and Council of Maryland in 1781 and pledged to support and maintain at their own expense the Barge *Experiment* so it can patrol the bay between Kent Point and Tilghman's Island in order to protect them against the enemy, stating in part, "whereas from the present exhausted state of the public treasury the government cannot immediately give that protection to every individual which is become necessary from the cruel and savage mode in which the war is now carried on against us" {Ref: Archives of Maryland 47:584-585}

MORNINGSTAR, ANGEL (Frederick County) received receipts from the Purchasing Agent for furnishing hay on 7 Jan and 12 Jan 1781 {Ref: Maryland State Archives MdHR-6636-23-2}; received a receipt for furnishing hay on 12 Feb 1781 {Ref: Maryland State Archives MdHR-6636-23-3}; received a receipt for furnishing hay on 15 Feb 1781 {Ref: Maryland State Archives MdHR-6636-23-30}

MORRIS, ANN (Charles County) received a receipt from the Purchasing Agent for furnishing wheat on 8 May 1783 {Ref: Maryland State Archives MdHR-6636-42-22}

MORRIS, CLEMENT (St. Mary's County) submitted an account of expenses for collecting and driving cattle on 27 Nov 1781 {Ref: Maryland State Archives MdHR-19970-3-17}

MORRIS, CORNELIUS (Caroline County) received a receipt from the Purchasing Agent for furnishing wheat on 1 Sep 1782 {Ref: Maryland State Archives MdHR-6636-42-7}

MORRIS, JACOB (Somerset County) received a receipt from the Purchasing Agent for furnishing bacon on 8 Aug 1780 {Ref: Maryland State Archives MdHR-6636-24-41}; received a receipt for furnishing bacon on 7 Jul 1781 {Ref: Maryland State Archives MdHR-6636-24-43}

MORRIS, SAMUEL (Baltimore County) submitted an account and received payment for stowing flour and measuring wheat for four days on 1 Feb 1780 {Ref: Maryland Historical Society MS.1814, Box 6}

MORRIS, WILLIAM (county not stated) pledged a loan in the amount of £180 to the State of Maryland under the Act for the Emission of Bills of Credit "to defray the expences of the present campaign" in June, 1781 {Ref: Archives of Maryland 47:327}

MORRISON, ELINOR (Baltimore Town) received payment for furnishing linen on 2 Oct 1779 {Ref: Maryland State Archives MdHR-19970-3-8}

MORRISON, JAMES (Frederick County) received a certificate from the Purchasing Agent for furnishing wheat on 6 Jul 1781 {Ref: Maryland State Archives MdHR-6636-23-28}

MORTON, WILLIAM (Prince George's County) received a receipt from the Purchasing Agent for furnishing wheat on 16 Aug 1781 {Ref: Maryland State Archives MdHR-6636-24-20}

MOSES, CONRAD (Frederick County) received a certificate from the Purchasing Agent for furnishing wheat on 17 Jun 1782 {Ref: Maryland State Archives

MdHR-6636-42-35}
MOTTER, HENRY (Frederick County) received a certificate from the Purchasing Agent for delivering flour on 30 Dec 1780 {Ref: Maryland State Archives MdHR-6636-23-29}
MOUNTICUE, JOHN (Caroline County) received a receipt from the Purchasing Agent for furnishing wheat on 1 Sep 1782 {Ref: Maryland State Archives MdHR-6636-42-7}
MUIR, ADAM (Baltimore County) received payment for furnishing corn on 6 Sep 1781 {Ref: Maryland State Archives MdHR-6636-43-38II}
MUIR, JOHN (Anne Arundel County) received a bond as Commissary of Stores in Annapolis on 20 Jun 1778 {Ref: Maryland State Archives MdHR-6636-11-128A}; appointed Purchaser of Clothing in his county by the Council of Maryland on 16 Jun 1781 {Ref: Archives of Maryland 45:476}
MULCAHY, DANIEL (Kent County) received a certificate from the Purchasing Agent for furnishing wheat on 14 Jan 1780 {Ref: Maryland State Archives MdHR-6636-23-41}
MULLAKIN, ANN (Montgomery County) received a receipt from the Purchasing Agent for furnishing wheat on 1 Aug 1780 {Ref: Maryland State Archives MdHR-6636-43-7}
MUMFORD, JOHN (Montgomery County) received a receipt from the Purchasing Agent for furnishing wheat on 18 Aug 1780 {Ref: Maryland State Archives MdHR-6636-24-6}
MUMFORD, MATT. OR MATHIAS (Worcester County) received a receipt from the Purchasing Agent for furnishing corn on 15 Feb 1780 {Ref: Maryland State Archives MdHR-6636-24-52}; his name appeared on "A List of Corn Purchased in Worcester County for the use of the State of Maryland" by the Commissary in July, 1780 {Ref: Archives of Maryland 45:9}
MUMMARD, JOHN (Montgomery County) received receipts from the Purchasing Agent for furnishing wheat on 13 Oct and 6 Nov 1780 {Ref: Maryland State Archives MdHR-6636-24-8}
MUNCASTER, JAMES (Charles County) received a receipt from the Purchasing Agent for furnishing wheat on 3 Aug 1782 {Ref: Maryland State Archives MdHR-6636-42-18}
MUNRO, DANIEL (Annapolis) received payment from the Council of Maryland "for riding Express" on 7 Jan and 20 Feb 1783 {Ref: Archives of Maryland 48:339, 363-364}
MUNSCHETT, MUNGO (Charles County) received a receipt from the Purchasing Agent for furnishing wheat on 11 Dec 1782 {Ref: Maryland State Archives MdHR-6636-42-20}
MURDOCK, GEORGE (Frederick County) was a colonel who was appointed by the Council of Maryland as one of thirty men to be "Agents for Purchasing

231

Provisions" on 30 Mar 1779 {Ref: Archives of Maryland 21:332}; commissioned an Assistant Deputy Commissary of Purchases on 10 Sep 1779 {Ref: Archives of Maryland 21:519}; delivered four cattle to the Purchasing Agent for the use of the State of Maryland in October, 1780 {Ref: Archives of Maryland 45:149}; received receipts for furnishing flour on 18 Dec and 27 Dec 1780 {Ref: Maryland State Archives MdHR-6636-23-29}; received a receipt for furnishing beef on 9 Mar 1781 {Ref: Maryland State Archives MdHR-6636-42-26}; received a receipt for furnishing corn meal on 12 Mar 1781 {Ref: Maryland State Archives MdHR-6636-23-4}; also see "Joseph Hall," q.v.

MURDOCK, JOHN (Montgomery County) received 80 musquets, 100 bayonetts, 50 cartridge boxes, 2550 cartridges, and 35 new locks from the Council of Maryland, delivered by John Beeden, and ordered that "the musquets you will direct to be repaired immediately" on 21 Jun 1781 {Ref: Archives of Maryland 45:481}; received certification for furnishing wheat on 14 Aug 1780 {Ref: Maryland State Archives MdHR-6636-43-7}

MURPHY, CHARLES (Queen Anne's County) submitted an account and receipt for hauling wheat from Sep 1782 to Feb 1783 {Ref: Maryland State Archives MdHR-6636-43-12}

MURPHY, MORGAN, see "Elizabeth Wilson," q.v.

MURPHY, PHILIP (Queen Anne's County) received a certificate from the Purchasing Agent for furnishing beef on 28 Sep 1781 {Ref: Maryland State Archives MdHR-6636-24-34}

MURPHY, HENRY (Harford County) furnished flour for the use of the state as reported to the Council of Maryland on a "Return of Provisions, Etc., received at the Head of Elk" on 6 Jun 1781 {Ref: Archives of Maryland 47:409}

MURPHY, WILLIAM (Montgomery County) received a receipt from the Purchasing Agent for furnishing wheat on 24 Aug 1780 {Ref: Maryland State Archives MdHR-6636-24-6}

MURPHY, ZACHARIAH (Charles County) received a receipt from the Purchasing Agent for furnishing wheat on 28 Dec 1782 {Ref: Maryland State Archives MdHR-6636-42-21}

MURRAY, HENRY PATRICK (Queen Anne's County) received a certificate of payment due for hauling on 9 Apr 1780 {Ref: Maryland State Archives MdHR-6636-24-28}

MURRAY, JAMES (Annapolis) was a doctor who served on a committee for the establishment of a firearms factory in 1776, became a colonel in the medical services in 1776, and served as physician to the State Dispensary in 1780 and in various capacities in the State Hospitals in 1781 {Ref: Maryland Genealogical Society Bulletin 19:4 (1978), pp. 303-307}; received flannel from the Commissary of Stores "for his assistance to the soldiery" on 17 Dec 1779 {Ref: Archives of Maryland 43:38}; received a receipt for repairing a hospital bucket on 4 Jul 1781 {Ref: Maryland State Archives MdHR-6636-31-120}; received payment from the Council of Maryland "for the purpose of procuring Necessaries for the Sick French Sailors in this City" on 4 Mar 1783 {Ref: Archives of Maryland 48:373}

MURRAY, JAMES (Dorchester County) was appointed by the Council of Safety to collect all the gold and silver coin that could be procured in the county in compliance with the Resolve of Congress on 27 Jan 1776 {Ref: Archives of Maryland 11:132}

MURRAY, JAMES, Esquire (Anne Arundel County) received a loan certificate for £459.12.10 due from the Council of Maryland "agreeable to the Act proposing to the Citizens of this State, Creditors of Congress on Loan Office Certificates, Etc." on 16 May 1783 for services rendered during the war {Ref: Archives of Maryland 48:415}

MURROW, RICHARD, see "William Jacob," q.v.

MURSHETT, JOHN (Charles County) was a captain who received a receipt from the Purchasing Agent for furnishing wheat on 1 Sep 1781 {Ref: Maryland State Archives MdHR-6636-42-15}

MURSHETT, MUNGO (Charles County) received a receipt from the Purchasing Agent for furnishing wheat on 1 Sep 1781 {Ref: Maryland State Archives MdHR-6636-42-15}

MUSCHETT, JOHN (Charles County) received a certificate from the Purchasing Agent for furnishing corn on 17 Jun 1780 {Ref: Maryland State Archives MdHR-6636-42-10}

MUSGROVE, JOHN (Montgomery County) received receipts from the Purchasing Agent for furnishing wheat on 4 May and 17 May 1781 {Ref: Maryland State Archives MdHR-6636-42-11}

MYRE, CHRISTOPHER (Frederick County) received a certificate from the Purchasing Agent for furnishing wheat on 6 Jun 1782 {Ref: Maryland State Archives MdHR-6636-42-35}

MYRES, JOSEPH (Frederick County) received a certificate from the Purchasing Agent for furnishing wheat on 23 May 1782 {Ref: Maryland State Archives MdHR-6636-42-34}

NABB, CHARLES (Talbot County) received a receipt from the Purchasing Agent for furnishing wheat on 25 Mar 1780 {Ref: Maryland State Archives MdHR-6636-24-50}; received a receipt for furnishing beef on 16 Feb 1781 {Ref: Maryland State Archives MdHR-6636-24-49}

NABB, JOHN (Talbot County) received a receipt from the Purchasing Agent for furnishing wheat on 28 Apr 1780 {Ref: Maryland State Archives MdHR-6636-24-50}

NAIRNE, JAMES (Worcester County) submitted an account and receipt for pickling beef on 20 May 1782 {Ref: Maryland State Archives MdHR-6636-43-

28T}; submitted an account and receipt for feeding a steer on 9 Aug 1782 {Ref: Maryland State Archives MdHR-6636-43-28N}

NALLEY, DENNIS (Charles County) received a receipt from the Purchasing Agent for furnishing wheat on 5 Nov 1781 {Ref: Maryland State Archives MdHR-6636-42-15}

NALLY, DENEY (Charles County) received a receipt from the Purchasing Agent for furnishing wheat on 29 Apr 1783 {Ref: Maryland State Archives MdHR-6636-42-22}

NAVE, BOSTIAN (Frederick County) received a certificate from the Purchasing Agent for furnishing wheat on 13 May 1782 {Ref: Maryland State Archives MdHR-6636-42-35}

NEAFF, JOHN (Frederick County) received a certificate from the Purchasing Agent for furnishing wheat on 31 Jul 1782 {Ref: Maryland State Archives MdHR-6636-42-36}

NEAL, RALPH (Charles County) received a receipt from the Purchasing Agent for furnishing wheat on 29 Dec 1782 {Ref: Maryland State Archives MdHR-6636-42-21}

NEAL, WILLIAM (Frederick County) received a receipt from the Purchasing Agent for furnishing pork on 20 Feb 1781 {Ref: Maryland State Archives MdHR-6636-23-3}

NEALE, ANN (Charles County) received a loan certificate for £117.14.5 due from the Council of Maryland "agreeable to the Act proposing to the Citizens of this State, Creditors of Congress on Loan Office Certificates, Etc." on 9 Oct 1783 for services rendered during the war {Ref: Archives of Maryland 48:461}

NEALE, JAMES, Youngest (Charles County) received a loan certificate for £98.16.3 due from the Council of Maryland "agreeable to the Act proposing to the Citizens of this State, Creditors of Congress on Loan Office Certificates, Etc." on 13 May 1783 for services rendered during the war {Ref: Archives of Maryland 48:412}

NECESSARY, THOMAS (Caroline County) received a receipt from the Purchasing Agent for furnishing wheat on 1 Sep 1782 {Ref: Maryland State Archives MdHR-6636-42-7}

NEDLE, RAPHAEL (Charles County) received a receipt from the Purchasing Agent for furnishing wheat on 31 Dec 1781 {Ref: Maryland State Archives MdHR-6636-42-15}

NEEDLES, JOHN (Talbot County) received a receipt from the Purchasing Agent for purchasing bacon on 19 May 1778 {Ref: Maryland State Archives MdHR-6636-12-15}

NEGRO CHARLES (Caroline County) furnished bacon on 20 Apr 1781 for the use of the State of Maryland {Ref: Archives of Maryland 47:250}

NEIDE, JOHN (Cecil County) received a receipt from the Purchasing Agent for storing wheat on 2 Aug 1782 and submitted an account for hauling wheat on 17 Dec 1782 {Ref: Maryland State Archives MdHR-6636-42-9}

NEILE, SAMUEL (Caroline County) received a receipt from the Purchasing Agent for furnishing wheat on 17 Aug 1782 {Ref: Maryland State Archives MdHR-6636-42-7}

NEILL, WILLIAM (Baltimore county) received a loan certificate for £2367.19.7 due from the Council of Maryland "agreeable to the Act proposing to the Citizens of this State, Creditors of Congress on Loan Office Certificates, Etc." on 23 Aug 1783 for services rendered during the war {Ref: Archives of Maryland 48:449}

NELMS, EDMUND N. (Worcester County) received a receipt from the Purchasing Agent for furnishing corn on 9 Mar 1780 {Ref: Maryland State Archives MdHR-6636-24-52}; his name appeared on "A List of Corn Purchased in Worcester County for the use of the State of Maryland" by the Commissary in July, 1780 {Ref: Archives of Maryland 45:10}

NELMS, EDWARD N. (Worcester County) received receipts from the Purchasing Agent for furnishing beef on 30 Sep and 15 Oct 1780 {Ref: Maryland State Archives MdHR-6636-24-54}

NELMS, JOHN (Worcester County) received a loan certificate for £169.3.3 due from the Council of Maryland "agreeable to the Act proposing to the Citizens of this State, Creditors of Congress on Loan Office Certificates, Etc." on 17 May 1783 for services rendered during the war {Ref: Archives of Maryland 48:416}

NELSON, ARTHUR (Frederick County) received a receipt from the Purchasing Agent for furnishing pork on 30 Mar 1781 {Ref: Maryland State Archives MdHR-6636-23-4}

NELSON, HENRY (Montgomery County) received a receipt from the Purchasing Agent for furnishing wheat on 22 Oct 1781 {Ref: Maryland State Archives MdHR-6636-24-15}

NELSON, JOHN (Frederick County) was a doctor who was appointed by the Council of Maryland to serve as "Surgeon of the Sixth Regiment" on 9 May 1777 {Ref: Archives of Maryland 16:245}

NELSON, JOSEPH (Charles County) received a receipt from the Purchasing Agent for furnishing wheat on 8 May 1783 {Ref: Maryland State Archives MdHR-6636-42-22}

NELSON, MOSES (Worcester County) submitted an account and receipt for furnishing salting beef on 1 Oct 1781 {Ref: Maryland State Archives MdHR-6636-43-27}

NELSON, VALENTINE (Baltimore County) submitted an account and received payment for driving seven wagons to Susquehanna Ferry with flour for the Continental Army on 22 Jan 1780 {Ref: Maryland Historical Society MS.1814,

Box 6}; submitted an account and receipt of flour at Susquehanna Lower Ferry for the Continental Army on 23 Jan 1780 {Ref: Maryland State Archives MdHR-6636-23-37}

NERVILLE, ROBERT (Caroline County) received a receipt from the Purchasing Agent for furnishing wheat on 20 Sep 1782 {Ref: Maryland State Archives MdHR-6636-42-7}

NESMITH, JOHN (Talbot County) received receipts from the Purchasing Agent for furnishing wheat on 14 Oct and 18 Oct 1780 {Ref: Maryland State Archives MdHR-6636-24-49}; he was one of twenty-six people who contacted the Governor and Council of Maryland in 1781 and pledged to support and maintain at their own expense the Barge *Experiment* so it can patrol the bay between Kent Point and Tilghman's Island in order to protect them against the enemy, stating in part, "whereas from the present exhausted state of the public treasury the government cannot immediately give that protection to every individual which is become necessary from the cruel and savage mode in which the war is now carried on against us" {Ref: Archives of Maryland 47:584-585}

NEWCOME, ROBERT (Talbot County) was one of twenty-six people who contacted the Governor and Council of Maryland in 1781 and pledged to support and maintain at their own expense the Barge *Experiment* so it can patrol the bay between Kent Point and Tilghman's Island in order to protect them against the enemy, stating in part, "whereas from the present exhausted state of the public treasury the government cannot immediately give that protection to every individual which is become necessary from the cruel and savage mode in which the war is now carried on against us" {Ref: Archives of Maryland 47:584-585}

NEWTON, ARNOLD (Frederick County) submitted an account for boarding services on 4 Apr 1777 {Ref: Maryland State Archives MdHR-19970-2-4}

NEWTON, SELBY (Worcester County) submitted an account and receipt for herding cattle on 25 Sep 1782 {Ref: Maryland State Archives MdHR-6636-43-28E}

NEWTON, WILLIAM (Montgomery County) received a receipt from the Purchasing Agent for furnishing wheat on 1 Sep 1780 {Ref: Maryland State Archives MdHR-6636-24-7}

NEWTON, WILLIAM (Dorchester County) received a receipt from the Purchasing Agent for furnishing wheat on 25 Mar 1783 {Ref: Maryland State Archives MdHR-6636-42-24}

NEWTON, WILLIS (Dorchester County) received a receipt from the Purchasing Agent for furnishing wheat on 3 Sep 1782 {Ref: Maryland State Archives MdHR-6636-42-23}

NEZDORFF, SAMUEL (Frederick County) submitted an account for repairing the scales of the warehouse on 20 Apr 1781 {Ref: Maryland State Archives

MdHR-6636-23-5}

NICHOLAS, JOHN (Frederick County) received a certificate from the Purchasing Agent for furnishing wheat on 29 Jul 1782 {Ref: Maryland State Archives MdHR-6636-42-36}

NICHOLAS, SAMUEL (Montgomery County) received a receipt from the Purchasing Agent for furnishing wheat on 1 Sep 1780 {Ref: Maryland State Archives MdHR-6636-24-7}

NICHOLAS, THOMAS (Montgomery County) received a receipt from the Purchasing Agent for furnishing wheat on 7 Sep 1780 {Ref: Maryland State Archives MdHR-6636-24-7}

NICHOLLS, EDWARD (Montgomery County) received a receipt from the Purchasing Agent for furnishing wheat on 20 Apr 1781 {Ref: Maryland State Archives MdHR-6636-42-11}

NICHOLLS, SAMUEL (Montgomery County) received a receipt from the Purchasing Agent for furnishing wheat on 12 Aug 1780 {Ref: Maryland State Archives MdHR-6636-24-6}; received a receipt for furnishing wheat on 7 Apr 1781 {Ref: Maryland State Archives MdHR-6636-24-18}; received a receipt for furnishing wheat on 26 May 1781 {Ref: Maryland State Archives MdHR-6636-24-18}

NICHOLLS, SIMON (Montgomery County) submitted an account for delivering wheat on 19 Mar 1782 {Ref: Maryland State Archives MdHR-6636-43-8}; received receipts from the Purchasing Agent for hauling wheat on 29 Apr and 21 May 1783 {Ref: Maryland State Archives MdHR-6636-50-141}; also see "Elias Burgess," q.v.

NICHOLLS, WILLIAM (Montgomery County) received a loan certificate for £18.3.6 due from the Council of Maryland "agreeable to the Act proposing to the Citizens of this State, Creditors of Congress on Loan Office Certificates, Etc." on 25 Oct 1783 for services rendered during the war {Ref: Archives of Maryland 48:473}

NICHOLS, ARCHIBALD (Prince George's County) received a receipt from the Purchasing Agent for furnishing wheat in 1782 {Ref: Maryland State Archives MdHR-6636-50-135}

NICHOLS, JEREMIAH (Talbot County) received a receipt from the Purchasing Agent for furnishing wheat on 9 Oct 1780 {Ref: Maryland State Archives MdHR-6636-24-47}

NICHOLS, SAMUEL (Montgomery County) received a receipt from the Purchasing Agent for furnishing wheat on 1 Aug 1780 {Ref: Maryland State Archives MdHR-6636-43-7}

NICHOLS, SIMON (Montgomery County) received a receipt from the Purchasing Agent for furnishing wheat on 14 Aug 1780 {Ref: Maryland State Archives MdHR-6636-43-7}

NICHOLS, THOMAS (Montgomery County) received a receipt from the Purchasing Agent for shelling corn on 20 Aug 1780 {Ref: Maryland State Archives MdHR-6636-24-2}; received a receipt for furnishing wheat on 24 Aug 1780 {Ref: Maryland State Archives MdHR-6636-24-6}

NICHOLS, THOMAS (Frederick County) received payment by order of the Council of Maryland for providing waggonage on 25 Mar 1778 {Ref: Archives of Maryland 16:551}; received receipts from the Purchasing Agent for furnishing flour and corn on 28 Apr and 26 May 1780 {Ref: Maryland State Archives MdHR-6636-24-1}

NICHOLSON, ALICE (county not stated) received a loan certificate for £26.14.2 due from the Council of Maryland "agreeable to the Act proposing to the Citizens of this State, Creditors of Congress on Loan Office Certificates, Etc." on 15 Aug 1783 for services rendered during the war {Ref: Archives of Maryland 48:447}

NICHOLSON, JOHN (Montgomery County) received a receipt from the Purchasing Agent for furnishing wheat on 9 Apr 1781 {Ref: Maryland State Archives MdHR-6636-42-11}

NICHOLSON, JOSEPH (Montgomery County) received a receipt from the Purchasing Agent for furnishing wheat on 4 May 1781 {Ref: Maryland State Archives MdHR-6636-42-11}

NICHOLSON (NICHOLDSON), JOSEPH (Kent County) received payment from the Purchasing Agent for furnishing cattle and pasturage for the public use in September, 1781 {Ref: Maryland State Archives MdHR-6636-43-3}

NICHOLSON, THOMAS (Baltimore County) received a receipt from the Purchasing Agent for furnishing flour on 5 Sep 1779 {Ref: Maryland State Archives MdHR-6636-21-67}

NICOLLS, DANIEL (Dorchester County) received a receipt from the Purchasing Agent for furnishing wheat on 1 Nov 1782 {Ref: Maryland State Archives MdHR-6636-42-23}; received a receipt for furnishing wheat on 25 Mar 1783 {Ref: Maryland State Archives MdHR-6636-42-24}

MELVIL, DAVID (Dorchester County) received a receipt from the Purchasing Agent for furnishing wheat on 25 Mar 1783 {Ref: Maryland State Archives MdHR-6636-42-24}

NICOLLS, JOHN (Dorchester County) received a receipt from the Purchasing Agent for furnishing wheat on 1 Oct 1782 {Ref: Maryland State Archives MdHR-6636-42-23}

NIELSON, JOHN (Somerset County) received a receipt from the Purchasing Agent for furnishing pork on 20 May 1782 {Ref: Maryland State Archives MdHR-6636-43-21}

NIESWINGER, CHRISTIAN (Anne Arundel County) received a receipt from the Purchasing Agent for furnishing powder on 16 Apr 1777 {Ref: Maryland State

Archives MdHR-6636-9-14A}

NIFE, MICHAEL (Frederick County) received a certificate from the Purchasing Agent for furnishing wheat on 10 Jun 1782 {Ref: Maryland State Archives MdHR-6636-42-35}

NIVEN (NEVIN), WILLIAM (Anne Arundel County) received payment from the Maryland Council of Safety for furnishing steel ramrods on 9 Apr 1776 {Ref: Archives of Maryland 11:317}; received payment "for the use of Mrs. Priscilla Pinkney ... for the use of his house for barracks" on 23 Jul 1776 and received payment "for the use of Mrs. Pinkney ... for rent of her house for barracks" on 23 Sep 1776 {Ref: Archives of Maryland 12:96, 293}

NIXON, CATHARINE (Anne Arundel County) received payment by order of the Council of Safety for attending the hospital on 25 Sep and 14 Oct 1776 {Ref: Archives of Maryland 12:298, 349}

NIXON (NIXSON), HUGH OR HEUGH (Montgomery County) received a receipt from the Purchasing Agent for furnishing wheat on 27 Jul 1780 {Ref: Maryland State Archives MdHR-6636-24-5}; received a receipt for furnishing wheat on 1 Aug 1780 {Ref: Maryland State Archives MdHR-6636-43-7}

NOBLE, JONATHAN (Dorchester County) received a receipt from the Purchasing Agent for furnishing wheat on 1 Oct 1782 {Ref: Maryland State Archives MdHR-6636-42-23}

NOBLE, LEVIN (Caroline County) received a receipt from the Purchasing Agent for furnishing wheat on 17 Aug 1782 {Ref: Maryland State Archives MdHR-6636-42-7}

NOBLE, RHODA (Caroline County) received a receipt from the Purchasing Agent for furnishing wheat on 5 Aug 1782 {Ref: Maryland State Archives MdHR-6636-42-7}

NOEL, SEPTIMUS (Baltimore County) received payment for the hire of his boat in transporting troops to the Head of Elk in Cecil County on 18 Jul 1776 {Ref: Archives of Maryland 12:71}

NOLAND (NOLAN), THOMAS (Frederick County) received a receipt from the Purchasing Agent for furnishing corn on 13 Mar 1781 {Ref: Maryland State Archives MdHR-6636-23-4}; received a receipt for furnishing corn on 4 Apr 1781 {Ref: Maryland State Archives MdHR-6636-23-5}; received a certificate for furnishing wheat on 17 Sep 1781 {Ref: Maryland State Archives MdHR-6636-23-28}

NOLAND, THOMAS (Baltimore County) received a certificate from the Purchasing Agent for furnishing corn on 18 Mar 1780 {Ref: Maryland State Archives MdHR-6636-23-33}

NOLEE, WILLIAM (Caroline County) received receipts from the Purchasing Agent for furnishing wheat on 31 Aug and 20 Sep 1782 {Ref: Maryland State Archives MdHR-6636-42-7}

NORARD, STEPHEN (Montgomery County) received a receipt from the Purchasing Agent for furnishing wheat on 24 Apr 1781 {Ref: Maryland State Archives MdHR-6636-42-11}

NORRIS, BENJAMIN (Prince George's County) received receipts from the Purchasing Agent for furnishing wheat on 12 Nov 1782 and 21 Mar 1783 {Ref: Maryland State Archives MdHR-6636-50-135}

NORRIS, BENJAMIN BRADFORD (Harford County) was appointed by the Committee of Safety "to ride in Bush Lower, Gunpowder Upper and Lower Hundreds and purchase guns and blankets agreeable to the request of the [Maryland] Council of Safety" on 19 Aug 1776 and submitted his account on 2 Sep 1776 {Ref: Preston's History of Harford County, pp. 333-334, 336}; pledged a loan in the amount of £100 to the State of Maryland under the Act for the Emission of Bills of Credit "to defray the expences of the present campaign" in June, 1781 {Ref: Archives of Maryland 47:327}

NORRIS, GEORGE (Prince George's County) received receipts from the Purchasing Agent for furnishing wheat in 1782 and on 5 Sep 1783 {Ref: Maryland State Archives MdHR-6636-50-135}

NORRIS, JAMES (Harford County) offered to make cartouch boxes for the Committee of Safety and they "agreed to employ him should they want any" on 18 Mar 1776 {Ref: Preston's History of Harford County, p. 321}

NORRIS, JOHN (Frederick County) received a certificate from the Purchasing Agent for furnishing wheat on 29 Jul 1782 {Ref: Maryland State Archives MdHR-6636-42-36}

NORRIS, MARTIN (Calvert County) received payment by order of the Council of Maryland "for expences in bringing cloathing from Calvert County for the army" on 9 Feb 1778 {Ref: Archives of Maryland 16:483}; submitted an account for collecting beef on 1 Jan 1781 and payment for driving cattle on 27 Feb 1782 {Ref: Maryland State Archives MdHR-6636-50-37}; received payment by order of the Council of Maryland "to be delivered over to Patrick Sim Smith, Commissary of Calvert County" on 17 Jan 1782 {Ref: Archives of Maryland 48:43}

NORRIS, SAMUEL (Frederick County) received a receipt from the Purchasing Agent for delivering flour on 26 Dec 1780 {Ref: Maryland State Archives MdHR-6636-23-29}; received receipts from the Purchasing Agent for delivering flour on 5 Jan, 12 Feb, 1 Mar and 21 Mar 1781 {Ref: Maryland State Archives MdHR-6636-23-30}

NORRIS, WILLIAM (Prince George's County) received receipts from the Purchasing Agent for furnishing wheat on 20 Apr 1782 and 13 Feb 1783 {Ref: Maryland State Archives MdHR-6636-50-135}

NORTHCRAFT, RICHARD (Montgomery County) received a receipt from the Purchasing Agent for furnishing wheat on 11 Apr 1781 {Ref: Maryland State

Archives MdHR-6636-42-11}

NORTHSINGER, SAMUEL (Frederick County) received a certificate from the Purchasing Agent for furnishing wheat on 14 Jun 1782 {Ref: Maryland State Archives MdHR-6636-42-35}

NORWOOD, JEREMIAH (Frederick County) received a certificate from the Purchasing Agent for furnishing wheat on 23 Jan 1782 {Ref: Maryland State Archives MdHR-6636-42-38}

NOTT, JESSE (Charles County) received a receipt from the Purchasing Agent for furnishing wheat on 10 May 1783 {Ref: Maryland State Archives MdHR-6636-42-22}

NOTT, WILLIAM (Montgomery County) received a receipt from the Purchasing Agent for furnishing wheat on 10 Apr 1781 {Ref: Maryland State Archives MdHR-6636-42-11}

NOWLAND, MATTHIAS (Caroline County) received a receipt from the Purchasing Agent for furnishing wheat on 1 Sep 1782 {Ref: Maryland State Archives MdHR-6636-42-7}

NULE, BENNETT (Charles County) received a receipt from the Purchasing Agent for furnishing wheat on 29 Dec 1782 {Ref: Maryland State Archives MdHR-6636-42-21}

NUNAR, JACOB (Caroline County) received a receipt from the Purchasing Agent for furnishing wheat on 5 Aug 1782 {Ref: Maryland State Archives MdHR-6636-42-7}

O'BRYAN, PAT (Queen Anne's County) received payment by order of the Council of Maryland via Charles Downes "for waggoning, etc." on 21 May 1778 {Ref: Archives of Maryland 21:102}

ODEN, DAVID JOHN (Montgomery County) received a receipt from the Purchasing Agent for furnishing wheat on 1 Aug 1780 {Ref: Maryland State Archives MdHR-6636-43-7}; received a receipt for furnishing wheat on 4 Aug 1780 {Ref: Maryland State Archives MdHR-6636-24-6}

ODEN, JOSIAS (Montgomery County) received a receipt from the Purchasing Agent for furnishing wheat on 10 Apr 1781 {Ref: Maryland State Archives MdHR-6636-24-15}

O'DONNELL, MICHAEL (Montgomery County) received a receipt from the Purchasing Agent for furnishing wheat on 23 Sep 1780 {Ref: Maryland State Archives MdHR-6636-24-7}

OFFUTT, JAMES (Montgomery County) received a receipt from the Purchasing Agent for furnishing wheat on 16 May 1781 {Ref: Maryland State Archives MdHR-6636-24-14}

OFFUTT, NATHANIEL (Montgomery County) received a receipt from the Purchasing Agent for furnishing wheat on 24 Aug 1780 {Ref: Maryland State Archives MdHR-6636-24-6}

OFFUTT, SAMUEL (Montgomery County) received a receipt from the Purchasing Agent for furnishing wheat on 30 Aug 1780 {Ref: Maryland State Archives MdHR-6636-24-6}; received a receipt for furnishing wheat on 5 Jun 1781 {Ref: Maryland State Archives MdHR-6636-24-18}

OFFUTT, WILLIAM (Montgomery County) received a receipt from the Purchasing Agent for furnishing wheat on 1 Aug 1780 {Ref: Maryland State Archives MdHR-6636-43-7}; received a receipt for furnishing wheat on 9 Aug 1780 {Ref: Maryland State Archives MdHR-6636-24-6}

OFFUTT, WILLIAM M. (Montgomery County) received receipts from the Purchasing Agent for furnishing wheat on 5 Sep and 6 Sep 1780 {Ref: Maryland State Archives MdHR-6636-24-7}

OFFUTT, ZADOCK (Montgomery County) received a receipt from the Purchasing Agent for furnishing wheat on 1 Aug 1780 {Ref: Maryland State Archives MdHR-6636-43-7}; received a receipt for furnishing wheat on 31 Aug 1780 {Ref: Maryland State Archives MdHR-6636-24-6}; received a receipt for furnishing wheat on 16 May 1781 {Ref: Maryland State Archives MdHR-6636-24-14}

OGDEN, ANANIS (Montgomery County) received a receipt from the Purchasing Agent for furnishing wheat on 19 Apr 1781 {Ref: Maryland State Archives MdHR-6636-24-18}

OGLE, AGNES (Frederick County) received a certificate from the Purchasing Agent for furnishing wheat on 27 Sep 1781 {Ref: Maryland State Archives MdHR-6636-23-28}

OGLE, ALEXANDER (Frederick County) received a receipt from the Purchasing Agent for delivering flour on 27 Dec 1780 {Ref: Maryland State Archives MdHR-6636-23-29}; received a certificate for delivering flour on or about 1 Jan 1781 {Ref: Maryland State Archives MdHR-6636-42-26}; received a receipt for furnishing corn meal and plank on 13 Jan 1781 {Ref: Maryland State Archives MdHR-6636-23-2}; received receipts from the Purchasing Agent for delivering flour on 9 Feb, 12 Feb and 2 Mar 1781 {Ref: Maryland State Archives MdHR-6636-23-30}; submitted an account for furnishing pork on 21 May 1781 {Ref: Maryland State Archives MdHR-6636-23-6}

OGLE, BENJAMIN (Frederick County) received a certificate from the Purchasing Agent for furnishing wheat on 14 Jun 1782 {Ref: Maryland State Archives MdHR-6636-42-35}; received a certificate for furnishing wheat on 16 Jun 1782 {Ref: Maryland State Archives MdHR-6636-42-36}

OGLE, BENJAMIN (Baltimore County) received a certificate from the Purchasing Agent for furnishing beef on 24 Mar 1781 {Ref: Maryland State Archives MdHR-6636-43-37}

OGLE, BENJAMIN (Frederick County) received payment by order of the Council of Safety for cartage on 28 Aug 1776 {Ref: Archives of Maryland 12:245}

OGLE, JOSEPH (Frederick County) received a certificate from the Purchasing Agent for furnishing wheat on 25 May 1781 {Ref: Maryland State Archives MdHR-6636-23-28}

OGLE, THOMAS (Frederick County) received loan certificates for £11.15.6 and £23.16.0 due from the Council of Maryland "agreeable to the Act proposing to the Citizens of this State, Creditors of Congress on Loan Office Certificates, Etc." on 20 May and 20 Dec 1783 for services rendered during the war {Ref: Archives of Maryland 48:418, 495}

OMENSETTER, JOHN (Baltimore County) contracted with and received payment by order of the Council of Safety for furnishing cartouch belts, bayonet belts and gun straps on 28 Mar and 6 Jun 1776 {Ref: Archives of Maryland 11:294, 466}

O'NEALE, HENRIETTA (Prince George's County) received a receipt from the Purchasing Agent for furnishing wheat in 1783 {Ref: Maryland State Archives MdHR-6636-50-135}

O'NEALE, LAURENCE (county not stated) pledged a loan in the amount of £300 to the State of Maryland under the Act for the Emission of Bills of Credit "to defray the expences of the present campaign" in June, 1781 {Ref: Archives of Maryland 47:327}

O'NEALE, LAWRENCE (Montgomery County) received a receipt from the Purchasing Agent for furnishing wheat on 18 May 1781 {Ref: Maryland State Archives MdHR-6636-24-18}

O'NEALE, LAWRENCE (Frederick County) received a receipt from the Purchasing Agent for furnishing corn on 4 May and 26 May 1780 {Ref: Maryland State Archives MdHR-6636-24-1}

O'NEIL, LAURENCE (Prince George's County) received a receipt from the Purchasing Agent for furnishing wheat on 24 May 1782 and 25 Apr 1783 {Ref: Maryland State Archives MdHR-6636-50-135}

O'NEILL, JOHN (Montgomery County) received a receipt from the Purchasing Agent for furnishing wheat on 28 Jul 1780 {Ref: Maryland State Archives MdHR-6636-24-5}; received a receipt for furnishing wheat on 1 Aug 1780 {Ref: Maryland State Archives MdHR-6636-43-7}

O'NEILL, JOHN (Baltimore County) received payment for furnishing beef on 13 Jun 1781 {Ref: Maryland State Archives MdHR-6636-43-38UU}

O'NEILL, JOSHUA (Montgomery County) received a receipt from the Purchasing Agent for furnishing wheat on 31 Aug 1780 {Ref: Maryland State Archives MdHR-6636-24-6}

O'NEILL, LAWRENCE (Montgomery County) received a receipt from the Purchasing Agent for furnishing wheat on 13 Nov 1780 {Ref: Maryland State Archives MdHR-6636-24-8}; received a receipt for furnishing wheat on 3 Sep 1781 {Ref: Maryland State Archives MdHR-6636-24-16}

243

O'NEILL, WILLIAM (Montgomery County) received a receipt from the Purchasing Agent for furnishing wheat on 1 Aug 1780 {Ref: Maryland State Archives MdHR-6636-43-7}; received a receipt for furnishing wheat on 8 Aug and 30 Aug 1780 {Ref: Maryland State Archives MdHR-6636-24-6}; received a receipt for furnishing wheat on 23 Oct and 27 Oct 1780 {Ref: Maryland State Archives MdHR-6636-24-8}

ORME, ARCHIBALD (Montgomery County) delivered cattle to the Purchasing Agent for the use of the State of Maryland in October, 1780 {Ref: Archives of Maryland 45:149}; received a certificate from the Purchasing Agent for furnishing wheat on 25 Mar 1781 {Ref: Maryland State Archives MdHR-6636-24-18}

ORME, JAMES (Montgomery County) received a receipt from the Purchasing Agent for furnishing wheat on 31 Mar 1781 {Ref: Maryland State Archives MdHR-6636-24-18}

ORME, LUCY (Montgomery County) received a receipt from the Purchasing Agent for furnishing bacon on 27 Jun 1781 {Ref: Maryland State Archives MdHR-6636-24-16}

ORME, MOSES (Montgomery County) received a receipt from the Purchasing Agent for furnishing wheat on 1 Aug 1780 {Ref: Maryland State Archives MdHR-6636-43-7}; received a receipt for furnishing wheat on 9 Aug 1780 {Ref: Maryland State Archives MdHR-6636-24-6}

ORNDOFF, PETER (Frederick County) received a certificate from the Purchasing Agent for furnishing wheat on 16 May 1782 {Ref: Maryland State Archives MdHR-6636-42-34}

ORRELL, ALICE (Caroline County) submitted an account of wheat received on 27 May 1782 and received a receipt from the Purchasing Agent for furnishing wheat on 17 Aug 1782 {Ref: Maryland State Archives MdHR-6636-42-7}

ORRELL, FRANCIS (Caroline County) received a receipt from the Purchasing Agent for furnishing wheat on 1 Sep 1782 {Ref: Maryland State Archives MdHR-6636-42-7}

ORRELL, ROBERT (Caroline County) received receipts from the Purchasing Agent for furnishing wheat on 17 Aug and 1 Sep 1782 {Ref: Maryland State Archives MdHR-6636-42-7}

ORRELL, THOMAS (Caroline County) received receipts from the Purchasing Agent for furnishing wheat on 17 Aug and 1 Sep 1782 {Ref: Maryland State Archives MdHR-6636-42-7}

OSBORN, MARY (Montgomery County) received a receipt from the Purchasing Agent for furnishing wheat on 4 Apr 1781 {Ref: Maryland State Archives MdHR-6636-24-14}

O'TOOLES, JESSE (Baltimore County) received payment for furnishing pork on 4 Oct 1781 {Ref: Maryland State Archives MdHR-6636-43-38W}

OTT, GEORGE (Frederick County) received a certificate from the Purchasing Agent for furnishing wheat on 23 May 1782 {Ref: Maryland State Archives MdHR-6636-42-35}

OTT, PHILIP (Frederick County) received a certificate from the Purchasing Agent for furnishing wheat on 23 May 1782 {Ref: Maryland State Archives MdHR-6636-42-35}

OTTO, WILLIAM (Frederick County) received a certificate from the Purchasing Agent for hauling flour on 11 Apr 1782 {Ref: Maryland State Archives MdHR-6636-42-33}

OVELMAN, HENRY (Frederick County) received payment by order of the Council of Safety for providing waggonage on 6 Aug 1776 {Ref: Archives of Maryland 12:175}

OWDEN, NATHAN (Montgomery County) received a receipt from the Purchasing Agent for furnishing wheat on 10 Oct 1781 {Ref: Maryland State Archives MdHR-6636-42-11}

OWEN, JOHN (Montgomery County) received a receipt from the Purchasing Agent for furnishing wheat on 4 Apr 1781 {Ref: Maryland State Archives MdHR-6636-42-11}

OWEN, LARANCE (Montgomery County) received a receipt from the Purchasing Agent for furnishing wheat on 5 Apr 1781 {Ref: Maryland State Archives MdHR-6636-42-11}

OWEN, ROBERT (Montgomery County) was a major who served as Purchaser of Provisions by 14 May 1778 {Ref: Archives of Maryland 21:81}; received receipts from the Purchasing Agent for furnishing wheat on 19 Apr, 13 Sep and 1 Oct 1781 {Ref: Maryland State Archives MdHR-6636-42-11}

OWEN, WILLIAM (Montgomery County) received a receipt from the Purchasing Agent for furnishing wheat on 6 Apr 1781 {Ref: Maryland State Archives MdHR-6636-42-11}; received a certificate of employment by the commissary of purchases on 18 Mar 1782 {Ref: Maryland State Archives MdHR-6636-50-91}

OWENS, ROBERT (Montgomery County) received a receipt from the Purchasing Agent for furnishing wheat on 21 Sep 1780 {Ref: Maryland State Archives MdHR-6636-24-7}

OWINGS, JOHN COCKEY (Baltimore County) received a certificate from the Purchasing Agent for furnishing beef on 22 Dec 1781 {Ref: Maryland State Archives MdHR-6636-49-56}

OXENHAM, PETER (Caroline County) received a receipt from the Purchasing Agent for wheat on 16 Sep 1782 {Ref: Maryland State Archives MdHR-6636-42-7}

OYLER, FREDERICK (Frederick County) received a certificate from the Purchasing Agent for furnishing beef on 21 Sep 1782 {Ref: Maryland State

245

Archives MdHR-6636-42-37}

OZMAN, ARCHIBALD (Montgomery County) received a receipt from the Purchasing Agent for furnishing wheat on 10 Oct 1780 {Ref: Maryland State Archives MdHR-6636-24-13}

OZMAN (OZMANT), RICHARD (Caroline County) received receipts from the Purchasing Agent for furnishing wheat on 5 Aug and 22 Aug 1782 {Ref: Maryland State Archives MdHR-6636-42-7}

PACA, AQUILA (Harford County) was appointed by the Council of Safety to collect all the gold and silver coin that could be procured in the county in compliance with the Resolve of Congress on 27 Jan 1776 {Ref: Archives of Maryland 11:132}

PACA, WILLIAM, Esquire (Talbot County) received a receipt from the Purchasing Agent for furnishing a steer on 1 Apr 1778 {Ref: Maryland State Archives MdHR-4587-40}; received a receipt for furnishing wheat on 30 Sep 1780 {Ref: Maryland State Archives MdHR-6636-24-49}; he was one of twenty-six people who contacted the Governor and Council of Maryland in 1781 and pledged to support and maintain at their own expense the Barge *Experiment* so it can patrol the bay between Kent Point and Tilghman's Island in order to protect them against the enemy, stating in part, "whereas from the present exhausted state of the public treasury the government cannot immediately give that protection to every individual which is become necessary from the cruel and savage mode in which the war is now carried on against us" {Ref: Archives of Maryland 47:584-585}; received a loan certificate for £506.1.2 due from the Council of Maryland "agreeable to the Act proposing to the Citizens of this State, Creditors of Congress on Loan Office Certificates, Etc." on 30 Aug 1783 for services rendered during the war {Ref: Archives of Maryland 48:451}

PACK, MARY (Montgomery County) received a receipt from the Purchasing Agent for furnishing wheat on 17 Jul 1781 {Ref: Maryland State Archives MdHR-6636-42-11}

PADDOCK, SETH (Baltimore County) received payment by order of the Council of Safety on 26 Jun 1776 "for detention of the sloop *Mayflower* and wages" when said vessel was sunk at Whetstone Point for the defence of Baltimore Town (which occurred in March, 1776 for the purpose of preventing any of the British Ships of War from coming up to Baltimore Town) {Ref: Archives of Maryland 11:521}

PADGETT, HENRY (Charles County) received a receipt from the Purchasing Agent for furnishing wheat on 20 Dec 1782 {Ref: Maryland State Archives MdHR-6636-42-20}

PAGE, AQUILLA (Kent County) received payment from the Purchasing Agent for furnishing cattle for the public use in September, 1781 {Ref: Maryland State

Archives MdHR-6636-43-3}

PAGE, JOHN (Kent County) received certificates from the Purchasing Agent for furnishing and hauling wheat on 14 Jan and 1 Jun 1780 {Ref: Maryland State Archives MdHR-6636-23-41}; received a certificate for furnishing wheat on 24 Jan 1780 {Ref: Maryland State Archives MdHR-6636-23-47}; received certificates from the Purchasing Agent for furnishing wheat and flour on 14 Apr and 20 Apr 1780 {Ref: Archives of Maryland 43:475; Maryland State Archives MdHR-6636-23-46}; received payment from the Purchasing Agent for furnishing cattle for the public use in September, 1781 {Ref: Maryland State Archives MdHR-6636-43-3}

PAGETT, WILLIAM (Charles County) received a receipt from the Purchasing Agent for furnishing wheat on 31 Oct 1782 {Ref: Maryland State Archives MdHR-6636-42-19}

PAINE, ISAAC (Caroline County) received a receipt from the Purchasing Agent for furnishing wheat on 1 Sep 1782 {Ref: Maryland State Archives MdHR-6636-42-7}

PAINE (PAIN), JOHN (Caroline County) received receipts from the Purchasing Agent for furnishing wheat on 22 Aug and 1 Sep 1782 {Ref: Maryland State Archives MdHR-6636-42-7}

PAINE, RAPHAEL (St. Mary's County) received payment from the Purchasing Agent on 26 Dec 1781 for collecting and driving public cattle for 16 days {Ref: Maryland State Archives MdHR-6636-43-23}

PALFREY, HUNLOCK (Baltimore County) received payment by order of the Council of Maryland "for flour purchased according to the direction of the Convention" on 26 Jun 1776 {Ref: Archives of Maryland 11:521}

PALMORE, ELENER (Montgomery County) received a receipt from the Purchasing Agent for furnishing wheat on 29 Jul 1781 {Ref: Maryland State Archives MdHR-6636-42-11}

PARK, JOHN (Harford County) received payment by order of the Council of Safety for furnishing a gun on 27 Aug 1776 {Ref: Archives of Maryland 12:242}

PARKER, DANIEL (Dorchester County) received a loan certificate for £74.7.7 due from the Council of Maryland "agreeable to the Act proposing to the Citizens of this State, Creditors of Congress on Loan Office Certificates, Etc." on 17 Oct 1783 for services rendered during the war {Ref: Archives of Maryland 48:470}

PARKER, DERRICK (Kent County) received a receipt from the Purchasing Agent for furnishing wheat on 11 Aug 1780 {Ref: Maryland State Archives MdHR-6636-23-49}

PARKER, DOCTOR (Montgomery County) received a receipt from the Purchasing Agent for furnishing wheat on 2 Oct and 5 Oct 1780 {Ref:

Maryland State Archives MdHR-6636-24-13}

PARKER, EDWARD (Cecil County) shipped coarse tenting linen manufactured to the Maryland Council of Safety in Annapolis for the use of the province and the army on 2 May 1776; received payment on 15 Jul 1776 {Ref: Archives of Maryland 11:400, 12:47}; received payment for furnishing blankets on 6 Sep 1776 {Ref: Archives of Maryland 12:259}

PARKER, JOHN (Worcester County) received a receipt from the Purchasing Agent for furnishing beef and pork on 18 Jun 1782 {Ref: Maryland State Archives MdHR-6636-43-27}; received a receipt for furnishing pork and bacon on 16 Aug 1782 {Ref: Maryland State Archives MdHR-6636-43-27}

PARKER, JOHN (county not stated) received payments by order of the Council of Safety for furnishing a gun on 2 Sep 1776 and a musquet on 23 Sep 1776 {Ref: Archives of Maryland 12:252, 293}

PARKER, JONATHAN (Annapolis) received payment by order of the Council of Safety for riding express on 16 Sep 1776 {Ref: Archives of Maryland 12:273}; received payment "for going express to Baltimore" on 27 Mar 1778 {Ref: Archives of Maryland 16:554}; received payment "for going express to Pennsylvania and the Delaware States on public business" on 16 Dec 1778 {Ref: Archives of Maryland 21:266}; submitted an account for riding express on 20 Mar 1780 {Ref: Maryland State Archives MdHR-6636-17-110}; received payment by order of the Council of Maryland "of the New Emission of this State to be delivered over to Baruch Williams, Commissary for Cecil County [and] to John Voorhees, Commissary for Kent County [and] to Nathaniel Potter, Commissary for Caroline County" on 6 Oct 1780 {Ref: Archives of Maryland 43:315}; received payment for riding express on 11 Apr, 12 Jul, 17 Jul and 10 Aug 1781 {Ref: Archives of Maryland 45:391, 498, 553; Maryland State Archives MdHR-6636-33-10}; received payment by order of the Council of Maryland on 29 Oct 1781 "for riding Express to Congress" (i.e., to deliver the news of the surrender of Gen. Cornwallis at Yorktown on 12 Oct 1781, which trip he made just before Tench Tilghman made his memorable ride for that same purpose). {Ref: Archives of Maryland 45:655}; received payment for riding express on 10 Apr and 7 Dec 1782 and 20 Feb 1783 {Ref: Archives of Maryland 48:127, 316, 363}

PARKER, THOMAS (Worcester County) submitted an account and receipt for collecting cattle on 7 Nov 1781 {Ref: Maryland State Archives MdHR-6636-43-27}

PARKER, WILLIAM (Montgomery County) received a receipt from the Purchasing Agent for furnishing wheat on 14 Nov 1780 {Ref: Maryland State Archives MdHR-6636-24-13}

PARKER, WILLIAM (Worcester County) submitted an account and receipt for hauling pork on 9 Aug 1782 {Ref: Maryland State Archives MdHR-6636-43-

28H}

PARKER, WILLIAM A. (Worcester County) submitted an account and receipt for furnishing barrels on 15 Mar 1782 {Ref: Maryland State Archives MdHR-6636-43-28NN}; submitted an account and receipt for furnishing pork barrels on 1 Apr 1782 {Ref: Maryland State Archives MdHR-6636-43-28KK}

PARKS, ANDREW (Kent County) received a certificate from the Purchasing Agent for furnishing corn on 17 Mar 1780 {Ref: Maryland State Archives MdHR-6636-43-1}

PARRAN, THOMAS (Calvert County) was a doctor who received payment by order of the Council of Safety for the hire of his boat on 28 Aug 1776 {Ref: Archives of Maryland 12:245}; received payment by order of the Council of Maryland for services rendered (not specified) on 26 May 1780 {Ref: Archives of Maryland 43:182}

PARRE, ALEXANDER (Montgomery County) received a receipt from the Purchasing Agent for furnishing wheat on 24 Apr 1781 {Ref: Maryland State Archives MdHR-6636-42-11}

PARROTT, JOHN (Talbot County) received a receipt from the Purchasing Agent for purchasing bacon on 19 May 1778 {Ref: Maryland State Archives MdHR-6636-12-15}

PARROTT, PERRY (Talbot County) submitted an account and receipt for hauling and purchasing bacon on 30 May 1778 {Ref: Maryland State Archives MdHR-6636-12-15}; received a certificate from the Purchasing Agent for furnishing wheat on 13 Mar 1780 {Ref: Maryland State Archives MdHR-6636-24-46}

PARROTT, RICHARD (Talbot County) submitted an account and receipt for purchasing and transporting bacon on 6 Jun and 9 Jun 1778 {Ref: Maryland State Archives MdHR-6636-12-15}; received a receipt for furnishing beef on 5 Oct 1780 {Ref: Maryland State Archives MdHR-6636-24-49}

PARROTT, WILLIAM (Caroline County) received a receipt from the Purchasing Agent for furnishing wheat on 1 Sep 1782 {Ref: Maryland State Archives MdHR-6636-42-7}

PARRY, JOHN (Baltimore County) submitted an account and received payment for hauling three loads of flour for use of the army and for one and a half days drayage on 28 Jan 1780 {Ref: Maryland Historical Society MS.1814, Box 6}

PARSON, JAMES (county not stated) received payment by order of the Council of Safety for furnishing boatage on 18 Sep 1776 {Ref: Archives of Maryland 12:280}

PARSONS, GEORGE JR. (Worcester County) received a receipt from the Purchasing Agent for furnishing bacon on 15 Oct 1780 {Ref: Maryland State Archives MdHR-6636-24-54}

PARTOR, BASIL (Montgomery County) received a receipt from the Purchasing Agent for furnishing wheat on 7 Sep 1780 {Ref: Maryland State Archives

249

MdHR-6636-24-7}

PATISON, ATHOWAY (Dorchester County) received a receipt from the Purchasing Agent for furnishing wheat on 25 Mar 1783 {Ref: Maryland State Archives MdHR-6636-42-24}

PATRIDGE, JONATHAN (Dorchester County) received a receipt from the Purchasing Agent for furnishing wheat on 12 Aug 1782 {Ref: Maryland State Archives MdHR-6636-42-23}

PATTEN, MATTHEW (Baltimore County) received payment by order of the Council of Safety for furnishing scabbards on 6 Sep 1776 {Ref: Archives of Maryland 12:259}

PATTERSON, JOHN (Talbot County) received a receipt from the Purchasing Agent for purchasing bacon on 13 Jun 1778 {Ref: Maryland State Archives MdHR-6636-12-15}

PATTEY, POWELL (Worcester County) received a receipt from the Purchasing Agent for furnishing cattle on 21 Sep 1782 {Ref: Maryland State Archives MdHR-6636-43-27}

PAYNE, DANIEL JR. (Dorchester County) received a receipt from the Purchasing Agent for furnishing wheat on 1 Nov 1782 {Ref: Maryland State Archives MdHR-6636-42-23}

PAYNE, JOHN (Caroline County) received a receipt from the Purchasing Agent for furnishing wheat on 5 Aug 1782 {Ref: Maryland State Archives MdHR-6636-42-7}

PEACK, THOMAS (Montgomery County) received a receipt from the Purchasing Agent for furnishing wheat on 1 Aug 1780 {Ref: Maryland State Archives MdHR-6636-43-7}

PEACOCK, JOHN (Harford County) received a receipt from the Purchasing Agent for furnishing wheat on 24 Mar 1780 {Ref: Maryland State Archives MdHR-6636-17-116}

PEACOCK, LUKE (Harford County) received a receipt from the Purchasing Agent for furnishing wheat on 10 Mar 1780 {Ref: Maryland State Archives MdHR-6636-23-39}

PEACOCK, RICHARD (Kent County) received a certificate from the Purchasing Agent for furnishing corn on 30 Jan 1780 {Ref: Maryland State Archives MdHR-6636-23-43}; received a certificate for grinding wheat on 10 Mar 1780 {Ref: Maryland State Archives MdHR-6636-43-1}

PEALE, JOHN (Baltimore County) received a receipt from the Purchasing Agent for furnishing flour on 15 Jan 1780 {Ref: Maryland State Archives MdHR-6636-23-37}

PEARCE, HENRY WARD (Cecil County) was appointed by the Council of Safety to collect all the gold and silver coin that could be procured in the county in compliance with the Resolve of Congress on 27 Jan 1776 {Ref: Archives of

Maryland 11:132}

PEARCE, JAMES (Kent County) received a certificate from the Purchasing Agent for furnishing wheat on 29 Jan 1780 {Ref: Maryland State Archives MdHR-6636-23-41}; received payment for furnishing flour on 30 Dec 1780 {Ref: Maryland State Archives MdHR-6636-23-49}; received payment from the Purchasing Agent for furnishing cattle for the public use in September, 1781 {Ref: Maryland State Archives MdHR-6636-43-3}; submitted an account and receipt for hauling in 1781-1782 {Ref: Maryland State Archives MdHR-6636-43-5}

PEARCE, WILLIAM (Prince George's County) received a receipt from the Purchasing Agent for furnishing wheat in 1782 {Ref: Maryland State Archives MdHR-6636-50-135}

PECK, ANDREW (Frederick County) received a certificate from the Purchasing Agent for furnishing wheat on 10 Jun 1782 {Ref: Maryland State Archives MdHR-6636-42-35}

PECK, SARAH (Charles County) received a receipt from the Purchasing Agent for furnishing wheat on 1 Sep 1781 {Ref: Maryland State Archives MdHR-6636-42-15}

PECK, THOMAS (Montgomery County) received a receipt from the Purchasing Agent for furnishing wheat on 21 Oct 1780 {Ref: Maryland State Archives MdHR-6636-24-8}

PECKINBAUGH, LEONARD (Frederick County) received a receipt from the Purchasing Agent for delivering flour on 27 Dec 1780 {Ref: Maryland State Archives MdHR-6636-23-29}

PEDDICOURT, NICHOLAS (Frederick County) received a receipt from the Purchasing Agent for furnishing corn on 23 Jan 1781 {Ref: Maryland State Archives MdHR-6636-23-2}

PEEK, THOMAS (Montgomery County) received a receipt from the Purchasing Agent for furnishing wheat on 7 Aug and 30 Aug 1780 {Ref: Maryland State Archives MdHR-6636-24-6}

PENCE, JACOB (Frederick County) received payment by order of the Council of Maryland for furnishing pasturage, hay and wood on 25 Mar 1778 {Ref: Archives of Maryland 16:551}

PENDAR, THOMAS (Caroline County) received a receipt from the Purchasing Agent for furnishing wheat on 31 Aug 1782 {Ref: Maryland State Archives MdHR-6636-42-7}

PENKIND (PENKEND), VINCENT OR VINSON (Caroline County) received a receipt from the Purchasing Agent for furnishing wheat on 1 Sep and 20 Sep 1782 {Ref: Maryland State Archives MdHR-6636-42-7}

PENN, BENJAMIN (Montgomery County) received a receipt from the Purchasing Agent for furnishing wheat on 21 Jun 1781 {Ref: Maryland State Archives

PENN, CALEB (Montgomery County) received a receipt from the Purchasing Agent for furnishing wheat on 29 May 1781 {Ref: Maryland State Archives MdHR-6636-42-11}

PENN, CHARLES (Montgomery County) received a receipt from the Purchasing Agent for furnishing wheat on 29 May 1781 {Ref: Maryland State Archives MdHR-6636-42-11}

PENN, JOHN (Montgomery County) received receipts from the Purchasing Agent for furnishing wheat on 29 May and 6 Aug 1781 {Ref: Maryland State Archives MdHR-6636-42-11}

PENN, TEYREEL OR TEYEERL (Charles County) received a receipt from the Purchasing Agent for furnishing wheat on 30 Apr 1782 {Ref: Maryland State Archives MdHR-6636-42-18}; received a receipt for furnishing wheat on 29 Dec 1782 {Ref: Maryland State Archives MdHR-6636-42-21}; received a receipt for furnishing wheat on 10 May 1783 {Ref: Maryland State Archives MdHR-6636-42-22}

PENNINGTON, HENRY (Kent County) received payment from the Purchasing Agent for furnishing cattle for the public use in September, 1781 {Ref: Maryland State Archives MdHR-6636-43-3}

PENNINGTON, JOSEPH (Kent County) received payment from the Purchasing Agent for driving cattle on 27 Oct 1780 {Ref: Maryland State Archives MdHR-6636-23-49}; received payment for collecting cattle for the public use in November, 1782 {Ref: Maryland State Archives MdHR-6636-43-3}

PENNY, ROBERT (Baltimore Town) received payment receipts for furnishing linen on 2 Oct, 9 Oct, 14 Oct and 23 Oct 1779 {Ref: Maryland State Archives MdHR-19970-3-8}

PERKINS, ISAAC (Kent County) was a colonel who was appointed by the Council of Maryland as one of thirty men to be "Agents for Purchasing Provisions" on 30 Mar 1779 {Ref: Archives of Maryland 21:332}; received a commission as Purchaser of Provisions on 16 Apr 1779 {Ref: Maryland State Archives MdHR-6636-13-116}; received a certificate for hauling supplies on 14 Apr 1780 {Ref: Maryland State Archives MdHR-6636-23-41}; received a certificate and receipt for a loan repayment on 18 Jun 1780 {Ref: Maryland State Archives MdHR-19970-19-27}; received payment for furnishing cattle for the public use in September, 1781 and for purchasing beef cattle for the public use in October, 1782 {Ref: Maryland State Archives MdHR-6636-43-3}

PERL, CHARLES (Frederick County) received a certificate from the Purchasing Agent for furnishing wheat on 28 Nov 1782 {Ref: Maryland State Archives MdHR-6636-42-37}

PERMARR, WILLIAM (Caroline County) received a receipt from the Purchasing Agent for wheat on 16 Sep 1782 {Ref: Maryland State Archives MdHR-6636-

42-7}

PERRY, ALEXANDER (Prince George's County) received receipts from the Purchasing Agent for furnishing wheat on 6 Aug 1782 and 25 Feb 1783 {Ref: Maryland State Archives MdHR-6636-50-135}

PERRY, CHARLES (Montgomery County) received a receipt from the Purchasing Agent for furnishing wheat on 22 Jul 1780 {Ref: Maryland State Archives MdHR-6636-24-5}; received a certificate for purchasing a horse on 2 Aug 1780 {Ref: Maryland State Archives MdHR-6636-24-50}

PERRY, ERASMUS (Montgomery County) received a receipt from the Purchasing Agent for furnishing wheat on 1 Aug 1780 {Ref: Maryland State Archives MdHR-6636-43-7}

PERRY, FRANCIS (Charles County) received a receipt from the Purchasing Agent for furnishing wheat on 18 Sep 1781 {Ref: Maryland State Archives MdHR-6636-23-24}

PERRY, JAMES (Montgomery County) received a receipt from the Purchasing Agent for furnishing wheat on 9 Apr 1781 {Ref: Maryland State Archives MdHR-6636-42-11}

PERRY, JOHN SR. (Charles County) received a receipt from the Purchasing Agent for furnishing wheat on 10 May 1783 {Ref: Maryland State Archives MdHR-6636-42-22}

PERRY, JOSEPH (Prince George's County) received a receipt from the Purchasing Agent for furnishing wheat on 16 Aug 1781 {Ref: Maryland State Archives MdHR-6636-24-20}

PERRY, SAMUEL (Frederick County) received a receipt from the Purchasing Agent for furnishing pork delivery on 9 May 1781 {Ref: Maryland State Archives MdHR-6636-23-31}; received a certificate for furnishing wheat on 10 Feb 1783 {Ref: Maryland State Archives MdHR-6636-42-38}

PERRY, WILLIAM (Prince George's County) received a loan certificate for £18.3.6 due from the Council of Maryland "agreeable to the Act proposing to the Citizens of this State, Creditors of Congress on Loan Office Certificates, Etc." on 29 Apr 1783 for services rendered during the war {Ref: Archives of Maryland 48:403}

PERRY, ZADOCK (Frederick County) received a receipt from the Purchasing Agent for furnishing corn on 2 May 1780 {Ref: Maryland State Archives MdHR-6636-24-1}; received a receipt for shelling corn on 7 May 1780 {Ref: Maryland State Archives MdHR-6636-24-2}

PETERS, JAMES (Frederick County) received a certificate from the Purchasing Agent for furnishing pork on 14 Mar 1781 {Ref: Maryland State Archives MdHR-6636-23-4}

PETERS (PETER), ROBERT (Montgomery County) received a receipt from the Purchasing Agent for furnishing wheat on 11 Aug 1780 {Ref: Maryland State

Archives MdHR-6636-24-6}; received a receipt for furnishing wheat on 9 Sep 1780 {Ref: Maryland State Archives MdHR-6636-24-7}

PETTICOAT, JASPER (Montgomery County) received a receipt from the Purchasing Agent for furnishing wheat on 29 Jun 1781 {Ref: Maryland State Archives MdHR-6636-24-15}

PETTICOAT, JOSEPH (Montgomery County) received a receipt from the Purchasing Agent for furnishing wheat on 10 Apr 1781 {Ref: Maryland State Archives MdHR-6636-24-15}

PETTICOAT, NICHOLAS (Prince George's County) received a receipt from the Purchasing Agent for furnishing wheat on 12 Jun 1782 {Ref: Maryland State Archives MdHR-6636-50-135}

PETTIT, EDWARD (Worcester County) appeared on "A List of Sundry Persons Corn Purchased of for the use of the State of Maryland" by the Commissary on 19 Jun 1780 {Ref: Archives of Maryland 45:9}; submitted an account and receipt for furnishing pork on 10 Oct 1782 {Ref: Maryland State Archives MdHR-6636-43-30H}

PHACALL, JOHN (county not stated) received a loan certificate for £42.1.0 due from the Council of Maryland "agreeable to the Act proposing to the Citizens of this State, Creditors of Congress on Loan Office Certificates, Etc." on 18 Oct 1783 for services rendered during the war {Ref: Archives of Maryland 48:471}

PHILLIPS, BEDDER (Prince George's County) received a receipt from the Purchasing Agent for furnishing wheat on 29 Mar 1783 {Ref: Maryland State Archives MdHR-6636-50-135}

PHILLIPS, ELISABETH (Caroline County) received a receipt from the Purchasing Agent for furnishing wheat on 1 Sep 1782 {Ref: Maryland State Archives MdHR-6636-42-7}

PHILLIPS, JAMES, see "Thomas Smith" and "Henry Stump," q.v.

PHILLIPS, JOSEPH (Dorchester County) received a receipt from the Purchasing Agent for furnishing wheat on 1 Nov 1782 {Ref: Maryland State Archives MdHR-6636-42-23}

PHILPOT, BARTON (Frederick County) received payment by order of the Council of Maryland via Dr. Philip Thomas for the hire of his wagon on 20 Apr 1778 {Ref: Archives of Maryland 21:42}

PHILPOTT, BENJAMIN (Charles County) received a receipt from the Purchasing Agent for furnishing wheat on 29 Dec 1782 {Ref: Maryland State Archives MdHR-6636-42-21}

PHIPS, JOHN (Anne Arundel County) received a loan certificate for £23.2.2 due from the Council of Maryland "agreeable to the Act proposing to the Citizens of this State, Creditors of Congress on Loan Office Certificates, Etc." on 14 Oct 1783 for services rendered during the war {Ref: Archives of Maryland 48:464}

PICKRON, JOSEPH (Charles County) received a receipt from the Purchasing

Agent for furnishing wheat on 3 May 1783 {Ref: Maryland State Archives MdHR-6636-42-22}

PIERCE, HENRY CULVER (Montgomery County) received a receipt from the Purchasing Agent for furnishing wheat on 3 Nov 1780 {Ref: Maryland State Archives MdHR-6636-24-8}

PILE, RALPH (Harford County) received a receipt from the Purchasing Agent for furnishing wheat on 23 Mar and 28 Jun 1780 {Ref: Maryland State Archives MdHR-6636-23-35}

PINOR, BARTUS (Kent County) received payment from the Purchasing Agent for furnishing cattle for the public use in September, 1781 {Ref: Maryland State Archives MdHR-6636-43-3}

PINOR (PINER), SARAH (Kent County) received a certificate from the Purchasing Agent for furnishing wheat on 14 Jan 1780 {Ref: Maryland State Archives MdHR-6636-23-41}; received payment for furnishing cattle and pasturage for the public use in September, 1781 {Ref: Maryland State Archives MdHR-6636-43-3}

PINKNEY, PRISCILLA, see "William Niven," q.v.

PITT, HILLARY (Worcester County) received a receipt from the Purchasing Agent for furnishing corn on 3 May 1780 {Ref: Maryland State Archives MdHR-6636-24-53}

PITT, JOHN (Dorchester County) received a receipt from the Purchasing Agent for furnishing wheat on 1 Nov 1782 {Ref: Maryland State Archives MdHR-6636-42-23}

PITT, JOHN (Baltimore County) received payment by order of the Council of Safety for the hire of his look out boat for the Flying Camp on 16 Aug 1776 {Ref: Archives of Maryland 12:208}; received flour from the commissary in Baltimore Town for delivery to Col. Henry Hollingsworth on 15 Jul 1780 {Ref: Archives of Maryland 45:85}

PITTS, HILLERY, (Worcester County) appeared on "A List of Corn Purchased in Worcester County for the use of the State of Maryland" by the Commissary in July, 1780 {Ref: Archives of Maryland 45:10}

PLACE, LEWIS (Baltimore County) received a certificate from the Purchasing Agent for furnishing corn on 16 Feb 1780 {Ref: Maryland State Archives MdHR-6636-23-33}

PLASTER, JOHN (Frederick County) received a certificate from the Purchasing Agent for furnishing wheat on 1 Jun 1782 {Ref: Maryland State Archives MdHR-6636-42-35}

PLATER, GEORGE (St. Mary's County) was a colonel who was appointed by the Council of Safety to collect all the gold and silver coin that could be procured in the county in compliance with the Resolve of Congress on 27 Jan 1776 {Ref: Archives of Maryland 11:132}; received payment "for expences incurred in erecting beacons on the River Patowmack" on 19 Jun 1776 {Ref: Archives of Maryland 11:499}

PLOWDEN, EDMUND (St. Mary's County) pledged a loan in the amount of £500 to the State of Maryland under the Act for the Emission of Bills of Credit "to defray the expences of the present campaign" in June, 1781 {Ref: Archives of Maryland 47:326}; received a loan certificate for £8.2.2 due from the Council of Maryland "agreeable to the Act proposing to the Citizens of this State, Creditors of Congress on Loan Office Certificates, Etc." on 21 Mar 1783 for services rendered during the war {Ref: Archives of Maryland 48:387}

PLOWDEN, FRANCIS (St. Mary's County) received payment from the Council of Maryland on 16 May 1783 "for 5,865 pounds of nett Tobacco at Coles Creek Warehouse in St. Mary's County, for the like Quantity lent the State by Henrietta Plowden in July 1780" {Ref: Archives of Maryland 48:414}

PLUMMER, JEREMIAH (Prince George's County) received a receipt from the Purchasing Agent for furnishing wheat in 1783 {Ref: Maryland State Archives MdHR-6636-50-135}

PLUMMER, JOHN (Frederick County) received a certificate from the Purchasing Agent for furnishing wheat on 4 Jun 1782 {Ref: Maryland State Archives MdHR-6636-42-35}

PLUMMER, PHILEMON (Montgomery County) received a receipt from the Purchasing Agent for furnishing wheat on 15 Apr and 20 Apr 1781 {Ref: Maryland State Archives MdHR-6636-42-11}

PLUMMER, THOMAS (Frederick County) received a certificate from the Purchasing Agent for furnishing wheat on 2 Jan 1782 {Ref: Maryland State Archives MdHR-6636-42-37}; received a certificate for furnishing wheat on 31 Jan 1783 {Ref: Maryland State Archives MdHR-6636-42-38}

POE, DAVID (Baltimore Town) received a receipt from the Purchasing Agent for furnishing pork on 5 Jun 1780 {Ref: Maryland State Archives MdHR-6636-21-133}; received a receipt for furnishing beef and pork on 10 May 1780 {Ref: Maryland State Archives MdHR-6636-40-46F}; received payment by order of the Council of Maryland "of the New Emission of this State to be delivered over to Thomas Donellan of Baltimore" on 25 Sep 1780 {Ref: Archives of Maryland 43:302}; served as Deputy Quartermaster in 1781 {Ref: Maryland State Archives MdHR-6636-26-18}; also see "John Butler," q.v.

POE, GEORGE (Baltimore Town) submitted an account and received payment for eight days service as wagon master on 29 Feb 1780 {Ref: Maryland Historical Society MS.1814, Box 6}; received payment for furnishing corn on 21 Apr 1781 {Ref: Maryland State Archives MdHR-6636-43-38DDDD}

POLK, BENJAMIN (Somerset County) received a receipt from the Purchasing Agent for furnishing pork on 30 Apr and 14 May 1782 {Ref: Maryland State Archives MdHR-6636-43-21}

POLK, GILLIS (Somerset County) received certificates from the Purchasing Agent for furnishing corn and flour on 29 Jan, 1 Feb, 9 Feb, 10 Feb, 26 Feb, 4 Mar, 20 Mar, 25 Mar, 28 Mar, 1 Apr and 8 Apr 1780 {Ref: Maryland State Archives MdHR-6636-24-39}; received a certificate for furnishing ground wheat on 6 Sep 1782 {Ref: Maryland State Archives MdHR-6636-43-21}

POLK, JAMES (Somerset County) received a receipt from the Purchasing Agent for furnishing bacon on 18 Aug 1780 {Ref: Maryland State Archives MdHR-6636-24-41}

POLK, JOSIAH (Somerset County) received a receipt from the Purchasing Agent for furnishing pork on 28 May 1782 {Ref: Maryland State Archives MdHR-6636-43-21}

POLK, WILLIAM (Somerset County) received a receipt from the Purchasing Agent for furnishing pork on 7 Aug 1780 {Ref: Maryland State Archives MdHR-6636-24-41}

POLL, JOSEPH (Prince George's County) received a receipt from the Purchasing Agent for furnishing wheat in 1782 {Ref: Maryland State Archives MdHR-6636-50-135}

POLLITT, GEORGE (Somerset County) received a receipt from the Purchasing Agent for furnishing bacon on 8 Aug 1780 {Ref: Maryland State Archives MdHR-6636-24-41}

POLLITT, JOHN JR. (Somerset County) received a receipt from the Purchasing Agent for furnishing bacon on 3 Aug 1780 {Ref: Maryland State Archives MdHR-6636-24-41}

POLLITT, THOMAS JR. (Somerset County) received a receipt from the Purchasing Agent for furnishing pork on 30 Aug 1780 {Ref: Maryland State Archives MdHR-6636-24-41}; received a receipt for furnishing pork on 14 May 1782 {Ref: Maryland State Archives MdHR-6636-43-21}

POLLOCK, JOHN (county not stated) received a loan certificate for £28.19.10½ due from the Council of Maryland "agreeable to the Act proposing to the Citizens of this State, Creditors of Congress on Loan Office Certificates, Etc." on 16 May 1783 for services rendered during the war {Ref: Archives of Maryland 48:414}

POOL, JOHN (Caroline County) received a receipt from the Purchasing Agent for furnishing wheat on 5 Aug 1782 {Ref: Maryland State Archives MdHR-6636-42-7}

POOL (POOLE), JOHN (Prince George's County) received payment by order of the Council of Maryland "to be delivered over to John Smith Brookes, Esqr., Commissary of Prince George's County" on 8 Jan 1782 {Ref: Archives of Maryland 48:39}; received a receipt from the Purchasing Agent for furnishing wheat in 1783 {Ref: Maryland State Archives MdHR-6636-50-135}

POORE, WALTER (Charles County) received a receipt from the Purchasing

Agent for furnishing wheat on 14 Feb 1782 {Ref: Maryland State Archives MdHR-6636-42-16}

PORTER, ANDREW (Cecil County) submitted an account for storing wheat on 28 Jan 1783 {Ref: Maryland State Archives MdHR-6636-48-2}; received a receipt for furnishing flour on 2 Jul 1783 {Ref: Maryland State Archives MdHR-6636-42-9}

PORTER, GEORGE (Caroline County) received a receipt from the Purchasing Agent for furnishing wheat on 1 Sep 1782 {Ref: Maryland State Archives MdHR-6636-42-7}

PORTER, JAMES (Caroline County) received a receipt from the Purchasing Agent for furnishing wheat on 31 Aug 1782 {Ref: Maryland State Archives MdHR-6636-42-7}

PORTER, MARY (Caroline County) received a receipt from the Purchasing Agent for furnishing wheat on 1 Sep 1782 {Ref: Maryland State Archives MdHR-6636-42-7}

PORTER, McKIMMEY (Somerset County) received a certificate from the Purchasing Agent for furnishing corn on 20 Jan 1780 {Ref: Maryland State Archives MdHR-6636-24-38}

PORTER, LAWRENCE (Dorchester County) received a receipt from the Purchasing Agent for furnishing wheat on 1 Oct 1782 {Ref: Maryland State Archives MdHR-6636-42-23}

PORTER, ROBERT (Dorchester County) received a receipt from the Purchasing Agent for furnishing wheat on 1 Oct 1782 {Ref: Maryland State Archives MdHR-6636-42-23}

PORTER, ROBERT JR. (Baltimore County) received payment for furnishing beef on 30 Apr 1781 {Ref: Maryland State Archives MdHR-6636-43-38NNN}

PORTTEUS, ROBERT (Baltimore Town) submitted a bill and receipt for furnishing thread on 30 Oct 1779 {Ref: Maryland State Archives MdHR-19970-3-8}

POSEY, BELAIN (Charles County) received a certificate for a loan to the state on 14 Jun 1780 {Ref: Maryland State Archives MdHR-6636-41-84}; received a receipt for furnishing wheat on 23 Oct 1781 {Ref: Maryland State Archives MdHR-6636-43-45H}; received a receipt for furnishing wheat on 30 Apr 1782 {Ref: Maryland State Archives MdHR-6636-42-18}; received a receipt for furnishing wheat on 8 May 1783 {Ref: Maryland State Archives MdHR-6636-42-22}

POSEY, BENJAMIN (Charles County) received a receipt from the Purchasing Agent for furnishing wheat on 16 Oct 1781 {Ref: Maryland State Archives MdHR-6636-23-24}

POSEY, BURDIT (Charles County) received a receipt from the Purchasing Agent for furnishing wheat on 20 Dec 1782 {Ref: Maryland State Archives MdHR-

6636-42-20}

POSEY, FRANCIS (Charles County) received a receipt from the Purchasing Agent for furnishing wheat on 1 Dec 1781 {Ref: Maryland State Archives MdHR-6636-42-15}

POSEY, HUMPHERY (Charles County) received a receipt from the Purchasing Agent for furnishing wheat on 10 May 1783 {Ref: Maryland State Archives MdHR-6636-42-22}

POSEY, THOMAS (Charles County) received a receipt from the Purchasing Agent for furnishing wheat on 26 Jan 1782 {Ref: Maryland State Archives MdHR-6636-42-16}; received a receipt for furnishing wheat on 9 Apr 1782 {Ref: Maryland State Archives MdHR-6636-42-18}

POSTLY (POSTLEY), JOHN (Worcester County) was a captain who was appointed by the Council of Maryland to be one of three Purchasers of Cattle for his county on 7 Jan 1778 {Ref: Archives of Maryland 16:456}; received receipts from the Purchasing Agent for furnishing corn on 29 Mar and 1 Jun 1780 {Ref: Maryland State Archives MdHR-6636-24-52&53}; his name appeared on "A List of Corn Purchased in Worcester County for the use of the State of Maryland" by the Commissary in July, 1780 {Ref: Archives of Maryland 45:9}

POSTON (POSTEN), PRISELA, PRICILLA OR PRISCILLA (Charles County) received a receipt from the Purchasing Agent for furnishing wheat on 27 Jul 1782 {Ref: Maryland State Archives MdHR-6636-42-18}; received a receipt for furnishing wheat on 20 Dec 1782 {Ref: Maryland State Archives MdHR-6636-42-20}; received a receipt for furnishing wheat on 15 Apr 1783 {Ref: Maryland State Archives MdHR-6636-42-22}

POSTON, PRISCILLA (Charles County) received a receipt from the Purchasing Agent for furnishing wheat on 7 Jul 1781 {Ref: Maryland State Archives MdHR-6636-42-15}

POTTER, NATHANIEL (Caroline County) was appointed by the Council of Maryland on 25 Mar 1778 as one of eighteen men to be "Agents for Purchasing Provisions for the Army of the United States Agreeable to an Act of Assembly passed the 23rd Inst." {Ref: Archives of Maryland 16:551}; submitted an account of purchases on 23 May 1778 {Ref: Maryland State Archives MdHR-4586-51}; commissioned an Assistant Deputy Commissary of Purchases on 10 Sep 1779 {Ref: Archives of Maryland 21:518}; appointed Commissary of Purchases for Caroline County by the Council of Maryland on 8 Jul 1780 {Ref: Archives of Maryland 43:215}; contracted for purchasing provisions on 23 Jul 1780 {Ref: Maryland State Archives MdHR-6636-19-41}; also see "Jonathan Parker," q.v.

POTTER, ZEBDIEL OR ZABDIEL (Caroline County) was a doctor and Commissary Agent who submitted accounts of wheat received on 22 Aug and

15 Sep 1782 {Ref: Maryland State Archives MdHR-6636-42-7}

POULSON, ANDREW (Frederick County) received a receipt from the Purchasing Agent for furnishing beef on 19 Jan 1781 {Ref: Maryland State Archives MdHR-6636-23-2}

POWEL, NATHANIEL (Frederick County) received a certificate from the Purchasing Agent for furnishing wheat on 8 Jun 1782 {Ref: Maryland State Archives MdHR-6636-42-35}

POWELL, GEORGE (Caroline County) received a receipt from the Purchasing Agent for wheat on 17 Sep 1782 {Ref: Maryland State Archives MdHR-6636-42-7}

POWELL, JAMES (Caroline County) received a receipt from the Purchasing Agent for furnishing wheat on 1 Sep 1782 {Ref: Maryland State Archives MdHR-6636-42-7}

POWELL, JESSE (Somerset County) received a receipt from the Purchasing Agent for furnishing beef on 6 Nov and 5 Dec 1781 {Ref: Maryland State Archives MdHR-6636-24-44}

POWELL (POWEL), JOHN (Worcester County) received a receipt from the Purchasing Agent for furnishing corn on 3 May 1780 {Ref: Maryland State Archives MdHR-6636-24-53}; his name appeared on "A List of Corn Purchased in Worcester County for the use of the State of Maryland" by the Commissary in July, 1780 {Ref: Archives of Maryland 45:10}

PRALL, EDWARD (Harford County) received a certificate from the Purchasing Agent for furnishing flour on 24 Apr 1780 {Ref: Maryland State Archives MdHR-6636-23-34}

PRATHAR, JOHN (Montgomery County) received a receipt from the Purchasing Agent for furnishing wheat on 28 Apr 1781 {Ref: Maryland State Archives MdHR-6636-42-11}

PRATHER, RICHARD (Montgomery County) received a loan certificate for £75.18.11 due from the Council of Maryland "agreeable to the Act proposing to the Citizens of this State, Creditors of Congress on Loan Office Certificates, Etc." on 16 May 1783 for services rendered during the war {Ref: Archives of Maryland 48:414}

PRATOR, BARUCH OR BARRUCK (Montgomery County) received a receipt from the Purchasing Agent for furnishing wheat on 28 Jul 1780 {Ref: Maryland State Archives MdHR-6636-24-5}; received a receipt for furnishing wheat on 1 Aug 1780 {Ref: Maryland State Archives MdHR-6636-43-7}

PRATOR, BASIL (Montgomery County) received a receipt from the Purchasing Agent for furnishing wheat on 7 Sep 1780 {Ref: Maryland State Archives MdHR-6636-24-7}

PRATOR, SAMUEL (Frederick County) received a certificate from the Purchasing Agent for furnishing wheat on 16 Aug 1782 {Ref: Maryland State Archives

MdHR-6636-42-37}

PRATT, HENRY (Queen Anne's County) received a receipt from the Purchasing Agent for furnishing bacon on 1 Apr 1778 {Ref: Maryland State Archives MdHR-4587-46}; submitted an account and receipt for hauling salt and wheat on 17 Sep 1782 {Ref: Maryland State Archives MdHR-6636-43-12}

PRATT, SARAH (Queen Anne's County) received a certificate from the Purchasing Agent for furnishing wheat on 2 Nov 1781 {Ref: Maryland State Archives MdHR-6636-24-34}

PRESTON, BARNARD JR. (Harford County) received a receipt from the Purchasing Agent for furnishing wheat on 22 Mar 1780 {Ref: Maryland State Archives MdHR-6636-23-35}

PRESTON, BARNARD SR. (Harford County) received a receipt from the Purchasing Agent for furnishing wheat on 10 Mar 1780 {Ref: Maryland State Archives MdHR-6636-23-35}

PREW, WILLIAM (Annapolis) served as messenger for the Council of Maryland in February and March, 1778 and was paid for his services on 17 Mar 1778 {Ref: Archives of Maryland 16:539}

PRICE, ANDREW (Caroline County) received a receipt from the Purchasing Agent for furnishing beef on 20 Dec 1782 {Ref: Maryland State Archives MdHR-6636-42-7}

PRICE, HUGH (Talbot County) received a certificate from the Purchasing Agent for furnishing wheat on 20 Mar 1780 {Ref: Maryland State Archives MdHR-6636-24-46}

PRICE, JAMES (Caroline County) received a receipt from the Purchasing Agent for furnishing wheat on 1 Sep 1782 {Ref: Maryland State Archives MdHR-6636-42-7}

PRICE, JOHN (Cecil County) submitted an account for hauling wheat on 10 Mar 1783 {Ref: Maryland State Archives MdHR-6636-42-9}

PRICE, JOHN (Queen Anne's County) received a certificate from the Purchasing Agent for furnishing wheat on 18 Jan 1780 {Ref: Maryland State Archives MdHR-6636-24-30}; received a certificate for furnishing beef on 8 Oct 1781 {Ref: Maryland State Archives MdHR-6636-24-34}

PRICE, JOSIAH (Washington County) received a receipt from the Purchasing Agent for furnishing wheat on 19 Dec 1782 {Ref: Maryland State Archives MdHR-6636-43-26}

PRICE, NEAL (Caroline County) received a receipt from the Purchasing Agent for wheat on 12 Sep 1782 {Ref: Maryland State Archives MdHR-6636-42-7}

PRICE, RICHARD (Charles County) received a receipt from the Purchasing Agent for furnishing wheat on 9 May 1783 {Ref: Maryland State Archives MdHR-6636-42-22}

PRICE, RUSSELL (Somerset County) received a receipt from the Purchasing

Agent for furnishing pork on 16 May 1782 {Ref: Maryland State Archives MdHR-6636-43-21}

PRICE, THOMAS (Worcester County) submitted an account and receipt for hauling on 6 Oct 1782 {Ref: Maryland State Archives MdHR-6636-43-30A}

PRICE, THOMAS (Frederick County) was a colonel who was appointed Commissary of Purchases for Frederick County by the Council of Maryland on 8 Jul 1780 {Ref: Archives of Maryland 43:215}; submitted an account for house rental and pasturing cattle in 1781 {Ref: Maryland State Archives MdHR-6636-23-32}; received a receipt for furnishing pork on 3 Apr 1781 {Ref: Maryland State Archives MdHR-6636-42-26}; received a certificate for grinding wheat on 27 Jan 1782 {Ref: Maryland State Archives MdHR-6636-42-37}; also see "Joseph Dowson," q.v.

PRICHETT (PRITCHETT), ELIAS (Montgomery County) received a receipt from the Purchasing Agent for furnishing wheat on 11 Sep 1780 {Ref: Maryland State Archives MdHR-6636-24-7}; received a receipt for furnishing wheat on 5 May 1781 {Ref: Maryland State Archives MdHR-6636-24-18}

PRICHETT, WILLIAM (Montgomery County) received a receipt from the Purchasing Agent for furnishing wheat on 29 May 1781 {Ref: Maryland State Archives MdHR-6636-24-18}

PRICKERS, CHARLES (Montgomery County) received a receipt from the Purchasing Agent for furnishing wheat on 17 May 1781 {Ref: Maryland State Archives MdHR-6636-24-18}

PRIESTLY, MARY (Baltimore Town) received payment by order of the Council of Maryland for nursing and boarding the crew of the state ship *Defence* on 13 Apr 1778 {Ref: Archives of Maryland 21:33}

PRIG, EDWARD (Harford County) received payment for furnishing a gun to the Committee of Safety on 2 Sep 1776 {Ref: Preston's History of Harford County, pp. 335-336}

PRIMROSE, JOHN (Queen Anne's County) received a certificate from the Purchasing Agent for furnishing beef on 28 Sep 1781 {Ref: Maryland State Archives MdHR-6636-24-34}

PRITCHETT, EDWARD (Caroline County) received a receipt from the Purchasing Agent for furnishing wheat on 5 Aug 1782 {Ref: Maryland State Archives MdHR-6636-42-7}

PROTHELS, SYLVANUS (Caroline County) received a receipt from the Purchasing Agent for furnishing wheat on 1 Sep 1782 {Ref: Maryland State Archives MdHR-6636-42-7}

PUGH, JOHN (Cecil County) received a receipt from the Purchasing Agent for furnishing wheat on 20 Jan 1783 {Ref: Maryland State Archives MdHR-6636-42-9}

PURDOM, JOHN (Montgomery County) received a receipt from the Purchasing

Agent for shelling corn on 19 Jul 1780 {Ref: Maryland State Archives MdHR-6636-24-2}

PURNAL, WILLIAM (Caroline County) received a receipt from the Purchasing Agent for furnishing wheat on 1 Sep 1782 {Ref: Maryland State Archives MdHR-6636-42-7}

PURNELL, BENJAMIN (Worcester County) received a loan certificate for £108.6.2 due from the Council of Maryland "agreeable to the Act proposing to the Citizens of this State, Creditors of Congress on Loan Office Certificates, Etc." on 17 May 1783 for services rendered during the war {Ref: Archives of Maryland 48:416}

PURNELL, ELISHA (Worcester County) submitted an account and receipt for furnishing salt on 1 Apr 1782 {Ref: Maryland State Archives MdHR-6636-43-28JJ}

PURNELL, MARY (Worcester County) submitted an account and receipt of payment due for beef on 20 Sep 1781 {Ref: Maryland State Archives MdHR-6636-43-27}

PURNELL, SARAH (Worcester County) received a receipt from the Purchasing Agent for furnishing corn on 15 Feb 1780 {Ref: Maryland State Archives MdHR-6636-24-52}; her name appeared on "A List of Corn Purchased in Worcester County for the use of the State of Maryland" by the Commissary in July, 1780 {Ref: Archives of Maryland 45:9}; received payment for furnishing beef on 10 Oct 1781 {Ref: Maryland State Archives MdHR-6636-43-28KKK}

PURNELL, THOMAS (Worcester County) was a captain who received a receipt from the Purchasing Agent for furnishing corn on 19 Mar 1780 {Ref: Maryland State Archives MdHR-6636-24-52}; received a receipt for furnishing corn on 14 Jun 1780 {Ref: Maryland State Archives MdHR-6636-24-53}; his name appeared on "A List of Corn Purchased in Worcester County for the use of the State of Maryland" by the Commissary in July, 1780 {Ref: Archives of Maryland 45:10}; received a receipt for furnishing beef on 19 Sep 1780 {Ref: Maryland State Archives MdHR-6636-24-54}; received payment for furnishing beef on 20 Sep 1781 {Ref: Maryland State Archives MdHR-6636-43-28YYY}; received a receipt for furnishing salt on 25 Feb 1782 {Ref: Maryland State Archives MdHR-6636-43-27}

PURNELL, WILLIAM (Worcester County) received a receipt from the Purchasing Agent for furnishing corn on 28 Apr 1780 {Ref: Maryland State Archives MdHR-6636-24-52}; his name appeared on "A List of Corn Purchased in Worcester County for the use of the State of Maryland" by the Commissary in July, 1780 {Ref: Archives of Maryland 45:10}

PURNELL, ZADOCK OR ZADOK (Worcester County) received a receipt from the Purchasing Agent for furnishing corn on 14 Jun 1780 {Ref: Maryland State Archives MdHR-6636-24-53}; his name appeared on "A List of Corn

Purchased in Worcester County for the use of the State of Maryland" by the Commissary in July, 1780 {Ref: Archives of Maryland 45:9}; received payment for furnishing pork on 20 Sep 1781 {Ref: Maryland State Archives MdHR-6636-43-28CCCC}

PURVIANCE, ROBERT (Baltimore County) submitted an account for furnishing oil casks and blubber on 4 Oct 1777 {Ref: Maryland State Archives MdHR-19970-10-24}; Robert and Samuel Purviance received a loan certificate for £1242.1.2 due from the Council of Maryland "agreeable to the Act proposing to the Citizens of this State, Creditors of Congress on Loan Office Certificates, Etc." on 18 Dec 1783 for services rendered during the war {Ref: Archives of Maryland 48:491}

PURVIANCE, SAMUEL (Baltimore County) was appointed by the Council of Safety to collect all the gold and silver coin that could be procured in the county in compliance with the Resolve of Congress on 27 Jan 1776 {Ref: Archives of Maryland 11:131}; submitted an account for furnishing oil casks and blubber on 4 Oct 1777 {Ref: Maryland State Archives MdHR-19970-10-24}; also see "Robert Purviance," q.v.

PYE, WALTER (Charles County) received a receipt from the Purchasing Agent for furnishing wheat on 14 Aug and 14 Sep 1782 {Ref: Maryland State Archives MdHR-6636-42-18}

PYPER, THOMAS (Queen Anne's County) submitted an account and receipt of payment due for supplies on 17 Aug 1781 {Ref: Maryland State Archives MdHR-6636-41-89}

QUEEN, FRANCIS (Charles County) received a receipt from the Purchasing Agent for furnishing wheat on 27 Jul 1782 {Ref: Maryland State Archives MdHR-6636-42-18}

QUEEN, JOHN (Frederick County) received a receipt from the Purchasing Agent for furnishing corn on 7 Jan 1781 {Ref: Maryland State Archives MdHR-6636-23-2}

QUEEN, RICHARD (Montgomery County) received a receipt from the Purchasing Agent for furnishing wheat on 5 Dec 1780 {Ref: Maryland State Archives MdHR-6636-24-13}

QUINTON, DIXON (Worcester County) submitted an account and receipt for furnishing bacon on 11 Sep 1781 {Ref: Maryland State Archives MdHR-6636-43-28E}

QUINTON, JAMES (Worcester County) submitted an account and receipt for furnishing salt in or about 1781 {Ref: Maryland State Archives MdHR-19970-4-1}

QUIRNEL, LAURENCE (Baltimore County) submitted an account and received payment for driving a wagon for five days to transport flour to the Susquehanna for the use of the army on 1 Jan 1780 {Ref: Maryland Historical Society

MS.1814, Box 6}

QUYNN, ALLEN (Anne Arundel County) received payment by order of the Council of Safety for cartage of wood on 28 Aug 1776 {Ref: Archives of Maryland 12:245}; pledged a loan in the amount of £100 to the State of Maryland under the Act for the Emission of Bills of Credit "to defray the expences of the present campaign" in June, 1781 {Ref: Archives of Maryland 47:327}; submitted an account for delivery of candles on 23 Feb 1783 {Ref: Maryland State Archives MdHR-6636-48-36}; received a loan certificate for £74.15.0 due from the Council of Maryland "agreeable to the Act proposing to the Citizens of this State, Creditors of Congress on Loan Office Certificates, Etc." on 4 Jul 1783 for services rendered during the war {Ref: Archives of Maryland 48:436}

RABRECK (REHBRECK), CHRISTOPHER (Baltimore Town) received payments by order of the Council of Safety for furnishing priming wires and brushes on 10 Aug and 18 Sep 1776 {Ref: Archives of Maryland 12:192, 280}

RACKLIFFE, CHARLES (Worcester) County) received a receipt from the Purchasing Agent for furnishing beef on 18 Sep 1780 {Ref: Maryland State Archives MdHR-6636-24-54}

RACKLIFFE, JOHN (Worcester County) received payment for furnishing pork on 15 Sep 1781 {Ref: Maryland State Archives MdHR-6636-43-28DDDD}

RACKLIFFE, NATHANIEL (Worcester County) received a receipt from the Purchasing Agent for furnishing pork on 18 Sep 1780 {Ref: Maryland State Archives MdHR-6636-24-54}

RADISH, HIRAM (Somerset County) received a receipt from the Purchasing Agent for furnishing bacon on 7 Jul 1781 {Ref: Maryland State Archives MdHR-6636-24-43}

RADISH, JOSEPH (Somerset County) received a receipt from the Purchasing Agent for furnishing bacon on 18 Jul 1781 {Ref: Maryland State Archives MdHR-6636-24-43}

RAGAN, DANIEL (Baltimore County) received payment by order of the Council of Maryland for ferriage on 28 Mar 1778 {Ref: Archives of Maryland 16:557}

RAIT, JOHN (Frederick County) received a certificate from the Purchasing Agent for furnishing wheat on 27 Jul 1782 {Ref: Maryland State Archives MdHR-6636-42-36}

RAMSAY, THOMAS (Cecil County) appeared on 19 Feb 1781 on a "Return [of] Flour forwarded and Delivered at the Head of Elk the Purchase of different Persons for the use of the United States" in the year 1780 {Ref: Archives of Maryland 47:77}; also see "Edward Wright," q.v.

RAMSEY, MRS. (Worcester County) received a receipt from the Purchasing Agent for furnishing beef on 13 Oct 1780 {Ref: Maryland State Archives MdHR-6636-24-54}

RANDALL, JOHN (Annapolis) was appointed Commissary by the Council of Maryland on 13 Feb 1778 to procure supplies and distribute them to the Quota of Troops of the American Army agreeable to a Resolve of the General Assembly passed on 13 Dec 1777 {Ref: Archives of Maryland 16:493}

RANDALL, JOHN (Baltimore County) submitted an account for coffee on 18 May 1780 {Ref: Maryland State Archives MdHR-6636-18-92}

RANDALL, WILLIAM (Baltimore County) received payment by order of the Council of Maryland for the hire of his wagon on 23 Jun 1778 {Ref: Archives of Maryland 21:147}

RANDELL, JOHN (Kent County) received payment from the Purchasing Agent for furnishing cattle and pasturage for the public use in September, 1781 {Ref: Maryland State Archives MdHR-6636-43-3}

RANSBURGH, GEORGE (Frederick County) received payment by order of the Council of Maryland for furnishing pasturage, hay and wood on 25 Mar 1778 {Ref: Archives of Maryland 16:550-551}

RANSBURGH, JOHN (Frederick County) received a loan certificate for £64.15.6 due from the Council of Maryland "agreeable to the Act proposing to the Citizens of this State, Creditors of Congress on Loan Office Certificates, Etc." on 30 Apr 1783 for services rendered during the war {Ref: Archives of Maryland 48:404}

RANSBURGH, STEPHEN (Frederick County) received a certificate from the Purchasing Agent for furnishing wheat on 18 Jul 1782 {Ref: Maryland State Archives MdHR-6636-42-36}

RASIN, JOSEPH (Kent County) received payment for hauling flour on 15 Jan 1781 {Ref: Maryland State Archives MdHR-6636-23-49}

RASIN, WILLIAM (Kent County) received a certificate from the Purchasing Agent for furnishing wheat on 26 Jan 1780 {Ref: Maryland State Archives MdHR-6636-43-1}; received payment from the Purchasing Agent for furnishing cattle for the public use in September, 1781 {Ref: Maryland State Archives MdHR-6636-43-3}

RATHELL (RAITHEL), JOSEPH (Talbot County) received a receipt from the Purchasing Agent for furnishing wheat on 6 Oct 1781 {Ref: Maryland State Archives MdHR-6636-24-51}

RAWLEY, WALTER (Dorchester County) received a receipt from the Purchasing Agent for furnishing wheat on 1 Nov 1782 {Ref: Maryland State Archives MdHR-6636-42-23}

RAWLINGS, FRANCIS (Anne Arundel County) received payment by order of the Council of Maryland "for beef purchased of him for the State" on 31 Jan 1778 {Ref: Archives of Maryland 16:481}

RAWLINGS, JOHN (Queen Anne's County) submitted an account for furnishing grain and barrels on 1 Jun 1780 {Ref: Maryland State Archives MdHR-6636-

24-26}

RAWLINGS, JOHN (Kent County) received a certificate from the Purchasing Agent for grinding wheat on 1 Apr 1780 {Ref: Maryland State Archives MdHR-6636-43-1}

RAWLINGS, JOHN (Montgomery County) received a receipt from the Purchasing Agent for furnishing wheat on 6 Sep 1781 {Ref: Maryland State Archives MdHR-6636-24-15}

RAWLINGS, MOSES (Frederick and Washington Counties) was a colonel who was commissioned an Assistant Deputy Commissary of Purchases on 10 Sep 1779 {Ref: Archives of Maryland 21:518}; appointed Commissary of Purchases for Washington County by the Council of Maryland on 8 Jul 1780 {Ref: Archives of Maryland 43:215}; received a receipt from the Purchasing Agent for hauling flour on 13 Sep 1783 {Ref: Maryland State Archives MdHR-6636-46-71B}

RAY, BENJAMIN (Montgomery County) received a receipt from the Purchasing Agent for furnishing wheat on 18 Oct 1780 {Ref: Maryland State Archives MdHR-6636-24-8}; received a receipt for furnishing wheat on 18 Apr 1781 {Ref: Maryland State Archives MdHR-6636-24-18}; received a receipt for furnishing wheat on 1 Oct 1781 {Ref: Maryland State Archives MdHR-6636-42-11}

RAY, CHARLES (Charles County) received a receipt from the Purchasing Agent for furnishing wheat on 29 Sep 1781 {Ref: Maryland State Archives MdHR-6636-42-15}; received a receipt for furnishing wheat on 28 Dec 1782 {Ref: Maryland State Archives MdHR-6636-42-21}

RAY, JAMES (Montgomery County) received a receipt from the Purchasing Agent for furnishing wheat on 27 Sep 1780 {Ref: Maryland State Archives MdHR-6636-24-7}

RAY, JOHN (Montgomery County) received a receipt from the Purchasing Agent for furnishing wheat on 1 Aug 1780 {Ref: Maryland State Archives MdHR-6636-43-7}; received a receipt for furnishing wheat on 1 Oct 1781 {Ref: Maryland State Archives MdHR-6636-24-15}

RAY, NICHOLAS (Montgomery County) received a receipt from the Purchasing Agent for furnishing wheat on 6 Apr 1781 {Ref: Maryland State Archives MdHR-6636-42-11}; received a certificate and oath of employment as a cattle collector by the commissary of purchases on 5 Feb and 18 Mar 1782 {Ref: Maryland State Archives MdHR-6636-50-91}

RAY, THOMAS (Talbot County) received a receipt from the Purchasing Agent for furnishing bacon for the use of the army on 4 May 1778 {Ref: Maryland State Archives MdHR-4587-82}

RAY, WILLIAM (Montgomery County) received a receipt from the Purchasing Agent for furnishing wheat on 1 Oct 1781 {Ref: Maryland State Archives

MdHR-6636-24-15}

RAYMER, MICHAEL (Frederick County) was appointed by the Council of Safety to collect all the gold and silver coin that could be procured in the county in compliance with the Resolve of Congress on 27 Jan 1776 {Ref: Archives of Maryland 11:132}

RAYNOR, WILLIAM (Frederick County) received a receipt from the Purchasing Agent for furnishing pork on 18 Jan 1781 {Ref: Maryland State Archives MdHR-6636-23-4}; received a receipt for furnishing pork on 10 Mar 1781 {Ref: Maryland State Archives MdHR-6636-23-4}

RAZIN, HENRY (Charles County) received a receipt from the Purchasing Agent for furnishing wheat on 29 Dec 1782 {Ref: Maryland State Archives MdHR-6636-42-21}

REA, GEORGE W. (Baltimore County) submitted an account and received payment for furnishing nails on 24 Feb 1780 {Ref: Maryland Historical Society MS.1814, Box 6}; submitted an account for coopering (receipt by William Rea) on 28 Sep 1781 {Ref: Maryland State Archives MdHR-6636-43-38X}; submitted an account and receipt for furnishing provisions on 1 Oct 1781 {Ref: Maryland State Archives MdHR-6636-43-38R}

REA, WILLIAM (Baltimore County) received a receipt from the Purchasing Agent for coopering, account of George W. Rea on 28 Sep 1781 {Ref: Maryland State Archives MdHR-6636-43-38X}

REASER (RAZOR), JACOB (Frederick County) was a gunsmith who contracted to make arms for the Council of Maryland on 15 Sep 1777 and agreed to finish 100 musquets fixed with bayonets, steel rammers, swivels, priming wires and brushes, and deliver them at the rate of twelve per month {Ref: Archives of Maryland 16:376}; he was still manufacturing arms on 12 Jan 1781 {Ref: Archives of Maryland 47:14}

REDDISH, HIRON (Somerset County) received a certificate from the Purchasing Agent for furnishing corn on 22 Jan 1780 {Ref: Maryland State Archives MdHR-6636-24-38}

REDER, RICHARD R. (Charles County) received a receipt from the Purchasing Agent for furnishing wheat on 26 Apr 1783 {Ref: Maryland State Archives MdHR-6636-42-22}

REDGRAVE, JAMES (Kent County) received payment for furnishing cattle and wheat on 7 Nov 1780 {Ref: Maryland State Archives MdHR-6636-23-49}

REDMAN, ALICE (Montgomery or Prince George's County) received payments by order of the Council of Maryland for services rendered (not specified) on 31 Aug 1781 and 26 Apr 1782 {Ref: Archives of Maryland 45:593, 48:148}

REDMAN, BENJAMIN (Montgomery County) received a receipt from the Purchasing Agent for furnishing wheat on 28 Jul 1781 {Ref: Maryland State Archives MdHR-6636-42-11}

REDMAN, FRANCES (Montgomery County) received a receipt from the Purchasing Agent for furnishing wheat on 3 Jul 1781 {Ref: Maryland State Archives MdHR-6636-24-15}

REDMAN, JOSEPH (Montgomery County) received a receipt from the Purchasing Agent for furnishing wheat on 25 Jul 1781 {Ref: Maryland State Archives MdHR-6636-42-11}

REDMAN, WILLIAM (Montgomery County) received a receipt from the Purchasing Agent for furnishing wheat on 28 Jul 1781 {Ref: Maryland State Archives MdHR-6636-24-15}

REED, JASPER (Queen Anne's County) received a certificate from the Purchasing Agent for furnishing wheat on 11 Jan 1780 {Ref: Maryland State Archives MdHR-6636-24-31}

REED, JEREMIAH (Queen Anne's County) received a certificate from the Purchasing Agent for furnishing wheat on 11 Jan 1780 {Ref: Maryland State Archives MdHR-6636-24-31}

REED (READ), JESSE (Queen Anne's County) received a loan certificate for £38.18.7 due from the Council of Maryland "agreeable to the Act proposing to the Citizens of this State, Creditors of Congress on Loan Office Certificates, Etc." on 31 Oct 1783 for services rendered during the war {Ref: Archives of Maryland 48:476}

REED, JOHN (Anne Arundel County) received payment by order of the Council of Maryland "for furnishing horses to the express from Virginia" on 4 Nov 1777 {Ref: Archives of Maryland 16:408}

REED, JONATHAN (Prince George's County) received a receipt from the Purchasing Agent for furnishing wheat on 23 Dec 1782 {Ref: Maryland State Archives MdHR-6636-50-142}

REED, MATHEW (Prince George's County) received a receipt from the Purchasing Agent for furnishing wheat in 1782 {Ref: Maryland State Archives MdHR-6636-50-135}; received receipts for furnishing wheat on 17 Dec 1782 and 12 Jan 1783 {Ref: Maryland State Archives MdHR-6636-50-142}

REED, RACHEL (Queen Anne's County) received a receipt from the Purchasing Agent for furnishing bacon on 1 Apr 1778 {Ref: Maryland State Archives MdHR-4587-44}

REEDER, HEZEKIAH (Charles County) received a receipt from the Purchasing Agent for furnishing beef on 23 Aug 1781 {Ref: Maryland State Archives MdHR-6636-43-37L}; submitted an account for purchasing cattle from 16 Jul to 4 Sep 1781 {Ref: Maryland State Archives MdHR-6636-23-23}

REEDER, RICHARD R. (Charles County) received a receipt from the Purchasing Agent for furnishing wheat on 16 Nov 1781 {Ref: Maryland State Archives MdHR-6636-42-15}; submitted an account for furnishing wheat on 21 Sep 1782 {Ref: Maryland State Archives MdHR-6636-43-45B}

REGISTER, SAMUEL (Talbot County) received a receipt from the Purchasing Agent for furnishing bacon for the use of the army on 15 May 1778 {Ref: Maryland State Archives MdHR-4587-86}

REID (READ), ROBERT (county not stated) contracted with the Council of Maryland to make guns on or about 15 Apr 1777 and furnished 30 musquets "in consequence of a former agreement" on 29 Jul 1777 {Ref: Archives of Maryland 16:212, 320}

REILY, BENJAMIN (Somerset County) received a receipt from the Purchasing Agent for furnishing wheat on 11 Oct 1781 {Ref: Maryland State Archives MdHR-6636-24-44}

REILY, ELIZABETH (Montgomery County) received a receipt from the Purchasing Agent for furnishing wheat on 4 May 1781 {Ref: Maryland State Archives MdHR-6636-42-11}

REILY, HUGH (Montgomery County) received a receipt from the Purchasing Agent for furnishing wheat on 14 Sep 1780 {Ref: Maryland State Archives MdHR-6636-24-7}; received a receipt for furnishing wheat on 9 Feb 1781 {Ref: Maryland State Archives MdHR-6636-24-9}

REILY, NINIAN (Montgomery County) received a certificate from the Purchasing Agent for furnishing wheat on 18 Jul 1780 {Ref: Maryland State Archives MdHR-6636-24-5}

REILY, ZACHARIAH (Montgomery County) received a receipt from the Purchasing Agent for furnishing wheat on 25 Jul 1781 {Ref: Maryland State Archives MdHR-6636-24-15}

REITH, ROBERT (Annapolis) served as messenger for the Governor and Council of Maryland from September, 1778 until his death circa February, 1781 {Ref: Archives of Maryland 21:210, 253, 272, 283, 309, 327, 364; 43:51, 159, 244, 275; 45:244, 302}

REMINGTON, JOHN (Montgomery County) received a receipt from the Purchasing Agent for furnishing wheat on 5 Sep 1780 {Ref: Maryland State Archives MdHR-6636-24-7}; received a receipt for furnishing wheat on 25 Apr 1781 {Ref: Maryland State Archives MdHR-6636-24-14}

RENCHAR, JOHN (Somerset County) received a certificate from the Purchasing Agent for furnishing corn on 26 Feb 1780 {Ref: Maryland State Archives MdHR-6636-24-39}

RENICHHOUSER, GEORGE (Frederick County) received a certificate from the Purchasing Agent for furnishing wheat on 10 Jun 1781 {Ref: Maryland State Archives MdHR-6636-23-28}

RENSBURG, STEPHEN (Frederick County) submitted an account for furnishing hay on 18 Nov 1780 {Ref: Maryland State Archives MdHR-6636-23-5}; received a receipt for furnishing hay on 28 Feb 1781 {Ref: Maryland State Archives MdHR-6636-23-3}

RETTLEMOSER, MICHAEL (Frederick County) received a certificate from the Purchasing Agent for furnishing wheat on 29 May 1782 {Ref: Maryland State Archives MdHR-6636-42-34}

REYMINGEN, GEORGE (Montgomery County) received a receipt from the Purchasing Agent for furnishing wheat on 20 Mar 1781 {Ref: Maryland State Archives MdHR-6636-24-18}

REYNER, EBENEZER (Kent County) received payment from the Purchasing Agent for furnishing cattle for the public use in September, 1781 {Ref: Maryland State Archives MdHR-6636-43-3}

REYNOLDS, HUGH (Frederick County) received a receipt from the Purchasing Agent for delivering flour on 27 Dec 1780 {Ref: Maryland State Archives MdHR-6636-23-29}; received a receipt for delivering flour on 25 Jan 1781 {Ref: Maryland State Archives MdHR-6636-23-2}; received receipts for hauling and delivering flour on 4 Jan, 23 Feb, 1 Mar and 28 Mar 1781 {Ref: Maryland State Archives MdHR-6636-23-30}

REYNOLDS, WILLIAM (Anne Arundel County) received payment by order of the Council of Safety for the hire of his horse on 9 Apr 1776 {Ref: Archives of Maryland 11:316}

RIAN, BURNETT (Frederick County) received a certificate from the Purchasing Agent for furnishing wheat on 26 May 1782 {Ref: Maryland State Archives MdHR-6636-42-33}

RICARDS, ARCHILAS (Somerset County) received a receipt from the Purchasing Agent for furnishing beef on 21 Nov 1781 {Ref: Maryland State Archives MdHR-6636-24-44}

RICH, PETER (Queen Anne's County) was an assistant purchasing agent who submitted an account of clothing purchased on 16 Feb 1778 {Ref: Maryland State Archives MdHR-6636-10-82B}

RICHARDS, CAESAR OR CASAR (Charles County) received a receipt from the Purchasing Agent for furnishing wheat on 3 Oct 1781 {Ref: Maryland State Archives MdHR-6636-42-15}; received a receipt for furnishing wheat on 2 Nov 1782 {Ref: Maryland State Archives MdHR-6636-42-19}

RICHARDS, HENRY (Caroline County) received a receipt from the Purchasing Agent for furnishing wheat on 5 Aug 1782 {Ref: Maryland State Archives MdHR-6636-42-7}

RICHARDS, JOHN (Montgomery County) received a receipt from the Purchasing Agent for furnishing wheat on 22 Oct 1781 {Ref: Maryland State Archives MdHR-6636-24-15}

RICHARDS, NATHANIEL (Worcester County) submitted an account and receipt for driving cattle on 30 Sep 1781 {Ref: Maryland State Archives MdHR-6636-43-27}

RICHARDSON, BENJAMIN (Harford County) was appointed by the Council of

Maryland to be one of five men in Harford County "to carry the Act to prohibit for a limited time the Exportation of Indian Corn, Etc., by Land" on 22 Dec 1780 {Ref: Archives of Maryland 45:251}

RICHARDSON, CHARLES (Caroline County) received a receipt from the Purchasing Agent for furnishing wheat on 1 Sep 1782 {Ref: Maryland State Archives MdHR-6636-42-7}

RICHARDSON, DANIEL (Caroline County) received a receipt from the Purchasing Agent for furnishing wheat on 1 Sep 1782 {Ref: Maryland State Archives MdHR-6636-42-7}

RICHARDSON, DANIEL (Queen Anne's County) received payments by order of the Council of Safety for furnishing boatage on 30 Aug 1776 {Ref: Archives of Maryland 12:247}

RICHARDSON, JOHN (Worcester County) was appointed by the Council of Maryland to be one of three Purchasers of Cattle for his county on 7 Jan 1778 {Ref: Archives of Maryland 16:456}; submitted an account and receipt for hauling pork on 8 Sep 1781 and for grazing and driving cattle on 15 Oct 1781 {Ref: Maryland State Archives MdHR-6636-43-27}

RICHARDSON, JOHN (Caroline County) received a receipt from the Purchasing Agent for furnishing wheat on 5 Aug 1782 {Ref: Maryland State Archives MdHR-6636-42-7}

RICHARDSON, JOSEPH (Caroline County) was appointed by the Council of Maryland to be one of two men in Caroline County "to carry the Act to prohibit for a limited time the Exportation of Indian Corn, Etc., by Land" on 22 Dec 1780 {Ref: Archives of Maryland 45:251}

RICHARDSON, PHILEMON (Caroline County) received a receipt from the Purchasing Agent for furnishing wheat on 1 Sep 1782 {Ref: Maryland State Archives MdHR-6636-42-7}

RICHARDSON, ROBERT M. (Worcester County) submitted an account and receipt for furnishing salt on 10 Feb 1782 {Ref: Maryland State Archives MdHR-6636-43-28CCC}

RICHARDSON, SAMUEL (Frederick County) received a certificate from the Purchasing Agent for furnishing wheat on 3 Feb 1783 {Ref: Maryland State Archives MdHR-6636-42-38}

RICHARDSON, SHADWICK OR SHADRICK (Worcester County) received payment from the Council of Maryland "for Bounty on Salt manufactured by him" on 8 Jul 1782 {Ref: Archives of Maryland 48:208}

RICHARDSON, THOMAS (Frederick County) received a certificate from the Purchasing Agent for furnishing wheat on 13 May 1782 {Ref: Maryland State Archives MdHR-6636-42-34}

RICHARDSON, THOMAS (Montgomery County) was a Deputy Commissary General by 15 Sep 1777 {Ref: Maryland State Archives MdHR-4576-120};

purchased provisions on 15 Jan 1778 {Ref: Maryland State Archives MdHR-6636-10-29}; served as Acting Commissary and requested delivery of salt on 3 Feb 1778 {Ref: Maryland State Archives MdHR-6636-10-59}; served as Commissary of Purchases and transported military supplies on 15 Apr 1778 {Ref: Maryland State Archives MdHR-5429-61GG}; from Valley Forge he requested provisions to be sent to the army on 20 May 1778 {Ref: Maryland State Archives MdHR-4588-67}; from Georgetown he requested provisions at Potomac to be sent to Head of Elk in Cecil County on 5 Jul 1778 {Ref: Maryland State Archives MdHR-4570-29}; appointed by the Council of Maryland as one of thirty men to be "Agents for Purchasing Provisions" on 30 Mar 1779 {Ref: Archives of Maryland 21:332}; commissioned an Assistant Deputy Commissary of Purchases for Prince George's, Charles, St. Mary's, and Montgomery Counties on 10 Sep 1779 {Ref: Archives of Maryland 21:518}; purchased wheat and flour on 13 May 1779 {Ref: Maryland State Archives MdHR-6636-14-19}; appointed Commissary of Purchases for Montgomery County by the Council of Maryland on 8 Jul 1780 {Ref: Archives of Maryland 43:215}; received a receipt for furnishing wheat on 7 Aug 1780 {Ref: Maryland State Archives MdHR-6636-24-6}; received a receipt for furnishing wheat on 1 Sep 1780 {Ref: Maryland State Archives MdHR-6636-24-7}; listed as "captain" when he received payment for wheat on 17 Sep 1780 {Ref: Maryland State Archives MdHR-6636-24-13}; listed as "Tho. Richardson & Co." when he delivered two barrels of pork for the use of the State of Maryland in October, 1780 {Ref: Archives of Maryland 45:149}; received a receipt for furnishing wheat on 28 Oct 1780 {Ref: Maryland State Archives MdHR-6636-24-8}; received a receipt for furnishing wheat on 28 Mar 1781 {Ref: Maryland State Archives MdHR-6636-24-14}; received a loan certificate for £93.7.6 due from the Council of Maryland "agreeable to the Act proposing to the Citizens of this State, Creditors of Congress on Loan Office Certificates, Etc." on 25 Mar 1783 for services rendered during the war {Ref: Archives of Maryland 48:389}; also see "George Adams" and "William Robertson," q.v.

RICHARDSON, WILLIAM (Charles County) received a receipt from the Purchasing Agent for furnishing wheat on 15 Apr 1783 {Ref: Maryland State Archives MdHR-6636-42-22}

RICHARDSON, WILLIAM (Worcester County) submitted an account and receipt for furnishing salt on 27 Dec 1781 {Ref: Maryland State Archives MdHR-6636-43-27}

RICHARDSON, WILLIAM (Caroline County) was a colonel who was appointed by the Council of Safety to collect all the gold and silver coin that could be procured in the county in compliance with the Resolve of Congress on 27 Jan 1776 {Ref: Archives of Maryland 11:132}; received a receipt for furnishing wheat on 31 Aug 1782 {Ref: Maryland State Archives MdHR-6636-42-7};

received a loan certificate for £105.7.1 due from the Council of Maryland "agreeable to the Act proposing to the Citizens of this State, Creditors of Congress on Loan Office Certificates, Etc." on 15 May 1783 for services rendered during the war {Ref: Archives of Maryland 48:413}

RICHARDSON, WILLIAM (Frederick County) received a certificate from the Purchasing Agent for furnishing wheat on 10 May 1782 {Ref: Maryland State Archives MdHR-6636-42-34}

RICHMOND, WILLIAM (Queen Anne's County) received a certificate from the Purchasing Agent for furnishing wheat on 24 Jan 1780 {Ref: Maryland State Archives MdHR-6636-24-29}; received a certificate for storage and delivery of wheat on 17 Mar 1780 {Ref: Maryland State Archives MdHR-6636-24-28}

RICKER, FREDERICK (Cecil County) submitted an account for storing wheat on 28 Jan 1783 {Ref: Maryland State Archives MdHR-6636-42-9}

RICKETTS (RICKETS), ANTHONY (Montgomery County) received a receipt from the Purchasing Agent for furnishing wheat on 1 Aug 1780 {Ref: Maryland State Archives MdHR-6636-43-7}; received a receipt from the Purchasing Agent for furnishing wheat on 9 Aug 1780 {Ref: Maryland State Archives MdHR-6636-24-6}; received a receipt for furnishing wheat on 10 Apr 1781 {Ref: Maryland State Archives MdHR-6636-42-11}

RICKETTS, BENJAMIN (Montgomery County) received a receipt from the Purchasing Agent for furnishing wheat on 15 Apr 1781 {Ref: Maryland State Archives MdHR-6636-42-11}

RICKETTS, DAVID (Cecil County) pledged a loan in the amount of £100 to the State of Maryland under the Act for the Emission of Bills of Credit "to defray the expences of the present campaign" in October, 1781 {Ref: Archives of Maryland 47:533}

RICKETTS, MARCH (Montgomery County) received a receipt from the Purchasing Agent for furnishing wheat on 30 May 1781 {Ref: Maryland State Archives MdHR-6636-42-11}

RICKETTS (RICKETS), RICHARD (Montgomery County) received a receipt from the Purchasing Agent for furnishing wheat on 1 Aug 1780 {Ref: Maryland State Archives MdHR-6636-43-7}; received receipts from the Purchasing Agent for furnishing wheat on 26 May and 30 May 1781 {Ref: Maryland State Archives MdHR-6636-42-11}

RICKETTS (RICKETS), RICHARD JR. (Montgomery County) received a receipt from the Purchasing Agent for furnishing wheat on 1 Aug 1780 {Ref: Maryland State Archives MdHR-6636-43-7}

RICKETTS (RUKETTS?), SAMUEL (Harford County) received payment for furnishing four guns to the Committee of Safety on 18 Jun 1776 {Ref: Preston's History of Harford County, p. 330}

RICKETTS, SARAH (Montgomery County) received receipts from the Purchasing

274

Agent for furnishing wheat on 21 Jun and 10 Oct 1781 {Ref: Maryland State Archives MdHR-6636-24-15}

RICKETTS, WILLIAM (Montgomery County) received a receipt from the Purchasing Agent for furnishing wheat on 16 May 1781 {Ref: Maryland State Archives MdHR-6636-24-18}

RIDDLE, BENJAMIN (Frederick County) received a certificate from the Purchasing Agent for furnishing wheat on 10 Jun 1782 {Ref: Maryland State Archives MdHR-6636-42-34}

RIDDLE, ELEANOR (Harford County) received payment by order of the Council of Maryland to be delivered over to James Webster for furnishing provisions to the county militia on 17 Mar 1778 {Ref: Archives of Maryland 16:539}

RIDGERS, JOHN (Caroline County) received a receipt from the Purchasing Agent for furnishing wheat on 1 Sep 1782 {Ref: Maryland State Archives MdHR-6636-42-7}

RIDGERS, JOSHUA (Caroline County) received receipts from the Purchasing Agent for furnishing wheat on 1 Sep 1782 {Ref: Maryland State Archives MdHR-6636-42-7}

RIDGELY, CHARLES OF WILLIAM (Baltimore and Anne Arundel Counties) pledged a loan in the amount of £300 to the State of Maryland under the Act for the Emission of Bills of Credit "to defray the expences of the present campaign" in June, 1781 {Ref: Archives of Maryland 47:326}

RIDGELY, HENRY (Anne Arundel County) received a loan certificate for £91.3.8 due from the Council of Maryland "agreeable to the Act proposing to the Citizens of this State, Creditors of Congress on Loan Office Certificates, Etc." on 18 Dec 1783 for services rendered during the war {Ref: Archives of Maryland 48:491}

RIDGELY, HENRY JR. (Anne Arundel County) received payment by order of the Council of Safety for furnishing a musquet and bayonet on 13 Aug 1776 {Ref: Archives of Maryland 12:198}

RIDGELY, RICHARD (Baltimore Town) received a loan certificate for £141.11.10 due from the Council of Maryland "agreeable to the Act proposing to the Citizens of this State, Creditors of Congress on Loan Office Certificates, Etc." on 23 Oct 1783 for services rendered during the war {Ref: Archives of Maryland 48:472}; also see "Hercules Courtenay" and "Thomas Harrison," q.v.

RIDGEWAY, ISAAC (Montgomery County) received a receipt from the Purchasing Agent for furnishing wheat on 23 Aug 1780 {Ref: Maryland State Archives MdHR-6636-24-6}

RIDGEWAY, MASHAM (Montgomery County) received a receipt from the Purchasing Agent for furnishing wheat on 20 Oct 1780 {Ref: Maryland State Archives MdHR-6636-24-8}

RIDGEWAY (RIDGWAY), ROBERT (Montgomery County) received a receipt

275

from the Purchasing Agent for furnishing wheat on 1 Aug 1780 {Ref: Maryland State Archives MdHR-6636-43-7}

RIDGEWAY (RIDGWAY), SAMUEL (Queen Anne's County) was appointed by the Council of Maryland to be one of three men in Queen Anne's County "to carry the Act to prohibit for a limited time the Exportation of Indian Corn, Etc., by Land" on 22 Dec 1780 {Ref: Archives of Maryland 45:251}

RIDLEY & PRINGLE (Baltimore Town), merchants, were given permission by the Council of Maryland "to transport 1500 barrels of biscuit to Philadelphia for the use of the French Marine" on 25 May 1781 {Ref: Archives of Maryland 45:445}

RIDOUT, JOHN (Anne Arundel County) received a certificate from the Purchasing Agent for furnishing wheat on 14 May 1780 {Ref: Maryland State Archives MdHR-6636-18-86}

RIESER, FREDERICK (Frederick County) received a certificate from the Purchasing Agent for furnishing wheat on 3 Jun 1782 {Ref: Maryland State Archives MdHR-6636-42-35}

RIGDEN, THOMAS (Montgomery County) received a receipt from the Purchasing Agent for furnishing wheat on 9 Aug 1780 {Ref: Maryland State Archives MdHR-6636-43-7}

RIGDON, BAKER (Harford County) received receipts from the Purchasing Agent for furnishing wheat on 2 Mar and 29 Jun 1780 {Ref: Maryland State Archives MdHR-6636-23-39}

RIGEY, LAWRENCE (Prince George's County) received a receipt from the Purchasing Agent for furnishing wheat on 28 May 1782 {Ref: Maryland State Archives MdHR-6636-50-135}

RIGGEN, JEREMIAH (Somerset County) received a receipt from the Purchasing Agent for furnishing hogs on 6 Feb 1782 {Ref: Maryland State Archives MdHR-6636-43-21}

RIGGIN, TIMOTHY (Somerset County) received a receipt from the Purchasing Agent for furnishing beef on 5 Dec 1781 {Ref: Maryland State Archives MdHR-6636-24-44}

RIGGINBURG, CUTLEB (Frederick County) received payment by order of the Council of Maryland for riding express from Frederick on 8 Aug 1781 {Ref: Archives of Maryland 45:550}

RIGGS, AMON (Montgomery County) received a receipt from the Purchasing Agent for furnishing wheat on 1 Aug 1780 {Ref: Maryland State Archives MdHR-6636-43-7}; received a receipt for furnishing wheat on 10 Apr 1781 {Ref: Maryland State Archives MdHR-6636-42-11}

RIGGS, JOHN (Prince George's County) received a receipt from the Purchasing Agent for furnishing wheat on 17 Jan 1783 {Ref: Maryland State Archives MdHR-6636-50-135}

RIGH, HENRY (Frederick County), executor of Henry Righ, received a loan certificate for £29.19.8 due from the Council of Maryland "agreeable to the Act proposing to the Citizens of this State, Creditors of Congress on Loan Office Certificates, Etc." on 19 May 1783 for services rendered during the war {Ref: Archives of Maryland 48:417}

RIGHT, SAMUEL (Charles County) received a receipt from the Purchasing Agent for furnishing wheat on 2 Nov 1782 {Ref: Maryland State Archives MdHR-6636-42-19}

RIGNEY, TERRENCE (Montgomery County) received a receipt from the Purchasing Agent for shelling corn on 17 Jul 1780 {Ref: Maryland State Archives MdHR-6636-24-2}

RILY, BENJAMIN (Kent County) submitted an account for hauling flour and receipt by Nicholas Riley on 1 Dec 1781 {Ref: Maryland State Archives MdHR-6636-43-5}

RINER, EBENEZER (Kent County) received money by order of the Council of Maryland "to be delivered over to John Voorhees, Commissary of Purchases for Kent County, to be by him expended in the purchase of cattle and accounted for" on 16 Oct 1781 {Ref: Archives of Maryland 45:64}

RINGGOLD, ANN (Kent County) received a certificate from the Purchasing Agent for furnishing wheat on 18 Feb 1780 {Ref: Maryland State Archives MdHR-6636-23-41}

RINGGOLD, JAMES (Kent County) received a certificate from the Purchasing Agent for furnishing wheat on 14 Jan 1780 {Ref: Maryland State Archives MdHR-6636-23-44}; received payments from the Purchasing Agent for furnishing cattle and pasturage for the public use in September, 1781 {Ref: Maryland State Archives MdHR-6636-43-3}

RINGGOLD, MARY (Kent County) received a certificate from the Purchasing Agent for furnishing wheat on 18 Feb 1780 {Ref: Maryland State Archives MdHR-6636-23-46}

RINGGOLD, THOMAS (Kent County) was appointed by the Council of Safety to collect all the gold and silver coin that could be procured in the county in compliance with the Resolve of Congress on 27 Jan 1776 {Ref: Archives of Maryland 11:132}; received payment by order of the Council of Safety "to enable him to prosecute a Salt Works on his bond" on 23 May 1776 {Ref: Archives of Maryland 11:441}

RINGGOLD, WILLIAM (Eastern Neck, Kent County) was appointed by the Council of Safety to collect all the gold and silver coin that could be procured in the county in compliance with the Resolve of Congress on 27 Jan 1776 {Ref: Archives of Maryland 11:132}; received payment from the Purchasing Agent for furnishing cattle and pasturage for the public use in September, 1781 {Ref: Maryland State Archives MdHR-6636-43-3}

RINGGOLD, WILLIAM (Kent County) received payment from the Purchasing Agent for furnishing cattle and pasturage for the public use on 29 Oct 1781 {Ref: Maryland State Archives MdHR-6636-43-3}
RINGGOLD, WILLIAM (Queen Anne's County) received a receipt from the Purchasing Agent for furnishing steers on 29 Apr 1778 {Ref: Maryland State Archives MdHR-4587-35/50}; received a certificate for furnishing beef on 19 Sep 1781 {Ref: Maryland State Archives MdHR-6636-24-34}
RINGROSE, AARON (Anne Arundel County) was a captain who received a receipt from the Purchasing Agent for furnishing flour on 14 May 1780 {Ref: Maryland State Archives MdHR-6636-24-46}
RISON, GARRARD (Charles County) received a receipt from the Purchasing Agent for furnishing wheat on 3 May 1783 {Ref: Maryland State Archives MdHR-6636-42-22}
RISTEAU, ABRAHAM (Baltimore County) was appointed Commissary of Purchases for Baltimore County by the Council of Maryland on 8 Jul 1780 and resigned by 5 Sep 1780 {Ref: Archives of Maryland 43:215, 276}
RITCHEY, JAMES (Prince George's County) submitted an account of goods delivered for the use of the state on 7 Jan 1778 {Ref: Maryland State Archives MdHR-4570-53}
ROBERTS, BASIL (Frederick County) received a certificate from the Purchasing Agent for furnishing beef on 2 Mar 1781 {Ref: Maryland State Archives MdHR-6636-23-4}
ROBERTS, BENJAMIN (Talbot County) received a receipt from the Purchasing Agent for furnishing bacon for the use of the army on 4 May 1778 {Ref: Maryland State Archives MdHR-4587-81}; submitted an account and receipt for hauling on 4 May 1778 {Ref: Maryland State Archives MdHR-6636-12-15}
ROBERTS, BILLINGSLEY (Montgomery County) received a receipt from the Purchasing Agent for furnishing wheat on 20 Jul 1781 {Ref: Maryland State Archives MdHR-6636-24-18}
ROBERTS, JOHN (Annapolis) was furnished with five soldiers by order of the Council of Maryland "for the purpose of a Guard to be put on Board a Vessel to transport public Horses from Kent Island to this City" on 6 Dec 1781 {Ref: Archives of Maryland 48:16}
ROBERTS, RICHARD (Montgomery County) received a receipt from the Purchasing Agent for furnishing wheat on 20 Jul 1781 {Ref: Maryland State Archives MdHR-6636-24-18}
ROBERTS, ZACHARIAH (Frederick County) received a receipt from the Purchasing Agent for furnishing pork on 7 Mar 1781 {Ref: Maryland State Archives MdHR-6636-23-4}
ROBERTSON, ALEXANDER (Somerset County) received receipts from the

Purchasing Agent for furnishing bacon on 17 Aug and 5 Oct 1780 {Ref: Maryland State Archives MdHR-6636-24-41}

ROBERTSON, WILLIAM (Montgomery County) received money from the Council of Maryland "to be delivered over to Thomas Richardson, Commissary of Montgomery County, to be expended in the Purchase of Forage and Accounted for" on 6 Sep 1781 {Ref: Archives of Maryland 45:604}

ROBERTSON, WILLIAM (Talbot County) received a certificate from the Purchasing Agent for purchasing a horse on 12 Jul 1780 {Ref: Maryland State Archives MdHR-6636-24-50}

ROBERTSON, WILLIAM (county not stated) received a loan certificate for £9.8.9 due from the Council of Maryland "agreeable to the Act proposing to the Citizens of this State, Creditors of Congress on Loan Office Certificates, Etc." on 4 Nov 1783 for services rendered during the war {Ref: Archives of Maryland 48:477}

ROBEY, ABSALOM (Montgomery County) received a receipt from the Purchasing Agent for furnishing wheat on 21 Oct 1780 {Ref: Maryland State Archives MdHR-6636-24-13}; received a receipt for furnishing wheat on 29 Dec 1780 {Ref: Maryland State Archives MdHR-6636-24-13}; received a receipt for furnishing wheat on 29 Dec 1780 {Ref: Maryland State Archives MdHR-6636-24-8}

ROBEY, JOHN (Charles County) received a receipt from the Purchasing Agent for furnishing wheat on 3 Nov and 30 Nov 1781 {Ref: Maryland State Archives MdHR-6636-42-15}

ROBEY, JOHN A. (Charles County) received a receipt from the Purchasing Agent for furnishing wheat on 28 May 1782 {Ref: Maryland State Archives MdHR-6636-42-18}; received a receipt for furnishing wheat on 28 Sep 1782 {Ref: Maryland State Archives MdHR-6636-42-19}

ROBEY, JOHN N. (Charles County) received a receipt from the Purchasing Agent for furnishing wheat on 20 Dec 1782 {Ref: Maryland State Archives MdHR-6636-42-20}

ROBEY, PETER (Charles County) received a receipt from the Purchasing Agent for furnishing wheat on 20 Jul 1782 {Ref: Maryland State Archives MdHR-6636-42-18}

ROBEY, RICHARD (Charles County) received a receipt from the Purchasing Agent for furnishing wheat on 28 Sep 1781 {Ref: Maryland State Archives MdHR-6636-42-15}

ROBEY, SAMUEL (Charles County) received a receipt from the Purchasing Agent for furnishing wheat on 24 Nov 1781 {Ref: Maryland State Archives MdHR-6636-42-15}

ROBEY, THOMAS (Charles County) received a receipt from the Purchasing Agent for furnishing wheat on 18 Aug 1782 {Ref: Maryland State Archives

MdHR-6636-42-18}

ROBINET, RICHARD (Cecil County) received a receipt from the Purchasing Agent for furnishing wheat on 6 May 1783 {Ref: Maryland State Archives MdHR-6636-42-9}

ROBINS, JOHN (Queen Anne's County) received a certificate from the Purchasing Agent for storing and delivering wheat and corn on 20 Mar 1780 {Ref: Maryland State Archives MdHR-6636-24-28}; received a certificate for furnishing wheat on 10 Jan 1780 {Ref: Maryland State Archives MdHR-6636-24-31}; submitted an account and receipt for hauling provisions from Jun 1782 to Feb 1783 {Ref: Maryland State Archives MdHR-6636-43-12}

ROBINS (ROBENS), JOHN (Worcester County) appeared on "A List of Sundry Persons Corn Purchased of for the use of the State of Maryland" by the Commissary on 19 Jun 1780 {Ref: Archives of Maryland 45:9}

ROBINSON, DANIEL (Caroline County) received a receipt from the Purchasing Agent for furnishing wheat on 24 Aug 1782 {Ref: Maryland State Archives MdHR-6636-42-7}

ROBINSON, DAVID (Anne Arundel County) received a loan certificate for £22.7.10 due from the Council of Maryland "agreeable to the Act proposing to the Citizens of this State, Creditors of Congress on Loan Office Certificates, Etc." on 10 Dec 1783 for services rendered during the war {Ref: Archives of Maryland 48:487}

ROBINSON, ELIJAH (Anne Arundel County) submitted his commissioner's account for furnishing grain in or about 1781 {Ref: Maryland State Archives MdHR-6636-23-9}

ROBINSON, JOHN (Talbot County) received a receipt from the Purchasing Agent for furnishing bacon for the use of the army on 27 Apr 1778 {Ref: Maryland State Archives MdHR-4587-72}; submitted an account and receipt for hauling on 28 Apr 1778 {Ref: Maryland State Archives MdHR-6636-12-15}

ROBINSON, JOHN (Caroline County) received receipts from the Purchasing Agent for furnishing wheat on 17 Aug and 1 Sep 1782 {Ref: Maryland State Archives MdHR-6636-42-7}

ROBINSON, LEONARD (Montgomery County) received a receipt from the Purchasing Agent for furnishing wheat on 9 Sep 1781 {Ref: Maryland State Archives MdHR-6636-42-11}

ROBINSON, LUKE (Caroline County) received a receipt from the Purchasing Agent for furnishing wheat on 5 Aug 1782 {Ref: Maryland State Archives MdHR-6636-42-7}

ROBINSON, RICHARD (Talbot County) submitted an account and receipt for hauling on 13 Jun 1778 {Ref: Maryland State Archives MdHR-6636-12-15}

ROBINSON, SOLOMON (Talbot County) received a receipt from the Purchasing Agent for furnishing bacon for the use of the army on 2 May 1778 {Ref:

Maryland State Archives MdHR-4587-79}

ROBINSON, THOMAS (Somerset County) received a receipt from the Purchasing Agent for furnishing beef on 1 Nov 1781 {Ref: Maryland State Archives MdHR-6636-24-44}

ROBINSON, WILLIAM (Baltimore County) received a certificate from the Purchasing Agent for furnishing rye on 19 Nov 1780 {Ref: Maryland State Archives MdHR-6636-23-33}

ROBISON, ABRAM (Frederick County) received a certificate from the Purchasing Agent for furnishing wheat on 23 May 1782 {Ref: Maryland State Archives MdHR-6636-42-34}

ROBSON, JOHN (Talbot County) received a receipt from the Purchasing Agent for furnishing bacon on 29 May 1778 {Ref: Maryland State Archives MdHR-6636-12-15}

ROBSON, THOMAS (Talbot County) received a receipt from the Purchasing Agent for furnishing bacon on 29 May 1778 {Ref: Maryland State Archives MdHR-6636-12-15}

ROCHESTER, FRANCES (Queen Anne's County) received a receipt from the Purchasing Agent for furnishing bacon on 2 May 1778 {Ref: Maryland State Archives MdHR-4587-39}

ROCHESTER, FRANCIS (Queen Anne's County) received a certificate from the Purchasing Agent for furnishing beef on 9 Oct 1781 {Ref: Maryland State Archives MdHR-6636-24-34}

RODENPEELER, PHILIP (Frederick County) received a certificate from the Purchasing Agent for furnishing whiskey on 7 Nov 1781 {Ref: Maryland State Archives MdHR-6636-23-28}

RODGERS, JOHN (Harford County) was a captain who received payment from the Committee of Safety "for ferriage of four waggon load of Arms and Ammunitions" on 5 Aug 1776 {Ref: Preston's History of Harford County, p. 332}

ROE, ABNER (Caroline County) received a receipt from the Purchasing Agent for furnishing wheat on 31 Aug 1782 {Ref: Maryland State Archives MdHR-6636-42-7}

ROEDEN, THOMAS (Kent County) received a certificate from the Purchasing Agent for furnishing wheat on 28 May 1780 {Ref: Maryland State Archives MdHR-6636-23-46}

ROENS, JOSEPH (Caroline County) received a receipt from the Purchasing Agent for furnishing wheat on 5 Aug 1782 {Ref: Maryland State Archives MdHR-6636-42-7}

ROGERS, PHILIP (Baltimore Town) was appointed by the Council of Maryland to be one of three "Superintendants of the Press, or Presses in Baltimore Town, employed in printing the Continental Bills of Credit" on 28 May 1777 {Ref:

Archives of Maryland 16:261}

ROGERS, ROBERT (Charles County) received a receipt from the Purchasing Agent for furnishing wheat on 10 May 1783 {Ref: Maryland State Archives MdHR-6636-42-22}

ROGERS, THOMAS (Montgomery County) received payment by order of the Council of Maryland "for three Days Forage for sixteen Horses to George Town" and also received from the Issuing Commissary "provisions for four men 3 Days in Waggoning Stores to George Town" on 29 Sep 1781 {Ref: Archives of Maryland 45:629}

ROGERS, WILLIAM (Baltimore Town) received payments for furnishing hats on 27 Oct and 18 Nov 1779 {Ref: Maryland State Archives MdHR-19970-3-8}

ROLAND, JACOB (Anne Arundel County) received a receipt from the Purchasing Agent for furnishing powder on 16 Apr 1777 {Ref: Maryland State Archives MdHR-6636-9-14B}

ROLAND, THOMAS (Charles County) received a receipt from the Purchasing Agent for furnishing wheat on 8 Dec 1781 {Ref: Maryland State Archives MdHR-6636-42-15}

ROLLINGS, JOHN (Queen Anne's County) submitted an account for grinding wheat on 12 Mar 1780 {Ref: Maryland State Archives MdHR-6636-24-22}; also see "John Thompson," q.v.

ROLLISON, CHARLES (Kent County) submitted an evaluation by the commissary for hauling wheat on 20 Apr 1780 {Ref: Maryland State Archives MdHR-6636-43-1}

ROSENSTEEL, GEORGE (Frederick County) received a receipt from the Purchasing Agent for furnishing pork on 27 Dec 1780 {Ref: Maryland State Archives MdHR-6636-23-1}

ROSIER, HENRY (Charles County) received a receipt from the Purchasing Agent for furnishing wheat on 11 Apr 1782 {Ref: Maryland State Archives MdHR-6636-42-18}; received a receipt for furnishing wheat on 29 Dec 1782 {Ref: Maryland State Archives MdHR-6636-42-21}

ROSS, ANTHONY (Caroline County) received a receipt from the Purchasing Agent for furnishing wheat on 17 Aug 1782 {Ref: Maryland State Archives MdHR-6636-42-7}

ROSS, JAMES JR. (Caroline County) received a receipt from the Purchasing Agent for furnishing wheat on 5 Aug 1782 {Ref: Maryland State Archives MdHR-6636-42-7}

ROSS, JAMES SR. (Caroline County) received a receipt from the Purchasing Agent for furnishing wheat on 5 Aug 1782 {Ref: Maryland State Archives MdHR-6636-42-7}

ROSS, JOHN (Dorchester County) received a receipt from the Purchasing Agent for furnishing wheat on 1 Nov 1782 {Ref: Maryland State Archives MdHR-

6636-42-23}

ROSS, JOHN (Queen Anne's County) received a receipt from the Purchasing Agent for furnishing bacon on 1 Apr 1778 {Ref: Maryland State Archives MdHR-4587-43}; received a receipt for furnishing bacon on 29 Apr 1778 {Ref: Maryland State Archives MdHR-4587-50}

ROSS, LEWIS (Caroline County) received a receipt from the Purchasing Agent for furnishing wheat on 5 Aug 1782 {Ref: Maryland State Archives MdHR-6636-42-7}

ROSS, NATHANIEL (Baltimore County) received a receipt from the Purchasing Agent for furnishing flour on 8 Nov 1781 {Ref: Maryland State Archives MdHR-6636-43-38P}

ROSS, PEGGY (Caroline County) received a receipt from the Purchasing Agent for furnishing wheat on 5 Aug 1782 {Ref: Maryland State Archives MdHR-6636-42-7}

ROSSITER, JOHN (Queen Anne's County) received a certificate from the Purchasing Agent for furnishing pork on 23 Feb 1782 {Ref: Maryland State Archives MdHR-6636-43-11}

ROUND, JOHN (Worcester County) submitted an account and receipt for furnishing pork barrels on 1 Mar 1782 {Ref: Maryland State Archives MdHR-6636-43-28UU}

ROUND (ROUNDS, ROWND), WILLIAM (Worcester County) received a receipt from the Purchasing Agent for furnishing corn on 19 Jun 1780 {Ref: Maryland State Archives MdHR-6636-24-53}; his name appeared on "A List of Corn Purchased in Worcester County for the use of the State of Maryland" by the Commissary in July, 1780 {Ref: Archives of Maryland 45:10}; received a receipt for furnishing bacon on 20 Sep 1780 {Ref: Maryland State Archives MdHR-6636-24-54}

ROWE, JOHN (Dorchester County) received a receipt from the Purchasing Agent for furnishing wheat on 1 Nov 1782 {Ref: Maryland State Archives MdHR-6636-42-23}

ROWE, JOHN JR. (Charles County) received a receipt from the Purchasing Agent for furnishing wheat on 31 Oct 1782 {Ref: Maryland State Archives MdHR-6636-42-19}

ROWINGS, WILLIAM (Dorchester County) received a receipt from the Purchasing Agent for furnishing wheat on 1 Nov 1782 {Ref: Maryland State Archives MdHR-6636-42-23}

ROWLAND, WILLIAM (Baltimore County) received a loan certificate for £110.1.2 due from the Council of Maryland "agreeable to the Act proposing to the Citizens of this State, Creditors of Congress on Loan Office Certificates, Etc." on 16 May 1783 for services rendered during the war {Ref: Archives of Maryland 48:414}

ROXBURGH, ALEXANDER (Somerset County) was a major who received a receipt from the Purchasing Agent for furnishing bacon on 20 Jun 1781 {Ref: Maryland State Archives MdHR-6636-24-43}

ROZIER, HENRY (Charles County) received a loan certificate for £80.11.4 due from the Council of Maryland "agreeable to the Act proposing to the Citizens of this State, Creditors of Congress on Loan Office Certificates, Etc." on 18 Dec 1783 for services rendered during the war {Ref: Archives of Maryland 48:491}

RUBEL, PETER (Frederick County) received a certificate from the Purchasing Agent for furnishing wheat on 15 Jul 1782 {Ref: Maryland State Archives MdHR-6636-42-36}

RUDULPH, TOBIAS (Cecil County) submitted a statement of account due for storing wheat at Head of Elk in 1782 and received payment on 6 Dec 1782 {Ref: Maryland State Archives MdHR-6636-41-74}

RUHOR, PETER (Frederick County) received a certificate from the Purchasing Agent for furnishing wheat on 3 Jun 1782 {Ref: Maryland State Archives MdHR-6636-42-35}

RUKETTS, SAMUEL, see "Samuel Ricketts," q.v.

RULOFF, GILBERT (Frederick County) received a certificate from the Purchasing Agent for furnishing wheat on 1 Aug 1782 {Ref: Maryland State Archives MdHR-6636-42-36}

RULY, NIN. (Montgomery County) received a receipt from the Purchasing Agent for furnishing wheat on 1 Aug 1780 {Ref: Maryland State Archives MdHR-6636-43-7}

RUMSEY, BENJAMIN (Harford County) submitted an account for storage of flour on 20 Jul 1779 and a request to pay Isaac Van Bibber {Ref: Maryland State Archives MdHR-6636-21-67}; received a loan certificate for £659.5.1 due from the Council of Maryland "agreeable to the Act proposing to the Citizens of this State, Creditors of Congress on Loan Office Certificates, Etc." on 23 May 1783 for services rendered during the war {Ref: Archives of Maryland 48:420}

RUMSEY, JOHN (Harford County) received a loan certificate for £3.19.4 due from the Council of Maryland "agreeable to the Act proposing to the Citizens of this State, Creditors of Congress on Loan Office Certificates, Etc." on 23 May 1783 for services rendered during the war {Ref: Archives of Maryland 48:420}

RUMSEY, WILLIAM (Cecil County) was appointed by the Council of Safety to collect all the gold and silver coin that could be procured in the county in compliance with the Resolve of Congress on 27 Jan 1776 {Ref: Archives of Maryland 11:132}

RUSK, DAVID (Baltimore County) received payment for furnishing hay on 18

Sep 1781 {Ref: Maryland State Archives MdHR-6636-43-38Z}
RUSK, WILLIAM (Baltimore County) received payment for furnishing beef on 11 Nov 1780 {Ref: Maryland State Archives MdHR-6636-43-38DDDDD}
RUSSEL, SOLOMON (Dorchester County) received a receipt from the Purchasing Agent for furnishing wheat on 1 Nov 1782 {Ref: Maryland State Archives MdHR-6636-42-23}
RUSSOM, JOHN (Caroline County) received a receipt from the Purchasing Agent for wheat on 17 Sep 1782 {Ref: Maryland State Archives MdHR-6636-42-7}
RUSSOM, WILLIAM (Caroline County) received a receipt from the Purchasing Agent for furnishing wheat on 1 Sep 1782 {Ref: Maryland State Archives MdHR-6636-42-7}
RUTLAND, THOMAS (Anne Arundel County) submitted an account of provisions for vessels on 25 Apr 1781 {Ref: Maryland State Archives MdHR-6636-30-92B}; ordered by the Council of Maryland "that John Bullen, Quartermaster, discharge Mr. Rutland's sloop from the service of the public" on 10 May 1781 {Ref: Archives of Maryland 45:429}; received payment "due him for cattle delivered per Account" on 6 Aug 1781 {Ref: Archives of Maryland 45:545}; received an order for the delivery of flour on 16 May 1782 {Ref: Maryland State Archives MdHR-6636-43-35C}; received loan certificates for £189.9.10 and £80.4.4 due from the Council of Maryland "agreeable to the Act proposing to the Citizens of this State, Creditors of Congress on Loan Office Certificates, Etc." on 7 Apr and 14 May 1783 for services rendered during the war {Ref: Archives of Maryland 48:395, 412}
RUTTERS, JAMES, see "James Butters," q.v.
RYE, WALTER (Charles County) received a receipt from the Purchasing Agent for furnishing wheat on 26 Apr 1782 {Ref: Maryland State Archives MdHR-6636-42-18}
RYER, HENRY (Frederick County) received a receipt from the Purchasing Agent for furnishing beef on 30 Mar 1781 {Ref: Maryland State Archives MdHR-6636-23-4}; submitted an account for furnishing beef on 28 Apr 1781 {Ref: Maryland State Archives MdHR-6636-23-5}
RYLAND, FRIDUS (Cecil County) submitted an account for hauling wheat on 6 Sep 1783 {Ref: Maryland State Archives MdHR-6636-42-9}
RYLET, EDWARD (Frederick County) submitted an account for furnishing corn on 2 Nov 1780 {Ref: Maryland State Archives MdHR-6636-23-8}
SADLER, SAMUEL (Baltimore Town) received payment by order of the Council of Maryland via Lt. William Judah "to be expended in the State Hospital in Baltimore" on 23 Dec 1778 {Ref: Archives of Maryland 21:271}
SADLER, THOMAS (Somerset County) received a receipt from the Purchasing Agent for furnishing pork on 12 May 1782 {Ref: Maryland State Archives MdHR-6636-43-21}; received a loan certificate for £30.16.1 due from the

Council of Maryland "agreeable to the Act proposing to the Citizens of this State, Creditors of Congress on Loan Office Certificates, Etc." on 24 Sep 1783 for services rendered during the war {Ref: Archives of Maryland 48:456}

SAER, JAMES (Prince George's County) received a receipt from the Purchasing Agent for furnishing wheat in 1783 {Ref: Maryland State Archives MdHR-6636-50-135}

SAER, WILLIAM (Prince George's County) received a receipt from the Purchasing Agent for furnishing wheat in 1783 {Ref: Maryland State Archives MdHR-6636-50-135}

SAFFELL, CHARLES (Montgomery County) received a receipt from the Purchasing Agent for furnishing wheat on 44 Aug 1781 {Ref: Maryland State Archives MdHR-6636-24-15}

SAFFELL, JAMES (Montgomery County) received a receipt from the Purchasing Agent for furnishing wheat on 25 Jul 1781 {Ref: Maryland State Archives MdHR-6636-42-11}

SAFFELL (SAFFAL), JOSHUA (Montgomery County) received a receipt from the Purchasing Agent for furnishing wheat on 15 May 1781 {Ref: Maryland State Archives MdHR-6636-42-11}

SAFFELL (SAFFEL), WILLIAM (Montgomery County) received a receipt from the Purchasing Agent for furnishing wheat on 12 May 1781 {Ref: Maryland State Archives MdHR-6636-42-11}

SAILOR, CHRISTIAN (Frederick County) received a certificate from the Purchasing Agent for furnishing wheat on 22 Aug 1781 {Ref: Maryland State Archives MdHR-6636-23-28}

SAILOR, DANIEL (Frederick County) received a certificate from the Purchasing Agent for furnishing wheat on 23 May 1782 {Ref: Maryland State Archives MdHR-6636-42-35}

SALISBERRY, JAMES (Caroline County) received a receipt from the Purchasing Agent for furnishing wheat on 27 May 1782 {Ref: Maryland State Archives MdHR-6636-42-7}

SALISBURY, JOHN (Caroline County) received a receipt from the Purchasing Agent for furnishing wheat on 27 May 1782 {Ref: Maryland State Archives MdHR-6636-42-7}

SALSBURY, JOHN JR. (Caroline County) received a receipt from the Purchasing Agent for furnishing wheat on 31 May 1782 {Ref: Maryland State Archives MdHR-6636-42-7}

SALSBURY, NEHEMIAH (Caroline County) received a receipt from the Purchasing Agent for furnishing wheat on 5 Aug 1782 {Ref: Maryland State Archives MdHR-6636-42-7}

SALSBURY, WILLIAM (Caroline County) received a receipt from the Purchasing Agent for furnishing wheat on 31 Aug 1782 {Ref: Maryland State Archives

MdHR-6636-42-7}

SANDERS, EDWARD (Charles County) received a receipt from the Purchasing Agent for delivering wheat on 23 Oct 1781 {Ref: Maryland State Archives MdHR-6636-42-15}; received a receipt for furnishing wheat on 15 Feb 1782 {Ref: Maryland State Archives MdHR-6636-42-16}; received a receipt for furnishing wheat on 14 Sep 1782 {Ref: Maryland State Archives MdHR-6636-42-18}

SANDERS, JOHN (Charles County) received a receipt from the Purchasing Agent for furnishing wheat on 26 Apr 1783 {Ref: Maryland State Archives MdHR-6636-42-22}

SANDERS, WILLIAM (Dorchester County) received a loan certificate for £18.7.8 due from the Council of Maryland "agreeable to the Act proposing to the Citizens of this State, Creditors of Congress on Loan Office Certificates, Etc." on 18 Dec 1783 for services rendered during the war {Ref: Archives of Maryland 48:491}

SANDERSON, FRANCIS (Baltimore Town) contracted with the Council of Safety on 3 Jul 1776 to furnish copper camp kettles and received payment on 17 Sep 1776 {Ref: Archives of Maryland 11:540, 11:545, 12:276}

SANDS, ANNE, Mrs. (Anne Arundel County) received payment by order of the Council of Maryland for making shirts on 27 Mar 1777 {Ref: Archives of Maryland 16:191}

SANDS, JOHN (Queen Anne's County) received a certificate from the Purchasing Agent for furnishing wheat on 14 Mar 1780 {Ref: Maryland State Archives MdHR-6636-24-32}; received a certificate for furnishing beef on 19 Sep 1781 {Ref: Maryland State Archives MdHR-6636-24-34}

SANKGO, JAMES DEVEREYS (Montgomery County) received a receipt from the Purchasing Agent for furnishing wheat on 20 Feb 1781 {Ref: Maryland State Archives MdHR-6636-24-18}

SANNEMS (LANNEMS?), JACOB (Baltimore County) submitted an account and received payment for hauling three loads of flour for the use of the army and for one and a half days drayage on 28 Jan 1780 {Ref: Maryland Historical Society MS.1814, Box 6}

SAPPINGTON, RICHARD (Anne Arundel and Harford Counties) was a doctor who received payment by order of the Council of Maryland "for going express to Philadelphia" on or about 3 Nov 1777 {Ref: Archives of Maryland 16:408}

SATERFIELD, SOLOMON (Caroline County) received a receipt from the Purchasing Agent for furnishing wheat on 1 Sep 1782 {Ref: Maryland State Archives MdHR-6636-42-7}

SAUL, ARTHUR (Montgomery County) received a receipt from the Purchasing Agent for shelling corn on 7 Apr 1780 {Ref: Maryland State Archives MdHR-6636-24-2}

287

SAUNDERS, THOMAS (Kent County) received a certificate from the Purchasing Agent for furnishing wheat on 26 Jan 1780 {Ref: Maryland State Archives MdHR-6636-43-1}

SAVATEER, JOHN (Baltimore County) submitted an account and received payment for stowing flour for one and a half days on 23 Mar 1780 {Ref: Maryland Historical Society MS.1814, Box 6}

SAVIN, THOMAS (Cecil County) requested compensation for procuring provisions on 28 Feb 1781 {Ref: Maryland State Archives MdHR-4601-54}

SCAGGS, JOHN (Kent County) received payment for furnishing flour on 1 Oct 1780 {Ref: Maryland State Archives MdHR-6636-23-49}

SCAGGS, RICHARD (Frederick County) received a receipt from the Purchasing Agent for furnishing corn on 13 Mar 1781 {Ref: Maryland State Archives MdHR-6636-23-4}

SCANLON, EDWARD (Kent County) received a certificate from the Purchasing Agent for hauling flour on 11 Apr 1780 {Ref: Maryland State Archives MdHR-6636-23-42}

SCARBARY, JOHN (Harford County) received a receipt from the Purchasing Agent for furnishing wheat on 30 Jun 1780 {Ref: Maryland State Archives MdHR-6636-23-35}

SCHLEY, GEORGE JACOB (Frederick County) received a receipt from the Purchasing Agent for furnishing beef on 7 Feb 1781 {Ref: Maryland State Archives MdHR-6636-23-3}

SCHLEY, JACOB (Frederick County) received payment by order of the Council of Safety for repairing musquets and contracted to supply ten large rifles carrying a ball of four ounces weight on 19 Apr 1776 {Ref: Archives of Maryland 11:353, 356}; he was still manufacturing arms on 12 Jan 1781 {Ref: Archives of Maryland 47:14}

SCHNEBELY, HENRY (Washington County) was a doctor who received payment by order of the Council of Maryland on 27 Jun 1777 for boarding soldiers {Ref: Archives of Maryland 16:301}; served as Commissary Agent and submitted an account of purchase of grain for the use of the state on 31 Mar 1780 {Ref: Maryland State Archives MdHR-4590-76}; submitted an account of purchase of grain on 16 Apr 1780 {Ref: Maryland State Archives MdHR-4590-74}; his name was listed as "Henry Snively" when he delivered flour to the commissary at Baltimore Town for the use of the State of Maryland in the summer of 1780 {Ref: Archives of Maryland 45:84}; received payment by order of the Council of Maryland for his use as Contractor for Wagons and Teams in Washington County on 2 Sep 1780 {Ref: Archives of Maryland 43:274}; submitted an account of purchase of supplies and wagons on 7 Oct 1780 {Ref: Maryland State Archives MdHR-6636-20-85}; received a receipt for furnishing flour on 8 Jan 1781 {Ref: Maryland State Archives MdHR-6636-

43-37P}; submitted an account and report on condition of horses on 6 May 1781 {Ref: Maryland State Archives MdHR-4597-7}

SCHNERTZELL, GEORGE (Montgomery County) submitted an account and receipt for furnishing linen on 15 Apr 1780 {Ref: Maryland State Archives MdHR-6636-24-2}

SCHOFIELD, HENRY (Somerset County) received a receipt from the Purchasing Agent for furnishing beef on 5 Dec 1781 {Ref: Maryland State Archives MdHR-6636-24-44}

SCHOOLFIELD, DAVID (Frederick County) received a receipt from the Purchasing Agent for furnishing mutton on 24 Mar 1781 {Ref: Maryland State Archives MdHR-6636-23-4}

SCHOOLFIELD, JOHN (Worcester County) received a receipt from the Purchasing Agent for furnishing wheat on 21 May 1781 {Ref: Maryland State Archives MdHR-6636-24-14}; submitted an account and receipt for furnishing pork on 3 May 1782 {Ref: Maryland State Archives MdHR-6636-43-28BB}

SCHRIVER, DAVID (Frederick County) received a loan certificate for £160.16.3 due from the Council of Maryland "agreeable to the Act proposing to the Citizens of this State, Creditors of Congress on Loan Office Certificates, Etc." on 20 May 1783 for services rendered during the war {Ref: Archives of Maryland 48:418}

SCOTT, BENJAMIN, OF JAMES (Harford County) was appointed by the Council of Maryland as one of thirty men to be "Agents for Purchasing Provisions" on 30 Mar 1779 {Ref: Archives of Maryland 21:332}

SCOTT, DANIEL, OF AQUILA (Harford County) received a loan certificate for £503.5.8 due from the Council of Maryland "agreeable to the Act proposing to the Citizens of this State, Creditors of Congress on Loan Office Certificates, Etc." on 23 Oct 1783 for services rendered during the war {Ref: Archives of Maryland 48:472}

SCOTT, GEORGE (Frederick County) solicited money for use by the state on 6 Jun 1780 {Ref: Maryland State Archives MdHR-6636-18-132}

SCOTT, HUGH (Frederick County) received a certificate from the Purchasing Agent for furnishing wheat on 30 May 1782 {Ref: Maryland State Archives MdHR-6636-42-35}

SCOTT, JOHN (Dorchester County) received a receipt from the Purchasing Agent for furnishing wheat on 25 Mar 1783 {Ref: Maryland State Archives MdHR-6636-42-24}

SCOTT, JOHN (Kent County) received payment from the Purchasing Agent for furnishing cattle and pasturage for the public use in September, 1781 {Ref: Maryland State Archives MdHR-6636-43-3}

SCRIVER, HENRY (Anne Arundel County) received a receipt from the Purchasing Agent for furnishing powder on 16 Apr 1777 {Ref: Maryland State

Archives MdHR-6636-9-14A}

SEARES, WILLIAM (Cecil County) submitted an account for storing wheat on 10 Apr 1783 {Ref: Maryland State Archives MdHR-6636-42-9}

SEARS, WILLIAM (Prince George's County) received a receipt from the Purchasing Agent for furnishing wheat on 15 Mar 1783 {Ref: Maryland State Archives MdHR-6636-50-135}

SEARS, WILLIAM (Montgomery County) received payment by order of the Council of Safety for furnishing a musquet and bayonet on 6 Oct 1777 {Ref: Archives of Maryland 16:392}

SEERS, PETER (Dorchester County) received a receipt from the Purchasing Agent for furnishing wheat on 1 Nov 1782 {Ref: Maryland State Archives MdHR-6636-42-23}

SEFTON, JOHN (Anne Arundel County) received a loan certificate for £12.17.9 due from the Council of Maryland "agreeable to the Act proposing to the Citizens of this State, Creditors of Congress on Loan Office Certificates, Etc." on 24 May 1783 for services rendered during the war {Ref: Archives of Maryland 48:420-421}

SELBY, ANN, see "Joseph Selby," q.v.

SELBY, JAMES (Worcester County) received a receipt from the Purchasing Agent for furnishing corn on 7 Apr 1780 {Ref: Maryland State Archives MdHR-6636-24-52}

SELBY, JOHN (Worcester County) received a receipt from the Purchasing Agent for furnishing beef on 10 Oct 1780 {Ref: Maryland State Archives MdHR-6636-24-54}; received a receipt for furnishing beef on 10 Oct 1782 {Ref: Maryland State Archives MdHR-6636-43-27}

SELBY, JOSEPH (Anne Arundel County) contracted with the Council of Safety for the making of cartouch belts, bayonet belts and gun slings on 24 Sep 1776 {Ref: Archives of Maryland 12:297}; on 19 Jan 1781 the Council of Maryland requested "that Mr. John Shaw receive of Mrs. Ann Selby, Widow of the late Joseph Selby, all the Cartridge Boxes which had been finished by Selby and Howard according to their Contract with the State" {Ref: Archives of Maryland 45:280}

SELBY, PARKER (Worcester County) submitted an account and receipt for grazing cattle and cattle driver's wages on 10 Sep 1781 {Ref: Maryland State Archives MdHR-6636-43-27}; received payment for furnishing beef on 20 Sep 1781 {Ref: Maryland State Archives MdHR-6636-43-28BBBB}

SELBY, RICHARD (Montgomery County) received a receipt from the Purchasing Agent for furnishing wheat on 1 Aug 1780 {Ref: Maryland State Archives MdHR-6636-43-7}; received a receipt for furnishing wheat on 9 Aug 1780 {Ref: Maryland State Archives MdHR-6636-24-6}; received a receipt for furnishing wheat on 20 May 1781 {Ref: Maryland State Archives MdHR-6636-

42-11}

SELBY, SAMUEL (Frederick County) received a receipt from the Purchasing Agent for furnishing corn on 19 Jan 1781 {Ref: Maryland State Archives MdHR-6636-23-2}

SELBY, THOMAS (Montgomery County) received a receipt from the Purchasing Agent for furnishing wheat on 1 Aug 1780 {Ref: Maryland State Archives MdHR-6636-43-7}

SELBY, THOMAS JR. (Montgomery County) received a receipt from the Purchasing Agent for furnishing wheat on 17 May 1781 {Ref: Maryland State Archives MdHR-6636-42-11}

SELBY, THOMAS SR. (Montgomery County) received a receipt from the Purchasing Agent for furnishing wheat on 7 Aug 1780 {Ref: Maryland State Archives MdHR-6636-24-6}; received a receipt for furnishing wheat on 20 May 1781 {Ref: Maryland State Archives MdHR-6636-42-11}

SELBY, WILLIAM (Worcester County) submitted an account and receipt for feeding a steer on 13 Jul 1782 {Ref: Maryland State Archives MdHR-6636-43-28/O}

SELLMAN, JOHN (Anne Arundel County) received payment by order of the Council of Maryland "for beef purchased of him by John Crysall" on 4 Feb 1778 {Ref: Archives of Maryland 16:483}

SERGEANT, BENJAMIN (Prince George's County) received a certificate from the Purchasing Agent for furnishing corn on 17 Jun 1780 {Ref: Maryland State Archives MdHR-6636-42-10}

SERGEANT, JAMES JR. (Frederick County) received a receipt from the Purchasing Agent for furnishing wheat on 29 May 1782 {Ref: Maryland State Archives MdHR-6636-42-34}

SERGEANT, SNOWDEN (Frederick County) received receipts from the Purchasing Agent for furnishing wheat on 2 Aug and 20 Oct 1781 {Ref: Maryland State Archives MdHR-6636-23-28}

SETH, JAMES (Queen Anne's County) received a certificate from the Purchasing Agent for furnishing beef on 10 Oct 1781 {Ref: Maryland State Archives MdHR-6636-24-34}

SETH, JAMES (Caroline County) received a receipt from the Purchasing Agent for furnishing wheat on 27 Jul 1782 {Ref: Maryland State Archives MdHR-6636-42-7}

SEVERE, PETER (Kent County) submitted an account and receipt for furnishing flour barrels on 12 Mar 1782 {Ref: Maryland State Archives MdHR-6636-43-5}

SEWELL, CLEMENT (Queen Anne's County) received a receipt from the Purchasing Agent for furnishing wheat on 30 Sep 1780 {Ref: Maryland State Archives MdHR-6636-24-33}; received a certificate of payment due for pasturing state cattle on 22 Nov 1781 {Ref: Maryland State Archives MdHR-6636-24-34}

SEXTON, BENJAMIN (Queen Anne's County) received a certificate from the Purchasing Agent for furnishing pork on 23 Feb 1782 {Ref: Maryland State Archives MdHR-6636-43-11}

SEYER, RICHARD (Montgomery County) received a receipt from the Purchasing Agent for furnishing wheat on 15 Sep 1780 {Ref: Maryland State Archives MdHR-6636-24-7}

SHANAHAN, JOHN (Talbot County) received a loan certificate for £153.17.10 due from the Council of Maryland "agreeable to the Act proposing to the Citizens of this State, Creditors of Congress on Loan Office Certificates, Etc." on 16 May 1783 for services rendered during the war {Ref: Archives of Maryland 48:415}

SHANKS, JOHN (Anne Arundel County) received a loan certificate for £23.5.8 due from the Council of Maryland "agreeable to the Act proposing to the Citizens of this State, Creditors of Congress on Loan Office Certificates, Etc." on 9 Oct 1783 for services rendered during the war {Ref: Archives of Maryland 48:461}

SHARON, GEORGE (Anne Arundel County) received a receipt from the Purchasing Agent for furnishing powder on 16 Apr 1777 {Ref: Maryland State Archives MdHR-6636-9-14A}

SHARMAN, BENJAMIN (Dorchester County) received a receipt from the Purchasing Agent for furnishing wheat on 1 Oct 1782 {Ref: Maryland State Archives MdHR-6636-42-23}

SHARP, HENRY (Caroline County) received receipts from the Purchasing Agent for furnishing wheat on 1 Sep 1782 {Ref: Maryland State Archives MdHR-6636-42-7}

SHARP, SAMUEL (Talbot County) was a Purchasing Agent who submitted an account and receipt for furnishing bacon and purchasing provisions for the use of the army on 23 Apr and 14 Jul 1778 {Ref: Maryland State Archives MdHR-6636-12-15}

SHARPE, ELIZABETH (Baltimore Town) received payments by order of the Council of Safety for nursing the sick at the hospital on 5 Sep 1776 and for attending the hospital on 5 Oct 1776 {Ref: Archives of Maryland 12:257, 321}

SHAVER, HENRY (Frederick County) received a receipt from the Purchasing Agent for delivering flour on 28 Apr 1781 {Ref: Maryland State Archives MdHR-6636-23-31}

SHAW, JAMES (Somerset County) submitted an account for providing corn and fodder for the Dorchester County militia in Somerset County on 18 Mar 1781 {Ref: Maryland State Archives MdHR-6636-43-15}

SHAW, JAMES (Montgomery County) received a receipt from the Purchasing

Agent for furnishing wheat on 5 Nov and 6 Nov 1780 {Ref: Maryland State Archives MdHR-6636-24-8}

SHAW, JAMES (Dorchester County) received a receipt from the Purchasing Agent for furnishing wheat on 1 Nov 1782 {Ref: Maryland State Archives MdHR-6636-42-23}

SHAW, JOHN (Montgomery County) received a receipt from the Purchasing Agent for furnishing wheat on 10 Apr 1781 {Ref: Maryland State Archives MdHR-6636-42-11}

SHAW, JOHN (Baltimore County) received an order for the delivery of flour on 22 Aug 1782 {Ref: Maryland State Archives MdHR-6636-43-37C}

SHAW, JOHN (Anne Arundel County) received payments by order of the Council of Safety for stocking musquets on 16 Apr and 8 May 1776 {Ref: Archives of Maryland 11:333, 417}; also see "Joseph Selby," q.v.

SHAW, JOHN JR. (Anne Arundel County) received a receipt from the Purchasing Agent for furnishing powder on 16 Apr 1777 {Ref: Maryland State Archives MdHR-6636-9-14A}

SHAW, MARY (Caroline County) received receipts from the Purchasing Agent for furnishing wheat on 1 Sep 1782 {Ref: Maryland State Archives MdHR-6636-42-7}

SHAW, PETER (Baltimore County) received payment by order of the Council of Safety for furnishing boatage on 16 Sep 1776 {Ref: Archives of Maryland 12:274}

SHECKELS, RICHARD (Frederick County) received a receipt from the Purchasing Agent for furnishing beef on 7 Mar 1781 {Ref: Maryland State Archives MdHR-6636-23-4}

SHEEHEE, DANIEL (Dorchester County) received a receipt from the Purchasing Agent for furnishing wheat on 1 Nov 1782 {Ref: Maryland State Archives MdHR-6636-42-23}

SHEINER, VALENTINE (Frederick County) received a certificate from the Purchasing Agent for furnishing wheat on 27 May 1782 {Ref: Maryland State Archives MdHR-6636-42-33}

SHEKELL, ABRAHAM (Montgomery County) received a receipt from the Purchasing Agent for furnishing wheat on 9 Apr 1781 {Ref: Maryland State Archives MdHR-6636-42-11}

SHELL, CHRISTIAN (Frederick County) received a receipt from the Purchasing Agent for furnishing whiskey on 13 Jan 1781 {Ref: Maryland State Archives MdHR-6636-23-2}

SHELLMAN, JOHN (Frederick County) received a receipt from the Purchasing Agent for furnishing corn on 19 Feb 1781 {Ref: Maryland State Archives MdHR-6636-23-3}; submitted an account for furnishing whiskey on 21 May 1781 {Ref: Maryland State Archives MdHR-6636-23-6}

293

SHEPPARD, FRANCIS, see "Gabriel Vanhorn," q.v.

SHEPPARD (SHEPHERD), PHILIP (Calvert County) received payment from the Council of Maryland as "appropriated for the payment of Expresses due him per Account passed by the Auditor General" on 20 Jul 1781 {Ref: Archives of Maryland 45:511}; submitted an account for collecting cattle for the use of the state in October, 1781 {Ref: Maryland State Archives MdHR-6636-50-37}

SHEPPARD, THOMAS (Montgomery County) received a receipt from the Purchasing Agent for furnishing wheat on 28 May 1781 {Ref: Maryland State Archives MdHR-6636-24-18}

SHEPPARD (SHEPARD), WILLIAM (Caroline County) received a receipt from the Purchasing Agent for furnishing wheat on 20 Sep 1782 {Ref: Maryland State Archives MdHR-6636-42-7}

SHERMAN, JOHN (Caroline County) received receipts from the Purchasing Agent for furnishing wheat on 11 Jun and 17 Aug 1782 {Ref: Maryland State Archives MdHR-6636-42-7}

SHERTEL, ERHARD (Frederick County) submitted an account and receipt for supplies on 23 Oct 1779 {Ref: Maryland State Archives MdHR-19970-3-8}

SHERWOOD, THOMAS, Esquire (Talbot County) received a loan certificate for £122.1.11 due from the Council of Maryland "agreeable to the Act proposing to the Citizens of this State, Creditors of Congress on Loan Office Certificates, Etc." on 16 May 1783 for services rendered during the war {Ref: Archives of Maryland 48:415}

SHERWOOD, WILLIAM (Talbot County) submitted an account and receipt for storage of bacon on 19 Jun 1778 {Ref: Maryland State Archives MdHR-6636-12-15}

SHIPLY, WILLIAM (Caroline County) was a captain who received a certificate from the Purchasing Agent for hauling corn on 24 Jun 1780 {Ref: Maryland State Archives MdHR-6636-23-20}

SHOEMAKER, JOSHUA (Montgomery County) received a receipt from the Purchasing Agent for furnishing wheat on 7 Feb 1781 {Ref: Maryland State Archives MdHR-6636-24-9}

SHOOT, GEORGE (Frederick County) received a receipt from the Purchasing Agent for furnishing rye in 1780 {Ref: Maryland State Archives MdHR-6636-23-33}

SHOUP, MARTIN (Frederick County) received a certificate from the Purchasing Agent for furnishing wheat on 12 Feb 1783 {Ref: Maryland State Archives MdHR-6636-42-38}

SHOVER, HENRY (Frederick County) received payment by order of the Council of Maryland for furnishing a gun on 28 Mar 1778 {Ref: Archives of Maryland 16:557}

SHOVER, PETER (Frederick County) received a certificate from the Purchasing

Agent for furnishing wheat on 29 May 1782 {Ref: Maryland State Archives MdHR-6636-42-34}

SHRIVER, WILLIAM (Frederick County) received a certificate from the Purchasing Agent for furnishing wheat on 24 Jan 1783 {Ref: Maryland State Archives MdHR-6636-42-38}

SHROP, MATTHIAS (Frederick County) received a certificate from the Purchasing Agent for purchasing bacon on 16 Apr 1778 {Ref: Maryland State Archives MdHR-4586-11}

SHRYOCK, HENRY (Washington County) was appointed by the Council of Maryland as one of thirty men to be "Agents for Purchasing Provisions" on 30 Mar 1779 {Ref: Archives of Maryland 21:332}; submitted an account of purchase of grain for the use of the state on 31 Mar 1780 {Ref: Maryland State Archives MdHR-4590-76}; submitted an account of purchase of grain on 16 Apr 1780 {Ref: Maryland State Archives MdHR-4590-74}; delivered flour to the commissary at Baltimore Town for the use of the State of Maryland in the summer of 1780 {Ref: Archives of Maryland 45:84}; received payment by order of the Council of Maryland for his use as Contractor for Horses in Washington County on 2 Sep 1780 {Ref: Archives of Maryland 43:274}

SHUSH, ANDREW (Frederick County) received a certificate from the Purchasing Agent for furnishing wheat on 11 Jun 1782 {Ref: Maryland State Archives MdHR-6636-42-35}

SILVESTER, DAVID (Caroline County) received a receipt from the Purchasing Agent for furnishing wheat on 1 Sep 1782 {Ref: Maryland State Archives MdHR-6636-42-7}

SIM, PHILIP (Anne Arundel County) received a receipt from the Purchasing Agent for furnishing powder on 16 Apr 1777 {Ref: Maryland State Archives MdHR-6636-9-14A}

SIMM, JOSEPH (Montgomery County) received a receipt from the Purchasing Agent for furnishing wheat on 1 Aug 1780 {Ref: Maryland State Archives MdHR-6636-43-7}

SIMMES, WILLIAM (Charles County) received a receipt from the Purchasing Agent for furnishing wheat on 23 Nov 1781 {Ref: Maryland State Archives MdHR-6636-42-15}

SIMMONS (SIMMONDS), ISAAC (Prince George's County) received payment by order of the Council of Maryland on 30 Jul 1777 for erecting a salt works {Ref: Archives of Maryland 16:322}; received payment by order of the Council of Safety for furnishing two guns on 13 Aug 1776 {Ref: Archives of Maryland 12:198}

SIMMONS, JAMES (Frederick County) received a receipt from the Purchasing Agent for delivering flour on 25 Jan 1781 {Ref: Maryland State Archives MdHR-6636-23-30}

295

SIMMONS, SAMUEL (Frederick County) received receipts from the Purchasing Agent for furnishing corn and rye on 6 Apr, 28 Apr and 9 Jun 1780 {Ref: Maryland State Archives MdHR-6636-24-1}

SIMMS, IGNATIUS (Charles County) received a receipt from the Purchasing Agent for furnishing wheat on 20 Dec 1782 {Ref: Maryland State Archives MdHR-6636-42-20}

SIMMS, JOSEPH (Charles County) received a receipt from the Purchasing Agent for furnishing wheat on 24 Nov 1781 {Ref: Maryland State Archives MdHR-6636-23-24}

SIMMS, MARMADUKE (Charles County) received a receipt from the Purchasing Agent for furnishing wheat on 10 May 1783 {Ref: Maryland State Archives MdHR-6636-42-22}

SIMPKINS, SILAS (Washington County) received payment by order of the Council of Maryland "for express from Old Town in Washington County" on 16 May 1778 {Ref: Archives of Maryland 21:86}

SIMPSON, ANNE, Mrs. (Baltimore Town) was a nurse who submitted accounts for rendering nursing services on the state ship *Defence* on 18 Mar 1777 and for boarding ill people on 12 Apr 1777 {Ref: Maryland State Archives MdHR-19970-2-1}

SIMPSON, CHARLES (Charles County) received a receipt from the Purchasing Agent for furnishing wheat on 28 Sep 1782 {Ref: Maryland State Archives MdHR-6636-42-19}

SIMPSON, JAMES (Charles County) received a receipt from the Purchasing Agent for furnishing wheat on 28 Sep 1782 {Ref: Maryland State Archives MdHR-6636-42-19}

SIMPSON, JOSEPH (Charles County) received a receipt from the Purchasing Agent for furnishing wheat on 10 Jan 1782 {Ref: Maryland State Archives MdHR-6636-42-16}

SIMPSON, SOLOMON (Montgomery and Prince George's Counties) was a colonel and Commissary of Provisions who submitted an account for purchasing grain on 5 Feb 1780 {Ref: Maryland State Archives MdHR-6636-17-42}; submitted an account of purchases and waggonage on 13 Mar 1780 {Ref: Maryland State Archives MdHR-6636-17-96}; received payment by order of the Council of Maryland (which misspelled his name as "Col. Solomon Stympson") for his use as Contractor for Wagons and Teams in Montgomery County on 12 Sep 1780 {Ref: Archives of Maryland 43:286}; received a receipt for furnishing wheat and shelling corn on 30 Jun and 20 Oct 1780 {Ref: Maryland State Archives MdHR-6636-24-2}; received receipts for furnishing wheat on 25 Jul 1782 and 9 Aug 1783 {Ref: Maryland State Archives MdHR-6636-50-135}

SIMS, ALEXIUS (Montgomery County) received a certificate of employment by the commissary of purchases on 16 Apr 1782 {Ref: Maryland State Archives MdHR-6636-50-91}

SIMS, JOSEPH (Montgomery County) received a receipt from the Purchasing Agent for furnishing wheat on 2 Aug 1780 {Ref: Maryland State Archives MdHR-6636-24-6}

SINCLAIR, WILLIAM (Baltimore County) received a receipt from the Purchasing Agent for furnishing flour on 2 Mar 1780 {Ref: Maryland State Archives MdHR-6636-23-15}

SINEGIN, PHILLIP (Somerset County) received a receipt from the Purchasing Agent for furnishing pork on 16 May 1782 {Ref: Maryland State Archives MdHR-6636-43-21}

SINN, PHILIP (Frederick County) received a receipt from the Purchasing Agent for delivering flour on 19 Apr 1781 {Ref: Maryland State Archives MdHR-6636-23-31}

SKINNER, JOHN (county not stated) received a loan certificate for £3469.18.9 due from the Council of Maryland "agreeable to the Act proposing to the Citizens of this State, Creditors of Congress on Loan Office Certificates, Etc." on 25 Sep 1783 for services rendered during the war {Ref: Archives of Maryland 48:456}

SKINNER, MORDECAI (Talbot County) received a receipt from the Purchasing Agent for furnishing bacon on 29 May 1778 {Ref: Maryland State Archives MdHR-6636-12-15}

SKINNER, TRUEMAN (Prince George's County) was a colonel who was listed in possession of some gunpowder on a "Return of Armes and Ammunition in Prince George's County Belonging to the Publick" on 3 Jul 1780 {Ref: Archives of Maryland 45:4}

SLACK, JOSEPH (Caroline County) received a receipt from the Purchasing Agent for furnishing wheat on 5 Aug 1782 {Ref: Maryland State Archives MdHR-6636-42-7}

SLATER, JONATHAN (Montgomery County) received a receipt from the Purchasing Agent for furnishing wheat on 21 Oct and 27 Nov 1780 {Ref: Maryland State Archives MdHR-6636-24-13}

SLATOR, JOHN (Charles County) received a receipt from the Purchasing Agent for furnishing wheat on 8 Aug 1781 {Ref: Maryland State Archives MdHR-6636-42-15}

SLATOR, THOMAS (Montgomery County) received a receipt from the Purchasing Agent for furnishing wheat on 24 Jul 1781 {Ref: Maryland State Archives MdHR-6636-42-11}

SLAUGHTER, JOHN (Caroline County) received a receipt from the Purchasing Agent for furnishing wheat on 20 Sep 1782 {Ref: Maryland State Archives MdHR-6636-42-7}

297

SLOSS, THOMAS (Somerset County) received a receipt from the Purchasing Agent for furnishing bacon on 8 Aug 1780 {Ref: Maryland State Archives MdHR-6636-24-41}; received a loan certificate for £112 due from the Council of Maryland "agreeable to the Act proposing to the Citizens of this State, Creditors of Congress on Loan Office Certificates, Etc." on 20 May 1783 for services rendered during the war {Ref: Archives of Maryland 48:418}

SLYE (SLIGH), CLARE (Charles County) received a receipt from the Purchasing Agent for furnishing wheat on 21 Sep 1781 {Ref: Maryland State Archives MdHR-6636-43-45/O}; received receipts for furnishing wheat on 29 Sep and 3 Nov 1781 {Ref: Maryland State Archives MdHR-6636-42-15}; received a receipt for furnishing wheat on 13 Feb 1782 {Ref: Maryland State Archives MdHR-6636-42-16}; received receipts for furnishing wheat on 26 Jul and 3 Aug 1782 {Ref: Maryland State Archives MdHR-6636-42-18}; received a receipt for furnishing wheat on 15 Nov 1782 {Ref: Maryland State Archives MdHR-6636-42-19}; received a receipt for furnishing wheat on 8 May 1783 {Ref: Maryland State Archives MdHR-6636-42-22}; received payment from the Council of Maryland on 9 Oct 1783 for services rendered (not specified) during the war {Ref: Archives of Maryland 48:461}

SLYE, WILLEY, Miss (Charles County) received a loan certificate for £13.9.4 due from the Council of Maryland "agreeable to the Act proposing to the Citizens of this State, Creditors of Congress on Loan Office Certificates, Etc." on 2 Jul 1783 for services rendered during the war {Ref: Archives of Maryland 48:436}

SMALL, CHARLOTTE (Baltimore County) received payment by order of the Council of Maryland for services rendered (not specified) on 17 Feb 1781 {Ref: Archives of Maryland 45:314}

SMALL, THOMAS (Baltimore County) received a receipt from the Purchasing Agent for furnishing beef on 19 Apr 1781 {Ref: Maryland State Archives MdHR-6636-43-37M}

SMALLWOOD, ANN (Charles County) received a receipt from the Purchasing Agent for furnishing wheat on 28 Dec 1782 {Ref: Maryland State Archives MdHR-6636-42-21}

SMALLWOOD, BAYNE (Charles County) received a receipt from the Purchasing Agent for furnishing wheat on 8 May 1783 {Ref: Maryland State Archives MdHR-6636-42-22}

SMALLWOOD, MARY (Charles County) received a receipt from the Purchasing Agent for furnishing wheat on 8 May 1783 {Ref: Maryland State Archives MdHR-6636-42-22}

SMALLWOOD, PRESILA (Charles County) received a receipt from the Purchasing Agent for furnishing wheat on 30 May 1782 {Ref: Maryland State Archives MdHR-6636-42-18}

SMALLWOOD, PRYOR (Charles County) received a receipt from the Purchasing

Agent for furnishing wheat on 15 Apr 1783 {Ref: Maryland State Archives MdHR-6636-42-22}

SMALLWOOD, SAMUEL (Charles County) received a receipt from the Purchasing Agent for furnishing wheat on 26 Apr 1783 {Ref: Maryland State Archives MdHR-6636-42-22}; also see "John Halkerston," q.v.

SMALLWOOD, THOMAS (Charles County) received a receipt from the Purchasing Agent for furnishing wheat on 8 May 1783 {Ref: Maryland State Archives MdHR-6636-42-22}

SMALLWOOD, WILLIAM (Charles County) received a receipt from the Purchasing Agent for furnishing wheat on 5 Dec 1782 {Ref: Maryland State Archives MdHR-6636-42-20}

SMITH, ADAM (Frederick County) received a certificate from the Purchasing Agent for furnishing wheat on 30 May 1782 {Ref: Maryland State Archives MdHR-6636-42-34}

SMITH, ANDREW (Frederick County) received a certificate from the Purchasing Agent for furnishing wheat on 14 Jul 1782 {Ref: Maryland State Archives MdHR-6636-42-36}

SMITH, ANTHONY (Montgomery County) received a receipt from the Purchasing Agent for furnishing wheat on 15 Apr 1781 {Ref: Maryland State Archives MdHR-6636-42-11}

SMITH, ARCHIBALD (Somerset County) received a receipt from the Purchasing Agent for furnishing bacon on 20 Jul 1781 {Ref: Maryland State Archives MdHR-6636-24-43}

SMITH, BASIL OR BASEL (St. Mary's County) received a certificate from the Purchasing Agent for furnishing wheat on 5 Oct 1780 {Ref: Maryland State Archives MdHR-6636-24-36}; his name appeared on "A Return of Beef on the Hoof Purchased by Joseph Ford Commissary of Purchases" on 6 Oct 1780 when he delivered a steer for the use of the state {Ref: Archives of Maryland 45:156}

SMITH, BENJAMIN (Worcester County) received a receipt from the Purchasing Agent for furnishing corn on 7 Sep 1780 {Ref: Maryland State Archives MdHR-6636-24-54}

SMITH, BENJAMIN (Harford County) received payment for furnishing a gun to the Committee of Safety on 2 Sep 1776 {Ref: Preston's History of Harford County, p. 335}

SMITH, DAVID (Cecil County) pledged a loan in the amount of £100 to the State of Maryland under the Act for the Emission of Bills of Credit "to defray the expences of the present campaign" in October, 1781 {Ref: Archives of Maryland 47:533}

SMITH, JAMES (Caroline County) received a receipt from the Purchasing Agent for furnishing wheat on 17 Aug 1782 {Ref: Maryland State Archives MdHR-

6636-42-7}

SMITH, JOHN (Baltimore County) received a receipt from the Purchasing Agent for rental of a warehouse on 4 Sep 1779 {Ref: Maryland State Archives MdHR-6636-21-67}

SMITH, JOHN (Harford County) received a receipt from the Purchasing Agent for furnishing wheat on 2 Mar 1780 {Ref: Maryland State Archives MdHR-6636-23-39}

SMITH, JOHN (Somerset County) received a receipt from the Purchasing Agent for furnishing bacon on 6 Sep 1780 {Ref: Maryland State Archives MdHR-6636-24-41}; received a receipt for furnishing beef on 8 Nov 1781 {Ref: Maryland State Archives MdHR-6636-24-44}

SMITH, JOHN (Prince George's County) was a tanner who received a receipt from the Purchasing Agent for money lent to the state on 9 Feb 1779 {Ref: Maryland State Archives MdHR-6636-50-94}

SMITH, JOHN (Caroline County) received a receipt from the Purchasing Agent for furnishing wheat on 1 Sep 1782 {Ref: Maryland State Archives MdHR-6636-42-7}

SMITH, JOHN (St. Mary's County) appeared on "A Return of Beef on the Hoof Purchased by Joseph Ford Commissary of Purchases" on 6 Oct 1780 when he delivered a steer for the use of the state {Ref: Archives of Maryland 45:156}

SMITH, JOSEPH (Frederick County) received a certificate from the Purchasing Agent for furnishing wheat on 5 Aug 1782 {Ref: Maryland State Archives MdHR-6636-42-36}

SMITH, LEVIN (Caroline County) received a receipt from the Purchasing Agent for furnishing wheat on 5 Aug 1782 {Ref: Maryland State Archives MdHR-6636-42-7}

SMITH, MARTHA (Harford County) received a receipt from the Purchasing Agent for furnishing wheat on 25 Feb 1780 {Ref: Maryland State Archives MdHR-6636-23-35}

SMITH, NICHOLAS (Frederick County) received a receipt from the Purchasing Agent for furnishing bulls on 1 Feb 1781 {Ref: Maryland State Archives MdHR-6636-23-3}

SMITH, OLIVER (Kent County) received payment for furnishing wheat on 7 Nov 1780 {Ref: Maryland State Archives MdHR-6636-23-49}

SMITH, PATRICK SIM (Calvert County) was appointed by the Council of Safety to collect all the gold and silver coin that could be procured in the county in compliance with the Resolve of Congress on 27 Jan 1776 {Ref: Archives of Maryland 11:132}; appointed by the Council of Maryland on 25 Mar 1778 as one of eighteen men to be "Agents for Purchasing Provisions for the Army of the United States Agreeable to an Act of Assembly passed the 23rd Inst." {Ref: Archives of Maryland 16:551}; purchased provisions for the army on 9 Apr

1778 {Ref: Maryland State Archives MdHR-4587-61}; purchased provisions for troops in the county on 12 May 1778 {Ref: Maryland State Archives MdHR-4587-68}; appointed Commissary of Purchases for Calvert County by the Council of Maryland on 8 Jul 1780 {Ref: Archives of Maryland 43:215}; submitted an account for wheat purchased for the army on 29 Dec 1780 {Ref: Maryland State Archives MdHR-6636-21-126}; submitted an account for collecting beef in 1781 {Ref: Maryland State Archives MdHR-6636-50-37}; appointed Purchaser of Clothing in his county by the Council of Maryland on 5 Jun 1781 {Ref: Archives of Maryland 45:462}; also see "Martin Norris" and "John Woolfe," q.v.

SMITH, PATT. (Baltimore Town) submitted an account and receipt of payment due for furnishing linen on 16 Oct and 30 Oct 1779 {Ref: Maryland State Archives MdHR-19970-3-8}

SMITH, RALPH (Caroline County) received receipts from the Purchasing Agent for furnishing wheat on 5 Aug 1782 {Ref: Maryland State Archives MdHR-6636-42-7}

SMITH, REBECCA (Montgomery County) received a receipt from the Purchasing Agent for furnishing wheat on 9 Jun 1781 {Ref: Maryland State Archives MdHR-6636-24-18}

SMITH, REBECCA (Caroline County) received a receipt from the Purchasing Agent for furnishing wheat on 5 Aug 1782 {Ref: Maryland State Archives MdHR-6636-42-7}

SMITH, REBECCAH (Caroline County) received a receipt from the Purchasing Agent for furnishing wheat on 17 Aug 1782 {Ref: Maryland State Archives MdHR-6636-42-7}

SMITH, RICHARD (Montgomery County) received a receipt from the Purchasing Agent for furnishing wheat on 28 Nov 1780 {Ref: Maryland State Archives MdHR-6636-24-8}

SMITH, RICHARD (Frederick County) received a receipt from the Purchasing Agent for furnishing beef on 20 Apr 1781 {Ref: Maryland State Archives MdHR-6636-23-5}

SMITH, RICHARD (county not stated) was a doctor who received a loan certificate for £28.7.3 due from the Council of Maryland "agreeable to the Act proposing to the Citizens of this State, Creditors of Congress on Loan Office Certificates, Etc." on 26 May 1783 for services rendered during the war {Ref: Archives of Maryland 48:421}

SMITH, ROBERT (Harford County) received a receipt from the Purchasing Agent for furnishing wheat on 28 Jun 1780 {Ref: Maryland State Archives MdHR-6636-23-39}

SMITH, ROBERT (Anne Arundel County) received a receipt from the Purchasing Agent for furnishing powder on 16 Apr 1777 {Ref: Maryland State Archives

MdHR-6636-9-14F}

SMITH, SAMUEL (Baltimore Town) was a colonel and commissary who received a receipt from the Purchasing Agent for munitions and supplies on 18 Nov 1780 {Ref: Maryland State Archives MdHR-6636-21-36}; received a receipt for flour and meal on 31 Aug 1781 (Ref: Courtesy of the Maryland State Archives MdHR-6636-43-38CC}; submitted an account and receipt for furnishing rum on 5 Mar 1781 {Ref: Maryland State Archives MdHR-6636-43-38JJJJ}; received payment for furnishing pork and beef on 1 May 1781 {Ref: Maryland State Archives MdHR-6636-43-38LLL}; received a receipt for furnishing flour and meal on 1 Jun 1781 {Ref: Maryland State Archives MdHR-6636-43-38/OO}; appointed Purchaser of Clothing in his county by the Council of Maryland on 5 Jun 1781 {Ref: Archives of Maryland 45:462}; submitted an account for forwarding clothing and other supplies on 29 Jun 1781 {Ref: Maryland State Archives MdHR-4597-45}; submitted a list of deliveries for the use of the state on 21 Jul 1781 {Ref: Maryland State Archives MdHR-4597-57}

SMITH, SAMUEL (Kent County) received payment from the Purchasing Agent for furnishing cattle and pasturage for the public use in September, 1781 {Ref: Maryland State Archives MdHR-6636-43-3}

SMITH, THOMAS (Frederick County) received a certificate from the Purchasing Agent for furnishing wheat on 28 May 1782 {Ref: Maryland State Archives MdHR-6636-42-34}

SMITH, THOMAS (Caroline County) received a receipt from the Purchasing Agent for furnishing wheat on 5 Aug 1782 {Ref: Maryland State Archives MdHR-6636-42-7}

SMITH, THOMAS (Harford County) received payment by order of the Council of Maryland via James Phillips for the hire of his wagon on 20 May 1778 {Ref: Archives of Maryland 21:97}

SMITH, THOMAS (Perkins Ferry, Harford County) was appointed by the Council of Maryland to be one of five men in Harford County "to carry the Act to prohibit for a limited time the Exportation of Indian Corn, Etc., by Land" on 22 Dec 1780 {Ref: Archives of Maryland 45:251}

SMITH, THOMAS (Kent County) was appointed Purchaser of Clothing in his county by the Council of Maryland on 5 Jun 1781 {Ref: Archives of Maryland 45:462}

SMITH, WILLIAM (Bay Side, Harford County) was appointed by the Council of Maryland to be one of five men in Harford County "to carry the Act to prohibit for a limited time the Exportation of Indian Corn, Etc., by Land" on 22 Dec 1780 {Ref: Archives of Maryland 45:251}

SMITH, WILLIAM (Baltimore County) procured food for the troops and shipped food to the fleet on 6 Oct 1779 {Ref: Maryland State Archives MdHR-4589-

78}; offered to ship freight in his vessels on 23 Dec 1779 {Ref: Maryland State Archives MdHR-4589-74}; received flour from the commissary in Baltimore Town "for the Marine of France" on 26 Jul 1780 and also received wheat circa 5 Oct 1780 {Ref: Archives of Maryland 45:85, 45:135}

SMITH, WILLIAM (Montgomery County) received a receipt from the Purchasing Agent for furnishing wheat on 12 Oct 1780 {Ref: Maryland State Archives MdHR-6636-24-8}; received a receipt for furnishing wheat on 14 Oct 1780 {Ref: Maryland State Archives MdHR-6636-24-8}

SMITH, WILLIAM (Frederick County) received a receipt from the Purchasing Agent for furnishing corn meal on 17 Mar 1781 {Ref: Maryland State Archives MdHR-6636-23-4}; received a certificate for furnishing wheat on 28 May 1782 {Ref: Maryland State Archives MdHR-6636-42-34}

SMITH, WILLIAM (Somerset County) received a receipt from the Purchasing Agent for furnishing pork on 14 Jul 1781 {Ref: Maryland State Archives MdHR-6636-24-43}

SMITH, WILLIAM (Caroline County) received a receipt from the Purchasing Agent for furnishing wheat on 5 Aug 1782 {Ref: Maryland State Archives MdHR-6636-42-7}

SMITH, WILLIAM (county not stated) received a loan certificate for £5200.19.2 due from the Council of Maryland "agreeable to the Act proposing to the Citizens of this State, Creditors of Congress on Loan Office Certificates, Etc." on 18 Dec 1783 for services rendered during the war {Ref: Archives of Maryland 48:491}

SMITH, WILLIAM JR. (Caroline County) received a receipt from the Purchasing Agent for furnishing wheat on 5 Aug 1782 {Ref: Maryland State Archives MdHR-6636-42-7}

SMITH, WILLIAM SR. (Caroline County) received receipts from the Purchasing Agent for furnishing wheat on 5 Aug 1782 {Ref: Maryland State Archives MdHR-6636-42-7}

SMITH & DORSEY (Baltimore County) received payment by order of the Council of Maryland for furnishing wood for the matrosses at Baltimore on 10 Dec 1777 {Ref: Archives of Maryland 16:433}

SMITHSON, THOMAS (Harford County) was given permission by the Council of Maryland on 12 Dec 1782 "to go into New York by Dobb's Ferry to carry Necessaries to his son a naval Prisoner" {Ref: Archives of Maryland 48:320}

SMITHSON, WILLIAM (Harford County) submitted "his account against the Province for Wagonedge of Powder" and received payment from the Committee of Safety on 6 May 1776 {Ref: Preston's History of Harford County, p. 326}

SMOCK, JOHN (Worcester County) submitted an account and receipt for hauling corn on 1 Sep 1781 {Ref: Maryland State Archives MdHR-6636-43-27};

submitted an account and receipt for hauling pork on 19 Jul 1782 {Ref: Maryland State Archives MdHR-6636-43-28K}

SMOCK, KENDALL (Worcester County) submitted an account and receipt for collecting cattle on 18 Sep 1781 {Ref: Maryland State Archives MdHR-6636-43-27}

SMOOT, EDWARD (Dorchester County) received a receipt from the Purchasing Agent for furnishing wheat on 1 Nov 1782 {Ref: Maryland State Archives MdHR-6636-42-23}

SMOOT, ELIZABETH (Charles County) received a receipt from the Purchasing Agent for furnishing wheat on 11 Sep 1781 {Ref: Maryland State Archives MdHR-6636-43-45Q}; received a receipt for furnishing wheat on 18 Sep 1781 {Ref: Maryland State Archives MdHR-6636-42-15}

SMOOT, ISAAC (Charles County) received a receipt from the Purchasing Agent for furnishing wheat on 6 Sep 1782 {Ref: Maryland State Archives MdHR-6636-42-18}

SMOOT, JOHN (Dorchester County) received a receipt from the Purchasing Agent for furnishing wheat on 1 Nov 1782 {Ref: Maryland State Archives MdHR-6636-42-23}

SMOOT, JOSIAS (Charles County) received a receipt from the Purchasing Agent for furnishing wheat on 19 Jan 1782 {Ref: Maryland State Archives MdHR-6636-42-16}

SMOOT, PETER (Frederick County) received a receipt from the Purchasing Agent for furnishing flour on 27 Feb 1781 {Ref: Maryland State Archives MdHR-6636-23-3}

SMOOT, THOMAS (Charles County) received a receipt from the Purchasing Agent for furnishing wheat on 17 Jun 1782 {Ref: Maryland State Archives MdHR-6636-42-18}

SMOOT, WILLIAM B. (Charles County) received a receipt from the Purchasing Agent for furnishing wheat on 2 Nov 1782 {Ref: Maryland State Archives MdHR-6636-42-19}

SMULLING, NATHANIEL (Somerset County) received a receipt from the Purchasing Agent for furnishing pork on 3 Jul 1781 {Ref: Maryland State Archives MdHR-6636-24-45}

SMYTH, FRANCIS (Kent or Queen Anne's County) received payment from the Maryland Council of Safety for furnishing leather breeches for the troops on 6 Jun 1776 {Ref: Archives of Maryland 11:466}

SMYTH, JOHN GREEN (Queen Anne's County) received a receipt from the Purchasing Agent for furnishing wheat on 30 Sep 1780 {Ref: Maryland State Archives MdHR-6636-24-33}

SMYTH, THOMAS (Kent County) received payment by order of the Council of Safety to defray the expense of the carriage of gunpowder from Indian River to

Chester Town and for ten musquets purchased by him for the use of the province on 1 Jun 1776 {Ref: Archives of Maryland 11:458}; received payment "to defray the expense of the carriage of war-like stores from Chinkotegue to Chester Town" on 17 Jul 1776 {Ref: Archives of Maryland 12:63}; received a certificate from the Purchasing Agent for furnishing wheat on 14 Jan 1780 {Ref: Maryland State Archives MdHR-6636-23-43}; received a certificate for furnishing wheat on 24 Jan 1780 {Ref: Maryland State Archives MdHR-6636-23-46}; received a certificate for hauling flour on 15 May 1780 {Ref: Maryland State Archives MdHR-6636-23-41}

SNIVELY, HENRY, see "Henry Schnebely," q.v.

SOMERHILL, JAMES (St. Mary's County) received payment from the Purchasing Agent on 2 Jan 1782 for collecting and driving public cattle for 17 days {Ref: Maryland State Archives MdHR-6636-43-23}

SOMERS, VALENTINE (Frederick County) submitted an account for furnishing beef on 12 May 1781 {Ref: Maryland State Archives MdHR-6636-23-6}

SOMERVILL, ALEXANDER (Calvert County) was appointed by the Council of Safety to collect all the gold and silver coin that could be procured in the county in compliance with the Resolve of Congress on 27 Jan 1776 {Ref: Archives of Maryland 11:132}

SOMERVILLE, WILLIAM (Calvert County) received a loan certificate for £269.10.5 due from the Council of Maryland "agreeable to the Act proposing to the Citizens of this State, Creditors of Congress on Loan Office Certificates, Etc." on 3 Dec 1783 for services rendered during the war {Ref: Archives of Maryland 48:485}

SOMMERS, HEZEKIAH (Montgomery County) received a receipt from the Purchasing Agent for furnishing wheat on 10 Aug 1780 {Ref: Maryland State Archives MdHR-6636-24-6}

SOPER, BASIL (Montgomery County) received a receipt from the Purchasing Agent for furnishing wheat on 9 Apr 1781 {Ref: Maryland State Archives MdHR-6636-42-11}

SOUTHERLY, SAMUEL (Caroline County) received a receipt from the Purchasing Agent for furnishing wheat on 20 Sep 1782 {Ref: Maryland State Archives MdHR-6636-42-7}

SOUTHWELL, JOHN (Charles County) received a receipt from the Purchasing Agent for furnishing wheat on 12 Oct 1782 {Ref: Maryland State Archives MdHR-6636-42-19}

SPALDEN, BASIL (Charles County) received a receipt from the Purchasing Agent for furnishing wheat on 20 Dec 1782 {Ref: Maryland State Archives MdHR-6636-42-20}; received a receipt for furnishing wheat on 28 Dec 1782 {Ref: Maryland State Archives MdHR-6636-42-21}

SPALDING, PHILIP (Charles County) received a receipt from the Purchasing

305

Agent for furnishing wheat on 15 Apr 1783 {Ref: Maryland State Archives MdHR-6636-42-22}; also see "John Halkerston," q.v.

SPARROW, SOLOMON (Anne Arundel County) contracted to manufacture clothing for soldiers on 19 Mar 1782 {Ref: Maryland State Archives MdHR-6636-40-33}

SPEAK, FRANCIS (Charles County) received a receipt from the Purchasing Agent for furnishing wheat on 29 Dec 1782 {Ref: Maryland State Archives MdHR-6636-42-21}

SPEAK, HENERITA (Charles County) received a receipt from the Purchasing Agent for furnishing wheat on 5 Dec 1782 {Ref: Maryland State Archives MdHR-6636-42-20}

SPEAK (SPEAKE), HENRY (Charles County) received a receipt from the Purchasing Agent for furnishing wheat on 24 Oct 1781 {Ref: Maryland State Archives MdHR-6636-23-24}; received a receipt for furnishing wheat on 1 Nov 1781 {Ref: Maryland State Archives MdHR-6636-42-15}

SPEAK, JOSEPH (Charles County) received a receipt from the Purchasing Agent for furnishing wheat on 28 Dec 1782 {Ref: Maryland State Archives MdHR-6636-42-21}

SPEAR, WILLIAM (Baltimore County) received a certificate of purchase and delivery of corn on 1 Feb 1780 {Ref: Maryland State Archives MdHR-6636-17-33B}; submitted an account and receipt for furnishing bread on 14 Nov 1780 {Ref: Maryland State Archives MdHR-6636-43-38XXXX}; submitted an account and receipt for baking bread and for coopering on 6 Mar 1781 {Ref: Maryland State Archives MdHR-6636-43-38HHHH}

SPEARS, JOHN (Montgomery County) received a receipt from the Purchasing Agent for furnishing wheat on 19 May and 20 Sep 1781 {Ref: Maryland State Archives MdHR-6636-24-15}

SPECKET, CHARLES (Frederick County) received payment by order of the Council of Maryland for riding express from Frederick Town to Annapolis and "for the purpose of bearing his expences on his return" on 13 Feb 1781 {Ref: Archives of Maryland 45:309}

SPENCE, JOHN (Worcester County) appeared on "A List of Sundry Persons Corn Purchased of for the use of the State of Maryland" by the Commissary on 19 Jun 1780 {Ref: Archives of Maryland 45:9}

SPENCER, ISAAC (Kent County) received a certificate from the Purchasing Agent for furnishing rye on 14 Feb 1780 {Ref: Maryland State Archives MdHR-6636-43-1}; received payment from the Purchasing Agent for furnishing cattle for the public use in September, 1781 {Ref: Maryland State Archives MdHR-6636-43-3}

SPINNIG, SAMUEL (Baltimore County) received payment for furnishing beef on 24 Apr 1781 {Ref: Maryland State Archives MdHR-6636-43-38QQQ}

SPRIGG, ELIZABETH (Prince George's County) received a loan certificate for £21.3.10 due from the Council of Maryland "agreeable to the Act proposing to the Citizens of this State, Creditors of Congress on Loan Office Certificates, Etc." on 20 Dec 1783 for services rendered during the war {Ref: Archives of Maryland 48:494}

SPRIGG, JOSEPH (Prince George's County) received a loan certificate for £1383.3.0 due from the Council of Maryland "agreeable to the Act proposing to the Citizens of this State, Creditors of Congress on Loan Office Certificates, Etc." on 25 Oct 1783 for services rendered during the war {Ref: Archives of Maryland 48:474}

SPRIGG, RICHARD (Prince George's County) received payment by order of the Council of Safety for furnishing a cannon on 17 Sep 1776 {Ref: Archives of Maryland 12:276}

SPRIGG, THOMAS (Prince George's County) received a receipt from the Purchasing Agent for furnishing wheat on 10 Feb 1783 {Ref: Maryland State Archives MdHR-6636-50-135}

SPRINGER, JACOB (Frederick County) received a certificate from the Purchasing Agent for furnishing wheat on 15 Jun 1782 {Ref: Maryland State Archives MdHR-6636-42-35}

SPROGAL, LODWICK (Queen Anne's County) received a receipt from the Purchasing Agent for furnishing bacon on 8 May 1778 {Ref: Maryland State Archives MdHR-4587-45}

SPRY, JOHN (Talbot County) received a receipt from the Purchasing Agent for purchasing bacon on 6 Jun 1778 {Ref: Maryland State Archives MdHR-6636-12-15}

STABLEFORD, DANIEL (Caroline County) received a receipt from the Purchasing Agent for furnishing wheat on 27 May 1782 {Ref: Maryland State Archives MdHR-6636-42-7}

STACK, PATRICK (Dorchester County) received a receipt from the Purchasing Agent for furnishing wheat on 1 Nov 1782 {Ref: Maryland State Archives MdHR-6636-42-23}

STACY, WILLIAM (Baltimore County) received receipts from the Purchasing Agent for furnishing barrels on 21 May, 22 Jul and 16 Aug 1779 {Ref: Maryland State Archives MdHR-6636-21-67}

STAFFORD, JAMES (Caroline County) received a receipt from the Purchasing Agent for furnishing wheat on 5 Aug 1782 {Ref: Maryland State Archives MdHR-6636-42-7}

STAFFORD, JOHN (Caroline County) received a receipt from the Purchasing Agent for furnishing wheat on 5 Aug 1782 {Ref: Maryland State Archives MdHR-6636-42-7}

STAILY, JACOB (Frederick County) received a receipt from the Purchasing

307

Agent for delivering flour on 18 Apr 1781 {Ref: Maryland State Archives MdHR-6636-23-31}

STAILY, JOSEPH (Frederick County) received a receipt from the Purchasing Agent for delivering flour on 18 Apr 1781 {Ref: Maryland State Archives MdHR-6636-23-31}

STAILY, MELCHOR (Frederick County) received a receipt from the Purchasing Agent for delivering flour on 18 Apr 1781 {Ref: Maryland State Archives MdHR-6636-23-31}

STAINTON, BENSON (Caroline County) was appointed by the Council of Safety to collect all the gold and silver coin that could be procured in the county in compliance with the Resolve of Congress on 27 Jan 1776 {Ref: Archives of Maryland 11:132}

STALLIONS, THOMAS (Montgomery County) received a receipt from the Purchasing Agent for furnishing wheat on 29 Jan 1781 {Ref: Maryland State Archives MdHR-6636-24-13}

STANFORD, DAVID (Somerset County) received a receipt from the Purchasing Agent for furnishing bacon on 15 Jul 1781 {Ref: Maryland State Archives MdHR-6636-24-43}

STANFORD, THOMAS (Somerset County) received a receipt from the Purchasing Agent for furnishing hogs on 4 Feb 1782 {Ref: Maryland State Archives MdHR-6636-43-21}

STANTON, BENSON (Caroline County) was a miller who received a certificate of employment by the commissary for milling on 3 Jun 1780 {Ref: Maryland State Archives MdHR-6636-23-20}

STASEY, SAMUEL (Montgomery County) received a receipt from the Purchasing Agent for furnishing wheat on 22 Aug 1780 {Ref: Maryland State Archives MdHR-6636-24-13}

STASEY, WILLIAM (Montgomery County) received a receipt from the Purchasing Agent for furnishing wheat on 22 Aug 1780 {Ref: Maryland State Archives MdHR-6636-24-13}

STATIA, WILLIAM (Baltimore County) submitted an account and received payment for lining, nailing, hooping and driving of casks on 24 Jan and 1 Feb 1780 {Ref: Maryland Historical Society MS.1814, Box 6}

STEELE, HENRY (Dorchester County) was appointed by the Council of Safety to collect all the gold and silver coin that could be procured in the county in compliance with the Resolve of Congress on 27 Jan 1776 {Ref: Archives of Maryland 11:132}

STEERE, JOHN (Frederick County) received a receipt from the Purchasing Agent for furnishing pork on 17 Jan 1781 {Ref: Maryland State Archives MdHR-6636-23-2}

STEPHEN, WILLIAM (Frederick County) received a certificate from the

Purchasing Agent for furnishing wheat on 10 Aug 1782 {Ref: Maryland State Archives MdHR-6636-42-36}

STEPHENS, GEORGE (Somerset County) received a receipt from the Purchasing Agent for furnishing barrels and a tub on 4 May 1782 {Ref: Maryland State Archives MdHR-6636-43-20}

STEPHENS, MARGARET (Somerset County) received a receipt from the Purchasing Agent for furnishing pork on 20 Mar 1782 {Ref: Maryland State Archives MdHR-6636-43-21}

STEPHENS, RICHARD (Montgomery County) received a receipt from the Purchasing Agent for furnishing wheat on 1 Aug 1780 {Ref: Maryland State Archives MdHR-6636-43-7}

STEPHENS, THOMAS (Kent County) submitted an account and receipt for grinding wheat and for furnishing flour barrels on 1 Mar 1782 {Ref: Maryland State Archives MdHR-6636-43-5}

STEPHENS, WILLIAM (county not stated) received a loan certificate for £16.16.10 due from the Council of Maryland "agreeable to the Act proposing to the Citizens of this State, Creditors of Congress on Loan Office Certificates, Etc." on 22 Dec 1783 for services rendered during the war {Ref: Archives of Maryland 48:495}

STEPHENSON, DANIEL (Frederick County) received a certificate from the Purchasing Agent for furnishing wheat on 12 Jun 1782 {Ref: Maryland State Archives MdHR-6636-42-35}

STERETT, JOHN, Esquire (Baltimore County) was appointed by the Council of Maryland on 25 Mar 1778 as one of eighteen men to be "Agents for Purchasing Provisions for the Army of the United States Agreeable to an Act of Assembly passed the 23rd Inst." and noted in the record as "removed" {Ref: Archives of Maryland 16:551}; received a loan certificate for £510.3.10 due from the Council of Maryland "agreeable to the Act proposing to the Citizens of this State, Creditors of Congress on Loan Office Certificates, Etc." on 10 Dec 1783 for services rendered during the war {Ref: Archives of Maryland 48:487}

STEUARD, JAMES (county not stated) received payment by order of the Council of Safety for furnishing a baggage wagon for the Flying Camp on 26 Aug 1776 {Ref: Archives of Maryland 12:240}

STEUART, JOHN (Worcester County) submitted an account and receipt for hauling pork on 10 Jul 1782 {Ref: Maryland State Archives MdHR-6636-43-28L}

STEVENS, ELEANOR (Worcester County) received a receipt from the Purchasing Agent for renting a house and for storing corn on 15 Oct 1780 {Ref: Maryland State Archives MdHR-6636-24-54}

STEVENS, EPHRAIM (Somerset County) was appointed by the Council of Maryland to be one of three Purchasers of Cattle for his county on 7 Jan 1778

{Ref: Archives of Maryland 16:456}; received a receipt for furnishing beef on 15 Mar 1781 {Ref: Maryland State Archives MdHR-6636-24-43}

STEVENS, JOHN (Talbot County) submitted an account and receipt for hauling on 17 Jun 1778 {Ref: Maryland State Archives MdHR-6636-12-15}

STEVENS, JOHN 3RD (Caroline County) received a receipt from the Purchasing Agent for furnishing wheat on 5 Aug 1782 {Ref: Maryland State Archives MdHR-6636-42-7}

STEVENS, LEVIN (Dorchester County) received a loan certificate for £16.16.10 due from the Council of Maryland "agreeable to the Act proposing to the Citizens of this State, Creditors of Congress on Loan Office Certificates, Etc." on 22 Dec 1783 for services rendered during the war {Ref: Archives of Maryland 48:495}

STEVENS, ROBERTSON (Dorchester County) was a commissary of purchases who submitted an account of wheat received on 12 Aug 1782 {Ref: Maryland State Archives MdHR-6636-42-23}

STEVENS, THOMAS (Talbot County) received a receipt from the Purchasing Agent for furnishing bacon for the use of the army on 2 May 1778 {Ref: Maryland State Archives MdHR-4587-77}; submitted an account and receipt for hauling on 2 May 1778 {Ref: Maryland State Archives MdHR-6636-12-15}

STEVENS, WILLIAM (Talbot County) received a receipt from the Purchasing Agent for purchasing bacon on 12 Jun 1778 {Ref: Maryland State Archives MdHR-6636-12-15}

STEVENSON, DANIEL (Baltimore County) received a receipt from the Purchasing Agent for furnishing veal on 18 May 1781 {Ref: Maryland State Archives MdHR-6636-43-38ZZ}

STEVENSON, HUGH (Worcester County) received a certificate from the Purchasing Agent for processing beef on or about 1 Jan 1781 {Ref: Maryland State Archives MdHR-6636-23-1}

STEVENSON, JAMES (Worcester County) submitted an account and receipt for butchering cattle on 15 Oct 1781 and for conveying horses on 8 Nov 1781 {Ref: Maryland State Archives MdHR-6636-43-27}; received a receipt for hauling salt and pork barrels on 1 Jan 1782 {Ref: Maryland State Archives MdHR-6636-43-28H}

STEVENSON, JOHN (Baltimore County) received a certificate from the Purchasing Agent for furnishing flour on 11 Jan 1780 {Ref: Maryland State Archives MdHR-6636-23-15}; received a loan certificate for £18.2.3 due from the Council of Maryland "agreeable to the Act proposing to the Citizens of this State, Creditors of Congress on Loan Office Certificates, Etc." on 24 Dec 1783 for services rendered during the war {Ref: Archives of Maryland 48:499}

STEVENSON, JOSHUA (Baltimore County) submitted an account of wheat procured for the army in 1780 {Ref: Maryland State Archives MdHR-6636-23-14}; delivered flour to the commissary at Baltimore Town for the use of the State of Maryland in the summer of 1780 {Ref: Archives of Maryland 45:84}

STEVENSON, WILLIAM (Worcester County) was appointed by the Council of Maryland as one of thirty men to be "Agents for Purchasing Provisions" on 30 Mar 1779 {Ref: Archives of Maryland 21:332}

STEWARD, DANIEL (Caroline County) received a receipt from the Purchasing Agent for furnishing wheat on 1 Sep 1782 {Ref: Maryland State Archives MdHR-6636-42-7}

STEWARD, STEPHEN (Baltimore County) received a receipt from the Purchasing Agent for furnishing provisions on 31 May 1781 {Ref: Maryland State Archives MdHR-19970-3-15}

STEWART, ALEXANDER (Frederick County) received a receipt from the Purchasing Agent for furnishing wheat on 29 May 1782 {Ref: Maryland State Archives MdHR-6636-42-34}

STEWART, ATHOL (Caroline County) received a receipt from the Purchasing Agent for wheat on 16 Sep 1782 {Ref: Maryland State Archives MdHR-6636-42-7}

STEWART, CHARLES (county not stated) received a loan certificate for £75.17.11 due from the Council of Maryland "agreeable to the Act proposing to the Citizens of this State, Creditors of Congress on Loan Office Certificates, Etc." on 21 May 1783 for services rendered during the war {Ref: Archives of Maryland 48:418-419}

STEWART, JOHN (Worcester County) was Contractor for Horses who received payment by order of the Council of Maryland on 9 Aug 1780 {Ref: Archives of Maryland 43:250}; submitted an account and receipt for driving cattle on 20 Dec 1781 {Ref: Maryland State Archives MdHR-6636-43-27}

STEWART, JOHN (Somerset County) was appointed by the Council of Maryland on 25 Mar 1778 as one of eighteen men to be "Agents for Purchasing Provisions for the Army of the United States Agreeable to an Act of Assembly passed the 23rd Inst." {Ref: Archives of Maryland 16:551}; received a receipt from the Purchasing Agent for furnishing bacon on 8 Aug 1780 {Ref: Maryland State Archives MdHR-6636-24-41}; received a loan certificate for £72.14.0 due from the Council of Maryland "agreeable to the Act proposing to the Citizens of this State, Creditors of Congress on Loan Office Certificates, Etc." on 19 Dec 1783 for services rendered during the war {Ref: Archives of Maryland 48:493}3

STEWART, JOHN (county not stated) was a captain who received a loan certificate for £59.18.1 due from the Council of Maryland "agreeable to the Act proposing to the Citizens of this State, Creditors of Congress on Loan Office Certificates, Etc." on 14 Jun 1783 for services rendered during the war {Ref:

Archives of Maryland 48:431}

STEWART, MORDECAI (Montgomery County) received a receipt from the Purchasing Agent for furnishing wheat on 1 Aug 1780 {Ref: Maryland State Archives MdHR-6636-43-7}; received a receipt for furnishing wheat on 2 Aug 1780 {Ref: Maryland State Archives MdHR-6636-24-6}; received a receipt for furnishing wheat on 18 May 1781 {Ref: Maryland State Archives MdHR-6636-24-18}

STEWART, WALTER (Charles County) received a receipt from the Purchasing Agent for furnishing wheat on 8 May 1783 {Ref: Maryland State Archives MdHR-6636-42-22}

STIEN, JACOB (Prince George's County) received receipts from the Purchasing Agent for furnishing wheat on 15 Apr and 20 May 1782 {Ref: Maryland State Archives MdHR-6636-50-135}

STIEN, JACOB (Montgomery County) received a receipt from the Purchasing Agent for shelling corn on 7 Jul 1780 {Ref: Maryland State Archives MdHR-6636-24-2}

STILES, JOSEPH (Harford County) agreed to take care of a mare for riding expresses for the Committee of Safety on 3 May 1775 {Ref: Preston's History of Harford County, p. 297}

STILES, WILLIAM (Montgomery County) received a receipt from the Purchasing Agent for furnishing wheat on 16 Aug 1781 {Ref: Maryland State Archives MdHR-6636-24-14}

STILLY, PETER (Frederick County) submitted an account for furnishing hay on 20 Nov 1780 {Ref: Maryland State Archives MdHR-6636-23-5}; received a certificate from the Purchasing Agent for furnishing wheat on 15 May 1782 {Ref: Maryland State Archives MdHR-6636-42-34}

STINCHICOMB, NATHANIEL (Baltimore County) received payment by order of the Council of Safety for furnishing boatage on 12 Sep 1776 {Ref: Archives of Maryland 12:267}

STOCKMAN, GEORGE (Frederick County) received a certificate from the Purchasing Agent for furnishing wheat on 27 May 1782 {Ref: Maryland State Archives MdHR-6636-42-34}

STODDERT, BENJAMIN, Esquire (Charles County) received a loan certificate for £30.5.6 due from the Council of Maryland "agreeable to the Act proposing to the Citizens of this State, Creditors of Congress on Loan Office Certificates, Etc." on 23 Jun 1783 for services rendered during the war {Ref: Archives of Maryland 48:433}

STODDERT, ELIZABETH (Charles County) received a receipt from the Purchasing Agent for furnishing wheat on 11 Apr 1782 {Ref: Maryland State Archives MdHR-6636-42-18}

STODDERT, LETTY (Charles County) received a receipt from the Purchasing

Agent for furnishing wheat on 11 Apr 1782 {Ref: Maryland State Archives MdHR-6636-42-18}

STODDERT (STODERT), SALLY (Charles County) received a receipt from the Purchasing Agent for furnishing wheat on 31 Oct 1782 {Ref: Maryland State Archives MdHR-6636-42-19}

STODDERT, WILLIAM (Charles County) received a receipt from the Purchasing Agent for furnishing wheat on 14 Aug 1782 {Ref: Maryland State Archives MdHR-6636-42-18}

STODDERT (STODERT), WILLIAM T. (Charles County) was a major who received a receipt from the Purchasing Agent for furnishing wheat on 29 Dec 1782 {Ref: Maryland State Archives MdHR-6636-42-21}; received a receipt for furnishing wheat on 10 May 1783 {Ref: Maryland State Archives MdHR-6636-42-22}

STOKER, MICHAEL (Frederick County) received a certificate from the Purchasing Agent for furnishing wheat on 6 Oct 1781 {Ref: Maryland State Archives MdHR-6636-23-28}

STONE, JOHN (Charles County) received a receipt from the Purchasing Agent for furnishing wheat on 28 Dec 1782 {Ref: Maryland State Archives MdHR-6636-42-21}; received a receipt for furnishing wheat on 8 May 1783 {Ref: Maryland State Archives MdHR-6636-42-22}

STONE, MARY (Charles County) received a receipt from the Purchasing Agent for furnishing wheat on 16 Nov 1781 {Ref: Maryland State Archives MdHR-6636-42-15}

STONE, MATTHEW (Charles County) received a receipt from the Purchasing Agent for furnishing wheat on 20 Dec 1782 {Ref: Maryland State Archives MdHR-6636-42-20}

STONE, MICHAEL T. (Charles County) received a receipt from the Purchasing Agent for furnishing wheat on 20 Dec 1782 {Ref: Maryland State Archives MdHR-6636-42-20}

STONE, NEHEMIAH (Prince George's County) received a receipt from the Purchasing Agent for furnishing wheat on 12 Feb 1782 {Ref: Maryland State Archives MdHR-6636-50-135}

STONE, SAMUEL (Charles County) received a receipt from the Purchasing Agent for furnishing wheat on 12 Nov 1782 {Ref: Maryland State Archives MdHR-6636-42-19}

STONE, WILLIAM (Somerset County) received a receipt from the Purchasing Agent for furnishing pork on 20 May 1782 {Ref: Maryland State Archives MdHR-6636-43-21}

STONE, WILLIAM (Charles County) received a receipt from the Purchasing Agent for furnishing wheat on 12 Nov 1782 {Ref: Maryland State Archives MdHR-6636-42-19}

STONER, ELIZABETH (Frederick County) received payment by order of the Council of Maryland for services rendered (not specified) on 22 Apr 1779 {Ref: Archives of Maryland 21:361}

STONER, JACOB (Frederick County) received a certificate from the Purchasing Agent for furnishing wheat on 27 Jul 1782 {Ref: Maryland State Archives MdHR-6636-42-36}

STONER, JOHN (Frederick County) was a captain who received receipts from the Purchasing Agent for furnishing corn meal on 12 Mar and 17 Mar 1781 {Ref: Maryland State Archives MdHR-6636-23-4}; received a receipt for delivering flour on 24 Feb 1781 {Ref: Maryland State Archives MdHR-6636-23-30}; received a receipt for delivering flour on 5 May 1781 {Ref: Maryland State Archives MdHR-6636-23-31}

STOREY, HENRY (Montgomery County) received a receipt from the Purchasing Agent for furnishing wheat on 10 Apr 1781 {Ref: Maryland State Archives MdHR-6636-42-11}

STORY, HENRY (Prince George's County) received a receipt from the Purchasing Agent for furnishing wheat on 7 Jun 1782 {Ref: Maryland State Archives MdHR-6636-50-135}

STOVER, BARBARY (Frederick County) received a certificate from the Purchasing Agent for furnishing wheat on 27 Nov 1782 {Ref: Maryland State Archives MdHR-6636-42-37}

STOVER, CHRISTIAN (Frederick County) submitted an account for furnishing beef on 16 May 1782 {Ref: Maryland State Archives MdHR-6636-23-6}

STOW, WILLIAM (Somerset County) received a receipt from the Purchasing Agent for furnishing pork on 15 Jul 1781 {Ref: Maryland State Archives MdHR-6636-24-43}

STRAWBRIDGE, WILLIAM (Somerset County) was a doctor who received a receipt from the Purchasing Agent for furnishing pork on 15 Aug 1780 {Ref: Maryland State Archives MdHR-6636-24-41}; received a receipt for furnishing pork on 4 Jun 1781 {Ref: Maryland State Archives MdHR-6636-24-43}

STRICKER, GEORGE (Frederick County) was a colonel who served as Collector of Horses in his county by 15 Jul 1781 {Ref: Maryland State Archives MdHR-4597-55}; receipt money from the Council of Maryland (which listed his name as "Col. George Streaker") as "appropriated for the present Campaign to be by him Accounted for" in procuring horses on 1 Aug 1781 {Ref: Archives of Maryland 45:531}; received a certificate from the Purchasing Agent for furnishing wheat on 11 Jun 1782 {Ref: Maryland State Archives MdHR-6636-42-35}; also see "Henry Yost" and "John Unseld" and "George Bane," q.v.

STRINGER, RICHARD (Frederick County) received certificates from the Purchasing Agent for furnishing wheat on 15 Nov and 20 Dec 1782 {Ref: Maryland State Archives MdHR-6636-42-37}

STROWN, THOMAS (Caroline County) received a receipt from the Purchasing Agent for furnishing wheat on 1 Sep 1782 {Ref: Maryland State Archives MdHR-6636-42-7}

STUART, ASA (Kent County) received payment from the Purchasing Agent for furnishing cattle for the public use in September, 1781 {Ref: Maryland State Archives MdHR-6636-43-3}

STUART, WILLIAM (Kent County) received payment for furnishing wheat on 29 Jul 1780 {Ref: Maryland State Archives MdHR-6636-23-49}

STUBBS, JOHN JR. (Caroline County) received a receipt from the Purchasing Agent for furnishing wheat on 17 Aug 1782 {Ref: Maryland State Archives MdHR-6636-42-7}

STUBBS, JOHN SR. (Caroline County) received a receipt from the Purchasing Agent for furnishing wheat on 17 Aug 1782 {Ref: Maryland State Archives MdHR-6636-42-7}

STUBBS, NICHOLAS (Dorchester County) received a receipt from the Purchasing Agent for furnishing wheat on 1 Nov 1782 {Ref: Maryland State Archives MdHR-6636-42-23}

STULL, CHRISTOPHER (Frederick County) received certificates from the Purchasing Agent for furnishing wheat on 20 Apr 1782 and wintering and pasturing of cattle on 23 May 1782 {Ref: Maryland State Archives MdHR-6636-42-33}

STUMP, HENRY (Harford County) received payment by order of the Council of Maryland via James Phillips for the hire of his wagon on 20 May 1778 {Ref: Archives of Maryland 21:97}

STUMP, JOHN (Cecil County) received a certificate from the Purchasing Agent for furnishing wheat on 20 Mar 1780 {Ref: Maryland State Archives MdHR-6636-23-22}

STUMP, JOHN JR. (Cecil County), son of John Stump, entered into a partnership for purchasing wheat for the public use with John Stump 3rd, son of Henry Stump who lives in Harford County, and Col. Henry Hollingsworth, on 24 Aug 1780, operating as John Stump, Jr. & Company until 15 Jan 1781; a pricing dispute arose and it was presented to the Council of Maryland that hundreds of bushels of wheat were "now on hand and stored in the dwelling house of Nathaniel Giles, lately deceased and under the care of Benjamin Fleetwood" on 29 Jan 1781 {Ref: Archives of Maryland 45:292-293}

STURGES (STURGIS), ABRAHAM (Worcester County) submitted an account and receipt for collecting cattle on 25 Sep 1781 {Ref: Maryland State Archives MdHR-6636-43-27}

STURGES (STURGIS), JOHN (Kent County) submitted an account and receipt for furnishing flour barrels, Dec 1781 to Jan 1782 {Ref: Maryland State Archives MdHR-6636-43-5}

STURGES (STURGIS), JOHN (Worcester County) submitted an account for processing pork in 1782 {Ref: Maryland State Archives MdHR-6636-43-28B}; received a receipt for processing pork on 1 May 1782 {Ref: Maryland State Archives MdHR-6636-43-28C}

STURGES (STURGIS), JOSHUA (Worcester County) received a receipt from the Purchasing Agent for furnishing corn on 7 Mar 1780 {Ref: Maryland State Archives MdHR-6636-24-52}; his name appeared on "A List of Corn Purchased in Worcester County for the use of the State of Maryland" by the Commissary in July, 1780 {Ref: Archives of Maryland 45:10}

STURGES (STURGIS), LEVIN (Worcester County) submitted an account and receipt for furnishing pork barrels in 1782 {Ref: Maryland State Archives MdHR-6636-43-28V}

STURGES (STURGIS), OUTTON (Worcester County) received a receipt from the Purchasing Agent for furnishing corn on 8 Mar 1780 {Ref: Maryland State Archives MdHR-6636-24-52}; his name appeared on "A List of Corn Purchased in Worcester County for the use of the State of Maryland" by the Commissary in July, 1780 {Ref: Archives of Maryland 45:10}

STURGES (STURGIS), ZADOCK (Worcester County) submitted an account and receipt for collecting cattle on 25 Oct 1781 {Ref: Maryland State Archives MdHR-6636-43-27}

SUDLER, JOHN (Kent County) submitted an account and receipts for furnishing nails on 8 Dec 1781, 26 Dec 1781 and 4 Feb 1782 {Ref: Maryland State Archives MdHR-6636-43-5}

SULLIVAN, FLETCHER (Caroline County) received a receipt from the Purchasing Agent for furnishing wheat on 5 Aug 1782 {Ref: Maryland State Archives MdHR-6636-42-7}

SULLIVAN (SULLIVANE), JAMES (Dorchester County) was appointed by the Council of Maryland on 25 Mar 1778 as one of eighteen men to be "Agents for Purchasing Provisions for the Army of the United States Agreeable to an Act of Assembly passed the 23rd Inst." {Ref: Archives of Maryland 16:551}; submitted an account for provisions purchased for the army on 23 Apr 1778 {Ref: Maryland State Archives MdHR-4588-2}; appointed Purchaser of Clothing in his county by the Council of Maryland on 5 Jun 1781 {Ref: Archives of Maryland 45:462}

SULLIVAN, JOHN (Caroline County) received a receipt from the Purchasing Agent for furnishing wheat on 5 Aug 1782 {Ref: Maryland State Archives MdHR-6636-42-7}

SULLIVAN, JOHN, OF JOHN (Caroline County) received a receipt from the Purchasing Agent for furnishing wheat on 15 Jun 1782 {Ref: Maryland State Archives MdHR-6636-42-7}

SULLIVAN, WILLIAM (Caroline County) received a receipt from the Purchasing

Agent for furnishing wheat on 5 Aug 1782 {Ref: Maryland State Archives MdHR-6636-42-7}

SULLIVANE, DANIEL, Esquire (Dorchester County) received a loan certificate for £33.8.10 due from the Council of Maryland "agreeable to the Act proposing to the Citizens of this State, Creditors of Congress on Loan Office Certificates, Etc." on 10 Dec 1783 for services rendered during the war {Ref: Archives of Maryland 48:487}

SUMMERS, DENT (Montgomery County) received a receipt from the Purchasing Agent for furnishing wheat on 10 Aug 1780 {Ref: Maryland State Archives MdHR-6636-24-6}

SUMMERS, HEZEKIAH (Montgomery County) received a receipt from the Purchasing Agent for furnishing wheat on 10 Aug 1780 {Ref: Maryland State Archives MdHR-6636-24-6}

SUMMERS, SARAH (Somerset County) received a certificate from the Purchasing Agent for lodging provided for the Dorchester County militia in Somerset County on 7 Mar 1781 {Ref: Maryland State Archives MdHR-6636-43-15}

SUMMERS, WILLIAM (Montgomery County) received a receipt from the Purchasing Agent for furnishing wheat on 16 Aug 1780 {Ref: Maryland State Archives MdHR-6636-24-6}; received a receipt for furnishing wheat on 13 Oct 1781 {Ref: Maryland State Archives MdHR-6636-24-15}; received a receipt for furnishing wheat on 26 Aug 1783 {Ref: Maryland State Archives MdHR-6636-50-135}

SUTER, GEORGE (Montgomery County) received a receipt from the Purchasing Agent for furnishing wheat on 29 May 1781 {Ref: Maryland State Archives MdHR-6636-42-11}; received a receipt for furnishing wheat on 5 Oct 1781 {Ref: Maryland State Archives MdHR-6636-24-15}

SUTER, JAMES (Montgomery County) received a certificate from the Purchasing Agent for furnishing wheat on 28 Jul 1780 {Ref: Maryland State Archives MdHR-6636-24-5}; received a receipt for furnishing wheat on 1 Aug 1780 {Ref: Maryland State Archives MdHR-6636-43-7}

SUTER, JOHN (Montgomery County) received a receipt from the Purchasing Agent for furnishing wheat on 28 Jul 1780 {Ref: Maryland State Archives MdHR-6636-24-5}; received a receipt for furnishing wheat on 1 Aug 1780 {Ref: Maryland State Archives MdHR-6636-43-7}; received a receipt for furnishing wheat on 11 Sep 1780 {Ref: Maryland State Archives MdHR-6636-24-7}

SUTHERIN, DANIEL (Caroline County) received a receipt from the Purchasing Agent for furnishing wheat on 5 Aug 1782 {Ref: Maryland State Archives MdHR-6636-42-7}

SUTHERLAND, JOHN (Prince George's County) received a receipt from the

Purchasing Agent for furnishing wheat on 9 Aug 1783 {Ref: Maryland State Archives MdHR-6636-50-135}; received receipts for furnishing wheat on 12 Feb, 24 Feb and 1 May 1783 {Ref: Maryland State Archives MdHR-6636-50-142}

SWAIN, THOMAS (Prince George's County) received a receipt from the Purchasing Agent for furnishing wheat on 9 May 1783 {Ref: Maryland State Archives MdHR-6636-43-9}

SWAN, JAMES (Charles County) received a receipt from the Purchasing Agent for furnishing wheat on 8 May 1783 {Ref: Maryland State Archives MdHR-6636-42-22}

SWAN, JAMES (Kent County) submitted an account and receipt for furnishing hay on 1 Dec 1781 {Ref: Maryland State Archives MdHR-6636-43-5}

SWAN, MATTHEW (Baltimore County) delivered barrels of shad and herring to the commissary at Baltimore Town for the use of the State of Maryland in the summer of 1780 {Ref: Archives of Maryland 45:84, 45:119}; received a receipt from the Purchasing Agent for furnishing flour on 18 Aug 1781 {Ref: Maryland State Archives MdHR-6636-28-121B}

SWEARINGEN, THOMAS (Montgomery County) received a receipt from the Purchasing Agent for furnishing wheat on 6 Sep 1780 {Ref: Maryland State Archives MdHR-6636-24-7}

SWEARINGEN, VAN (Frederick County) was a commissioner who submitted an account for grain purchased for the Continental Army on 9 Mar and 8 Apr 1780 {Ref: Maryland State Archives MdHR-6636-17-86A&B}; received a receipt for furnishing corn on 15 Feb and 17 Mar 1780 {Ref: Maryland State Archives MdHR-6636-23-33}; received a receipt for furnishing flour, corn meal and rye on 19 Nov 1780 and 28 Mar 1781 {Ref: Maryland State Archives MdHR-6636-23-33}; received a receipt for grinding wheat on 27 Jan 1782 {Ref: Maryland State Archives MdHR-6636-42-37}; received a receipt for furnishing wheat on 27 May 1782 {Ref: Maryland State Archives MdHR-6636-42-33}

SWIFT, LUKE (Harford County) received payment for furnishing a gun to the Committee of Safety on 18 Jun 1776 {Ref: Preston's History of Harford County, p. 330}

SWIFT, SAMUEL (Caroline County) received a receipt from the Purchasing Agent for furnishing wheat on 1 Sep 1782 {Ref: Maryland State Archives MdHR-6636-42-7}

SWIGATE, BEN (Caroline County) received a receipt from the Purchasing Agent for furnishing wheat on 5 Aug 1782 {Ref: Maryland State Archives MdHR-6636-42-7}

SYLVESTER, BENJAMIN (Caroline County) received a certificate from the Purchasing Agent for furnishing wheat on 12 Feb 1780 {Ref: Maryland State Archives MdHR-6636-23-19}; received a certificate for storing wheat on 3 Jun

1780 {Ref: Maryland State Archives MdHR-6636-23-20}
TABBS, BARTON (Charles County) was a doctor who received payment by order of the Council of Safety for his medical attendance at St. George's Camp on 16 Sep 1776 {Ref: Archives of Maryland 12:274}; received payment for his services on 28 Apr 1777 {Ref: Archives of Maryland 16:231}
TALBOT, EDWARD (Harford County) received a certificate from the Purchasing Agent for furnishing wheat on 31 Jan 1780 {Ref: Maryland State Archives MdHR-6636-23-36}
TALBOTT, THOMAS (Prince George's County) received a receipt from the Purchasing Agent for furnishing wheat in 1782 {Ref: Maryland State Archives MdHR-6636-50-135}
TALBOTT, WILLIAM (Montgomery County) received a receipt from the Purchasing Agent for furnishing wheat on 21 Aug 1780 {Ref: Maryland State Archives MdHR-6636-24-6}; received a receipt for furnishing wheat on 30 Aug 1780 {Ref: Maryland State Archives MdHR-6636-24-6}; received a receipt for furnishing wheat on 9 Sep 1780 {Ref: Maryland State Archives MdHR-6636-24-7}
TALBUT, WILLIAM (Montgomery County) received a receipt from the Purchasing Agent for furnishing wheat on 1 Aug 1780 {Ref: Maryland State Archives MdHR-6636-43-7}
TALLBOY, WILLIAM (Caroline County) received a receipt from the Purchasing Agent for furnishing wheat on 20 Sep 1782 {Ref: Maryland State Archives MdHR-6636-42-7}
TARGO, JACOB (Frederick County) received a receipt from the Purchasing Agent for furnishing hay on 19 Dec 1780 {Ref: Maryland State Archives MdHR-6636-23-1}
TARLTON, JEREMIAH (St. Mary's County) received payment from the Purchasing Agent on 23 Dec 1781 for collecting and driving public cattle for 11 days {Ref: Maryland State Archives MdHR-6636-43-23}
TARLTON, JOHN (St. Mary's County) appeared on "A Return of Beef on the Hoof Purchased by Joseph Ford Commissary of Purchases" on 8 Oct 1780 when he delivered a steer for the use of the state {Ref: Archives of Maryland 45:156}
TATE, JOHN (Prince George's County) received a receipt from the Purchasing Agent for furnishing wheat on 25 Mar 1783 {Ref: Maryland State Archives MdHR-6636-50-135}
TAYLOR, JAMES (county not stated) received payments by order of the Council of Safety for making gun carriages on 1 May and 18 Jul 1776 and for furnishing a musquet on 6 Aug 1776 {Ref: Archives of Maryland 11:395, 12:71, 12:174}
TAYLOR, JESSE JR. (Charles County) received payment from the Council of

319

Maryland for clothing goods furnished to the Purchaser of Clothing on 4 Sep 1781 and said money to be delivered over to his father Jesse Taylor, Sr. {Ref: Archives of Maryland 45:600}

TAYLOR, JNO. (Baltimore County) submitted an account and received payment for hauling flour for the use of the army on 28 Jan 1780 {Ref: Maryland Historical Society MS.1814, Box 6}

TAYLOR, JOHN (Charles County) received a receipt from the Purchasing Agent for furnishing wheat on 11 Dec 1781 {Ref: Maryland State Archives MdHR-6636-42-15}

TAYLOR, JOHN (Baltimore County) submitted an account and received payment for one day's drayage of flour for the use of the army on 28 Jan 1780 {Ref: Maryland Historical Society MS.1814, Box 6}

TAYLOR, JOHN (Prince George's County) received a receipt from the Purchasing Agent for furnishing wheat on 12 Jun 1782 {Ref: Maryland State Archives MdHR-6636-50-135}

TAYLOR, PHILLIP (Kent County) received payment from the Purchasing Agent for furnishing cattle and pasturage for the public use in September, 1781 and for purchasing beef cattle for the public use in October, 1782 {Ref: Maryland State Archives MdHR-6636-43-3}

TAYLOR, RICHARD (Baltimore County) received a receipt from the Purchasing Agent for hauling wheat on 23 Jul 1779 {Ref: Maryland State Archives MdHR-6636-21-67}

TAYLOR, RICHARD (Worcester County) received payment for furnishing beef on 26 Sep 1781 {Ref: Maryland State Archives MdHR-6636-43-28UUU}

TAYLOR, THOMAS (Kent County) submitted an account and receipt for riding express and for furnishing flour barrels and nails on 20 Dec to 26 Dec 1781 {Ref: Maryland State Archives MdHR-6636-43-5}; received payment for collecting cattle for the public use in November, 1782 {Ref: Maryland State Archives MdHR-6636-43-3}

TAYLOR, WILLIAM (Montgomery County) received a receipt from the Purchasing Agent for furnishing wheat on 9 Feb 1781 {Ref: Maryland State Archives MdHR-6636-24-9}

TENCH, JOSHUA (Charles County) received a receipt from the Purchasing Agent for furnishing wheat on 20 Dec 1782 {Ref: Maryland State Archives MdHR-6636-42-20}

TENLY, THOMAS (Frederick County) received a receipt from the Purchasing Agent for furnishing corn on 12 Jan 1781 {Ref: Maryland State Archives MdHR-6636-23-2}

THAWLEY, EDWARD (Caroline County) received a receipt from the Purchasing Agent for furnishing wheat on 1 Sep 1782 {Ref: Maryland State Archives MdHR-6636-42-7}

THAWLEY, JOHN (Caroline County) received a receipt from the Purchasing Agent for furnishing wheat on 1 Sep 1782 {Ref: Maryland State Archives MdHR-6636-42-7}

THOMAS, CLEMENT (Charles County) received a receipt from the Purchasing Agent for furnishing wheat on 20 Dec 1782 {Ref: Maryland State Archives MdHR-6636-42-20}

THOMAS, EDWARD (Frederick County) received a receipt from the Purchasing Agent for furnishing pork delivery on 14 Mar 1781 {Ref: Maryland State Archives MdHR-6636-23-30}; received a certificate for furnishing beef on 16 Jun 1781 {Ref: Maryland State Archives MdHR-6636-42-32}

THOMAS, FRANCIS (Frederick County) received a receipt from the Purchasing Agent for furnishing beef on 18 Feb 1781 {Ref: Maryland State Archives MdHR-6636-23-3}; submitted an account for furnishing beef and bacon on 29 May 1781 {Ref: Maryland State Archives MdHR-6636-23-6}

THOMAS, HENRY (Harford County) received a receipt from the Purchasing Agent for furnishing wheat on 22 Mar and 27 Jun 1780 {Ref: Maryland State Archives MdHR-6636-23-35}

THOMAS, ISAAC (Cecil County) received a receipt from the Purchasing Agent for furnishing wheat on 20 Jan 1783 {Ref: Maryland State Archives MdHR-6636-42-9}

THOMAS, JACOB (Frederick County) received a certificate from the Purchasing Agent for furnishing wheat on 27 May 1782 {Ref: Maryland State Archives MdHR-6636-42-33}

THOMAS, JOHN (Dorchester County) received a receipt from the Purchasing Agent for furnishing wheat on 1 Oct 1782 {Ref: Maryland State Archives MdHR-6636-42-23}

THOMAS, JOHN (Talbot County) received a receipt from the Purchasing Agent for furnishing wheat on 29 Oct and 5 Nov 1780 {Ref: Maryland State Archives MdHR-6636-24-47}

THOMAS, JOHN ALLEN (St. Mary's County) was a captain who was requested by the Maryland Council of Safety to purchase all the buckshot he could procure in St. Mary's County on 22 Apr 1776 {Ref: Archives of Maryland 11:367}; appointed one of eighteen Collectors of Clothing by the Council of Maryland under "An Act to Procure Cloathing for the Quota of this State of the American Army" on 27 Nov 1777 {Ref: Archives of Maryland 16:426}; appointed by the Council of Maryland on 25 Mar 1778 as one of eighteen men to be "Agents for Purchasing Provisions for the Army of the United States Agreeable to an Act of Assembly passed the 23rd Inst." and was listed in the record as "Capt. John Thomas" {Ref: Archives of Maryland 16:551}

THOMAS, NATHANIEL (Caroline County) received a receipt from the Purchasing Agent for furnishing wheat on 24 Aug 1782 {Ref: Maryland State

Archives MdHR-6636-42-7}

THOMAS, PHILIP (Frederick County) was a doctor who received money from the Council of Maryland to be expended in the purchase of wagons on 1 Sep 1781 {Ref: Archives of Maryland 45:595}; received a certificate from the Purchasing Agent for wintering a cow on 30 May 1782 {Ref: Maryland State Archives MdHR-6636-42-36}; received a certificate for furnishing wheat on 17 Jun 1782 {Ref: Maryland State Archives MdHR-6636-42-35}; received a certificate for furnishing wheat on 21 Oct 1782 {Ref: Maryland State Archives MdHR-6636-42-37}; also see "Barton Philpot," q.v.

THOMAS, ROBERT (Montgomery County) received a receipt from the Purchasing Agent for furnishing wheat on 9 Aug 1780 {Ref: Maryland State Archives MdHR-6636-24-6}

THOMAS, SALISBURY (Charles County) received a receipt from the Purchasing Agent for furnishing wheat on 20 Dec 1782 {Ref: Maryland State Archives MdHR-6636-42-20}

THOMAS, SAMUEL (Cecil County) pledged a loan in the amount of £200 to the State of Maryland under the Act for the Emission of Bills of Credit "to defray the expences of the present campaign" in October, 1781 {Ref: Archives of Maryland 47:533}

THOMAS, SAMUEL (Frederick County) received a receipt from the Purchasing Agent for furnishing corn, rye and flour on 14 Jun 1781 {Ref: Maryland State Archives MdHR-6636-24-1}

THOMAS, SAMUEL (Talbot County) submitted an account and a receipt for the hire of his wagon on 6 May 1778 and for hauling bacon on 15 May 1778 {Ref: Maryland State Archives MdHR-6636-12-15}; received a certificate from the Purchasing Agent for furnishing wheat on 7 Apr 1780 {Ref: Archives of Maryland 43:475; Maryland State Archives MdHR-6636-24-50}; received a certificate for furnishing wheat on 7 Dec 1781 {Ref: Maryland State Archives MdHR-6636-24-34}

THOMAS, SAMUEL (Montgomery County) collected and transported grain for the use of the state on 21 Feb 1780 {Ref: Maryland State Archives MdHR-6636-17-62}; received a certificate and receipts for furnishing wheat on 25 Mar, 7 Apr and 28 Apr 1780 {Ref: Maryland State Archives MdHR-6636-24-50}; received a receipt for furnishing wheat on 29 Jul 1780 {Ref: Maryland State Archives MdHR-6636-24-5}; received a receipt for furnishing wheat on 1 Aug 1780 {Ref: Maryland State Archives MdHR-6636-43-7}; received a receipt for furnishing wheat on or about 1 Jan 1781 {Ref: Maryland State Archives MdHR-6636-42-11}

THOMAS, SAMUEL 3RD (Montgomery County) served as Contractor for Horses by appointment from the Council of Maryland in 1780 {Ref: Archives of Maryland 43:321}

THOMAS, TRISTRAM (Queen Anne's County) received a certificate from the Purchasing Agent for furnishing wheat on 18 Jan 1780 {Ref: Maryland State Archives MdHR-6636-24-31}; received a certificate for furnishing beef on 8 Oct 1781 {Ref: Maryland State Archives MdHR-6636-24-34}

THOMAS, WILLIAM (Frederick County) received a certificate from the Purchasing Agent for furnishing wheat on 17 Sep 1781 {Ref: Maryland State Archives MdHR-6636-23-28}

THOMAS, WILLIAM (Talbot County) received a receipt from the Purchasing Agent for furnishing beef on 5 Oct 1780 {Ref: Maryland State Archives MdHR-6636-24-49}

THOMAS, WILLIAM (county not stated) received payments by order of the Council of Safety for the hire of his boat and furnishing boatage for the Flying Camp on 15 Aug, 23 Aug and 30 Aug 1776 {Ref: Archives of Maryland 12:205, 233, 247}

THOMAS, WILLIAM (county not stated) received a loan certificate for £36.11.9 due from the Council of Maryland "agreeable to the Act proposing to the Citizens of this State, Creditors of Congress on Loan Office Certificates, Etc." on 19 Dec 1783 for services rendered during the war {Ref: Archives of Maryland 48:494}

THOMPSON, BASIL (Prince George's County) received a receipt from the Purchasing Agent for furnishing wheat in 1782 {Ref: Maryland State Archives MdHR-6636-50-135}

THOMPSON, EDWARD (Dorchester County) received a receipt from the Purchasing Agent for furnishing wheat on 1 Nov 1782 {Ref: Maryland State Archives MdHR-6636-42-23}

THOMPSON, JOHN (Cecil County) received a receipt from the Purchasing Agent for furnishing flour on 12 Mar 1780 {Ref: Maryland State Archives MdHR-6636-24-25}

THOMPSON, JOHN (Queen Anne's County) was a colonel who was appointed by the Council of Maryland as one of thirty men to be "Agents for Purchasing Provisions" on 30 Mar 1779 {Ref: Archives of Maryland 21:332}; received a receipt from the commissary for furnishing bacon on 8 May 1778 {Ref: Maryland State Archives MdHR-4587-34}; submitted an account of flour from John Rolling's mill on 12 Mar 1780 {Ref: Maryland State Archives MdHR-6636-24-22}; submitted his account for grain and barrels on 1 Jun 1780 {Ref: Maryland State Archives MdHR-6636-24-26}

THOMPSON, JOHN (St. Mary's County) received payment from the Purchasing Agent on 23 Dec 1781 for collecting and driving public cattle for 26 days {Ref: Maryland State Archives MdHR-6636-43-23}

THOMPSON, JOHN BAPTIST (Montgomery County) received receipts from the Purchasing Agent for furnishing wheat on 10 Apr and 8 Oct 1781 {Ref:

Maryland State Archives MdHR-6636-24-15}

THOMPSON, JOHN D. (Cecil County) requested compensation for procuring provisions on 28 Feb 1781 {Ref: Maryland State Archives MdHR-4601-54}

THOMPSON, RICHARD (county not stated) received payment by order of the Council of Maryland "for rent of houses per account passed" on 4 Feb 1778 {Ref: Archives of Maryland 16:483}

THOMPSON, SAMUEL JR. (Queen Anne's County) was appointed by the Council of Safety to collect all the gold and silver coin that could be procured in the county in compliance with the Resolve of Congress on 27 Jan 1776 {Ref: Archives of Maryland 11:132}

THOMPSON, WILLIAM (Montgomery County) received a receipt from the Purchasing Agent for furnishing wheat on 1 May 1781 {Ref: Maryland State Archives MdHR-6636-24-18}

THRASHER, ROBERT (Montgomery County) received a receipt from the Purchasing Agent for furnishing wheat on 24 Aug 1780 {Ref: Maryland State Archives MdHR-6636-24-6}

THRASHER, THOMAS (Montgomery County) received a loan certificate for £23.17.8 due from the Council of Maryland "agreeable to the Act proposing to the Citizens of this State, Creditors of Congress on Loan Office Certificates, Etc." on 17 Jun 1783 for services rendered during the war {Ref: Archives of Maryland 48:432}

THRIFT, JOHN (Kent County) received receipts from the Purchasing Agent for furnishing wheat on 25 Oct and 7 Nov 1780 {Ref: Maryland State Archives MdHR-6636-23-49}

THULKIELD, HUGH (Montgomery County) received a receipt from the Purchasing Agent for furnishing wheat on 29 Nov 1780 {Ref: Maryland State Archives MdHR-6636-24-13}

TIAN, CHARLES (Charles County) received a receipt from the Purchasing Agent for furnishing wheat on 18 May 1782 {Ref: Maryland State Archives MdHR-6636-42-18}

TIAN, JOSEPH (Charles County) received a receipt from the Purchasing Agent for furnishing wheat on 14 Sep 1782 {Ref: Maryland State Archives MdHR-6636-42-18}

TIAN, WILLIAM (Charles County) received a receipt from the Purchasing Agent for furnishing wheat on 18 Nov 1782 {Ref: Maryland State Archives MdHR-6636-42-19}

TIBBETS (TIBBELS?), HENRY (Talbot County) was one of twenty-six people who contacted the Governor and Council of Maryland in 1781 and pledged to support and maintain at their own expense the Barge *Experiment* so it can patrol the bay between Kent Point and Tilghman's Island in order to protect them against the enemy, stating in part, "whereas from the present exhausted state of the public treasury the government cannot immediately give that protection to every individual which is become necessary from the cruel and savage mode in which the war is now carried on against us" {Ref: Archives of Maryland 47:584-585}

TIBBETS (TIBBELS?), THOMAS (Talbot County) was one of twenty-six people who contacted the Governor and Council of Maryland in 1781 and pledged to support and maintain at their own expense the Barge *Experiment* so it can patrol the bay between Kent Point and Tilghman's Island in order to protect them against the enemy, stating in part, "whereas from the present exhausted state of the public treasury the government cannot immediately give that protection to every individual which is become necessary from the cruel and savage mode in which the war is now carried on against us" {Ref: Archives of Maryland 47:584-585}

TIBELL, HENRY (Talbot County) received payment by order of the Council of Safety for boarding sick soldiers on 17 Aug 1776 {Ref: Archives of Maryland 12:215}

TILDEN (TILDON), CHARLES (Kent County) received payment from the Purchasing Agent for furnishing cattle and pasturage for the public use in September, 1781 {Ref: Maryland State Archives MdHR-6636-43-3}

TILDEN, WILLIAM (Kent County) received a certificate from the Purchasing Agent for furnishing wheat on 20 Feb 1780 {Ref: Maryland State Archives MdHR-6636-43-1}

TILGHMAN, EDWARD (Queen Anne's County) received a certificate from the Purchasing Agent for furnishing wheat on 18 Jan 1780 {Ref: Maryland State Archives MdHR-6636-24-32}

TILGHMAN, EDWARD JR. (Queen Anne's County) received a certificate from the Purchasing Agent for furnishing wheat on 18 Jan 1780 {Ref: Maryland State Archives MdHR-6636-24-32}

TILGHMAN, JAMES (Queenstown, Queen Anne's County) received a receipt from the Purchasing Agent for furnishing beef on 22 Dec 1779 {Ref: Maryland State Archives MdHR-6636-17-73}

TILGHMAN, JAMES (Talbot County) was one of twenty-six people who contacted the Governor and Council of Maryland in 1781 and pledged to support and maintain at their own expense the Barge *Experiment* so it can patrol the bay between Kent Point and Tilghman's Island in order to protect them against the enemy, stating in part, "whereas from the present exhausted state of the public treasury the government cannot immediately give that protection to every individual which is become necessary from the cruel and savage mode in which the war is now carried on against us" {Ref: Archives of Maryland 47:584-585}

TILGHMAN, JAMES JR. (Talbot County) received a certificate from the

Purchasing Agent for furnishing wheat on 29 Jan 1780 {Ref: Maryland State Archives MdHR-6636-24-46}

TILGHMAN, MATTHEW (Talbot County) was a colonel who received payment by order of the Council of Safety for the hire of his boat for the Flying Camp on 22 Aug 1776 {Ref: Archives of Maryland 12:232}; received a receipt for meat purchased on 22 May 1778 {Ref: Maryland State Archives MdHR-6636-12-15}; received payment for furnishing beef on 23 Sep 1780 {Ref: Maryland State Archives MdHR-6636-24-49}; received payment for a delivery of provisions on 2 May 1781 {Ref: Maryland State Archives MdHR-19969-3-20}; submitted an account of purchase and storage of provisions on 16 Oct 1781 {Ref: Maryland State Archives MdHR-4603-32}; he was one of twenty-six people who contacted the Governor and Council of Maryland in 1781 and pledged to support and maintain at their own expense the Barge *Experiment* so it can patrol the bay between Kent Point and Tilghman's Island in order to protect them against the enemy, stating in part, "whereas from the present exhausted state of the public treasury the government cannot immediately give that protection to every individual which is become necessary from the cruel and savage mode in which the war is now carried on against us" {Ref: Archives of Maryland 47:584-585}

TILGHMAN, PEREGRINE (Talbot County) was a colonel who was appointed by the Council of Maryland on 25 Mar 1778 as one of eighteen men to be "Agents for Purchasing Provisions for the Army of the United States Agreeable to an Act of Assembly passed the 23rd Inst." and noted in the record as "resigned" {Ref: Archives of Maryland 16:551}; received certificates and receipts for furnishing wheat, flour, rye and corn on 16 Jan, 29 Jan, 1 Feb, 1 Mar, 2 Mar, 7 Mar, 25 Mar, 7 Apr, 10 Apr, 1 May, 3 May and 27 May 1780 {Ref: Archives of Maryland 43:475; Maryland State Archives MdHR-6636-24-46}; submitted an account for transportation, storage and seizure of corn on 7 Mar 1780 {Ref: Maryland State Archives MdHR-6636-17-80}; he was one of twenty-six people who contacted the Governor and Council of Maryland in 1781 and pledged to support and maintain at their own expense the Barge *Experiment* so it can patrol the bay between Kent Point and Tilghman's Island in order to protect them against the enemy, stating in part, "whereas from the present exhausted state of the public treasury the government cannot immediately give that protection to every individual which is become necessary from the cruel and savage mode in which the war is now carried on against us" {Ref: Archives of Maryland 47:584-585}

TILGHMAN, RICHARD JR. (Queen Anne's County) received a certificate from the Purchasing Agent for furnishing wheat on 26 Jan 1780 {Ref: Maryland State Archives MdHR-6636-24-30}

TILGHMAN, RICHARD IV (Queen Anne's County) received a certificate from the Purchasing Agent for furnishing bacon on 19 Mar 1781 {Ref: Maryland State Archives MdHR-6636-24-34}

TILGHMAN, TENCH, see "Jonathan Parker," q.v.

TILGHMAN, WILLIAM JR. (Queen Anne's County) received a certificate from the Purchasing Agent for furnishing wheat on 21 Feb 1780 {Ref: Maryland State Archives MdHR-6636-24-29}

TIMMINS (TIMMONS, TIMMONDS), EDWARD (Harford County) contracted with the Maryland Council of Safety for making steel ramrods on 21 Mar 1776 {Ref: Archives of Maryland 11:272}; received payment by order of the Council of Safety for repairing guns for the militia on 19 Jul, 23 Jul and 3 Oct 1776 {Ref: Archives of Maryland 12:77, 233, 317}; received payment for furnishing a gun on 15 Feb 1777 {Ref: Archives of Maryland 16:138}

TIPLETT, MARY (Baltimore Town) received payment by order of the Council of Safety for attending the barracks on 24 Aug 1776 {Ref: Archives of Maryland 12:234}; also see "Mary Tripolett," q.v.

TODD, NATHAN (Caroline County) received a receipt from the Purchasing Agent for furnishing wheat on 4 Jun 1782 {Ref: Maryland State Archives MdHR-6636-42-7}

TOLLAN, THOMAS (Prince George's County) received a receipt from the Purchasing Agent for furnishing wheat on 10 Dec 1782 {Ref: Maryland State Archives MdHR-6636-50-135}

TOLSON, THOMAS (Baltimore County) received payment for hauling bread on 4 Jul 1781 {Ref: Maryland State Archives MdHR-6636-43-38MM}

TOMLINSON, HUGH (Frederick County) received receipts from the Purchasing Agent for furnishing corn on 1 Apr, 7 Apr, 11 Apr, 14 Apr, 18 Apr, 25 Apr, 28 Apr, 5 May, 12 May, 16 May, 23 May and 20 Oct 1780, and a receipt for furnishing corn and rye on 13 Jun 1780 {Ref: Maryland State Archives MdHR-6636-24-1&2}; received a receipt for furnishing wheat on 20 Oct 1780 {Ref: Maryland State Archives MdHR-6636-24-8}

TOOTLE (TOOTELL), JAMES (Anne Arundel County) was a captain who received payment by order of the Council of Safety for building a magazine near Annapolis on 15 May 1776 {Ref: Archives of Maryland 11:427, 439}; appointed one of eighteen Collectors of Clothing by the Council of Maryland under "An Act to Procure Cloathing for the Quota of this State of the American Army" on 27 Nov 1777 {Ref: Archives of Maryland 16:426}

TOOTLE (TOOTELL), RICHARD (Anne Arundel County) was a doctor who was requested to remove any soldiers of infectious disorders to be nursed in private houses by order of the Council of Safety on 17 Sep 1776 {Ref: Archives of Maryland 12:276}; Mrs. Tootell and Robert Couden, executors of Dr. Richard Tootell, received a loan certificate for £76.19.6 due from the Council of Maryland "agreeable to the Act proposing to the Citizens of this State,

327

Creditors of Congress on Loan Office Certificates, Etc." on 4 Mar 1783 for services rendered during the war {Ref: Archives of Maryland 48:373}

TOPPING, JAMES (Montgomery County) received a receipt from the Purchasing Agent for furnishing wheat on 1 Nov 1781 {Ref: Maryland State Archives MdHR-6636-24-14}

TOULSON, JOHN (Cecil County) received a certificate for money loaned to the state on 5 Aug 1780 {Ref: Maryland State Archives MdHR-6636-54-21}

TOWERS, JAMES (Caroline County) received receipts from the Purchasing Agent for furnishing wheat on 5 Aug and 22 Aug 1782 {Ref: Maryland State Archives MdHR-6636-42-7}

TOWERS, SOLOMON (Caroline County) received a receipt from the Purchasing Agent for furnishing wheat on 17 Aug 1782 {Ref: Maryland State Archives MdHR-6636-42-7}

TOWERS, THOMAS (Caroline County) received receipts from the Purchasing Agent for furnishing wheat on 5 Aug 1782 {Ref: Maryland State Archives MdHR-6636-42-7}

TOWNLEY, BRUCE (Prince George's County) received a receipt from the Purchasing Agent for furnishing wheat on 9 Aug 1783 {Ref: Maryland State Archives MdHR-6636-50-135}

TOWNSAND, BENJAMIN (Caroline County) received a receipt from the Purchasing Agent for furnishing wheat on 17 Aug 1782 {Ref: Maryland State Archives MdHR-6636-42-7}

TOWNSEND, JOHN (Worcester County) submitted an account and receipt for driving cattle on 30 Nov 1781 {Ref: Maryland State Archives MdHR-6636-43-27}

TOWNSEND, JOSHUA (Worcester County) was a major who received a receipt from the Purchasing Agent for furnishing corn on 21 Apr 1780 {Ref: Maryland State Archives MdHR-6636-24-52}; his name appeared on "A List of Corn Purchased in Worcester County for the use of the State of Maryland" by the Commissary in July, 1780 {Ref: Archives of Maryland 45:10}; submitted an account for procurement of provisions on 21 May 1781 {Ref: Maryland State Archives MdHR-6636-43-27}; submitted an account and receipt for furnishing provisions on 1 Oct 1781 {Ref: Maryland State Archives MdHR-6636-43-28X}; received a receipt for processing cattle on 1 Jan 1782 {Ref: Maryland State Archives MdHR-6636-43-28E}; submitted an account and receipt for furnishing salt in 1782 {Ref: Maryland State Archives MdHR-6636-43-28Q}; submitted an account and receipt for furnishing pork on 1 Oct 1782 {Ref: Maryland State Archives MdHR-6636-43-30J}; submitted an account for storing and packing pork on 1 Dec 1782 {Ref: Maryland State Archives MdHR-6636-43-28R}; submitted an account for storing provisions on 1 Dec 1782 {Ref: Maryland State Archives MdHR-6636-43-28G}

TOWNSEND, LEVIN (Worcester County) submitted an account and receipt for driving cattle on 30 Nov 1781 {Ref: Maryland State Archives MdHR-6636-43-27}

TOWNSHEND, ROSE (Charles County) received a receipt from the Purchasing Agent for furnishing wheat on 3 Aug 1782 {Ref: Maryland State Archives MdHR-6636-42-18}

TOWSON, WILLIAM (Baltimore County) submitted an account and receipt of flour for General Washington on 20 Jan 1780 {Ref: Maryland State Archives MdHR-6636-23-37}; submitted an account and received payment on 1 Feb 1780 for twelve days service as wagon master from 10 Jan to 22 Jan 1780 {Ref: Maryland Historical Society MS.1814, Box 6}

TRAIL, BASIL (Montgomery County) received a receipt from the Purchasing Agent for furnishing wheat on 15 Apr 1781 {Ref: Maryland State Archives MdHR-6636-42-11}

TRAIL, DAVID JR. (Montgomery County) received a receipt from the Purchasing Agent for furnishing wheat on 17 Apr 1781 {Ref: Maryland State Archives MdHR-6636-42-11}

TRAIL, DAVID SR. (Frederick and Montgomery Counties) received a receipt from the Purchasing Agent for furnishing wheat on 4 Sep 1780 {Ref: Maryland State Archives MdHR-6636-24-7}; received a receipt for furnishing wheat on 14 Apr 1781 {Ref: Maryland State Archives MdHR-6636-42-11}; submitted an account for furnishing pork on 1 May 1781 {Ref: Maryland State Archives MdHR-6636-23-5}

TRAIL, JAMES JR. (Montgomery County) received a receipt from the Purchasing Agent for furnishing wheat on 1 Aug 1780 {Ref: Maryland State Archives MdHR-6636-43-7}

TRALE, FRANCES (Montgomery County) received a receipt from the Purchasing Agent for furnishing wheat on 1 Aug 1780 {Ref: Maryland State Archives MdHR-6636-43-7}

TRAPNALL, JAMES (Harford County) received a receipt from the Purchasing Agent for furnishing flour at Susquehanna Lower Ferry on 23 Jan 1780 {Ref: Maryland State Archives MdHR-6636-23-37}

TRIGOE (TRIGGY), JOSHUA (Talbot County) received payment by order of the Council of Safety for carrying troops to the Head of Elk in Cecil County on 17 Aug 1776 {Ref: Archives of Maryland 12:215}; received payment by order of the Council of Safety for furnishing boatage on 9 Sep 1776 {Ref: Archives of Maryland 12:262}

TRINDEL, JOHN (Anne Arundel County) received a receipt from the Purchasing Agent for furnishing powder on 16 Apr 1777 {Ref: Maryland State Archives MdHR-6636-9-14G}

TRIPOLET, MAGDALEN (Baltimore Town) received payment by order of the

329

Council of Maryland "for the rent of her houses for barracks" on 14 Mar 1778 {Ref: Archives of Maryland 21:81}

TRIPOLETT, MARY (Baltimore Town) received payment by order of the Council of Maryland "due for damages of her houses, etc. per account allowed by the House of Delegates" on 27 Jul 1779 {Ref: Archives of Maryland 21:480}; also see "Mary Tiplett," q.v.

TRIPPE, ANNE (Talbot County) received a loan certificate for £15.2.10 due from the Council of Maryland "agreeable to the Act proposing to the Citizens of this State, Creditors of Congress on Loan Office Certificates, Etc." on 29 Apr 1783 for services rendered during the war {Ref: Archives of Maryland 48:403}

TRIPPE, EDWARD (Talbot County) submitted an account and receipt for storing and transporting meat on 14 Jul 1778 {Ref: Maryland State Archives MdHR-6636-12-15}

TRIPPE, ELIZABETH (Talbot County) received a receipt from the Purchasing Agent for furnishing bacon for the use of the army on 13 May 1778 {Ref: Maryland State Archives MdHR-4587-84}; submitted an account and receipt for delivery of bacon on 13 May 1778 {Ref: Maryland State Archives MdHR-6636-12-15}; received a loan certificate for £33.2.8 due from the Council of Maryland "agreeable to the Act proposing to the Citizens of this State, Creditors of Congress on Loan Office Certificates, Etc." on 29 Apr 1783 for services rendered during the war {Ref: Archives of Maryland 48:403}

TRIPPE, JOHN (Talbot County) submitted an account and receipt for furnishing bacon on 24 Apr 1778 {Ref: Maryland State Archives MdHR-6636-12-15}

TRIPPE, MARGARET (Dorchester County) received a receipt from the Purchasing Agent for furnishing wheat on 1 Nov 1782 {Ref: Maryland State Archives MdHR-6636-42-23}

TROTH, HENRY (Kent County) received a certificate from the Purchasing Agent for furnishing wheat on 22 Jan 1780 {Ref: Maryland State Archives MdHR-6636-23-42}

TROUT, JACOB (Frederick County) submitted an account for furnishing hay on 20 Nov 1780 {Ref: Maryland State Archives MdHR-6636-23-5}

TROXIE, PETER (Frederick County) received a certificate from the Purchasing Agent for furnishing wheat on 8 Jul 1782 {Ref: Maryland State Archives MdHR-6636-42-36}

TRUEMAN, ISAAC (Kent County) received a certificate from the Purchasing Agent for furnishing bacon on 24 Jul 1780 {Ref: Maryland State Archives MdHR-6636-23-48}

TRUITT, ELI (Worcester County) submitted an account and receipt for driving cattle on 20 Nov 1781 {Ref: Maryland State Archives MdHR-6636-43-27}; submitted an account and receipt for rounding up cattle in or about 1782 {Ref: Maryland State Archives MdHR-6636-43-28J}

TRUITT, HENRY (Worcester County) submitted an account for slaughtering beef and a receipt for a negro's wages on 24 Apr 1781 {Ref: Maryland State Archives MdHR-6636-43-27}; submitted an account and receipt for furnishing pork on 1 Dec 1782 {Ref: Maryland State Archives MdHR-6636-43-28D}
TRUITT, WILLIAM (Worcester County) submitted an account and receipt for cattle collector's wages on 10 Sep 1781 {Ref: Maryland State Archives MdHR-6636-43-27}
TRUMAN, ALEXANDER, see "George P. Keeports," q.v.
TRUMELL, SAMBON (Montgomery County) received a receipt from the Purchasing Agent for furnishing wheat on 25 May 1781 {Ref: Maryland State Archives MdHR-6636-24-18}
TRUNDLE, JOHN (Montgomery County) received a receipt from the Purchasing Agent for furnishing wheat on 9 Aug 1780 {Ref: Maryland State Archives MdHR-6636-24-6}; received a receipt for furnishing wheat on 14 Oct 1780 {Ref: Maryland State Archives MdHR-6636-24-8}; received a receipt for furnishing wheat on 6 Jan 1781 {Ref: Maryland State Archives MdHR-6636-24-9}
TRUNELL, THOMAS (Montgomery County) received a receipt from the Purchasing Agent for furnishing wheat on 10 Apr and 31 Oct 1781 {Ref: Maryland State Archives MdHR-6636-24-14}
TRYALL, EDWARD (Queen Anne's County) received a certificate from the Purchasing Agent for furnishing wheat on 26 Jan 1780 {Ref: Maryland State Archives MdHR-6636-24-32}
TUBMAN, ELINOR (Charles County) received a receipt from the Purchasing Agent for furnishing wheat on 28 Dec 1782 {Ref: Maryland State Archives MdHR-6636-42-21}
TUBMAN, GEORGE (Charles County) received a receipt from the Purchasing Agent for furnishing wheat on 28 Dec 1782 {Ref: Maryland State Archives MdHR-6636-42-21}; received a receipt for furnishing wheat on 10 May 1783 {Ref: Maryland State Archives MdHR-6636-42-22}
TUBMAN, RICHARD (Charles County) received a receipt from the Purchasing Agent for furnishing wheat on 8 May 1783 {Ref: Maryland State Archives MdHR-6636-42-22}
TUCK, WILLIAM (Anne Arundel County) received payment by order of the Council of Safety for furnishing a gun on 28 Aug 1776 and for riding express on 13 Sep and 19 Sep 1776 {Ref: Archives of Maryland 12:245, 269, 280}; received payment by order of the Council of Maryland "for the use of Mrs. Elizabeth Tuck per account passed" on 20 Nov 1779 {Ref: Archives of Maryland 43:22}; received payment from the Council of Maryland as "appropriated for the payment of Expresses, Etc., his allowance on the Journal of May Session 1781" on 16 Jul 1781 {Ref: Archives of Maryland 45:503}

331

TUCKER, EDWARD (Montgomery County) received a receipt from the Purchasing Agent for furnishing wheat on 1 Aug 1780 {Ref: Maryland State Archives MdHR-6636-43-7}; received a receipt for furnishing wheat on 9 Aug 1780 {Ref: Maryland State Archives MdHR-6636-24-6}

TUCKER, JONATHAN (Frederick County) received payment by order of the Council of Maryland for the hire of his wagon on 14 Apr 1778 {Ref: Archives of Maryland 21:34}; received receipts from the Purchasing Agent for furnishing corn on 23 Mar, 24 Mar, 29 Mar, 30 Mar and 6 May 1780 {Ref: Maryland State Archives MdHR-6636-24-1}

TUCKER, JONATHAN (Prince George's County) received receipts from the Purchasing Agent for furnishing wheat on 12 Nov 1782, 2 Mar 1783 and 24 Mar 1783 {Ref: Maryland State Archives MdHR-6636-50-135}; received receipts for furnishing wheat on 4 Dec and 28 Dec 1782 {Ref: Maryland State Archives MdHR-6636-50-142}

TUCKER, JOSEPH (Montgomery County) received a receipt from the Purchasing Agent for furnishing wheat on 8 Sep 1780 {Ref: Maryland State Archives MdHR-6636-24-13}; received a receipt for furnishing wheat on 18 May 1781 {Ref: Maryland State Archives MdHR-6636-24-14}

TUCKER, LEVI (Caroline County) received a receipt from the Purchasing Agent for furnishing wheat on 17 Jun 1782 {Ref: Maryland State Archives MdHR-6636-42-7}

TUCKER, MARTHA (Montgomery County) was a widow who received a receipt from the Purchasing Agent for furnishing wheat on 14 Nov 1781 {Ref: Maryland State Archives MdHR-6636-24-14}

TUCKER, SELE (Anne Arundel County) received a receipt from the Purchasing Agent for freight of provisions on 16 Apr 1778 {Ref: Maryland State Archives MdHR-6636-11-36C}

TUCKER, WALTER (Montgomery County) received a receipt from the Purchasing Agent for furnishing wheat on 8 Sep 1780 {Ref: Maryland State Archives MdHR-6636-24-13}; received a receipt for furnishing wheat on 9 Apr 1781 {Ref: Maryland State Archives MdHR-6636-24-14}

TUCKER, WILLIAM (Montgomery County) received a receipt from the Purchasing Agent for furnishing wheat on 10 Aug 1780 {Ref: Maryland State Archives MdHR-6636-24-6}

TURK, ANDREW (Frederick County) received a certificate from the Purchasing Agent for furnishing corn on 18 Dec 1780 {Ref: Maryland State Archives MdHR-6636-23-33}

TURNER, GEORGE (Caroline County) received a receipt from the Purchasing Agent for furnishing wheat on 1 Sep 1782 {Ref: Maryland State Archives MdHR-6636-42-7}

TURNER, JOHN B., see "John Halkerston," q.v.

TURNER, JOSEPH, see "John Halkerston," q.v.

TURNER, RANDOLPH (Charles County) received a receipt from the Purchasing Agent for furnishing wheat on 12 Oct 1781 {Ref: Maryland State Archives MdHR-6636-42-15}; received a receipt for furnishing wheat on 29 Dec 1782 {Ref: Maryland State Archives MdHR-6636-42-21}

TURNER, SAMUEL (Montgomery County) received a receipt from the Purchasing Agent for furnishing wheat on 3 May and 20 Jul 1781 {Ref: Maryland State Archives MdHR-6636-24-18}

TURNER, WILLIAM (Baltimore County) submitted an account and received payment for hauling eight loads of flour on 28 Jan 1780 {Ref: Maryland Historical Society MS.1814, Box 6}

TURNER, ZADOCK (Worcester County) submitted an account and receipt for furnishing bacon on 15 Aug 1781 {Ref: Maryland State Archives MdHR-6636-43-27}

TURPIN, JOSHUA (Somerset County) received a receipt from the Purchasing Agent for furnishing beef on 9 Nov 1781 {Ref: Maryland State Archives MdHR-6636-24-44}

TURPIN, NEHEMIAH (Somerset County) received a receipt from the Purchasing Agent for furnishing beef on 8 Nov 1781 {Ref: Maryland State Archives MdHR-6636-24-44}

TUTTERER, BATTIS (Frederick County) received a certificate from the Purchasing Agent for furnishing wheat on 22 May 1782 {Ref: Maryland State Archives MdHR-6636-42-33}; received a certificate for furnishing wheat on 28 May 1782 {Ref: Maryland State Archives MdHR-6636-42-34}

TWILLY, GEORGE (Somerset County) received a receipt from the Purchasing Agent for furnishing pork on 12 May 1782 {Ref: Maryland State Archives MdHR-6636-43-21}

TYAN, CHARLES (Charles County) received a receipt from the Purchasing Agent for furnishing wheat on 29 Dec 1782 {Ref: Maryland State Archives MdHR-6636-42-21}

TYER, JOHN (Charles County) received a receipt from the Purchasing Agent for furnishing wheat on 29 Dec 1782 {Ref: Maryland State Archives MdHR-6636-42-21}

TYER, JOSEPH (Charles County) received a receipt from the Purchasing Agent for furnishing wheat on 30 Apr 1782 {Ref: Maryland State Archives MdHR-6636-42-18}

TYER, RALPH (Charles County) received a receipt from the Purchasing Agent for furnishing wheat on 29 Dec 1782 {Ref: Maryland State Archives MdHR-6636-42-21}

TYLER, WILLIAM (Charles County) received a receipt from the Purchasing Agent for furnishing wheat on 28 Dec 1782 {Ref: Maryland State Archives

MdHR-6636-42-21}

TYSON, ELIJAH (Baltimore County) proposed to the Council of Safety on 28 Jun 1776 "to erect a mill for manufacturing gunpowder at the Little Falls of Gunpowder River in Baltimore County about eighteen miles distance from Baltimore Town and three from Joppa in Harford County [and] he will engage to manufacture at as cheap a rate as it is in the Province of Pennsylvania and in equal quantities in proportion to the quantity of materials found him for the use of the Province of Maryland" {Ref: Archives of Maryland 11:531-532}

UMSTAD (UMSTATTD), ABRAHAM (Montgomery County) received a receipt from the Purchasing Agent for furnishing wheat on 7 Nov 1780 {Ref: Maryland State Archives MdHR-6636-24-8}; received a receipt for furnishing wheat on 28 Apr 1781 {Ref: Maryland State Archives MdHR-6636-42-11}

UNSELD (UNSILD), JOHN (Frederick County) was ordered by the Council of Safety to deliver to Capt. George Stricker all the musquets and bullet moulds which are now finished by him and Henry Yost for the use of the province on 4 Apr 1776 {Ref: Archives of Maryland 11:308, 400}

VAIN, WILLIAM (Charles County) received a receipt from the Purchasing Agent for furnishing wheat on 15 Apr 1783 {Ref: Maryland State Archives MdHR-6636-42-22}

VANBIBBER, ABRAHAM (Baltimore County) received a loan certificate for £9799.18.3 due from the Council of Maryland "agreeable to the Act proposing to the Citizens of this State, Creditors of Congress on Loan Office Certificates, Etc." on 12 May 1783 for services rendered during the war {Ref: Archives of Maryland 48:411}

VANBIBBER, ISAAC (Baltimore County) received loan certificates for £7003.9.2½ and £634.2.1 due from the Council of Maryland "agreeable to the Act proposing to the Citizens of this State, Creditors of Congress on Loan Office Certificates, Etc." on 6 May and 7 May 1783 for services rendered during the war {Ref: Archives of Maryland 48:406, 409}; also see "Benjamin Rumsey," q.v.

VANBIBBER & HARRISON, see "Monsieur Dhugé," q.v.

VANCE, DAVID (Somerset County) received a certificate from the Purchasing Agent for furnishing corn on 25 Jan 1780 {Ref: Maryland State Archives MdHR-6636-24-38}

VANDERFORD, JOHN (Queen Anne's County) received a certificate from the Purchasing Agent for furnishing beef on 8 Oct 1781 {Ref: Maryland State Archives MdHR-6636-24-34}

VANHORN (VANHORNE), GABRIEL (Harford County) made an agreement to ride express between Harford Town and Head of Elk on 14 Jun 1780 {Ref: Maryland State Archives MdHR-6636-21-116B}; certification by Lt. Francis Sheppard at Harford Town that Col. Gabriel Vanhorn gave pasturage to horses on 24 Aug 1780 {Ref: Maryland State Archives MdHR-6636-19-140}

VANSANT, EPHRAIM (Kent County) received payment from the Purchasing Agent for collecting cattle for the public use in November, 1782 {Ref: Maryland State Archives MdHR-6636-43-3}

VANSANT, GARRETT (Kent County) received payment for furnishing pork on 11 Nov 1780 {Ref: Maryland State Archives MdHR-6636-23-49}; submitted an account and receipt for furnishing barrels and hauling supplies on 30 Mar 1782 {Ref: Maryland State Archives MdHR-6636-43-5}

VANSANT, GEORGE (Kent County) submitted an account and receipt for carting supplies on 30 Mar 1782 {Ref: Maryland State Archives MdHR-6636-43-5}

VANSICLE, GILBERT (Dorchester County) received a receipt from the Purchasing Agent for furnishing wheat on 1 Nov 1782 {Ref: Maryland State Archives MdHR-6636-42-23}

VARDIN, JOHN, see "John Verden," q.v.

VAUX, EBAN (Caroline County) received a receipt from the Purchasing Agent for furnishing wheat on 5 Aug 1782 {Ref: Maryland State Archives MdHR-6636-42-7}

VAUX, EBENEZAR (Caroline County) received a receipt from the Purchasing Agent for furnishing wheat on 5 Aug 1782 {Ref: Maryland State Archives MdHR-6636-42-7}

VAUX, JOHN (Caroline County) received a receipt from the Purchasing Agent for furnishing wheat on 5 Aug 1782 {Ref: Maryland State Archives MdHR-6636-42-7}

VAUX, SALATHIEL (Caroline County) received a receipt from the Purchasing Agent for furnishing wheat on 5 Aug 1782 {Ref: Maryland State Archives MdHR-6636-42-7}

VAUX, WILLIAM (Caroline County) received a receipt from the Purchasing Agent for furnishing wheat on 5 Aug 1782 {Ref: Maryland State Archives MdHR-6636-42-7}

VEACH (VEATCH), HEZEKIAH (Prince George's County) received a receipt from the Purchasing Agent for furnishing wheat on 8 May on 12 Aug and 20 Dec 1782 {Ref: Maryland State Archives MdHR-6636-50-135}

VEACH, JOHN (Prince George's County) received a receipt from the Purchasing Agent for furnishing wheat on 20 Nov 1782 {Ref: Maryland State Archives MdHR-6636-50-135}

VEACH, SOLOMON (Prince George's County) received a receipt from the Purchasing Agent for furnishing wheat on 20 Nov 1782 {Ref: Maryland State Archives MdHR-6636-50-135}

VEACH, THOMAS (Prince George's County) received a receipt from the Purchasing Agent for furnishing wheat on 11 Sep 1783 {Ref: Maryland State Archives MdHR-6636-50-135}; received a receipt for hauling wheat on 7 Nov

1783 {Ref: Maryland State Archives MdHR-6636-50-141}

VEACH, VINCENT (Prince George's County) received a receipt from the Purchasing Agent for furnishing wheat on 20 Nov 1782 {Ref: Maryland State Archives MdHR-6636-50-135}

VEACH, WILLIAM (Prince George's County) received a receipt from the Purchasing Agent for furnishing wheat on 11 Mar 1783 {Ref: Maryland State Archives MdHR-6636-50-135}

VEARS, DANIEL (Montgomery County) received a receipt from the Purchasing Agent for furnishing wheat on 18 Jun 1781 {Ref: Maryland State Archives MdHR-6636-24-15}

VEAZEY, JOHN WARD (Cecil County) was appointed by the Council of Maryland as one of thirty men to be "Agents for Purchasing Provisions" on 30 Mar 1779 {Ref: Archives of Maryland 21:332}

VENABLES, BENJAMIN SR. (Somerset County) received a receipt from the Purchasing Agent for furnishing bacon on 10 Jul 1781 {Ref: Maryland State Archives MdHR-6636-24-43}; received a loan certificate for £45.11.8 due from the Council of Maryland "agreeable to the Act proposing to the Citizens of this State, Creditors of Congress on Loan Office Certificates, Etc." on 18 Dec 1783 for services rendered during the war {Ref: Archives of Maryland 48:491}

VENABLES, JOHN (Montgomery County) received a receipt from the Purchasing Agent for furnishing wheat on 3 Jul 1781 {Ref: Maryland State Archives MdHR-6636-42-11}

VENABLES, RACHEL (Somerset County) received a receipt from the Purchasing Agent for furnishing pork on 23 Apr 1782 {Ref: Maryland State Archives MdHR-6636-43-21}

VERDEN (VARDIN), JOHN (Charles County) delivered cattle to Annapolis for the use of the state by request of the Commissary of Charles County circa 6 Oct 1780 {Ref: Archives of Maryland 45:135}; received payment from the Council of Maryland as "appropriated for the payment of Expresses, Etc., per Account passed by the Auditor General" on 9 Aug 1781 {Ref: Archives of Maryland 45:551}; submitted an account and receipt for express riders on 30 Aug 1781 {Ref: Maryland State Archives MdHR-6636-23-25}; submitted an account and receipt for collecting cattle on 29 Oct 1781 {Ref: Maryland State Archives MdHR-6636-42-12}

VERDEN (VERDIN), RICHARD (Charles County) delivered powder and muskets from the Armourer to Francis Ware, county lieutenant, for the use of the militia by order of the Council of Maryland who also ordered "that the Issuing Commissary deliver to the said Richard Verdin one Beeves hide to cover powder and arms sent to Col. Ware" on 26 Jan 1781 {Ref: Archives of Maryland 45:289}

VICKERS, SARAH (Talbot County) received a receipt from the Purchasing Agent for furnishing wheat on 6 Oct 1781 {Ref: Maryland State Archives MdHR-6636-24-51}

VIERS, JOHN (Montgomery County) received a receipt from the Purchasing Agent for furnishing wheat on 16 Aug 1780 {Ref: Maryland State Archives MdHR-6636-24-6}

VIERS, WILLIAM (Montgomery County) received a receipt from the Purchasing Agent for furnishing wheat on 9 Aug 1780 {Ref: Maryland State Archives MdHR-6636-24-6}

VILEY, GEORGE (Montgomery County) received a receipt from the Purchasing Agent for furnishing wheat on 2 Jan 1782 {Ref: Maryland State Archives MdHR-6636-43-8}

VOORHEES, JOHN (Kent County) was appointed Commissary of Purchases for Kent County by the Council of Maryland on 8 Jul 1780 {Ref: Archives of Maryland 43:215}; submitted an account and receipt for military supplies in 1781 {Ref: Maryland State Archives MdHR-6636-43-2A/2Z}; submitted an account of wheat received for assessments on 30 Mar 1782 {Ref: Maryland State Archives MdHR-6636-43-4}; also see "Jonathan Parker" and "Ebenezer Riner," q.v.

WADE, ROBERT (Charles County) received a receipt from the Purchasing Agent for furnishing corn meal on 13 Apr 1781 {Ref: Maryland State Archives MdHR-19970-3-16}

WAIGHT, THOMAS (Baltimore County) submitted an account and received payment for one day's drayage of flour for the use of the army on 28 Jan 1780 {Ref: Maryland Historical Society MS.1814, Box 6}

WAILES, BENJAMIN (Somerset County) received a receipt from the Purchasing Agent for furnishing bacon on 18 Jul 1781 {Ref: Maryland State Archives MdHR-6636-24-43}

WAILES, LEVIN (Somerset County) received a receipt of wages for delivering cattle on 3 Jan 1782 {Ref: Maryland State Archives MdHR-6636-43-15}

WAINWRIGHT, GEORGE (Worcester County) submitted an account and receipt for hauling pork on 12 Sep 1781 {Ref: Maryland State Archives MdHR-6636-43-27}; submitted an account and receipt for furnishing salt on 5 Jan 1782 {Ref: Maryland State Archives MdHR-6636-43-28FFF}; submitted an account and receipt for hauling pork on 25 Jul 1782 {Ref: Maryland State Archives MdHR-6636-43-28J}

WALES, ANDREW (Bladensburgh, Prince George's County) received payment from the Purchasing Agent for furnishing clothing ("duffle and felt hatts") on 11 Jun 1781 {Ref: Archives of Maryland 47:287}

WALES, BENJAMIN (Worcester County) received a receipt from the Purchasing Agent for storing corn on 10 Oct 1780 {Ref: Maryland State Archives MdHR-

6636-24-54}

WALKER, JOHN (Caroline County) received a receipt from the Purchasing Agent for furnishing wheat on 22 Aug 1782 {Ref: Maryland State Archives MdHR-6636-42-7}

WALKER, JOSEPH (Marlbro, Prince George's County) received payment from the Purchasing Agent for furnishing material for clothing ("oznaburgs") on 11 Jun 1781 {Ref: Archives of Maryland 47:287}

WALKER, WILLIAM BANFIELD (county not stated) received payment by order of the Council of Maryland "for salt purchased of him for the State" on 30 Jan 1778 {Ref: Archives of Maryland 16:480}

WALLACE, CHARLES, Esquire (Baltimore County) received payment by order of the Council of Safety to enable him and William Lux to carry on a Salt Work on 8 Jun 1776 {Ref: Archives of Maryland 11:472}; received a loan certificate for £2407.5.4 due from the Council of Maryland "agreeable to the Act proposing to the Citizens of this State, Creditors of Congress on Loan Office Certificates, Etc." on 11 Oct 1783 for services rendered during the war {Ref: Archives of Maryland 48:463}

WALLACE, DAVID (Cecil County) received receipts from the Purchasing Agent for furnishing flour on 20 Feb, 21 Feb and 7 Mar 1783 {Ref: Maryland State Archives MdHR-6636-42-9}

WALLACE, FRANCES (Kent County) received payment from the Purchasing Agent for furnishing cattle for the public use in September, 1781 {Ref: Maryland State Archives MdHR-6636-43-3}

WALLACE, HENRY (Kent County) received payment from the Purchasing Agent for furnishing cattle for the public use in September, 1781 {Ref: Maryland State Archives MdHR-6636-43-3}

WALLACE, JAMES (Montgomery County) received a receipt from the Purchasing Agent for furnishing wheat on 1 Aug 1780 {Ref: Maryland State Archives MdHR-6636-43-7}

WALLACE, JOHN (Baltimore County) submitted an account and received payment for coopering, nailing and hooping on 26 Jan 1780 and for four days trimming thirty casks on 25 Feb 1780 {Ref: Maryland Historical Society MS.1814, Box 6}; received payment for furnishing casks on 4 Mar 1781 {Ref: Maryland State Archives MdHR-6636-43-38BBBB}

WALLACE, JOHN (Kent County) received payment from the Purchasing Agent for furnishing cattle on 17 Oct 1780 {Ref: Maryland State Archives MdHR-6636-23-49}; received payment for furnishing cattle for the public use on 11 Oct 1781 {Ref: Maryland State Archives MdHR-6636-43-3}

WALLACE, JOHN (Charles County) received a receipt from the Purchasing Agent for furnishing wheat on 10 May 1783 {Ref: Maryland State Archives MdHR-6636-42-22}

WALLACE, MICHAEL (Baltimore Town) was a doctor who was appointed by the Council of Safety to serve as "Surgeon's Mate to the Battalion" on 7 Mar 1776 {Ref: Archives of Maryland 11:207}

WALLCART, JOHN (Kent County) received a certificate from the Purchasing Agent for hauling wheat on 6 Jun 1780 {Ref: Maryland State Archives MdHR-6636-23-42}

WALLER, WILLIAM (Anne Arundel County) received payment by order of the Council of Safety for sounding the depth of the river between Greenbury's Point and Horn Point on 11 Apr 1776 {Ref: Archives of Maryland 11:326}

WALLEY, ZEDEKIAH (Worcester County) submitted an account for furnishing brandy on 1 Aug 1781 {Ref: Maryland State Archives MdHR-6636-24-56}

WALLS, JOHN MILBORN (Caroline County) received a receipt from the Purchasing Agent for furnishing wheat on 1 Sep 1782 {Ref: Maryland State Archives MdHR-6636-42-7}

WALSH, EDMUND (Baltimore County) submitted an account and received payment for turning out and stowing flour for one and three quarter days on 28 Jan and 1 Feb 1780 {Ref: Maryland Historical Society MS.1814, Box 6}

WALSH, MARY (Queen Anne's County) received a receipt from the Purchasing Agent for furnishing wheat on 29 Sep 1780 {Ref: Maryland State Archives MdHR-6636-24-33}

WALTER, DAVID (Prince George's County) received a receipt from the Purchasing Agent for furnishing wheat on 10 Aug 1783 {Ref: Maryland State Archives MdHR-6636-50-135}

WALTER, GEORGE (Prince George's County) received a receipt from the Purchasing Agent for furnishing wheat on 8 Jun 1782 {Ref: Maryland State Archives MdHR-6636-50-135}; received a receipt for furnishing wheat on 9 Aug 1783 {Ref: Maryland State Archives MdHR-6636-50-135}

WALTER, HENRY (Frederick County) submitted an account for boarding services on 3 Apr 1777 {Ref: Maryland State Archives MdHR-19970-2-4}

WALTER, LEVY (Frederick County) received a receipt from the Purchasing Agent for furnishing corn on 3 May 1780 {Ref: Maryland State Archives MdHR-6636-24-1}

WALTER, WILLIAM (St. Mary's County) submitted an account of expenses for collecting and driving cattle on 26 Nov 1781 {Ref: Maryland State Archives MdHR-19970-3-17}

WALTERS, DAVID (Montgomery County) received a receipt from the Purchasing Agent for furnishing wheat on 17 May 1781 {Ref: Maryland State Archives MdHR-6636-24-18}

WALTERS, EDWARD (Somerset County) received a receipt from the Purchasing Agent for furnishing pork on 20 Jul 1781 {Ref: Maryland State Archives MdHR-6636-24-43}

WALTERS, GEORGE (Montgomery County) received a receipt from the Purchasing Agent for furnishing wheat on 19 May 1781 {Ref: Maryland State Archives MdHR-6636-24-18}

WALTERS, JAMES (Somerset County) was a captain who received a receipt from the Purchasing Agent for furnishing pork on 10 Jun 1781 {Ref: Maryland State Archives MdHR-6636-24-43}

WALTERS, JOSEPH (Worcester County) submitted an account and receipt for furnishing salt on 20 Dec 1781 {Ref: Maryland State Archives MdHR-6636-43-27}

WALTERS, ROBERT (Queen Anne's County) was a Commissary of Purchases who submitted an account of supplies in 1780 {Ref: Maryland State Archives MdHR-6636-21-140}; received a certificate for furnishing wheat on 5 Jan 1780 {Ref: Maryland State Archives MdHR-6636-24-21C}; received a certificate for furnishing wheat on 18 Mar 1780 {Ref: Maryland State Archives MdHR-6636-24-21A}; received a receipt for furnishing corn on 1 Apr 1780 {Ref: Maryland State Archives MdHR-6636-24-21B}

WALTERS, SARAH (Montgomery County) received a receipt from the Purchasing Agent for furnishing wheat on 31 May 1781 {Ref: Maryland State Archives MdHR-6636-24-18}

WALTERS, THOMAS (Somerset County) was a captain who received a receipt from the Purchasing Agent for furnishing pork on 10 Jun 1781 {Ref: Maryland State Archives MdHR-6636-24-43}

WANES, ISAAC (Frederick County) received a certificate from the Purchasing Agent for furnishing wheat on 22 May 1782 {Ref: Maryland State Archives MdHR-6636-42-33}

WARD, ACHILLES (Charles County) received a receipt from the Purchasing Agent for furnishing wheat on 18 May 1782 {Ref: Maryland State Archives MdHR-6636-42-18}

WARD, GEORGE (Baltimore County) submitted an account and received payment for stowing flour for two days on 24 Mar 1780 {Ref: Maryland Historical Society MS.1814, Box 6}

WARD, IGNATIUS (Charles County) received a receipt from the Purchasing Agent for furnishing wheat on 26 Jan 1782 {Ref: Maryland State Archives MdHR-6636-42-16}; received a receipt for furnishing wheat on 15 Apr 1783 {Ref: Maryland State Archives MdHR-6636-42-22}

WARD, JAMIE (Somerset County) received a receipt from the Purchasing Agent for furnishing beef on 5 Nov 1781 {Ref: Maryland State Archives MdHR-6636-24-44}

WARD, JOHN (Charles County) received a receipt from the Purchasing Agent for furnishing wheat on 28 Dec 1782 {Ref: Maryland State Archives MdHR-6636-42-21}; received a receipt for furnishing wheat on 12 Apr 1783 {Ref: Maryland

State Archives MdHR-6636-42-22}
WARD, JOHN (Caroline County) received a receipt from the Purchasing Agent for furnishing wheat on 22 Aug 1782 {Ref: Maryland State Archives MdHR-6636-42-7}
WARD, JOHN (county not stated) pledged a loan in the amount of £100 to the State of Maryland under the Act for the Emission of Bills of Credit "to defray the expences of the present campaign" in June, 1781 {Ref: Archives of Maryland 47:327}
WARD, NANNY (Somerset County) received a receipt from the Purchasing Agent for furnishing beef on 5 Nov 1781 {Ref: Maryland State Archives MdHR-6636-24-44}
WARD, RICHARD (Caroline County) received a receipt from the Purchasing Agent for furnishing wheat on 1 Sep 1782 {Ref: Maryland State Archives MdHR-6636-42-7}
WARD, STEPHEN (Somerset County) received a receipt from the Purchasing Agent for furnishing pork on 1 May 1781 {Ref: Maryland State Archives MdHR-6636-24-43}; received a receipt for furnishing beef on 5 Dec 1781 {Ref: Maryland State Archives MdHR-6636-24-44}
WARD, THOMAS (Somerset County) received a receipt from the Purchasing Agent for furnishing beef on 6 Nov 1781 {Ref: Maryland State Archives MdHR-6636-24-44}
WARD, WILLIAM (Charles County) received a receipt from the Purchasing Agent for furnishing wheat on 14 Feb 1782 {Ref: Maryland State Archives MdHR-6636-42-16}
WARDEN, ELIJAH (Charles County) received a receipt from the Purchasing Agent for furnishing wheat on 13 May and 22 Jul 1782 {Ref: Maryland State Archives MdHR-6636-42-18}
WARDER, JOSEPH (Charles County) received a receipt from the Purchasing Agent for furnishing wheat on 16 Feb 1782 {Ref: Maryland State Archives MdHR-6636-42-16}
WARE, FRANCIS (Charles County) was a colonel who received a loan certificate for £99.4.3 due from the Council of Maryland "agreeable to the Act proposing to the Citizens of this State, Creditors of Congress on Loan Office Certificates, Etc." on 24 Dec 1783 for services rendered during the war {Ref: Archives of Maryland 48:499}
WARFIELD, ALEXANDER (Anne Arundel County) received a loan certificate for £31.9.3 due from the Council of Maryland "agreeable to the Act proposing to the Citizens of this State, Creditors of Congress on Loan Office Certificates, Etc." on 7 Apr 1783 for services rendered during the war {Ref: Archives of Maryland 48:395}
WARFIELD, AZEL (Anne Arundel County) was a gunsmith who received

payment by order of the Council of Maryland for furnishing a gun on 9 Sep 1777 and received 12 gun barrels and locks from the Armourer to be stocked by him at that time {Ref: Archives of Maryland 16:367}

WARFIELD, CHARLES ALEXANDER (Anne Arundel County) was a doctor who contracted with the Maryland Council of Safety to carry on a crude nitre manufactory on 23 Jul 1776 {Ref: Archives of Maryland 12:96}

WARFIELD, JOHN WORTHINGTON (Montgomery County) received a receipt from the Purchasing Agent for furnishing wheat on 10 Oct 1780 {Ref: Maryland State Archives MdHR-6636-24-8}; received a receipt for furnishing wheat on 10 Apr 1781 {Ref: Maryland State Archives MdHR-6636-42-11}

WARFIELD, VACHEL (Anne Arundel County) received payment by order of the Council of Safety via Reubin Meriwether for the hire of his wagon on 9 Dec 1777 {Ref: Archives of Maryland 16:431}

WARFIELD, WALTER (Anne Arundel County) was a doctor who was appointed by the Council of Maryland to serve as "Surgeon's Mate to Dr. Ephraim Howard" in Col. Thomas Dorsey's Battalion of Marching Militia on 3 Sep 1777 {Ref: Archives of Maryland 16:359}

WARNER, CUTHBERT (Harford County) received money from the Committee of Safety to carry on the business of gun making in partnership with Isaiah Boulderson on 27 Nov 1775 {Ref: Preston's History of Harford County, p. 317}

WARREN, CLARK (Caroline County) received a receipt from the Purchasing Agent for furnishing wheat on 20 Sep 1782 {Ref: Maryland State Archives MdHR-6636-42-7}

WARREN, JOHN (Caroline County) received a loan certificate for £44.12.7 due from the Council of Maryland "agreeable to the Act proposing to the Citizens of this State, Creditors of Congress on Loan Office Certificates, Etc." on 26 May 1783 for services rendered during the war {Ref: Archives of Maryland 48:421}

WARREN, SOLOMON (Caroline County) received receipts from the Purchasing Agent for furnishing wheat on 5 Aug 1782 {Ref: Maryland State Archives MdHR-6636-42-7}

WARRING, BASIL (Prince George's County) received a certificate from the Purchasing Agent for delivery of wheat on 27 Dec 1782 {Ref: Maryland State Archives MdHR-6636-50-137}

WARTERS, JOSEPH (Montgomery County) received receipts from the Purchasing Agent for furnishing wheat on 4 Jun and 4 Oct 1781 {Ref: Maryland State Archives MdHR-6636-42-11}

WARTERS, ZACHARIAH (Montgomery County) received a receipt from the Purchasing Agent for furnishing wheat on 20 Apr 1781 {Ref: Maryland State Archives MdHR-6636-42-11}

WARTHEN, BENNETT (Charles County) received a receipt from the Purchasing Agent for furnishing wheat on 28 Dec 1782 {Ref: Maryland State Archives MdHR-6636-42-21}

WASHINGTON, GENERAL, see "William Towson" and "Monsieur Dhugé," q.v.

WATERMAN, PHILIS (Annapolis) received payment by order of the Council of Safety (which misspelled her name as "Philis Waterland") for attending the sick at the hospital on 5 Sep 1776, and received payment for attending the hospital on 5 Oct 1776 {Ref: Archives of Maryland 12:257, 321}

WATERS, HENRY (Charles County) received a receipt from the Purchasing Agent for furnishing wheat on 31 Oct 1781 {Ref: Maryland State Archives MdHR-6636-43-45L}

WATERS, HEZEKIAH (Baltimore County) submitted an account and received payment for furnishing nails on 23 Mar 1780 {Ref: Maryland Historical Society MS.1814, Box 6}

WATERS, ISAAC (Montgomery County) received a receipt from the Purchasing Agent for furnishing wheat on 1 Aug 1780 {Ref: Maryland State Archives MdHR-6636-43-7}; received a receipt for furnishing wheat on 10 Aug 1780 {Ref: Maryland State Archives MdHR-6636-24-6}

WATERS, JAMES (Charles County) received a receipt from the Purchasing Agent for furnishing wheat on 16 Nov 1781 {Ref: Maryland State Archives MdHR-6636-42-15}

WATERS, JOSEPH (Montgomery County) received a receipt from the Purchasing Agent for furnishing wheat on 1 Aug 1780 {Ref: Maryland State Archives MdHR-6636-43-7}; received a receipt for furnishing wheat on 4 Oct 1781 {Ref: Maryland State Archives MdHR-6636-24-15}

WATERS, NANCY (Dorchester County) received a receipt from the Purchasing Agent for furnishing wheat on 1 Oct 1782 {Ref: Maryland State Archives MdHR-6636-42-23}

WATERS, PATRICK (Worcester County) submitted an account and receipt for furnishing salt on 15 Sep 1781 {Ref: Maryland State Archives MdHR-6636-43-27}

WATERS, RICHARD (Baltimore County) received a receipt from the Purchasing Agent for furnishing corn on 16 Feb 1780 {Ref: Maryland State Archives MdHR-6636-23-33}

WATERS, RICHARD (Somerset County) was a captain who received a receipt from the Purchasing Agent for furnishing beef on 29 Oct 1781 {Ref: Maryland State Archives MdHR-6636-24-44}; received a loan certificate for £288.13.11 due from the Council of Maryland "agreeable to the Act proposing to the Citizens of this State, Creditors of Congress on Loan Office Certificates, Etc." on 23 Sep 1783 for services rendered during the war {Ref: Archives of Maryland 48:455}

343

WATERS, RICHARD JR. (Frederick County) received a certificate from the Purchasing Agent for furnishing corn on 15 Feb 1780 {Ref: Maryland State Archives MdHR-6636-42-33}

WATERS, RICHARD SR. (Montgomery County) received a receipt from the Purchasing Agent for furnishing wheat on 9 Sep 1781 {Ref: Maryland State Archives MdHR-6636-24-15}; received a loan certificate for £46.10.0 due from the Council of Maryland "agreeable to the Act proposing to the Citizens of this State, Creditors of Congress on Loan Office Certificates, Etc." on 24 Sep 1783 for services rendered during the war {Ref: Archives of Maryland 48:456}

WATERS, ROBERT (Queen Anne's County) received a certificate from the Purchasing Agent for furnishing wheat on 2 May 1780 {Ref: Archives of Maryland 43:475; Maryland State Archives MdHR-6636-40-46E}

WATERS, ROSE, Mrs. (Somerset County) received a receipt from the Purchasing Agent for furnishing beef on 29 Oct 1781 {Ref: Maryland State Archives MdHR-6636-24-44}

WATERS, SARAH, Mrs. (Somerset County) submitted an account for furnishing beef on 29 Oct 1781 {Ref: Maryland State Archives MdHR-6636-43-15}

WATERS, THOMAS (Somerset County) received a loan certificate for £91.6.0 due from the Council of Maryland "agreeable to the Act proposing to the Citizens of this State, Creditors of Congress on Loan Office Certificates, Etc." on 22 May 1783 for services rendered during the war {Ref: Archives of Maryland 48:419}

WATERS, WILLIAM (Montgomery County) was appointed by the Council of Maryland on 25 Mar 1778 as one of eighteen men to be "Agents for Purchasing Provisions for the Army of the United States Agreeable to an Act of Assembly passed the 23rd Inst." but was noted in the record as "refused to act" {Ref: Archives of Maryland 16:551}; received a receipt from the Purchasing Agent for furnishing wheat on 1 Aug 1780 {Ref: Maryland State Archives MdHR-6636-43-7}

WATERS, WILLIAM (Worcester County) submitted an account and receipt of wages for loading tobacco on 20 Jun 1781 {Ref: Maryland State Archives MdHR-6636-43-27}

WATERS, WILLIAM, OF WILLIAM (Somerset County) received a loan certificate for £13.8.1 due from the Council of Maryland "agreeable to the Act proposing to the Citizens of this State, Creditors of Congress on Loan Office Certificates, Etc." on 22 May 1783 for services rendered during the war {Ref: Archives of Maryland 48:419}

WATERS, WILLIAM SR. (Somerset County) received a receipt from the Purchasing Agent for furnishing beef on 29 Oct 1781 {Ref: Maryland State Archives MdHR-6636-24-44}

WATERS, ZACHARIAH (Baltimore County) received payment for furnishing beef on 17 Mar 1781 {Ref: Maryland State Archives MdHR-6636-43-38IIII}

WATKINS, JOHN B. (Charles County) submitted an account and receipt for taking care of a sick steer on 1 Sep 1781 {Ref: Maryland State Archives MdHR-6636-23-25}

WATKINS, NICHOLAS (Anne Arundel County) received a loan certificate for £3.19.4 due from the Council of Maryland "agreeable to the Act proposing to the Citizens of this State, Creditors of Congress on Loan Office Certificates, Etc." on 23 May 1783 for services rendered during the war {Ref: Archives of Maryland 48:420}

WATKINS (WALKINS?), THOMAS (Caroline County) received a receipt from the Purchasing Agent for furnishing wheat on 5 Aug 1782 {Ref: Maryland State Archives MdHR-6636-42-7}

WATSON, SAMUEL (Montgomery County) received a receipt from the Purchasing Agent for shelling corn in 1780. {Ref: Maryland State Archives MdHR-6636-24-2}

WATSON, WILLIAM (Caroline County) received a receipt from the Purchasing Agent for furnishing wheat on 5 Aug 1782 {Ref: Maryland State Archives MdHR-6636-42-7}

WATTS, HENRY (Charles County) received a receipt from the Purchasing Agent for furnishing wheat on 27 Oct 1781 {Ref: Maryland State Archives MdHR-6636-42-15}

WATTS, JOHN (Montgomery County) received a receipt from the Purchasing Agent for furnishing wheat on 7 May 1781 {Ref: Maryland State Archives MdHR-6636-42-11}

WATTS, WILLIAM (Talbot County) was one of twenty-six people who contacted the Governor and Council of Maryland in 1781 and pledged to support and maintain at their own expense the Barge *Experiment* so it can patrol the bay between Kent Point and Tilghman's Island in order to protect them against the enemy, stating in part, "whereas from the present exhausted state of the public treasury the government cannot immediately give that protection to every individual which is become necessary from the cruel and savage mode in which the war is now carried on against us" {Ref: Archives of Maryland 47:584-585}

WAYMAN, EDMOND OR EDMUND (Montgomery and Prince George's Counties) received a receipt from the Purchasing Agent for furnishing wheat on 30 May 1781 {Ref: Maryland State Archives MdHR-6636-24-15}; received a receipt for furnishing wheat on 24 Jun 1782 and 1783 {Ref: Maryland State Archives MdHR-6636-50-135}

WAYMAN, JOHN (Frederick County) received a certificate from the Purchasing Agent for furnishing beef and pork on 15 Mar 1781 {Ref: Maryland State Archives MdHR-6636-23-4}

WAYNE, ISAAC (Frederick County) submitted an account for furnishing beef on

4 May 1781 {Ref: Maryland State Archives MdHR-6636-23-6}

WAYNE, JOHN (Harford County) delivered a shipment of powder, lead and gun flints for the Harford County Militia from the Commissary of Stores in Baltimore by order of the Council of Maryland on 29 Aug 1777 {Ref: Archives of Maryland 16:347}

WEATHERLY, JESSE (Somerset County) received a receipt from the Purchasing Agent for furnishing beef on 10 Nov 1781 {Ref: Maryland State Archives MdHR-6636-24-44}

WEBB, FRANCIS (Dorchester County) received a receipt from the Purchasing Agent for furnishing salt pork on 1 Oct 1782 {Ref: Maryland State Archives MdHR-6636-42-23}

WEBB, GEORGE (Caroline County) received a receipt from the Purchasing Agent for furnishing wheat on 1 Sep 1782 {Ref: Maryland State Archives MdHR-6636-42-7}

WEBB, PETER (Talbot County) received a loan certificate for £76.5.1 due from the Council of Maryland "agreeable to the Act proposing to the Citizens of this State, Creditors of Congress on Loan Office Certificates, Etc." on 24 Dec 1783 for services rendered during the war {Ref: Archives of Maryland 48:499}

WEBB, WILLIAM (Harford County) was appointed by the Committee of Safety "to ride all the north side of Deer Creek and purchase guns and blankets agreeable to the request of the [Maryland] Council of Safety" on 19 Aug 1776 and submitted his account on 2 Sep 1776 {Ref: Preston's History of Harford County, pp. 333-334, 336}

WEBSTER, CATHARINE (Dorchester County) received a receipt from the Purchasing Agent for furnishing wheat on 1 Oct 1782 {Ref: Maryland State Archives MdHR-6636-42-23}

WEBSTER, ISAAC (Harford County) received a loan certificate for £95.1.4 due from the Council of Maryland "agreeable to the Act proposing to the Citizens of this State, Creditors of Congress on Loan Office Certificates, Etc." on 10 Dec 1783 for services rendered during the war {Ref: Archives of Maryland 48:487}

WEBSTER, JAMES, see "Eleanor Riddle," q.v.

WEBSTER, JOHN (Caroline County) received receipts from the Purchasing Agent for furnishing wheat on 5 Aug 1782 {Ref: Maryland State Archives MdHR-6636-42-7}

WEBSTER, RICHARD (Caroline County) received a receipt from the Purchasing Agent for furnishing wheat on 5 Aug 1782 {Ref: Maryland State Archives MdHR-6636-42-7}

WEDDING, THOMAS (Charles County) received a receipt from the Purchasing Agent for furnishing wheat on 8 Aug 1781 {Ref: Maryland State Archives MdHR-6636-42-15}; received a receipt for furnishing wheat on 15 Feb 1782

{Ref: Maryland State Archives MdHR-6636-42-16}
WEDDLE, PETER (Frederick County) received a certificate from the Purchasing Agent for furnishing wheat on 28 May 1782 {Ref: Maryland State Archives MdHR-6636-42-34}
WEDERSTRANDT, CONRAD T. OR CONROD THEODORE (Queen Anne's County) submitted an account and receipt for furnishing beef on 20 Dec 1779 {Ref: Maryland State Archives MdHR-6636-15-153}; commissioned an Assistant Deputy Commissary Purchases for Queen Anne's County, Talbot County and below on 10 Sep 1779 {Ref: Archives of Maryland 21:518, 43:20}; submitted an account and receipt for furnishing beef on 2 Mar 1780 {Ref: Maryland State Archives MdHR-6636-17-73}; appointed Commissary of Purchases by the Council of Maryland on 8 Jul 1780 and resigned by 18 Jul 1780 {Ref: Archives of Maryland 43:215, 223}; received payment by order of the Council of Maryland "of the New Emission of this State to be delivered over to Charles Blake, Commissary for Queen Anne's County" on 23 Sep 1780 {Ref: Archives of Maryland 43:301}; received a loan certificate for £128.2.4 due from the Council of Maryland "agreeable to the Act proposing to the Citizens of this State, Creditors of Congress on Loan Office Certificates, Etc." on 17 Oct 1783 for services rendered during the war {Ref: Archives of Maryland 48:470}
WEEKS, SIMON (Kent County) received payment from the Purchasing Agent for furnishing cattle and pasturage for the public use in September, 1781 {Ref: Maryland State Archives MdHR-6636-43-3}
WEEMS, JAMES (Calvert County) received certificates for loans to the Continental Congress on 28 Feb, 23 Mar, 30 May and 8 Jun 1778 {Ref: Maryland State Archives MdHR-6636-11-119A/C/E/F}
WEEMS, JOHN (Anne Arundel County) was appointed by the Council of Safety to collect all the gold and silver coin that could be procured in the county in compliance with the Resolve of Congress on 27 Jan 1776 {Ref: Archives of Maryland 11:132}
WELCH, HENRY O'NEAL (county not stated) received a loan certificate for £195.19.8 due from the Council of Maryland "agreeable to the Act proposing to the Citizens of this State, Creditors of Congress on Loan Office Certificates, Etc." on 9 Dec 1783 for services rendered during the war {Ref: Archives of Maryland 48:486}
WELLEMEN, WILLIAM (Montgomery County) received a receipt from the Purchasing Agent for furnishing wheat on 1 Aug 1780 {Ref: Maryland State Archives MdHR-6636-43-7}
WELLING, JOHN (Montgomery County) received a receipt from the Purchasing Agent for furnishing wheat on 24 Apr 1781 {Ref: Maryland State Archives MdHR-6636-42-11}

347

WELLS, CYPRIAN (Baltimore Town) received payment by order of the Council of Safety for furnishing ten reams of paper on 1 Jun 1776 {Ref: Archives of Maryland 11:476}

WELSH, WILLIAM (Charles County) received a receipt from the Purchasing Agent for furnishing wheat on 3 May 1783 {Ref: Maryland State Archives MdHR-6636-42-22}

WELSH, WILLIAM (Somerset County) received a certificate from the Purchasing Agent for furnishing corn on 26 Feb 1780 {Ref: Maryland State Archives MdHR-6636-24-39}

WERTS, PETER (Frederick County) received a certificate from the Purchasing Agent for furnishing wheat on 16 May 1782 {Ref: Maryland State Archives MdHR-6636-42-34}

WERTZ, JASPER (Montgomery County) received a receipt from the Purchasing Agent for furnishing wheat on 20 Sep 1780 {Ref: Maryland State Archives MdHR-6636-24-13}

WEST, BASIL OR BAZIL (Montgomery County) received a receipt from the Purchasing Agent for furnishing wheat on 17 Jul 1780 {Ref: Maryland State Archives MdHR-6636-24-5}; received a receipt for furnishing wheat on 1 Aug 1780 {Ref: Maryland State Archives MdHR-6636-43-7}; received a receipt for furnishing wheat on 11 Jun 1781 {Ref: Maryland State Archives MdHR-6636-42-11}

WEST, JAMES (county not stated) received payments by order of the Council of Safety for furnishing boatage on 7 Sep and 17 Sep 1776 {Ref: Archives of Maryland 12:260, 276}

WEST, JOHN (Caroline County) received a certificate from the Purchasing Agent for hauling flour on 24 Jun 1780 {Ref: Maryland State Archives MdHR-6636-23-20}

WEST, JOSEPH (Frederick County) received a certificate from the Purchasing Agent for furnishing wheat on 8 Jun 1782 {Ref: Maryland State Archives MdHR-6636-42-35}

WEST, OSBORN (Montgomery County) received a receipt from the Purchasing Agent for furnishing wheat on 29 Jul 1780 {Ref: Maryland State Archives MdHR-6636-24-5}; received a receipt for furnishing wheat on 11 Jun 1781 {Ref: Maryland State Archives MdHR-6636-42-11}

WEST, OZMAN (Montgomery County) received a receipt from the Purchasing Agent for furnishing wheat on 1 Aug 1780 {Ref: Maryland State Archives MdHR-6636-43-7}

WEST, RICHARD (Montgomery County) received a receipt from the Purchasing Agent for furnishing wheat on 31 Jul 1780 {Ref: Maryland State Archives MdHR-6636-24-5}; received a receipt for furnishing wheat on 1 Aug 1780 {Ref: Maryland State Archives MdHR-6636-43-7}; received a receipt for furnishing wheat on 8 Aug 1780 {Ref: Maryland State Archives MdHR-6636-24-6}; received a receipt for furnishing wheat on 7 Sep and 8 Sep 1780 {Ref: Maryland State Archives MdHR-6636-24-7}

WEST, STEPHEN (Prince George's County) was appointed by the Council of Safety to collect all the gold and silver coin that could be procured in the county in compliance with the Resolve of Congress on 27 Jan 1776 {Ref: Archives of Maryland 11:132}; his name appeared as "Stephen Wests Store Marlbro 13 qr. caskes computed" when he was listed in possession of some gunpowder on a "Return of Armes and Ammunition in Prince George's County Belonging to the Publick" on 3 Jul 1780 {Ref: Archives of Maryland 45:4}

WEST, WILLIAM (Montgomery County) received a receipt from the Purchasing Agent for furnishing wheat on 19 Jul 1780 {Ref: Maryland State Archives MdHR-6636-24-5}; received a receipt for furnishing wheat on 1 Aug 1780 {Ref: Maryland State Archives MdHR-6636-43-7}; received a receipt for furnishing wheat on 11 Jun 1781 {Ref: Maryland State Archives MdHR-6636-42-11}

WEST, WILLIAM, see "Thomas Harrison," q.v.

WESTINGBERGER, PAUL (Anne Arundel County) received a receipt from the Purchasing Agent for furnishing powder on 16 Apr 1777 {Ref: Maryland State Archives MdHR-6636-9-14A}

WETHERED, JOHN (Kent County) received payment from the Purchasing Agent for furnishing cattle for the public use in September, 1781 {Ref: Maryland State Archives MdHR-6636-43-3}; John and William Wethered (misspelled as "Weathero") received a loan certificate for £182.3.11 due from the Council of Maryland "agreeable to the Act proposing to the Citizens of this State, Creditors of Congress on Loan Office Certificates, Etc." on 19 May 1783 for services rendered during the war {Ref: Archives of Maryland 48:417}

WEYAR, PETER (Frederick County) received a certificate from the Purchasing Agent for furnishing wheat on 30 May 1782 {Ref: Maryland State Archives MdHR-6636-42-34}

WHADMAN, WHEATLY (Caroline County) received receipts from the Purchasing Agent for wheat on 17 Aug and 16 Sep 1782 {Ref: Maryland State Archives MdHR-6636-42-7}

WHALAND, DANIEL (Montgomery County) received a receipt from the Purchasing Agent for shelling corn on 17 Jul 1780 {Ref: Maryland State Archives MdHR-6636-24-2}

WHANRIGHT, GEORGE (Worcester County) received a receipt from the Purchasing Agent for hauling corn on 24 Sep and 30 Sep 1780 {Ref: Maryland State Archives MdHR-6636-24-54}

WHEALAND, JANE (Dorchester County) received a receipt from the Purchasing Agent for furnishing wheat on 1 Nov 1782 {Ref: Maryland State Archives

349

MdHR-6636-42-23}

WHEALING, MICHAEL (Montgomery County) received a receipt from the Purchasing Agent for furnishing wheat on 16 Nov 1780 {Ref: Maryland State Archives MdHR-6636-24-8}

WHEALTON, WILLIAM (Dorchester County) received a receipt from the Purchasing Agent for furnishing wheat on 1 Oct 1782 {Ref: Maryland State Archives MdHR-6636-42-23}

WHEAT, JOSEPH (Montgomery County) received a receipt from the Purchasing Agent for furnishing wheat on 28 Apr 1781 {Ref: Maryland State Archives MdHR-6636-42-11}

WHEATLEY, WILLIAM (Caroline County) was appointed one of eighteen Collectors of Clothing by the Council of Maryland under "An Act to Procure Cloathing for the Quota of this State of the American Army" on 27 Nov 1777 {Ref: Archives of Maryland 16:426}

WHEATTY, FRANCIS (Charles County) received a receipt from the Purchasing Agent for furnishing wheat on 16 Jul 1781 {Ref: Maryland State Archives MdHR-6636-42-15}

WHEELER, BENEDICT (Charles County) received a receipt from the Purchasing Agent for furnishing wheat on 8 May 1783 {Ref: Maryland State Archives MdHR-6636-42-22}

WHEELER, BENJAMIN (Harford County) received a receipt from the Purchasing Agent for furnishing wheat on 13 Apr 1780 {Ref: Maryland State Archives MdHR-6636-23-35}

WHEELER, CLEMENT (Charles County) received a receipt from the Purchasing Agent for furnishing wheat on 10 May 1783 {Ref: Maryland State Archives MdHR-6636-42-22}

WHEELER, CLEMENT (Prince George's County) received a receipt from the Purchasing Agent for furnishing wheat on 20 May 1783 {Ref: Maryland State Archives MdHR-6636-43-9}

WHEELER, HEZEKIAH (Montgomery County) received a certificate from the Purchasing Agent for wood on 4 Jul 1781 {Ref: Maryland State Archives MdHR-6636-31-127}

WHEELER, IGNATIUS (Harford County) received payment by order of the Council of Maryland for his use as Contractor for Horses in Harford County on 2 Oct 1780 {Ref: Archives of Maryland 43:310}

WHEELER, IGNATIUS JR. (Harford County) submitted his account to the Committee of Safety for collecting blankets on 2 Sep 1776 {Ref: Preston's History of Harford County, p. 336}; received a certificate from the Purchasing Agent for furnishing wheat on 9 Mar 1780 {Ref: Maryland State Archives MdHR-6636-23-34}

WHEELER, JOHN (Caroline County) received a receipt from the Purchasing

Agent for furnishing wheat on 1 Sep 1782 {Ref: Maryland State Archives MdHR-6636-42-7}

WHEELER, JOSEPH (Charles County) received a receipt from the Purchasing Agent for furnishing wheat on 31 Oct 1782 {Ref: Maryland State Archives MdHR-6636-42-19}

WHEELER, LUKE (Charles County) received a receipt from the Purchasing Agent for furnishing wheat on 11 Apr 1782 {Ref: Maryland State Archives MdHR-6636-42-18}; received a receipt for furnishing wheat on 31 Oct 1782 {Ref: Maryland State Archives MdHR-6636-42-19}

WHEELER, ZADOCK (Somerset County) received a receipt from the Purchasing Agent for furnishing beef on 5 Dec 1781 {Ref: Maryland State Archives MdHR-6636-24-44}

WHEELING, RICHARD (Montgomery County) received a receipt from the Purchasing Agent for furnishing wheat on 11 Sep 1780 {Ref: Maryland State Archives MdHR-6636-24-7}

WHELAN, ANN (Charles County) received a receipt from the Purchasing Agent for furnishing wheat on 28 Dec 1782 {Ref: Maryland State Archives MdHR-6636-42-21}

WHELAN, THOMAS (Charles County) received a receipt from the Purchasing Agent for furnishing wheat on 26 Jun 1782 {Ref: Maryland State Archives MdHR-6636-42-18}

WHELAN, WILLIAM (Charles County) received a receipt from the Purchasing Agent for furnishing wheat on 11 Apr 1782 {Ref: Maryland State Archives MdHR-6636-42-18}

WHELAND, DANIEL (Montgomery County) received a receipt from the Purchasing Agent for furnishing wheat on 22 May 1781 {Ref: Maryland State Archives MdHR-6636-24-18}

WHIDDON (WEEDON), OLIVER (Anne Arundel County) received payment by order of the Council of Safety for stocking musquets on 6 Apr 1776 {Ref: Archives of Maryland 11:314}; received payments for repairing guns on 30 Aug and 3 Sep 1776 and musquets on 13 Sep, 18 Sep, 21 Sep, 2 Oct and 10 Oct 1776 {Ref: Archives of Maryland 12:248, 255, 269, 280, 293, 316, 330}

WHIP, BARBARY (Frederick County) received a certificate from the Purchasing Agent for furnishing wheat on 21 Sep 1781 {Ref: Maryland State Archives MdHR-6636-23-28}

WHIP, JOHN (Frederick County) received a certificate from the Purchasing Agent for furnishing wheat on 31 Jul 1782 {Ref: Maryland State Archives MdHR-6636-42-36}

WHITAKER, ROBERT (Prince George's County) received a loan certificate for £11.8.2 due from the Council of Maryland "agreeable to the Act proposing to the Citizens of this State, Creditors of Congress on Loan Office Certificates,

351

Etc." on 18 Dec 1783 for services rendered during the war {Ref: Archives of Maryland 48:491}

WHITAOF(?), WILLIAM (county not stated) contracted with and received payment from the Council of Safety to erect a slitting mill on 29 Jul 1776 {Ref: Archives of Maryland 11:465}

WHITBY, BENJAMIN (Caroline County) received a receipt from the Purchasing Agent for furnishing wheat on 31 Aug 1782 {Ref: Maryland State Archives MdHR-6636-42-7}

WHITBY, NATHAN (Caroline County) received a receipt from the Purchasing Agent for furnishing wheat on 31 Aug 1782 {Ref: Maryland State Archives MdHR-6636-42-7}

WHITCROFT, BURTON (Annapolis) received payment "for four Days assisting the Council Coppying" on 4 May 1782 {Ref: Archives of Maryland 48:155}

WHITE, BENJAMIN (Prince George's County) received a receipt from the Purchasing Agent for furnishing wheat on 10 May 1783 {Ref: Maryland State Archives MdHR-6636-43-9}

WHITE, HENRY (Worcester County) submitted an account and a receipt for collecting, herding and grazing cattle on 1 Sep and 19 Sep 1781 {Ref: Maryland State Archives MdHR-6636-43-27}

WHITE, JAMES (Caroline County) received a receipt from the Purchasing Agent for furnishing wheat on 29 May 1782 {Ref: Maryland State Archives MdHR-6636-42-7}

WHITE, JAMES (Harford County) received payment for furnishing a gun to the Committee of Safety on 18 Jun 1776 {Ref: Preston's History of Harford County, p. 330}

WHITE, JOHN (Caroline County) received receipts from the Purchasing Agent for furnishing wheat on 31 Aug and 1 Sep 1782 {Ref: Maryland State Archives MdHR-6636-42-7}

WHITE, JOHN (Worcester County) received a receipt from the Purchasing Agent for furnishing corn on 1 May 1780 {Ref: Maryland State Archives MdHR-6636-24-53}; his name appeared on "A List of Corn Purchased in Worcester County for the use of the State of Maryland" by the Commissary in July, 1780 {Ref: Archives of Maryland 45:10}

WHITE, JONATHAN (Montgomery County) was a captain who received a receipt from the Purchasing Agent for furnishing wheat on 11 Dec 1780 {Ref: Maryland State Archives MdHR-6636-24-13}

WHITE, JOSEPH (Worcester County) was a major who received payment for furnishing beef on 10 Oct 1781 {Ref: Maryland State Archives MdHR-6636-43-28MMM}

WHITE, JULIUS (Frederick County) submitted an account for furnishing beef on 21 May 1781 {Ref: Maryland State Archives MdHR-6636-23-6}

352

WHITE, MAJOR (Worcester County) submitted an account and receipt for killing beef on 1 Oct 1781 {Ref: Maryland State Archives MdHR-6636-43-27}

WHITE, NANNY, Mrs. (Somerset County) received a receipt from the Purchasing Agent for furnishing beef on 6 Dec 1781 {Ref: Maryland State Archives MdHR-6636-24-44}

WHITE, NICHOLAS (Frederick Town) was a gunsmith who received payment by order of the Council of Safety for furnishing or repairing a gun on 1 Oct 1776 {Ref: Archives of Maryland 12:313}; Council of Maryland "ordered that the Armourer deliver to Adam Coile for the use of N. White of Frederick Town 110 musquet gun barrels, 110 setts of brass mounting and 110 musquet bayonets" on 18 Jun 1777 {Ref: Archives of Maryland 16:293}; contracted with the Council of Maryland to completely finish 200 stands of arms supplied by the State (and to be returned at the rate of 48 stands per month) on 20 Nov 1777 {Ref: Archives of Maryland 16:419}; he was still manufacturing arms on 12 Jan 1781 {Ref: Archives of Maryland 47:14}

WHITE, OLIVER (Baltimore County) requested payment by order of the Council of Safety on 10 Oct 1776 "for sinkage of vessels at *Otter* alarm" at Whetstone Point in March, 1776 for the purpose of preventing any of the British Ships of War from coming up to Baltimore Town {Ref: Archives of Maryland 12:333}

WHITE, RICHARD (Harford County) received payment for making cartouch boxes for the Committee of Safety on 29 Apr 1776 {Ref: Preston's History of Harford County, p. 325}

WHITE, RICHARD (Prince George's County) received a receipt from the Purchasing Agent for furnishing wheat on 18 Apr 1783 {Ref: Maryland State Archives MdHR-6636-43-9}

WHITE, SAMUEL JR. (Montgomery County) received a receipt from the Purchasing Agent for furnishing wheat on 1 Aug 1780 {Ref: Maryland State Archives MdHR-6636-43-7}

WHITE, THOMAS (county not stated) received payment by order of the Council of Safety for furnishing boatage for the Flying Camp on 2 Sep 1776 {Ref: Archives of Maryland 12:252}

WHITE, THOMAS (county not stated) received a loan certificate for £52.9.3 due from the Council of Maryland "agreeable to the Act proposing to the Citizens of this State, Creditors of Congress on Loan Office Certificates, Etc." on 10 Dec 1783 for services rendered during the war {Ref: Archives of Maryland 48:487}

WHITE, TRUMAN (Frederick County) received a receipt from the Purchasing Agent for furnishing corn on 2 Jun 1780 {Ref: Maryland State Archives MdHR-6636-24-1}

WHITE, WALTER (Montgomery County) received a receipt from the Purchasing Agent for shelling corn on 9 Jul 1780 {Ref: Maryland State Archives MdHR-

6636-24-2}
WHITE, WALTER (Prince George's County) received a receipt from the Purchasing Agent for furnishing wheat in 1782 {Ref: Maryland State Archives MdHR-6636-50-135}
WHITELY (WHITELEY), ARTHUR (Dorchester County) pledged a loan in the amount of £200 to the State of Maryland under the Act for the Emission of Bills of Credit "to defray the expences of the present campaign" in June, 1781 {Ref: Archives of Maryland 47:326}; received a loan certificate for £26.7.7 due from the Council of Maryland "agreeable to the Act proposing to the Citizens of this State, Creditors of Congress on Loan Office Certificates, Etc." on 22 Dec 1783 for services rendered during the war {Ref: Archives of Maryland 48:495}
WHITLEY, MRS. (Somerset County) received a receipt from the Purchasing Agent for furnishing beef on 6 Nov 1781 {Ref: Maryland State Archives MdHR-6636-24-44}
WHITTEN, WILLIAM (Charles County) received a receipt from the Purchasing Agent for a wheat certificate on 27 Oct 1781 {Ref: Maryland State Archives MdHR-6636-23-25}; received a receipt for furnishing wheat on 8 Dec 1781 {Ref: Maryland State Archives MdHR-6636-42-15}
WHITTINGTON, ISAAC (Somerset County) received a receipt from the Purchasing Agent for furnishing beef on 6 Nov 1781 {Ref: Maryland State Archives MdHR-6636-24-44}
WICKES, JOSEPH (Kent County) received a certificate from the Purchasing Agent for furnishing flour on 16 Jan 1780 {Ref: Maryland State Archives MdHR-6636-23-43}
WICKES, SIMON (Kent County) received a certificate from the Purchasing Agent for furnishing flour on 16 Jan 1780 {Ref: Maryland State Archives MdHR-6636-23-43}
WIESENTHAL, CHARLES FREDERICK (Baltimore Town) was a doctor who was appointed by the Council of Safety to serve as "Surgeon to the Battalion" on 2 Mar 1776 {Ref: Archives of Maryland 11:197}; received payment by order of the Council of Maryland "for oil purchased by him for the State" on 5 Nov 1777 {Ref: Archives of Maryland 16:409}; received payment "to be expended in necessaries for the Hospital in Baltimore Town" on 28 Jul 1781 {Ref: Archives of Maryland 45:524}
WIGLY, WILLIAM (Baltimore County) submitted an account and received payment for turning out and stowing flour for one and three quarter days on 28 Jan 1780 {Ref: Maryland Historical Society MS.1814, Box 6}
WILCOXON, JESSE (Montgomery County) received a receipt from the Purchasing Agent for furnishing wheat on 21 Jul 1780 {Ref: Maryland State Archives MdHR-6636-24-5}; received a certificate for furnishing wheat on 21

Jul 1780 {Ref: Maryland State Archives MdHR-6636-24-5}

WILCOXON, WILLIAM (Montgomery County) received a receipt from the Purchasing Agent for furnishing wheat on 8 Aug 1780 {Ref: Maryland State Archives MdHR-6636-24-6}; received a receipt for furnishing wheat on 10 Apr 1781 {Ref: Maryland State Archives MdHR-6636-24-15}

WILEY, AQUILA (Macamson's Mill, Harford County) was appointed by the Council of Maryland to be one of five men in Harford County "to carry the Act to prohibit for a limited time the Exportation of Indian Corn, Etc., by Land" on 22 Dec 1780 {Ref: Archives of Maryland 45:251}

WILEY, JAMES (Frederick County) received a certificate from the Purchasing Agent for furnishing wheat on 7 Jun 1782 {Ref: Maryland State Archives MdHR-6636-42-34}

WILEY, JOSHUA (Baltimore County) received a receipt from the Purchasing Agent for furnishing flour on 19 Jun and 8 Aug 1779 {Ref: Maryland State Archives MdHR-6636-21-67}

WILFE, ADAM (Frederick County) received a certificate from the Purchasing Agent for hauling on 30 Sep 1781 {Ref: Maryland State Archives MdHR-6636-42-32}

WILKINS, WILLIAM (Anne Arundel County) was appointed by the Council of Maryland to be one of the two "Supervisors of the Press for superintending the printing of the [Continental] Bills of Credit" on 5 Sep 1780 {Ref: Archives of Maryland 43:276}; appointed by the Council of Maryland to be one of the "Signers of the New Bills of Credit emitted by Congress" on 11 Sep 1780 {Ref: Archives of Maryland 43:285}

WILKINSON, ALEXANDER (Charles County) received a receipt from the Purchasing Agent for furnishing wheat on 15 Apr 1783 {Ref: Maryland State Archives MdHR-6636-42-22}

WILKINSON, JOSEPH (Calvert County) was appointed one of eighteen Collectors of Clothing by the Council of Maryland under "An Act to Procure Cloathing for the Quota of this State of the American Army" on 27 Nov 1777 {Ref: Archives of Maryland 16:426}

WILKINSON, WALTER (Charles County) received a receipt from the Purchasing Agent for furnishing wheat on 15 Apr 1783 {Ref: Maryland State Archives MdHR-6636-42-22}

WILKINSON, WILLIAM (Montgomery County) received a receipt from the Purchasing Agent for shelling corn on 17 Apr 1780 {Ref: Maryland State Archives MdHR-6636-24-2}

WILLABEY, EDWARD (Caroline County) received a receipt from the Purchasing Agent for furnishing wheat on 5 Aug 1782 {Ref: Maryland State Archives MdHR-6636-42-7}

WILLABY, SOLOMON (Caroline County) received a receipt from the Purchasing

Agent for furnishing wheat on 1 Sep 1782 {Ref: Maryland State Archives MdHR-6636-42-7}

WILLET, GRIFFITH (Prince George's County) received a receipt from the Purchasing Agent for furnishing wheat on 13 Jan 1783 {Ref: Maryland State Archives MdHR-6636-50-135}

WILLET, RICHARD (Charles County) received a receipt from the Purchasing Agent for furnishing wheat on 11 Feb 1782 {Ref: Maryland State Archives MdHR-6636-42-16}

WILLETT, BENJAMIN (Montgomery County) received a receipt from the Purchasing Agent for furnishing wheat on 8 Sep 1780 {Ref: Maryland State Archives MdHR-6636-24-13}; received a receipt for furnishing wheat on 11 May 1781 {Ref: Maryland State Archives MdHR-6636-24-18}

WILLETT, NINIAN (Montgomery County) received a receipt from the Purchasing Agent for furnishing wheat on 18 Sep 1780 {Ref: Maryland State Archives MdHR-6636-24-7}; received a receipt for furnishing wheat on 5 Oct 1780 {Ref: Maryland State Archives MdHR-6636-24-8}

WILLETT, RICHARD (Charles County) received a receipt from the Purchasing Agent for furnishing wheat on 25 May 1782 {Ref: Maryland State Archives MdHR-6636-42-18}; received a receipt for furnishing wheat on 28 Sep 1782 {Ref: Maryland State Archives MdHR-6636-42-19}

WILLIAM, THOMAS (Frederick County) received a certificate from the Purchasing Agent for furnishing wheat on 28 May 1782 {Ref: Maryland State Archives MdHR-6636-42-33}

WILLIAM, WALTER (Prince George's County) received a receipt from the Purchasing Agent for furnishing wheat in 1782 {Ref: Maryland State Archives MdHR-6636-50-135}

WILLIAMS, AMOS (Montgomery County) received a receipt from the Purchasing Agent for furnishing wheat on 1 Aug 1780 {Ref: Maryland State Archives MdHR-6636-43-7}; received a receipt for furnishing wheat on 7 Sep 1780 {Ref: Maryland State Archives MdHR-6636-24-7}; received a receipt for furnishing wheat on 28 Oct 1780 {Ref: Maryland State Archives MdHR-6636-24-8}; received a receipt for furnishing wheat on 10 Oct 1781 {Ref: Maryland State Archives MdHR-6636-24-15}

WILLIAMS, BARUCH OR BARRUCH (Cecil County) was appointed Commissary of Purchases for Cecil County by the Council of Maryland on 8 Jul 1780 {Ref: Archives of Maryland 43:215}; submitted an account of shipment of provisions on 17 Oct 1780 {Ref: Maryland State Archives MdHR-6636-20-116}; submitted an account of cattle and bacon delivered to Col. Hollingsworth on 22 Nov 1780 {Ref: Maryland State Archives MdHR-6636-21-46}; appointed by the Council of Maryland to be one of five men in Cecil County "to carry the Act to prohibit for a limited time the Exportation of Indian

Corn, Etc., by Land" on 22 Dec 1780 {Ref: Archives of Maryland 45:250}; submitted his settlement of accounts and payments due on 7 Apr 1781 {Ref: Maryland State Archives MdHR-6636-26-93}; appointed Purchaser of Clothing in his county by the Council of Maryland on 5 Jun 1781 {Ref: Archives of Maryland 45:462}; also see "Jonathan Parker," q.v.

WILLIAMS, BENJAMIN (Montgomery County) received a receipt from the Purchasing Agent for furnishing wheat on 28 Jun 1781 {Ref: Maryland State Archives MdHR-6636-24-15}

WILLIAMS, CHARLES (Montgomery County) received a receipt from the Purchasing Agent for furnishing wheat on 28 Jul 1780 {Ref: Maryland State Archives MdHR-6636-24-5}; received a receipt for furnishing wheat on 1 Aug 1780 {Ref: Maryland State Archives MdHR-6636-43-7}; received a receipt for furnishing wheat on 7 Sep 1780 {Ref: Maryland State Archives MdHR-6636-24-7}; received a receipt for furnishing wheat on 5 Oct 1781 {Ref: Maryland State Archives MdHR-6636-42-11}

WILLIAMS, ELY (Washington County) was appointed Purchaser of Clothing in his county by the Council of Maryland on 5 Jun 1781 {Ref: Archives of Maryland 45:462}

WILLIAMS, FRANCES, Miss (Calvert County) received a certificate for a loan to the Continental Congress on 4 Jun 1778 {Ref: Maryland State Archives MdHR-6636-11-119H}

WILLIAMS, HENRY (Frederick County) received a receipt from the Purchasing Agent for furnishing mutton on 19 Jan 1781 {Ref: Maryland State Archives MdHR-6636-23-2}; received a certificate for furnishing wheat on 16 May 1782 {Ref: Maryland State Archives MdHR-6636-42-33}

WILLIAMS, JACOB (Montgomery County) received a receipt from the Purchasing Agent for shelling corn on 18 May 1780 {Ref: Maryland State Archives MdHR-6636-24-2}; received a receipt for furnishing wheat on 4 Sep and 7 Sep 1780 {Ref: Maryland State Archives MdHR-6636-24-7}

WILLIAMS, JOHN (Charles County) received receipts from the Purchasing Agent for furnishing wheat on 24 Nov and 8 Dec 1781 {Ref: Maryland State Archives MdHR-6636-42-15}

WILLIAMS, JOHN (Montgomery County) received a receipt from the Purchasing Agent for shelling corn on 20 Apr 1780 {Ref: Maryland State Archives MdHR-6636-24-2}

WILLIAMS, JOSEPH (Kent County) received a certificate from the Purchasing Agent for furnishing wheat on 26 Jan 1780 {Ref: Maryland State Archives MdHR-6636-43-1}

WILLIAMS, MARTHA, Mrs. (Somerset County) received a receipt from the Purchasing Agent for furnishing beef on 6 Dec 1781 {Ref: Maryland State Archives MdHR-6636-24-44}

WILLIAMS, MARY, Mrs. (Somerset County) received a receipt from the Purchasing Agent for furnishing beef on 31 Oct 1781 {Ref: Maryland State Archives MdHR-6636-24-44}

WILLIAMS, PLANNER (Somerset County) received a receipt from the Purchasing Agent for furnishing bacon on 5 Oct 1780 {Ref: Maryland State Archives MdHR-6636-24-41}; received a receipt for furnishing pork on 3 Jul 1781 {Ref: Maryland State Archives MdHR-6636-24-45}; submitted an account for furnishing beef on 1 Nov 1781 {Ref: Maryland State Archives MdHR-6636-43-15}

WILLIAMS, THOMAS (Somerset County) received a receipt from the Purchasing Agent for furnishing pork on 1 May 1781 {Ref: Maryland State Archives MdHR-6636-24-43}; received a receipt for furnishing beef on 1 Nov 1781 {Ref: Maryland State Archives MdHR-6636-24-44}

WILLIAMS, THOMAS (Caroline County) received a receipt from the Purchasing Agent for furnishing wheat on 20 Sep 1782 {Ref: Maryland State Archives MdHR-6636-42-7}

WILLIAMS, WILLIAM (Montgomery County) received a receipt from the Purchasing Agent for furnishing wheat on 4 Sep and 30 Sep 1780 {Ref: Maryland State Archives MdHR-6636-24-7}; received a receipt for furnishing wheat on 7 Oct and 10 Oct 1781 {Ref: Maryland State Archives MdHR-6636-24-15}

WILLIAMS, WILLIAM PRATOR (Montgomery County) received a receipt from the Purchasing Agent for furnishing wheat on 20 Oct 1780 {Ref: Maryland State Archives MdHR-6636-24-8}

WILLIAMSON, ALEXANDER (Montgomery County) received a receipt from the Purchasing Agent for furnishing wheat on 7 Apr 1781 {Ref: Maryland State Archives MdHR-6636-24-14}

WILLIS, ELIJAH (Caroline County) received a receipt from the Purchasing Agent for furnishing wheat on 5 Aug 1782 {Ref: Maryland State Archives MdHR-6636-42-7}

WILLIS, JABEZ (Worcester County) submitted an account and receipt for furnishing pork on 23 Apr 1782 {Ref: Maryland State Archives MdHR-6636-43-28FF}

WILLIS, JERVIZ (Dorchester County) received a receipt from the Purchasing Agent for furnishing wheat on 1 Oct 1782 {Ref: Maryland State Archives MdHR-6636-42-23}

WILLIS, THOMAS (Caroline County) received receipts from the Purchasing Agent for furnishing wheat on 5 Aug 1782 {Ref: Maryland State Archives MdHR-6636-42-7}

WILLIS, WILLIAM (Caroline County) received a receipt from the Purchasing Agent for furnishing wheat on 5 Aug 1782 {Ref: Maryland State Archives

MdHR-6636-42-7}

WILLIX(?), WILLIAM (county not stated) received payment by order of the Council of Maryland for furnishing a gun on 13 Sep 1776 {Ref: Archives of Maryland 16:375}

WILLS, MATTHEW (Anne Arundel County) made an agreement to deliver bacon and pork to Col. Henry Hollingsworth in Cecil County on 12 Jun 1780 {Ref: Maryland State Archives MdHR-6636-18-141}

WILLSON, ALEXANDER (Montgomery County) received a receipt from the Purchasing Agent for furnishing wheat on 1 Aug 1780 {Ref: Maryland State Archives MdHR-6636-43-7}

WILLSON, BENJAMIN (Caroline County) received a receipt from the Purchasing Agent for furnishing wheat on 1 Sep 1782 {Ref: Maryland State Archives MdHR-6636-42-7}

WILLSON, CHRISTOPHER (Caroline County) received a receipt from the Purchasing Agent for furnishing wheat on 1 Aug 1782 {Ref: Maryland State Archives MdHR-6636-42-7}

WILLSON, EXANDER (Montgomery County) received a receipt from the Purchasing Agent for furnishing wheat on 19 May 1781 {Ref: Maryland State Archives MdHR-6636-42-11}

WILLSON, BENJAMIN (Caroline County) received a receipt from the Purchasing Agent for furnishing wheat on 1 Sep 1782 {Ref: Maryland State Archives MdHR-6636-42-7}

WILLSON, JAMES (Caroline County) received a receipt from the Purchasing Agent for wheat on 20 Sep 1782 {Ref: Maryland State Archives MdHR-6636-42-7}

WILLSON, JOHN (Caroline County) received a receipt from the Purchasing Agent for furnishing wheat on 1 Sep 1782 {Ref: Maryland State Archives MdHR-6636-42-7}

WILLSON, JOHN (Montgomery County) received a receipt from the Purchasing Agent for furnishing wheat on 12 Mar 1781 {Ref: Maryland State Archives MdHR-6636-24-15}

WILLSON, RICHARD (Cecil County) submitted an account for storing and hauling wheat on 1 Aug 1782 {Ref: Maryland State Archives MdHR-6636-42-9}

WILLSON, ROBERT (Montgomery County) received a receipt from the Purchasing Agent for furnishing wheat on 11 Aug 1781 {Ref: Maryland State Archives MdHR-6636-24-15}

WILLSON, SAMUEL (Caroline County) received a receipt from the Purchasing Agent for furnishing wheat on 31 Aug 1782 {Ref: Maryland State Archives MdHR-6636-42-7}

WILLSON, THOMAS (Montgomery County) received a receipt from the

Purchasing Agent for furnishing wheat on 20 Oct 1780 {Ref: Maryland State Archives MdHR-6636-24-13}

WILLSON, THOMAS (Frederick County) received a certificate from the Purchasing Agent for furnishing wheat on 10 Feb 1783 {Ref: Maryland State Archives MdHR-6636-42-38}

WILLSON, WILLIAM (Caroline County) received a receipt from the Purchasing Agent for wheat on 20 Sep 1782 {Ref: Maryland State Archives MdHR-6636-42-7}

WILMER, JOHN L. (Kent County) received payment for furnishing beef on 14 Nov 1780 {Ref: Maryland State Archives MdHR-6636-23-49}

WILMER, SIMON (Kent County) received a certificate from the Purchasing Agent for furnishing wheat on 26 Jan 1780; received a certificate for hauling flour on 12 May 1780 {Ref: Maryland State Archives MdHR-6636-23-41}

WILMOTT, JOHN (Baltimore County) received payment for the hire of his wagon on 8 Jan 1778 {Ref: Maryland State Archives MdHR-6636-10-53}

WILMOTT, JOHN JR. (Baltimore County) received payments by order of the Council of Maryland "for riding express on Continental business" on 31 Jan and 25 Feb 1778 {Ref: Archives of Maryland 16:481, 520}; received payment "for going express to Queen Anne's County" on 25 May 1778 {Ref: Archives of Maryland 21:109}

WILSON, ALEXANDER (Montgomery County) received a receipt from the Purchasing Agent for furnishing wheat on 10 Aug 1780 {Ref: Maryland State Archives MdHR-6636-24-6}

WILSON, CHARITY (Montgomery County) received a receipt from the Purchasing Agent for furnishing wheat on 7 Oct 1780 {Ref: Maryland State Archives MdHR-6636-24-8}

WILSON, DENWOOD (Somerset County) received a receipt from the Purchasing Agent for furnishing bacon on 1 Jul 1780 {Ref: Maryland State Archives MdHR-6636-24-41}; received a loan certificate for £343.8.6 due from the Council of Maryland "agreeable to the Act proposing to the Citizens of this State, Creditors of Congress on Loan Office Certificates, Etc." on 19 Dec 1783 for services rendered during the war {Ref: Archives of Maryland 48:493}

WILSON, ELIZABETH (Baltimore Town) submitted an account for boarding services rendered to Morgan Murphy, a marine on the state ship *Defence*, and other guests on 18 Mar and 4 Apr 1777 {Ref: Maryland State Archives MdHR-19970-2-1}

WILSON, GEORGE (Kent County) received payment from the Purchasing Agent for furnishing cattle for the public use in September, 1781 {Ref: Maryland State Archives MdHR-6636-43-3}

WILSON, JAMES (Harford County) received payment for furnishing a gun to the Committee of Safety on 18 Jun 1776 {Ref: Preston's History of Harford

County, p. 330}

WILSON, JAMES (Kent County) received payment for furnishing a cart, horses, and a negro man on 27 Oct 1780 {Ref: Maryland State Archives MdHR-6636-23-49}

WILSON, JAMES (Somerset County) received receipts from the Purchasing Agent for furnishing bacon on 9 Jul and 29 Jul 1780 {Ref: Maryland State Archives MdHR-6636-24-41}; received a receipt for furnishing pork on 20 Mar 1781 {Ref: Maryland State Archives MdHR-6636-24-43}

WILSON, JAMES (Montgomery County) received a receipt from the Purchasing Agent for shelling corn on 7 Apr 1780 {Ref: Maryland State Archives MdHR-6636-24-2}

WILSON, JOHN (Harford County) received payment from the Committee of Safety for furnishing powder and lead on 24 Oct 1775 and for two casks of brimstone on 27 Aug 1776 {Ref: Preston's History of Harford County, pp. 314, 334}

WILSON, JOHN (Prince George's County) received receipts from the Purchasing Agent for furnishing wheat on 3 Dec 1782 and 31 Jul 1783 {Ref: Maryland State Archives MdHR-6636-50-135}

WILSON, JOHN (Montgomery County) received a receipt from the Purchasing Agent for furnishing linen on 26 Apr 1780 {Ref: Maryland State Archives MdHR-6636-24-2}

WILSON, JOHN (Kent County) submitted an account and receipt for grinding wheat on 30 Mar 1782 {Ref: Maryland State Archives MdHR-6636-43-5}

WILSON, JOHN SR. (Kent County) received payment from the Purchasing Agent for furnishing cattle for the public use in September, 1781 {Ref: Maryland State Archives MdHR-6636-43-3}

WILSON, JOSEPH (Montgomery County) received receipts from the Purchasing Agent for furnishing wheat on 2 Oct and 31 Oct 1780 {Ref: Maryland State Archives MdHR-6636-24-8}

WILSON, LEVIN (Somerset County) received a receipt from the Purchasing Agent for furnishing pork on 29 Apr 1782 {Ref: Maryland State Archives MdHR-6636-43-21}

WILSON, MARTHA (Somerset County) received a loan certificate for £37.4.10 due from the Council of Maryland "agreeable to the Act proposing to the Citizens of this State, Creditors of Congress on Loan Office Certificates, Etc." on 2 May 1783 for services rendered during the war {Ref: Archives of Maryland 48:405}

WILSON, RICHARD (Worcester County) was a Commissary Agent who submitted an account for storing wheat on 13 May 1783 {Ref: Maryland State Archives MdHR-6636-43-13}

WILSON, ROBERT (Montgomery County) received a receipt from the Purchasing

Agent for furnishing wheat on 7 Apr 1781 {Ref: Maryland State Archives MdHR-6636-42-11}

WILSON, ROBERT (Queen Anne's County) received a receipt from the Purchasing Agent for furnishing wheat on 25 Jul 1780 {Ref: Maryland State Archives MdHR-6636-24-33}

WILSON, SAMUEL (Somerset County) was appointed by the Council of Safety to collect all the gold and silver coin that could be procured in the county in compliance with the Resolve of Congress on 27 Jan 1776 {Ref: Archives of Maryland 11:132}; received a receipt for furnishing corn, brandy and fodder on 21 Aug 1781 {Ref: Maryland State Archives MdHR-6636-43-15}; received a receipt for furnishing pork on 21 May 1782 {Ref: Maryland State Archives MdHR-6636-43-21}; received a receipt for furnishing wheat on 10 Oct 1782 {Ref: Maryland State Archives MdHR-6636-43-21}

WILSON, THOMAS (Charles County) received a receipt of repayment of money lent during the war to the state on 22 Dec 1784 {Ref: Maryland State Archives MdHR-6636-50-71}

WILSON, WADSWORTH (Frederick County) received a receipt from the Purchasing Agent for furnishing pork on 9 Mar 1781 {Ref: Maryland State Archives MdHR-6636-23-4}

WILSON, WILLIAM (Caroline County) received a receipt from the Purchasing Agent for furnishing wheat on 1 Sep 1782 {Ref: Maryland State Archives MdHR-6636-42-7}

WILSON, WILLIAM (Kent County) received payment from the commissary for traveling expenses on 28 Aug 1780 {Ref: Maryland State Archives MdHR-6636-23-49}

WILSON, WILLIAM (Somerset County) received a receipt from the Purchasing Agent for furnishing beef on 6 Nov 1781 {Ref: Maryland State Archives MdHR-6636-24-44}

WILSON, ZADOCK (Montgomery County) received a certificate from the Purchasing Agent for indebtedness owed to him by the state for services rendered to the commissary of purchases on 18 Mar 1782 {Ref: Maryland State Archives MdHR-6636-50-91}

WINCHESTER, JACOB (Caroline County) received a receipt from the Purchasing Agent for furnishing wheat on 24 Aug 1782 {Ref: Maryland State Archives MdHR-6636-42-7}

WINCHESTER, MARY (county not stated) received a loan certificate for £62.7.6 due from the Council of Maryland "agreeable to the Act proposing to the Citizens of this State, Creditors of Congress on Loan Office Certificates, Etc." on 15 Oct 1783 for services rendered during the war {Ref: Archives of Maryland 48:464}

WINDER, JOHN (Somerset County) pledged a loan in the amount of £200 to the

State of Maryland under the Act for the Emission of Bills of Credit "to defray the expences of the present campaign" in June, 1781 {Ref: Archives of Maryland 47:326}

WINDER, WILLIAM (Somerset County) received payment by order of the Council of Safety for guarding powder on 7 May 1776 {Ref: Archives of Maryland 11:414}; appointed by the Council of Maryland to be one of three Purchasers of Cattle for Somerset County on 7 Jan 1778 {Ref: Archives of Maryland 16:456}; received a receipt for storing pork and corn on 7 Oct 1780 {Ref: Maryland State Archives MdHR-6636-24-54}; received a receipt for furnishing wheat on 29 Dec 1781 {Ref: Maryland State Archives MdHR-6636-24-44}

WINDER, WILLIAM JR. (Worcester County) was ordered by the Maryland Council to buy or seize cattle on 7 Jan 1778 {Ref: Maryland State Archives MdHR-6636-10-12}; received a receipt for storing corn on 10 Oct 1780 {Ref: Maryland State Archives MdHR-6636-24-54}

WINDSOM, WILLIAM (Montgomery County) received a receipt from the Purchasing Agent for furnishing wheat on 31 Aug 1780 {Ref: Maryland State Archives MdHR-6636-24-6}

WINDSOR, THOMAS (Montgomery County) received a receipt from the Purchasing Agent for furnishing wheat on 4 Oct 1781 {Ref: Maryland State Archives MdHR-6636-24-15}

WINGAR, IGNATIUS (Montgomery County) received a receipt from the Purchasing Agent for furnishing wheat on 1 Aug 1780 {Ref: Maryland State Archives MdHR-6636-43-7}

WINGER, JOHN STEPHENS (Montgomery County) received a receipt from the Purchasing Agent for furnishing wheat on 1 Aug 1780 {Ref: Maryland State Archives MdHR-6636-43-7}

WINN, JOHN (Prince George's County) contracted with the commissary of purchases to supply fish for the use of the state on 1 Sep 1779 {Ref: Maryland State Archives MdHR-6636-15-52B}

WINTER, CHARLES (Charles County) received a receipt from the Purchasing Agent for furnishing wheat on 20 Oct 1781 {Ref: Maryland State Archives MdHR-6636-42-15}

WINTER, WILLIAM SR. (Charles County) received a receipt from the Purchasing Agent for furnishing wheat on 20 Dec 1782 {Ref: Maryland State Archives MdHR-6636-42-20}

WINTERS, ELISHA (Chestertown, Kent County) contracted with the Maryland Council of Safety to repair guns, bayonets, ramrods, etc. for the Flying Camp on 12 Jul 1776; ordered by the Council "to deliver all the musquets he has ready made for the public service" on 24 Sep 1776 {Ref: Archives of Maryland 12:30-31, 12:97}

WINTERS, GEORGE (county not stated) received a loan certificate for £5.1.6 due from the Council of Maryland "agreeable to the Act proposing to the Citizens of this State, Creditors of Congress on Loan Office Certificates, Etc." on 19 Aug 1783 for services rendered during the war {Ref: Archives of Maryland 48:448}

WISE, JOHN ADAM (Frederick County) received a receipt from the Purchasing Agent for furnishing beef on 10 Jan 1781 {Ref: Maryland State Archives MdHR-6636-23-2}

WISE, WILLIAM (Worcester County) was appointed by the Council of Maryland to be one of three Purchasers of Cattle for his county on 7 Jan 1778 {Ref: Archives of Maryland 16:456}

WITCH, RICHARD (Prince George's County) received a receipt from the Purchasing Agent for furnishing wheat on 11 Feb 1783 {Ref: Maryland State Archives MdHR-6636-50-135}

WODWARDS, REUBIN (Dorchester County) received a receipt from the Purchasing Agent for furnishing wheat on 1 Oct 1782 {Ref: Maryland State Archives MdHR-6636-42-23}

WOLFE, ADAM (Frederick County) received a certificate from the Purchasing Agent for hauling on 30 Sep 1781 {Ref: Maryland State Archives MdHR-6636-42-32}

WOLFE, HENRY (Frederick County) received a certificate from the Purchasing Agent for furnishing wheat on 28 May 1782 {Ref: Maryland State Archives MdHR-6636-42-33}

WOOD, JACOB (Caroline County) received a receipt from the Purchasing Agent for furnishing wheat on 16 Aug 1782 {Ref: Maryland State Archives MdHR-6636-42-7}

WOOD, JOHN (Prince George's County) received a receipt from the Purchasing Agent for furnishing wheat in 1783 {Ref: Maryland State Archives MdHR-6636-50-135}

WOOD, JOSEPH (Frederick County) was a colonel who received a receipt from the Purchasing Agent for delivering flour on 3 Jan 1780 {Ref: Maryland State Archives MdHR-6636-23-30}; received a receipt for furnishing whiskey on 26 Dec 1780 {Ref: Maryland State Archives MdHR-6636-23-1}; received a receipt for whiskey on 4 Apr 1781 {Ref: Maryland State Archives MdHR-6636-23-5}; submitted an account for whiskey on 29 May 1781 {Ref: Maryland State Archives MdHR-6636-23-6}

WOOD, JOSEPH JR. (Frederick County) received a receipt from the Purchasing Agent for hauling flour on or about 1 Jan 1781 {Ref: Maryland State Archives MdHR-6636-23-31}; received a receipt for hauling provisions and hiring two men on 9 Jun 1781 {Ref: Maryland State Archives MdHR-6636-23-31}

WOOD, JOSEPH SR. (Frederick County) received a certificate from the

Purchasing Agent for furnishing wheat on 3 Sep 1782 {Ref: Maryland State Archives MdHR-6636-42-37}

WOOD, LEONARD (Charles County) received a receipt from the Purchasing Agent for furnishing wheat on 28 Dec 1782 {Ref: Maryland State Archives MdHR-6636-42-21}

WOOD, WILLIAM (Worcester County) was a captain who received a receipt from the Purchasing Agent for hauling corn on 30 Mar 1780 {Ref: Maryland State Archives MdHR-6636-24-52}

WOOD, WILLIAM (Frederick County) received a certificate from the Purchasing Agent for furnishing wheat on 1 Aug 1782 {Ref: Maryland State Archives MdHR-6636-42-36}

WOODLAND, ABM. (Kent County) received payment from the Purchasing Agent for furnishing cattle for the public use in September, 1781 {Ref: Maryland State Archives MdHR-6636-43-3}

WOODLAND, JOHN (Kent County) received a certificate from the Purchasing Agent for furnishing wheat on 18 Jan 1780 {Ref: Maryland State Archives MdHR-6636-43-1}; received payment for furnishing cattle on 20 Oct 1780 {Ref: Maryland State Archives MdHR-6636-23-49}; submitted an account and a receipt for grinding wheat and for carting flour and nails on 1 Dec 1781 and 1 Feb 1782 {Ref: Maryland State Archives MdHR-6636-43-5}

WOODWARD, FRANCIS (Montgomery County) received a receipt from the Purchasing Agent for furnishing wheat on 21 Apr 1781 {Ref: Maryland State Archives MdHR-6636-24-14}

WOODWARD, JOSEPH (St. Mary's County) submitted an account and receipt of pay for driving cattle on 18 Oct 1781 {Ref: Maryland State Archives MdHR-19970-3-17}

WOODWARD, SAMUEL (Charles County) received a receipt from the Purchasing Agent for furnishing wheat on 23 Oct 1781 {Ref: Maryland State Archives MdHR-6636-23-24}; received a receipt for furnishing wheat on 10 May 1783 {Ref: Maryland State Archives MdHR-6636-42-22}

WOOLFE, JOHN (Calvert County) received money from the Council of Maryland "to be delivered over to Patrick Sim Smith, Commissary of Calvert County, for the use of his Department Accounted" on 7 Sep 1781 {Ref: Archives of Maryland 45:607}

WOOLFORD, LEVIN (Somerset County) was appointed by the Council of Maryland to be one of three Purchasers of Cattle for his county on 7 Jan 1778 {Ref: Archives of Maryland 16:456}

WOOLSEY, GEORGE (Baltimore Town) received payment for supplying demurrage for the brigantine *Rogers* on 22 Jul 1776 {Ref: Archives of Maryland 12:88-89}

WOOLTON, RICHARD (Montgomery County) received a receipt from the

Purchasing Agent for furnishing wheat on 3 Aug 1780 {Ref: Maryland State Archives MdHR-6636-24-6}

WOOTTON, SINGLETON (Queen Ann, Prince George's County) received payment from the Purchasing Agent for furnishing material for clothing ("oznaburgs and jermon dowlass") on 11 Jun 1781 {Ref: Archives of Maryland 47:287}

WOOTTON, WILLIAM TURNER (Prince George's County) was appointed by the Council of Safety to collect all the gold and silver coin that could be procured in the county in compliance with the Resolve of Congress on 27 Jan 1776 {Ref: Archives of Maryland 11:132}

WORLAND, JOHN (Montgomery County) received a receipt from the Purchasing Agent for furnishing wheat on 4 Sep 1781 {Ref: Maryland State Archives MdHR-6636-24-15}

WORMAN, ANDREW (Frederick County) received a certificate from the Purchasing Agent for furnishing beef on 13 Apr 1780 {Ref: Maryland State Archives MdHR-6636-23-27}; received a receipt for driving cattle on 16 Apr 1781 {Ref: Maryland State Archives MdHR-6636-23-31}

WORMAN, JOHN (Montgomery County) received a receipt from the Purchasing Agent for furnishing wheat on 2 May 1781 {Ref: Maryland State Archives MdHR-6636-24-18}

WORTERS, JOSEPH (Prince George's County) received receipts from the Purchasing Agent for furnishing wheat on 21 May and 8 Jun 1782 {Ref: Maryland State Archives MdHR-6636-50-135}

WORTH, ANDREW (Montgomery County) received a receipt from the Purchasing Agent for furnishing wheat on 27 Oct 1780 {Ref: Maryland State Archives MdHR-6636-24-13}

WORTH, WILLIAM (Kent County) received payment by order of the Council of Safety on 10 Oct 1776 "for sinkage of vessels at *Otter* alarm" at Whetstone Point in March, 1776 for the purpose of preventing any of the British Ships of War from coming up to Baltimore Town {Ref: Archives of Maryland 12:330}

WORTHEN, BENNET (Charles County) received a receipt from the Purchasing Agent for furnishing wheat on 28 Sep 1782 {Ref: Maryland State Archives MdHR-6636-42-19}

WORTHINGTON, CHARLES (Harford County) received a receipt from the Purchasing Agent for furnishing wheat on 13 Apr 1780 {Ref: Maryland State Archives MdHR-6636-23-35}

WORTHINGTON, CHARLES (Anne Arundel County) received payment by order of the Council of Maryland via Vachel Worthington for the hire of his wagon on 15 Apr 1778 {Ref: Archives of Maryland 21:35}; he was a doctor who received payment "out of the money approp. for the Barges to purchase Medicines & Hospital Stores on Account" on 21 Sep 1782 {Ref: Archives of

Maryland 48:265}

WORTHINGTON, ELIZABETH, see "Vachel Worthington," q.v.

WORTHINGTON, JOHN (Baltimore County) received payment for furnishing beef on 14 Apr 1781 {Ref: Maryland State Archives MdHR-6636-43-38YYY}; also see "Edward Gaither," q.v.

WORTHINGTON, NICHOLAS (Anne Arundel County) pledged a loan in the amount of £100 to the State of Maryland under the Act for the Emission of Bills of Credit "to defray the expences of the present campaign" in June, 1781 {Ref: Archives of Maryland 47:326}; received a loan certificate for £212.5.9 due from the Council of Maryland "agreeable to the Act proposing to the Citizens of this State, Creditors of Congress on Loan Office Certificates, Etc." on 9 Dec 1783 for services rendered during the war {Ref: Archives of Maryland 48:486}

WORTHINGTON, SAMUEL (Baltimore County) received a certificate from the Purchasing Agent for furnishing flour on 8 Jan 1780 {Ref: Maryland State Archives MdHR-6636-17-8}

WORTHINGTON, VACHEL (Anne Arundel County) and Elizabeth Worthington received payment from the Council of Maryland for services rendered (not specified) on 17 Dec 1781 {Ref: Archives of Maryland 48:27}; also see "Charles Worthington," q.v.

WOTKINS, PETER (Frederick County) received a certificate from the Purchasing Agent for furnishing wheat on 14 Jun 1782 {Ref: Maryland State Archives MdHR-6636-42-35}

WRIGHT, EDWARD (Queen Anne's County) received a receipt from the Purchasing Agent for furnishing corn on 1 Apr 1780 {Ref: Archives of Maryland 43:475; Maryland State Archives MdHR-6636-24-21B}; his name appeared with Thomas Ramsay on 19 Feb 1781 on a "Return [of] Flour forwarded and Delivered at the Head of Elk the Purchase of different Persons for the use of the United States" in the year 1780 {Ref: Archives of Maryland 47:77}

WRIGHT, HENRY (Frederick County) received a certificate from the Purchasing Agent for furnishing wheat on 30 Jul 1782 {Ref: Maryland State Archives MdHR-6636-42-36}

WRIGHT, JACOB (Somerset County) received a receipt from the Purchasing Agent for furnishing pork on 23 Apr 1782 {Ref: Maryland State Archives MdHR-6636-43-21}

WRIGHT, JACOB (Dorchester County) received a receipt from the Purchasing Agent for furnishing wheat on 25 Mar 1783 {Ref: Maryland State Archives MdHR-6636-42-24}

WRIGHT, JOHN L. (Charles County) received a receipt from the Purchasing Agent for furnishing wheat on 9 Feb 1782 {Ref: Maryland State Archives

MdHR-6636-42-16}

WRIGHT, JOSHUA (Caroline County) received a receipt from the Purchasing Agent for furnishing wheat on 5 Aug 1782 {Ref: Maryland State Archives MdHR-6636-42-7}

WRIGHT, NATHANIEL (Worcester County) received a receipt from the Purchasing Agent for furnishing wheat on 15 Sep 1780 {Ref: Maryland State Archives MdHR-6636-24-33}

WRIGHT, NATHANIEL (Cecil County) received a receipt from the Purchasing Agent for furnishing wheat on 13 Sep 1782 {Ref: Maryland State Archives MdHR-6636-42-9}

WRIGHT, NATHANIEL (Queen Anne's County) received a certificate from the Purchasing Agent for furnishing beef on 21 Sep 1781 {Ref: Maryland State Archives MdHR-6636-24-34}

WRIGHT, SAMUEL (Dorchester County) received a receipt from the Purchasing Agent for furnishing wheat on 1 Oct 1782 {Ref: Maryland State Archives MdHR-6636-42-23}

WRIGHT, SOLOMON, Esquire (Queen Anne's County) received a loan certificate for £11.2.4 due from the Council of Maryland "agreeable to the Act proposing to the Citizens of this State, Creditors of Congress on Loan Office Certificates, Etc." on 14 Oct 1783 for services rendered during the war {Ref: Archives of Maryland 48:464}

WRIGHT, THOMAS (Queen Anne's County) received a receipt from the Purchasing Agent for furnishing beef on 22 Dec 1779 {Ref: Maryland State Archives MdHR-6636-17-73}; received a certificate for furnishing wheat on 6 Feb 1780 {Ref: Maryland State Archives MdHR-6636-24-30}; received a certificate for furnishing bacon on 10 Apr 1781 {Ref: Maryland State Archives MdHR-6636-24-34}

WRIGHT, TRUEMAN (Montgomery County) received a certificate from the Purchasing Agent for hauling corn on 2 Jun 1780 {Ref: Maryland State Archives MdHR-6636-50-91}

WRIGHT, TURBUTT (Queen Anne's County) was appointed by the Council of Safety to collect all the gold and silver coin that could be procured in the county in compliance with the Resolve of Congress on 27 Jan 1776 {Ref: Archives of Maryland 11:132}

WRIGHT, WALTER (Dorchester County) received payment by order of the Council of Safety for supplying six cords of wood on 24 Jul 1776 {Ref: Archives of Maryland 12:109}

WRIGHT, WILLIAM (Queen Anne's County) was licensed Assistant Commissary of Purchases by the Council of Maryland on 19 Nov 1779 {Ref: Archives of Maryland 43:20}; appointed by the Council of Maryland to be one of three men in Queen Anne's County "to carry the Act to prohibit for a limited time the

Exportation of Indian Corn, Etc., by Land" on 22 Dec 1780 {Ref: Archives of Maryland 45:251}

WYE, POLLY (Baltimore Town) received payment by order of the Council of Maryland for services rendered [not specified, but possibly for making shirts] on 28 Feb 1777 {Ref: Archives of Maryland 16:153}

WYET, JOHN (Caroline County) received a receipt from the Purchasing Agent for furnishing wheat on 1 Sep 1782 {Ref: Maryland State Archives MdHR-6636-42-7}

WYNN, JOHN (Prince George's County) received payment by order of the Council of Maryland "agreeable to his and Abraham Coxe's bond to erect a salt works" on 3 Nov 1777 {Ref: Archives of Maryland 16:408}

YATES, JOHN (Charles County) received a receipt from the Purchasing Agent for furnishing wheat on 17 Nov 1781 {Ref: Maryland State Archives MdHR-6636-43-45D}; received a receipt for furnishing wheat on 24 Nov 1781 {Ref: Maryland State Archives MdHR-6636-42-15}; received a receipt for furnishing wheat on 29 Dec 1782 {Ref: Maryland State Archives MdHR-6636-42-21}

YEARING, HENRY (Frederick County) received a certificate from the Purchasing Agent for furnishing wheat on 10 Feb 1783 {Ref: Maryland State Archives MdHR-6636-42-38}

YEARLEY, JOHN (Kent County) received a certificate from the Purchasing Agent for furnishing corn on 9 Feb 1780 {Ref: Maryland State Archives MdHR-6636-23-41}

YEARLING, SARAH (Prince George's County) received a receipt from the Purchasing Agent for furnishing wheat in 1782 {Ref: Maryland State Archives MdHR-6636-50-135}

YEATES, DONALDSON (Kent County) was a colonel and Deputy Quartermaster General by 1778 {Ref: Maryland State Archives MdHR-6636-21-24}; submitted an invoice for the purchase of provisions on 3 Feb 1778 {Ref: Maryland State Archives MdHR-6636-12-28C}; received a receipt of pork and beef for the Continental Army on 12 Sep 1778 {Ref: Maryland State Archives MdHR-6636-12-28B}

YIELDHALL, BENJAMIN (Anne Arundel County) received a receipt from the Purchasing Agent for furnishing cattle on 31 Aug 1781 {Ref: Maryland State Archives MdHR-6636-31-120}

YIELDHALL (YELDHALL), GILBERT (Anne Arundel County) received payment by order of the Council of Safety for furnishing a gun on 24 Sep 1776 {Ref: Archives of Maryland 12:297}

YIELDHALL (YELDEL), THOMAS (Anne Arundel County) delivered 300 musquets, 287 bayonets, and 265 cartridge boxes on his boat from Baltimore to the Council of Maryland in Annapolis on 2 Sep 1781 {Ref: Archives of Maryland 47:472}

YIELDHALL (YIELDELL), WILLIAM (Anne Arundel County) received payment from the Council of Maryland as "appropriated for the payment of Expresses, Etc., per Accounts passed by the Auditor General" on 17 Jul 1781 {Ref: Archives of Maryland 45:506}; received a receipt for furnishing cattle on 31 Aug 1781 {Ref: Maryland State Archives MdHR-6636-31-120}; submitted an account and receipt for provisions and the hire of his boat for transportation of flour on 24 May 1782 {Ref: Maryland State Archives MdHR-6636-40-90}

YIELDING, WILLIAM (Anne Arundel County) was ordered by the Council of Maryland to deliver to John Bullen, the Issuing Commissary, "all of the bran in his possession belonging to this state" on 17 Aug 1780 {Ref: Archives of Maryland 43:257}

YOE, ANNA (Queen Anne's County) received a receipt from the Purchasing Agent for furnishing bacon on 1 Apr 1778 {Ref: Maryland State Archives MdHR-4587-42}

YORK, GEORGE (Harford County) received payment for furnishing a gun to the Committee of Safety on 18 Jun 1776 {Ref: Preston's History of Harford County, p. 330}

YOST, HENRY (Frederick County) was ordered by the Council of Safety to deliver to Capt. George Stricker all the musquets and bullet moulds which are now finished by him and John Unseld for the use of the province on 4 Apr 1776 {Ref: Archives of Maryland 11:308, 400}; received payment from the Council of Maryland for repairing muskets on 30 Jan 1781 {Ref: Archives of Maryland 45:294}

YOST, JOHN (Frederick County) received payment by order of the Council of Safety to enable him to carry on his gun manufactory on 13 May 1776 {Ref: Archives of Maryland 11:421}; from George Town he informed the Council on 13 Sep 1776 that he had erected a horse mill for boring gun barrels, that he had the workmen needed to make locks, screws, mounting and forging barrels ready for boring, that if he could get the necessary materials from Head of Elk that he ordered from Philadelphia he could proceed, and he would be glad to furnish 300 ready forged locks to the gun manufactory at Frederick Town if the Council might be of service to hasten their conveyance; ordered by the Council "to deliver all the musquets he has ready made for the public service" on 24 Sep 1776 {Ref: Archives of Maryland 12:271}; he was still manufacturing arms on 12 Jan 1781 {Ref: Archives of Maryland 47:14}; also see "John Youst," q.v.

YOST, MARGARET (Frederick County) received a certificate from the Purchasing Agent for furnishing wheat on 21 Mar 1782 {Ref: Maryland State Archives MdHR-6636-42-37}

YOUNG, HUGH (Baltimore Town) submitted an account for the delivery of cannon on 1 Jul 1780 {Ref: Maryland State Archives MdHR-4600-7}

YOUNG, JOHN (Prince George's County) received receipts from the Purchasing

Agent for furnishing wheat on 12 Jun 1782 and 11 Feb 1783 {Ref: Maryland State Archives MdHR-6636-50-135}

YOUNG, JOHN (Caroline County) received a receipt from the Purchasing Agent for furnishing wheat on 5 Aug 1782 {Ref: Maryland State Archives MdHR-6636-42-7}

YOUNG, JOHN TULLY (Baltimore County) received a loan certificate for £16.9.8 due from the Council of Maryland "agreeable to the Act proposing to the Citizens of this State, Creditors of Congress on Loan Office Certificates, Etc." on 9 Oct 1783 for services rendered during the war {Ref: Archives of Maryland 48:460}

YOUNG, NOTLEY (Prince George's County) received receipts from the Purchasing Agent for furnishing wheat on 11 May, 16 May and 17 Sep 1781 {Ref: Maryland State Archives MdHR-6636-24-14}; received a receipt for furnishing wheat on 28 Apr 1781 {Ref: Maryland State Archives MdHR-6636-24-20}; received a loan certificate for £78.14.5 due from the Council of Maryland "agreeable to the Act proposing to the Citizens of this State, Creditors of Congress on Loan Office Certificates, Etc." on 2 Jul 1783 for services rendered during the war {Ref: Archives of Maryland 48:436}

YOUNG, WILLIAM (Frederick County) received a receipt from the Purchasing Agent for furnishing wheat on 21 Apr 1781 {Ref: Maryland State Archives MdHR-6636-50-91}

YOUNG, WILLIAM (Prince George's County) received a receipt from the Purchasing Agent for furnishing wheat on 23 Jul 1782 {Ref: Maryland State Archives MdHR-6636-50-135}

YOUST, JOHN (Montgomery County) received a supply of gunpowder from the Council of Safety "to prove the musquets made by him for the use of this province" on 20 Jan 1776 {Ref: Archives of Maryland 11:99}; received a receipt from the Purchasing Agent for furnishing wheat on 7 May 1781 {Ref: Maryland State Archives MdHR-6636-24-18}; also see "John Yost," q.v.

YOUTSE, PETER (Frederick County) received a certificate from the Purchasing Agent for furnishing wheat on 26 May 1782 {Ref: Maryland State Archives MdHR-6636-42-33}

ZIMMERMAN, JACOB (Frederick County) received a receipt from the Purchasing Agent for caring for cattle on 29 Apr 1781 {Ref: Maryland State Archives MdHR-6636-23-31}; received a certificate for furnishing wheat on 15 Jun 1782 {Ref: Maryland State Archives MdHR-6636-42-35}

Other books by the author:

A Closer Look at St. John's Parish Registers [Baltimore County, Maryland], 1701-1801
A Collection of Maryland Church Records
A Guide to Genealogical Research in Maryland: 5th Edition, Revised and Enlarged
Abstracts of the Ledgers and Accounts of the Bush Store and Rock Run Store, 1759-1771
Abstracts of the Orphans Court Proceedings of Harford County, 1778-1800
Abstracts of Wills, Harford County, Maryland, 1800-1805
Baltimore City [Maryland] Deaths and Burials, 1834-1840
Baltimore County, Maryland, Overseers of Roads, 1693-1793
Bastardy Cases in Baltimore County, Maryland, 1673-1783
Bastardy Cases in Harford County, Maryland, 1774-1844
Bible and Family Records of Harford County, Maryland Families: Volume V
Children of Harford County: Indentures and Guardianships, 1801-1830
Colonial Delaware Soldiers and Sailors, 1638-1776
Colonial Families of the Eastern Shore of Maryland
Volumes 5, 6, 7, 8, 9, 11, 12, 13, 14, and 16
Colonial Maryland Soldiers and Sailors, 1634-1734
Dr. John Archer's First Medical Ledger, 1767-1769, Annotated Abstracts
Early Anglican Records of Cecil County
Early Harford Countians, Individuals Living in Harford County, Maryland in Its Formative Years
Volume 1: A to K, Volume 2: L to Z, and Volume 3: Supplement
Harford County Taxpayers in 1870, 1872 and 1883
Harford County, Maryland Divorce Cases, 1827-1912: An Annotated Index
Heirs and Legatees of Harford County, Maryland, 1774-1802
Heirs and Legatees of Harford County, Maryland, 1802-1846
Inhabitants of Baltimore County, Maryland, 1763-1774
Inhabitants of Cecil County, Maryland, 1649-1774
Inhabitants of Harford County, Maryland, 1791-1800
Inhabitants of Kent County, Maryland, 1637-1787
Joseph A. Pennington & Co., Havre De Grace, Maryland Funeral Home Records:
Volume II, 1877-1882, 1893-1900
Maryland Bible Records, Volume 1: Baltimore and Harford Counties
Maryland Bible Records, Volume 2: Baltimore and Harford Counties
Maryland Bible Records, Volume 3: Carroll County
Maryland Bible Records, Volume 4: Eastern Shore
Maryland Deponents, 1634-1799
Maryland Deponents: Volume 3, 1634-1776
Maryland Public Service Records, 1775-1783: A Compendium of Men and Women of Maryland Who Rendered Aid in Support of the American Cause against Great Britain during the Revolutionary War
Marylanders to Carolina: Migration of Marylanders to North Carolina and South Carolina prior to 1800

Marylanders to Kentucky, 1775-1825

Methodist Records of Baltimore City, Maryland: Volume 1, 1799-1829

Methodist Records of Baltimore City, Maryland: Volume 2, 1830-1839

Methodist Records of Baltimore City, Maryland: Volume 3, 1840-1850 (East City Station)

More Maryland Deponents, 1716-1799

More Marylanders to Carolina: Migration of Marylanders to North Carolina and South Carolina prior to 1800

More Marylanders to Kentucky, 1778-1828

Outpensioners of Harford County, Maryland, 1856-1896

Presbyterian Records of Baltimore City, Maryland, 1765-1840

Quaker Records of Baltimore and Harford Counties, Maryland, 1801-1825

Quaker Records of Northern Maryland, 1716-1800

Quaker Records of Southern Maryland, 1658-1800

Revolutionary Patriots of Anne Arundel County, Maryland

Revolutionary Patriots of Baltimore Town and Baltimore County, 1775-1783

Revolutionary Patriots of Calvert and St. Mary's Counties, Maryland, 1775-1783

Revolutionary Patriots of Caroline County, Maryland, 1775-1783

Revolutionary Patriots of Cecil County, Maryland

Revolutionary Patriots of Charles County, Maryland, 1775-1783

Revolutionary Patriots of Delaware, 1775-1783

Revolutionary Patriots of Dorchester County, Maryland, 1775-1783

Revolutionary Patriots of Frederick County, Maryland, 1775-1783

Revolutionary Patriots of Harford County, Maryland, 1775-1783

Revolutionary Patriots of Kent and Queen Anne's Counties

Revolutionary Patriots of Lancaster County, Pennsylvania

Revolutionary Patriots of Maryland, 1775-1783: A Supplement

Revolutionary Patriots of Maryland, 1775-1783: Second Supplement

Revolutionary Patriots of Montgomery County, Maryland, 1776-1783

Revolutionary Patriots of Prince George's County, Maryland, 1775-1783

Revolutionary Patriots of Talbot County, Maryland, 1775-1783

Revolutionary Patriots of Worcester and Somerset Counties, Maryland, 1775-1783

Revolutionary Patriots of Washington County, Maryland, 1776-1783

St. George's (Old Spesutia) Parish, Harford County, Maryland: Church and Cemetery Records, 1820-1920

St. John's and St. George's Parish Registers, 1696-1851

Survey Field Book of David and William Clark in Harford County, Maryland, 1770-1812

The Crenshaws of Kentucky, 1800-1995

The Delaware Militia in the War of 1812

Union Chapel United Methodist Church Cemetery Tombstone Inscriptions, Wilna, Harford County, Maryland

www.ingramcontent.com/pod-product-compliance
Lightning Source LLC
Chambersburg PA
CBHW050330230426
43663CB00010B/1802